A DOCUMENTARY HISTORY
of RELIGION *in* AMERICA

To 1877

A DOCUMENTARY HISTORY
of RELIGION *in* AMERICA

To 1877

THIRD EDITION

Edited by

Edwin S. Gaustad

with revisions by

Mark A. Noll

WILLIAM B. EERDMANS PUBLISHING COMPANY
GRAND RAPIDS, MICHIGAN / CAMBRIDGE, U.K.

© 1982, 1993, 2003 Wm. B. Eerdmans Publishing Co.
All rights reserved

Wm. B. Eerdmans Publishing Co.
255 Jefferson Ave. S.E., Grand Rapids, Michigan 49503 /
P.O. Box 163, Cambridge CB3 9PU U.K.

Printed in the United States of America

08 07 06 05 04 03   7 6 5 4 3 2 1

Library of Congress Cataloging-in-Publication Data

Gaustad, Edwin Scott.
    A documentary history of religion in America.
    Bibliography: passim
    Includes index.
    1. United States — Religion — Sources. 1. Title.
    BL2530.U6G38   291'.0973   82-7398
    ISBN 0-8028-2229-0 (v. 1)   AACR2

www.eerdmans.com

For Layna J.

Contents

CHAPTER FIVE

Evangelical Empire: Rise and Fall   405

Preface to the Third Edition

The scholarship of Edwin Gaustad that lay behind earlier editions of this documentary history was as impeccable for that purpose as it has been for all of his other major interpretations of American religion. As reviser, I have tried to do the minimum of necessary refurbishing in order to preserve the cohesion and breadth of those earlier editions. That refurbishing has meant an update of the bibliographical essays for the individual chapters, a new set of documents for the dozen or so years since the second edition was prepared, and a few additions to reflect recent scholarly concerns. Those additions include a little more on the Civil War as a religious event, a few more documents reporting religious developments among women and people of color, and one or two new contributions related to research interests of my own. By way of compensation a few documents from the second edition have been dropped, but Professor Gaustad's major, and even secondary, emphases still prevail. The conceptualization, organization, and flow of this edition remain his. I have been privileged to lend a hand in updating this work for what I hope will be another generation of readers as grateful as I have been for Ed Gaustad's discerning guidance through the past. I am also pleased to acknowledge the great help I have received from research assistant, Luke Harlow.

MARK A. NOLL

Preface to the Second Edition

The very first thing that needs to be expressed is a word of gratitude for the fine reception that has been granted to the *Documentary*. This is reassuring in many ways, not least in its implication that love's labor has not been lost. So to all faculty and students that have utilized the work, my warmest thanks.

Second, since the world of scholarship continues its steady productivity, this volume has taken note of those studies thought to be potentially useful to readers relying on the titles noted at the conclusion of each chapter. Graduate student James D. LeShana has ably assisted me in this latter endeavor.

E.S.G.

Preface to the First Edition

When asked how the writing of history differed from other literary activity, prize-winning historian Barbara Tuchman replied: "I feel the creativity of a historian is somewhat more disciplined. . . . A historian has to work, to begin with, with verifiable facts, as far as he can find them, documented, if possible . . ." (*The Quarterly Journal* of the Library of Congress [Winter, 1981], p. 24). And the farther away one moves from documents, the less disciplined the historical reconstruction, the less reliable the generalizations, the less satisfactory the long-term results. With documents close at hand, it is possible for every man and woman to be his or her own historian. This is the first aim of the present work: to enable the "amateur" to reconstruct the religious history of America with the building blocks provided here. (Of course, not every voice from the past has been reproduced here; to attempt that would be to abandon discipline in another way, and the alternative to some selectivity is hopeless chaos.)

A second aim has been to be faithful (again, within disciplined limits) to America's religious variety. Not a phenomenon exclusively of the twentieth century, pluralism on the North American continent is as old as the nation, as old as Jamestown or Quebec, and indeed much older than that. When countless native American tribes, of countless and obscure migrations, traversed the unbounded land, religious variety was already present in bountiful profusion. That variety, augmented by immigration from Europe and Africa, from Asia and Latin America, only grew. Europe was, of course, not a single entity, but only a convenient label for many languages and nations. To speak of Africa was to allude to widely dispersed tribes and ancient cultures. Powerfully enduring religions and enormous religious literatures emanated from Asia, while Latin American history interacted with that of the North at varying times and at several cultural levels. Can one be faithful to all the layers, all the divisions, to each and every enclave of religious and cultural life in what was to become the United States of America?

If the record of the past is treated as infinitely divisible, the result is more catalogue or collection than history. It is neither possible nor appropriate to think in terms of precise mathematical segments of "equal time" for all actors or institutions in the national past. Not appropriate because ideas, events, personalities, and structures are not of equal moment; and not possible because surviving records do not spread themselves evenly across centuries, classes, or creeds. One might wish for as much testimony from the Indian to whom the missionary preached as we have from the preacher, but the wish is not the father of the document. One might weigh the works of William Penn beside those of Mary Dyer, but the scales will never balance. Or one might, in all fairness, search for the response to an angry Anglican attack upon illiterate frontier religion, but fail to find any such "other side." So every calculus of equal documentation eludes, but the principle remains: to be wholly responsive to a pluralism that is totally and originally American — Indian and European, slave and free, Jew and Gentile, male and female, dogmatist and agnostic, conformist and eccentric, politically powerful and politically disinherited, sinner and saint.

A third aim has been to allow, as often as possible, the private and passionate voices to be heard. "Document," in other words, has by no means been limited to the pontifical pronouncement, the ecclesiastical resolution, the minutes of the previous meeting (was *any* meeting ever as dull as its official minutes regularly suggest?), or the pale consensus arrived at after reckless name-calling and vituperative debate (here the latter will receive more attention than the former). What is written by a committee often deserves to be read only by same. So, whenever a lively option existed between the cry of the heart and the impersonal thud of bureaucracy, the editorial choice was clear. Those options were of course not always present; thus, from time to time the voice of officialdom must be heard. On the whole, however, it has been assumed that history could only acquire flesh and blood — that is, life — from documents enlivened by passion, from letters or diaries or polemics or pleas that reveal men and women in all their vulnerable humanity.

The courtesy of specific publishers and repositories is acknowledged elsewhere. Here may I express appreciation to those scholars who have pointed the way in providing documentary histories directed toward specific groups: Roman Catholics, Jews, blacks, women, pacifists, abolitionists, and others. Citation is provided at appropriate points in the book to these valuable guides. And while the documentary edited two decades ago by H. Shelton Smith, Robert T. Handy, and Lefferts A. Loetscher is confined to American Christianity, those two volumes have never been far from my side. A special word of appreciation is due the library staff of the University of California, Riverside, and especially to those bearing up under the burden of incessant interlibrary loan requests. As an extraordinarily helpful graduate student, Leigh Johnsen assisted me in the identification and location of many of the documents for Volume I. Finally, I express gratitude to my wife who typed not a word herein; however, she did provide me with a new typewriter so that I might with less difficulty do it all myself.

E.S.G.

Illustrations

Acknowledgments

We gratefully acknowledge the kindness of the following publishers, persons, or institutions for their permission to utilize material under their copyright or control. Gratitude is also expressed here to those publishers who, through a modern reprinting, have made older works no longer under copyright readily accessible again.

Abingdon Press. *Journals and Letters of Francis Asbury* (1958). *Life Experience and Gospel Labors of the Rt. Rev. Richard Allen* (1960).

AMS Press. L. F. Greene, ed., *The Writings of the Late Elder John Leland* . . . (1969). W. S. Perry, ed., *Historical Collections Relating to the American Colonial Church* (1969). M. D. Conway, ed., *Writings of Thomas Paine* (1967). J. H. Noyes, *Bible Communism* . . . (1973). F. W. Evans, *Compendium of the Origin* . . . (1975).

Anderson, Gates & Wright. Benjamin Drake, *Life of Tecumseh, and his brother the prophet* (1858).

Arno Press. *American Tract Society Documents* (1972). *Lyman Beecher and the Reform of Society* (1972). O. A. Brownson, *Essays and Reviews* (1972). Alexander Campbell, *The Christian System* (1969). L. F. Greene, ed., *Writings of the Late Elder John Leland* (1969). A. E. Grimké, *Appeal to the Christian Women* . . . (1969). R. A. Guild, *Early History of Brown University* (1980). I. T. Hecker, *Questions of the Soul* (1978). David Humphreys, *An Historical Account of the SPG* (1969). J. and O. Lovejoy, *Memoirs of the Rev. Elijah P. Lovejoy* (1969). Jonathan Mayhew, *Observations on the Charter and Conduct of the SPG* (1972). Samuel F. B. Morse, *Imminent Dangers* . . . (1969). Lucy Mack Smith, *Biographical Sketches of Joseph Smith* (1969). Adolph Spaeth, *Charles Porterfield Krauth* (1969). Daniel Alexander Payne, *Sermons and Addresses, 1853-1891* (1972). M. J. Spalding, *Sketches of Early Catholic Missions* (1972). E. M. Stone, *Biography of Rev. Elhanan Winchester* (1972).

Association for Study of Afro-American Life and History, Inc. *Journal of Negro History* (1967).

Roland H. Bainton. *Age of Reformation* (1956).

Beacon. John Henrik Clarke, ed., *William Styron's Nat Turner* (1968).

Bedford. Ida B. Wells in *Southern Horrors and Other Writings . . .*, ed. Jacqueline Jones Royster (1997).

Bethany Press. W. E. Tucker and L. G. McAllister, *Journey into Faith* (1975).

Bobbs-Merrill. Perry Miller, *Roger Williams* (1953). Gilbert Tennent in *The Great Awakening,* ed. Alan Heimert and Perry Miller (1967).

Carlson. Richard Newman, ed., *Black Preacher to White America: The Collected Writings of Lemuel Haynes, 1774-1833* (1990).

Chelsea House. Roger Bruns, ed., *Am I Not a Man and a Brother . . .* (1977).

University of Chicago Press. *Papers of James Madison* (1973). Alexis de Tocqueville, *The Old Regime and the Revolution,* ed. François Furet and Françoise Mélonio, trans. Alan S. Kahan (1998).

Arthur H. Clark. C. M. Drury, ed., *First White Women over the Rockies* (1963).

Columbia University Press. J. L. Blau and S. W. Baron, eds., *Jews of the United States . . .* (1963).

Cooper Square Publishers. W. W. Sweet, ed., *Religion on the American Frontier* (1964).

Dawson's Book Shop. F. J. Weber, ed., *Documents of Catholic California History* (1965).

Deseret Book Company. B. H. Roberts, *History of the Church of Jesus Christ of Latter Day Saints* (1964).

Fortress Press. Martin Luther, *Three Treatises* (1947). T. G. Tappert and J. W. Doberstein, eds., *Journals of Henry Melchior Muhlenberg* (1942).

Garland Publishing Company. *Narrative of the Massacre . . . of Wife and Children of Thomas Baldwin* (1977).

University of Georgia Press. *Detailed Reports on the Salzburger Emigrants . . .* (1968).

Glencoe Publishing Company. J. T. Ellis, ed., *Documents of American Catholic History* (1956).

Greenwood Press. W. E. Washburn, ed., *The American Indian and the United States* (1973).

Harper & Row. W. H. Capps, ed., *Seeing with a Native Eye* (1976). Norman Cousins, *"In God We Trust" . . .* (1958). Perry Miller and T. H. Johnson, *The Puritans: A Sourcebook* (1963).

Harvard University Press. Barbara M. Cross, ed., *Autobiography of Lyman Beecher* (1961). Thomas Hutchinson, *History of the Colony and Province of Massachusetts Bay* (1936). W. G. McLoughlin, ed., *Lectures on Revivals of Religion . . .* (1960); and *Isaac Backus on Church, State, and Calvinism* (1968). O. Handlin and J. Clive, eds., *Journey to Pennsylvania* (1960). S. E. Morison, *Founding of Harvard College* (1935).

Herald Press. R. K. MacMaster et al., *Conscience in Crisis . . .* (1979).

Jewish Publication Society of America. J. R. Marcus, ed., *Memoirs of American Jews* (1955).

Louisiana State University Press. K. Silverman, ed., *Selected Letters of Cotton Mather* (1971).

Loyola University Press. F. X. Curran, S.J., ed., *Catholics in Colonial Law* (1963).

Massachusetts Historical Society. *Winthrop Papers* (1931).

University of New Mexico Press. G. P. Hammond and Agupito Ray, *Don Juan de Oñate . . .* Part II (1953).

University of North Carolina Press. L. J. Cappon, ed., *The Adams-Jefferson Correspondence* (1959). R. J. Hooker, ed., *The Carolina Backcountry . . .* (1953). E. W. Knight, ed., *Documentary History of Education in the South* (1949). *Poems of Phillis Wheatly* (1966).

University of Notre Dame Press. J. F. Gower and R. M. Leliaert, ed., *The Brownson-Hecker Correspondence* (1979).

Oxford University Press. Lawrence Foster, *Religion and Sexuality* . . . (1981). Willie Lee Rose, *Documentary History of Slavery in America* (1976). H. Shelton Smith, *Horace Bushnell* (1965).

Paulist Press. Peter Guilday, *Life and Times of John Carroll* (1954). Ellin Kelly and Annabelle Melville, eds., *Elizabeth Seton: Selected Writings* (1987).

Pickwick. John W. Nevin in *Catholic and Reformed: Selected Theological Writings of John Williamson Nevin,* ed. Charles Yrigoyen, Jr., and George H. Bricker (1978).

Princeton University Press. Julian P. Boyd, ed., *Papers of Thomas Jefferson* (1950).

Russell and Russell (Atheneum Press). *The Dial* (1961).

University of South Carolina Press. David B. Chesebrough, ed., *"God Ordained This War": Sermons on the Sectional Crisis, 1830-1865* (1991).

Syracuse University Press. Arthur C. Parker in *Parker on the Iroquois,* ed. William N. Fenton (1968).

Wesleyan University Press. R. Slotkin and J. K. Folsom, *So Dreadfull a Judgment* . . . (1978).

Westminster Press. M. W. Armstrong et al., *Presbyterian Enterprise* (1956). John Calvin, *Institutes of the Christian Religion* (1936).

William and Mary Quarterly. Michael J. Crawford in Vol. 33 (January, 1976).

Yale University Press. J. W. Blassingame, ed., *The Frederick Douglass Papers* (1979). D. E. Stanford, ed., *Poems of Edward Taylor* (1960). Carol F. Karlsen and Laurie Crumpacker, eds., *The Journal of Esther Edwards Burr, 1754-1757* (1984).

CHAPTER ONE

The Old World and the New

The sixteenth and seventeenth centuries saw the transplanting of both European nationalism and European religion into the Western Hemisphere. Colonists and soldiers from any nation were pawns in an intricate game of international chess; or, to change the figure, territorial claims made on behalf of either church or state (or both) were often only bold bluffs in a game of considerable chance. Whatever the game, the New World saw many winners and losers, high rollers and quitters, the quick and the dead. And along with the Europeans seeking to make their mark were an increasing number of Africans, unwilling participants in the entire venture, and a diminishing number of Indians, unbelieving witnesses to a trickle turning to flood. Before rushing on to the newcomers, however, it is good to dwell on the religion of the land's first inhabitants.

Natural Religion

In the Age of Exploration, western Europe's imperialism was theological no less than political. As Europeans would export to the New World their government, soldiers, traders, settlers, and modes of civilization, they would also dispatch their religion. Never mind that the New World already possessed armies and economies, cities and cultures, those of Europe were "higher" and therefore endowed with a preemptive right to prevail.

And prevail of course they did. So effectively indeed have they prevailed that the very memory of an earlier, pre-European age is virtually obliterated. To write of "American religion," therefore, is to write of European religion transplanted to America. None would deny that this is a very large part of the story; upon reflection, few would argue that it is the whole story.

Our history thus begins with an attempt to document something of the religion to be found among America's native peoples. In the absence of abundant literary remains, persisting oral traditions and tribal memories offer pas-

1

sage into a long-buried past. And the richness of that past becomes more evident as one pauses to consider the nature of religion itself.

Religious phenomena, well-nigh universal so far as can be determined, display a common pattern not of detail but of essential structure. This is not so surprising when one considers that life itself poses widely shared problems, provoking human beings to raise similar questions and probe for similarly satisfying answers. Nonetheless, the term "religion" defies simple and universally acceptable definition. Description may be easier than definition, and the characteristic features of religion offered long ago by George Foot Moore may serve as a point of departure. Man, Moore observed, believes that there are powers upon which he is dependent; that those powers are motivated in ways similar to his own actions; that those powers are therefore pliable, susceptible to being influenced by petition, offering, flattery, or other means; and, finally, that men and women act upon these beliefs.

Not even as description will these observations meet every objection or every lexicographical demand. But Moore's comment has the virtue of emphasizing two fundamental ingredients present in religion: beliefs (historical, mythological, theological, philosophical) and actions related to those beliefs (ethical, liturgical, social, political). So in all folk religions, one finds both myth (something believed) and ritual (something done). Thus in primitive Hawaii, the Polynesian deities of sky and earth, of war and harvest, inspired awe and evoked belief; the powerful, pervading *mana* thus required ceremonies designed to appropriate its fearful force for good, or to ward off its equally powerful potential for evil. Likewise, in the religion of the several tribes of native Americans, Indians believe in powers beyond the realm of ordinary common sense and control; they also act on or act out these beliefs.

Similarity in structure, however, does not imply uniformity in expression. Too readily we indulge in the imaginary construct called "the American Indian" or "the religion of the Indian." The vast geographical and chronological spread of those peoples who crossed the Bering Strait land bridge some thirty to forty thousand years ago allows for no such single entity as "the American Indian." Enormous variety in both time and space characterizes the native populations of the Western Hemisphere. And much lies beyond our present power to recover. The modern American can look, for example, at Ohio's great Serpent Mound built thousands of years ago or at Georgia's Rock Eagle Effigy Mound erected hundreds of years ago only to wonder at the achievements of those cultures and the probable complexities of their religions. Even in more modern times one hesitates to generalize about cultural similarities among the desert-dwelling Zuni, the forest-roaming Iroquois, the Sioux of the open plains, and the Salishan of the Pacific Northwest. "The religion" of the American Indians turns out to be the multi-colored, many-layered religious patterns of hundreds of discrete Indian tribes and villages.

Many modern students first became conscious of Indian literature and beliefs from reading the enormously popular *Black Elk Speaks*. From Black Elk himself (a holy man of the Oglala Sioux) emerged a dignity, a solemnity, a profundity perhaps not widely anticipated. In a modern edition of this "religious classic, perhaps the only religious classic of this century," Vine Deloria, Jr., notes that the book spoke not only to those unfamiliar with Indian cultures and traditions; for the young Indians searching for their roots, "the book has become a North American bible of all tribes." And in a different way, the several books of Carlos Castaneda on the Yaqui Indians of northern Mexico have given old patterns of thought and behavior new relevance and rapt interest.

In presenting the Indians' oral traditions, anthropologists regularly employ the term "myth." This is not a derogatory word. Rather, it points to a different use of language than that found in, say, science or history. Myth treats that which lies beyond science and before history, probes for that which is true not for one time and place (for example, Columbus discovered America in 1492) but for all time and all space. Because myths (anyone's myths) do not lend themselves to empirical verification, it is appropriate to speak not of facts but of beliefs. And should one ask, "Why believe when there are no (or insufficient) facts?", the answer is that life won't wait until all the facts come in. All mankind is like the impatient, curious four-year-old, wanting to know: "Where did I come from? Why will I die? Who made me? the world? the sky so blue?" While there are many kinds of myths, the documents below will concentrate on one kind: myths of origin, specifically the origin of the world.

While there are also many kinds of religious ceremonies, the focus below will be on the pervasive rites of passage: that is, on those ceremonies which help usher one across difficult and dangerous thresholds (birth, puberty, marriage, childbirth, death). Major world religions all give attention to these vulnerable and critical junctures of life, but so too do the world's "minor" religions, those of tribe and village and obscure or forgotten microcultures. These also call upon all the resources and accumulated tradition of the group in order to guide the perplexed, comfort the afflicted, and strengthen those who could not make life's journey alone.

New Spain

Spain's storied conquests are more often told of Central and South America than of that disappointing continent farther north. In the former, civilizations were higher (Aztec, Inca, Maya), the riches far greater, and the victories for church and state more enduring. But "conquistadores" entered North America too, even if their ultimate fates can scarcely be labeled as "conquests."

Florida — the very name of course is Spanish — early felt the European boot wedged into its sandy soil. That peninsula stretched out into the Caribbean so far that the first Spanish explorers understandably took it for another large island — comparable, for example, to Cuba. Before abandoning her Florida efforts, however, Spain discovered that Florida was a mere vestibule to another great mass of land. Soldiers and missionaries ventured as far north as the Chesapeake Bay before retreat beckoned as the only sensible course. The unplanned trek of Cabeza de Vaca from Florida to Texas and Mexico as well as the more or less planned expedition of Hernando de Soto in the southeastern corner of the continent stumbled upon no treasures of gold, no fabled capital cities. Undismayed, other Spanish explorers pursued their dreams, now farther west, and specifically into what was later to be called New Mexico.

In all of this marching, searching, and wandering, agents of Spain's church accompanied agents of the state. Those "agents" were invariably members of the great orders: Dominicans, Franciscans, Jesuits. The Dominicans (or Order of Preachers) arrived in the New World in direct response to the appeal of one of their number, Bartholomew de Las Casas, that Indians be converted rather than slaughtered, that they be regarded as human beings rather than animals. The Jesuits (or Society of Jesus) responded to appeals to enter Florida; they did so, then continued at tragic cost to push farther north along the Atlantic Coast. The Franciscans (or Order of Friars Minor), latest to arrive, also waded onto Florida's beaches, but labored with more lasting effect west of the Mississippi and Pecos Rivers.

New France

Decades before France established permanent settlements in North America, fishermen from that nation had plumbed the riches off Newfoundland's bountiful banks. But if fish constituted France's initial commercial interest across the Atlantic, fur led her far beyond those coastal shores. French penetration of the continent proceeded initially via the great St. Lawrence River, the modern cities of Montreal and Quebec being monuments to that seventeenth-century effort. On the secular side, the name of Samuel Champlain (c. 1567-1635) is inseparable from France's forts (Quebec in 1608), trading posts, villages, and enduring influence. On the religious side, the Society of Jesus above all other names is marked from the mouth of the St. Lawrence to and throughout the Great Lakes, then south along the Mississippi all the way to that river's broad basin at New Orleans.

While other Catholic orders do appear in New France, the Jesuits emerge as the spiritual right arm of the national conquest. The seventy-three volumes of Jesuit reports or *relationes* stand, moreover, as the indispensable source for all of New France's history. Since French population did not swiftly follow upon the heels of French exploration, Jesuit missionaries worked chiefly with the Indian tribes of interior America. And the clash of cultures and of wills has rarely — if ever — been more fully documented, more poignantly revealed. Converts came slowly, sometimes not at all; however, one of them, Kateri Tekakwitha, was beatified in 1980, this being the three hundredth anniversary of the Mohawk maiden's death.

Jesuits managed to be intrepid explorers as well as reporters, cartographers, translators, catechizers, and preachers. Father Jacques Marquette (1637-75) left his name upon the land, his fame especially linked to the exploration of the Mississippi River in 1673. Other Frenchmen ultimately found their way to the river's mouth, discovering not (as some hoped) a new route to Asia but the lifeline of mid-America. In the eighteenth century, Jesuit mission stations dotted the river banks, bays, and lakes from Quebec to New Orleans, forming a broad arc of French Catholicism west of the Appalachian range. The abrupt end of Jesuit labors in North America belongs to a later chapter, but here we observe one and one-half centuries during which members of Loyola's faithful band gave labor and life to a western wilderness they thought to tame.

New Netherland and New Sweden

Under the direction of the West India Company (chartered in 1621), the Dutch began arriving in the New World, around the mouth of the Hudson River, in 1623. Three years later Peter Minuit made his famous twenty-four dollar purchase of Manhattan Island from the Indians. While Holland generally and certainly the Company in particular were more interested in commerce than in colonization, Dutch settlers and Dutch clergy did arrive in sufficient force to flavor the region along the Hudson. Even though the Dutch flag came down in 1664, yielding to an English one, the imprint of New Netherland was never totally erased by New York.

Clergy of Holland's national church found the New World an unnerving place. Besides the "entirely savage and wild" Indian population, one encountered imported diversity and variety of every imaginable sort. Lutherans, Jews, Papists, Mennonites, Quakers — these and others seemed drawn by some powerful magnet to a region that should have been filled only with orderly Dutch towns. New Netherland bore disappointingly little resemblance to Old. Fortunately for all those not members of Holland's Reformed (Calvinist) Church, there was a dumping ground nearby: Rhode Island. But many stubbornly refused to be dumped. We shall, one pastor lamented, "soon become a Babel of confusion, instead of remaining a united and peaceful people." That was to become the American lament from Maine to Georgia: how expect order and unity when there is so much mixture and variety?

Even more ephemeral than New Netherland was New Sweden, located only a short distance to the south. In 1638 Swedes sailed up the Delaware River to establish Fort Christina (near the present site of Wilmington, Delaware). Though Sweden's king, "Lion of the North" Gustavus Adolphus, had died six years earlier, his vision and his aggressive Protestantism shaped this western venture. The Protestantism was of course Lutheran, that being the official religion of Sweden and all Scandinavia. And one of the Lutheran clergy, John Campanius, learned the language of the Delaware Indians well enough to translate the catechism of Martin Luther into "American-Virginian." Squeezed between the Dutch to the north and the English to the south, New Sweden fell initially to Holland in 1654. A decade later, as noted above, the Dutch themselves surrendered with the result that England's claim stretched in unbroken line from the French far removed in Canada's north to the Spanish clinging to Florida's south.

England Anew

For all of North America, England more than Europe's other powers came to stay. Though by no means among the first to cross that treacherous "ocean sea," England did plant colonies in sufficient numbers and win land with sufficient force to endure. Not that her "planting" resulted from some smoothly functioning, centrally synchronized English colonial office. Quite the contrary: in this instance as in many others, England muddled through. In richly varied ways — joint stock companies, adventurers, proprietors, royal advisors, and governors — English men and women did come, did cultivate, did marry and multiply. Others came from Scotland and Germany in significant numbers, and still others from Africa directly or by way of islands in the Caribbean.

In Virginia, and by extension throughout the South, the Church of England saw itself as entitled to all of the official recognition and support there that this national church enjoyed at home. Many steps were taken in an effort to see that this would be so. Parish boundaries were legally fixed, taxes for the support of the clergy were duly levied, generous acreage (glebe lands) was faithfully set aside, and parish vestries were granted broad privileges and powers. But nothing seemed to go according to plan. And English clergy, like the Dutch clergy noted above, found little in the New World which bore a comforting resemblance to the Old. The re-creation of English village life in seventeenth-century Virginia defied the best effort. Geography dictated much of the irreconcilable divergence, while economic necessities (and failures), political wrangles (and weaknesses), and population patterns (and diversity) dictated the rest. Virginia might name its rivers and towns after English kings, might furnish its houses with English linen and glass, and might demand that England's Book of Common Prayer be faithfully followed in all respects; yet no Englishman, searching in vain for that quiet village green, would mistake Virginia for home.

In Massachusetts, and by extension throughout New England, a different drummer marched. There the religious priorities outranked the economic ones, and there religion was less an attempted transplant of the National Church than a careful cultivation of a church newly formed and reformed. Pilgrims and Puritans alike brought with them a vision of what Christ's true church should be, of how society should be ordered and a biblical commonwealth constructed. Their errand into the wilderness was above all else a religious errand, and all institutions — town meeting, school, church, family, law — must faithfully reflect that central fact. Here geography permitted towns and parishes to be laid out in a manner closer to the patterns left behind. Here farmers and merchants could assume roles not sharply different from those known before. And here a new college could actually aspire to follow in Cambridge, Massachusetts, the pattern set by the university long established in Cambridge, England.

So in the 1620s the Pilgrims and in the 1630s the Puritans brought into being, respectively, the Plymouth Colony and the Massachusetts Bay Colony, the latter being much the larger of the two. Though initially differing on their relationship with England's mother church, the two colonies soon merged ecclesiastically into "the way Congregational" as opposed to "the way National." And before the century was over, the two colonies had merged politically as well. The "New England Way" came to stand as a model which, it was fervently hoped, Old England would behold in admiration and respond to with imitation. During the first half of the seventeenth century, Massachusetts and Connecticut kept one eye over their shoulders to see how the Church at home responded to the effort abroad to bring Christ's pure church into being. When England under Oliver Cromwell underwent its own Puritan revolution, the delicate experiment being conducted three thousand miles away lost some of its relevance and some of its intensity.

Three of the thirteen colonies followed such distinctive religious paths as to require separate treatment as "special cases": Maryland, Rhode Island, and Pennsylvania. Initially, Maryland cannot be included in the generalizations above concerning an Anglican south — though Anglican it eventually became. In its early years, however, it stood apart from England's other colonies, north or south, as having been launched under the auspices of a Roman Catholic proprietor, Lord Baltimore. One of the few sentiments binding the British colonies together was their profound anti-Catholicism, an inevitable part of their intellectual baggage brought over from bloodied England. Yet in 1634 the Crown encouraged and made possible the Catholic colony of Maryland — clearly a "special case."

Rhode Island, as noted above, had its special character thrust upon it: as a dumping ground, as the latrine of New England (at least as contemporaries were fond of saying). The reason for such undisguised contempt was simple to see: Rhode Island imposed no religious requirements, made no religious demands, enforced no religious uniformity. And in the early seventeenth century, such libertine behavior on the part of a government was as unthinkable as it was intolerable. Not that Rhode Islanders were indifferent to religion; most were not. But in that small space south of Massachusetts and east of Connecticut, men and women were free to be as religious, or as irreligious, as they pleased.

Between the microcosms of Maryland and Rhode Island, the macrocosm of Pennsylvania came into being a half-century later. The grant of land given to William Penn was huge, and there on a vast scale experiments of several sorts were tried — none more notable than Penn's explicit dedication to liberty of conscience. Because so many took Penn so literally, Pennsylvania presents a picture of greatest diversity: ethnic, linguistic, religious. Indeed, Maryland, Rhode Island, and Pennsylvania shared two common features: they all experimented with religious liberty, and the initial experimenters all were overwhelmed by it.

The final section relating to England examines that nation's encounter with the Indian, especially in the realm of religion.

1. Natural Religion

Ceremonies (things done)

Hopi

A contemporary member of the Hopi tribe and currently on the anthropology faculty of the University of Arizona, Emory Sekaquaptewa offers keen insight into the nature of religious ceremony in general. At the same time, he locates the abstract very specifically in the Hopi's involvement with the kachina doll. The document likewise reveals the intimate bond between things done and things believed.

I was born and raised in a small Hopi village. My first language, of course, was Hopi. In the world I first came to know, I had various experiences which resulted in images by which I knew the world around me. One of these very significant and prominent images, as I recall my early childhood, is the kachina doll. It developed particular meaning for me.

In Hopi practice the kachina is represented as a real being. From the time children are able to understand and to verbalize, until they are eight or ten years old, they are taught that the kachina is real. Every exposure the child has to the kachina is to a spiritual being which is real. There are a variety of ways in which the Hopis attempt to demonstrate this realism to the child. The kachina is all goodness and all kindness. The kachina also gives gifts to children in all of its appearances. Thus it is rather difficult for me to agree with the descriptions of the kachina that often appear in literature. The kachina is fre-

[Source: Walter H. Capps, ed., *Seeing with a Native Eye: Essays on Native American Religion* (New York: Harper and Row, 1976), pp. 36-39.]

quently described as being grotesque, but the Hopi child does not perceive the kachina as grotesque.

By his conduct toward the child, the kachina demands good behavior. As children we were taught that all things that come from the kachina hold certain spiritual gifts of reproduction. That is to say, when we received a bowl of fruit or something else, the gift was brought home and placed in the middle of the room. We were then given cornmeal and asked to go outside the house and pray in our childish fashion for an abundance of what we had received. And when we came back into the house, there was more than we had actually received from the hand of the kachina. This kind of practice builds in Hopi children the notion of the kachina as the symbol of ideal goodness.

Then there are times when the kachina is the symbol of admonition. When the child misbehaves he or she is threatened either with the idea that the kachinas will withhold their kindness from them, or even that the kachinas will come and deprive them of their person. There are various ways to dramatize this. I recall a little skit, which was performed to appease the kachina *soya*. The soya has been described as an ogre, but this is a misnomer. The soya is used to threaten the child because of bad behavior, but it certainly does not appear as an ogre to the child. So I prefer to say soya, which is the name of this kachina. He appears at a certain time of the year; and in preparation for his appearance certain children are given a warning. If they do not behave, straighten up, the kachina will come and take them. But threats as such are never effective unless there is some mechanism by which the child can appreciate and understand how one can get out of this predicament. So, in preparation for the appearance of the soya to the child, the parents plan or design a scheme by which they are going to save the child at the very last moment. The one which was used in the case I am talking about was this: the child, barely six years old, had misbehaved and was threatened with the appearance of the soya, who would come and take him away because he had misbehaved. So on the day of the arrival of the kachina, the parents had planned that when the kachinas came to the door, they would send the child outside, and the mother would appear with the child and inform the kachina in all seriousness that it was not right and timely for them to come after him, because he was going to be married. He was a groom and until this very important ceremony was completed he was not available. So the kachinas demanded some proof. They were very persistent, so after much drama and emotion the bride was brought out to show that there really was a marriage ceremony going on. The bride turned out to be the old grandmother, who was dressed in the full paraphernalia of a bride. Then bride and groom appealed as a pair to the kachinas that this was indeed an important ceremony. Obviously when there is a marriage, the relations on both sides are very interested in the preservation of the union. So all the relatives intervened, and

Hopi women's dance, Oraibi, Arizona, 1879
(National Archives)

soon they outnumbered the kachinas, and thus the child was saved. The child not only learned the importance of good behavior, but this drama also strengthened his security by showing him that there are people who do come to his aid.

This is just an attempt to point out the various ways the child is brought up to feel and know security. Security comes from knowing one's place within the prevailing kinship relationship; within the community. But it also involves learning the cultural norms or the community ethic.

Then comes a time when the child has demonstrated a certain degree of responsibility and understanding, when he or she shows the ability to comprehend a little more of the spiritual world. At this time they are ready to be initiated into the kachina ceremony. This ceremony is quite elaborate and is intended to expose the young person[1] to what the kachina is in fact and in spirit, attempting to help him discern the difference between the spirit and the fact. He learns that he has become eligible to participate in the kachina dance like his father, his brothers, his uncles, whom he has held in high regard. Now he is going to participate as one of them. He learns to identify with the adult world in this fashion. Because this is done in such a dramatic way he has a good foundation. When it is revealed to him that the kachina is just an impersonation, an impersonation which possesses a spiritual essence, the child's security is not destroyed. Instead the experience strengthens the individual in another phase of his life in the community.

Since the kachina has been so prominent in the child's life, most of the child's fantasies involve the kachina. Before his initiation most of his fantasies have consisted in emulating the kachina. Children go around the corner of the house; they enact their feelings about the kachina, they dance and sing like the kachina. At this early age they begin to feel the sense of projection into this spiritual reality. When the child is initiated and becomes eligible to participate as a kachina, it is not difficult to fantasize now as a participant in the real kachina ceremony, and that is the essence of the kachina ceremony. The fantasizing continues, then, in spite of the initiation which seems to have the effect of revealing to the child that this is just a plaything, that now we are grown up and we don't believe. This idea of make-believe continues with the Hopi man and woman as they mature, and as far as I am concerned it must continue throughout life. For the kachina ceremonies require that a person project oneself into the spirit world, into the world of fantasy, or the world of make-believe. Unless one can do this, spiritual experience cannot be achieved.

Zuni

"Nowhere in the New World," Ruth L. Bunzel declared, "except in the ancient civilizations of Mexico and Yucatan, has ceremonialism been more highly developed" than among the Zuni. Much of that ceremony orients itself toward the sun, which is understood as the source of all life. The first rite of passage is appropriately one which surrounds the child's entry into the world.

---

1. While I describe this initiation from my own experience as a young boy, both girls and boys participate in this ceremony.

[Source: *Forty-Seventh Annual Report of the Bureau of American Ethnology, 1929-1930* (Washington: Government Printing Office, 1932), pp. 635-36; quotations above are from p. 480 and p. 511.]

Presenting an Infant to the Sun

On the eighth day of life an infant's head is washed by his "aunts" — that is, women of his father's clan, his most important ceremonial relatives. Corn meal is placed in his hand and he is taken outdoors, facing the east, at the moment of sunrise. Corn meal is sprinkled to the rising sun with the following prayer, spoken by the paternal grandmother.

> Now this is the day.
> Our child,
> Into the daylight
> You will go out standing.
> Preparing for your day,
> We have passed our days,
> When all your days were at an end,
> When eight days were past,
> Our sun father
> Went in to sit down at his sacred place.
> And our night fathers
> Having come out standing to their sacred place,
> Passing a blessed night
> We came to day.
> Now this day
> Our father,
> Dawn priests,
> Have come out standing to their sacred place.
> Our sun father
> Having come out standing to his sacred place,
> Our child,
> It is your day.
> This day,
> The flesh of white corn,
> Prayer meal,
> To our sun father
> This prayer meal we offer.
> May your road be fulfilled
> Reaching to the road of your sun father,
> When your road is fulfilled
> In your thoughts (may we live).
> May we be the ones whom your thoughts will embrace,
> For this, on this day
> To our sun father.

We offer prayer meal.
To this end:
May you help us all to finish our roads.

Chinook

*Toward the end of the nineteenth century, the well-known anthropologist
Franz Boas gathered tribal traditions and texts (oral) from one of the few remaining Chinooks. Two ceremonies are presented from this once powerful
tribe of the Northwest: (1) the first is related to puberty, and (2) the second to
childbirth (this latter now being seen from the perspective not of the infant's
welfare but that of the parents). The difficult transition from childhood to
adulthood and from the status of a married adult to that of a parent — these
too called for the assistance of religion, for the rites of passage.*

1.

When a chief's daughter is menstruating for the first time, she is hidden [from
the view of the people]. Only an [old] woman takes care of her. Cedar bark is
tied to her arms [above the elbows and at the wrists], to her legs, and around her
waist. She fasts sometimes five days, sometimes ten days, or four or six days. Now
the people are invited and a potlatch is made for the girl. She remains hidden five
days. Now she is taken out [of her hiding place] and the cedar bark which is tied
around her [arms, legs, and waist] is taken off. Then strings of dentaha are tied
around her arms and legs, and a buckskin strap is tied around her waist. This remains tied around her for one hundred days, then it is taken off. Now an old
woman washes her face. Another old woman paints her; still another one combs
her. When this is finished the people are paid for dancing for her. Now these old
women are paid and the girl is hidden again. She has a separate door. She bathes
in a creek far [from the village]. For fifty days she does not eat fresh food. When
she is menstruant for the second time her father gives another potlatch. She
must not warm herself. She must never look at the people. She must not look at
the sky, she must not pick berries. It is forbidden. When she looks at the sky it
becomes bad weather. When she picks berries it will rain. She hangs up her
[towel of] cedar bark on [a certain] spruce tree. The tree dries up at once. After
one hundred days she may eat fresh food, she may pick berries and warm herself.

[Source: *Chinook Texts*, Bulletin No. 20, Bureau of Ethnology (Washington: Government
Printing Office, 1894), pp. 246-47; p. 241.]

If the people move from one place to another, she is carried into the canoe. She must not paddle and is carried on the back into the canoe. She must not step into salt water. When it is night she must go to bathe. She must rise earlier than the birds. If the birds should rise first she will not live long. If she does everything in the right way she will get old before she dies.

2.

When a woman is with child she does not sleep long. She awakes early in the morning and arises at once. She opens the door. She does not stay in the doorway, but goes out at once. When a woman who is with child sits down, nobody must stand back of her and nobody must lie down crosswise [at her feet]. It is the same at night [when she lies down]. When a person lies down near her, his head must point in the same direction as her feet are turned. When she comes to a creek she jumps across twice. She does not lie down outside the house, else the sun would make her sick. It is forbidden. She does not wear a necklace, else the navel-string would be wound around the child's neck. She does not wear bracelets, else the navel-string would be tied around the child's arm. She does not look at a corpse. She does not look at anything that is dead. It is forbidden. She does not look at a raccoon nor at an otter. She does not look at anything that is rotten. She does not blow up a [seal] bladder. She does not eat anything that has been found. It is forbidden. She does not eat trout nor steel-head salmon. It is forbidden. Her husband does not eat anything that has been found. He does not kill raccoons. He does not singe seals. He does not shoot birds. He does not look at a corpse. He does not kill otters, else the child would get sick by sympathy. It is the same with the raccoon. When the child should fall sick and nearly die it would have a hard struggle against death, like the otter. It is the same with a bird or a raccoon. It would obtain sickness by sympathy.

Kwakiutl

Of all the "passages," death is the most threatening to those left behind. For it seems to represent the victory of evil's powerful force, the unleashing of elements inimical to the family and the community. The recently dead, moreover, may need to be sacrificed to or even threatened in order that they not return to haunt or otherwise harm those that remain. The Kwakiutl cere-

[Source: *Thirty-Fifth Annual Report of the Bureau of American Ethnology, 1913-1914*, part 1 (Washington: Government Printing Office, 1921), pp. 705-9.]

mony is designed first of all to forestall death; when that fails, however, the effort is then intended to insulate death, to control or limit the damage which it may do.

When a beloved child is dying, the parents keep on praying to the spirit not to try to take away their child. "I will pay you with these clothes of this my child, Sitting-on-Fire." Thus they say, while they put on the fire the clothes of the one who is lying there sick.

Then the parents of the one who is lying there sick pay Sitting-on-Fire, that he may pray to the souls of the grandparents of the one who lies sick, that they may not wish to call their grandson. And the parents of the one who lies there sick take four kinds of food, dry salmon first. They break it into four pieces. When it is ready, they take cinquefoil-roots and fold them up in four pieces. And when that is ready, they take dried berry-cakes and break them into four pieces. And when that is ready, they take viburnum-berries, four spoonfuls. When all this is ready, the father of the one who is lying sick in bed takes the dry salmon and throws the pieces into the fire, one by one. And the mother of the one who lies sick in bed says, "O Sitting-on-Fire! now eat, and protect my child, Sitting-on-Fire!"

Then the father of the one who lies sick in bed takes also cinquefoil roots; he takes one (root) and dips it into the oil. And the mother of the one who lies

Arapaho ghost dance, western plains, c. 1900
(National Archives)

sick in bed says again, "O Sitting-on-Fire! go on, and pray to the spirits, that they may have mercy on my child!" Thus she says.

Then the father takes also one of the dried berry-cakes, dips it into oil, and throws it into the fire. Then he himself says, "O Sitting-on-Fire! now do have mercy on me, and keep alive my child here, Sitting-on-Fire! Have mercy and press back my child here, spirit, and I will take care of this, supernatural one, that I may still have for a while my son here! Long-Life-Maker!"

And when he has put all the berry-cakes on the fire of the house, then he takes one of the spoonfuls of viburnum-berries, and three times he aims at the fire of the house. The fourth time he pours them on the fire; and he says, "Take this, Sitting-on-Fire! and pray to the spirits of those behind us that they have mercy on me and my wife here! Pray to the Long-Life-Maker that he may come and take away the sickness of my child here! Take pity on me, and ask the supernatural one to come! Wa!" Thus says the father to Sitting-on-Fire. Then that is finished. . . .

In the morning, when day comes, the hearts of the parents of the one who lies sick abed feel bad, for they know that their child will die. Then the one who is lying sick abed is growing weak very fast. His parents now take all the best kinds of food and the best clothing for the one who is sick abed, who is dying.

As soon as (the breath) of the one lying sick abed breaks, the parents take the best clothing and put it on the one who had been sick abed. After the parents have done so, the mother kicks her dead child four times. And when she first kicks him, she says, "Don't turn your head back to me." Then she turns around, and again she kicks him. And as she kicks him, she says, "Don't come back again." Then she turns around again. She kicks him; and she says as she kicks him, "Just go straight ahead." And then she kicks him again; and says, "Only protect me and your father from sickness." Thus she says, and she leaves him.

Myths (things believed)

Tsimshian

All documents reproduced under the heading of "myth" relate to the universally asked question, "Where did the world come from?" These cosmogonic myths personify the forces of creation, thereby bringing them within reach of

[Source: *Thirty-First Annual Report of the Bureau of American Ethnology, 1909-1910* (Washington: Government Printing Office, 1916), pp. 113-16.]

*human comprehension and thereby usually making them a focus of religious
ceremony no less than of religious philosophy.*

It was in the beginning, before anything that lives in our world was created.
There was only the chief in heaven. There was no light in heaven. There were
only emptiness and darkness.

The chief had two sons and one daughter. His people were numerous. Indeed, they were the tribe of the chief.

These were the names of his three children. The name of the eldest one
was Walking About Early; the name of the second, The One Who Walks All
Over The Sky. The name of the girl was Support Of Sun. They were very strong.
The younger boy was wiser and abler than the elder one. Therefore one day he
was sad, and he pondered why darkness was continuing all the time. Therefore
one day he spoke to his sister, "Let us go and get pitch wood!" They went and
they cut very good pitch wood. They made a ring of a slender cedar twig, and
measured it according to the size of a face. Then they tied pitch wood all round
it, so that it looked like a mask. After they had finished, they told their sister,
who was accompanying them while they were getting pitch wood, not to tell the
people about what they were doing. Then The One Who Walks All Over The
Sky went to where the Sun rises and showed himself to the people. The pitch
wood that was tied around his face was burning.

Suddenly the people saw the great light rising in the east. They were glad
when they saw the light. Then he ran in full sight across the sky. He came from
the east and went westward. He was carrying the pitch mask. That is the reason
why he was running quickly, because else the pitch wood would have been
burned up. Therefore he was running quickly across the sky. Then the chief's
tribe assembled. They sat down together to hold a council, and said, "We are
glad because your child has given us light, but he is running too quickly. He
ought to go a little more slowly, so that we may enjoy the light for a longer
time." Therefore the chief told his son what the people had said. His son replied,
asking him what he should do, since the pitch wood would burn before he
could reach the west. Therefore he went that way every day.

The people assembled again and held a council, and requested him to go
slowly along the sky. That is what they asked of him; and therefore his sister
said, "I will hold him when he is running along the sky."

Then the people blessed the woman, and the father also blessed his
daughter. Next time when The One Who Walks All Over The Sky started on his
journey, Support Of Sun started too. She went southward. Her brother rose in
the east, and then the girl turned back and ran to meet her brother.

The woman said, "Wait for me until I catch up with you!" She ran as fast
as she could, and held her brother in the middle of the sky. For this reason the
Sun stops for a little while in the middle of the sky.

Mogollon Bowl. The figures represent the contrast between male and female, night and day, darkness and light, death and life.
(Werner Forman, Art Resource, NY)

The woman stood firm, holding her brother. Therefore we see the Sun stopping for a little while in the middle of the sky. . . .

When The One Who Walks All Over The Sky was asleep, sparks flew out of his mouth. Those are the stars; and at night the moon receives its light from the shining face of the Sun, who is asleep when he is tired and when his light shoots out of the smoke hole.

Sometimes when the Sun is glad he adorns himself. He takes his sister's red ocher to paint his face. Then the people know what kind of weather it is going to be on the following day. When the people see the red sky in the evening, they know that it will be good weather the following day; and when they see the red sky in the morning, they know that the weather is going to be bad the whole day. That is what the people say.

Pima

In the Pima account below, the "thing believed" is itself in the form of a "thing done." In this instance, however, the ceremony occurred not on earth, but before "all that we see" came into being.

In the beginning there was nothing where now are earth, sun, moon, stars, and all that we see. Ages long the darkness was gathering, until it formed a great mass in which developed the spirit of Earth Doctor, who, like the fluffy wisp of cotton that floats upon the wind, drifted to and fro without support or place to fix himself. Conscious of his power, he determined to try to build an abiding place, so he took from his breast a little dust and flattened it into a cake. Then he thought within himself, "Come forth, some kind of plant," and there appeared the creosote bush. Placing this in front of him, he saw it turn over as soon as his grasp upon it relaxed. Advancing toward it, he again set it upright, and again it fell. A third and yet a fourth time he placed it, and then it remained standing. When the flat dust cake was still he danced upon it, singing:

> Earth Magician shapes this world.
>> Behold what he can do!
> Round and smooth he molds it.
>> Behold what he can do!

> Earth Magician makes the mountains.
>> Heed what he has to say!
> He it is that makes the mesas.
>> Heed what he has to say.

> Earth Magician shapes this world;
>> Earth Magician makes its mountains;
> Makes all larger, larger, larger.
>> Into the earth the magician glances;
> Into its mountains he may see.

[Source: *Twenty-Sixth Annual Report of the Bureau of American Ethnology, 1904-1905* (Washington: Government Printing Office, 1908), pp. 206-7.]

Cherokee

In a free translation provided by James Mooney, the Cherokee story (possibly influenced by biblical accounts introduced via Christian missionaries) describes in great detail not the heavenly bodies but life on earth — and under the earth.

The earth is a great island floating in a sea of water, and suspended at each of the four cardinal points by a cord hanging down from the sky vault, which is of solid rock. When the world grows old and worn out, the people will die and the cords will break and let the earth sink down into the ocean, and all will be water again. The Indians are afraid of this.

When all was water, the animals were above . . . beyond the arch; but it was very much crowded, and they were wanting more room. They wondered what was below the water, and at last . . . "Beaver's Grandchild," the little Water-beetle, offered to go and see if it could learn. It darted in every direction over the surface of the water, but could find no firm place to rest. Then it dived to the bottom and came up with some soft mud, which began to grow and spread on every side until it became the island which we call the earth. It was afterward fastened to the sky with four cords, but no one remembers who did this.

At first the earth was flat and very soft and wet. The animals were anxious to get down, and sent out different birds to see if it was yet dry, but they found no place to alight and came back again to [the world above]. At last it seemed to be time, and they sent out the Buzzard and told him to go and make ready for them. This was the Great Buzzard, the father of all the buzzards we see now. He flew all over the earth, low down near the ground, and it was still soft. When he reached the Cherokee country, he was very tired, and his wings began to flap and strike the ground, and wherever they struck the earth there was a valley, and where they turned up again there was a mountain. When the animals above saw this, they were afraid that the whole world would be mountains, so they called him back, but the Cherokee country remains full of mountains to this day.

When the earth was dry and the animals came down, it was still dark, so they got the sun and set it in a track to go every day across the island from east to west, just overhead. It was too hot this way, and . . . the Red Crawfish had his shell scorched a bright red, so that his meat was spoiled; and the Cherokee do not eat it. The conjurers put the sun another hand-breadth higher in the air, but it was still too hot. They raised it another time, and another, until it was seven

[Source: *Nineteenth Annual Report of the Bureau of American Ethnology, 1897-1898* (Washington: Government Printing Office, 1900), pp. 239-40.]

hand-breadths high and just under the sky arch. Then it was right, and they left it so. . . .

There is another world under this, and it is like ours in everything — animals, plants, and people — save that the seasons are different. The streams that come down from the mountains are the trails by which we reach this underworld, and the springs at their heads are the doorways by which we enter it, but to do this one must fast and go to water and have one of the underground people for a guide. We know that the seasons in the underworld are different from ours, because the water in the springs is always warmer in winter and cooler in summer than the outer air.

When the animals and plants were first made — we do not know by whom — they were told to watch and keep awake for seven nights, just as young men now fast and keep awake when they pray to their medicine. They tried to do this, and nearly all were awake through the first night, but the next night several dropped off to sleep, and the third night others were asleep, and then others, until, on the seventh night, of all the animals only the owl, the panther, and one or two more were still awake. To these were given the power to see and to go about in the dark, and to make prey of the birds and animals which must sleep at night. Of the trees only the cedar, the pine, the spruce, the holly, and the laurel were awake to the end, and to them it was given to be always green and to be greatest for medicine, but to the others it was said: "Because you have not endured to the end you shall lose your hair every winter."

Men came after the animals and plants. At first there were only a brother and sister until he struck her with a fish and told her to multiply, and so it was. In seven days a child was born to her, and thereafter every seven days another, and they increased very fast until there was danger that the world could not keep them. Then it was made that a woman should have only one child in a year, and it has been so ever since.

Salmon carving. Many tribes in the Pacific Northwest regarded salmon as supernatural creatures willing to sacrifice themselves for the sake of humans.
(Werner Forman, Art Resource, NY)

Zuni

Among the Zuni, more than one explanation is offered for the origin of the world. Several brief set pieces can then be placed in ceremonial sequence, "yet all making a connected strand" (F. H. Cushing). The account that follows may also have accommodated itself to some degree to the teachings of the Spanish missionaries.

Before the beginning of the new making, Áwonawílona (the Maker and Container of All, the All-father Father), solely had being. There was nothing else whatsoever throughout the great space of the ages save everywhere black darkness in it, and everywhere void desolation.

In the beginning of the new-made, Áwonawílona conceived within himself and thought outward in space, whereby mists of increase, steams potent of growth, were evolved and uplifted. Thus, by means of his innate knowledge, the All-container made himself in person and form of the Sun whom we hold to be our father and who thus came to exist and appear. With his appearance came the brightening of the spaces with light, and with the brightening of the spaces the great mist-clouds were thickened together and fell, whereby was evolved water in water; yea, and the world-holding sea.

With his substance of flesh . . . outdrawn from the surface of his person, the Sun-father formed the seed-stuff of twain worlds, impregnating therewith the great waters, and lo! in the heat of his light these waters of the sea grew green and scums . . . rose upon them, waxing wide and weighty until, behold! they became . . . the "Four-fold Containing Mother-earth," and . . . the "All-covering Father-sky."

[Source: *Thirteenth Annual Report of the Bureau of American Ethnology, 1891-1892* (Washington: Government Printing Office, 1896), p. 379; quotation above is from p. 375.]

2. New Spain

Ponce de León (c. 1460-1521)

Since Ponce de León accompanied Columbus on his second voyage in 1493, his claim to chronological priority in the New World would be difficult to dispute. His even better known priority, however, is as discoverer of Florida on Easter Sunday (in Spanish, Pascua Florida*) in 1513. The following year King Ferdinand appointed him* adelantado *(governor) of that newly discovered land. In Ferdinand's instructions to his governor, the references to the Indian merit special attention.*

The agreement that was made by Our command with you, Juan Ponce de Leon, for the expedition to colonize the island of Beniny and the island of Florida which you discovered by Our command, in addition to the articles and agreement that were made with you when you took action for discovery, is as follows:

First, whereas, in the said articles and agreement made with you by Our command, concerning the discovering and colonizing of the said islands, I gave license and authority, for the time and limitation of three years to commence from the day of delivery to you of the said articles, to conduct at your cost and charge the vessels that you might wish, provided that you stood obligated to begin the expedition of discovery within the first year; and because until now you have occupied yourself in matters of Our service and you have not had time to start the voyage of discovery, it is My will and pleasure that the said three years may commence to run and be reckoned from the day you may embark on your voyage to the said islands.

Item, that as soon as you embark [sic] at the said islands you may sum-

---

[Source: D. B. Quinn, ed., *New American World* (New York: Arno Press and Hector Bye, 1979), I, 238-39.]

mon the chiefs and Indians thereof, by the best device or devices there can be given them, to understand what should be said to them, conformably to a summons that has been drawn up by several learned men . . . by all the ways and means you may be able to devise, that they should come into the knowledge of Our Catholic Faith and should obey and serve as they are bound to do; and you will take down in signed form before two or three notaries, if such there be, and before as many witnesses and these the most creditable, as may be found there, in order that it may serve for Our justification, and you will send the said document; and the summons must be made once, twice, thrice.

And if after the aforesaid they do not wish to obey what is contained in the said summons, you can make war and seize them and carry them away for slaves; but if they do obey, give them the best treatment you can and endeavor, as is stated, by all the means at your disposal, to convert them to Our Holy Catholic Faith; and if by chance, after having once obeyed the said summons, they again rebel, I command that you again make the said summons before making war or doing harm or damage.

Bartholomew de Las Casas (1474-1566) and *Sublimis Deus,* 1537

The Dominican Las Casas, first priest to be ordained in the New World (1510), labored chiefly in the Caribbean and South America. He journeyed to Spain to protest the dehumanizing and enslaving of the Indians — even more the senseless torture and murder. "In Gods name, consider," he wrote, "what sort of deeds are these, and whether they do not surpass every imaginable cruelty and injustice, and whether it squares well with such Christians as these to call them devils; and whether it could be worse to give the Indians into the charge of the devils of hell than to the Christians of the Indies" (F. A. MacNutt, p. 409). Partly in response to such urgent pleas, Pope Paul III (pontificate, 1534-49) issued the bull excerpted below in 1537. Sublimis Deus tried to halt a senseless brutality that was by no means Spain's alone.

We . . . consider, however, that the Indians are truly men and that they are not only capable of understanding the catholic faith but, according to our information, they desire exceedingly to receive it. Desiring to provide ample remedy for these evils, we define and declare by these our letters, or by any translation thereof signed by any notary public and sealed with the seal of any ecclesiastical

---

[Source: F. A. MacNutt, *Bartholomew de Las Casas* . . . (New York: G. P. Putnam's Sons, 1909), p. 429.]

dignitary, to which the same credit shall be given as to the originals, that, not-withstanding whatever may have been or may be said to the contrary, the said Indians and all other people who may later be discovered by Christians, are by no means to be deprived of their liberty or the possession of their property, even though they be outside the faith of Jesus Christ; and that they may and should, freely and legitimately, enjoy their liberty and the possession of their property; nor should they be in any way enslaved; should the contrary happen, it shall be null and of no effect.

Dominicans in Florida

Converting the natives required careful preparation, especially if the Indians had already experienced brutality at the hands of other Europeans. Influenced by Las Casas, Friar Luis Cáncer and other Dominicans landed in Florida in 1549 — unfortunately without having made careful preparation. Debarking at Tampa Bay, Cáncer was slain almost immediately, this in full view of those still aboard the ship on which he had come. One of his associates who escaped left this account of North America's early martyr.

When I saw the Indians I sent ashore the interpreter, who was an Indian girl we had brought from Havana and came from those parts, and the good man Fuentes went with her. The Pilot would not let me go, but I was sure that with the interpreter and giving them something they would do no harm to the monk, so I lifted up my habit without telling the Pilot and plunged into the sea waist-deep, and the Lord knows the speed at which I went to stop them dealing with the monk before they heard the reason for our voyage. When I reached the shore I fell to my knees and begged for God's grace and help, then I went up to the flat bit where I found them all together; before I reached them I did again what I had done on the beach, and then got up and began to take out from my sleeve some things from Flanders, which may not seem very important or valu-able to Christians, but which they regarded as valuable and great gifts.

Then they came to me, and I gave them part of what I was carrying, then I went to the monk, who came to me, and I embraced him with great pleasure, and we both knelt down, with Fuentes and the Indian girl, took out the book and recited the litanies, commending ourselves to the Lord and His Saints. The Indians knelt, some of them squatting, which pleased me very much, and once they had got up I left the litanies in the middle and sat down with them on a log

---

[Source: D. B. Quinn, ed., *New American World* (New York: Arno Press and Hector Bye, 1979), II, 192, 194.]

and soon found out where the port and the bay we were looking for were, about a day and a half's journey by land from where we were; we told them of our aims and wishes.

When the Indian girl saw it was all so peaceful she was very pleased and said to me "Father, didn't I tell you that if I spoke to them they would not kill you? These people are from my land and this one speaks my language." Our Lord knows how pleased we were to see them as peaceful as they were being then; I was getting covered in their red dye from all the embracing that was going on, although I managed to get the worst of it on my habit to leave the skin untouched. To see if I was free to do so, if they would let me go to the launch, I was careful to tell them that I had more to give them and I was going back to get it, although in fact I had it already in my sleeve, but I had not wanted to give them all of it since I had intended to do this: I went, and came back, and found so many who wanted to embrace me that I could not get away from them. This friendship and affection was obviously based on what they thought they could get from us than on ourselves, but since this world is the route to the other, and as we all know from experience and say that love is good deeds and that gifts can break rocks, I was pleased that they should receive us so well for these material matters: the spiritual and true would come bit by bit, like the fear of being bad is considered a good thing because afterwards there enters the true and good. . . .

When we arrived at the ship, thinking we were carrying great news, we found others waiting both much better and much worse: they told us that there had come there one of the Spaniards that Soto had taken, who had fled from his master in a canoe. I was very pleased with such good news, and it would have been a great help to our purpose if he had not added other sadder and more terrible information, saying that the Indians who had taken the monk and his companion had killed them as soon as I left them, and that they were holding the seaman alive. When he was asked how he had found this out, he said "I have often heard it from other Indians who saw them being killed, and I also saw the skin from the head of the monk, which an Indian showed me who was taking it about as an exhibit, and he said that they were doing and saying many things when they killed them." All this is a most terrible thing and very distressing for us all, but even so it could be endured, and is the kind of event involved in these affairs of the faith, and I always used to think, whenever I considered the importance of this matter, that, as it was with the Apostles, it would be with our own blood that we would plant and establish the law and the faith of the one who even to give it and preach it to us suffered and died; and since this is the way it is, and is only to be expected in the preaching of so great a law, there is no reason to despair of future success because of something like this happening.

Pedro Menéndez de Avilés and the Jesuits

Governor of Florida from 1565 to 1574, Menéndez in 1565 moved against the French Protestants (Huguenots) who had established a small base at the mouth of the St. John River in northeastern Florida. Spain regarded all Florida — if not all North and South America — as her papally bestowed domain; thus the French, whether Protestant or Catholic, must go. When Menéndez drove the Huguenots out, he established a fortification which he called St. Augustine, though this oldest settlement of North America never developed as Florida's sixteenth-century governor envisioned. The following year, 1566, concerned about the meagre missionary activity in Florida, Menéndez wrote a letter to a Jesuit, urging that Jesuits of high character and firm dedication be sent to undertake the conversion of the Indians to Christianity.

On one hand I was delighted to see how well Our Lord the King helped us, and on the other I felt upset and thwarted to see that nobody of the Company was coming, nor even a learned man of religion; for in view of the many chiefs we have as friends, and the good understanding and sense of the natives of these provinces, and the great desire they have to be Christians and know the Law of Jesus Christ, six such men of religion will do more in a month than many thousands of us laymen will achieve in many years: for we needed them to explain the doctrine to ourselves. It is just a waste of time in a place like this to think of establishing the Holy Gospels here with soldiers alone. Your Honour should be sure that, unless I am much mistaken, the Word of Our Lord will spread in these areas. For most of the ceremonies of these people involve worshipping the sun and the moon, and they use dead game animals as idols, and other animals too: and each year they have three or four festivals for their devotions, in which they worship the sun, and go for three days without eating, without drinking and without sleeping, which is their fasting. And those who are weak and cannot endure this are considered bad Indians, and are thus despised by the noble people; and the one who comes best through these hardships is considered the most valiant, and he is shown the greatest respect.

They are people of great strength, fast and good swimmers; they are often fighting among themselves, and no chief is known to be powerful among them. I have not wanted to undertake friendship with any chief for the sake of making war on his enemy, even if he is my enemy too, for I am telling them that Our Lord is in Heaven and He is Chief of all the chiefs of the earth and of all creation, and that he is angry with them for making war and killing each other like

[Source: D. B. Quinn, ed., *New American World* (New York: Arno Press and Hector Bye, 1979), II, 536-37.]

wild beasts. And thus some of them have let me make peace between them, and have taken down their idols, and have asked me to give them crosses to worship at: I have already given them them, and they worship them, and I have given them some boys and soldiers to teach them Christian Doctrine.

They ask me to make them Christian as we are, and I have told them that I am waiting for Your Honours, so you can make wordlists, and quickly learn their language, and then tell them how they are to be Christians, and enlighten them that if they are not they are serving and having as their Lord the most evil creature of the world, which is the devil, who is deceiving them, and that if they are Christian, they will be enlightened and serve Our Lord, who is Chief of Heaven and earth; and then, being happy and content, they will be our true brothers, and we will give them whatever we may have.

And as I had told them that in this help that was coming were coming these men of religion, who would soon talk to them and teach them to be Christians, and then they did not come, they took me for a liar, and some of them have taken umbrage, saying I was having them on, and the chiefs who are my enemies are laughing at them and at me.

It has done a great deal of damage that there have not come any of Your Honours nor other learned men of religion to explain the doctrine to these people, for as they are highly treacherous and unreliable, if with time and firm foundations the peace I have made with them is not strengthened, to open the door to the Holy Gospels being preached, and to what the men of Religion have to say making sure of the chiefs, then we will be too late and achieve nothing, if they think we are deceiving them. May Our Lord encourage that good Company of Jesus to send to these parts up to six Companions, and may they be such, because they will be bound to achieve very much.

Franciscans and Indian Revolt

Franciscan missionaries had achieved some success among the Indians on St. Catherine Island (off Georgia's coast, south of the Savannah River) when in 1597 the natives rebelled against the disruption of their ancestral ways. The document below exposes the wide cultural chasm between Indian customs and European/Christian ones. The Island Indians seemed ready enough to become Christians until they learned that the new religion was not simply in addition to the old but was intended totally to replace the old. The year following the revolt saw Indian rebellion harshly suppressed.

[Source: D. B. Quinn, ed., *New American World* (New York: Arno Press and Hector Bye, 1979), V, 69-70.]

The friars of San Francisco busied themselves for two years in preaching to the Indians of Florida, separated into various provinces. In the town of Tolemaro or Tolemato lived the friar Pedro de Corpa, a notable preacher, and deputy of that doctrina, against whom rose the elder son and heir of the chief of the island of Guale, who was exceedingly vexed at the reproaches which Father Corpa made to him, because although a Christian, he lived worse than a Gentile, and he fled from the town because he was not able to endure them. He returned to it within a few days, at the end of September [1597], bringing many Indian warriors, with bows and arrows, their heads ornamented with great plumes, and entering in the night, in profound silence, they went to the house where the father lived; they broke down the feeble doors, found him on his knees, and killed him with an axe. This unheard-of atrocity was proclaimed in the town; and although some showed signs of regret, most, who were as little disturbed, apparently, as the son of the chief, joined him, and he said to them the day following: "Although the friar is dead he would not have been if he had not prevented us from living as before we were Christians: let us return to our ancient customs, and let us prepare to defend ourselves against the punishment which the governor of Florida will attempt to inflict upon us, and if this happens it will be as rigorous [on account of] this friar alone as if we had finished all; because he will pursue us in the same manner on account of the friar whom we have killed as for all."

Those who followed him in the newly executed deed approved; and they said that it could not be doubted that he would want to take vengeance for one as he would take it for all. Then the barbarian continued: "Since the punishment on account of one is not going to be greater than for all, let us restore the liberty of which these friars have robbed us, with promises of benefits which we have not seen, in hope of which they wish that those of us who call ourselves Christians experience at once the losses and discomforts: they take from us women, leaving us only one and that in perpetuity, prohibiting us from changing her: they obstruct our dances, banquets, feasts, celebrations, fires, and wars, so that by failing to use them we lose the ancient valor and dexterity inherited from our ancestors: they persecute our old people calling them witches; even our labor disturbs them, since they want to command us to avoid it on some days, and be prepared to execute all that they say, although they are not satisfied; they always reprimand us, injure us, oppress us, preach to us, call us bad Christians, and deprive us of all happiness, which our ancestors enjoyed, with the hope that they will give us heaven. These are deceptions in order to subject us, in holding us disposed after their manner; already what can we expect, except to be slaves. If now we kill all of them, we will remove such a heavy yoke immediately, and our valor will make the governor treat us well, if it happens that he does not come out badly." The multitude was convinced by his speech; and as a sign of their victory, they cut off Father Corpa's head, and they put it in the port on a lance, as a trophy of their victory, and the body they threw into a forest, where it was never found.

Franciscans in New Mexico

A thousand miles north of Mexico City, the imperial arm of Spain reached into what is now known as New Mexico. Beginning in 1595, Don Juan de Oñate as governor and colonizer led the advance. By 1610 the city of Santa Fe stood as a permanent Spanish outpost; there, a couple of generations later (1680) the Indians revolted, just as they had on St. Catherine Island. Seeds of that revolt had been planted long before, however, as the following account of a Franciscan friar makes clear. Writing to the Viceroy in 1601, Brother Juan de Escalona severely criticizes Oñate in particular, Spanish cruelty and exploitation in general. Having earlier observed, he now condemns "the great outrages against the Indians" committed "without rhyme or reason."

Would that I could have spoken to your lordship in person and have given you more directly the information that now I must of necessity put down in writing, lest I be an unfaithful servant of the Lord. I cannot help the situation as much in this way as by a personal conference and I would have preferred that someone else should make this report. As prelate and protector, however, sent to this land to prevent evil and to seek what is good for God's children, I must inform your lordship of what is and has been transpiring here, for although reports and communications have been sent from here about matters in this land, they do not tell the actual truth about what has been going on since the arrival of Governor Don Juan de Oñate in this province. I shall tell about these matters, not because I wish to meddle in the affairs of others, but because, as prelate, I am under obligation, by informing his majesty and your lordship, to seek a remedy for the difficulties and obstacles that prevent the preaching of the gospel and the conversion of these souls.

The first and foremost difficulty, from which have sprung all the evils and the ruin of this land, is the fact that this conquest was entrusted to a man of such limited resources as Don Juan de Oñate. The result was that soon after he entered the land, his people began to perpetrate many offenses against the natives and to plunder their pueblos of the corn they had gathered for their own sustenance; here corn is God, for they have nothing else with which to support themselves. Because of this situation and because the Spaniards asked the na-

[Source: G. P. Hammond and Agapito Rey, *Don Juan de Oñate, Colonizer of New Mexico, 1595-1628* (Albuquerque: University of New Mexico Press, 1953), Part II, pp. 692-95.]

tives for blankets as tribute, even before teaching them the meaning of God, the Indians began to get restless, abandon their pueblos, and take to the mountains.

The governor did not want to sow a community plot to feed his people, although we friars urged him to do so, and the Indians agreed to it so that they would not be deprived of their food. This effort was all of no avail, and now the Indians have to provide everything. As a result, all the corn they had saved for years past has been consumed, and not a kernel is left over for them. The whole land has thus been reduced to such need that the Indians drop dead from starvation wherever they live; and they eat dirt and charcoal ground up with some seeds and a little corn in order to sustain life. Any Spaniard who gets his fill of tortillas here feels as if he has obtained a grant of nobility. Your lordship must not believe that the Indians part willingly with their corn, or the blankets with which they cover themselves; on the contrary, this extortion is done by threats and force of arms, the soldiers burning some of the houses and killing the Indians. This was the cause of the Acoma war,[2] as I have clearly established after questioning friars, captains, and soldiers. And the war which was recently waged against the Jumanas started the same way. In these conflicts, more than eight hundred men, women, and children were killed, and three pueblos burned. Their supplies of food were also burned, and this at a time when there was such great need. . . .

In addition to the aforesaid, all of the provisions which the governor and his men took along on this new expedition they took from the Indians. I was to have gone on this journey, but on observing the great outrages against the Indians and the wars waged against them without rhyme or reason, I did not dare to accompany the governor; instead I sent two friars to go with him. This expedition would have been impossible if the Indians had not furnished him with the provisions and supplies needed, and if I, in the name of his majesty, had not provided him with sixty mules, six carts, and two negroes that your lordship had given us to come to this land. My reason for giving this assistance, even though your lordship had ordered just the opposite, was that the said exploration could not have been undertaken without it, nor could the gospel have been preached to these people; and this was important, especially when we were already at the borders of their lands and the church and his majesty had sent us for this purpose. Furthermore, if this expedition had not been made, all the soldiers would have run away, for all are here against their will, owing to the great privations they endure. To protect his majesty's interests, the governor assumed responsibility for the damages caused by his people and gave me three honor-

2. The pueblo of Acoma (in central New Mexico) responded to the military's demands by killing a dozen or more Spanish soldiers in November, 1598. Two months later Oñate punished the village harshly, cutting off one foot of each man over twenty-five years of age and sentencing him to twenty years of servitude.

able men with property in New Spain as guarantors. The soldiers and captains provided the rest of the arms and horses, as he had nothing of his own. For lack of these he left here some servants whom he could not take along.

I have told all this to make it clear that the governor does not have the resources to carry out the discovery of these lands. I do not hesitate to say that even if he were to stay here for twenty thousand years, he could never discover what there is to be discovered in this land, unless his majesty should aid him or take over the whole project. Moreover, the governor has oppressed his people so that they are all discontented and anxious to get away, both on account of the sterility of the land and of his harsh conduct toward them. I do not hesitate to say that his majesty could have discovered this land with fifty well-armed Christian men, giving them the necessary things for this purpose, and that what these fifty men might discover could be placed under the royal crown and the conquest effected in a Christian manner without outraging or killing these poor Indians, who think that we are all evil and that the king who sent us here is ineffective and a tyrant. By so doing we would satisfy the wishes of our mother church, which, not without long consideration and forethought and illuminated by the Holy Spirit, entrusted these conquests and the conversions of souls to the kings of Castile, our lords, acknowledging in them the means, Christianity, and holiness for an undertaking as heroic as is that of winning souls for God.

Because of these matters (and others that I am not telling), we cannot preach the gospel now, for it is despised by these people on account of our great offenses and the harm we have done them. At the same time it is not desirable to abandon this land, either for the service of God or the conscience of his majesty since many souls have already been baptized. Besides, this place where we are now established is a good stepping stone and site from which to explore this whole land.

3. New France

French Views of Native Americans

In 1611 Father Pierre Baird, S.J., reported to his Superior at a time when France had barely gained a foothold in the North American continent. Nor had the French missionary spirit yet made any significant advance. Concerning the conversion of the Indian, Baird recognized the grandeur of the challenge but also "the difficulties which beset it." Reliance upon God and king, however, would make it possible for Jesuits to reach and redeem those savages "poor and wretched in the extreme."

And now you have had, my Reverend Father, an account of our voyage, of what happened in it, and before it, and since our arrival at this settlement. It now remains to tell you that the conversion of this country, to the Gospel, and of these people to civilization, is not a small undertaking nor free from great difficulties; for, in the first place, if we consider the country, it is only a forest, without other conveniences of life than those which will be brought from France, and what in time may be obtained from the soil after it has been cultivated. The nation is savage, wandering and full of bad habits; the people few and isolated. They are, I say, savage, haunting the woods, ignorant, lawless and rude: they are wanderers, with nothing to attach them to a place, neither homes nor relationship, neither possessions nor love of country; as a people they have bad habits, are extremely lazy, gluttonous, profane, treacherous, cruel in their revenge, and given up to all kinds of lewdness, men and women alike, the men having several wives and abandoning them to others, and the women only serving them as slaves, whom they strike and beat unmercifully,

---

[Source: D. B. Quinn, ed., *New American World* (New York: Arno Press and Hector Bye, 1979), IV, 392-94.]

and who dare not complain; and after being half killed, if it so please the murderer, they must laugh and caress him.

With all these vices, they are exceedingly vainglorious: they think they are better, more valiant and more ingenious than the French; and, what is difficult to believe, richer than we are. They consider themselves, I say, braver than we are, boasting that they have killed Basques and Malouins, and that they do a great deal of harm to the ships, and that no one has ever resented it, insinuating that it was from a lack of courage. They consider themselves better than the French; "For," they say, "you are always fighting and quarreling among yourselves; we live peaceably. You are envious and are all the time slandering each other; you are thieves and deceivers: you are covetous, and are neither generous nor kind; as for us, if we have a morsel of bread we share it with our neighbor."

They are saying these and like things continually, seeing the above-mentioned imperfections in some of us, and flattering themselves that some of their own people do not have them so conspicuously; not realizing that they all have much greater vices, and that the better part of our people do not have even these defects, they conclude generally that they are superior to all christians. It is self-love that blinds them, and the evil one who leads them on, no more nor less than in our France; we see those who have deviated from the faith holding themselves higher and boasting of being better than the catholics, because in some of them they see many faults; considering neither the virtues of the other catholics, nor their own still greater imperfections; wishing to have, like Cyclops, only a single eye, and to fix that one upon the vices of a few catholics, never upon the virtues of the others, nor upon themselves, unless it be for the purpose of self-deception.

Also they [the savages] consider themselves more ingenious, inasmuch as they see us admire some of their productions as the work of people so rude and ignorant; lacking intelligence, they bestow very little admiration upon what we show them, although much more worthy of being admired. Hence they regard themselves as much richer than we are, although they are poor and wretched in the extreme. . . .

All these things, added to the difficulty of acquiring the language, the time that must be consumed, the expenses that must be incurred, the great distress, toil and poverty that must be endured, fully proclaim the greatness of this enterprise and the difficulties which beset it. Yet many things encourage me to continue in it. . . .

In conclusion, we hope in time to make them susceptible of receiving the doctrines of the faith and of the christian and catholic religion, and later, to penetrate farther into the regions beyond, which they say are more populous and better cultivated. We base this hope upon Divine goodness and mercy, upon the zeal and fervent charity of all good people who earnestly desire the kingdom of God, particularly upon the holy prayers of Your Reverence and of our Reverend Fathers and very dear Brothers, to whom we most affectionately commend ourselves.

From Port Royal, New France, this tenth day of June, one thousand six hundred and eleven.

[Signed] PIERRE BAIRD

Advice to those "whom it shall please God to call to New France," 1636

A bright star in the Jesuit firmament, Jean de Brébeuf, S.J. (1593-1649), engaged in mission activity chiefly among the Hurons. He began his work there (the Lake bearing their name indicates the general location) in 1625, learning the Hurons' language and customs. He learned patience as well, for in two years he had not made a single convert. When France briefly fell before English power, Brébeuf returned to his native land. By 1633, however, he was back in New France and the next year back among the Hurons. In the document below, he would discourage any who might accept the vocation of the missionary under the dangerous illusion that it would be simple or easy. Not much romanticizing of wild men in a wild country survived this realist's sober advice.

Easy as may be a trip with the Savages, there is always enough to greatly cast down a heart not well under subjection. The readiness of the Savages does not shorten the road, does not smooth down the rocks, does not remove the dangers. Be with whom you like, you must expect to be, at least, three or four weeks on the way, to have as companions persons you have never seen before; to be cramped in a bark Canoe in an uncomfortable position, not being free to turn yourself to one side or the other; in danger fifty times a day of being upset or of being dashed upon the rocks. During the day, the Sun burns you; during the night, you run the risk of being a prey to Mosquitoes. You sometimes ascend five or six rapids in a day; and, in the evening, the only refreshment is a little corn crushed between two stones and cooked in fine clear water; the only bed is the earth, sometimes only the rough, uneven rocks, and usually no roof but the stars; and all this in perpetual silence. If you are accidentally hurt, if you fall sick, do not expect from these Barbarians any assistance, for whence could they obtain it? And if the sickness is dangerous, and if you are remote from the vil-

---

[Source: R. G. Thwaites, ed., *Jesuit Relations and Allied Documents* (Cleveland: Burrows Brothers, 1896-1901), X, 89, 91, 93, 97, 99.]

lages, which are here very scattered, I would not like to guarantee that they would not abandon you, if you could not make shift to follow them.

When you reach the Hurons, you will indeed find hearts full of charity; we will receive you with open arms as an Angel of Paradise, we shall have all the inclination in the world to do you good; but we are so situated that we can do very little. We shall receive you in a Hut, so mean that I have scarcely found in France one wretched enough to compare it with; that is how you will be lodged. Harassed and fatigued as you will be, we shall be able to give you nothing but a poor mat, or at most a skin, to serve as a bed; and, besides, you will arrive at a season when miserable little insects that we call here *Taouhac,* and, in good French, *pulces* [fleas], will keep you awake almost all night, for in these countries they are incomparably more troublesome than in France; the dust of the Cabin nourishes them, the Savages bring them to us, we get them in their houses; and this petty martyrdom, not to speak of Mosquitoes, Sandflies, and other like vermin, lasts usually not less than three or four months of the Summer.

Instead of being a great master and great Theologian as in France, you must reckon on being here a humble Scholar, and then, good God! with what masters! — women, little children, and all the Savages, — and exposed to their laughter. The Huron language will be your saint Thomas and your Aristotle; and clever man as you are, and speaking glibly among learned and capable persons, you must make up your mind to be for a long time mute among the Barbarians. You will have accomplished much, if, at the end of a considerable time, you begin to stammer a little.

And then how do you think you would pass the Winter with us? After having heard all that must be endured in wintering among the Montagnets Savages, I may say that that is almost the life we lead here among the Hurons. I say it without exaggeration, the five and six months of Winter are spent in almost continual discomforts, — excessive cold, smoke, and the annoyance of the Savages. . . .

"But is that all?" some one will exclaim. "Do you think by your arguments to throw water on the fire that consumes me, and lessen ever so little the zeal I have for the conversion of these Peoples? I declare that these things have served only to confirm me the more in my vocation; that I feel myself more carried away than ever by my affection for New France, and that I bear a holy jealousy towards those who are already enduring all these sufferings; all these labors seem to me nothing, in comparison with what I am willing to endure for God; if I knew a place under Heaven where there was yet more to be suffered, I would go there." Ah! whoever you are to whom God gives these sentiments and this light, come, come, my dear Brother, it is workmen such as you that we ask for here; it is to souls like yours that God has appointed the conquest of so many other souls whom the Devil holds yet in his power; apprehend no difficulties,

— there will be none for you, since it is your whole consolation to see yourself crucified with the Son of God.

Brébeuf's Instructions to Missionaries, 1637

If, despite Brébeuf's portrayal of mission life in its grosser reality, a few missionaries did actually appear, then this hardy Jesuit has specific instructions to give. With sensitivity as well as good sense, Jean de Brébeuf offered the kind of practical counsel that might well make the difference between a modest success and a dismal failure. Brébeuf's own missionary endeavor came to a tragic and brutal end when in 1649 he was tortured and finally put to death by the Iroquois of upstate New York. The Iroquois were longtime enemies of the more pacific Hurons and sometime enemies of the French.

You must have sincere affection for the Savages, — looking upon them as ransomed by the blood of the son of God, and as our brethren, with whom we are to pass the rest of our lives.

To conciliate the Savages, you must be careful never to make them wait for you in embarking.

You must provide yourself with a tinder box or with a burning mirror, or with both, to furnish them fire in the daytime to light their pipes, and in the evening when they have to encamp; these little services win their hearts.

You should try to eat their sagamité or salmagundi in the way they prepare it, although it may be dirty, half-cooked, and very tasteless. As to the other numerous things which may be unpleasant, they must be endured for the love of God, without saying anything or appearing to notice them.

It is well at first to take everything they offer, although you may not be able to eat it all; for, when one becomes somewhat accustomed to it, there is not too much.

You must try and eat at daybreak unless you can take your meal with you in the canoe; for the day is very long, if you have to pass it without eating. The Barbarians eat only at Sunrise and Sunset, when they are on their journeys.

You must be prompt in embarking and disembarking; and tuck up your gowns so that they will not get wet, and so that you will not carry either water or sand into the canoe. To be properly dressed, you must have your feet and legs bare; while crossing the rapids, you can wear your shoes, and, in the long portages, even your leggings.

[Source: R. G. Thwaites, ed., *Jesuit Relations and Allied Documents* (Cleveland: Burrows Brothers, 1896-1901), XII, 117, 119, 121.]

You must so conduct yourself as not to be at all troublesome to even one of these Barbarians.

It is not well to ask many questions, nor should you yield to your desire to learn the language and to make observations on the way; this may be carried too far. You must relieve those in your canoe of this annoyance, especially as you cannot profit much by it during the work. Silence is a good equipment at such a time. . . .

Be careful not to annoy any one in the canoe with your hat; it would be better to take your nightcap. There is no impropriety among the Savages.

Do not undertake anything unless you desire to continue it; for example, do not begin to paddle unless you are inclined to continue paddling. Take from the start the place in the canoe that you wish to keep; do not lend them your garments, unless you are willing to surrender them during the whole journey. It is easier to refuse at first than to ask them back, to change, or to desist afterwards.

Martyrdom of Isaac Jogues, S.J., 1646

Like Brébeuf, Jogues (1607-46) worked first among the Hurons. Accompanying a group of Hurons in 1642 back to Quebec, he and his party were ambushed by some Mohawks and carried off into captivity in upstate New York. After almost a year of deprivation and detention, he managed to escape into Fort Orange (Albany) where the Dutch Reformed minister (Johannes Megapolensis; see below, pp. 47-48) befriended him and ultimately helped to arrange his passage back to France. But in 1644, the persistent Jesuit returned to New France and to that vocation which he would not renounce. In serving as a peace envoy between Hurons and Mohawks, Jogues was again seized and tortured by the latter, eventually being put to death on October 18, 1646. The account excerpted below, written a year later by a younger colleague, incorporates Jogues's own description of his earlier suffering.

Eight days after our departure from the shores of the great river of saint Lawrence, we met two hundred Hiroquois, who were coming in pursuit of the French and of the Savages, our allies. At this encounter we were obliged to sustain a new shock. It is a belief among those Barbarians that those who go to war

---

[Source: R. G. Thwaites, ed., *Jesuit Relations and Allied Documents* (Cleveland: Burrows Brothers, 1896-1901), XXXI, 31, 33, 35.]

are the more fortunate in proportion as they are cruel toward their enemies; I assure you that they made us thoroughly feel the force of that wretched belief.

Accordingly, having perceived us, they first thanked the Sun for having caused us to fall into the hands of their Fellow-countrymen; they next fired a salute with a volley of arquebus shots, by way of congratulation for their victory. That done, they set up a stage on a hill; then, entering the woods, they seek sticks or thorns, according to their fancy. Being thus armed, they form in line, — a hundred on one side, and a hundred on the other, — and make us pass, all naked, along that way of fury and anguish; there is rivalry among them to discharge upon us the most and the heaviest blows; they made me march last, that I might be more exposed to their rage. I had not accomplished the half of this course when I fell to the earth under the weight of that hail and of those redoubled blows. I did not strive to rise again, — partly because of my weakness, partly because I was accepting that place for my sepulchre. . . . Seeing me prostrate, they rush upon me; God alone knows for how long a time and how many were the blows that were dealt on my body; but the sufferings undertaken for his love and his glory are filled with joy and honor. Seeing, then, that I had not fallen by accident, and that I did not rise again for being too near death, they entered upon a cruel compassion; their rage was not yet glutted, and they wished to conduct me alive into their own country; accordingly, they embrace me, and carry me all bleeding upon that stage they have prepared. When I am restored to my senses, they make me come down, and offer me a thousand and one insults, making me the sport and object of their reviling; they begin their assaults over again, dealing upon my head and neck, and all my body, another hailstorm of blows. I would be too tedious if I should set down in writing all the rigor of my sufferings. They burned one of my fingers, and crushed another with their teeth, and those which were already torn, they squeezed and twisted with a rage of Demons; they scratched my wounds with their nails; and, when strength failed me, they applied fire to my arms and thighs. My companions were treated very nearly as I was. One of those Barbarians, having advanced with a large knife in his right hand, took my nose in his left hand, wishing to cut it off; but he stopped suddenly, and as if astonished, withdrawing without doing aught to me. He returns a quarter of an hour later, as if indignant with himself for his cowardice; he again seizes me at the same place, you know, my God, what I said to you at that moment, in the depth of my heart. In fine, I know not what invisible force repulsed him for the second time. It was over with my life if he had proceeded; for they are not accustomed to leave long on the earth those who are notably mutilated.

New France Proclaimed, June 4, 1671

At Sault Ste. Marie (originally a mission station founded by Isaac Jogues), "the most solemn ceremony . . . ever observed in these regions" laid claim to a vast territory in the name of the King of France and for the purpose of "subjecting these nations to Jesus Christ's dominion." That land mass so dedicated extended all the way from Hudson Bay to Mexico. A military officer, the Sieur de Saint-Lusson, invited Indian tribes from all around to witness the ceremony and be duly impressed with the advantages of doing business with the French. (This in opposition to the English with whom the French had recently waged a disastrous war.) An ecclesiastical officer, Claude Jean Allouez, S.J. (1622-89), at the same time impressed upon those assembled the superior virtues of Christianity. Indeed, Allouez, baptizing thousands, was among France's most successful evangelists to interior America. His words follow below.

For this purpose, after wintering on the Lake of the Hurons, Monsieur de saint Lusson repaired to sainte Marie du Sault early in May of this year, sixteen hundred and seventy-one. First, he summoned the surrounding tribes living within a radius of a hundred leagues, and even more; and they responded through their Ambassadors, to the number of fourteen Nations. After making all necessary preparations for the successful issue of the whole undertaking to the honor of France, he began, on June fourth of the same year, with the most solemn ceremony ever observed in these regions.

For, when all had assembled in a great public council, and a height had been chosen well adapted to his purpose, — overlooking, as it did, the Village of the people of the Sault, — he caused the Cross to be planted there, and then the King's standard to be raised, with all the pomp that he could devise.

The Cross was publicly blessed, with all the ceremonies of the Church, by the Superior of these Missions; and then, when it had been raised from the ground for the purpose of planting it, the *Vexilla* was sung. Many Frenchmen there present at the time joined in this hymn, to the wonder and delight of the assembled Savages; while the whole company was filled with a common joy at sight of this glorious standard of Jesus Christ, which seemed to have been raised so high only to rule over the hearts of all these poor peoples.

Then the French Escutcheon, fixed to a Cedar pole, was also erected, above the Cross; while the *Exaudiat* was sung, and prayer for his Majesty's Sacred person was offered in that faraway corner of the world. After this, Mon-

---

[Source: R. G. Thwaites, ed., *Jesuit Relations and Allied Documents* (Cleveland: Burrows Brothers, 1896-1901), LV, 107, 109, 111.]

sieur de saint Lusson, observing all the forms customary on such occasions, took possession of those regions, while the air resounded with repeated shouts of "Long live the King!" and with the discharge of musketry, — to the delight and astonishment of all those peoples, who had never seen anything of the kind.

After this confused uproar of voices and muskets had ceased, perfect silence was imposed upon the whole assemblage; and Father Claude Allouez began to Eulogize the King, in order to make all those Nations understand what sort of a man he was whose standard they beheld, and to whose sovereignty they were that day submitting. Being well versed in their tongue and in their ways, he was so successful in adapting himself to their comprehension as to give them such an opinion of our incomparable Monarch's greatness that they have no words with which to express their thoughts upon the subject.

"Here is an excellent matter brought to your attention, my brothers," said he to them, — "a great and important matter, which is the cause of this council. Cast your eyes upon the Cross raised so high above your heads: there it was that Jesus Christ, the Son of God, making himself man for the love of men, was pleased to be fastened and to die, in atonement to his Eternal Father for our sins. He is the master of our lives, of Heaven, of Earth, and of Hell. Of him I have always spoken to you, and his name and word I have borne into all these countries. But look likewise at that other post, to which are affixed the armorial bearings of the great Captain of France whom we call King. He lives beyond the sea; he is the Captain of the greatest Captains, and has not his equal in the world. All the Captains you have ever seen, or of whom you have ever heard, are mere children compared with him. He is like a great tree, and they, only like little plants that we tread under foot in walking."

4. New Netherland and New Sweden

Jonas Michaelius (1577-?)

The first Dutch Reformed minister to arrive in Manhattan, Michaelius stepped on shore in 1628 after a difficult crossing, only to face even greater difficulty on land. Soon after debarkation, his wife of more than sixteen years of marriage died, leaving him "with three children very much discommoded. . . ." Of Michaelius's three-year period of service in America, not a great deal is known; however, his own initial reaction to this primitive land survives in a valuable letter dated August 11, 1628 — only four months after his arrival. This epistle, addressed to a fellow pastor back in Amsterdam, suggests that its author was not really prepared for the challenges of the New World. Indeed, when later back in Holland he applied to return to New Netherland, the decision of the West India Company was "no."

The favorable opportunity which now presents itself of writing to your Reverence I cannot let pass, without embracing it, according to my promise. And, first to unburden myself in this communication of a sorrowful circumstance, it pleased the Lord, seven weeks after we arrived in this country, to take from me my good partner, who had been to me, for more than sixteen years, a virtuous, faithful, and altogether amiable yokefellow; and I now find myself alone with three children, very much discommoded, without her society and assistance. But what have I to say? The Lord himself has done this, against whom no one can oppose himself. And why should I even wish to, knowing that all things must work together for good to them that love God? I hope therefore to bear

---

[Source: J. F. Jameson, ed., *Narratives of New Netherland, 1609-1664* (New York: Charles Scribner's Sons, 1909), pp. 122-25, 126-27.]

my cross patiently, and by the grace and help of the Lord, not to let the courage fail me which in my duties here I so especially need. . . .

Our coming here was agreeable to all, and I hope, by the grace of the Lord, that my service will not be unfruitful. The people, for the most part, are rather rough and unrestrained, but I find in almost all of them both love and respect towards me; two things with which hitherto the Lord has everywhere graciously blessed my labors, and which in our calling, as your Reverence well knows and finds, are especially desirable, in order to make our ministry fruitful. . . .

At the first administration of the Lord's Supper which was observed, not without great joy and comfort to many, we had fully fifty communicants — Walloons and Dutch; of whom, a portion made their first confession of faith before us, and others exhibited their church certificates. Others had forgotten to bring their certificates with them, not thinking that a church would be formed and established here; and some who brought them, had lost them unfortunately in a general conflagration, but they were admitted upon the satisfactory testimony of others to whom they were known, and also upon their daily good deportment, since one cannot observe strictly all the usual formalities in making a beginning under such circumstances.

We administer the Holy Supper of the Lord once in four months, provisionally, until a larger number of people shall otherwise require. The Walloons and French have no service on Sundays, otherwise than in the Dutch language, for those who understand no Dutch are very few. A portion of the Walloons are going back to the Fatherland, either because their years here are expired, or else because some are not very serviceable to the Company. Some of them live far away and could not well come in time of heavy rain and storm, so that they themselves cannot think it advisable to appoint any special service in French for so small a number, and that upon an uncertainty. Nevertheless, the Lord's Supper is administered to them in the French language, and according to the French mode, with a sermon preceding, which I have before me in writing, so long as I can not trust myself extemporaneously. . . .

As to the natives of this country, I find them entirely savage and wild, strangers to all decency, yea, uncivil and stupid as garden poles, proficient in all wickedness and godlessness; devilish men, who serve nobody but the Devil, that is, the spirit which in their language they call Menetto; under which title they comprehend everything that is subtle and crafty and beyond human skill and power. They have so much witchcraft, divination, sorcery and wicked arts, that they can hardly be held in by any bands or locks. They are as thievish and treacherous as they are tall; and in cruelty they are altogether inhuman, more than barbarous, far exceeding the Africans.

Johannes Megapolensis (1603-70) and the Mohawks

In addition to their settlement of Manhattan at the mouth of the Hudson River, the Dutch moved up that river to establish Fort Orange (on the site of present Albany). The advantage of that location for fur traders was clear: the Mohawk River flowed from the West into the Hudson at that point, granting the Dutch access into interior America and the fur-trapping Indian tribes. Megapolensis and his family came to Fort Orange in 1642, remaining there for six years. When his time was up in America, he prepared to leave for home but was dissuaded from doing so by the now pastorless people in Manhattan. There he remained for the rest of his life, ministering to the Dutch but also trying to understand and be understood by the Indian.

The inhabitants of this country are of two kinds: first, Christians — at least so called; second, Indians. Of the Christians I shall say nothing; my design is to speak of the Indians only. These among us are again of two kinds: first, the [Mohawks] . . . ; second, the [Mohicans]. . . . These two nations have different languages, which have no affinity with each other, like Dutch and Latin. These people formerly carried on a great war against each other, but since the [Mohicans] were subdued by the [Mohawks], peace has subsisted between them, and the conquered are obliged to bring a yearly contribution to the others. We live among both these kinds of Indians; and when they come to us from their country, or we go to them, they do us every act of friendship. The principal nation of all the savages and Indians hereabouts with which we have the most intercourse, is the [Mohawks], who have laid all the other Indians near us under contribution. This nation has a very difficult language, and it costs me great pains to learn it, so as to be able to speak and preach in it fluently. There is no Christian here who understands the language thoroughly; those who have lived here long can use a kind of jargon just sufficient to carry on trade with it, but they do not understand the fundamentals of the language. I am making a vocabulary of the [Mohawks'] language, and when I am among them I ask them how things are called; but as they are very stupid, I sometimes cannot make them understand what I want. Moreover when they tell me, one tells me the word in the infinitive mood, another in the indicative; one in the first, another in the second person; one in the present, another in the preterit. So I stand oftentimes and look, but do not know how to put it down. And as they have declensions and conjugations also, and have their augments like the Greeks, I am like one distracted, and frequently cannot tell what to do, and

---

[Source: J. F. Jameson, ed., *Narratives of New Netherland, 1609-1664* (New York: Charles Scribner's Sons, 1909), pp. 172, 177-78.]

there is no one to set me right. I shall have to speculate in this alone, in order to become in time an Indian grammarian. . . .

If they are sick, or have a pain or soreness anywhere in their limbs, and I ask them what ails them they say that the Devil sits in their body, or in the sore places, and bites them there; so that they attribute to the Devil at once the accidents which befall them; they have otherwise no religion. When we pray they laugh at us. Some of them despise it entirely; and some, when we tell them what we do when we pray, stand astonished. When we deliver a sermon, sometimes ten or twelve of them, more or less, will attend, each having a long tobacco pipe, made by himself, in his mouth, and will stand awhile and look, and afterwards ask me what I am doing and what I want, that I stand there alone and make so many words, while none of the rest may speak. I tell them that I am admonishing the Christians, that they must not steal, nor commit lewdness, nor get drunk, nor commit murder, and that they too ought not to do these things; and that I intend in process of time to preach the same to them and come to them in their own country and castles (about three days' journey from here, further inland), when I am acquainted with their language. Then they say I do well to teach the Christians; but immediately add . . . "Why do so many Christians do these things?" They call us *Assirioni,* that is, cloth-makers, or *Charistooni,* that is, iron-workers, because our people first brought cloth and iron among them.

They will not come into a house where there is a menstruous woman, nor eat with her. No woman may touch their snares with which they catch deer, for they say the deer can scent it.

The other day an old woman came to our house, and told my people that her forefathers had told her "that *Tharonhij-Jagon,* that is, God, once went out walking with his brother, and a dispute arose between them, and God killed his brother." I suppose this fable took its rise from Cain and Abel. They have a droll theory of the Creation, for they think that a pregnant woman fell down from heaven, and that a tortoise, (tortoises are plenty and large here, in this country, two, three and four feet long, some with two heads, very mischievous and addicted to biting) took this pregnant woman on its back, because every place was covered with water; and that the woman sat upon the tortoise, groped with her hands in the water, and scraped together some of the earth, whence it finally happened that the earth was raised above the water. They think that there are more worlds than one, and that we came from another world.

Megapolensis and the Jews, 1655

In a famous passage from his letter to the Classis (or Synod) of Amsterdam, Megapolensis revealed his strong resistance to allowing Jews to remain on the island of Manhattan. He clearly objected to Jews as Jews, but also to many others not safely within the Dutch Calvinist fold, namely, "Atheists and various other servants of Baal. . . ." Holland's West India Company, however, turned out to favor a policy less exclusivist, less parochial.

Some Jews came from Holland last summer, in order to trade. Later a few Jews came upon the same ship as De Polheymius; they were healthy, but poor. It would have been proper, that they should have been supported by their own people, but they have been at our charge, so that we have had to spend several hundred guilders for their support. They came several times to my house, weeping and bemoaning their misery. If I directed them to the Jewish merchants, they said, that they would not even lend them a few stivers. Some more have come from Holland this spring. They report that still more of the same lot would follow, and then they would build here a synagogue. This causes among the congregation here a great deal of complaint and murmuring. These people have no other God than the unrighteous Mammon, and no other aim than to get possession of christian property, and to win all other merchants by drawing all trade towards themselves. Therefore we request your Reverences to obtain from the Lords-Directors, that these godless rascals, who are of no benefit to the country, but look at everything for their own profit, may be sent away from here. For as we have here Papists, Mennonites and Lutherans among the Dutch; also many Puritans or Independents, and many Atheists and various other servants of Baal among the English under this Government, who conceal themselves under the name of Christians; it would create a still greater confusion, if the obstinate and immovable Jews came to settle here.

Megapolensis and Isaac Jogues

As noted above (p. 39), Megapolensis befriended Jogues before the latter's trip back to Europe and subsequent return to Canada — and to his death. Here in a 1658 letter to the Amsterdam Classis, Megapolensis writes first

[Source for Megapolensis and the Jews, 1655: Hugh Hastings, ed., *Ecclesiastical Records, State of New York* (Albany, 1901), I, 335-36.]

[Source for Megapolensis and Isaac Jogues: J. F. Jameson, ed., *Narratives of New Netherland, 1609-1664* (New York: Charles Scribner's Sons, 1909), pp. 403-4.]

*about Jogues, then about a second Jesuit, Giuseppe Bressani (1612-72).
Megapolensis was himself a Catholic in his youth. Now, as a Dutch Reformed minister his prejudices ran high against popery as well as much besides; nevertheless, his humanity sometimes eclipsed his dogmatism.*

It happened in the year 1642, when I was minister in the colony of
Rensselaerswyck, that our Indians in the neighborhood, who are generally
called [Mohawks] . . . , were at war with the Canadian or French Indians.
Among the prisoners whom our Indians had taken from the French, was this
Jesuit, whom they according to their custom had handled severely. When he
was brought to us, his left thumb and several fingers on both hands had been
cut off, either wholly or in part, and the nails of the remaining fingers had been
chewed off. As this Jesuit had been held in captivity by them for some time, they
consented that he should go among the Dutch, but only when accompanied by
some of them. At last the Indians resolved to burn him. Concerning this he
came to me with grievous complaint. We advised him that next time the Indians were asleep, he should run away and come to us, and we would protect and
secure him, and send him by ship to France. This was done. After concealing
him and entertaining him for six weeks, we sent him to the Manhattans and
thence to England and France, as he was a Frenchman, born at Paris.

Afterward this same Jesuit came again from France to Canada. As our Indians had made peace with the French, he again left Canada, and took up his
residence among the Mohawks. He indulged in the largest expectations of converting them to popery, but the Mohawks with their hatchets put him to a violent death. They then brought and presented to me his missal and breviary together with his underclothing, shirts and coat. When I said to them that I would
not have thought that they would have killed this Frenchman, they answered,
that the Jesuits did not consider the fact, that their people (the French) were always planning to kill the Dutch.

In the year 1644 our Indians again took captive a Jesuit, who had been
treated in the same manner as to his hands and fingers as the above mentioned.
The Jesuit was brought to us naked, with his maimed and bloody fingers. We
clothed him, placed him under the care of our surgeon, and he almost daily fed
at my table. This Jesuit, a native of Rouen, was ransomed by us from the Indians, and we sent him by ship to France. He also returned again from France to
Canada. He wrote me a letter, as the previously mentioned one had done,
thanking me for the benefits I had conferred on him. He stated also that he had
not argued, when with me, on the subject of religion, yet he had felt deeply interested in me on account of my favors to him; that he was anxious for the life
of my soul, and admonished me to come again into the Papal Church from
which I had separated myself. In each case I returned such a reply that a second
letter was never sent me.

John Printz (1592-1663) of New Sweden

While the first group of Swedish Lutherans arrived at Fort Christina (Wilmington) in Delaware in 1638, the "second colony" came five years later under the leadership of John Printz. Governor of New Sweden for a decade (1643-53), Printz was a harsh but effective ruler of the short-lived colony. Printz's instructions, issued to him in August of 1642 in the name of the seventeen-year-old Queen Christina, reveal how New Sweden — like New Spain, New France, and New Netherland — hoped to combine commercial success with religious dedication.

Inasmuch as some of the subjects of Her Royal Majesty and of the Crown of Sweden have, for some time past, undertaken to sail to the coasts of the West Indies, and have already succeeded in conquering and purchasing a considerable tract of land, and in promoting commerce, with the especial object of extending the jurisdiction and greatness of Her Royal Majesty and of the Swedish crown, and have called the country New Sweden; wherefore, and inasmuch as Her Royal Majesty approves and finds this their undertaking and voyaging not only laudable in itself, but reasonable, and likely, in the course of time, to benefit and strengthen Her Royal Majesty and the Swedish throne: So has Her Royal Majesty, for the promotion of that work, and for the assistance of those who participate therein, furnished them for the making of that important voyage, and also for the confirming and strengthening of that important work thus begun in New Sweden, for said voyage, two ships, named the *Fama* and the *Swan,* as well as some other means necessary thereto, under a certain Governor, whom Her Majesty has provided with sufficient and necessary powers, having thereunto appointed and legitimated Lieutenant-Colonel John Printz, whom she has, accordingly, seen good to instruct upon the points following. . . .

12. Next to this, he shall pay the necessary attention to the culture of tobacco, and appoint thereto a certain number of laborers, so arranging that the produce may be large, more and more being set out and cultivated from time to time, so that he can send over a good quantity of tobacco on all ships coming hither.

13. That better arrangements may be made for the production of cattle, both great and small, the Governor shall at once exert himself to obtain a good breed of cattle of all kinds, and especially of that which is sent out from this country, and also seek to obtain a supply from the neighboring English, dividing everything with those who will use and employ it in agriculture in exchange

[Source: Israel Acrelius, *A History of New Sweden* . . . (Philadelphia: Historical Society of Pennsylvania, 1874 [originally published in Swedish in 1759]), pp. 30, 36-38, 39-40.]

for seed, and with such prudence as he shall find most serviceable to the members of the Company.

14. Among and above other things, he shall direct his attention to sheep, to obtain them of good kinds, and as soon as may be seek to arrange as many sheep-folds as he conveniently can, so that presently a considerable supply of wool of good quality may be sent over to this country. . . .

17. And as almost everywhere in the forests wild grapevines and grapes are found, and the climate seems to be favorable to the production of wine, so shall the Governor also direct his thoughts to the timely introduction of this culture, and what might herein be devised and effected.

18. He can also have careful search made everywhere as to whether any

"Old Swedes' Church," Wilmington, Delaware
(Keystone-Mast Collection, University of California, Riverside)

metals or minerals are to be found in the country, and, if any are discovered, send hither correct information, and then await further orders from this place.

19. Out of the abundant forests, the Governor shall examine and consider how and in what manner profit may be derived from the country; especially what kind of advantages may be expected from oak-trees and walnut-trees, and whether a good quality of them might be sent over here as ballast. So also it might be examined whether oil might not be advantageously pressed out of the walnuts. . . .

26. Above all things, shall the Governor consider and see to it that a true and due worship, becoming honor, laud, and praise be paid to the Most High God in all things, and to that end all proper care shall be taken that divine service be zealously performed according to the unaltered Augsburg Confession, the Council of Upsala, and the ceremonies of the Swedish Church; and all persons, but especially the young, shall be duly instructed in the articles of their Christian faith; and all good church discipline shall in like manner be duly exercised and received. But so far as relates to the Holland colonists that live and settle under the government of Her Royal Majesty and the Swedish Crown, the Governor shall not disturb them in the indulgence granted them as to the exercise of the Reformed religion according to the aforesaid Royal Charter.

Dutch Surrender, 1664

The Dutch Reformed minister, Samuel Drisius, reported to his ecclesiastical superiors in 1664 on the fall of New Netherland to the English. His letter, dated September 15 of that year, offers graphic, even poignant detail of the end of Holland's forty-year adventure in North America. When New Netherland became New York, this did not bring about the end of Dutch population or of an influence — especially in New York and New Jersey — exercised by Holland's national church. For while England in 1664 was no great devotee of religious liberty (the Declaration of Toleration was still a quarter-century away), that nation was prepared to extend courtesy toward the national church of another, especially Protestant, nation. The Dutch Reformed pastors and people continued, therefore, as a significant feature of the colonial landscape.

I cannot refrain from informing you of our present situation, namely, that we have been brought under the government of the King of England. On the 26th of August there arrived in the Bay of the North River, near Staten Island, four great men-of-war, or frigates, well manned with sailors and soldiers. They were

[Source: Hugh Hastings, ed., *Ecclesiastical Records, State of New York* (Albany, 1901), I, 560-62.]

The Dutch surrender New Amsterdam, 1664
(© New York Public Library/Art Resource, NY)

provided with a patent or commission from the King of Great Britain to demand and take possession of this province, in the name of his majesty. If this could not be done in an amicable way, they were to attack the place, and everything was to be thrown open for the English soldiers to plunder, rob and pillage. We were not a little troubled by the arrival of these frigates.

Our Director-General and Council, with the municipal authorities of the city, took the matter much to heart and zealously sought, by messages between them and General Richard Nicolls, to delay the decision. They asked that the whole business should be referred to his Majesty of England, and the Lords, the States General of Holland; but every effort was fruitless. They landed their soldiers about two (Dutch) miles from here, (six English miles,) at Gravezandt, (Gravesend) and marched them over Long Island to the Ferry opposite this place. The frigates came up under full sail on the 4th of September with guns trained to one side. They had orders, and intended, if any resistance was shown to them, to give a full broadside on this open place, then take it by assault, and make it a scene of pillage and bloodshed.

Our Hon. rulers of the (West India) Company, and the municipal authorities of the city, were inclined to defend the place, but found that it was impossible, for the city was not in a defensible condition. And even if fortified, it could not have been defended, because every man posted on the circuit of it would have been four rods distant from his neighbor. Besides the store of powder in the fort, as well as in the city, was small. No relief or assistance could be expected, while daily great numbers on foot and on horseback, from New England, joined the English, hotly bent upon plundering the place. Savages and privateers also offered their services against us. Six hundred Northern Indians with one hundred and fifty French privateers, had even an English commission. Therefore upon the earnest request of our citizens and other inhabitants, our authorities found themselves compelled to come to terms, for the sake of avoiding bloodshed and pillage. The negotiations were concluded on the 6th of September. The English moved in on the 8th, according to agreement.

After the surrender of the place several Englishmen, who had lived here a long time and were our friends, came to us, and said that God had signally overruled matters, that the affair had been arranged by negotiations; else nothing but pillage, bloodshed and general ruin would have followed. This was confirmed by several soldiers who said that they had come here from England hoping for booty, but that now, since the matter turned out so differently, they desired to return to England.

The Articles of Surrender stipulate, that our religious services and doctrines, together with the preachers shall remain and continue unchanged. Therefore we could not separate ourselves from our congregation and hearers, but consider it our duty to remain with them for some time yet, that they may not scatter and run wild.

5. England Anew

Virginia

John Rolfe (1585-1622) and Pocahantas (c. 1595-1617)

Rolfe's claim to a page in American history rests upon his introduction of to-bacco cultivation into Virginia in 1612, but even more upon his marriage to the Indian "princess," Pocahantas, in 1614. The marriage itself helped to maintain peace with the Indians (Powhatans) for some years, but Pocahantas's early death threatened the uneasy calm. Ironically, Rolfe himself was slain in the major Indian uprising of 1622. In his letter to Virginia's governor excerpted below, Rolfe tries to unsort the mixture of motives that led to his decision to marry Pocahantas. Despite the great emphasis upon a religious motivation, his observation that his heart and his thoughts were hopelessly "enthralled in so intricate a labyrinth" makes him sound like just any other man in love.

But to avoid tedious preambles, and to come neerer the matter: first suffer me with your patence, to sweepe and make cleane the way wherein I walke, from all suspicions and doubts, which may be covered therein, and faithfully to reveale unto you, what should move me hereunto.

Let therefore this my well advised protestation, which here I make betweene God and my own conscience, be a sufficient witnesse, at the dreadfull day of judgement (when the secret of all mens harts shall be opened) to condemne me herein, if my chiefest intent and purpose be not, to strive with all

---

[Source: Leon G. Tyler, ed., *Narratives of Early Virginia, 1606-1625* (New York: Charles Scribner's Sons, 1907), pp. 240-42, 243-44.]

my power of body and minde, in the undertaking of so mightie a matter, no way led (so farre forth as mans weakenesse may permit) with the unbridled desire of carnall affection: but for the good of this plantation, for the honour of our countrie, for the glory of God, for my owne salvation, and for the converting to the true knowledge of God and Jesus Christ, an unbeleeving creature, namely Pokahuntas. To whom my hartie and best thoughts are, and have a long time bin so intangled, and inthralled in so intricate a laborinth, that I was even awearied to unwinde my selfe thereout. But almighty God, who never faileth his, that truely invocate his holy name hath opened the gate, and led me by the hand that I might plainely see and discerne the safe paths wherein to tread. . . .

I never failed to offer my daily and faithfull praiers to God, for his sacred and holy assistance. I forgot not to set before mine eies the frailty of mankinde, his prone[ness] to evill, his indulgencie of wicked thoughts, with many other imperfections wherein man is daily insnared, and oftentimes overthrowne, and them compared to my present estate. Nor was I ignorant of the heavie displeasure which almightie God conceived against the sonnes of Levie and Israel for marrying strange wives, nor of the inconveniences which may thereby arise, with other the like good motions which made me looke about warily and with good circumspection, into the grounds and principall agitations, which thus should provoke me to be in love with one whose education hath bin rude, her manners barbarous, her generation accursed, and so discrepant in all nurtriture from my selfe, that oftentimes with feare and trembling, I have ended my private controversie with this: surely these are wicked instigations, hatched by him who seeketh and delighteth in mans destruction; and so with fervent praiers to be ever preserved from such diabolical assaults (as I tooke those to be) I have taken some rest.

Thus when I had thought I had obtained my peace and quietnesse, beholde another, but more gracious tentation hath made breaches into my holiest and strongest meditations; with which I have bin put to a new triall, in a straighter manner then the former: for besides the many passions and sufferings which I have daily, hourely, yea and in my sleepe indured, even awaking mee to astonishment, taxing mee with remisnesse, and carelesnesse, refusing and neglecting to performe the duetie of a good Christian, pulling me by the eare, and crying: why dost not thou indevour to make her a Christian? And these have happened to my greater wonder, even when she hath bin furthest seperated from me, which in common reason (were it not an undoubted worke of God) might breede forgetfulnesse of a farre more worthie creature. Besides, I say the holy spirit of God hath often demaunded of me, why I was created, If not for transitory pleasures and worldly vanities, but to labour in the Lords vineyard, there to sow and plant, to nourish and increase the fruites thereof, daily adding with the good husband in the Gospell, somewhat to the tallent, that in the end the fruites may be reaped, to the comfort of the laborer in this life, and his salvation in the world to come? And if this be, as undoubtedly this is, the service Jesus Christ requireth of his best servant: wo unto him that hath these instruments of pietie put into his hands, and wilfully despiseth to worke with them. Likewise, adding hereunto her great apparance of love to me, her desire to be taught and instructed in the knowledge of God, her capablenesse of understanding, her aptnesse and willingnesse to receive anie good impression, and also the spirituall, besides her owne incitements stirring me up hereunto.

What should I doe? shall I be of so untoward a disposition, as to refuse to leade the blind into the right way? Shall I be so unnaturall, as not to give bread to the hungrie? or uncharitable, as not to cover the naked? Shall I despise to ac-tuate these pious dueties of a Christian? Shall the base feare of displeasing the world, overpower and with holde mee from revealing unto man these spirituall workes of the Lord, which in my meditations and praiers, I have daily made knowne unto him, God forbid. . . .

Now if the vulgar sort, who square all mens actions by the base rule of their own filthinesse, shall taxe or taunt me in this my godly labour: let them know, it is not any hungry appetite, to gorge my selfe with incontinency; sure (if I would, and were so sensually inclined) I might satisfie such desire, though not without a seared conscience, yet with Christians more pleasing to the eie, and lesse fearefull in the offence unlawfully committed. Nor am I in so desper-ate an estate, that I regard not what becommeth of mee; nor am I out of hope

Baptism of Pocahantas
(Library of Congress)

but one day to see my Country, nor so void of friends, nor mean in birth, but there to obtain a mach to my great content: nor have I ignorantly passed over my hopes there, or regardlesly seek to loose the love of my friends, by taking this course: I know them all, and have not rashly over-slipped any.

But shal it please God thus to dispose of me (which I earnestly desire to fulfill my ends before sette down) I will heartely accept of it as a godly taxe appointed me, and I will never cease, (God assisting me) untill I have accomplished, and brought to perfection so holy a worke, in which I will daily pray God to blesse me, to mine, and her eternall happines. And thus desiring no longer to live, to enjoy the blessings of God, then [than] this my resolution doth tend to such godly ends, as are by me before declared: not doubting of your favourable acceptance, I take my leave. . . .

Anti-Catholicism, 1641

One of the constants of colonial American history is the pervading fear of the Roman Catholic Church — of "popery," in the language of the time. Virginia's English men and women simply reflected in this regard the anxieties of England's own citizens concerning papal plots and papal imperialism. Roman Catholics in seventeenth-century England who refused to conform to the National Church — "recusants" they were called — lived under the gravest suspicions with respect to their political loyalty. The colony of Virginia was unlikely to receive any prominent Catholic emigrants, but should it do so, the young government made it unmistakably clear that such persons were barred from political office as well as from proselytizing activity.

It is enacted by the authority aforesaid, that according to a Statute made in the third year of the reign of our sovereign Lord King James, of blessed memory, no popist [sic] recusant shall at any time hereafter exercise the place or places of secretary, counsellor, register, commissioner, surveyor or sheriff, or any other public place, but be utterly disabled for the same;

And further, be it enacted by the authority aforesaid, that none shall be admitted into any of the aforesaid offices or places before he or they have taken the oaths of supremacy and allegiance. And if any person or persons whatsoever shall by any sinister or secret means contrive to himself any of the aforesaid places, or any other public office whatsoever, and refuse to take the aforesaid oaths, he or they so convicted before any assembly shall be dismissed of his

---

[Source: Francis X. Curran, S.J., ed., *Catholics in Colonial Law* (Chicago: Loyola University Press, 1963), p. 22.]

said office, and for his offense herein, forfeit a thousand pounds weight of tobacco, to be disposed of by the next grand assembly after conviction.

And it is enacted by the authority aforesaid that the statutes in force
against popish recusants be duly executed in the government; and that it shall
not be lawful, under the penalty aforesaid, for any popish priest that shall hereafter arrive here to remain above five days, after warning given for his departure
by the governor or commander of that place where he or they shall be, if wind
and weather hinder not his departure; this act to be in force after ten days from
the publication here at James City.

Church Establishment

*As early as 1619, the Virginia legislature made provision for governmental
support of the Anglican clergy. Yet not then or later were the problems of official establishment of the Church of England so readily solved. The country
was poor, the population scattered, the interests varied. Repeatedly, governors and lawmakers tried to buttress an ecclesiastical structure that seemed
ever on the verge of collapse, or perhaps of never being built at all. In 1642
Virginia's Assembly gave explicit instructions for the appointment of clergy
and, twenty years later, for the creation of local parish vestries.*

Ministers to Be Inducted.

That for the Preservation of Purity & Unity of Doctrine & Discipline in the
Church, & the right Administration of the Sacraments, no ministers be admitted to officiate in this Country but such as shall produce to the Governor a Testimonial that he hath receiv'd his Ordination from some Bishop in England, &
shall then subscribe to be conformable to the Orders & Constitutions of the
Church of England & the Laws there establish'd, upon which the Governor is
hereby requested to induct the s^d minister into any parish, that shall make Presentation of him; And if any other person pretending himself a minister, shall
contrary to this Act presume to teach or preach publickly or privately, the Governor & Council are hereby desir'd and impowered to suspend & silence the
Person so offending, & upon his obstinate persistence, to compell him to depart
the Country with the first Convenience as it hath been formerly provided by
the 77th Act made at James City the 2^d March, 1642.

[Source: W. S. Perry, *Historical Collections Relating to the American Colonial Church* (New
York: AMS Press, 1969 [1870]), I, 243-44.]

Vestrys Appointed.

That for the making & proportioning of the Levys & Assessments, for building & repairing the Churches & Chappels, Provision for the poor, maintenance of the ministers & each other necessary Uses, & for the more orderly managing all parochial Affairs; *Be it exacted* that 12 of the most able men of each parish be by the major part of the s^d parish chose to be a Vestry out of which number the minister & Vestry to make choice of two Church Wardens yearly, & in Case of the Death of any Vestryman or his Departure out of the parish, that the s^d Minister and Vestry make Choice of another to supply his room; *And be it further enacted,* that none shall be admitted to be of the Vestry, that doth not take the Oaths of Allegiance & Supremacy to His Majesty, & subscribe to be conformable to the Doctrine & Discipline of the Church of England.

Virginia's Cure, 1662

To any clear-eyed observer, the problems of simply picking up England's Church and setting it down in England's colony were readily apparent. Clergy were scarce and often of poor quality: so how does one make Virginia more attractive to better ministers? Towns were nonexistent and population was scattered: so how, and even more where, does one build a church? People were impoverished, uneducated, and indifferent: so where does one begin? The author of the pamphlet quoted below, perhaps Roger Green, saw his proposals as the "only true remedy" for the "Churches Unhappinness" in Virginia. In portraying that unhappiness, the author exaggerates only slightly the parlous state of a church desperately trying to become "established." His remedies, however appropriate, proved beyond the means or the will of seventeenth-century Virginians, and beyond the capacity of the Bishop of London — to whom these remarks are addressed.

To shew the unhappy State of the Church in Virginia, and the true Remedy of it, I shall first give a brief Description of the Manner of our Peoples scatter'd Habitations there; next shew the sad unhappy consequents of such their scatter'd Living both in reference to themselves and the poor Heathen that are about them, and by the way briefly set down the cause of scattering their Habitations, then proceed to propound the Remedy, and means of procuring it; next assert the Benefits of it in reference both to themselves and the Heathen; set down the

---

[Source: George M. Brydon, *Virginia's Mother Church* (Richmond: Virginia Historical Society, 1947), I, 492-93, 494, 497-98.]

cause why this Remedy hath not been hitherto compassed: and lastly, till it can be procured, give directions for the present supply of their Churches.

That part of Virginia which hath at present craved your Lordships Assistance to preserve the Christian Religion, and to promote the Building Gods Church among them, by supplying them with sufficient Ministers of the Gospel, is bounded on the North by the great River Patomek, on the South by the River Chawan, including also the Land inhabited on the East side of the Chesipiack Bay, called Accomack, and contains above half as much Land as England; it is divided into several Counties, and those Counties contain in all about Fifty Parishes, the Families whereof are dispersedly and scatteringly seated upon the sides of Rivers; some of which running very far into the Country, bear the English Plantations above a hundred Miles, and being very broad, cause the Inhabitants of either side to be listed in several Parishes. Every such Parish is extended many Miles in length upon the Rivers side and usually not above a mile in Breadth backward from the River, which is the common stated breadth of every Plantation belonging to each Particular Proprietor, of which Plantations, some extend themselves half a mile, some a mile, some two miles, some three miles, and upward upon the sides of those Rivers, many of them are parted from each other by small Rivers and Creeks, which small Rivers and Creeks are seated after the manner of the great Rivers. The Families of such Parishes being seated after this manner, at such distances from each other, many of them are very remote from the House of God, though placed in the middest of them. Many Parishes as yet want both Churches and Gleabes, and I think not above a fifth part of them are supplyed with Ministers, where there are Ministers the People meet together Weekly, but once upon the Lords day, and sometimes not at all, being hindred by Extremities of Wind and Weather; and divers of the more remote Families being discouraged, by the length or tediousness of the way, through extremities of heat in Summer, frost and Snow in Winter, and tempestuous weather in both, do seldome repair thither.

By which brief Description of their manner of seating themselves in that Wildernesse, Your Lordship may easily apprehend that their very manner of Planting themselves, hath caused them hitherto to rob God in a great measure of that publick Worship and Service, which as a Homage due to his great name, he requires to be constantly paid to him, at the times appointed for it, in the publick Congregations of his people in his House of Prayer. . . .

But though this be the saddest Consequence of their dispersed manner of Planting themselves (for what Misery can be greater than to live under the Curse of God?) yet this hath a very sad Train of Attendants which are likewise consequents of their scatter'd Planting. For, hence is the great want of Christian Neighbourhood, or brotherly admonition, of holy Examples of religious Persons, of the Comfort of theirs, and their Ministers Administrations in Sicknesse, and Distresse, of the Benefit of Christian and Civil Conference and Commerce.

And hence it is, that the most faithfull and vigilant Pastors, assisted by the most careful Church-wardens, cannot possibly take notice of the Vices that reign in their families, of the spiritual defects in their Conversations, or if they have notice of them, and provide Spiritual Remedies in their public Ministery, it is a hazard if they that are most concerned in them be present at the application of them: and if they should spend time in visiting their remote and far distant habitations, they would have little or none left for their necessary Studies, and to provide necessary spiritual food for the rest of their Flocks. And hence it is that through the licentious lives of many of them, the Christian Religion is like still to be dishonored, and the Name of God to be blasphemed among the Heathen, who are near them, and oft among them, and consequently their Conversion hindred.

Lastly, their almost general want of Schooles, for the education of their Children, is another consequent of their scattered planting, of most sad consideration, most of all bewailed of Parents there, and therefore the arguments drawn from thence, most likely to prevail with them chearfuly to embrace the Remedy. This want of Schooles, as it renders a very numerous generation of Christians Children born in Virginia (who naturally are of beautiful and comely Persons, and generally of more ingenious Spirits then these in England) unserviceable for any great Employments either in Church or State, so likewise it obstructs the hopefullest way they have, for the Conversion of the Heathen, which is, by winning the Heathen to bring in their Children to be taught and instructed in our Schooles, together with the Children of Christians. . . .

. . . I shall humbly in obedience to your Lordships command endeavour to contribute towards the compassing this Remedy by propounding,

1. That your Lordship would be pleased to acquaint the King with the necessity of promoting the building of Towns in each County of Virginia, upon the consideration of the fore-mentioned sad Consequents of their present manner of living there.

2. That your Lordship upon the foregoing consideration, be pleased to move the pitiful, and charitable heart of His Gracious Majesty (considering the Poverty and needs of Virginia) for a Collection to be made in all the Churches of his three Kingdomes (there being considerable numbers of each Kingdome) for the promoting of a work of so great Charity to the Souls of many thousands of his Loyal Subjects, their Children, and the Generations after them, and of numberlesse poor Heathen, and that the Ministers of each Congregation be enjoyned with more than ordinary care, and pains to stirre up the people to a free and liberal Contribution towards it; or if this way be not thought sufficient, then some other way be taken to do it.

3. That the way of dispencing such collections for sending Work-men over for the building of Towns and Schooles, and the assistance the persons that shall inhabit them shall contribute towards them may be determin'd here, by

the advice of Virginia's present or late Honourable Govenours if in London; and whom they shall make choice of for their assistants (who have formerly lived in Virginia); and that the King (if he shall approve what is so determined) may be humbly Petitioned to authorize it by his special command, lest what is duely ordered here, be perverted there.

Fourthly, That those Planters who have such a considerable number of Servants, as may be judged may enable them for it, if they be not willing (for I have heard some expresse their willingnesse and some their aversenesse) may by His Majesties Authority be enjoyned, to contribute the Assistance that shall be thought meet for them, to build themselves houses in the Towns nearest to them, and to inhabit them, for they having horses enough in that Country, may be convenienced, as their occasions require, to visit their Plantations. And the Masters who shall inhabit the Towns, having Families of Servants upon remote Plantations, may be ordered to take care, that upon Saturdays Afternoon (when by the Custome of Virginia, Servants are freed from their ordinary labour) their Servants (except one or two, left by turns to secure their Plantations) may repair to their Houses in the Towns, and there remain with their Masters, until the publick Worship and Service of the Lords Day be ended.

Fifthly, That for a continual supply of able Ministers for their Churches after a set term of years, Your Lordship would please to endeavour the procuring an Act of Parliament, whereby a certain number of Fellowships, as they happen to be next proportionably vacant in both the Universities, may bear the name of Virginia Fellowships, so long as the Needs of that Church shall require it; and none be admitted to them, but such as shall engage by promise to hold them seven years and no longer; and at the expiration of those seven years, transport themselves to Virginia, and serve that Church in the Office of the Ministery seven years more (the Church there providing for them) which being expired, they shall be left to their own Liberty to return or not: and if they perform not the Conditions of their Admittance, then to be uncapable of any Preferment.

These things being procured, I think Virginia will be in the most probable way (that her present condition can admit) of being cured of the forementioned evils of her scatter'd Planting.

Massachusetts

Reasons for Removal: The Pilgrims

Those Puritans who withdrew from the Church of England, who affirmed (in a famous phrase) a "reformation without tarrying for any," have come to be known in American history as "the pilgrims." These Separatists had fled England in 1609 for Holland, seeking there a refuge from England's rigid requirements of conformity to the Book of Common Prayer. After about a dozen years abroad, however, these pilgrims concluded that Holland was not the long-term solution to their religious problems. William Bradford (1590-1657), later Governor of Plymouth Plantation, relates the reasons why the dangerous and costly voyage was to be made across the Atlantic Ocean. In 1620 the Mayflower *made its two-month crossing from the coast of southern England to the northeastern shores of America.*

After they had lived in this citie [Leyden] about some 11. or 12. years, . . . and sundrie of them were taken away by death, and many others begane to be well striken in years, . . . those prudent governours with sundrie of the sagest members begane both deeply to apprehend their present dangers, and wisely to foresee the future, and thinke of timly remedy. In the agitation of their thoughts, and much discours of things hear aboute, at length they began to incline to this conclusion, of remooval to some other place. Not out of any newfanglednes, or other such like giddie humor, by which men are oftentimes transported to their great hurt and danger, but for sundrie weightie and solid reasons; some of the cheefe of which I will hear breefly touch. And first, they saw and found by experience the hardnes of the place and countrie to be such, as few in comparison would come to them, and fewer that would bide it out, and continew with them. For many that came to them, and many more that desired to be with them, could not endure that great labor and hard fare, with other inconveniences which they underwent and were contented with. . . . For many, though they desired to injoye the ordinances of God in their puritie, and the libertie of the gospell with them, yet, alass, they admitted of bondage, with danger of conscience, rather than to indure these hardships; yea, some preferred and chose the prisons in England, rather then this libertie in Holland, with these afflictions. But it was thought that if a better and easier place of living could be had, it would draw many, and take away these discouragments. Yea, their pastor

[Source: William T. Davis, ed., *Bradford's History of Plymouth Plantation* (New York: Charles Scribner's Sons, 1920), pp. 44-46.]

would often say, that many of those who both wrote and preached now against them, if they were in a place wher they might have libertie and live comfortably, they would then practise as they did.

2^{ly} They saw that though the people generally bore all these difficulties very cherfully, and with a resolute courage, being in the best and strength of their years, yet old age began to steale on many of them, (and their great and continuall labours, with other crosses and sorrows, hastened it before the time,) so as it was not only probably thought, but apparently seen, that within a few years more they would be in danger to scatter, by necessities pressing them, or sinke under their burdens, or both. . . .

Thirdly; as necessitie was a taskmaster over them, so they were forced to be such, not only to their servants, but in a sorte, to their dearest children; the which as it did not a litle wound the tender harts of many a loving father and mother, so it produced likwise sundrie sad and sorowful effects. For many of their children, that were of best dispositions and gracious inclinations, haveing lernde to bear the yoake in their youth, and willing to bear parte of their parents burden, were, often times, so oppressed with their hevie labours, that though their minds were free and willing, yet their bodies bowed under the weight of the same, and became decreped in their early youth; the vigor of nature being consumed in the very budd as it were. But that which was more lamentable, and of all sorowes most heavie to be borne, was that many of their children, by these occasions, and the great licentiousness of youth in that countrie, and the manifold temptations of the place, were drawne away by evill examples into extravagante and dangerous courses, getting the raines off their neks, and departing from their parents. Some became souldiers, others tooke upon them farr viages by sea, and other some worse courses, tending to dissolutnes and the danger of their soules, to the great greefe of their parents and dishonour of God. So that they saw their posteritie would be in danger to degenerate and be corrupted.

Lastly, (and which was not least), a great hope and inward zeall they had of laying some good foundation, or at least to make some way therunto, for the propagating and advancing the gospell of the kingdom of Christ in those remote parts of the world; yea, though they should be but even as stepping-stones unto others for the performing of so great a work.

These, and some other like reasons, moved them to undertake this resolution of their removall; the which they afterward prosecuted with so great difficulties, as by the sequell will appeare.

Persuading London, 1617

Since leaving England for Holland had been illegal, the Pilgrims had been obliged to make that move in secret. But a major expedition across the Atlantic, and to one of England's own colonies, could hardly be executed as a wholly private venture. The Pilgrims needed help, both politically and financially. To obtain such, they turned to the Virginia Company and especially to a sympathetic friend therein, Sir Edwin Sandys. The Leyden pastors, John Robinson and William Brewster, wrote Sandys, explaining why these earnest English folk living in Holland should be granted royal sufferance if not royal blessing in their colonization plans. They also thanked Sandys for his crucial assistance "in this weighty business about Virginia." While it was to Virginia they planned to go, it was Cape Cod they actually reached.

We veryly beleeve and trust the Lord is with us, unto whom and whose service we have given our selves in many trialls; and that he will graciously prosper our indeavours according to the simplicitie of our harts therin.

2^{ly}. We are well weaned from the delicate milke of our mother countrie, and enured to the difficulties of a strange and hard land, which yet in a great parte we have by patience overcome.

3^{ly}. The people are for the body of them, industrious, and frugall, we thinke we may safly say, as any company of people in the world.

4^{ly}. We are knite togeather as a body in a most stricte and sacred bond and covenante of the Lord, of the violation wherof we make great conscience, and by vertue wherof we doe hould our selves straitly tied to all care of each others good, and of the whole by every one and so mutually.

5. Lastly, it is not with us as with other men, whom small things can discourage, or small discontentments cause to wish them selves at home againe. We knowe our entertainmente in England, and in Holand; we shall much prejudice both our arts and means by removall; who, if we should be driven to returne, we should not hope to recover our present helps and comforts, neither indeed looke ever, for our selves, to attaine unto the like in any other place during our lives, which are now drawing towards their periods.

These motives we have been bould to tender unto you, which you in your wisdome may also imparte to any other our wor^{PP}: freinds of the Counsell with you; of all whose godly dispossition and loving towards our despised persons, we are most glad, and shall not faile by all good means to continue and increase the same. We will not be further troublesome, but doe, with the renewed re-

[Source: William T. Davis, ed., *Bradford's History of Plymouth Plantation* (New York: Charles Scribner's Sons, 1920), pp. 54-55.]

membrance of our humble duties to your Wor^PP: and (so farr as in modestie we may be bould) to any other of our wellwillers of the Counsell with you, we take our leaves, commiting your persons and counsels to the guidance and direction of the Almighty.

Yours much bounden in all duty,

Leyden, Desem: 15.   JOHN ROBINSON,
An°: 1617.   WILLIAM BREWSTER.

Reasons for Removal: The Puritans

The far larger migration to New England came in the 1630s under the aegis of the Massachusetts Bay Company. These immigrants, styled the "Puritans," regarded themselves as still part of the Church of England — but the reforming and purifying part. Dedicated to making that Church more thoroughly Protestant (or less compromised by popery), the Puritans hoped to create in Massachusetts a true Church of England. And in their bold vision, they even dared to hope that once old England perceived what new England had managed to achieve, then the whole National Church would accept that model erected in a "city set on a hill." The Bay Colony's first governor, John Winthrop (1588-1649), explained in 1629 why a large number of English yeomen and their families were prepared to make their leap of faith.

(1) It will be a service to the Church of great consequence to carry the Gospell into those parts of the world, to helpe on the comminge of the fullnesse of the Gentiles, and to raise a Bulworke against the kingdome of Ante-Christ which the Jesuites labour to reare vp in those parts.

(2) All other Churches of Europe are brought to desolation, and our sinnes, for which the Lord beginnes allreaddy to frowne vpon vs, and to cutte vs short doe threatne euill times to be comminge vpon vs, and whoe knowes, but that God hath provided this place to be a refuge for many whome he meanes to saue out of the generall callamity, and seeinge the Church hath noe place lefte to flie into but the wildernesse, what better worke can there be, then to goe and provide tabernacles and foode for her against she comes thether:

(3) This Land growes weary of her Inhabitantes, soe as man whoe is the most praetious of all creatures, is here more vile and base then the earth we treade vpon, and of lesse prise among vs then an horse or a sheepe, masters are

---

[Source: *Winthrop Papers, II, 1623-1630* (Boston: Massachusetts Historical Society, 1931), 138-40.]

forced by authority to entertaine servants, parents to maintaine there owne children, all townes complaine of the burthen of their poore, . . .

(6) The Fountaines of Learning and Religion are soe corrupted as (besides the vnsupportable charge of there education) most children (euen the best witts and of faierest hopes) are perverted, corrupted, and vtterlie ouerthrowne by the multitude of euill examples and the licentious gouernment of those Seminaries, where men straine at knatts, and swallowe camells, vse all severity for mainetaynance of cappes, and other accomplymentes, but suffer all ruffianlike fashions, and disorder in manners to passe vncontrolled. . . .

(9) It appeares to be a worke of God for the good of his Church in that he hath disposed the hartes of soe many of his wise and faithfull servantes both ministers, and others not onely to approue of the enterprise but to interest themselues in it, some in theire persons, and estates, other by there serious advise and helpe otherwise, and all by there praiers for the wealfare of it Amos 3: the Lord revealeth his secreat to his servantes the profits, it is likely he hath some great worke in hand which he hath revealed to his prophetts among vs whom he hath stirred vp to encourage his servantes to this Plantation, for he doeth not vse to seduce his people by his owne prophetts, but committe that office to the ministrie of false prophetts and heing speritses.

A Modell of Christian Charity, 1630

John Winthrop was a lawyer and layman, not a minister. But the Puritans believed all, pastors and people, to be of one spiritual estate. All of those persons elected or chosen by God to be his forever were equally responsible before God, equally called by him to worthy service in the world. So this layman composed a sermon aboard the ship that brought him to Massachusetts, a sermon that set down characteristic features of "the Puritan mind" and "the New England way." The concluding sentiments concerning the covenant made between God and his people are particularly noteworthy.

1. For the persons, we are a Company professing ourselves fellow members of Christ. In which respect only, though we were absent from each other many miles, and had our employments as far distant, yet we ought to account ourselves knit together by this bond of love, and live in exercise of it. . . .

2. For the work we have in hand, it is by a mutual consent through a spe-

[Source: Perry Miller and T. H. Johnson, *The Puritans: A Sourcebook of Their Writings* (New York: Harper and Row, 1963 [1938]), I, 197-98. Spelling and punctuation have been modernized.]

John Winthrop
(Library of Congress)

cial overruling providence, and a more than ordinary approbation of the
Churches of Christ, to seek out a place of Cohabitation and Consortship under
a due form of Government both civil and ecclesiastical. In such cases as this, the
care of the public must oversway all private respects, by which not only conscience, but mere Civil policy doth bind us. For it is a rule that particular estates
cannot subsist in the ruin of the public.

3. The end is to improve our lives to do more service to the Lord, the comfort and increase of the body of Christ, whereof we are members, that ourselves and posterity may be the better preserved from the Common corruptions of this evil world, to serve the Lord and work out our Salvation under the power and purity of his holy Ordinances.

4. For the means whereby this must be effected, they are twofold: a Conformity with the work and end we aim at — these we see are extraordinary; therefore, we must not content ourselves with usual ordinary means. Whatsoever we did or ought to have done when we lived in England, the same must we do, and more also, where we go. That which the most (in their Church) maintain as a truth in profession only, we must bring into familiar and constant practice. As in this duty of love, we must love brotherly without dissimulation. We must love one another with a pure heart fervently; we must bear one another's burdens; we must not look only on our own things, but also on the things of our brethren. Neither must we think that the Lord will bear with such failings at our hands as he doth from those among whom we have lived. . . .

Thus stands the cause between God and us: we are entered into Covenant with him for this work, we have taken out a Commission. The Lord hath given us leave to draw our own Articles. We have professed to enterprise these Actions upon these and these ends [and] we have hereupon besought him of favor and blessing. Now if the Lord shall please to hear us, and bring us in peace to the place we desire, then hath he ratified this Covenant and sealed our Commission [and] will expect a strict performance of the Articles contained in it. But if we shall neglect the observance of these Articles which are the ends we have propounded, and dissembling with our God, shall fall to embrace this present world and prosecute our carnal intentions, seeking great things for ourselves and our posterity, the Lord will surely break out in wrath against us [and] be revenged of such a perjured people and make us know the price of the breach of such a Covenant.

Puritan Poets

Anne Bradstreet (c. 1612-72), housewife, mother, and poet, came to Massachusetts aboard the same vessel that brought John Winthrop. Her poetry, long acclaimed as the outstanding example of that art in early America, also testifies to the Puritan theology with which it is embued. A later poet (as well

---

[Sources: For Bradstreet, Perry Miller and T. H. Johnson, *The Puritans: A Sourcebook of Their Writings* (New York: Harper and Row, 1963 [1938]), II, 579. For Taylor, D. E. Stanford, ed., *The Poems of Edward Taylor* (New Haven: Yale University Press, 1960), p. 1.]

*as one much later to be discovered), Edward Taylor (c. 1645-1729), was a Pu-
ritan pastor in Westfield, Massachusetts. His poetry, with its remarkable appeal to the senses, was written chiefly as a series of private meditations prior
to communion or the service of the Lord's Supper.*

[Longing for Heaven]
Anne Bradstreet

As weary pilgrim, now at rest,
 Hugs with delight his silent nest
His wasted limbes, now lye full soft
 That myrie steps, haue troden oft
Blesses himself, to think vpon
 his dangers past, and travalles done
The burning sun no more shall heat
 Nor stormy raines, on him shall beat.
The bryars and thornes no more shall scratch
 nor hungry wolues at him shall catch
He erring pathes no more shall tread
 nor wild fruits eate, in stead of bread,
for waters cold he doth not long
 for thirst no more shall parch his tongue
No rugged stones his feet shall gaule
 nor stumps nor rocks cause him to fall
All cares and feares, he bids farwell
 and meanes in safity now to dwell.
A pilgrim I, on earth, perplext
 wth sinns wth cares and sorrows vext
By age and paines brought to decay
 and my Clay house mouldring away
Oh how I long to be at rest
 and soare on high among the blest.
This body shall in silence sleep
 Mine eyes no more shall ever weep
No fainting fits shall me assaile
 nor grinding paines my body fralle
Wth cares and fears ne'r cumbred be
 Nor losses know, nor sorrowes see
What tho my flesh shall there consume
 it is the bed Christ did perfume
And when a few yeares shall be gone

this mortall shall be cloth'd vpon
A Corrupt Carcasse downe it lyes
    a glorious body it shall rise
In weaknes and dishonour sowne
    in power 'tis rais'd by Christ alone
Then soule and body shall vnite
    and of their maker haue the sight[.]

Prologue
Edward Taylor

Lord, Can a Crumb of Dust the Earth outweigh,
    Outmatch all mountains, nay the Chrystall Sky?
Imbosom in't designs that shall Display
    And trace into the Boundless Deity?
    Yea hand a Pen whose moysture doth guild ore
    Eternall Glory with a glorious glore.

If it its Pen had of an Angels Quill,
    And Sharpend on a Pretious Stone ground tite,
And dipt in Liquid Gold, and mov'de by Skill
    In Christall leaves should golden Letters write
    It would but blot and blur yea jag, and jar
    Unless thou mak'st the Pen, and Scribener.

I am this Crumb of Dust which is design'd
    To make my Pen unto thy Praise alone,
And my dull Pliancy I would gladly grinde
    Unto an Edge on Zions Pretious Stone.
    And Write in Liquid Gold upon thy Name
    My Letters till thy glory forth doth flame.

Let not th'attempts breake down my Dust I pray
    Nor laugh thou them to scorn but pardon give.
Inspire this Crumb of Dust till it display
    Thy Glory through't: and then thy dust shall live.
    Its failings then thou'lt overlook I trust,
    They being Slips slipt from thy Crumb of Dust.

Thy Crumb of Dust breaths two words from its breast,
    That thou wilt guide its pen to write aright

To Prove thou art, and that thou art the best
   And shew thy Properties to shine most bright.
   And then thy Works will shine as flowers on Stems
   Or as in Jewellary Shops, do Jems.

Special Cases: Maryland, Rhode Island, Pennsylvania

Maryland and Roman Catholics

Alone of Britain's thirteen colonies in North America, Maryland began with a Roman Catholic proprietor. Lord Baltimore (or George Calvert, c. 1580-1632) had the original idea, but his son Cecilius (1606-75) actually served as proprietor when the colony began in 1634. The question arises now, as it did then: why should England, a nation prevailingly anti-Catholic, grant land to a Catholic family, land that would likely be a Catholic refuge? In a pamphlet written in 1633 on the proprietor's behalf one finds answers to the query. The reasons set down offer a fascinating commentary on the times, as well as on the low esteem in which the New World was held. Whatever the reasons and rationalizations, the grant was made, the colony settled, and English Catholicism — despite repeated adversity and open hostility — firmly planted.

OBJECT. 1. It may be objected that the Lawes against the Roman Catholikes were made in order to their conformity to the Protestant Religion, for the good of their soules, and by that meanes to free this Kingdome of Popery, rather than of their persons, but such a licence for them to depart this Kingdome, and to go into Mariland, or any country where they may have free liberty of their Religion, would take away all hopes of their conformity to the Church of England.

ANSWER. It is evident that reason of State (for the safety of the King and Kingdome) more than of Religion was the cause and end of those Lawes, for there are no such against divers other professions of Religion in England, although they be as different from the doctrine of the Protestant Church, established by Law in this Kingdome, as that of the Roman Catholiques is. And this reason of State appeares also in the nature of most of those Lawes, for they expresse great doubts and jealousies of the said Roman Catholiques affection to, and dependence on a forraigne power, and tend therefore, most of them, to

---

[Source: Thomas Hughes, S.J., *History of the Society of Jesus in North America*, Documents, Vol. I, pt. 1 (New York: Longmans, Green and Co., 1908), pp. 10-12, 12-14.]

disinable them (by confining, disarming, etc.) from plotting or doing any mischiefe to the King or State, and to secure their allegiance to the King by oathes etc., and the penalties of divers of them are abjuration of the Realme, which puts them out of the way of conformity to the Church of England. Moreover conversion in matter of Religion, if it bee forced, should give little satisfaction to a wise State of the fidelity of such convertites, for those who for worldly respects will breake their faith with God doubtlesse will doe it, upon a fit occasion, much sooner with men; and for voluntary conversions such Lawes could be of no use. Wherefore certainely the safety of King and Kingdome was the sole ayme and end of them.

OBJECT. 2. Such a licence will seem to be a kind of tolleration of (at least a connivence at) Popery which some may find a scruple of Conscience to allow of in any part of the Kings Dominions, because they esteem it a kinde of idolatry, and may therefore conceive that it would scandalize their brethren and the common people here.

ANSWER. Such scrupulous persons may as well have a scruple to let the Roman Catholiques live here, although it be under persecution, as to give way to such a licence, because banishment from a pleasant, plentifull and ones owne native country, into a wildernesse among salvages and wild beasts, although it proceed (in a manner) from ones own election, yet, in this case, where it is provoked by other wayes of persecution, is but an exchange rather then a freedome of punishment, and perhaps in some mens opinions from one persecution to a worse. For divers malefactors in this Kingdome have chosen rather to be hanged, then to go into Virginia, when upon that condition they have bin offered their lives, even at the place of execution. . . .

OBJECT. 3. By it the Kings revenue will be impaired in loosing the benefit which the said Lawes give him, out of Recusants estates, while they continue in England of that profession of Religion.

ANSWER. The end of those Lawes was not the Kings profit, but (as is said before) the freeing of this Kingdome of Recusants which deprives the King of any benefit by them, so as his Majesty will have no wrong don him by such a licence, because he will loose nothing by it of what was intended him by the said Lawes; this is no ancient revenue of the Crowne, for it had inception but in Queene Elizabeths time, and conformity or alienation to a Protestant deprives the King of this revenue. If there were no crimes at all committed in England, the King would loose many fines and confiscations, whereby his revenue would also be impaired (which in the other as well as in this branch of it is but casuall), and yet without question the King and State would both desire it. The same reason holds in this, considering what opinion is had here of the Recusants, wherefore it cannot with good manners be doubted that his Majestie will in this businesse preferre his owne benefit, before that which the State shall conceive to be convenient for his safety, and the publique good.

OBJECT. 4. It would much prejudice this Kingdome by drawing considerable number of people, and transporting of a great deale of wealth, from hence.

ANSWER. The number of all the Recusants in England is not so great, as the departure of them all from hence would make any sensible diminution of people in it, and their profession in Religion would make them the lesse missed here. If the number were great, then consequently (according to the maximes of this State) they were the more dangerous, and there would be the more reason by this meanes to lessen it. And if it bee but small (as indeed it is) then their absence from hence would little prejudice the Kingdome in the decrease of people, nor will such a licence occasion the transportation of much wealth out of England, for they shal not need to carry any considerable summes of money with them, nor is it desired that they should have leave to do so, but only usefull things for a Plantation, as provisions for cloathing and building and planting tooles etc. which will advantage this Kingdome by increase of trade and vent of its Native Commodities, and transferre the rest of their Estates by Bills of Exchange into Bankes beyond Sea, which tends also to the advantage of the trade of England, for more stock by this meanes will be imployed in it.

OBJECT. 5. It may prove dangerous to Virginea and New England, where many English Protestants are planted, Maryland being scituated betweene them both, because it may be suspected that the said Roman Catholiques will bring in the Spaniards or some other forraigne enemy to suppresse the Protestants in those parts, or perhaps grow strong enough to doe it of themselves, or that in time (having the Government of that Province of Mariland in their hands) they may and will shake off any dependance on the Crowne of England.

ANSWER. The English Colonies in New England are at least 500 miles, and that of Virginea 100 miles distant from Mariland, and it will be a long time before planters can be at leisure to think of any such designe, and there is little cause to doubt, that any people as long as they may live peaceably under their owne Government, without oppression either in spiritualls or temporalls, will desire to bring in any forraigners to domineere over them, which misery they would undoubtedly fall into, if any considerable forraigne Prince or State (who are only in this case to be feared) had the possession of the English Collonies in Virginea or New England. But the number of English Protestants already in Virginea and New England, together with the poverty of those parts, makes it very improbable that any forraigne Prince or State will bee tempted to undergoe the charge and hazard of such a remote designe, it being well knowne that the Spanish Colonies in the West Indies are farther distant then Europe is from thence. . . . Much lesse cause is there to feare that they should grow strong enough of themselves to suppresse the Protestants in those parts; for there are already at least three times as many Protestants there, as there are Roman Catholiques in all England. And the Protestants in Virginea and New England

are like to increase much faster by new supplyes of people yearely from England, etc., then are the Roman Catholiques in Mariland. Moreover although
they should (which God forbid and which the English Protestants in those
parts will in all probability be still able to prevent) shake off any dependance on
the Crowne of England, yet first England would by this meanes be freed of so
many suspected persons now in it; secondly, it would loose little by it; and lastly,
even in that case, it were notwithstanding more for the honour of the English
Nation, that English men, although Roman Catholiques, and although not de-
pendant on the Crowne of England, should possesse that country then
forraigners, who otherwise are like to do it. . . .

English America's First Mass

*Andrew White, S.J. (1579-1656), was aboard one of the first two ships which
sailed up the Chesapeake in 1634 to launch Lord Baltimore's colony. As superior to the Jesuit mission in Maryland, Father White labored initially with
his fellow English but soon most earnestly with the Indians (Patuxent and
Piscataway tribes). Recognizing their minority status, Catholics under Baltimore invited Protestants to settle there; in 1649, the former even passed an
Act of Toleration to guarantee religious liberty to such Protestants. Unhappily, when Protestants later seized control of the colony, similar guaran-
tees were not extended to Catholics. Below, Father White describes this early
arrival, the ships touching briefly at Virginia before sailing on northward to
Maryland.*

At length, sailing from this place, we reached the *cape,* which they call *Point
Comfort,* in Virginia, on the 27th of February, full of apprehension, lest the English inhabitants, who were much displeased at our settling, should be plotting
something against us. Nevertheless the letters we carried from the King, and
from the high treasurer of England, served to allay their anger, and to procure
those things which would afterwards be useful to us. For the Governor of Virginia hoped, that by this kindness toward us, he would more easily recover from
the Royal treasury a large sum of money which was due him. They only told us
that a rumor prevailed, that six ships were coming to reduce everything under
the power of the Spaniards, and that for this reason, all the natives were in
arms; this we afterwards found to be true. Yet I fear the rumor had its origin
with the English.

[Source: *Relatio Itineris in Marylandiam; or, Narrative of a Voyage to Maryland* (Baltimore:
Maryland Historical Society, 1944), pp. 30-33.]

After being kindly treated for eight or nine days, we set sail on the third of March, and entering the Chesapeak Bay, we turned our course to the north to reach the *Potomeack* River. The Chesopeacke Bay, ten leagues (30 Italian miles) wide, flows gently between its shores: it is four, five and six fathoms deep, and abounds in fish when the season is favorable; you will scarcely find a more beautiful body of water. Yet it yields the palm to the Potomeack River, which we named after St. Gregory.

Having now arrived at the wished-for country, we allotted names according to circumstances. And indeed the Promontory, which is toward the south, we consecrated with the name of St. Gregory (now Smith Point,) naming the northern one (now Point Lookout) St. Michael's, in honor of all the angels. Never have I beheld a larger or more beautiful river. The Thames seems a mere rivulet in comparison with it; it is not disfigured with any swamps, but has firm land on each side. Fine groves of trees appear, not choked with briers or bushes and undergrowth, but growing at intervals as if planted by the hand of man, so that you can drive a four-horse carriage, wherever you choose, through the midst of the trees. Just at the mouth of the river, we observed the natives in arms. That night, fires blazed through the whole country, and since they had never seen such a large ship, messengers were sent in all directions, who reported that a *Canoe,* like an island had come with as many men as there were trees in the woods. We went on, however, to Herons' Islands, so called from the immense numbers of these birds. The first island we came to, [we called] St. Clement's Island, and as it has a sloping shore, there is no way of getting to it except by wading. Here the women, who had left the ship, to do the washing, upset the boat and came near being drowned, losing also a large part of my linen clothes, no small loss in these parts.

This island abounds in cedar and sassafras trees, and flowers and herbs, for making all kinds of salads, and it also produces a wild nut tree, which bears a very hard walnut with a thick shell and a small but very delicious kernel. Since, however, the island contains only four hundred acres, we saw that it would not afford room enough for the new settlement. Yet we looked for a suitable place to build only a Fort (perhaps on the island itself) to keep off strangers, and to protect the trade of the river and our boundaries; for this was the narrowest crossing-place on the river.

On the day of the Annunciation of the Most Holy Virgin Mary in the year 1634, we celebrated the mass for the first time, on this island. This had never been done before in this part of the world. After we had completed the sacrifice, we took upon our shoulders a great cross, which we had hewn out of a tree, and advancing in order to the appointed place, with the assistance of the Governor and his associates and the other Catholics, we erected a trophy to Christ the Saviour, humbly reciting, on our bended knees, the Litanies of the Sacred Cross, with great emotion.

Rhode Island and the Baptists

Massachusetts, as noted above, saw itself as pursuing a grand "errand into the wilderness," creating there a model community and a pure church. No one was to be allowed to frustrate that errand. When some tried, they were either exiled (Roger Williams in 1635, Anne Hutchinson in 1638) or hanged (four Quakers in Boston, 1659-61). Roger Williams (c. 1603-83), exiled for contending that the Puritans must separate themselves from the impure Church of England and must separate their civil from their ecclesiastical estates, left Massachusetts to found Rhode Island in 1636. That beleaguered little colony was to become a refuge for religious liberty, with Williams himself continuing to be (for nearly half a century) that liberty's leading advocate. Briefly a Baptist, Williams persisted in defense of Baptist rights and liberties, especially when these were denied by his old nemesis, Massachusetts. Bay Colony authorities especially resented Baptist attacks on infant baptism and on civil government's intrusion into religious affairs. When in 1651, three Baptists were arrested in Massachusetts (and one, Obadiah Holmes, publicly whipped), Williams's indignation knew no bounds. Here he would instruct Governor John Endicott concerning the noblest of all liberties: liberty of conscience.

Be pleased then (honored Sir) to remember that that thing which we call conscience is of such a nature (especially in Englishmen) as once a Pope of Rome, at the suffering of an Englishman in Rome, himself observed that although it be groundless, false, and deluded, yet it is not by any arguments or torments easily removed.

I speak not of the stream of the multitude of all nations, which have their ebbings; and flowings in religion (as the longest sword and strongest arm of flesh carries it), but I speak of conscience, a persuasion fixed in the mind and heart of man, which enforceth him to judge (as Paul said of himself a persecutor) and to do so and so with respect to God, His worship.

This conscience is found in all mankind, more or less: in Jews, Turks, Papists, Protestants, pagans. . . .

The Maker and Searcher of our hearts knows with what bitterness I write, as with bitterness of soul I have heard such language as to proceed from yourself and others, who formerly have fled from (with crying out against) persecutors: "You will say, this is your conscience; you will say, you are persecuted, and you are persecuted for your conscience. No, you are conventiclers, heretics, blasphemers, seducers. You deserve to be hanged; rather than one shall be

---

[Source: Perry Miller, *Roger Williams: His Contribution to the American Tradition* (Cleveland: Bobbs-Merrill, 1953), pp. 159, 161, 162-63, 163-64.]

wanting to hang him, I will hang him myself. I am resolved not to leave an heretic in the country. I had rather so many whores and whore-mongers and thieves came amongst us."

Oh Sir, you cannot forget what language and dialect this is, whether not the same unsavory and ungodly, blasphemous and bloody, which the Gardiners and Bonners,[3] both former and latter, used to all that bowed not the state golden image of what conscience soever they were. And indeed, Sir, if the most High be pleased to awaken you to render unto His holy Majesty His due praises, in your truly broken-hearted confessions and supplications, you will then proclaim to all the world, that what profession soever you made of the Lamb, yet these expressions could not proceed from the dragon's mouth. . . .

Oh, remember it is a dangerous combat for the potsherds of the earth to fight with their dreadful potter! It is a dismal battle for poor naked feet to kick against the pricks; it is a dreadful voice from the King of kings and Lord of lords: "Endecott, Endecott, why huntest thou me? why imprisonest thou me? why finest, why so bloodily whippest? why wouldst thou (did not I hold thy bloody hands) hang and burn me?" Yea, Sir, I beseech you remember that it is a dangerous thing to put this to the may-be, to the venture or hazard, to the possibility. "Is it possible," may you well say, "that since I hunt, I hunt not the life of my Savior and the blood of the Lamb of God? I have fought against many several sorts of consciences; is it beyond all possibility and hazard that I have not fought against God, that I have not persecuted Jesus in some of them?"

Sir, I must be humbly bold to say that 'tis impossible for any man or men to maintain their Christ by their sword and to worship a true Christ, to fight against all consciences opposite to theirs, and not to fight against God in some of them and to hunt after the precious life of the true Lord Jesus Christ. Oh, remember, whither your principles and consciences must in time and opportunity force you! . . .

Sir, I know I have much presumed upon your many weighty affairs and thoughts; I end with an humble cry to the Father of mercies, that you may take David's counsel, and silently commune with your own heart upon your bed, reflect upon your own spirit, and believe Him that said it to his overzealous disciples, "You know not what spirit you are of"; that no sleep may seize upon your eyes, nor slumber upon your eyelids, until your serious thoughts have seriously, calmly, and unchangeably (through help from Christ Jesus) fixed,

First, on a moderation towards the spirits and consciences of all mankind, merely differing from or opposing yours with only religious and spiritual opposition;

Secondly, a deep and cordial resolution (in these wonderful searching,

---

3. Bishops Stephen Gardiner (c. 1493-1555) and Edmund Bonner (c. 1500-69) were perceived as among the most vigorous persecutors of Protestants.

Roger Williams statue, U.S. Capitol
(Baptist Joint Committee on Public Affairs)

disputing, and dissenting times) to search, to listen, to pray, to fast, and more fearfully, more tremblingly to enquire what the holy pleasure and the holy mysteries of the most Holy are: in whom I humbly desire to be

Your poor fellow-servant, unfeignedly.
respective and faithful,
ROGER WILLIAMS

Pennsylvania and the Quakers

The Quakers, "above every tribe the most maliciously represented," seemed to the vast majority of their seventeenth-century fellows an example of religion gone mad. Quakers had no ministry, no sacraments, no liturgy, no structure, no weapons; yet, they confidently asserted that they and their precepts would soon take over the world. They honored neither man nor law if, in their judgment, either went against conscience. Originating in England in 1651 under the ministrations of George Fox, Quakerism found itself harshly treated on its home ground. When in 1681 the opportunity came to establish a roomy refuge in the New World, William Penn (1644-1718) seized and magnified that opportunity. Penn's preface to The Christian Quaker *(published in 1669) opened his defense of those modern world "Bereans": that is, those who "received the word with all readiness of mind, and searched the Scriptures daily, whether these things are so" (Acts 17:11).*

To the Noble Bereans of this Age.

When our dear Lord Jesus Christ, the blessed author of the Christian religion, first sent forth his disciples, to proclaim the happy approach of the heavenly kingdom, among several other things that he gave them in charge, it pleased him to make this one of their instructions; "Into whatsoever city or town ye shall enter, enquire who in it is worthy;" foreseeing the ill use unworthy persons would make of that message, and with what unweariness the implacable pharisee, and subtle scribe, would endeavour to pervert the right way of the Lord, and thereby prejudice the simple against the reception of that excellent testimony.

This being the case of the people called Quakers, who above every tribe of men are most maliciously represented, bitterly envied, and furiously oppugned by many of the scribes and pharisees of our time, for as impious wretches as those of that time reputed our blessed Saviour and his constant followers to be; it becometh us, in a condition so desperate, to provide ourselves with some worthy readers, men that dare trust their reason above reports, and be impartial in an age as biassed as this we live in; whose determinations shall not wait upon the sentence of ignorance nor interest, but a sincere and punctual examination of the matter.

And since there are none recorded in sacred writ, on whom the Holy

---

[Source: *The Select Works of William Penn,* 4th ed. (London: William Phillips, 1825), I, 225-26.]

Ghost conferred so honourable a character, but the Bereans of that age (for that they both searched after truth impartially, and when they found it, embraced it readily, for which they were entitled noble); therefore it is that to you, the off-spring of that worthy stock, and noble Bereans of our age, I, in behalf of the so much calumniated abettors of the cause of truth, chose to dedicate this defence of our holy profession from the injurious practices of a sort of men, who, not unlike to the Jews of Thessalonica, that, envying the prosperity of the gospel among your ancestors, made it their business to stir up the multitude against the zealous promoters of it. And no matter what it be, provided they can but obtain their end of fixing an odium upon the Quakers: they do not only boldly condemn what they esteem worst in us (how deservedly we will not now say) but insinuate what is best to be criminal.

The sobriety of our lives, they call a cheat for custom; and our incessant preachings and holy living, a decoy to advance our party: if we say nothing to them when they interrogate us, it is sullenness or inability; if we say something to them, it is impertinency, or equivocation. We must not believe as we do believe, but as they would have us believe, which they are sure to make obnoxious enough, that they may the more securely inveigh against us. Nor must our writings mean what we say we mean by them, but what they will have them to mean, lest they should want proofs for their charges. It was our very case that put David upon that complaint, "Every day they wrest my words: all their thoughts are against me for evil." But to David's God we commit our slandered cause, and to you the Bereans of our age.

Degenerate not from the example of your progenitors; if you do, you are no longer true Bereans, and to such we inscribe this work: if you do not, we may assure ourselves of the justice of a fair enquiry and an equal judgment.

The God and Father of our Lord Jesus Christ augment your desire after truth, give you clearer discerning of the truth, and enable you both more readily to receive, and with greater resolution to maintain the truth. I am

A christian Quaker, and your christian friend,

WILLIAM PENN.

Penn and Liberty of Conscience, 1686

Penn's Holy Experiment rested upon the conviction that men and women were not to be coerced in matters of religion, for true religion flourished best

[Source: *The Select Works of William Penn,* 4th ed. (London: William Phillips, 1825), II, 507-8.]

where force was found least. Philadelphia, literally "brotherly love," was so named because on that principle, extended to all persons, a noble society can be built. Even when Penn had problems — and he had many — he continued to argue that religious persecution was a costly as well as a bloody business. Here, three years before England's Act of Toleration, Penn issues "A Persuasive to Moderation to Church Dissenters in Prudence and Conscience." The brief segment below is followed by thirty-five pages of unconventional argumentation against the conventional wisdom of the day.

Moderation, the subject of this discourse, is, in plainer English, liberty of conscience to church-dissenters: a cause I have, with all humility, undertaken to plead, against the prejudices of the times.

That there is such a thing as conscience, and the liberty of it, in reference to faith and worship towards God, must not be denied, even by those that are most scandalized at the ill use some seem to have made of such pretences. But to settle the terms: by conscience, I understand, the apprehension and persuasion a man has of his duty to God: by liberty of conscience, I mean, a free and open profession and exercise of that duty; especially in worship: but I always premise this conscience to keep within the bounds of morality, and that it be neither frantic or mischievous, but a good subject, a good child, a good servant, in all the affairs of life; as exact to yield to Caesar the things that are Caesar's, as jealous of withholding from God the thing that is God's. — In brief, he that acknowledges the civil government under which he lives, and that maintains no principle hurtful to his neighbour in his civil property. For he that in any thing violates his duty to these relations, cannot be said to observe it to God, who ought to have his tribute out of it. Such do not reject their prince, parent, master, or neighbour, but God, who enjoins that duty to them. Those pathetic words of Christ will naturally enough reach the case, "In that ye did it not to them, ye did it not to me:" for duty to such relations hath a divine stamp; and divine right runs through more things of the world, and acts of our lives, than we are aware of; and sacrilege may be committed against more than the church. Nor will a dedication to God, of the robbery from man, expiate the guilt of disobedience: for though zeal could turn gossip to theft, his altars would renounce the sacrifice.

The conscience then that I state, and the liberty I pray, carrying so great a salvo and deference to public and private relations, no ill design can, with any justice, be fixed upon the author, or reflection upon the subject, which by this time, I think, I may venture to call a toleration.

But to this so much craved, as well as needed, toleration, I meet with two objections of weight, the solving of which will make way for it in this kingdom. And the first is, a disbelief of the possibility of the thing. 'Toleration of dissenting worships from that established, is not practicable,' say some, 'without danger to the state, with which it is interwoven.' This is political. The other objection is, 'That admitting dissenters to be in the wrong, (which is always premised by the national church) such latitude were the way to keep up the disunion, and instead of compelling them into a better way, leave them in the possession and pursuit of their old errors.' This is religious. I think I have given the objections fairly; it will be my next business to answer them as fully.

The English and the Indian

Indian Missions in Massachusetts

The most famous of New England's missionaries to the Indians, John Eliot (1604-90), graduate of Cambridge University, spent most of his professional life as the Congregational (Puritan) minister of the church in Roxbury, Massachusetts. Eliot's enduring achievement, the translation of the entire Bible into the language of the Algonkian, reached completion in 1663. With the Bible in their own language and in their own hands, native Americans — Eliot fervently hoped — would be prepared to instruct their own people, train their own clergy, and free themselves of European intrusion. Something of Eliot's method in preaching to the Indians can be gleaned from this 1647 entry in John Winthrop's Journal.

Mention was made before of some beginning to instruct the Indians, etc. Mr. John Eliot, teacher of the church of Roxbury, found such encouragement, as he took great pains to get their language, and in a few months could speak of the things of God to their understanding; and God prospered his endeavors, so as he kept a constant lecture to them in two places, one week at the wigwam of one Wabon, a new sachem near Watertown mill, and the other the next week in the wigwam of Cutshamekin near Dorchester mill. And for the furtherance of the work of God, divers of the English resorted to his lecture, and the governor and other of the magistrates and elders sometimes; and the Indians began to repair thither from other parts. His manner of proceeding was thus; he would persuade one of the other elders or some magistrate to begin the exercise with prayer in English; then he took a text, and read it first in the Indian language, and after in English; then he preached to them in Indian about an hour; (but first I should have spoke of the catechising their children, who were soon

[Source: James K. Hosmer, ed., *Winthrop's Journal* (New York: Charles Scribner's Sons, 1908), pp. 318-21.]

brought to answer him some short questions, whereupon he gave each of them an apple or a cake) then he demanded of some of the chiefs, if they understood him; if they answered, yea, then he asked of them if they had any questions to propound. And they had usually two or three or more questions, which he did resolve. At one time (when the governor was there and about two hundred people, Indian and English, in one wigwam of Cutshamekin's) an old man asked him, if God would receive such an old man as he was; to whom he answered by opening the parable of the workmen that were hired into the vineyard; and when he had opened it, he asked the old man, if he did believe it, who answered he did, and was ready to weep. A second question was, what was the reason, that when all Englishmen did know God, yet some of them were poor. His answer was, 1. that God knows it is better for his children to be good than to be rich; he knows withal, that if some of them had riches, they would abuse them, and wax proud and wanton, etc., therefore he gives them no more riches than may be needful for them, that they may be kept from pride, etc., to depend upon him, 2. he would hereby have men know, that he hath better blessings to bestow upon good men than riches, etc., and that their best portion is in heaven, etc. A third question was, if a man had two wives, (which was ordinary with them,) seeing he must put away one, which he should put away. To this it was answered, that by the law of God the first is the true wife, and the other is no wife; but if such a case fell out, they should then repair to the magistrates, and they would direct them what to do, for it might be, that the first wife might be an adulteress, etc., and then she was to be put away. When all their questions were resolved, he concluded with prayer in the Indian language.

The Indians were usually very attentive, and kept their children so quiet as caused no disturbance. Some of them began to be seriously affected, and to understand the things of God, and they were generally ready to reform whatsoever they were told to be against the word of God, as their sorcery, (which they call powwowing,) their whoredoms, etc., idleness, etc. The Indians grew very inquisitive after knowledge both in things divine and also human, so as one of them, meeting with an honest plain Englishman, would needs know of him, what were the first beginnings (which we call principles) of a commonwealth. The Englishman, being far short in the knowledge of such matters, yet ashamed that an Indian should find an Englishman ignorant of any thing, bethought himself what answer to give him, at last resolved upon this, viz. that the first principle of a commonwealth was salt, for (saith he) by means of salt we can keep our flesh and fish, to have it ready when we need it, whereas you lose much for want of it, and are sometimes ready to starve. A second principle is iron, for thereby we fell trees, build houses, till our land, etc. A third is ships, by which we carry forth such commodities as we have to spare, and fetch in such as we need, as cloth, wine, etc. Alas! (saith the Indian) then I fear, we shall never be a commonwealth, for we can neither make salt, nor iron, nor ships.

King Philip's War, 1675

In addition to the labors of Eliot, the Mayhew family (Thomas and his grandson, Experience) watched over a major mission station for the "Praying Indians" (i.e., converts) on Martha's Vineyard. A devastating blow to all mission effort in New England was King Philip's War. Erupting in 1675, the Wampanoags — soon joined by other tribes — burned and bloodied much of Massachusetts and Rhode Island. The loss of life and property was enormous. Eliot in a letter to the New England Company in London writes in the midst of this tragedy which he seeks to comprehend.

I must change my ditty now. I have much to write of lamentation over the work of Christ among our praying Indians, of which God hath called you to be nursing Fathers. The work (in our Patent) is under great sufferings. It is killed (in words, wishes & expression) but not in deeds as yet. It is (as it were) dead, but not buried, nor (I believe) shall be. . . . We needed through our corruptions & infirmities all that is come upon us & which the Lord hath performed all his work, his purging work upon us; he can easily and will lay by the rod. When the house is swept, he will lay away the broom. . . . I complain not of our sufferings, but meekly praise the Lord that they be now worse. Yet I cannot but say, they are greater than I can or in modesty & meekness is not for me to express. Be it so. It is the Lord that hath done it, & shall living man complain? . . .

There be 350 souls or therabout put upon a bleake bare Island, the fittest we have, where they suffer hunger & cold. There is neither food nor competent fuel to be had, & they are bare in clothing because they cannot be received to work for clothing, as they were wont to do. Our rulers are careful to order them food, but it is so hard to be performed that they suffer much. I beg your prayers, that the Lord would take care of them & provide for them. I cannot without difficulty, hardship & peril get unto them. I have been but twice with them, yet I praise God that they be put out of the way of greater perils, dangers & temptations. . . .

At another place there were a company making ready to go to the Island, but were surprised by the Enemy & carried away captive & we cannot hear anything of them. What is become of them, whether any of them be martyred we cannot tell. We cannot say how many there be of them, but more than an hundred, & sundry of them right Godly, both men and women. . . . All in Plymouth Patent are still in quiet & so are all our [Martha's Vineyard] Indians & all the Nantucket Indians. I beg prayers that they may be still preserved.

[Source: *Some Correspondence between the Governors and Treasurers of the New England Company in London and the Commissioners of the United Colonies in America* . . . (London: Spottiswoode & Co., 1896), pp. 52-54. Spelling and punctuation have been modernized.]

William Penn and the Indians, 1681

*Penn's 1701 treaty with the Indians, immortalized in the familiar painting of
Benjamin West's, had its foundation in the charity and humanity of Penn
himself and of the religious principles he espoused. Even before the first
Quakers arrived in Philadelphia from England, Penn sought an acceptable
agreement with the Indians regarding land. He also ordered his agents to
treat the native Americans with all possible decency and equity. By their
hands he dispatched this letter from London on October 18, 1681.*

My Friends,

There is a great God and power that hath made the world, and all things
therein, to whom you and I, and all people owe their being and well-being, and
to whom you and I must one day give an account for all that we do in the world.
This great God hath written his law in our hearts, by which we are taught and
commanded to love, and help, and do good to one another. Now this great God
hath been pleased to make me concerned in your part of the world, and the
king of the country, where I live, hath given me a great province therein; but I
desire to enjoy it *with your love and consent,* that we may always live together as
neighbours and friends; else what would the great God do to us, who hath
made us, not to devour and destroy one another, but to live soberly and kindly
together in the world? Now, I would have you well observe, that I am very sensible of the unkindness and injustice that have been too much exercised towards
you by the people of these parts of the world, who have sought themselves, and
to make great advantages by you, rather than to be examples of goodness and
patience unto you, which I hear hath been a matter of trouble to you, and
caused great grudgings and animosities, sometimes to the shedding of blood,
which hath made the great God angry. But I am not such a man, as is well
known in my own country. I have great love and regard towards you, and desire
to win and gain your love and friendship by a kind, just, and peaceable life; and
the people I send are of the same mind, and shall, in all things, behave themselves accordingly; and, if in anything any shall offend you or your people, you
shall have a full and speedy satisfaction for the same, by an equal number of just
men on both sides; that, by no means you may have just occasion of being offended against them.

I shall shortly come to you myself, at which time we may more largely and
freely confer and discourse of these matters, in the mean time I have sent my
commissioners to treat with you about land, and a firm league of peace. Let me

---

[Source: *Some Account of the Conduct of the Religious Society of Friends towards the Indian
Tribes . . .* (London: Edward Marsh, 1844), pp. 29-30.]

Penn's Treaty with the Indians by Benjamin West
(Pennsylvania Academy of Fine Arts)

desire you to be kind to them, and the people, and receive these *presents* and *tokens,* which I have sent you, as a testimony of my *good will* to you, and my resolution to live justly, peaceably, and friendly with you.

I am, your loving Friend,
WILLIAM PENN.

Virginia Indians and the College of William & Mary

While the 1622 Indian revolt dealt a severe blow to Virginia's missionary interest, the early idealism did not altogether disappear. When the College of William & Mary received its charter in 1693, part of the rationale for a college was to offer education (Christian, of course) to selected young Indian men. Here the colony's governor, Francis Nicholson, issues instructions in

[Source: W. S. Perry, *Historical Collections Relating to the American Colonial Church* (New York: AMS Press, 1969 [1870]), I, 123-24.]

1700 on approaching and informing the Indians concerning this new educational opportunity for their children. None responded, however, to this call.

You shall acquaint the s^d Indians that you have particular directions from me, (the chief Govr of Virginia) under the great King of Engl^d, &c. (my most sacred master), to discourse & treat with them, concerning the several particulars following.

ITEM. You shall acquaint them, that a great & good man who lately died in Engl^d (the hon^{ble} Robert Boyle, Esqr.), having a great love for the Indians, hath left money enough to the College here in Virginia, to keep 9 or 10 Indian children at it, & to teach them to read, write & all other arts & sciences, that the best Englishmen's sons do learn.

ITEM. You shall acquaint them that if they let their children be brought to the College & educated there, the Englishmen will teach them to know their great Almighty God who is able to do every thing for them & will give them all good things as he doth to the Englishmen.

ITEM. You shall acquaint them that this next Summer the rooms will be made ready at the College for their reception & accommodation & that if any one Great nation will send 3 or 4 of their children thither, they shall have good, valuable clothes, books & learning & shall be well look'd after both in health & sickness & when they are good scholars, shall be sent back to teach the same things to their own people. Let the children be young, about 7 or 8 years of age, seeing they are to be taught from the first beginning of letters & let them have a careful Indian man of their own country to wait upon them & to serve them & to talk continually with them in their language that they do not forget it, whilst they are amongst the English.

ITEM. You shall acquaint them that while their Children are at the College, their Fathers or other relations or Friends may come & see them as often as they please; they shall be made welcome themselves & will see how well their children are used.

ITEM. You shall take particular care to make the great men of the Indians thoroughly sensible of every particular part of these propositions, & you shall use your best Interest and endeavour to promote this good work & that no jealousy or apprehensions of danger may remain in the Indians, you shall assure them, that I am their very good friend & am very willing to have a trade and commerce with them & if they think fit some of them may safely come in & see the College & be satisfied of the truth of the aforementioned particulars.

ITEM. You shall in the name of the College, give them all imaginable assurance, that their Children shall have very good usage & all upon free cost.

Suggested Reading (Chapter One)

On the nature of religion itself, besides the older classics of G. F. Moore, *The Birth and Growth of Religion* (1924), A. N. Whitehead, *Religion in the Making* (1926), and Rudolf Otto, *The Idea of the Holy* (1923), it is now possible to consult the major reference work edited by Mircea Eliade, *The Encyclopedia of Religion,* 16 vols. (1987). For works particularly relevant to Native American experience, see Anthony F. C. Wallace, *Religion: An Anthropological View* (1966), and Vine Deloria, Jr., *For This Land: Writings on Religion in America* (1999).

Comprehensive orientation to the subjects treated in this documentary history is found in the three-volume *Encyclopedia of the American Religious Experience,* ed. Charles H. Lippy and Peter W. Williams (1988). For a classic narrative survey, see Sydney E. Ahlstrom, *A Religious History of the American People* (1972). Other broad narratives include Martin E. Marty, *Pilgrims in Their Own Land: 500 Years of Religion in America* (1984), Edwin S. Gaustad and Leigh Eric Schmidt, *The Religious History of America* (2002), and Mark A. Noll, *The Old Religion in a New World: The Story of North American Christianity* (2002). Geographical orientation over time is provided by E. S. Gaustad and Philip L. Barlow, *New Historical Atlas of Religion in America* (2000).

For general treatment of Native American religious practice, see Joel W. Marin, *The Land Looks After Us: A History of Native American Religion* (2001). Examples of Indian cosmology and ethics can be sampled in George Lankford, ed., *Native American Legends, Southeastern Legends: Tales from the Natchez, Caddo, Biloxi, Chickasaw, and Other Nations* (1987), Ray A. Williamson and Claire R. Farrer, eds., *Earth and Sky: Native American Cosmovision* (1993), and Barry O'Connell, ed., *On Our Own Ground: The Complete Writings of William Apess, a Pequot* (1992). The edition of Black Elk referred to in the text is that published by the University of Nebraska Press in 1979: *Black Elk Speaks: Being the Life Story of a Holy Man of the Oglala Sioux.* Carlos Castañeda's work includes these titles: *The Teachings of Don Juan* (1968), *The Second Ring of Power* (1977), *The Fire Within* (1984), and *The Art of Dreaming* (1993).

Indian religion is dealt with broadly in Sam D. Gill's *Native American Religions* (1982) and in Roger D. Kennedy's *Hidden Cities: The Discovery and Loss of Ancient North American Civilization* (1994), and more narrowly in Joel W. Martin's *Sacred Revolt: The Muskogees' Struggle for a New World* (1991), Lee Irwin's *The Dreamseekers: Native American Visionary Traditions of the Great Plains* (1994), and Judith Vander's *Shoshone Ghost Dance Religion: Poetry Songs and Great Basin Context* (1997). See also James Axtell, *The Indian Peoples of Eastern America* (1975), Axtell, *The Invasion Within* (1985), and Mark St. Pierre and Tilda Long Soldier, *Walking in a Sacred Manner: Healers, Dreamers, and Pipe Carriers — Medicine Women of the Plains Indians* (1995).

On the missionary efforts of the Spanish, French, and English among Native Americans, a fine general study is Henry W. Bowden, *American Indians and Christian Missions* (1981). More narrowly focused is Christopher Vecsey, *On the Padres' Trails* (1996). Treatments of missionary contact with Native Americans cannot avoid interpretive evaluation. For studies showing missionaries in a relatively positive light, see Alden T. Vaughan's *New England Frontier: Puritans and Indians, 1620-1675* (1965), and Richard W. Cogley, *John Eliot's Mission to the Indians Before King Philip's War* (1999). For the opposite perspective, see George E. Tinker, *Missionary Conquest: The Gospel and Native American Cultural Genocide* (1993), and Francis Jennings, *The Invasion of America* (1975). Treatment alert to the multivalent effects of Christianization in one Native American tradition is found in Michael D. McNally, *Ojibwe Singers: Hymns, Grief, and a Native Culture in Motion* (2000).

David Beers Quinn's five-volume work, *New American World* (1979), is an invaluable storehouse for the entire period of European exploration. Students who find this a useful resource will also be interested in Quinn's own works, including *North American Discovery to First Settlement* (1978) and *Set Fair for Roanoke* (1985). As comprehensive in its execution as in its conception is the three-volume *Encyclopedia of the North American Colonies,* ed. Jacob Ernest Cooke (1993). Useful surveys of the colonial period include C. O. Sauer's *Sixteenth Century North America* (1971), and especially Alan Taylor's *American Colonies* (2001). Orientation for religious history is provided by Charles H. Lippy, Robert Choquette, and Stafford Poole, *Christianity Comes to the Americas* (1992); Jon Butler, *Religion in Colonial America* (2000); and with special attention to recent trends in scholarship, "Religion in Early America," special issue of *William and Mary Quarterly* 54 (Oct. 1997): 693-848.

Charles Gibson's *Spain in America* (1966) is a classic in its field, while the religious dimensions of that topic (with treatment also of English and French colonies) are more explicitly detailed by John Tracy Ellis, *Catholics in Colonial America* (1963), and in the early chapters of James Hennesey, S.J., *American Catholics: A History of the Roman Catholic Community in the United States* (1981). Carlos E. Castañeda, *Our Catholic Heritage in Texas, 1519-1936* (7 vols., 1936-1958), is thorough for its region, while Ramón A. Gutiérrez, *When Jesus Came, the Corn Mothers Went Away: Marriage, Sexuality, and Power in New Mexico, 1500-1846* (1991), reflects more broadly on the mixture of Catholic and native cultures. Cornelius J. Jaenen has examined both the "missionary church" and the "colonial church" in *The Role of the Church in New France* (1967). All students of French colonial religion sustain a continued debt to the many volumes of *The Jesuit Relations and Allied Documents,* ed. R. G. Thwaites (1896-1901).

The Dutch effort in the New World to combine two competing interests is the subject of George L. Smith's *Religion and Trade in New Netherland* (1973).

Randall Balmer's *A Perfect Babel of Confusion: Dutch Religion and English Culture in the Middle Colonies* (new ed., 2002) reveals the depth of the continuing contest between Dutch and English in New York. But for all religious history in early New York the indispensable source is the six-volume work edited by Hugh Hastings, *Ecclesiastical Records, State of New York* (1901-05). No other state or colony has had its religious history documented on such a scale.

The early history of Virginia may be usefully approached first through the writings of its adventurer-governor: *Captain John Smith: A Select Edition of His Writings* (1988). For Virginia's established church, there is much on parish life in Dell Upton's engaging and well-illustrated *Holy Things and Profane* (1986). A broader survey, moving beyond Virginia, is provided by John F. Woolverton, *Colonial Anglicanism in North America* (1984). For New England in the seventeenth century, there is an ocean of useful scholarship. An excellent effort at linking new-world developments with ongoing history in the old world is Stephen Foster, *The Long Argument: English Puritanism and the Shaping of New England Culture* (1991). That transatlantic theme is well maintained by the essays in Francis J. Bremer, ed., *Puritanism* (1993). The leader who was to Massachusetts as John Smith was to Virginia is well served by *The Journal of John Winthrop, 1630-1649*, ed. Richard S. Dunn, *et al.* (1996, also available as an abridged paperback). Biographical studies by Edmund S. Morgan, *The Puritan Dilemma: The Story of John Winthrop* (1958), and Francis J. Bremer, *John Winthrop: America's Forgotten Founding Father* (2003), constitute a most useful pair. The edited volume, E. S. Morgan, *Puritan Political Ideas* (1965), remains very useful for orientation to New England's early history. For the pilgrims of southeastern Massachusetts there still is no better book than William Bradford's *Of Plimoth Plantation*, which is available in many modern editions, but see also John Demos, *A Little Commonwealth: Family Life in Plymouth Colony* (1970). On the Rhode Island story, consult E. S. Gaustad, *Liberty of Conscience: Roger Williams in America* (1991). The fullest account of Baptist development remains William G. McLoughlin, *New England Dissent, 1630-1833: The Baptists and Separation of Church and State*, 2 vols. (1971). For Pennsylvania and the Quakers, see Mary Maples Dunn, *William Penn: Politics and Conscience* (1967), Gary B. Nash, *Quakers and Politics: Pennsylvania, 1681-1726* (1968), Sally Schwarz, *"A Mixed Multitude": The Struggle for Toleration in Colonial Pennsylvania* (1988), and especially Mary Maples Dunn and Richard S. Dunn, eds., *The Papers of William Penn*, 5 vols. (1981-87). On Maryland, in addition to the Catholic histories noted above, see Ronald Hoffman and Sally D. Mason, *Princes of Ireland, Planters of Maryland: A Carroll Saga, 1500-1782* (2000).

TWO

Americanizing the Ways of Faith

By the middle of the eighteenth century, it was obvious to all (as it had been earlier to some) that Europe's religious patterns were not to be duplicated in America. Something was lost — or perhaps gained? — in transition. No state church ever dominated all of the thirteen colonies: not Spain's, not France's, not Holland's, and not even England's. No uniform liturgy prevailed, no official creed was sanctioned, no clerical class came into being. For many Americans in and around 1750, this palpable variety provoked more alarm than comfort, for the pervading assumption throughout Western civilization was that social and political stability rested on a foundation of religious uniformity. However widely that assumption was held, in fact only two groups in colonial America were strong enough to try to act upon it: Congregationalism and Anglicanism.

Religion and Social Order

In New England the Puritan or Congregational way enjoyed the advantages of an early start, a steady increase in population, an educated and disciplined ministry, a viable economy, and an intimate interaction on its own ground between political and ecclesiastical authority. Yet, religious uniformity seemed impossible to achieve or maintain; or, if not impossible, the cost of such maintenance seemed extraordinarily high. For one hundred years or more, New England nonetheless banned, whipped, harangued, and hanged in its determined effort to preserve and protect a given social order. Many still hoped that what had come to be called "the New England Way" need not be limited to New England alone. And if by 1700 or 1750 Old England no longer cared, this was no reason to assume that Puritan principles could not spread southward and — someday — even to an unopened West.

The course of Anglican development was less steady, even if in the long run (with England's overt backing) it seemed to be more sure. For *this* colonial

church, after all, was but the counterpart of *the* Church, England's own. Powerful lords and bishops, wealthy patrons and endowed societies, conspired to advance the episcopal cause whenever and wherever possible throughout North
America. Royal pressures thrust Anglicanism upon an unwilling Boston, over-
turned a Catholic proprietorship in Maryland, thwarted the irregular and unlicensed advances of dissent, and bestowed privilege after privilege upon a
Church synonymous with social stability and good form. Yet here too, as with
Congregationalism, the cost of conformity came high. Ultimately, colonial anxieties and resentments outweighed all those legal advantages that Anglicanism
enjoyed.

Religious and Racial Variety

Thus, variety and dissent more than quiet conformity and sober decorum came
to characterize the American scene. The diversity resulted, in part, from the several doors opened to Europe's religiously oppressed. Refugees from Germany's
Palatinate settled along the Hudson River valley, in New York. Lutherans fleeing
from persecution in Salzburg, Austria, found their way to Savannah, Georgia.
The Atlantic crossing, however filled with tragedy and terror, seemed less fearful than the horrors left behind. But in one respect, diversity in the eighteenth
century declined: France's Jesuits were forced to withdraw from their stations
all across North America and, in their withdrawing, religion on this continent
was forever after altered.

Europe, however, accounted for only a small part of the religious diversity
growing more evident decade after decade. The empty lands themselves encouraged experimentation and novelty, especially when in a colony such as
Pennsylvania no heavy-handed laws oppressed the experimenters. For colonial
churches, far removed from ecclesiastical courts and spiritual overlords, the
tendency to become their own masters was almost beyond resisting. And those
who moved farther inland, away from even civil overlords, moved beyond experimentation to wild fanaticism, at least in the eyes of some beholders:
". . . People's Brains are turn'd and bewilder'd." Not yet had a nation come into
being nor a law proclaiming religious liberty to all been adopted, but the unof-
ficial practice of the 1750s and 60s helped shape the official policy of the 1780s
and 90s.

The most striking diversity, as well as the most troubling, was racial
rather than religious. Yet religion spoke, however feebly or ineffectively, to that
difference. Blackness posed the question of human rights, while slavery posed
the issue of property rights. When those two fundamental concerns knitted
themselves confoundedly together, it took more political and theological acumen than most possessed to cut the gnarled knot. Even before Jefferson's egali-

tarian Declaration, however, religious voices attacked slavery as an institution, deplored dehumanization as a demonstrable fact. The Indian raised the question of property in a different way: not that he *was* property (like the slave) but that he interfered with property (of the whites). The Indian did not even have to claim any parcel of land as his own; he had only to roam through it or forage from it or live too near it. The cultural clash of the earlier period continued as the drums of death relentlessly beat on.

Passions and Intellect

While men and women of varying ethnic, religious, and racial identifications often saw nothing but their differences, some commonalities and some hope for community did exist. If the circumstances were right, the unities could even count for more than the varieties. In that wave of religious excitement known as the Great Awakening, many found the depths of religious feeling more meaningful than the superficiality of denomination or language or even race. Ecclesiastical divisions melted before the powerful and often extemporaneous preaching of such diverse voices as Jonathan Edwards (Congregational), Gilbert Tennent (Presbyterian), Theodore Frelinghuysen (Dutch Reformed), and George Whitefield (Anglican, never quite Methodist). In the course of this mass movement of the 1740s and beyond, bonds were forged for another mass movement a generation later: the American Revolution. Also, the Awakening intensified the concern for a zealous ministry and for an education appropriate thereto. Finally, the revivalism of this period stimulated and in large degree directed the thinking of colonial America's most profound philosopher-theologian, Jonathan Edwards.

By the time of the Revolution, the European and English churches transplanted to America's river banks and rocky shores had begun to take on a character and style appropriate to their new locale. The very fact of overwhelming and apparently ineradicable diversity made a new style inevitable, but so did geography and expediency, Old World irrelevance and New World hope.

1. Religion and Social Order

Congregationalism (Puritanism)

Anne Hutchinson (1591-1643)

As noted in Chapter One, Massachusetts in its effort to maintain a homoge-
neous social order found it expedient in 1635 to exile Roger Williams. That
action seemed to enlarge the Bay Colony's problems more than solve them.
For in succeeding years, dissenters continued to speak and continued to
threaten. Shortly after Williams's departure, Anne Hutchinson, "a woman
of ready wit and bold spirit" (the words are John Winthrop's), raised Puri-
tan anxieties and troubled the still waters. She, it was charged, did not be-
lieve good works to be a sign of salvation, such demotion of morality threat-
ening the whole moral order of New England. She also asserted that the
Holy Spirit granted direct and immediate inspiration to the true believer,
such elevation of private communication with God challenging ministerial
authority within this Bible commonwealth. Anne Hutchinson presumed too
much, talked too much, knew too much; in short, she did things not "fitting
for your sex." In a trial that verged on a farce, this mother, wife, midwife,
and theologian was examined in November of 1637; to the surprise of few,
she was found guilty. Like Roger Williams, she fled for refuge first to Rhode
Island, later to Long Island where she and several young children were slain
by Indians.

[Source: Thomas Hutchinson, *The History of the Colony and Province of Massachusetts Bay*
(Cambridge: Harvard University Press, 1936), II, 366, 383-84.]

The Examination of Anne Hutchinson

John Winthrop, Governor (JW): Mrs. Hutchinson, you are called here as one of those that have troubled the peace of the commonwealth and the churches here; you are known to be a woman that hath had a great share in the promoting and divulging of those opinions that are causes of this trouble, and to be nearly joined not only in affinity and affection with some of those the court had taken notice of and passed censure upon, but you have spoken diverse things (as we have been informed) very prejudicial to the honour of the churches and ministers thereof[.] [A]nd you have maintained a meeting and an assembly in your house that hath been condemned by the general assembly as a thing not tolerable nor comely in the sight of God nor fitting for your sex. . . .

Anne Hutchinson (AH): I am called here to answer before you, but I hear no things laid to my charge.

JW: I have told you some already and more I can tell you.

AH: Name one, Sir.

JW: Have I not named some already?

AH: What have I said or done?

JW: Why for your doings, this you did harbour and countenance those that are parties in this faction that you have heard of.

AH: That's matter of conscience, Sir.

JW: Your conscience you must keep, or it must be kept for you. . . .

AH: If you please to give me leave, I shall give you the ground of what I know to be true. Being much troubled to see the falseness of the constitution of the church of England, I had like to have turned separatist[.] [W]hereupon I kept a day of solemn humiliation and pondering, this scripture was brought unto me — he that denies Jesus Christ is the antichrist[.] This I considered of and in considering found that the papists did not deny him to be come in the flesh, nor we did not deny him: who then was antichrist? Was the Turk antichrist only? The Lord knows that I could not open scripture; he must by his prophetical office open it unto me. So after that being unsatisfied in the thing, the Lord was pleased to bring this scripture out of the Hebrews. He that denies the testament denies the testator, and in this did open unto me and give me to see that those which did not teach the new covenant had the spirit of antichrist, and upon this he did discover the ministry unto me; and, ever since, I bless the Lord, he hath let me see which was the clear ministry and which the wrong. Since that time I confess I have been more choice and he hath left me to distinguish between the voice of my beloved and the voice of Moses, the voice of John Baptist and the voice of antichrist, for all those voices are spoken of in scripture. Now if you do condemn me for speaking what in my conscience I know to be truth, I must commit myself unto the Lord.

Second Officer of the Court: How do you know that that was the spirit?

AH: How did Abraham know that it was God that bid him offer his son, being a breach of the sixth commandment?

Third Officer: By an immediate voice.

AH: So to me by an immediate revelation.

Third Officer: How! an immediate revelation.

AH: By the voice of his own spirit to my soul. I will give you another scripture, Jer. 46: 27, 28 — out of which the Lord showed me what he would do for me and the rest of his servants. But after he was pleased to reveal himself to me I did presently like Abraham run to Hagar. And after that he did let me see the atheism of my own heart, for which I begged of the Lord that it might not remain in my heart, and being thus, he did show me this (a twelvemonth after) which I told you of before. . . . Therefore, I desire you to look to it, for you see this scripture fulfilled this day and therefore I desire you that as you tender the Lord and the church and commonwealth to consider and look what you do. You have power over my body but the Lord Jesus hath power over my body and soul; and assure yourselves thus much, you do as much as in you lies to put the Lord Jesus Christ from you, and if you go on in this course you begin, you will bring a curse upon you and your posterity, and the mouth of the Lord hath spoken it.

Mary Dyer (?-1660)

Quakers had a special capacity for unnerving New England. As in the case of Anne Hutchinson, so with the Quakers: the claim to direct inspiration from God (the Inner Light dwelling in all persons) bid fair to undermine all authority, be it biblical, political, clerical. The similarity between Anne Hutchinson and Mary Dyer is not just theoretical. When the former was excommunicated from her church in 1638, the latter also left the church and also fled to Rhode Island. Mary along with her husband William lived in Newport, but they traveled to England in the 1650s where Mary heard and heeded the teaching of George Fox, founder of the Society of Friends. Upon returning to New England as a Quaker in 1657, Mary Dyer quickly ran afoul of Boston's unrelenting opposition to her "Enthusiastick" preaching. She was jailed, expelled, and warned — but to no avail. Told that a return to Boston would result in her death, Mary Dyer nonetheless returned in May, 1660 — to be hanged. The hanging took place despite husband William's poignant plea to Governor John Endicott: "O, do not deprive me of her, but I pray give

---

[Source: Horatio Rogers, *Mary Dyer of Rhode Island* . . . (Providence: Preston and Rounds, 1896), pp. 84- 86; for her husband's letter, see pp. 94-97.]

her me once again & I shall be so much obliged forever." Below is a portion of Mary Dyer's address to the General Court of Massachusetts after the sentence of death had been passed.

To the General Court now in Boston.

Whereas I am by many charged with the Guiltiness of my own Blood; if you mean, in my coming to Boston, I am therein clear, and justified by the Lord, in whose Will I came, who will require my Blood of you, be sure, who have made a Law to take away the Lives of the Innocent Servants of God, if they come among you, who are called by you, *Cursed Quakers;* altho' I say, and am a living Witness for them and the Lord, that he hath Blessed them, and sent them unto you: Therefore be not found Fighters against God, but let my Counsel and Request be accepted with you, To Repeal all such Laws, that the Truth and Servants of the Lord may have free Passage among you, and you be kept from shedding Innocent Blood, which I know there are many among you would not do, if they knew it so to be: Nor can the Enemy that stirreth you up thus to destroy this Holy Seed, in any measure countervail the great Damage that you will by thus doing procure: Therefore, seeing the Lord hath not hid it from me, it lyeth upon me, in Love to your Souls, thus to persuade you: I have no self-ends, the Lord knoweth, for if my Life were freely granted by you, it would not avail me, nor could I expect it of you, so long as I should daily hear or see the Sufferings of these People, my dear Brethren and Seed, with whom my Life is bound up, as I have done these two Years; and now it is like to encrease, even unto Death, for no evil Doing, but coming among you: Was ever the like Laws heard of, among a People that profess Christ come in the Flesh? And have such no other Weapons, but such Laws, to fight against Spiritual Wickedness withall, as you call it, Wo is me for you! Of whom take you Counsel? Search with the Light of Christ in ye, and it will shew you of whom, as it hath done me and many more, who have been disobedient and deceived, as now you are; which Light, as you come into, and obeying what is made manifest to you therein, you will not Repent, that you were kept from shedding Blood, tho' it were from a woman.

Witchcraft at Salem: Trial of George Burroughs, 1692

More unnerving even than those who pretended to speak for God were those thought to work for the devil. Witches and wizards were as much a part of the ordinary assumption of seventeenth-century Europeans and Americans

[Source: G. L. Burr, *Narratives of the Witchcraft Cases, 1648-1706* (New York: Charles Scribner's Sons, 1914), pp. 215-19.]

as are split personalities and psychic phenomena in a later age. What is star-
tling is not that New England hanged witches, but that it hanged so few
(probably not more than forty all told; this compared with Europe's thou-
sands hanged or more often burned). Hysteria erupted, but one must also
note that hysteria was soon checked and corrected. For a time, however, Sa-
lem Village was afire with accusation and counter-accusation, with grudges
aired and hurts revenged, with struggles by the all-too-human to cope with
and fathom the all-too-mysterious. In Salem alone, nineteen were hanged,
with one pressed to death. The Reverend George Burroughs (c. 1650-92),
Harvard graduate and pastor in Salem Village from 1680 to 1683, had moved
on to a church in Maine when he was called back to Salem for trial in early
August of 1692. Found guilty of witchcraft, he was hanged on August 19. The
evidence for such a conviction, utilizing the words of Cotton Mather, is pre-
sented below.

Glad should I have been, if I had never known the Name of this man; or never
had this occasion to mention so much as the first Letters of his Name. But the
Government requiring some Account of his Trial to be Inserted in this Book, it
becomes me with all Obedience to submit unto the Order.

I. This G. B. was indicted for Witch-crafts, and in the Prosecution of the
Charge against him, he was Accused by five or six of the Bewitched, as the Author of their Miseries; he was Accused by eight of the Confessing Witches, as
being an Head Actor at some of their Hellish Randezvouzes, and one who had
the promise of being a King in Satans Kingdom, now going to be Erected: he
was Accused by nine persons for extraordinary Lifting, and such Feats of
Strength, as could not be done without a Diabolical Assistance. And for other
such Things he was Accused, until about Thirty Testimonies were brought in
against him. . . .

II. The Court being sensible, that the Testimonies of the Parties Bewitched use to have a Room among the Suspicions or Presumptions, brought in
against one Indicted for Witch-craft, there were now heard the Testimonies of
several Persons, who were most notoriously Bewitched, and every day Tortured
by Invisible Hands, and these now all charged the Spectres of G. B. to have a
share in their Torments. At the Examination of this G. B. the Bewitched People
were grievously harassed with Preternatural Mischiefs, which could not possibly be Dissembled; and they still ascribed it unto the Endeavours of G. B. to kill
them. And now upon his Trial, one of the Bewitched Persons testify'd, That in
her Agonies, a little Black hair'd man came to her, saying his Name was B. and
bidding her set her hand unto a Book which he show'd unto her; and bragging
that he was a Conjurer, above the ordinary Rank of Witches; That he often persecuted her with the offer of that Book, saying, She should be well, and need
fear no body, if she would but Sign it; but he inflicted cruel Pains and Hurts

upon her, because of her Denying so to do. The Testimonies of the other Sufferers concurred with these; and it was Remarkable, that whereas Biting was one of the ways which the Witches used for the vexing of the Sufferers, when they cry'd out of G. B. biting them, the print of the Teeth would be seen on the Flesh of the Complainers, and just such a sett of Teeth as G. B's would then appear upon them, which could be distinguished from those of some other mens. Others of them testify'd, That in their Torments, G. B. tempted them to go unto a Sacrament, unto which they perceived him with a sound of Trumpet Summoning of other Witches, who quickly after the Sound would come from all Quarters unto the Rendezvouz. One of them falling into a kind of Trance, afterwards affirmed, That G. B. had carried her into a very high Mountain, where he show'd her mighty and glorious Kingdoms, and said, He would give them all to her, if she would write in his Book; but she told him, They were none of his to give; and refused the motions, enduring of much misery for that Refusal.

It cost the Court a wonderful deal of Trouble, to hear the Testimonies of the Sufferers; for when they were going to give in their Depositions, they would for a long time be taken with fitts, that made them uncapable of saying any thing. The Chief judge asked the prisoner, who he thought hindred these witnesses from giving their testimonies? and he answered, He supposed it was the Divel. That Honourable person then reply'd, How comes the Divel so loathe to have any Testimony born against you? Which cast him into very great confusion.

III. It has been a frequent thing for the Bewitched people to be entertained with Apparitions of Ghosts of murdered people, at the same time that the Spectres of the witches trouble them. These Ghosts do always affright the Beholders more than all the other spectral Representations; and when they exhibit themselves, they cry out, of being Murdered by the witchcrafts or other violences of the persons who are then in spectre present. It is further considerable, that once or twice, these Apparitions have been seen by others at the very same time that they have shewn them selves to the Bewitched; and seldom have there been these Apparitions but when something unusual and suspected had attended the Death of the party thus Appearing. . . .

Well, G. B. being now upon his Triall, one of the Bewitched persons was cast into Horror at the Ghosts of B's two deceased wives then appearing before him, and crying for Vengeance against him. Hereupon several of the Bewitched persons were successively called in, who all not knowing what the former had seen and said, concurred in their Horror of the Apparition, which they affirmed that he had before him. But he, tho' much appalled, utterly deny'd that he discerned any thing of it; nor was it any part of his Conviction.

IV. Judicious Writers have assigned it a great place in the Conviction of witches, when persons are Impeached by other Notorious witches, to be as Ill as themselves; especially, if the persons have been much noted for neglecting the

Worship of God. Now, as there might have been Testimonies Enough of G. B's Antipathy to Prayer and the other Ordinances of God, tho' by his profession singularly obliged thereunto; so, there now came in against the prisoner the Testimonies of several persons, who confessed their own having been Horrible Witches, and ever since their confessions had been themselves terribly Tortured by the Devils and other Witches, even like the other Sufferers; and therein undergone the pains of many Deaths for their Confessions.

These now Testify'd, that G. B. had been at Witch-meetings with them; and that he was the Person who had Seduc'd and Compell'd them into the snares of Witchcraft: That he promised them Fine Cloaths, for doing it; that he brought Poppets to them, and thorns to stick into those Poppets, for the afflicting of other People; And that he exhorted them, with the rest of the Crue, to bewitch all Salem-Village, but be sure to do it Gradually, if they would prevail in what they did.

Witchcraft at Salem:
Cotton Mather and Spectral Evidence

In the trial described above, one reads of the appearance of "spectres" — that is, ghosts or apparitions or likenesses. Many of the accused were found guilty on the basis of that person's "spectre" appearing to someone in a dream, for example, and inflicting harm or offering temptation. Such "evidence" was, of course, as impossible to refute as it was subject to abuse. Cotton Mather (1663-1728), pastor of Boston's Second Congregational Church and the colony's leading theologian, began to doubt the validity of such evidence. Eventually he and his father, Increase Mather (1639-1723), led in the discrediting of spectral evidence. Once such evidence was no longer so readily believed, the flood of accusations quickly dried up. In August of 1692 (the month when George Burroughs was hanged), Cotton Mather wrote to a friend: "I do still think that when there is no further evidence against a person but only this, that a specter in their shape does afflict a neighbor, that evidence is not enough to convict" one of witchcraft. Nearly three months earlier (May 31, 1692), in the letter excerpted below, Mather expressed caution as to the evidence, horror as to the crime.

And yet I must humbly beg you that in the management of the affair in your most worthy hands, you do not lay more stress upon pure specter testimony

---

[Source: Kenneth Silverman, ed., *Selected Letters of Cotton Mather* (Baton Rouge: Louisiana State University Press, 1971), pp. 36-37, 39-40; for the August letter, see pp. 41-43.]

than it will bear. When you are satisfied or have good, plain, legal evidence that the demons which molest our poor neighbors do indeed represent such and such people to the sufferers, tho' this be a presumption, yet I suppose you will not reckon it a conviction that the people so represented are witches to be immediately exterminated. It is very certain that the devils have sometimes represented the shapes of persons not only innocent, but also very virtuous, tho' I believe that the just God then ordinarily provides a way for the speedy vindication of the persons thus abused. Moreover, I do suspect that persons who have too much indulged themselves in malignant, envious, malicious ebullitions of their souls, may unhappily expose themselves to the judgment of being represented by devils, of whom they never had any vision, and with whom they have much less written any covenant. I would say this: if upon the bare supposal of a poor creature's being represented by a specter, too great a progress be made by the authority in ruining a poor neighbor so represented, it may be that a door may be thereby opened for the devils to obtain from the courts in the invisible world a license to proceed unto most hideous desolations upon the repute and repose of such as have yet been kept from the great transgression. If mankind have thus far once consented unto the credit of diabolical representations, the door is opened! Perhaps there are wise and good men that may be ready to style him that shall advance this caution, a witch advocate; but in the winding up, this caution will certainly be wished for. . . .

Albeit the business of this witchcraft be very much transacted upon the stage of imagination, yet we know that, as in treason there is an imagining which is a capital crime, and here also the business thus managed in imagination yet may not be called imaginary. The effects are dreadfully real. Our dear neighbors are most really tormented, really murdered, and really acquainted with hidden things, which are afterwards proved plainly to have been realities. I say, then, as that man is justly executed for an assassinate, who in the sight of men shall with a sword in his hand stab his neighbor into the heart, so suppose a long train laid unto a barrel of gunpowder under the floor where a neighbor is, and suppose a man with a match perhaps in his mouth, out of sight, set fire unto the further end of the train, tho' never so far off. This man also is to be treated as equally a malefactor. Our neighbors at Salem Village are blown up, after a sort, with an infernal gunpowder; the train is laid in the laws of the kingdom of darkness limited by God himself. Now the question is, who gives fire to this train? and by what acts is the match applied? . . .

I begin to fear that the devils do more easily proselyte poor mortals into witchcraft than is commonly conceived. When a sinful child of man distempers himself with some exorbitant motions in his mind (and it is to be feared the murmuring phrensies of late prevailing in the country have this way exposed many to sore temptations) a devil then soon presents himself unto him, and he demands, Are you willing that I should go do this or that for you? If the man once comply, the devil hath him now in a most horrid snare, and by a permission from the just vengeance of God he visits the man with buffetings as well as allurements, till the forlorn man at first only for the sake of quietness, but at length out of improved wickedness, will commission the devil to do mischief as often as he requires it. And for this cause 'tis worth considering, whether there be a necessity always by extirpations by halter or fagot every wretched creature that shall be hooked into some degrees of witchcraft. What if some of the lesser criminals be only scourged with lesser punishments, and also put upon some solemn, open, public, and explicit renunciation of the devil? I am apt to think that the devils would then cease afflicting the neighborhood whom these wretches have stood them upon, and perhaps they themselves would now suffer some impressions from the devils, which if they do, they must be willing to bear till the God that hears prayer deliver them.

Proposals of 1705

In their continuing effort to maintain control in New England, the Congregational churches had to do more than drive out heretics and hang witches: they had to discipline themselves. Pure Congregationalism, wherein each local church was a law unto itself, came to be seen as an invitation to anarchy. The churches must speak together, work together, and most of all together resist the forces that would transform New England into just another "mixed medley" of confused and rapacious humanity. In 1705 several Massachusetts ministerial associations met to consider the Proposals excerpted below. Three years later, the clergy of Connecticut agreed on what has come to be called the Saybrook Platform, utilizing often the very language of the 1705 Proposals. In both instances, church discipline and church polity were being strengthened while local liberty and perhaps even idiosyncrasy were being deliberately curtailed.

1st Part, It was Proposed,

1st, That the Ministers of the Country form themselves into Associations, that may meet at proper times to Consider such things as may properly lie before them, Relating to their own faithfulness towards each other, and the common Interest of the Churches; and that each of those Associations have a Moderator for a certain time, who shall continue till another be Chosen, who may call them together upon Emergencies.

[Source: Williston Walker, *The Creeds and Platforms of Congregationalism* (Boston: Pilgrim Press, 1960 [1893]), pp. 487-89.]

In these Associations,

2dly. That Questions and Cases of importance, either provided by themselves, or by others presented unto them, should be upon due deliberation Answered.

3dly, That Advice be taken by the Associated Pastors from time to time, e're they Proceed to any action in their Particular Churches, which be likely to produce any imbroilments. That the Associated Pastors do Carefully and Lovingly treat each other with that watchfulness which may be of Universal Advantage; and that if any Minister be accused to the Association whereto he belongs, of Scandal or Heresie, the matter shall be there examined, and if the Associated Ministers find just accusation for it, they shall direct to the Calling of a Council, by whom such an Offendor is to be proceeded against.

4thly, That the Candidates of the Ministry undergo a due Tryal by some one or other of the Associations, concerning their Qualifications for the Evangelical Ministry; and that no particular Pastor or Congregation Imploy any one in Occasional Preaching, who has not been Recommended by a Testimonial under the Hands of some Association. . . .

Second Part, It is Proposed,

1st. That these Associated Pastors, with a proper Number of Delegates from their several Churches, be formed into a standing or stated Council, which shall Consult, Advise and Determine all Affairs that shall be proper matter for the Consideration of an Ecclesiastical Council within their respective Limits, except always, the Cases are such as the Associated Pastors judge more convenient to fall under the Cognizance of some other Council. . . .

8thly, If a particular Church will not be Reclaimed by Council from such gross Disorders as plainly hurt the common Interest of *Christianity,* and are not meer tolerable differences in Opinion, but are plain Sins against the Command & Kingdom of our Lord Jesus Christ, the Council is to declare that Church no longer fit for Communion with the Churches of the Faithful; and the Churches represented in the Council, are to Approve, Confirm and Ratifie the Sentence, and with-draw from the Communion of the Church that would not be healed: Nevertheless, if any Members of the disorderly Church, do not justifie their Disorders, but suitably testifie against them, these are still to be received to the wonted Communion by the Churches; and if after due waiting, the Church be not recovered, they may upon [*Advice*] be actually taken in as Members of some other Church in the Vicinity.

Jonathan Mayhew (1720-66) and the Society for the Propagation of the Gospel

On a political level, keeping Congregationalism strong in New England meant, above all else, keeping Anglicanism out. England meddled in the affairs of Massachusetts far too much, from the latter's point of view. And that meddling certainly included English efforts on behalf of England's Church. Under Governor Edmund Andros, for example, and the ill-fated Dominion of New England, King's Chapel became Boston's first Anglican church — by fiat — in 1689. In 1701, a missionary society was formed in England: the Society for the Propagation of the Gospel in Foreign Parts (SPG). The chief purpose of the Society was to bring Christianity to those who did not already have it: Indians, blacks, unchurched colonists, etc. But when the SPG started to missionize already well-churched New England, this was clearly (at least to Mayhew) another English effort to subvert all liberty, civil and ecclesiastical, for all Americans. In the document presented below, Jonathan Mayhew, pastor of Boston's West Congregational Church, protests this utterly uncalled for invasion of New England by the SPG.

That the Society have chiefly sent their missionaries into those British plantations where they were much needed, according to the true design of their institution; and that they have hereby served the interest of religion in them, is by no means denied: It were very criminal to deny them the praise that is justly due to them in this respect. But, that they have deviated from their original plan according to the charter, in some other respects; and thereby left undone much of the good which they might probably have effected, with the ordinary blessing of God, may perhaps be equally evident from this and the following sections. Most of the following facts are very notorious, even from the anniversary sermons, abstracts, and other publications of the Society; so that they will not be denied.

1. For several years, I think about eight or nine, after the Society was founded, they sent no missionary into N. England. Which may naturally be looked on as one argument, that it was not originally considered among those plantations which were supposed to stand in need of their charity.

2. They have from time to time, since they began to send missionaries into these parts, been adding to their number, supporting episcopal schools, etc.

It is also to be observed, that a very large proportion of their missionaries have fallen to the share of N. England. . . . The gradual increase of the mission-

[Source: Jonathan Mayhew, *Observations on the Charter and Conduct of the Society for the Propagation of the Gospel* . . . (New York: Arno Press, 1972 [1763]), pp. 51-56.]

aries, catechists, etc. in N. England, appears from the abstracts to have been as follows, viz.

In	1718		3.
	1727		10.
	1730		14.
	1739		22.
	1745		24.
	1761	about	30.

I have seen no later abstract.

How large a proportion of missionaries, etc. this is for N. England, compared with the other colonies, especially when a due regard is had to their religious state respectively, may appear by the single cast of the eye on the table following. In the last mentioned year, 1761, according to the abstract, their numbers in the southern colonies; where they were so much needed, were,

In New-York	16.	S. Carolina	5.
New-Jersey	10.	Georgia	1.
Pennsylvania	9.	Bahama Islands	1.
N. Carolina	5.	Barbados	2.

It does not appear from the abstracts, that the Society have any missionaries at all in the other W. India Islands, where, as is commonly reported, there is hardly any show of public worship kept up, of any kind; and where there are so many thousands of Negro slaves in total ignorance of christianity. The true cause of this neglect may be seen hereafter.

3. It is notorious that the missionaries, instead of being sent to the frontier and other poor Towns in N. England, where the provision and accommodations for ministers were the meanest, have generally been station'd in the oldest, most populous and richest towns, where the best provision was before made for ministers; where the public worship of God was constantly and regularly upheld, and his word and sacraments duly administered according to the congregational and presbyterian modes. This will be evident to all that are in any measure acquainted with this country, from the bare mention of some of the places where the Society support missions and schools; viz. Boston, Cambridge, Salem, Marblehead, Newbury, Portsmouth in New-Hampshire, Braintree, Scituate, Bristow, Portsmouth in Rhode-Island, N. London, Stratford, Fairfield, Middletown, etc. . . .

5. To those who are well acquainted with N. England, and the manner and circumstances in which episcopal churches have been gathered and founded here, it appears that the Society have manifested a sufficient forwardness to en-

courage and increase small disaffected parties in our towns, upon an application to them; — in those towns, I mean, where a regular, legal and due provision was already made for the support of God's public worship. Some of these little parties, or rather factions, it is well known here, have taken their rise from no fixed principle of a conscientious dissent from our manner of worship, but from mere levity, petulance or avarice; — from some trifling, groundless dis-

Jonathan Mayhew
(National Portrait Gallery, Smithsonian Institution, Washington, D.C.)

gust at the stated minister; or a dissatisfaction about pews and rates; or at their being under, or likely to come under censure for their immoral practices. I do not affirm positively, that either of these has always been the case, without exception: But, that it often has been, is as well known amongst us, as a thing of that nature can be known. These people being thus affronted and angry without cause, presently declare for the church, without really knowing any thing of the state of the controversy; and apply to some missionary or missionaries, to recommend them to the charity of the Society. And divers of the missionaries have been much injured, (which there is no reason to suppose) if they have not been very busy in intrigues in order to foment these divisions and parties, for the good of the church; yea, been at the bottom of them. . . .

But from whatever cause these little discontented parties have generally taken their origin, in towns where there were learned and orthodox ministers duly supported; thus much is certain, that they have not only been recommended to the Society from time to time, but been encouraged thereby, and had missionaries sent to them. The number of these humble supplicants in a town, have sometimes not exceeded eight, ten or twelve heads of families; and this in towns consisting of two or three hundred families. It is commonly, and I believe truly said, that there are scarce so many as ten families in the town of Cambridge, which usually attend the service of the church lately set up therein, but about half a quarter of a mile from the College, and from the meeting-house there. What is this but setting up altar against altar?

The Anglican (Episcopal) Church

Maryland: Appeal to Bishop of London, 1696

As has been noted above, Maryland began under Roman Catholic proprietorship. In the final decade of the seventeenth century, however, when Maryland became a royal colony, the Church of England moved to displace Catholicism in prestige and legal favor. With the aid of Virginia's Governor Francis Nicholson, Anglican clergy in Maryland turned to the Bishop of London for help in establishing their church on firm footing "before we be overrun with enthusiasm, idolatry, and atheism. . . ." In the document below, the final reference to Thomas Bray (1656-1730) anticipates his arrival in

[Source: W. S. Perry, ed., *Historical Collections Relating to the American Colonial Church* (New York: AMS Press, 1969 [1878]), IV, 8-9, 11-13.]

Maryland four years later. Bray, founder of the SPG already mentioned (see pp. 106-9), also brought into being in 1699 the Society for Promoting Christian Knowledge (SPCK). Through the first two-thirds of the eighteenth century, these two societies led the way in furthering the Anglican cause in colonial America.

When His Excellency, Governor Nicholson, came into the Country in the year 1694, there were but 3 Clergymen in Episcopal Orders, besides 5 or 6 popish priests, who had perverted divers idle people from the Protestant Religion. There was also a sort of wandering pretenders to preaching that came from New England and other places; which deluded not only the Protestant Dissenters from our Church but many of the Churchmen themselves, by their extemporary prayers and preachments, for which they were admitted by the people and got money of them.

The 3 Episcopal Clergymen, having made a hard shift to live here some time after they came hither, did afterwards marry and maintain their families out of the plantations they had with their cures.

And tho' the better and most responsible persons of the neighbouring Plantations that owned themselves to be of the Communion of the Church of England subscribed their names to some small Contributions for their officiating amongst them, that those Clergymen could not get the half and sometimes not the fourth part of their subscriptions, notwithstanding they endeavoured to acquit themselves to the best of their powers, in a constant and conscientious discharge of their ministerial function. . . .

Should they obtain their petitions only for themselves, the incomes of some of the best Parishes, in respect of the Tobacco raised by the 40[1b1] . . . would be so impaired that there would not be left a tolerable subsistence for a single Clergyman and his horse, and one horse, at least, we must all of us, of necessity, keep ready by us, not only to ride to Church on Sundays, but to ride all over our Parishes to Christenings, Weddings, visiting the sick, and burials on the week days, when or wherever we are sent for.

Could the Quakers clear themselves of the 40[1] . . . the Papists might all pretend to do so too, because they have Priests of their own to provide for; and could both these parties effect their designs, the Clergy and Church of England would be left in a very naked and poor condition here, besides that we might expect many that have their religion still to choose, would turn either Papists or Quakers, and refuse to pay too, for many of them look upon the Sacraments as needless impositions, and go neither to the Papists' Mass nor the Quakers' meetings, and seldom or ever to Church.

Now we become most humble petitioners to your Lordship, that if there

1. Per head of household.

should be occasion (as we have reason to fear there is) your Lordship would be pleased to espouse our Cause, and intercede with His Most Gracious Majesty that we may not be wholly discouraged from staying in these parts of the English Empire, and preaching the Gospel here, as well as the Papists and Presbyterians and Quakers do after their manner, and our just hopes, and that we shall not be thought much worse by great good and wise persons, for the Quakers' insinuations against us behind our backs, which we doubt not have been as maliciously as cunningly contrived.

We hope your Lordship will be likewise pleased upon occasion to make such further intercession for us with His Majesty as that we may not be prejudged before we have each to answer for ourselves, both against Papists and Quakers, either by writing or by proxies, when we shall know the particulars of their pretended advances, and what may be falsely said against us by those two inveterate enemies to the Church of England.

May it please your Lordship, as far removed as the Quakers and Papists seem to be in their different sentiments about religion, they are jointly bent against our Church, and daily endeavour to draw people to their parties, by suggesting to them that Lord Baltimore will govern here again; than which nothing can be more pleasing news to libertines and loose persons, who call seldom or never be gotten to come to Church at all. And should my Lord rule as formerly, the insolence of the Romish Priests (who are somewhat curbed by his Excellency's great care and vigilance) would soon be intolerable in these parts, that are so remote from England.

Besides there being great numbers of Irish Papists brought continually into this province, and many Irish Priests being suspected to be coming incog. amongst us (as having no better place of refuge in the King's Dominions) upon their being banished from Ireland, there is great reason to fear there will be as much discouragement and danger coming upon all his Majesty's good Protestant subjects here as upon the English Clergy.

This expectation of the Lord Baltimore's being restored to the Government of Maryland animates the Priests and Jesuits to begin already to inveigle several ignorant people to turn to their religion. To which end they do (contrary to the Act of Parliament to deter them from perverting any of His Majesty's Protestant subjects to popery) introduce themselves into the Company of the sick, when they have no Ministers, that his Excellency hath been lately forced to issue out his proclamation against their so doing, to restrain them.

And now, may it please your Lordship, we, your Lordship's most dutiful Clergy, do humbly represent unto your Lordship the great and urgent necessity of an Ecclesiastical rule here, invested with such ample power and authority from your Lordship as may capacitate him to redress what is amiss, and to supply what is wanting in the Church.

We further humbly represent unto your Lordship that we conceive this to be the very crisis of time wherein (with the help of Divine Providence) to lay a firm foundation in this Country (which is yet in its infancy as to Church matters) for the establishment of the Church of England, before we be overrun with enthusiasm, idolatry, and atheism, which are already too rife and prevailing amongst us.

We most humbly beg your Lordship's pardon for our great presumption in troubling your Lordship with this long letter, and we hope ere long we shall be happy with the presence of The Reverend D^r. Bray, your Lordship's designed Commissary. In the mean time, we beg leave to make this thankful acknowledgment of your Lordship's care in providing such a worthy and deserving person to preside in the Church in Maryland.

New York: Against "Jesuits & Popish Priests," 1700

If in the political realm Anglicanism represented the greatest threat to Congregationalism, the traditional and powerful enemy of the former was Roman Catholicism. When England took over New York from the Dutch in 1664, she was prepared to accept Holland's national church as somewhat analogous to her own. But such concession was not to be granted to Catholics, be they French, Spanish, English, or Irish — especially Irish. The following act, passed in New York on August 9, 1700, leaves little to the imagination and nothing for negotiation.

Whereas divers Jesuits preists; and popish missionaries have of late, come and for Some time have had their residence in the remote parts of this Province and other his ma'tys adjacent Colonies, who by their wicked and Subtle Insinuations Industriously Labour to Debauch Seduce and w'thdraw the Indians from their due obedience unto his most Sacred ma'ty and to Excite and Stir them up to Sedition Rebellion and open Hostility against his ma'tys Goverm't for prevention whereof Bee it Enacted by his Excel the Gov'r Council and Representatives Convened in Generall Assembly and it is hereby Enacted by the Authority of the Same, That all and every Jesuit and Seminary Preist missionary or other Spirituall or Ecclesiasticall person made or ordained by any Authority power or Jurisdicon derived Challenged or p'tended from the Pope or See of Rome now resideing w'th in this province or any part thereof shall depart from and out of the Same at or before the first day of November next in this present year Seaventeen hundred.

[Source: Hugh Hastings, ed., *Ecclesiastical Records, State of New York* (Albany, 1901), II, 1368-70.]

And be it further Enacted by the authority aforesaid, That all and every Jesuit Seminary Preist Missionary or other Spirituall or Ecclesiasticall person made or Ordained by any Authority power or Jurisdiction derived Challenged or p'tended from the pope or See of Rome or that shall profess himself or otherwise appear to be Such by preaching & teaching of others to Say any popish prayers by Celebrating masses granting of absolutions or using any other of the Romish Ceremonies & Rites of worship by what name title or degree So ever such a person shall be called or known who shall Continue abide remaine or come into this province or any part thereof after ye first day of November aforesaid shall be deemed and Accounted an incendiary and disturber of the publick peace and Safety and an Enemy to the true Christian Religion and shal be adjudged to Suffer perpetuall Imprisonm't and if any person being So Sentenced and actually Imprisoned shall break prison and make his Escape and be afterwards retaken he shall Suffer such paines of Death penalties and forfeitures as in Cases of ffelony.

And it is further Enacted by the authority aforesaid, That every person that shall wittingly and willingly receive, harbour, Conceale aid Succour and releive any Jesuit preist missionary or other Ecclesiastical person of the Romish Clergy knowing him to be Such and be thereof lawfully Convicted before any of his ma'tys Courts of Records w'thin this Province w'ch Courts are hereby Impowered and Authorized to hear try and Determine the Same he shall forfeit the Sum of two hundred pounds Currant mony of this Province one half to his Maty for and towards the Support of the Governm't and the other half to the Informer who shall sue for ye Same in any Court of Record w'thin this province wherein no Essoyn protection or wager of Law shall be allowed and Such person shall be further punished by being Set in ye pillory on three Severall dayes and also be bound to the good behaviour at the discretion of the Court.

And be it further Enacted by the Authority aforesaid That it shall and may be Lawfull to and for every justice of the peace to cause any person or persons Suspected of being a Jesuit, Seminary Preist or of the Romish Clergy to be apprehended & Convented before himself & Some other of his ma'tys justices and if Such person do not give Sattisfactory acco't of himself he shall be committed to prison in order to a Tryall also it shall and may be Lawfull to and for any person or persons to app'rehend w'thout a warrant any Jesuit Seminary preist or other of the Romish Clergy as aforesaid and to Convent him before ye Gov'r or any two of the Council to be Examined and Imprisoned in order to a Tryall unless he give a Satisfactory acco't of himself and as it will be Esteemed and accepted as a good Service don for ye King by the person who shall Seiz & apprehend any Jesuit Preist missionary or Romish Ecclesiactick as aforesaid So the Gov'r of this province for ye time being w'th ye advice & Consent of the Council may Suitably reward him as they think fitt.

Provided this act shall not Extend, or be Construed to Extend unto any of the Romish Clergy, who shall happen to be Shipwrackt, or thro' other adversity shall be cast on shoure or driven into this province, So as he Continue or abide no Longer w'thin ye Same than untill he may have opportunity of passage for his Departure So also as Such person Immediately upon his arrivall shall forthw'th attend ye Gov'r if near to ye place of his Residence or otherwise on one or more of ye Council or next justices of the peace, & acquaint y'm w'th his Circumstances & observe ye Direccons w'ch they shall give him during his stay in ye province.

New York: Against the Presbyterians, 1707

Anglican struggle for control in New York was directed against more than Catholics alone. Presbyterian itinerant minister Francis Makemie (1658-1708) was arrested along with a companion for preaching without a license. Makemie, believing that the 1689 Declaration of Toleration issued by Sovereigns William and Mary made Anglican exclusivism illegal, defended his right to preach without hindrance. The Anglican governor, Edward Cornbury, believing otherwise, fined and jailed Makemie. In the end, however, Makemie was vindicated and Cornbury recalled.

Warrant for Arrest

Whereas I am informed, that one Mackennan, and one Hampton, two Presbyterian Preachers, who lately came to this City, have taken upon them to Preach in a Private House, without having obtained My Licence for so doing, which is directly contrary to the known Laws of England; and being likewise informed, that they are gone into Long-Island, with intent there to spread their Pernicious Doctrine and Principles, to the great disturbance of the Church by Law Established, and of the Government of this Province. You are therefore hereby Required and Commanded, to take into your Custody the Bodies of the said Mackennan and Hampton, and them to bring with all convenient speed before me, at Fort-Anne in New-York. And for so doing, this shall be your sufficient Warrant: Given under my Hand, at Fort Anne this 21st day of January, 1706, 7.

Cornbury.

[Source: Maurice W. Armstrong et al., *The Presbyterian Enterprise* (Philadelphia: Westminster Press, 1956), pp. 14-16.]

Interlocutory Conference

Lord Cornbury. How dare you take upon you to Preach in my Government, without my Licence?

Mr. Makemie. We have Liberty from an Act of Parliament, made the First Year of the Reign of King William and Queen Mary, which gave us Liberty, with which Law we have complied.

Ld. C. None shall Preach in my Government without my Licence.

F. M. If the Law for Liberty, my Lord, had directed us to any particular persons in Authority for Licence, we would readily have observed the same; but we cannot find any directions in said Act of Parliament, therefore could not take notice therof.

Ld. C. That Law does not extend to the American Plantations, but only to England.

F. M. My Lord, I humbly conceive, it is not a limited nor Local Act, and am well assured, it extends to other Plantations of the Queens Dominions, which is evident from Certificates from Courts of Record of Virginia, and Maryland, certifying we have complied with said Law.

Both Certificates were produced and read by Lord Cornbury, who was pleased to say, these Certificates extended not to New-York.

Ld. C. I know it is local and limited, for I was at making thereof.

F. M. Your Excellency might be at making thereof, but we are well assured, there is no such limiting clause therein, as is in Local Acts, and desire the Law may be produced to determine this point.

Ld. C. Turning to Mr. Attorney, Mr. Bekely, who was present, ask'd him, Is it not so, Mr. Attorney?

Mr. Attorney. Yes, it is Local, my Lord, and producing an Argument for it, further said, that all the Paenal Laws were Local, and limited, and did not extend to the Plantations, and the Act of Toleration being made to take off the edge of the Paenel Laws; therefore the Act of Toleration does not extend to any Plantations.

F. M. I desire the Law may be produced; for I am morally perswaded, there is no limitation or restriction in the Law to England, Wales, and Berwick on Tweed; for it extends to sundry Plantations of the Queens Dominions, as Barbadoes, Virginia, and Maryland; which was evident from the Certificates produced, which we could not have obtained, if the Act of Parliament had not extended to the Plantations.

And Mr. Makemie further said, that he presumed New-York was a part of Her Majesties Dominions also; and that sundry Ministers on the East-end of Long-Island, had complied with said Law, and qualifyed themselves at Court, by complying with the directions of said Law, and have no Licence from your Lordship.

Ld. C. Yes, New-York is of Her Majesties Dominions; but the Act of Toleration does not extend to the Plantations by its own intrinsick vertue, or any intention of the Legislators, but only by her Majesties Royal Instructions signifyed unto me, and that is from Her Prerogative and Clemency. And the Courts which have qualifyed those men, are in error, and I shall check them for it.

F. M. If the Law extends to the Plantations any manner of way, whether by the Queens Prerogative, Clemency, or otherwise, our Certificates were a demonstration we had complied therewith. . . .

Ld. C. That act of Parliament was made against Strowling Preachers, and you are such, and shall not Preach in my Government.

F. M. There is not one word, my Lord, mentioned in any part of the Law, against Travelling or Strowling Preachers, as Your Excellency is pleased to call them; and we are to judge that to be the true end of the Law, which is specifyed in the Preamble thereof, which is for the satisfaction of Scrupulous Consciences, and Uniting the Subjects of England, in interest and affection. And it is well known, my Lord, to all, that Quakers, who also have Liberty by this Law, have few or no fixed Teachers, but chiefly taught by such as Travel; and it is known to all such are sent forth by the Yearly Meeting at London, and Travel and Teach over the Plantations, and are not molested.

Ld. C. I have troubled some of them, and will trouble them more.

North Carolina: Anglicanism "over-toping its power," 1707

The Quaker John Archdale (c. 1642-1717), deputy governor of North Carolina, thought that Anglicans and non-Anglicans should be able to live peaceably side by side, with neither group dispossessing or dominating the other. "Unchristian Broils," Archdale argued, "will enfeeble the vital spirit" of the still young colony (not formally separated from South Carolina until 1712). Here in 1707, a year marked by the union between Scotland and England, should there not be a similar spirit of tolerance across the sea? Clearly, Archdale thought so, with the Quaker colony of Pennsylvania as his proof that such could be done in North Carolina — if the Anglicans would allow, it.

It is stupendious to consider, how passionate and preposterous Zeal, not only vails but stupifies, oftentimes, the Rational Powers: For cannot Dissenters Kill

---

[Source: Alexander S. Salley, Jr., *Narratives of Early Carolina, 1650-1750* (New York: Charles Scribner's Sons, 1911), pp. 305, 306-7.]

Wolves and Bears, etc., as well as Church-men; as also Fell Trees and Clear Ground for Plantations, and be as capable of defending the same generally as well as the other. Surely Pennsylvania can bear witness to what I write; and Carolina falls no way short of it in its Natural Production to the industrious Planter. . . . But it is not my Business to Open the Sore, but to Heal it, if possible; and now we are like to have some considerable Numbers of Scotch Britains, Men generally Ingenious and Industrious, who are like to disperse themselves into our American Colonies, who are a People generally zealous for Liberty and Property, and will by no Perswasion be attracted to any part where their Native Rights are invaded, or who rather expect an Enlargement thereof in a Wilderness Country, than an Abridgement thereof, as that prudent Management of William Penn hath establish'd in his Colony, and was first intended for Carolina, in a Scheme laid by the Earl of Shaftsbury, etc., but secretly over-thrown by that Party of High pretended Churchmen that have lain Latent from the Beginning, as I have before intimated. Our Colonies are very weak at this time, but the Divine Hand of Providence seems to be ready to supply our Deficiency by a Union, contrary to that Spirit that hath wrought the Dissentions in Carolina. . . .

Now as the Civil Power doth endanger it self by grasping at more than its Essential Right can justly and reasonably claim; so the High-Church by over-toping its Power in too great a Severity, in forsaking the Golden Rule of doing as they would be done by, may so weaken the Foundation of the Ecclesiastical and Civil State of that Country, that so they may both sink into a ruinous condition by losing their Main Sinews and Strength, which (as Solomon saith) lies in the multitude of its Inhabitants: And this I am satisfied in, and have some experimental reason for what I say, That if the extraordinary Fertility and Pleasantness of the Country had not been an alluring and binding Obligation to most Dissenters there settled, they had left the High-Church to have been a Prey to the Wolves and Bears, Indians and Foreign Enemies: But I hope now they will see their Folly, and embarque in one common Interest, and thereby they will reap the Benefit of our Union at Home, by Numbers of Industrious and Ingenious Scottish Britains, who otherwise will never come to be imposed upon by a High-flown Church Party; and without such a Strength I see not how it can stand long, let the Government be in any Hand whatsoever. I have discharged my Conscience in a Christian and truly British Spirit, that desires nothing more than the Spiritual and Temporal Welfare of Great Britain; and hope, pray for, and cordially desire the long and prosperous Reign of our most gracious Queen, whom the Divine Hand of Providence hath placed on the Throne, to be as a Nursing Mother to all Her Children committed to Her Charge. And I also heartily wish that the inferior Sphere of the Royal Power committed in Trust to the Lords Proprietors of that Province of Carolina, may Govern it with a measure of the same Prudence, justice, and truly Christian Affection, as She more imediately Governs the entire Body of Her Subjects.

South Carolina: Huguenot Quarrel, 1726

The Edict of Nantes, which had protected some Protestants in France, was revoked by Louis XIV in 1685. As a consequence, large numbers of French Calvinists (Huguenots) fled France for the Netherlands, or England, or the New World. Because South Carolina was being populated shortly after this Revocation, it appeared a natural refuge. But as the colony grew stronger, local Anglicans grew more assertive, especially under the leadership of Commissary Alexander Garden of Charleston. Garden (who later on opposed George Whitefield; see below, pp. 160-65) wanted nothing going on in his area in the name of religion that lacked his specific approval and blessing. All was to be done in good Anglican order, or not done at all. In the letter quoted below (and dated January 7, 1726), the Huguenot minister, John Lapierre, protests to the Bishop of London his exasperation over Garden's too precious concern regarding "canons and rubricks," "ecclesiastical laws and constitutions."

My Lord,

I have received your Lordship's admonition good advice and favourable wishes with all humility, respect and thankfulness — rather chusing to receive your checks than to be overlook'd among my brethren; but how much the happier would I count myself, My Lord, if I could obtain the same share in your favour and protection as I had once in that of your illustrious predecessor, by whome I was ordained and sent to the place wherein I am now officiating on the nineteenth year from my mission to a French colony, during which time I had the honour to wait upon several vaccant parishes of the English, besides my own parish of St. Dennis, without any molestation from the clergy or laity; but rather with all sorts of good encouragements, whereby upon recommendations, the honourable society was pleased to exstend their bounty upon me, having heard, withal of my helpless and chargeable family then consisting of five young children and my wife who lost her sight before our departure from England. The Reverend Mr. Garden was my first open adversary I had in this province, upon information that I had baptised a child of one of his parishioners, the case was this My Lord; the father of the child one Mr. Joseph Moor being at variance with his minister unknown to me, seeing me in his town on a certain day envited me to his house, and told me he had a young child to baptise if I would do it for him, whereupon I answered him that I thought it not convenient being in another minister's parish, he told me that Mr. Garden was

---

[Source: A. H. Hirsch, *The Huguenots of Colonial South Carolina* (Durham: Duke University Press, 1928), pp. 321-23.]

very willing I should perform that office, but this did not prevail upon me till he added further that it was his wife's earnest desire being a French woman and formerly one of my hearers, the assistants likewise being of the French nation, but the father I suffered to be over persuaded, for want of a timely consideration, My Lord, and not out of any evil intent or contempt: for after I saw my name brought into question by my brother Garden, I would have made him all reasonable satisfaction in a meeting of the clergy as our former custom was, without any need of troubling your Lordship: cases of obstinacy and stubbornness excepted. This so sudden and preposterous proceeding of Mr. Garden did lay upon me a necessity of vindicating and clearing myself before the people of this province by my appealing to a general arbitration and exposing to the light this slanderous lettre, which I make bold, My Lord, to propose here to your perusal in the following expressions:

Sir,

I have often heard of your insolent and disorderly practices in other parishes, but little suspected that I should have experienced them in my own. The following fact is so notorious that I am confident you will not dare to deny it: viz: that when you was last in my parish a few days ago, you did then and there: not only administer the Holy Sacrament of Baptism to a child of one of my parishioners without either my consent or privity, and whilst I was upon the spot and the child in good health, contrary to the express canons and rubricks of the Church; but also you did administer it in a public form and in a private house noless contrary to the said canons and rubricks and the known practice in my parish. This matter of fact Sir I charge you with which I am confident you will not dare to deny, so equally confident I am, that you can offer nothing tolerable either to justify or excuse, thus to break upon my charge is it to enter in by the door, or not rather to climb up some other way? is it the action of the shepherd or not rather of a thief and a robber thus to trample on the canons and rubricks of the church, is it the action of a faithful and obedient son and not rather of an apostate and faithless Traytor? I was in hopes that the late prevailing principles in your parish, of Dutarts I mean had been quite extinguish'd with those unhappy people, but alas, the reverend Mr. Lappierre daring thus to act in so open contempt and defiance of the ecclesiastical laws and constitutions savours so strongly of them that those hopes are almost choak'd and fears sprung up in their room. Pray Sir, could you flatter yourself either, that I shoud hear nothing of this clandestine piece of intrusion or that hearing of it I should yet pass it over in silence? Sure you are not so silly as to have flattered yourself of either of these. I heard of it the next day, I have already acquainted the Governor of it, and you may assure yourself that nothing but death shall prevent my transmitting it by him well attested in every circumstance to the Bishop of London and the honourable Society together of my complaint of it in the strongest terms. How little so ever you deserve it, yet I scorn to act any other than a fair and honourable part in this affair, and therefore give you this notice that I shall and to whom I shall complain that you may make such defence as you shall think proper against my complaint, I am your much provoak'd friend and servant.

Charlestown
April 7th 8th 1725.   A. GARDEN.

Your eyes may see My Lord how vile I am here made by a brother and I hope of your charity that if anything further should be alleged against me by the Reverend Mr. Garden, your Lordship will vouchsafe to hear me before I am condemned considering that I am as well as my adversary a labourer in the Lord's Vineyard under your inspection and patronage, and your Lordship, the most dutiful most humble and obedient servant,

JOHN LAPIERRE.

Episcopacy Issue: Pennsylvania (1707) and New England (1727)

While dissenting groups in America may have felt threatened by a state-sponsored Church of England, Anglicans themselves felt threatened — and cheated — by the lack of a bishop. Not only was a bishop required for the rites of confirmation and ordination, his very presence was deemed essential to the well-being of the entire community. A bishop could counsel, reprove, adjudicate, and — where necessary — discipline. No wonder that Anglican establishment came so hard in Virginia or Maryland, in Carolina or New York: without a bishop the American Church was a crippled church. Repeatedly, colonial Anglicans pleaded, prayed, schemed, and searched the ocean's horizons for a bishop. Without such, we are not a church, they said, only "a private Conventicle." Two excerpts reveal the strength of the arguments as well as the depth of the feelings: the first, dated September 18, 1707, is part of a report to the SPG by Evan Evans on "the State of the Church in Pennsylvania"; the second, dated July 20, 1727, and also addressed to the SPG, comes from the Anglican clergy of New England as a group.

[Source: W. S. Perry, ed., *Historical Collections Relating to the American Colonial Church* (New York: AMS Press, 1969 [1871, 1873]), II, 36-39; III, 224, 225, 226-27.]

Evan Evans to the SPG, September 18, 1707

I should now put an End to my memoriall, were it not y^t ye want of a B^P amongst us cannot be past over in Silence; 'tis a Dismall thing to Consider how much the want of one has retarded ye Progress of the true Religion in America.

The Spaniards were in the begining of their settlem^{ts} in these Indies sensible of these Disadvantages; and therefore they wisely remedied any Inconveniencies that might happen on this score, by Erecting Severall Bishopricks in their Dominions in y^t part of the world; and why we shou'd not Coppy after them, especially in soe usefull & necessary a point, I doe not understand? Since w^t is good for them in this Respect cannot be bad for us. . . . It can be noe shame for us to imitate their Prudence & Conduct & on this Occasion, & tho' we had no such instance or Example to direct or Influence in an affair of this kind, yet the Evident Necessity of ye thing it selfe loudly calls for Supply and Reliefe.

I will only mention a few things [which] points at this Defect, and then the Venerable Society will judge whether ye English Americans have not Reason to press for and Demand the Constant Residence of a Mitred head among them.

I take it for granted, that the Ends of the Mission can never be rightly answered without Establishing the Discipline, as well as the Doctrine of the Church of England in those parts, For ye One is a Fortress and Bullwark of Defence to the other, and once the Outworks of Religion come to be slighted and dismantled, it is easy to foresee wthout ye spirit of Prophecy w^t ye Consequence will be.

1st As to a Ready & constant Supply of Ministers or Missionaries (wch is of ye last consequence to the well Being of the American Churches), this can never be hoped for wthout a Resident Bishop among 'em to whom upon ye Death or notorious & scandalous immorality of any Clergy man, Application may in a little time be made, & the wants of each Cure may be supplied by his Ordaining such persons as shall be found capable of Labouring in God's Vineyard; Such I presume a Resident Bishop wou'd seldome or never want there. For to Establish a Bishoprick woul'd be in Effect ye Establishing a colledge in those Parts, Or at least it would draw many of our young Students thither from Great Brittain & Ireland in hopes both of Ordination and Preferment; whereas by sending to Great Brittaine, a vast Deal of time is lost; Nor can the true State of Ecclesiasticall things or Persons be Ever so well known, as by A Bishop, who lives upon ye Spott, and who consequently can best see into all the Secrett Causes, and Springs of things.

2^{ly}. A Bishop is absolutely necessary to Preside over the American Clergy, and to oblige them to doe their Duty, and to live in Peace and Unity, One with Another.

The Missionaries of America are like other men, & they may sometimes fall Out and Differ among themselves, and give great Offence thro' their unnecessary Heats and Animosities to the People.

The Contention between Paul and Barnabas was soe sharp, and grew so high, that they fell out, and parted upon it, and can wee thinke that the American Missionaries are better armed, or less Exposed to Accidents of this kind than those two great and holy men were.

And if this should be the Case of English Missionaries; as it has sometimes been, How fatall must ye Consequences of such an unhappy Strife and Contention be where there is no Superiour to Controul them, or to take a Cognizance of any affair of this kind, into his hands; Religion in this Case must bleed, and fall a victim to the Factions & unruly Humours of a few Turbulent and indiscreet persons, nor indeed humanly Speaking. Is it possible it shou'd be otherwise: When there was no King in Israeli, the Children of Israeli did that which was Right in their own Eyes, and can it be Expected, that it will be otherwise with the Clergy of America, where there is no Bishop to put a stop to their Career, or to keep 'em within those bounds of Decency, Respect, and mutuall forbearance; which they so much owe to One another; wheresoever Presbytery is established there they have the face and Appearance of an Ecclesiasticall Jurisdiction, and Authority, after their way, to Resort to, upon All Occasions.

But our Clergy in America are left naked, and destitute of any Advantage of this kind, and are exposed to the mercy and Conduct of their Own, Very often unreasonable Passions and Appetites, which are by many Degrees the worst Masters they can truckle under.

I will only in the third place mention ye Disadvantages, the Laity lie under, for want of A Bishop, and put an End to this tedious Memoriall.

The Ministers subsistance, and Livelyhood, being in all places, in America, more or less depending upon the Bounty of the People by Contributions, & Acts of Assembly: It is a difficult matter for them without the Countenance and Authority of a Bishop, to put a stop to ye Prophaness and Immorality of their severall parishioners, for to touch the more Topping, and Considerable men of them, either in Publique or Private is to draw the fury of the whole Congregation upon the Missionary, and to deprive himselfe of that Salary, or maintenance which he had from them.

It were to be wish'd that the Clergy's Sallarys, & maintenance in America were settled and adjusted by Act of Parliament in Great Brittaine, and then they would be the more bold and Resolute in Doeing their Duty, But as bad as things are in this Respect, yet a Bishop wou'd to a great Degree Remedy all Inconveniencies of this kind; for if the missionarie either could not, or Durst not doe his Duty, then the Bishop wou'd, and the Layty would be in a little time brought, to pay a greater Regard to their spirituall Guides, and then they would by Degrees, submit to Church Discipline, and Censures, without which, tho' a church may be planted, and gathered, yet it can never be of any long Growth or Continuance.

But now Nothing of that kind is heard of or attempted there and men Committ Adultery, and Polygamy, Incest, and A Thousand other Crimes, of which the Minister can hardly admonish them in Private, without manifest hazard and Disadvantage to himselfe, because there is no Ecclesiastical jurisdiction established in those parts, and tho' there were, there are no Laws, in being, which makes the Inhabitants of those Countreys lyable, and Obnoxious to it. . . .

Add to this that the want of a Bishop to Confirm in those parts is a great Trouble, to the American Clergy, for they are bound by the Rubrick not to administer the Sacrament of the Lord's Supper but to such as are Confirmed; which Prohibition notwithstanding they are forced to break thro', in this Case of Necessity; many other Reasons may be assigned for the Erecting a Bishoprick in the British America.

The Anglican Clergy of New England to the SPG, July 20, 1727

As to Religion in general & the state of our respective Churches, it is certain that in many places thro' the prevailing of the Gospel there is a great reformation in life & manners, & vice and immorality, rampant heretofore, do now begin to disappear, the Lord's Day free from former profanations is now observed with commendable strictness, and Swearing, Drinking and Debauchery are put under proper restraints, more from the awe of Religion than the Laws of Government, and that these things are owing to the settlement of the Church in these parts, is not only with Joy acknowledged by her friends but is plainly allowed by her Enemies both in principles and morals in their grief, envy and united opposition to it. But this brings us to the cause of it. . . .

As for Rhode Island, that fertile soil of Heresy & Schism, tho' in the main the Church doth triumph over those prostrate Enemies, yet still they endeavour to recover fresh strength & again finding encouragement from the commander in chief, an Anabaptist, & his Deputy, a Quaker, who, howfarsoever they disagree in principle, yet strenuously endeavour to promote what they have peculiarly espoused & if in nothing else concur in this to treat the Church with united indignities. . . .

And it moreover appearing to us by the frame of our Constitution impossible in the nature of the thing to observe our Rubrick or obey our Canons without a Bishop to whom we may have immediate recourse & whose frequent visitations of us is by them supposed, we pray to be heard, when we beg that without which our ministerial functions cannot be regularly discharged, namely, ye presence of a Bishop amongst us, for tho' no person can be more if so vigilant over us at the vast distance we have the unhappiness to be from him, than our R^t Rev^d & extremely beloved Diocesan, yet it being without the power

& bounds of any mortal to make us capable of discharging our dutys according to our Offices, our Orders & our Oaths, whilst he is so inaccessible to us, we would humbly represent the absolute necessity of being blessed with the favor we so earnestly pray for.

We are, &^c.,

TIMOTHY CUTLER,   JAMES M^cSPARRAN,
JAMES HONYMAN,   GEORGE PIGOT,
                    SAMUEL JOHNSON.

2. Religious and Racial Variety

Continental Diversity

The Palatines

Europe's bitter religious wars left a stain on Protestant-Catholic relations that decades, perhaps centuries, could not erase. A 1699 letter (published in England), purporting to offer "a true account of the sad condition of the Protestants in the Palatinate," commented as follows: "so inherent is persecution to popery that to be a Papist and a persecutor may be looked upon as controvertible terms that imply the same thing." When princes changed, religions changed — or at the very least they threatened to do so. When the fortunes of Catholic France waxed in the central Rhineland, the safety of German Protestants there waned — or at the very least was perceived to do so. England arranged for the rescue of some eight or nine thousand "poor distressed Palatines," moving them temporarily to England, then about half that number more permanently to New York and New Jersey in 1708 and 1710. In the document below, these Protestant (Lutheran and Reformed) farmers and artisans address their fellow laborers in England concerning their persecution and their rescue.

We the poor distressed Palatines, whose utter ruin was accomplished by the merciless cruelty of a bloody enemy the French whose prevailing power some years past, like a torrent rushed into our country and overwhelmed us at once,

---

[Source: Hugh Hastings, ed., *Ecclesiastical Records, State of New York* (Albany, 1902), III, 1823; quotation above is from 1454.]

and being not content with money and food necessary for their occasion, not only disposest us of all support, but inhumanly burnt our houses to the ground, whereby being deprived of all shelter, we were turned into the open fields, and there drove us, with our families to seek what shelter we could find, being obliged to make the cold earth our repository for rest, and the clouds was our canopy and covering. We poor wretches in this deplorable condition made our humble supplications and cries to Almighty God, whose omnisciency is extensive, and who has promised to relieve all those who make their humble supplications to him, that he will hear them, relieve them, and support them in what condition so ever, and likewise has promised to all those, who shall feed the hungry, clothe the naked, and comfort the distressed, they shall be received into his everlasting Kingdom, whereby they shall be rewarded with eternal life.

We magnifi the goodness of our Great God who heard our prayers, and in his good time disposed the hearts of good and pious princes to a Christian compassion and charity toward us in this deplorable state, by whose royal bounties, and the large donations of well disposed quality and Gentry, we and our children have been preserved from perishing from hunger, but especially since our arrival in this land of Canaan, abounding with all things necessary and convenient for human life.

Blessed Land! Govern'd by the Mother of Europe, and the best of Queens, in the steadiness and great alacrity in contributing largely, in all respects, toward all her allies abroad for the speedy reducing the exhorbitant power of France and our great enemy, and likewise her great piety and mild government and great charity toward all her distressed subjects at home, and not bounded here, but from afar hath gathered strangers and despicable creatures (as a hen her chickens under her wings) scattered abroad, destitute, hungry, naked and in want of every thing necessary for our support.

This great act of charity towards us obliges us, and our posterity to perpetuate her name in our families, and to render our hearty prayers to Almighty God, that he will be pleased to bless her sacred Majesty with long life and a prosperous reign, and this nation with a happy peace and plenty; and for the better obtaining of which, may he give her repeated victories over her enemies, which are the redundant rewards and blessings of God, upon her in this life, and may she be blessed with an immortal crown that never fades.

We humbly entreat all tradesmen not to repine at the good disposition of her sacred Majesty, and of the quality and gentry, but with great compassion join with them in their charitable disposition toward us, and with a cheerful readiness help us at this juncture, which we hope will be a means to redouble the blessing of God upon this nation. We entreat you to lay aside all reflections and imprecations, and ill language against us, for that is contradictory to a christian spirit, and we do assure you, it shall be our endeavor to act with great humility and gratitude, and to render our prayers for you, which is all the return that can be made by your

DISTRESSED BRETHREN, THE PALATINES

The Salzburgers

In 1731, the Roman Catholic archbishop of Salzburg, Austria, expelled all Lutherans from his ecclesiastical jurisdiction. Samuel Urlsperger, a Lutheran pastor in Augsburg, Germany, persuaded England's Society for Promoting Christian Knowledge to come to the rescue of these refugees. Since the colony of Georgia was then well along in its planning and since that colony needed pious, diligent emigrants, the solution seemed ready made. The "Salzburgers" would go to Georgia, first by way of Augsburg, then by way of Rotterdam. Their hope-filled, fear-filled ocean crossing in 1734 is described below in the words of their two clerical leaders. And as Pastor Urlsperger, who edited this journal, remarks, "Whoever takes the trouble to read this work with attention and in the right spirit will find ample material and opportunity to praise and glorify God with abundant thanks for His wise and benevolent guidance which He had gloriously shown in the affairs of the Georgia colonists."

On the 6th [of January, 1734] as the wind became favorable, we had to spend our time in Dover preparing for our departure.

The 7th. We were not able to leave yesterday because the wind again turned toward the west. And it seems that nothing will come of it today. The ship's crew does not want to start with a half-wind because they could not get through the Channel with it. Everything has been thrown into some confusion so that we will not be able to take Holy Communion as we had intended; but we are continuing with the preparation.

The 8th of Jan. After the north wind started blowing we experienced a hard freeze here, having had sunny weather and rain until now. With this wind we left Dover today in God's name, and we praised the Lord for all the kindness that was bestowed upon our bodies and souls in the English harbor.

The 9th. Just as most of the people became very sick at the beginning of the voyage, we too have become stricken by seasickness. But it is not as violent

---

[Source: *Detailed Reports on the Salzburger Emigrants Who Settled in America . . .* (Athens: University of Georgia Press, 1968), I, 39-40, 40-41, 43-44, 45-46, 47, 50, 51, 55-56, 58-59, 60-61; quotation above is from xxi.]

Salzburger emigration
Literally, the poem reads: "Nothing but the gospel forces us into exile.
Should we leave the Fatherland, we are still in God's hand."
(Library of Congress)

as it was on the trip from Rotterdam to Dover. Our true God has sent the most beautiful south-easterly wind which, it is hoped, will bring us through the English Channel in a few days. We are praising Him diligently for this kind deed.

The 10th. Today our bodies were strengthened again. With the favorable wind we passed this morning out of the English Channel, which is 300 English miles long. On the great ocean we considered the wonders of God, His omnipotence, and great wisdom. Our hearts were full of joy, and on the topdeck of the ship we all joined in the song: "Wondrous King," etc. We also edified ourselves with a good discourse which once again moved one of those present very much, so much that he definitely resolved to give himself over completely to our dear Saviour, for he can see what bliss it is to have a gracious God and a clear conscience. . . .

The 15th. Today the wind changed to southwest and almost completely west against us so that we could not maintain our course. Whenever something on our voyage goes contrary to our wishes, we diligently remind our congregation of the 27th chapter of the Acts of the Apostles. This we now not only understand better than before, but also consider it a great comfort that it is written in the Bible, as otherwise one might think of it as useless and superfluous. In the evening hour God heard our common prayer and again gave us a strong and rather favorable wind. During the day some of our company had remembered and had been very much impressed by the last words of James 5:17-18: "Elijah was a man," etc. When the favorable wind had come, each of them revealed his thoughts to the others, and great joy and praise of God arose. . . .

The 28th of Jan. This afternoon at two o'clock all of us aboard the ship had a great scare which impressed our hearts and our congregation's hearts very much (may God grant it to all aboard the ship!) and effected much good through God's grace. When the captain's dinner was cooking, the cabin boy who had to prepare it spilled the broth from the meat into the fire so that the steam penetrated throughout the ship and into the cabins. Since some sailors were in the powder magazine at that time, someone got the idea that the powder had caught on fire. He immediately called for water and came running on deck in great fear. Thereupon the captain and everybody ran to the bow of the ship and everyone thought his last hour had come. It is impossible to describe what a wretched sight this was and how miserably the old and the young were screaming. After the panic had passed, we called our congregation together and sang the hymn; "I shall, as long as I live here," etc. We praised God in prayer and reminded them briefly of the verse from the 13th Psalm which we had considered in this morning's prayer hour: I have trusted in Thy mercy. We closed with the verse: Let us come before His presence, etc. and reminded them briefly of the words contained therein: Fulfill your promised duty, etc. . . .

The 5th of Feb. Last night our dear Father gave us a good southeasterly wind which increased in strength during the day; for this we have already sung a song of praise to Him and shall do so again. He arranges it wisely to withdraw the favorable winds from us from time to time, for otherwise we would take them for granted and would give Him little prayer and thanks. Toward noon, one of us mingled with the congregation, pointed out the favorable wind to them, and asked whether they had prayed to God for it constantly. All of them not only confirmed this with a joyous YES, but one of them pulled from his pocket a prayer book in which he had a bookmark at a prayer for good wind. This he had dedicated diligently to the Lord whom wind and sea obey. Hereupon we roused them to give thanks for the favor received. . . .

The 10th. Our dear God graciously granted that today, Sunday, was spent by everybody on the ship, more so than usual, with the reading of the Bible and other useful books, even by the sailors. In this the Saltzburgers always led them with their good example. They are glad that God has heard their prayer and has made a certain individual much kinder and more friendly toward them. They have resolved to continue setting a good example and praying for him. We reminded them of the words of Solomon: "When a man's ways please the Lord, he maketh even," etc. . . .

The 19th. All day long the wind continued to blow so violently against us from west-north-west and the waves were so high that we could spread only two sails in the wind while the ship continued to be tossed from side to side.

When the Saltzburgers came on deck they were asked how it was with their confidence in God and to which verses of the Bible they had clung. Thereupon all the men and women not only quoted strength-giving verses but also showed happy confidence, which gave us much encouragement. At the evening prayer hour we sang: "Put your ways (in the hands of God)", etc.; and we reminded them of a few verses and led but one prayer, as the circumstances did not permit anything more. . . .

The 24th. This was Sunday. In the evening one of us chanced to think about the doxology in the Lord's Prayer, especially the words: THINE IS THE POWER, which we presented to God in prayer. He heard us, for the sake of His son, by sending a little east wind in the evening hours which started to move our ship and grew so beautiful and strong during the night that the next morning we could not praise the Lord enough for this benefit, which greatly strengthened us in our faith. Our congregation also were so delighted that we could hear many a "God be praised!" come from their mouths. Some said with Christian simplicity that, if they knew which hymn the Heavenly Father liked best, they would sing it with a thousand joys. . . .

The 5th of March. This morning about 9 o'clock our Father in Heaven let the sun rise. We had prayed for this since yesterday when we thought we had come close to land. After sunrise one of the sailors called from the mast that he had sighted land and not long afterwards we could recognize it clearly from the deck below. Hereupon we assembled and made good our vow to God with the hymn: LORD GOD WE PRAISE THEE. The 66th Psalm, which came next in order of our readings, brought us great pleasure because it fitted our circumstances exceedingly well. At last we read from the 5th chapter of Joshua, with the admonition that those who needed it should use the last few days at sea to open their hearts.

The 6th. Although we had seen the land, we were unable to reach it yesterday or today. Rather, we were driven further out to sea by contrary winds. God's ways with us are wondrous indeed. As soon as we sighted land an adverse wind arose, while until then we had had a calm. God is giving us time to drive out the false gods and to truly purify our hearts before landing. This we impressed upon ourselves and our listeners with diligence. During the prayer hour we also recalled what is written in the books of Moses about the Jews, who occasionally could see their land from a distance, but had to remain in one spot or wander from one place to another, in accordance with the orders God had given from the column of fire and smoke. A few days ago it was rather cold in this region but today we had a very lovely and warm day. God has heard our prayer and has again given us a favorable wind which, we hope, will bring us to Charleston soon. . . .

The 10th. Praise be to God who has let us spend this Reminiscere Sunday on the water. Again He has done great things for us. He refreshed our bodies

with sound food and drink; and everyone on the ship was in good spirits because we were lying off the shores of our dear Georgia on a beautifully calm sea
listening to the birds singing sweetly. It was very edifying for us to come to the
border of Georgia on this day, as the Gospel teaches us that Jesus went to the
border of the heathen lands after having suffered much discomfort and persecution from His own countrymen. Among other things, we compared with the
Gospel the 32nd chapter of Genesis, in which we find that, while traveling, Jacob (1) thankfully recalls the many good deeds of God (2), is afraid of his fierce
brother, yet finally (3) under prayer and tears (Compare Hosea 12:5) is freed
from all fear and wins the blessing of Christ (Compare Ephesians 1, entire). The
second point received special stress because some were worried that, as they
had been told, they might be none too safe from attack by the enemy in their
land. See Genesis 31:24 and compare v. 29. Likewise: "When a man's ways please
the Lord, He maketh even his enemies to be at peace with him."

The 11th of March. Our ship has struck a sandbar; and for this reason the
drinking water, which will no longer be needed, will be let out of the barrels in
order to lighten the ship.

The 12th. Last night, about ten o'clock, God helped us off the sandbar.
Thus it was possible to anchor the ship for the rest of the night at a better place.
If God had not sent an unusually high tide we would have been stuck much
longer and would have had to work the ship loose with much labor. This was
told us by some strangers who had come to see us from Georgia. All things of
this sort strengthen our faith: for God answers prayers. Since Sunday we have
been in the Savannah River, which presents a very gay view on both banks
where a great many birds can be seen and heard. The river itself is three times as
wide as the Saale at its widest point and is even wider than the Rhine. It is 16 to
25 feet deep and has many fish and oysters. . . .

The 13th of March. A tent was put up for our Saltzburgers, in which they
are to live until Mr. Oglethorpe[2] can come down from Charleston to see them.
A Jew [Benjamin Sheftal], who had also received some land here, took the
Saltzburgers in and treated them to breakfast with a good rice-soup. God has
awakened some people here so that they are very friendly toward us and show
great kindness. At times there are many large and small vermin here, among
others some very small black flies which fly in swarms around people's heads
and hands and sting them. So that they won't interfere with the work of the laborers, large fires are made upwind so that the smoke is blown over them and
drives the vermin away. According to the inhabitants, the land is very fertile.
There grows here a certain plant called myrtle, which has green berries. These
are boiled and from the extract, which floats on top, people make candles which
look very pretty and green but do not burn as well as the white candles.

---

2. James E. Oglethorpe (1696-1785), first governor of the colony of Georgia.

The 14th of March. Last night we held our first prayer hour on shore in the local church where we have permission to continue as long as we are here. The inhabitants of the town join us and prove themselves very devout. Also Jews, of which there are said to be twelve families, attend and listen attentively. They understand some German. The church is merely made of a few boards nailed together and has neither windows nor choir but only a roof and walls. Yet it suits us very well and the Saltzburgers like it. Also, instead of glass windows the houses have only paper, linen, or just the open window frame. This afternoon someone led us to the Indians who live in this neighborhood. We found them in circumstances which made our hearts bleed. The members of our congregation had been there shortly before, and the pitiful sight had filled them likewise with compassion and sorrow.

In this sad mood we assembled for prayers, and God led us to the verse: FOR GOD SO LOVED THE WORLD, etc., John 3:16. We were aroused to thankfulness toward God for the Holy Gospel, especially since we had seen among the Indians what a great pity it is not to have it. At the same time we gained hope that God will continue to show clearly that He loved the world, and still loves it. We were strengthened in the high hope of the 72nd Psalm, which followed in order, that God would show mercy to these poor heathens as He had done to others. We shall pray for them diligently. The counsel of man is very dear in this case, and it will not be easy to help them because their language is said to be extremely difficult to learn.

Mr. Oglethorpe arrived here today and received us and our Saltzburgers in very friendly fashion. He will now make arrangements to take our people to their destination. We had our midday meal with him.

The 15th of March. Mr. Oglethorpe is a man of exceptionally fine qualities. Since it means a great deal to him to bring true knowledge of God to the poor Indians as well, he urged us today to learn their language which has only about one thousand primitive words. Our Saltzburgers have been cautioned very much to refrain from drinking a certain sweet-tasting brandy, called rum, which is made in Jamaica from a sugar base, because this drink has already brought death to many. Intelligent people who have visited them these days were favorably impressed with their devotion and general deportment. Consequently they predict much good for the land.

Gottlieb Mittelberger and the Atlantic Crossing

Mittelberger is not a major figure in American religious history; however, for two reasons his voice deserves to be heard. First, he found religious liberty and laxity too much to his disliking to remain in America, and thus he speaks for the many who decided not to cast their lot with this untamed land. Second, he left an account of the Atlantic crossing so dismaying as to raise the question how the American colonies ever got settled at all. For the "lower sort" (indentured servants and the like, to say nothing of slaves), the voyage was a nightmare and the promise at the end of that horror more often than not a hoax. Mittelberger sailed in 1750 (as one of nearly five hundred passengers) to become an organist and schoolmaster near Philadelphia. In 1754 he returned to Germany, publishing two years later his unflattering account.

Because of contrary winds it sometimes takes the boats from two to four weeks to make the trip from Holland to Cowes. But, given favorable winds, that voyage can be completed in eight days or less. On arrival everything is examined once more and customs duties paid. It can happen that ships have to ride at anchor there from eight to fourteen days, or until they have taken on full cargoes. During this time everyone has to spend his last remaining money and to consume the provisions that he meant to save for the ocean voyage, so that most people must suffer tremendous hunger and want at sea where they really feel the greatest need. Many thus already begin their sufferings on the voyage between Holland and England.

When the ships have weighed anchor for the last time, usually off Cowes in Old England, then both the long sea voyage and misery begin in earnest. For from there the ships often take eight, nine, ten, or twelve weeks sailing to Philadelphia, if the wind is unfavorable. But even given the most favorable winds, the voyage takes seven weeks.

During the journey the ship is full of pitiful signs of distress — smells, fumes, horrors, vomiting, various kinds of sea sickness, fever, dysentery, headaches, heat, constipation, boils, scurvy, cancer, mouth-rot, and similar afflictions, all of them caused by the age and the highly-salted state of the food, especially of the meat, as well as by the very bad and filthy water, which brings about the miserable destruction and death of many. Add to all that shortage of food, hunger, thirst, frost, heat, dampness, fear, misery, vexation, and lamentation as well as other troubles. Thus, for example, there are so many lice, especially on the sick people, that they have to be scraped off the bodies. All this misery

---

[Source: Gottlieb Mittelberger, *Journey to Pennsylvania,* ed. and trans. by Oscar Handlin and John Clive (Cambridge: Harvard University Press, 1960), pp. 12-15, 16-18.]

reaches its climax when in addition to everything else one must also suffer through two to three days and nights of storm, with everyone convinced that the ship with all aboard is bound to sink. In such misery all the people on board pray and cry pitifully together.

In the course of such a storm the sea begins to surge and rage so that the waves often seem to rise up like high mountains, sometimes sweeping over the ship; and one thinks that he is going to sink along with the ship. All the while the ship, tossed by storm and waves, moves constantly from one side to the other, so that nobody aboard can either walk, sit, or lie down and the tightly packed people on their cots, the sick as well as the healthy, are thrown every which way. One can easily imagine that these hardships necessarily affect many people so severely that they cannot survive them.

I myself was afflicted by severe illness at sea, and know very well how I felt. These people in their misery are many times very much in want of solace, and I often entertained and comforted them with singing, praying, and encouragement. Also, when possible, and when wind and waves permitted it, I held daily prayer meetings with them on deck, and, since we had no ordained clergyman on board, was forced to administer baptism to five children. I also held services, including a sermon, every Sunday, and when the dead were buried at sea, commended them and our souls to the mercy of God.

Among those who are in good health impatience sometimes grows so great and bitter that one person begins to curse the other, or himself and the day of his birth, and people sometimes come close to murdering one another. Misery and malice are readily associated, so that people begin to cheat and steal from one another. And then one always blames the other for having undertaken the voyage. Often the children cry out against their parents, husbands against wives and wives against husbands, brothers against their sisters, friends and acquaintances against one another.

But most of all they cry out against the thieves of human beings! Many groan and exclaim: "Oh! If only I were back at home, even lying in my pigsty!" Or they call out: "Ah, dear God, if I only once again had a piece of good bread or a good fresh drop of water." Many people whimper, sigh, and cry out pitifully for home. Most of them become homesick at the thought that many hundreds of people must necessarily perish, die, and be thrown into the ocean in such misery. And this in turn makes their families, or those who were responsible for their undertaking the journey, oftentimes fall almost into despair — so that it soon becomes practically impossible to rouse them from their depression. In a word, groaning, crying, and lamentation go on aboard day and night; so that even the hearts of the most hardened, hearing all this, begin to bleed.

One can scarcely conceive what happens at sea to women in childbirth and to their innocent offspring. Very few escape with their lives; and mother and child, as soon as they have died, are thrown into the water. On board our ship, on a day on which we had a great storm, a woman about to give birth and unable to deliver under the circumstances, was pushed through one of the portholes into the sea because her corpse was far back in the stern and could not be brought forward to the deck.

Children between the ages of one and seven seldom survive the sea voyage; and parents must often watch their offspring suffer miserably, die, and be thrown into the ocean, from want, hunger, thirst, and the like. I myself, alas, saw such a pitiful fate overtake thirty-two children on board our vessel, all of whom were finally thrown into the sea. Their parents grieve all the more, since their children do not find repose in the earth, but are devoured by the predatory fish of the ocean. It is also worth noting that children who have not had either measles or smallpox usually get them on board the ship and for the most part perish as a result. . . .

When at last after the long and difficult voyage the ships finally approach land, when one gets to see the headlands for the sight of which the people on board had longed so passionately, then everyone crawls from below to the deck, in order to look at the land from afar. And people cry for joy, pray, and sing praises and thanks to God. The glimpse of land revives the passengers, especially those who are half-dead of illness. Their spirits, however weak they had become, leap up, triumph, and rejoice within them. Such people are now willing to bear all ills patiently, if only they can disembark soon and step on land. But, alas, alas!

When the ships finally arrive in Philadelphia after the long voyage only those are let off who can pay their sea freight or can give good security. The others, who lack the money to pay, have to remain on board until they are purchased and until their purchasers can thus pry them loose from the ship. In this whole process the sick are the worst off, for the healthy are preferred and are more readily paid for. The miserable people who are ill must often still remain at sea and in sight of the city for another two or three weeks — which in many cases means death. Yet many of them, were they able to pay their debts and to leave the ships at once, might escape with their lives. . . .

This is how the commerce in human beings on board ship takes place. Every day Englishmen, Dutchmen, and High Germans come from Philadelphia and other places, some of them very far away, sometime twenty or thirty or forty hours' journey, and go on board the newly arrived vessel that has brought people from Europe and offers them for sale. From among the healthy they pick out those suitable for the purposes for which they require them. Then they negotiate with them as to the length of the period for which they will go into service in order to pay off their passage, the whole amount of which they generally still owe. When an agreement has been reached, adult persons by written contract bind themselves to serve for three, four, five, or six years, according to their health and age. The very young, between the ages of ten and fifteen, have to serve until they are twenty-one, however.

Many parents in order to pay their fares in this way and get off the ship must barter and sell their children as if they were cattle. Since the fathers and mothers often do not know where or to what masters their children are to be sent, it frequently happens that after leaving the vessel, parents and children do not see each other for years on end, or even for the rest of their lives.

Henry Muhlenberg: A Typical Day, 1764

It was to Muhlenberg's church in Upper Providence (between Philadelphia and Reading) that Mittelberger (see above) came to install and give voice to an organ. Henry Melchior Muhlenberg (1711-87) came to Philadelphia in 1742, assuming pastoral duties there as well as in New Hanover and Upper Providence. Ultimately, Muhlenberg traveled from New York to Georgia in his one-man missionary movement to all colonial Lutherans — and to as many others as he could reach. Diversity he accepted as a challenge and religious liberty he embraced as an ally. Something of his breathless exuberance and boundless energy is evident in this excerpt from his Journals.

September 4, Tuesday. In the forenoon I went first to Squire J[ones] and spoke to him about the disorderly innkeeper in N[ew] H[anover]. However, nothing can be done about it because action should have been taken at the last court. Thence to Squire H[oc]k[ley], but found him not at home. At ten o'clock I went to the schoolhouse and sat with Mr. Handschue to receive announcements of intention to commune. After eleven o'clock I left and visited three sick families. Also stopped in to call on the late Mr. Gilbert Tennent's widow. When I got back home I found two men from Germantown waiting for me. They brought a letter from Brother Voigt in which he presented a *casus conscientiae* and desired an immediate reply. I replied and was immediately called away to confer with a trustee about the collectors from upcountry. Thence to the schoolhouse where I attended the registration of communicants until five o'clock. From five to six o'clock I visited the sick. From six to eight o'clock instructed the three confirmands. From eight to twelve o'clock I wrote letters to Virginia.

[Source: T. G. Tappert and J. W. Doberstein, eds., *The Journals of Henry Melchior Muhlenberg* (Philadelphia: The Muhlenberg Press, 1945), II, 116.]

Jesuit Banishment, 1764

As noted in the introduction to this chapter, one move in the latter half of the eighteenth century actually reduced Europe's religious variety in America instead of enlarging it. That radical and abrupt step was the recall of all France's Jesuit missionaries from their labors in North America. That action, part of a general suppression of an order grown too large and too influential, came first from France in 1761 and 1762. The shock waves reached the Western Hemisphere a year or two later; how they affected the individual is revealed in the account below by Father François P. Watrin, S.J. Watrin's dismay at the proceedings is all too evident, as is the sweeping nature of the accusations brought against the Society of Jesus in New France.

You write me, Monsieur, that you were surprised to learn of the arrival at Paris of Jesuits banished from Louisiana by a decree pronounced against them in that colony. You wish to know the reasons for this decree, and what followed its execution. I am familiar with the affair that interests you, and likewise with all that can in any way relate thereto. I lived for almost thirty years in Louisiana, and only departed thence at the beginning of this year. I am persuaded that your curiosity has no other motives than your love for religion and for truth. In the recital which I am about to give you, I shall be careful to say nothing which will depart in the least from these two rules.

In the month of June, 1763, the Jesuits of New Orleans, the capital of Louisiana, were still between hope and fear as to their future fate. As early as the preceding year, they had seen their enemies distribute with a triumphant air, manuscript copies of the decree given by the Parliament of Paris, August 6, 1761. But people worthy of respect had calmed their fears. They were expecting a great deal from the information given in their favor, and above all, from the petition addressed to the King by the bishops of France. They finally learned what they were to expect, at the arrival of the ship, which brought, with the news of peace, orders for their destruction.

There came upon the ship Monsieur d'Albadie, commissary-general of the navy and controller of Louisiana, and with him Monsieur de la Frenière, procurator-general of the superior council of this colony — both newly appointed to their positions. Monsieur the commissary did not delay to notify the superior of the Jesuits of what was brewing against them. "I believe," he said to him, "that Monsieur the procurator-general is charged with some order that concerns you." This was a sufficient warning, for any one who could have un-

---

[Source: R. G. Thwaites, ed., *Jesuit Relations and Allied Documents* (Cleveland: Burrows Brothers, 1896-1901), LXX, 213, 215, 217, 219, 221, 223.]

derstood him; but the Jesuits, too confident, were disposed to believe that, in spite of the example of so many Parliaments of France, nothing would be done against them in Louisiana; and, at a moment so critical, they did not take the slightest precaution about protecting their property.

Proceedings were begun. It was decreed that the Institute of the Jesuits should be brought to the council, to be examined. It was a great undertaking for this tribunal. All the judges who composed it ought at least to have studied theology and civil and ecclesiastical law. But, above all, they ought to have understood the language in which the institute is written. Now, this is not the kind of knowledge that is required from judges of colonies. In selecting them, search is not made for pupils of universities, but those among the habitants who show some capacity for business are chosen. Accordingly, one finds in these councils elderly shopkeepers, physicians, and officers of troops. Those who are best educated are usually the pupils of the naval bureaus; it is they who, up to the present, have been most often chosen, at least in Louisiana, as presidents of councils, an honor attached to the office of intendant or commissary-controller.

For these reasons, we are justified in saying that it was a great undertaking for the council of New Orleans to pronounce upon the Institute of the Jesuits. . . .

To these Gentlemen, it was enough to believe themselves well informed; one could not go astray while following such guides. . . .

The decree was declared on the 9th of July. It was said that the Institute of the Jesuits was hostile to the royal authority, the rights of the bishops, and the public peace and safety; and that the vows uttered according to this institute were null. It was prohibited to these Jesuits, hitherto thus styled, to take that name hereafter, or to wear their customary garb, orders being given them to assume that of secular ecclesiastics. Excepting their books and some wearing apparel which was allowed to them, all their property, real and personal, was to be seized and sold at auction. It was ordained that the chapel ornaments and the sacred vessels of New Orleans should be delivered up to the Reverend Capuchin Fathers; that the chapel ornaments and sacred vessels of the Jesuits living in the country of the Illinois should be delivered up to the Royal procurator for that country, and that the chapels should then be demolished; and that, finally, the aforesaid Jesuits, so-called, should return to France, embarking upon the first ships ready to depart — prohibiting them, meanwhile, from remaining together. A sum of six hundred livres was assigned to pay each one's passage, and another, of 1,500 francs, for their sustenance and support for six months. They were enjoined to present themselves, after that term, to Monsieur the duke de Choiseul, secretary of State in the department of marine, to ask him for the pensions which would be assigned from the proceeds of the sale of their property.

I have mentioned above the general motives for the condemnation of the Jesuits of Louisiana, motives copied from the decrees of the Parliaments of

France; but, in that which the council of New Orleans issued, it undertook to insert something special and new. It stated that the Jesuits established in the colony *had not taken any care of their missions; that they had thought only of making their estates valuable; and that they were usurpers of the vicariate-general of New Orleans.*

If their own interests alone had been at stake, the Jesuits of Louisiana, after the loss of their property, could still have borne in silence the attack upon their reputation made by this decree. But there are times when silence is an admission, and it is not permitted to admit the wrong imputed when a scandal would result therefrom. Now, what a scandal, if missionaries sent to America for the instruction of the French and the savages, missionaries subsisting there upon the benefactions of the King — if such men should be forced by the voice of conscience to acknowledge, at least tacitly, *that they took no care of their missions; that they only gave their attention to their estates; and, besides, that they are usurpers of the vicariate-general of an episcopate!* But no, conscience will not oblige the Jesuits of Louisiana to acknowledge what is imputed to them! It obliges them, on the contrary, to speak, and, in what they have to say for their justification, they do not fear to be convicted of falsehood; at least, they do not fear that anything true or substantial will be opposed to them.

British Diversity

Muhlenberg as Ecumenical Churchman

We have already met Pastor Muhlenberg as the vigorous minister to the European variety imported into Pennsylvania. But this Lutheran pastor also encountered and helpfully commented upon the sectarianism derived from Britain. Pennsylvania proved a real testing ground for religious liberty in the eighteenth century, a test for the sectarians themselves as well as for those of more churchly traditions. In this excerpt from Muhlenberg's Journals, one sees the German Lutheran himself passing the test quite handsomely as he tries to minister to all in an irenic spirit.

July 23 [1751]. Preached once more in Dutch, on the Beatitudes, Matthew 5. The two Reformed pastors and a large crowd of people were present. They all lis-

[Source: T. G. Tappert and J. W. Doberstein, eds., *The Journals of Henry Melchior Muhlenberg* (Philadelphia: The Muhlenberg Press, 1945), I, 299, 300, 665.]

tened very attentively. Several guileless Reformed people were sure that I was not a Lutheran preacher because I had not reviled and run down other denominations, but simply preached the order of salvation. One awakened Reformed man had ridden three miles from his home to the church and after the service, absorbed in sweet thoughts, walked all the way home before it finally occurred to him that he had left his horse standing near the church. Our poor scattered sheep were not a little encouraged and said they need no longer be ashamed of their religion when such praises were sung of their preacher, etc. Poor worms! . . .

Now that the Dutch language had become easier for me, and since it seemed to me to be a pity to spend Sunday for such a small group alone, I decided to conduct a brief English service or *Kinderlehre* on Sunday evenings, though it is rather difficult during the week to meditate and write out three sermons in three different languages along with house-catechizations and many other duties. . . .

[1763.] The new missionary [Alexander Murray] of the local English congregation came to visit me right after my arrival and engaged me in a long conversa-

Lutheran Church, Fifth Street, Philadelphia
(Library of Congress)

tion concerning the English Church. He deeply regretted that a *coalition* between the German Lutheran congregations and the English Church had not yet been effected. He expressed the opinion that this was just the most suitable period in which to establish a bishop in America. And if this were to come to pass, native German sons of good intelligence and piety could be educated in the English academies, ordained, and usefully employed for the best welfare of the Church of Christ in both the German and English languages, since, as it is, strife and factiousness prevail in the German Evangelical and Reformed congregations and the people are gradually joining with the Quakers or might even fall back into heathenism if preventive measures are not taken. I told him that I would think just as he did if I were in his place. I said that one could travel from one pole to the other in a few minutes on a map, but in practice things went much more slowly and laboriously.

Muhlenberg and the Baptists

In a manner both thoughtful and searching, Muhlenberg as pastoral counselor argued that one baptism is sufficient, that a rebaptism would cause "a great offense" against the "whole Christian church." Here Muhlenberg makes that point not on behalf of his own Lutheran church but on behalf of the Presbyterians with whom the woman described below had earlier been identified. Baptists migrated into Pennsylvania from both England proper and Wales, becoming sufficiently numerous to justify the formation of their first interchurch organization, the Philadelphia Association, in 1707. By 1765, the year of this excerpt, Baptists existed in largest numbers in Pennsylvania and Rhode Island.

In the evening I had to visit a German member of the congregation who had married an English woman. The woman's father was a member of the Baptist congregation and her mother was a Presbyterian. She had been baptized by a Presbyterian *minister* when she was nine years old and now she was insisting upon being baptized again in the Baptist congregation. The husband objected to this, and among other arguments he said that if she broke the baptismal covenant she had made with God when she was baptized at the age of nine years, then he, too, could break his marriage covenant with her. Several days previously she had had the *Baptist minister* at their home and he, setting forth all the usual arguments, declared that she would not be a communicant member of his

---

[Source: T. G. Tappert and J. W. Doberstein, eds., *The Journals of Henry Melchior Muhlenberg* (Philadelphia: The Muhlenberg Press, 1945), II, 161-63.]

church unless she submitted to Baptism. When the husband countered with the argument mentioned above, namely, that in that case he had an equal right to break his marriage vow, the *Baptist minister* advised them to secure my opinion. I therefore conferred with both of them. She claimed to be a member of her father's congregation and intimated that the covenant into which she had entered when she was nine years old was not sufficient because it had been contrived by her mother at a time when she herself had no conception or understanding of what it meant, etc. She also cited Acts 19 and other like texts. I replied:

1. That, according to our Saviour's mind and according to His teaching and that of His apostles, Holy Baptism is a rebirth which must not be confused with conversion. According to Christ's teaching, this rebirth consisted in being cut off from the guilty and corrupt family of Adam and being translated, ingrafted, or incorporated into Christ's kingdom of grace, into the Second Adam from heaven, the God-Man, the true Vine, into His family, thus receiving new sap and life, etc., etc. All heathen nations and people must in this way be consecrated into the one seed of Abraham. . . .

2. . . . [E]very son of Adam, whether his body be twelve inches or a yard in stature, has a right to the grace and righteousness obtained through Christ, because all races and peoples shall be blessed in Him, the one Seed.

3. Hence, no matter whether they are received by Baptism into Christ's kingdom and family on the day they are born or when they are nine years old, one Baptism is sufficient, and it is unnecessary to repeat it. Since no one can be cut off from the wild root and translated from death to life too early, it would be a great shame, pity, and folly to lose even a single minute of the time when the door of grace is open through which one might go as an accursed, condemnable child of Adam, without any merit or worthiness whatsoever, and be adopted as a child of God in Christ, the sole Mediator and Redeemer.

I told her that I would have no objection to the *Baptist minister's* receiving her as a communicant member without rebaptism. But if she permitted herself to be rebaptized, she would thereby be causing a great offense, and by that token would be declaring that Holy Baptism in the whole Christian church, and especially in the Presbyterian church, as a part of the whole, was invalid and insufficient; and she would some day regret it, if her conscience should ever be awakened. Ever since her Baptism at the age of nine, she had had free access and right to all the benefits of the salvation obtained by Christ; but if she permitted herself to be rebaptized into the Baptist congregation, she would be descending from Christ to men, from the Spirit to the flesh, from grace to works, and would be born, not of God, but of blood, the will of the flesh, and the will of man. I knew what she lacked — not Baptism, but a genuine conversion of heart and renewal of heart, mind, spirit, and all her powers. And this she must seek not in cisterns, but in the one, living fountain in Christ, according to His Word; only thus would she find rest unto her soul.

She told me of various awakenings and divine visitations of grace which God had made upon her soul, and also revealed a number of doubts she had concerning infant Baptism and sprinkling in Baptism, etc. I answered these and told her of several examples of persons who had allowed themselves to be baptized from one party into another and had become worse and worse, etc. She said, among other things, that her conscience would force her to join the Baptist congregation and be baptized if there was no other alternative. Answer: Christ's teaching and command would not be affected by her conscience. On the contrary, her conscience must conform itself to His command. In closing, I knelt with the husband and wife, and prayed in English, commending the matter to the Shepherd and Bishop of our souls. How it will turn out I do not know.

Muhlenberg and Quaker Pacifism

Western Pennsylvania was a dangerous frontier in the 1750s and 1760s, exposed as it was to Indian hostility and French encroachment. Those fighting for their lives and property on that frontier had little sympathy for the pacifist Quakers who lived, for the most part, in the relative security of eastern Pennsylvania. In the French and Indian War (1756-63), that pacifism grew particularly intolerable for those on the frontier. When aroused frontiersmen murdered twenty Conestoga Indians and later marched in armed rebellion on Philadelphia itself, then — according to Muhlenberg — even the pacifist Quakers decided to take up arms. But against their fellow colonists! The sordid events of 1764 mar both Pennsylvania's and America's early history, but Muhlenberg's trenchant observations throw a fascinating light upon the whole episode. They also leave no doubt as to their author's own sympathies.

It seems almost inconceivable, but a number of older and younger Quakers also formed themselves into companies and took up arms, etc. At any rate, it was a strange sight to the children on the streets. A whole *troup* of small boys followed a prominent Quaker down the street shouting in amazement, "Look, look! a Quaker carrying a musket on his shoulder!" Indeed, the older folks also looked upon it as a miraculous portent to see so many old and young Quakers arming themselves with flintlocks and daggers, or so-called murderous weapons! What heightened their amazement was this: that these pious sheep, who had such a tender conscience during the long Spanish, French, and Indian War, and would rather have died than lift a hand for defense against the most dan-

[Source: T. G. Tappert and J. W. Doberstein, eds., *The Journals of Henry Melchior Muhlenberg* (Philadelphia: The Muhlenberg Press, 1945), II, 20, 23.]

gerous enemies, were now all of a sudden willing to put on horns of iron like Zedekiah, the son of Chenaanah (I Kings 22), and shoot and smite a small group of their poor, oppressed, driven, and suffering fellow inhabitants and citizens from the frontier! . . .

The spokesman stated why they had come down with their weapons. (1) They, the backwoodsmen, had for years been left to cope with the distressing warfare on the frontiers without any help. They had been plundered by the Indians and had fought much and suffered much. Although they had repeatedly sent their *gravamina* to the government in Philadelphia, both in writing and by word of mouth, they had received neither help nor hearing. (2) After the Indians had been taken to Philadelphia, they, the backwoodsmen, were insulted by Quakers and other disorderly people who jeered at them, "See there! There are the murderers of Paxton who have slain the Indians!" (3) More than that, the leading Quakers took those Bethlehem Indians (among whom were murderers) into the city and treated them like lords at public expense. Meanwhile nothing at all was done for the suffering frontiersmen. On the contrary, it was said that they were nothing but a mixed crowd of Scotch-Irishmen and Germans; it did not matter whether they lived or died. (4) They were in a position to give assurances that they were loyal subjects of our king and friends of the province. In fact, they had proved this by risking life and limb against the enemy. They said that they had no intention of using their weapons against the government or of doing harm to loyal fellow citizens, but that they intended only to defend themselves against attack, to take the Indians out of the barracks, and to conduct them out of the province. They proposed to do this without killing them, and they were ready to offer an adequate guarantee to this effect. (5) Now, however, that they were informed that the Bethlehem Indians had been taken into custody not by private Quakers but by the government, and that they were being guarded by His Majesty's soldiers, they had no desire to use their weapons and even less to apply pressure to the government by force of arms. Instead, they would select three deputies from their midst and through these lay their grievances and remonstrances before the government.

Episcopal Order vs. "congregational" Chaos

The SPG missionary, Alexander Murray (noted above, p. 141), found quite intolerable the American tendency to let congregations run everything. Instead of orderly establishment and landed endowment, religion in Pennsyl-

---

[Source: W. S. Perry, ed., *Historical Collections Relating to the American Colonial Church* (New York: AMS Press, 1969 [1871]), II, 357-58.]

vania was subject to the "humor and caprice" of people who change their minds — and their preachers — as often as they do their clothes. Writing in that same dreary year of 1764, missionary Murray from his station in Reading addressed a letter to the secretary of the SPG. A portion of that letter is given below.

It is the unanimous opinion of all here who wish well to the preservation & enlargement of the Church, that in the Settlement of our late conquests in America application should be made in the very beginning for the allotment of Lands towards the support of a Clergy regularly ordained in our Church, after the example of the French, who constantly pursued this scheme in Canada, & thereby maintained a numerous Body of priests and Jesuits, who are over zealous and active in proselyting the Natives and sowing among them the seeds of prejudice and antipathy against the British as too providently appears from their singular attachment to the French still. It cannot be expected that the Society's funds can extend beyond the present limits they have set to them; and if they continue sufficient to preserve even the present Missions, it is all, at the utmost, can be hoped from them.

The Number of Papists in this county I have not got a more particular account of yet than what I sent you in my last, nor that of Dissenters of which we have some of every name. But the state of their several congregations are rather too evident from their scandalous differences and animosities, each within itself as well as with one another. The people are ever and anon quarrelling with their preachers, whom, of humor and caprice, they change much oftener than they renew their cloaths, so that it is a great deal if they are not all by the Ears in a twelvemonth. They are supported by annual contributions, which are made good the first year; then they are wearied, and both parties find it convenient to part, the Minister to find a fresh subsistence, & the people to get a new one in his place, no matter whether better or worse, so be their itch after novelty is gratified. In this perpetual round of changes and contentions, they sometimes move with a seeming gravity as they do at others with all the party Rage and violence of Men out of their senses, ending in provoking Libels and Lampoons and in Batteries and Bloodshed, twixt pastor and people, as here of late; which forms the most ludicrous and pitiable contrast imaginable, and has too manifest a tendency to expose the ministerial character to such obloquy and contempt without distinction as I could hardly have thought it could be loaded with in any Christian Country as I observe it generally is here. In the short time I have been here the Baptists, Lutherans and Calvinists (the most numerous Sects in this Town and Country adjacent), have changed their Ministers, and are still unprovided as they have been for some months past. In the midst of these convulsions & wildfire, I leave you to judge what state of mind I must necessarily be in; not knowing often what course to steer, that if possible, I may give no offence: and hitherto I have been abundantly happy to preserve the favor of my own people and have no share in the quarrels of the others. A Minister here must double his guard and deny himself many of the innocent comforts and liberties of life and undergo as many of its inconveniences, toils and troubles, if ever he would succeed in his work, particularly in the frontier Missions. . . .

Backcountry Baptists

Charles Woodmason (c. 1720-?), an Anglican itinerant from South Carolina, in 1766 toured his province's backcountry (i.e., the region west of the tidewater lands, into the foothills and mountains). Scandalized by what he saw of religious disorder and unchecked improvisation in religion, Woodmason wrote a report designed to demonstrate the absolute necessity for England's Church to rule and set all aright. It was not necessary to argue the point: just present the disturbing, horrifying facts. Of course, Woodmason is not an objective observer or reporter of the "facts" of religious life in the backcountry. But one can sense here, as perhaps nowhere else, what terror religious diversity (and the potential of religious liberty) held for those accustomed to a disciplined, hierarchically ruled national church. If this was what "Americanizing" of religion meant, Woodmason wanted none of it.

But let me say, that these Assemblies at Private Houses for Singing Hymns, is very reprehensible. First because People may assemble in this Place, and Sing, and then no Scandal would arise, and 2dly The Hymns commonly sung, had far better be thrown into the Fire. I have seen many of them — Which are not only execrable in Point of Versification, but withal full of Blasphemy Nonsense, and Incoherence. No Edification therefore can spring from such Singing. Withal should it be said, that they thus meet because these Hymns and Tunes are not permitted in the Church — I answer That as to the Tunes, the Clerk is the Person concern'd Who is both able and willing to gratify any in Choice of Tunes; And as for Hymns We do not disallow of them, provided they be Solemn, Sublime, Elegant and Devout — Fit to be offer'd up to the Throne of Grace — And such can be furnish'd to any Religious Society, desirous of them.

The best Things are most liable to Abuse — And these Singing Matches lie under the Imputation of being only Rendezvous of Idlers, under the Mask of Devotion. Meetings for Young Persons to carry on Intrigues and Amours. For

[Source: Richard J. Hooker, ed., *The Carolina Backcountry on the Eve of the Revolution* (Chapel Hill: University of North Carolina Press, 1953), pp. 97-99, 99-100, 102-3.]

all Classes of Villains, and the Vicious of both Sexes to make Assignations; and for others to indulge themselves in Acts of Intemperance and Wantoness, So that these Religious Societies are Evil spoken off, and therefore ought to be abolished conformable to what was done in the Primitive Times. The first Christians us'd to assemble at Nights, at the Tombs of the Martyrs, and there sing Hymns and perform Prayers. But as this gave Offence to the Heathens, and occasion'd the whole Body to be censur'd for the Irregularities of a Few it was judged proper to abolish these Nocturnal Meetings: And this Act of the Primitive Church ought to be a Rule to us at present: For it is rather better to decline an Innocent Duty that may be productive of some Good, rather than to have it perverted by base Minds to many Purposes of Evil:

But let us go on, and examine if in the General Corruption of Manners these New Lights have made any Reform in the Vice of Drunkenness? Truly, I wot not. There is not one Hogshead of Liquor less consum'd since their visiting us, or any Tavern shut up — So far from it, that there has been Great Increase of Both. Go to any Common Muster or Vendue, Will you not see the same Fighting, Brawling Gouging, Quarreling as ever? And this too among the Holy ones of our New Israele Are Riots, Frolics, Races, Games, Cards, Dice, Dances, less frequent now than formerly? Are fewer persons to be seen in Taverns, or reeling or drunk on the Roads? And have any of the Godly Storekeepers given up their Licences, or refus'd to retail Poison, If this can be made appear, I will yield the Point. But if [it] can be made apparent that a much greater Quantity of Rum is now expended in private families than heretofore — That the greater Part of these religious Assemblies are calculated for private Entertainments, where each brings his Quota and which often terminates in Intemperance and Intoxication of both Sexes, Young and Old: That one half of those who resort to these Assemblies Go more for sake of Liquor, than Instruction, or Devotion. That if it be proven that Liquor has been top'd about even in their very Meeting Houses, and the Preachers refreshed with Good Things, and after the Farce ended Stuff'd and Cramm'd almost to bursting, then it must be granted that little or no Reform has been made among the Vulgar in Point of Intemperance save only among some few Persons in some Places where the Mode only is chang'd and drinking in Public wav'd for the Indulgence of double the Consumption in Private. . . .

We will further enquire, if Lascivousness, or Wantoness, Adultery or Fornication [are] less common than formerly, before the Arrival of these *Holy* Persons, Are there fewer Bastards born? Are more Girls with their Virginity about them, Married, than were heretofore? The Parish Register will prove the Contrary. There are rather more Bastards, more Mullatoes born than before. Nor out of 100 Young Women that I marry in a Year have I seen, or is there seen, Six but what are with Child? And this as Common with the Germans on other Side the River, as among You on this Side: So that a Minister is accounted as a Scandalous Person for even coming here to marry such People, and for baptizing their Bastard Children as the Law obliges Me to register All Parties who are Married, and all Children Born. This occasions such Numbers (especially of the Saints) to fly into the next Province, and up to the German Ministers and any where to get Married, to prevent their being register'd, as therefrom the Birth of their Children would be trac'd: And as for Adulteries, the present State of most Persons around 9/10 of whom now labour under a filthy Distemper (as is well known to all) puts that Matter out of all Dispute and shews that the Saints however outwardly Precise and Reserved are not one Whit more Chaste than formerly, and possibly are more privately Vicious.

And nothing more leads to this Than what they call their Love Feasts and Kiss of Charity. To which Feasts, celebrated at Night, much Liquor is privately carried, and deposited on the Roads, and in Bye Paths and Places. The Assignations made on Sundays at the Singing Clubs, are here realized. And it is no wonder that Things are as they are, when many Young Persons have 3. 4. 5. 6 Miles to walk home in the dark Night, with Convoy, thro' the Woods', Or staying perhaps all Night at some Cabbin (as on Sunday Nights) and sleeping together either doubly or promiscuously? Or a Girl being mounted behind a Person to be carried home, or any wheres. All this indeed contributes to multiply Subjects for the King in this frontier Country, and so is wink'd at by the Magistracy and Parochial Officers but at same time, gives great Occasion to the Enemies of Virtue, to triumph, for Religion to be scandalized and brought into Contempt; For all Devotion to be Ridicul'd, and in the Sequel, will prove the Entire banishment and End of all Religion — Confusion — Anarchy and ev'ry Evil Work will be the Consequence of such Lewdness and Immorality.

But another vile Matter that does and must give Offence to all Sober Minds Is, what they call their *Experiences;* It seems, that before a Person be dipp'd, He must give an Account of his Secret Calls, Conviction, Conversion, Repentance &c &c. Some of these Experiences have been so ludicrous and ridiculous that *Democritus* in Spite of himself must have burst with Laughter. Others, altogether as blasphemous Such as their Visions, Dreams, Revelations — and the like; Too many, and too horrid to be mention'd. Nothing in the *Alcoran* Nothing that can be found in all the Miracles of the Church of Rome, and all the Reveries of her Saints can be so absurd, or so Enthusiastic, as what has gravely been recited in that *Tabernacle* Yonder — To the Scandal of Religion and Insult of Common Sense. And to heighten the Farce, To see two or three fellows with fix'd Countenances and grave Looks, hearing all this Nonsense for Hours together, and making particular Enquiries, when, How, Where, in what Manner, these Miraculous Events happen'd — To see, I say, a Sett of Mongrels under Pretext of Religion, Sit, and hear for Hours together a String of Vile, cook'd up, Silly and Senseless Lyes, What they know to be Such, What they are Sensible has not the least foundation in Truth or Reason, and to encourage Persons in such Gross Inventions must grieve, must give great Offence to ev'ry one that has the Honour of Christianity at Heart.

Then again to see them Divide and Sub divide, Split into Parties — Rail at and excommunicate one another — Turn out of Meeting, and receive into another — And a Gang of them getting together and gabbling one after the other (and sometimes disputing against each other) on Abstruse Theological Question — Speculative Points — Abstracted Notions, and Scholastic Subtelties, such as the greatest Metaph[ys]icians and Learned Scholars never yet could define, or agree on — To hear Ignorant Wretches, who can not write — Who never read ten Pages in any Book, and can hardly read the Alphabett discussing such Knotty Points for the Edification of their Auditors, is a Scene so farcical, so highly humoursome as excels any Exhibition of Folly that has ever yet appear'd in the World, and consequently must give High offence to all Inteligent and rational Minds.

If any Thing offensive beyond all This to greive the Hearts and Minds of serious Christians presents it Self to view among them, it is their Mode of Baptism, to which Lascivous Persons of both Sexes resort, as to a Public Bath. I know not whether it would not be less offensive to Modesty for them to strip wholly into Buff at once, than to be dipp'd with those very thin Linen Drawers they are equipp'd in — Which when wet, so closely adheres to the Limbs, as exposes the Nudities equally as if none at All, If this be not Offensive and a greivous Insult on all Modesty and Decency among Civiliz'd People I know not what can be term'd so.

African and Indian Diversity

Puritan Antislavery, 1700

The legal fact of slavery augmented by the physiological fact of blackness rendered social mobility virtually impossible for America's Negro population. That same conjunction rendered the Christian conscience virtually helpless for decades. Yet more than a hundred years before the Emancipation Proclamation or even before the abolitionist movement, some did question the very institution of slavery itself, raising those questions in the name of religion, even more in the name of Puritan allegiance to and understanding of

[Source: Roger Bruns, ed., *Am I Not a Man and a Brother* . . . (New York: Chelsea House, 1977), pp. 10-12.]

the Bible. Here the Puritan judge of the Superior Court of Massachusetts Colony, Samuel Sewall (1652-1730), argues that slavery is always and everywhere wrong, whether it is Joseph being sold into slavery in ancient Egypt, or men and women being so sold in modern America. "There is no proportion between Twenty pieces of Silver and Liberty." Sewall's tract, published in Boston in 1700, is entitled The Selling of Joseph a Memorial.

Forasmuch as Liberty *is in real value next unto* Life: *None ought to part with it themselves, or deprive others of it, but upon most mature consideration.*

The Numerousness of Slaves at this Day in the Province, and the Uneasiness of them under their Slavery, hath put many upon thinking whether the Foundation of it be firmly and well laid; so as to sustain the Vast Weight that is built upon it. It is most certain that all Men, as they are the Sons of Adam, are Co-heirs, and have equal Right unto Liberty, and all other outward Comforts of Life. God *hath given the Earth [with all its commodities] unto the Sons of Adam.* Psal. 115, 16. *And hath made of one Blood all Nations of Men, for to dwell on all the face of the Earth, and hath determined the Times before appointed, and the bounds of their Habitation: That they should seek the Lord. Forasmuch then as we are the Offspring of God, &c.* Acts 17. 26, 27, 29. Now, although the Title given by the last Adam doth infinitely better Men's Estates, respecting God and themselves; and grants them a most beneficial and inviolable Lease under the Broad Seal of Heaven, who were before only Tenants at Will; yet through the Indulgence of God to our First Parents after the Fall, the outward Estate of all and every of their Children, remains the same as to one another. So that Originally, and Naturally, there is no such thing as Slavery. Joseph was rightfully no more a Slave to his Brethren, than they were to him; and they had no more Authority to Sell him, than they had to Slay him. And if they had nothing to do to sell him; the Ishmaelites bargaining with them, and paying down Twenty pieces of Silver, could not make a Title. Neither could Potiphar have any better Interest in him than the Ishmaelities had. Gen. 37, 20, 27, 28. For he that shall in this case plead Alteration of Property, seems to have forfeited a great part of his own claim to Humanity. There is no proportion between Twenty Pieces of Silver and Liberty. The Commodity itself is the Claimer. If Arabian Gold be imported in any quantities, most are afraid to meddle with it, though they might have it at easy rates; lest it should have been wrongfully taken from the Owners, it should kindle a fire to the Consumption of their whole Estate. 'Tis pity there should be more Caution used in buying a Horse, or a little lifeless dust, than there is in purchasing Men and Women. . . .

And all things considered, it would concluce more to the Welfare of the Province, to have White Servants for a Term of Years, than to have Slaves for Life. Few can endure to hear of a Negro's being made free; and indeed they can seldom use their Freedom well; yet their continual aspiring after their forbidden Liberty, renders them Unwilling Servants. And there is such a disparity in their Conditions, Colour, and Hair, that they can never embody with us, & grow up in orderly Families, to the Peopling of the Land; but still remain in our Body Politick as a kind of extravasat Blood. As many Negro Men as there are among us, so many empty Places are there in our Train Bands, and the places taken up of Men that might make Husbands for our Daughters. And the Sons and Daughters of New England would become more like Jacob and Rachel, if this Slavery were thrust quite out of Doors. Moreover it is too well known what Temptations Masters are under, to connive at the Fornication of their Slaves; lest they should be obliged to find them Wives, or pay their Fines. It seems to be practically pleaded that they might be lawless; 'tis thought much of, that the Law should have satisfaction for their Thefts, and other Immoralities; by which means, Holiness to the Lord is more rarely engraven upon this sort of Servitude. It is likewise most lamentable to think, how in taking Negroes out of Africa, and selling of them here, That which God has Joined together, Men do boldly rend asunder; Men from their Country, Husbands from their Wives, Parents from their Children. How horrible is the Uncleanness, Mortality, if not Murder, that the Ships are guilty of that bring great Crouds of these miserable Men and Women. Methinks when we are bemoaning the barbarous Usage of our Friends and Kinsfolk in Africa, it might not be unreasonable to enquire whether we are not culpable in forcing the Africans to become Slaves amongst ourselves. And it may be a question whether all the Benefit received by Negro Slaves will balance the Accompt of Cash laid out upon them; and for the Redemption of our own enslaved Friends out of Africa.

Episcopal Frustration, 1730

The SPG had the instruction and conversion of the uprooted Negro as a principal purpose of its being. Yet obstacle after obstacle was thrown up in its path to obstruct and frustrate that purpose. David Humphreys, secretary of the SPG and author of its first history, reported candidly in 1730 concerning the Society's efforts and the pitiable results. He also explored the reasons for the record of failure.

The Negroe Slaves even in those Colonies, where the Society send Missionaries, amount to many Thousands of Persons, of both Sexes, and all Ages, and most of them are very capable of receiving Instruction. Even the grown Persons brought from Guinea, quickly learn English enough to be understood in ordi-

[Source: David Humphreys, *An Historical Account of the Incorporated Society for the Propagation of the Gospel in Foreign Parts* (New York: Arno Press, 1969 [1730]), pp. 232-36.]

nary Matters; but the Children born of Negroe Parents in the Colonies, are bred up entirely in the English Language.

The Society looked upon the Instruction and Conversion of the Negroes, as a principal Branch of their Care; esteeming it a great Reproach to the Christian Name, that so many Thousands of Persons should continue in the same State of Pagan Darkness, under a Christian Government, and living in Christian Families; as they lay before under, in their own Heathen Countries. The Society, immediately from their first Institution, strove to promote their Conversion; and inasmuch as their Income, would not enable them to send Numbers of Catechists, sufficient to instruct the Negroes; yet they resolved to do their utmost, and at least, to give this Work the Mark of their highest Approbation.

They wrote therefore to all their Missionaries, that they should use their best Endeavours, at proper Times, to instruct the Negroes; and should especially take Occasion, to recommend it zealously to the Masters, to order their Slaves, at convenient Times, to come to them, that they might be instructed. These Directions had a good Effect, and some Hundreds of Negroes have been instructed, received Baptism, and been admitted to the Communion, and lived very orderly Lives. The Reader may remember, there is frequently Mention made above, in the Account of the Labours of the Missionaries, of many Negroes at different Times instructed and baptized; to relate the Particulars here, would be too circumstantial, and altogether useless.

It is Matter of Commendation to the Clergy, that they have done thus much in so great and difficult a Work. But alas! what is the Instruction of a few Hundreds, in several Years, with respect to the many Thousands uninstructed, unconverted, living, dying, utter Pagans. It must be confessed, what hath been done is as nothing, with Regard to what a true Christian would hope to see effected. But the Difficulties the Clergy meet with in this good Work are exceeding great. The first is, the Negroes want Time to receive Instruction. Several Masters allow their Negroes Sunday only, for rest; and then the Minister of a Parish is fully employed in other Duties, and cannot attend them: Many Planters, in order to free themselves from the Trouble and Charge of Feeding and Cloathing their Slaves, allow them one Day in a Week, to clear Ground and plant it, to subsist themselves and Families. Some allow all Saturday, some half Saturday and Sunday; others allow, only Sunday. How can the Negroe attend for Instruction, who on half Saturday and Sunday is to provide Food and Rayment for himself and Family for the Week following? The Negroe will urge in his own Excuse, that the Support of himself, and all that is dear to him, doth absolutely depend upon this, his necessary Labour, on Saturday and Sunday. If this be not strictly justifiable, yet it is sure, the miserable Man's Plea, will engage the Reader's Compassion.

This is the Case in some Colonies, in others it differs: In some Places, the Slaves do the whole Labour of the Country, in the Field; in others, they are used only as House Servants. Another Difficulty arises from the Habitations and Set-tlements of the Masters, being at great Distances from each other in most Places in the Colonies; for which reason, neither can a Minister go to many Families, if the Negroes were allowed Time to attend him; nor can a proper Number of them assemble together at one Place, without considerable Loss of Time to their Masters. But the greatest Obstruction is, the Masters themselves do not consider enough, the Obligation which lies upon them, to have their Slaves in-structed. Some have been so weak as to argue, the Negroes had no Souls; others, that they grew worse by being taught, and made Christians: I would not men-tion these, if they were not popular Arguments now, because they have no Foundation in Reason or Truth.

Quaker Abolitionism, 1737

Even among socially sensitive Quakers, the eccentric Benjamin Lay was years ahead of his time. He condemned Quakers who themselves held slaves, doing so with such uncompromising vigor as to be ejected from the Philadel-phia Yearly Meeting in 1738. Decades later, however, in 1774 that same Yearly Meeting forbade all Quakers from holding slaves upon pain of being re-moved from their connection with the Society of Friends. Lay's rambling 278-page book, printed by Benjamin Franklin, bore the title All Slave-Keepers that Keep the Innocent in Bondage, Apostates. . . .

We pretend not to love fighting with carnal Weapons, nor to carry Swords by our sides, but carry a worse thing in the Heart, as will I believe appear by and by; what, I pray and beseech you, dear Friends, by the tender Mercies of our God, to consider, can be greater Hypocrisy, and plainer contradiction, than for us as a People, to refuse to bear Arms, or to pay them that do, and yet purchase the Plunder, the Captives, for Slaves at a very great Price, thereby Justifying their sell-ing of them, and the War, by which they were or are obtained; nor doth this sat-isfy, but their Children also are kept in Slavery, *ad infinitum;* is not this plainly and substantially trampling the most Blessed and Glorious Testimony that ever was or ever will be in the World, under our Feet, and committing of Iniquity with both Hands earnestly? Is this the way to convince the poor Slaves, or our Children, or Neighbours, or the World? Is it not the way rather to encourage and strengthen them in their Infidelity, and Atheism, and their Hellish Practice of Fighting, Murthering, killing and Robbing one another, to the end of the World.

[Source: Roger Bruns, ed., *Am I Not a Man and a Brother . . .* (New York: Chelsea House, 1977), pp. 48-49.]

Benjamin Lay
(National Portrait Gallery, Smithsonian Institution,
Washington, D.C. Gift of the James Smithson Society)

My dear Friends, I beg, I would intreat, in all Humility, with all earnestness of mind, on the bended Knees of my Body and Soul; willingly and with all readiness, sincerely, if that would do, that you would turn to the Lord, the Blessed Truth, in your Hearts, for Direction, for Counsel and Advice; that you may quit your selves like Men, honourably, of this so Hellish a Practice. Especially, you that have the Word of Reconciliation to preach to the Children of Men; and if you have any true tenderness of the Love of God in you, as I right well know, blessed be the Name of the Lord, all true Ministers have, you my dear Friends, consider waightily of these important concerns, and quit yourselves of your Slaves; for a good example in you might do a great deal of good, as a bad one will do, and has done a very great deal of mischief to the Truth; for the Eyes of the People are upon you, some for good, and some for Evil.

And my Friends, you that have Slaves, and do minister to others in our Meetings, consider I intreat and beseech you concerning this thing in particular. What Burthens and Afflictions, Bondage, and sore Captivity you bring upon your dear and tender Friends, and keep them in, which cannot touch with this vile and Hellish Practice, but are constrained to bear Testimony against it, as one of the greatest Sins in the World. . . .

Indian Captivity Narrative, 1682

A literary genre of great popularity in colonial America, narratives of Chris-
tians (often women) captured by Indians appeared throughout the eigh-
teenth and well into the nineteenth centuries. These narratives traditionally
tell how, in the providence of God, deliverance ultimately came, with good
miraculously and mysteriously emerging out of evil. In the course of King
Philip's War (see above, p. 85), Mary Rowlandson (c. 1635-78), a minister's
wife in Lancaster, Massachusetts, was captured along with her three children
in 1676. After four months in captivity, she and — later — two children were
ransomed, a third child having died as a result of injuries received in the ini-
tial capture. Mary Rowlandson's widely read and frequently reprinted nar-
rative was intended to show, as her title makes clear, The Sovereignty and
Goodness of God, together with the Faithfulness of His Promises Displayed *(1682).*

On the tenth of February 1675, came the Indians with great numbers upon Lancaster: Their first coming was about sun-rising; hearing the noise of some guns,
we looked out; several houses were burning, and the smoke ascending to
heaven. There were five persons taken in one house, the father, and the mother
and a sucking child, they knocked on the head; the other two they took and carried away alive. There were two others, who being out of their garrison upon
some occasion were set upon; one was knocked on the head, the other escaped:
another there was who running along was shot and wounded, and fell down; he
begged of them his life, promising them money (as they told me) but they
would not hearken to him but knocked him in the head, and stripped him naked, and split open his bowels. Another seeing many of the Indians about his
barn, ventured and went out, but was quickly shot down. There were three others belonging to the same garrison who were killed; the Indians getting up
upon the roof of the barn, had advantage to shoot down upon them over their
fortification. Thus these murderous wretches went on, burning, and destroying
before them.

    At length they came and beset our own house, and quickly it was the
dolefullest day that ever mine eyes saw. The house stood upon the edge of a hill;
some of the Indians got behind the hill, others into the barn, and others behind
any thing that could shelter them; from all which places they shot against the
house, so that the bullets seemed to fly like hail; and quickly they wounded one

---

[Source: Richard Slotkin and J. K. Folsom, *So Dreadfull a Judgment: Puritan Responses to*
King Philip's War, 1676-1677 (Middletown: Wesleyan University Press, 1978), pp. 323-25, 365-
66.]

man among us, then another, and then a third. About two hours (according to my observation, in that amazing time) they had been about the house before they prevailed to fire it (which they did with flax and hemp, which they brought out of the barn, and there being no defense about the house, only two flankers at two opposite corners and one of them not finished) they fired it once and one ventured out and quenched it, but they quickly fired again, and that took. Now is the dreadful hour come, that I have often heard of (in time of war, as it was the case of others) but now mine eyes see it. Some in our house were fighting for their lives, others wallowing in their blood, the house on fire over our heads, and the bloody heathen ready to knock us on the head, if we stirred out. Now might we hear mothers and children crying out for themselves, and one another, Lord, What shall we do? Then I took my children (and one of my sisters, hers) to go forth and leave the house: but as soon as we came to the door and appeared, the Indians shot so thick that the bullets rattled against the house, as if one had taken an handful of stones and threw them, so that we were fain to give back. We had six stout dogs belonging to our garrison, but none of them would stir, though another time, if any Indian had come to the door, they were ready to fly upon him and tear him down. The Lord hereby would make us the more to acknowledge his hand, and to see that our help is always in him. But out we must go, the fire increasing, and coming along behind us, roaring, and the Indians gaping before us with their guns, spears and hatchets to devour us. No sooner were we out of the house, but my brother-in-law (being before wounded, in defending the house, in or near the throat) fell down dead whereat the Indians scornfully shouted, and holloed, and were presently upon him, stripping off his clothes, the bullets flying thick, one went through my side, and the same (as would seem) through the bowels and hand of my dear child in my arms. One of my elder sister's children, named William, had then his leg broken, which the Indians perceiving, they knocked him on the head. Thus were we butchered by those merciless heathen, standing amazed, with the blood running down to our heels. My eldest sister being yet in the house, and seeing those woeful sights, the infidels haling mothers one way, and children another, and some wallowing in their blood: and her elder son telling her that her son William was dead, and myself was wounded, she said, And, Lord, let me die with them; which was no sooner said, but she was struck with a bullet, and fell down dead over the threshold. . . .

Oh the doleful sight that now was to behold at this house! *Come, behold the works of the Lord, what desolations he has made in the earth.* Of thirty-seven persons who were in this one house, none escaped either present death, or a bitter captivity, save only one, who might say as he, Job 1. 15, *And I only am escaped alone to tell the news.* There were twelve killed, some shot, some stabbed with their spears, some knocked down with their hatchets. When we are in prosperity, oh the little that we think of such dreadful sights, and to see our dear friends, and relations lie bleeding out their heart's blood upon the ground. There was one who was chopped into the head with a hatchet, and stripped naked, and yet was crawling up and down. It is a solemn sight to see so many Christians lying in their blood, some here, and some there, like a company of sheep torn by wolves. All of them stripped naked by a company of hell-hounds, roaring, singing, ranting and insulting, as if they would have torn our very hearts out; yet the Lord by his almighty power preserved a number of us from death, for there were twenty-four of us taken alive and carried captive.

I can remember the time, when I used to sleep quietly without workings in my thoughts, whole nights together, but now it is other ways with me. When all are fast about me, and no eye open, but His who ever waketh, my thoughts are upon things past, upon the awful dispensation of the Lord towards us; upon His wonderful power and might, in carrying of us through so many difficulties, in returning us in safety, and suffering none to hurt us. I remember in the night season, how the other day I was in the midst of thousands of enemies, and nothing but death before me: it is then hard work to persuade myself, that ever I should be satisfied with bread again. But now we are fed with the finest of the wheat, and, as I may say, with honey out of the rock: instead of the husk, we have the fatted calf. The thoughts of these things in the particulars of them, and of the love and goodness of God towards us, make it true of me, what David said of himself, Psalms 6. 6. *I watered my couch with my tears.* Oh! the wonderful power of God that mine eyes have seen, affording matter enough for my thoughts to run in, that when others are sleeping mine are weeping.

I have seen the extreme vanity of this world: one hour I have been in health, and wealth, wanting nothing: but the next hour in sickness and wounds, and death, having nothing but sorrow and affliction.

Before I knew what affliction meant, I was ready sometimes to wish for it. When I lived in prosperity, having the comforts of the world about me, my relations by me, my heart cheerful, and taking little care for anything; and yet seeing many, whom I preferred before myself, under many trials and afflictions, in sickness, weakness, poverty, losses, crosses, and cares of the world, I should be sometimes jealous lest I should not have my portion in this life, and that scripture would come to my mind, Hebrews 12. 6. *For whom the Lord loveth he chasteneth, and scourgeth every son whom he receiveth.* But now I see the Lord had his time to scourge and chasten me. The portion of some is to have their afflictions by drops, now one drop and then another; but the dregs of the cup, the wine of astonishment, like a sweeping rain that leaveth no food, did the Lord prepare to be my portion. Affliction I wanted, and affliction I had, full measure (I thought) pressed down and running over; yet I see, when God calls a person to anything, and through never so many difficulties, yet He is fully able to carry them through and make them see, and say they have been gainers thereby. And I hope I can say in some measure, as David did, *It is good for me that I have been afflicted.* The Lord hath showed me the vanity of these outward things. That they are the vanity of vanities, and vexation of spirit; that they are but a shadow, a blast, a bubble, and our whole dependence must be upon Him. If trouble from smaller matters begin to arise in me, I have something at hand to check myself with, and say, why am I troubled? It was but the other day that if I had had the world, I would have given it for my freedom, or to have been a servant to a Christian. I have learned to look beyond present and smaller troubles, and to be quieted under them, as Moses said, Exodus 14. 13. *Stand still and see the salvation of the Lord.*

Quaker Testimony on the Indian, 1722-63

From William Penn's early assurances to the Indian (see above, p. 85) through the eighteenth century, Quakers continued to work for some mode of accommodation with native Americans. Extermination always stood in the wings as a ready alternative, with many non-native Americans being too ready to apply that "solution." The Philadelphia Yearly Meeting of necessity returned again and again to this question which haunted and haunts all of American history. The document below recapitulates the views of the Meeting in 1722, 1759, and 1763.

When way was made for our worthy Friends, the proprietors and owners of lands in these provinces, to make their first settlement, it pleased Almighty God to influence the native Indians so as to make them very helpful to those early settlers, before they could raise stocks or provisions for their sustenance. And it being soon observed, that those people, when they got rum or other strong liquors, set no bounds to themselves, but were apt to be abusive, and sometimes even destroyed one another, there came a religious concern upon Friends to prevent those abuses; nevertheless, some people, preferring their filthy lucre before the common-good, continued in this evil practice, so that our Yearly Meeting, in the year 1687, testified, that the practice of selling rum or other strong liquors to the Indians, or exchanging the same for any goods or merchandize with them, is a thing displeasing to the Lord and a dishonour to truth; and, although this Testimony has been since renewed by several Yearly Meetings, it is yet notorious that the same hath not been duly observed by some persons; it therefore becomes the weighty concern of this meeting, earnestly to recommend that testimony to the strict observance of all Friends; and where any un-

---

[Source: *Some Account of the Conduct of the Religious Society of Friends Toward the Indian Tribes . . .* (London: Edward Marsh, 1844), pp. 88-89.]

der our profession act contrary thereto, let them be speedily dealt with and censured for such their evil practice. 1722.

In these provinces we may say, the Lord hath, as a gracious and tender parent, dealt bountifully with us, even from the days of our fathers; it was He who strengthened them to labour through the difficulties attending the improvement of a wilderness, and made way for them in the hearts of the Indian natives, so that by them they were comforted in times of want and distress; it was by the gracious influence of His Holy Spirit that they were disposed to work righteousness, and walk uprightly one towards another and towards the natives, and in life and conversation to manifest the excellency of the principles and doctrines of the Christian religion, and thereby they retained their esteem and friendship, which ought ever to be remembered with grateful thankfulness by us. 1759.

It is the solid sense and judgment of this meeting, that Friends should not purchase, or remove to settle on such lands as have not been fairly and openly first purchased of the Indians, by those persons who are or may be authorized by the government to make such purchases; and that Monthly Meetings should be careful to excite their members to the strict observance of this advice; and where any so remove contrary to the advice of their brethren, that they should not give certificates to such persons, but persuade them to avoid the danger to which they expose themselves, and to convince them of the inconsistency of their conduct with our Christian profession. 1763.

3. Passions and Intellect

Revivalism

George Whitefield (1714-70), Awakener

George Whitefield, the catalyst par excellence of religious passion in mid-eighteenth-century America, was a close friend of John and Charles Wesley; nonetheless, he was too committed to Calvinism ever to join their Methodist connexion. Though this Anglican irregular made many trips between England and America, none had greater impact than his second. Coming to the colonies in the fall of 1739, the twenty-five-year-old preacher hurried from town to town, from vacant hall to crowded church, from open field to busy market to declare the richness of God's boundless grace. His own journal, written in the same frenetic pace in which he traveled, reveals the excitement, the emotion, the public clamor. Whitefield was an event, as was the Great Awakening itself. Both changed the course of colonial history. Whitefield, in the excerpts below, recounts his initial visits in 1740 to (1) Boston, (2) Northampton, and (3) Philadelphia.

1.

Sunday, October 12 [1740]. Spoke to as many as I could, who came for spiritual advice. Preached, with great power, at Dr. Sewall's meeting-house, which was so exceedingly thronged, that I was obliged to get in at one of the windows. Dined

---

[Source: *George Whitefield's Journals* (London: Banner of Truth Trust, 1960), pp. 472-73, 476-77, 489-91.]

George Whitefield
(National Portrait Gallery, Smithsonian Institution, Washington, D.C.)

with the Governor, who came to me, after dinner, when I had retired, and earnestly desired my prayers. The Lord be with and in him, for time and eternity! Heard Dr. Sewall preach, in the afternoon. Was sick at meeting, and, also, after it was over. Went with the Governor, in his coach, to the common, where I preached my farewell sermon to near twenty thousand people, — a sight I have not seen since I left Blackheath, — and a sight, perhaps never seen before in America. It being nearly dusk before I had done, the sight was more solemn. Numbers, great numbers, melted into tears, when I talked of leaving them. I was very particular in my application, both to rulers, ministers, and people, and exhorted my hearers steadily to imitate the piety of their forefathers; so that I might hear, that with one heart and mind, they were striving together for the faith of the Gospel. After sermon, the Governor went with me to my lodgings. I stood in the passage, and spoke to a great company, both within and without doors; but they were so deeply affected, and cried so loud, that I was obliged to leave off praying. The Governor took his leave in the most affectionate manner, and said he would come and take me in his coach to Charleston ferry the next morning. . . .

Boston is a large, populous place, and very wealthy. It has the form of religion kept up, but has lost much of its power. I have not heard of any remarkable stir for many years. Ministers and people are obliged to confess, that the love of many is waxed cold. Both seem to be too much conformed to the world. There is much of the pride of life to be seen in their assemblies. Jewels, patches, and gay apparel are commonly worn by the female sex. The little infants who were brought to baptism, were wrapped up in such fine things, and so much pains taken to dress them, that one would think they were brought thither to be initiated into, rather than to renounce, the pomps and vanities of this wicked world. There are nine meeting-houses of the Congregational persuasion, one Baptist, one French, and one belonging to the Scots-Irish. There are two monthly, and one weekly lectures; and those, too, but poorly attended. I mentioned it in my sermons, and I trust God will stir up the people to tread more frequently the courts of His house. One thing Boston is very remarkable for, viz., the external observance of the Sabbath. Men in civil offices have a regard for religion. The Governor encourages them; and the ministers and magistrates seem to be more united than in any other place where I have been. Both were exceedingly civil during my stay. I never saw so little scoffing, and never had so little opposition. Still, I fear, many rest in a head-knowledge, are close Pharisees, and have only a name to live.

2.

Sunday, October 19. Felt great satisfaction in being at the house of Mr. [Jonathan] Edwards. A sweeter couple I have not yet seen. Their children were not dressed in silks and satins, but plain, as become the children of those who, in all things, ought to be examples of Christian simplicity. Mrs. Edwards is adorned with a meek and quiet spirit; she talked solidly of the things of God, and seemed to be such a helpmeet for her husband, that she caused me to renew those prayers, which, for some months, I have put up to God, that He would be pleased to send me a daughter of Abraham to be my wife. Lord, I desire to have no choice of my own. Thou knowest my circumstances; Thou knowest I only desire to marry in and for Thee. Thou didst choose a Rebecca for Isaac, choose one to be a helpmeet for me, in carrying on that great work which is committed to my charge. Preached this morning, and good Mr. Edwards wept during the whole time of exercise. The people were equally affected; and, in the afternoon, the power increased yet more. Our Lord seemed to keep the good wine till the last. I have not seen four such gracious meetings together since my arrival. Oh, that my soul may be refreshed with the joyful news, that Northampton people have recovered their first love; that the Lord has revived His work in their souls, and caused them to do their first works!

3.

Sunday, Nov. 9. Several came to see me, with whom I prayed. Preached at eleven in the morning, to several thousands, in a house built for that purpose since my departure from Philadelphia. It is a hundred feet long, and seventy feet broad. A large gallery is to be erected all round it. Both in the morning and the evening, God's glory filled the house. It was never preached in before. The roof is not yet up, but the people raised a convenient pulpit, and boarded the bottom. Great was the joy of most of the hearers when they saw me; but some still mocked. Between the services I received a packet of letters from England, dated in March last. May the Lord heal, and bring good out of the divisions which at present seem to be among the brethren there. Many friends being in the room, I kneeled down, prayed, and exhorted them all. I was greatly rejoiced to look round them, because there were some who had been marvellous offenders against God. . . . Whatever men's reasoning may suggest, if the children of God fairly examine their own experiences, — if they do God justice, they must acknowledge that they did not choose God, but that God chose them. And if He chose them at all, it must be from eternity, and that too without anything foreseen in them. Unless they acknowledge this, man's salvation must be in part owing to the free-will of man; and if so, unless men descend from other parents than I did, Christ Jesus might have died, and never have seen the travail of His soul in the salvation of one of His creatures. But I would be tender on this point, and leave persons to be taught it of God. I am of the martyr [John] Bradford's mind. Let a man go to the grammar school of faith and repentance, before he goes to the university of election and predestination. A bare head-knowledge of sound words availeth nothing. I am quite tired of Christless talkers. From such may I ever turn away. Amen.

Coming to Hear Whitefield

During his great tour of New England in the fall of 1740, George Whitefield attracted unusually eager listeners wherever he preached. A rare record of what it was like to take part in that experience was left by Nathan Cole (1711-

[Source: Michael J. Crawford, "The Spiritual Travels of Nathan Cole," *William and Mary Quarterly* 33 (Jan. 1976): 92-94.]

1783), who farmed and did carpentry near Middletown, Connecticut, one of the stops on that tour. Only shortly before, Whitefield had been at Northampton, Massachusetts, preaching for Jonathan Edwards. Both Edwards and his wife Sarah left extensive notes on how Whitefield had affected them. Now it was the turn of a layman to say what Whitefield's preaching was like. The following account details events from Thursday, October 23, 1740.

Now it pleased God to send Mr Whitefield into this land; and my hearing of his preaching at Philadelphia, like one of the Old apostles, and many thousands flocking to hear him preach the Gospel; and great numbers were converted to Christ; I felt the Spirit of God drawing me by conviction; I longed to see and hear him, and wished he would come this way. I heard he was come to New York and the Jerseys and great multitudes flocking after him under great concern for their Souls which brought on my Concern more and more hoping soon to see him but next I heard he was at long Island; then at Boston and next at Northampton.

Then on a Sudden, in the morning about 8 or 9 of the Clock there came a messenger and said Mr Whitfield preached at Hartford and Weathersfield yesterday and is to preach at Middletown this morning at ten of the Clock, I was in my field at Work, I dropt my tool that I had in my hand and ran home to my wife telling her to make ready quickly to go and hear Mr Whitfield preach at Middletown, then run to my pasture for my horse with all my might; fearing that I should be too late; having my horse I with my wife soon mounted the horse and went forward as fast as I thought the horse could bear, and when my horse got *much* out of breath I would get down and put my wife on the Saddle and bid her ride as fast as she could and not Stop or Slack for me except I bad her and so I would run untill I was *much* out of breath; and then mount my horse again, and so I did several times to favour my horse; we improved every moment to get along as if we were fleeing for our lives; all the while fearing we should be too late to hear the Sermon, for we had twelve miles to ride double in little more than an hour and we went round by the upper housen parish.[3]

And when we came within about half a mile or a mile of the Road that comes down from Hartford weathersfield and Stepney to Middletown; on high land I saw before me a Cloud or fogg rising; I first thought it came from the great River,[4] but as I came nearer the Road, I heard a noise something like a low rumbling thunder and presently found it was the noise of Horses feet coming down the Road and this Cloud was a Cloud of dust made by the Horses feet; it arose some Rods into the air over the tops of Hills and trees and when I came

3. Middletown Upper Houses Parish, the present town of Cromwell.
4. The Connecticut River.

within about 20 *rods* of the Road, I could see men and horses Sliping along in the Cloud like shadows and as I drew nearer it seemed like a steady Stream of horses and their riders, scarcely a horse more than his length behind another, all of a Lather and foam with sweat, their breath rolling out of their nostrils every Jump; every horse seemed to go with all his might to carry his rider to hear news from heaven for the saving of Souls, it made me tremble to see the Sight, how the world was in a Struggle; I found a Vacance between two horses to Slip in mine and my Wife said law our Cloaths will be all spoiled see how they look, for they were so Covered with dust, that they looked almost all of a Colour Coats, hats, Shirts, and horses.

We went down in the Stream but heard no man speak a word all the way for 3 miles but every one pressing forward in great haste and when we got to Middletown old meeting house there was a great Multitude *it was said to be 3 or 4000* of people Assembled together; we dismounted and shook of[f] our Dust; and the ministers were then Coming to the meeting house; I turned and looked towards the Great River and saw the ferry boats Running swift backward and forward bringing over loads of people and the Oars Rowed nimble and quick; every thing men horses and boats seemed to be Struggling for life; *The land and banks over the river looked black with people and horses* all along the 12 miles I saw no man at work in his field, but all seemed to be gone.

When I saw Mr Whitfield come upon the Scaffold he Lookt almost angelical; a young, Slim, slender, youth before some thousands of people with a bold undaunted Countenance, and my hearing how God was with him every where as he came along it Solemnized my mind; and put me into a trembling fear before he began to preach; for he looked as if he was Cloathed with authority from the Great God; *and a sweet sollome solemnity sat upon his brow* And my hearing him preach, gave me a heart wound; By Gods blessing: my old Foundation was broken up, and I saw that my righteousness would not save me; then I was convinced of the doctrine of Election: and went right to quarrelling with God about it; because that all I could do would not save me; and he had decreed from Eternity who should be saved and who not.

Timothy Cutler (1684-1765), Opposer

When The Great Awakening washed across the Atlantic seaboard colonies, it bound together those who found the vitality of immediate religious experience far more meaningful than traditional forms or received ways. In this

[Source: W. S. Perry, ed., *Historical Collections Relating to the American Colonial Church* (New York: AMS Press, 1969 [1873]), III, 345-48, 349-50, 350-51.]

way, the movement brought unity. But it also brought division and hostility,
especially among those who saw the revivalism as reckless zeal and nothing
more than an emotional binge. Boston's Anglican rector, Timothy Cutler,
found himself repelled by Whitefield in particular, by "Enthusiasm . . .
swell'd to much higher degrees of madness" in general. Cutler concluded that
the effect of all this raising of passion boded ill for the Anglican Church and
for all true religion. His sharp criticism is taken from three letters written in
the midst of that "madness": (1) Dec. 5, 1740, to the Bishop of London;
(2) Dec. 11, 1740, to the Secretary of the SPG; and (3) January 14, 1742, once
more to the Bishop of London.

1.

My Lord,

At Your Lordship's commands I presented You with the best Account I
could of our Northampton Enthusiasts, a considerable time ago; and tho' I am
not honor'd with that motive now, I beg leave to second it with the Progress of
another Enthusiast who has received Your Lordship's Animadversions, much to
the advantage of the Church. The General Expectations of M^r. Whitefield were
much raised by the large Encomiums the Dissenters bestowed on him; D^r.
Colman & M^r. Cooper^5 stile him the Wonder of the Age. Before that Panegyric I
presume to lay before Your Lordship, the Dissenters invited him here, and accordingly was He lodged in Town at D^r. Colman's Brother's.

His first landing in New England was at Rhode Island, Sept. 14. From
thence, after a few days, he rode to Bristol, where in the Rev^d M^r. Usher's^6 absence, He was by the Church Wardens invited into the Church, but refused
from a Preingagement by the Dissenters there, in whose Meeting House He
Prayed, *extempore*, and Preached; the Inferior Court, then sitting, adjourning to
attend him.

By Thursday night following He carne to this Town, welcomed by all our
Teachers. The next Morning the Secretary of the Province, a Dissenter, waited
on Him to conduct him to the Rev^d the Commissary's; but understanding He
was not at home, He found him at 11 O'Clock, at Prayers in his Church, where
were present 5 more Clergymen of us. After Prayers he saluted us all, whom
with him the Commissary invited to his House, where we had not been long
before he entered on Invectives against the Corruptions and Errors of the
Church, but was more temperate in the use of that Talent than he commonly
is. . . .

5. Congregational clergy in Boston.
6. Anglican clergyman.

Between 3 & 4 O'clock he left us, he was in D^r. Colman's Pulpit, in his Gown, (which he constantly wore in Town), before a large Audience of Teachers and People, Praying, *extempore,* and Preaching; commending the Faith and Purity of this Country, the Design and Lives of our Forefathers who settled it, And this was a Topic he never forgot upon all Public Occasions. He also reproved the People for their slack attendance on the Weekly Dissenters' Lectures — assign'd it to the late Fashionable Preaching among us. He also reproached the Church universally for her Corruptions in the Faith and Deviation from her Articles. . . .

He scarce ever omitted preaching twice a day, besides frequent Expounding in the Family, and some time after that, Family Prayer, with Multitudes that attended him and joined with him, within doors and without. He preach'd in this Town and many of the Towns adjacent, in Conventicles, Commons, and open Places, where he was always thronged, and seldom by less than Thousands 2, 5, 8, and at his Farewell, by not less than 20,000. Before his departure he made one excursion of 60 miles, Preaching all the way going and coming. He always minded us of the Orphan House at Georgia, and obtain'd a Collection in one Place and another of above £300 this Currency. . . .

While he was here, the face of things was quite altered; little Business went forward, People were always flocking to him, and he was the subject of all our Talk, and to speak against him was neither credible nor scarce safe. Governor & Council, and all Authority, Teachers & People, tryed to excel in showing Respect to him, nor do I know when things will subside into that easy condition they were in before he came.

The Variance he has caused remain in too great a degree. 1 tho't it my Duty, as mildly as I could, to bear witness against his opinion and Practices, and had no thanks from many within and without the Church, tho' I hope the Ferment is somewhat allay'd.

2.

The whole Church in this Town and the adjacent parts, with all the Church both at home and abroad, hath felt the ill effects of M^r. Whitefield's visits. Our sufferings here are very particular, being but an handful to the dissenters, who of all orders and degrees were highly fond of his coming, and gave him a most hearty and distinguishing welcome, and strived to excell one another in it, and to be cold or differently effected is with them a pretty strong mark of reprobation. The clergy of this Town never invited him into their Pulpits, nor did he ask them, nor ever attended any one of our Churches, saving one Friday at Prayers, upon his first entrance, to make himself known to us, tho' he tarried over three Sundays in Town, daily preaching in our Meeting Houses, and in open places, and was an hearer among the Dissenters on one part of two Sundays. Bishops,

Divines, Churchmen and Christians are with us, good or bad, as he describes them, and nothing but a conformity to his notions and rules will give us a shining character. The Idea he gives us of the present Church (and too many receive it) is Heterodoxy, Falsehood to our articles and rules, Persecution, and never more so. The principals, and books and practices of this Country are applauded and preferred to everything now in the Church, and People are exhorted to adhere to their Dissenting Pastors.

Too many unhappy Feuds and Debates are owing to M^r. Whitefield's being among us; and we have even disobliged the Dissenters in suffering them to engross him, but I hope the Fury and Ferment is subsiding, and that we shall at length be tolerably sweetened towards one another. What may hinder it are the enthusiastic Notions very much kindled among us and like to be propagated by his Writings, dispersed every where, with Antinomianism revived, and I fear also, Infidel and Libertine Principles, which some express a particular fondness for at this time. Our labours among our people would be very much assisted by suitable Books on these subjects, and the Society's bounty in this kind never wants good effects, tho' not so large as good men wish.

3.

[Since my earlier letter], Enthusiasm has swell'd to much higher degrees of madness; and nothing is too bad wherewith to stigmatize those who disapprove of it so that should the Friends of it encrease much more, their Bitterness, Fury & Rage might well make us tremble. They assemble People in Towns and frequently enter Meeting Houses without the knowledge or Liking of the Proper Teachers, who commonly think it safest for them to stifle their Resentments. Those who could not act that Prudence have many of them had Parties made among them to their great Vexation, and some Laymen or other have started up, and Strengthened the Schism in the Exercise of their Gifts of Praying and Preaching, and indeed the Times are fruitful of many such Ruling Elders, Deacons, and other illiterate Mechanics, who neglect or lay aside their callings for this Purpose, and are much admired and followed by the People. Two of them have enter'd this Town and affected multitudes; and one of them has had the Liberty of sundry Dissenting Pulpits; here as well as elsewhere, we have new Lectures in abundance, stated and occasional, by Day and Night. Here Children and Servants stroll, withdrawing themselves from Family care and Subjection; and Day Labourers spend much of their Time, expecting notwithstanding full Wages. In some Places (this Town not excepted), Lectures, especially Evening ones, are attended with hideous Yellings, and shameful Revels, continuing till Midnight, and till Break of Day, and much Wickedness is justly feared to be the Consequence of Them.

Gilbert Tennent's Warning to Ministers

Gilbert Tennent (1703-1764) was the son of the Presbyterians' leading pastor-educator in the first part of the eighteenth century. This father, William Tennent (1673-1746), had migrated to Pennsylvania from Ulster and then had established a classical academy in Neshaminy, where he instructed his sons and other young men in both the liberal arts and the principles of pious Calvinism. When William became the pastor of the Presbyterian church in New Brunswick, New Jersey, in the mid-1720s, he came under the influence of Theodore Frelinghuysen, a Dutch Reformed minister who had been touched by the pietistic revivals of continental Europe. Under Frelinghuysen's guidance Tennent too began to preach strongly against sin, to urge repentance upon his hearers, and to mobilize a drive for "true religion" among his fellow Presbyterians. Tennent became one of the chief sponsors of George Whitefield when he passed through the middle colonies, and Tennent would later preach in New England and other locations in the wake of Whitefield and with his same revivalistic goals in view. On March 8, 1740, Tennent preached a widely noted sermon in Nottingham, Pennsylvania, which encapsulated the awakeners' ardor for a lively, evangelical ministry. Later he would retract some of the harshness of this address, but for both friends and foes of the colonial revival, it was a landmark. No one had to ask twice why Tennent so feared "The Danger of an Unconverted Ministry."

MARK VI. 34.
And Jesus, when he came out, saw much People and was moved with Compassion towards them, because they were as Sheep not having a Shepherd.

As a faithful Ministry is a great Ornament, Blessing and Comfort, to the Church of GOD; even the Feet of such Messengers are beautiful: So on the contrary, an ungodly Ministry is a great Curse and Judgment: Those Caterpillars labour to devour every green Thing.

There is nothing that may more justly call forth our saddest Sorrows, and make all our Powers and Passions mourn, in, the most doleful Accents, the most incessant, insatiable, and deploring Agonies; than the melancholly Case of

[Source: Gilbert Tennent, *The Danger of an Unconverted Ministry, Considered in a Sermon on Mark VI.34* (2nd ed., Philadelphia, 1741); reprinted from *The Great Awakening: Documents Illustrating the Crisis and Its Consequences,* ed. Alan Heimert and Perry Miller (Indianapolis: Bobbs-Merrill, 1967), pp. 72-75.]

such, who have no faithful Ministry! This Truth is set before our Minds in a strong Light, in the Words that I have chosen now to insist upon! in which we have an Account of our LORD's Grief with the Causes of it.

We are informed, That our dear Redeemer was moved with Compassion towards them. The original Word signifies the strongest and most vehement Pity, issuing from the innermost Bowels.

But what was the Cause of this great and compassionate Commotion in the Heart of Christ? It was because he saw much People as Sheep, having no Shepherd. Why, had the People then no Teachers? O yes! they had Heaps of Pharisee-Teachers, that came out, no doubt after they had been at the Feet of *Gamaliel* the usual Time, and according to the Acts, Cannons, and Traditions of the Jewish Church. But notwithstanding of the great Crowds of these Ortho-dox, Letter-learned and regular Pharisees, our Lord laments the unhappy Case of that great Number of People, who, in the Days of his Flesh, had no-better Guides: Because that those were as good as none (in many Respects) in our Sav-iour's judgment. For all them, the People were as Sheep without a Shepherd. . . .

First I am to enquire into the *Characters of the Old Pharisee-Teachers.* Now I think the most notorious Branches of their Character, were these, viz. *Pride, Policy, Malice, Ignorance, Covetousness,* and *Bigotry to human Inventions in religious Matters.*

The old Pharisees were very proud and conceity; they loved the upper-most Seats in the Synagogues, and to be called Rabbi, Rabbi; they were masterly and positive in their Assertions, as if forsooth Knowledge must die with them; they look'd upon others that differed from them, and the common People with an Air of Disdain; and especially any who had a Respect for JESUS and his Doc-trine, and dislik'd them; they judged such accursed.

The old Pharisee-Shepherds were as crafty as Foxes; they tried by all Means to ensnare our Lord by their captious Questions, and to expose him to the Displeasure of the State; while in the mean Time, by sly and sneaking Methods, they tried to secure for themselves the Favour of the Grandees, and the People's Applause; and this they obtained to their Satisfaction. *John 7. 48.*

But while they exerted the Craft of Foxes, they did not forget to breathe forth the Cruelty of Wolves, in a malicious Aspersing the Person of Christ, and in a violent Opposing of the Truths, People and Power of his Religion. Yea, the most stern and strict of them were the Ring-leaders of the Party: Wit-ness *Saul's* Journey to *Damascus,* with Letters from the Chief-Priest, to bring bound to *Jerusalem* all that he could find of that Way. It's true the Pharisees did not proceed to violent Measures with our Saviour and his Disciples just at first; but that was not owing to their good Nature, but their Policy; for they feared the People. They must keep the People in their Interests: Ay, that was the main Chance, the Compass that directed all their Proceedings; and there-fore such sly cautious Methods must be pursued as might consist herewith.

They wanted to root vital Religion out of the World; but they found it beyond their Thumb.

Although some of the old Pharisee-Shepherds had a very fair and strict Out-side; yet were they ignorant of the New-Birth: Witness Rabbi *Nicodemus,* who talked like a Fool about it. Hear how our LORD cursed those plaister'd Hypocrites, Mat. 23. 27, 28. *Wo unto you, Scribes and Pharisees, Hypocrites; for ye are like whited Sepulchres, which indeed appear beautiful outward, but are within full of dead Bones, and of all Uncleanness. Even so ye also appear righteous unto Men, but within ye are full of Hypocrisy and Iniquity.* Ay, if they had but a little of the Learning then in Fashion, and a fair Outside, they were presently put into the Priest's Office, though they had no Experience of the New-Birth. O Sad!

The old Pharisees, for all their long Prayers and other pious Pretences, had their Eyes, with *Judas,* fixed upon the Bag. Why, they came into the Priest's Office for a Piece of Bread; they took it up as a Trade, and therefore endeavoured to make the best Market of it they could. O Shame!

David Brainerd's Diary

Unlike their Roman Catholic counterparts, Protestants made relatively few attempts at missions to Native Americans during the colonial period. Among the few to take up that task was Connecticut native David Brainerd (1718-1747), who in 1739 had experienced an evangelical "New Light" conversion while a student at Yale. Although he did not complete his college education, he was nonetheless appointed as a missionary in 1742 by the Society in Scotland for Propagating Christian Knowledge; in 1744 he was ordained for the ministry by the Presbytery of New York. From 1743 to 1747, Brainerd worked among Indians in New York, New Jersey, and Pennsylvania; in 1745 and 1746 he presided over a revival among the Delaware near Trenton. Brainerd died prematurely in 1747 from tuberculosis, but he gained renown when Jonathan Edwards, the father of his fiancée, published his journal. Later generations looked to this record, which was both a missionary story and an account of inner spirituality, as a model of evangelical piety.

Tuesday, Oct. 26, 1742. [At West-Suffield] Underwent the most dreadful, distresses, under a sense of my own unworthiness. It seemed to me, I deserved rather to be driven out of the place, than to have any body treat me with any

---

[Source: *The Life and Diary of the Rev. David Brainerd* in *The Works of President Edwards,* vol. 3 (New York: Burt Franklin, 1968 [London, 1817]), pp. 124, 125-26, 332-33.]

kindness, or come to hear me preach. And verily my spirits were so depressed at this time, (as at many others,) that it was impossible I should treat immortal souls with faithfulness. I could not deal closely and faithfully with them, I felt so infinitely vile in myself. Oh, what *dust and ashes* I am, to think of preaching the gospel to others! Indeed I never can be faithful for one moment, but shall certainly "daub with untempered mortar," if God do not grant me special help. — In the evening I went to the meeting-house, and it looked to me near as easy for one to rise out of the grave and preach, as for me. However, God afforded me some life and power, both in prayer and sermon; and was pleased to lift me up, and shew me that he could enable me to preach. O the wonderful goodness of God to so vile a sinner! — Returned to my quarters; and enjoyed some sweetness in prayer alone, and mourned that I could not live more to God.

Thursday, Nov. 4, 1742. [At Lebanon] Saw much of my nothingness most of this day: but felt concerned that I had no more sense of my insufficiency and unworthiness. O it is sweet *lying in the dust!* But it is distressing to feel in my soul that hell of corruption, which still remains in me. — In the afternoon, had a sense of the sweetness of a strict, close, and constant devotedness to God, and my soul was comforted with his consolations. My soul felt a pleasing, yet painful concern, lest I should spend some moments *without God.* O may I always *live to God!* — In the evening, I was visited by some friends, and spent the time in prayer and such conversation as tended to our edification, It was a comfortable season to my soul: I felt an intense desire to spend every moment for God. God is unspeakably gracious to me continually. In times past, he has given me inexpressible sweetness in the performance of duty. Frequently my soul has enjoyed much of God; but has been ready to say, "Lord, it is good to be here;" and so to indulge sloth, while I have lived on the sweetness of my feelings. But of late, God has been pleased to keep my soul *hungry,* almost continually; so that I have been filled with a kind of pleasing pain. When I really enjoy God, I feel my desires of him the more insatiable, and my thirstings after holiness the more unquenchable; and the Lord will not allow me to feel as though I were fully supplied and satisfied, but keeps me still reaching forward. I feel barren and empty, as though I could not live, without more of God; I feel ashamed and guilty *before him.* Oh! I see, that "the law is spiritual, but I am carnal." I do not, I cannot live to God. Oh for holiness! Oh for more of God in my soul! Oh this pleasing pain! It makes my soul press after God; the language of it is, "Then shall I be satisfied, when I awake in God's likeness," (Psal. xvii. *ult.*); but never, never before: and consequently I am engaged to "press towards the mark," day by day. O that I may feel this continual hunger, and not be retarded, but rather animated by every cluster from Canaan, to reach forward in the narrow way, for the full enjoyment and possession of the heavenly inheritance! O that I may never loiter in my heavenly journey!

Aug. 9, 1745. Spent almost the whole day with the Indians, the former part of it in discoursing to many of them privately, and especially to some who had lately received comfort, and endeavouring to inquire into the grounds of it, as well as to give them some proper instrustions, cautions, and directions.

In the afternoon discoursed to them publicly. There were now present about seventy persons, old and young. I opened and applied the parable of the sower, Matt. xiii. Was enabled to discourse with much plainness, and found afterwards that this discourse was very instructive to them. There were many tears among them while I was discoursing publicly, but no considerable cry: yet some were much affected with a few words spoken from Matt. xi. 28. *Come unto me, all ye that labour, &c.* with which I concluded my discourse. But while I was discoursing near night to two or three of the awakened persons, a divine influence seemed to attend what was spoken to them in a powerful manner, which caused the persons to cry out in anguish of soul, although I spoke not a word of terror; but, on the contrary, set before them the fulness and all-sufficiency of Christ's merits, and his willingness to save all that came to him; and thereupon pressed them to come without delay.

The cry of these was soon heard by others, who, though scattered before, immediately gathered round. I then proceeded in the same strain of gospel-invitation, till they were all melted into tears and cries, except two or three; and seemed in the greatest distress to find and secure an interest in the great Redeemer. — Some who had but little more than a *ruffle* made in their *passions* the day before, seemed now to be deeply affected and wounded at heart: and the concern in general appeared near as prevalent as it was the day before. There was indeed a very *great mourning* among them, and yet every one seemed to *mourn apart.* For so great was their concern, that almost every one was praying and crying for himself, as if none had been near. *Guttummaukalummeh, guttummaukalummeh,* i.e. "Have mercy upon me, have mercy upon me;" was the common cry.

It was very affecting to see the poor Indians, who the other day were halooing and yelling in their *idolatrous* feasts and *drunken* frolics, now crying to God with such importunity for an interest in his dear Son! — Found two or three persons, who, I had reason to hope, had taken comfort upon good grounds since the evening before: and these, with others that had obtained comfort, were together, and seemed to rejoice much that God was carrying on his work with such power upon others.

Letters of Esther Edwards Burr

Esther Edwards Burr (1732-1758) was the wife of one famous clergyman (Aaron Burr) and the daughter of an even more famous pastor-theologian (Jonathan Edwards). In her short life, she passed through many difficulties. The death of her husband in 1757 left her a widow with two very young children (including Aaron Burr, Jr., who would become famous for his misadventures in the early American republic). Throughout her married life, she oversaw the activities of a very busy household, since Aaron Burr, Sr., was president of the College of New Jersey when it moved to its permanent home at Princeton and since the president's household received a ceaseless parade of guests. Esther Burr was unusual in her day because of her literary efforts, especially her correspondence with a contemporary, Sarah Prince of Boston, which she prepared in the form of a diary. From that diary and her letters, mostly sent to family members, we are able to see how one young adherent to revival religion lived out her days. Shortly before her own death on April 7, 1758, she wrote the letters to her father and mother that are excerpted below.

No doubt, dear madam, it will be some comfort to you to hear, that God has not utterly forsaken, although he has cast down. I would speak it to the glory of God's name, that I think he has, in an uncommon degree, discovered himself to be an all-sufficient God, a full fountain of all good. Although all streams were cut off, yet the fountain is left full. I think I have been enabled to cast my care upon him, and have found great peace and calmness in my mind, such as this world cannot give nor take. I have had uncommon freedom, and nearness to the throne of grace. God has seemed sensibly near, in such a supporting and comfortable manner, that I think I have never experienced the like. God has helped me to review my past and present mercies, with some heart-affecting degree of thankfulness.

I think God has given me such a sense of the vanity of the world, and uncertainty of all sublunary enjoyments, as I never had before. The world vanishes out of my sight! Heavenly and eternal things appear much more real and important, than ever before. I feel myself to be under much greater obligations to be the Lord's than before this sore affliction. The way of salvation, by faith in Jesus Christ, has appeared more clear and excellent; and I have been constrained to venture my all upon him; and have found great peace of soul, in what I hope have been the actings of faith. Some parts of the Psalms have been very comforting and refreshing to my soul. I hope God has helped me to eye his hand, in

---

[Source: *The Journal of Esther Edwards Burr, 1754-1757,* ed. Carol F. Karlsen and Laurie Crumpacker (New Haven: Yale University Press, 1984), pp. 293-296.]

this awful dispensation; and to see the infinite right he has to his own, and to dispose of them as he pleases.

Thus, dear madam, I have given you some broken hints of the exercises and supports of my mind, since the death of him, whose memory and example will ever be precious to me as my own life. O, dear madam! I doubt not but I have your, and my honoured father's prayers, daily, for me; but, give me leave to entreat you both, to request earnestly of the Lord, that I may never despise his chastenings, nor faint under this his severe stroke; of which I am sensible there is great danger, if God should only deny me the supports, that he has hitherto graciously granted.

Since I wrote my Mothers Letter God has carried me throu new tryals and given new supports — My little Son has been sick with [the] slow Fever ever since my Brother left us, and has been brought to the Brink of the Grave but I hope in mercy God is bringing off him back again — I was innabled to Resighn the Ch[ild] (after a severe strugle with Nature) with the gre[at]est freedom — God shewed me that the Child w[as] not my own but His, that he had a right to recall what he had lent when ever he thought fit, and I had no reason to complain or say God was hard with me. This silenced me. But O how good is God! He not only kept me from complaining but comforted me by ennabling me to offer up the Child by Faith, I think if ever I acted Faith. I saw the fullness there was in Christ for little Infants, and his willingness to accept of such as were offered to him — suffer little Children to come unto me and forbid them not, were comforting words — God also shewed me in such a lively manner the fullness there was in himself of all spiritual Blessings, that I said altho all streams were cut off yet so long as my God lives I have enough — He enabled me to say that altho' thou slay me yet will I trust in thee — In this time of tryal I was lead to enter into a renewed and explissit Covenant [wi]th . . God . . in a more solemn manner then ever before with the greatest freedom and delight, after much self examminnation and prayer I did give my self and Children to God with my whole Heart — never untill now had I a sense of the privilage we are allowed in love — [starting?] with God — This act of soul left my mind [with] a great calm and steady trust in God — a few days after this one Eve in talking of the glorious state my dear departed Husband must be in, my soul was carried out in such longing desires after this glorious state that I was forced to retire from the Famaly to conceal my joy. When alone I was so transported and my soul carried out in such Eager desires after Perfection and the full injoyment of God and to serve him uninterruptedly that I think my Nature could not have borne much more — I think dear Sir I had that Night a foretaste of Heaven — this frame continued in some good degree the whole Night. I slept but little, and when I did my Dreams were all of Heavenly and divine things — Frequently [since] I have felt the same in kind tho' not in degree. This was about the time that God called me to give up my Child — Thus a kind and gracious God h[asl been with me in six Troubles and in seven.

But O Sir what cause of deep Humiliation [and] abasement of soul have I on account of remaining Corruption which I see working continually, especually Pride — O how many shapes does Pride Cloak it self in — Satan is also bang shoting hi[s] Dar[ts]. [B]ut blessed be God those temptations of his that used to overthro' me, as yet hant touched me — I will just hint at one or two if I ant two Tedious in length. When I was about to renew my Covenant with God it seemed as if one spoak it to me and said tis better that you should not renew it then to Break it when you have. What a dreadfull thing will it be if you dont keep it — My reply was I did not do it in my own strength. Then the temptation would return, how do you know that God will help you keep it — but it did not shake me in the least — O to be delivered from the power of Satan as well as sin! I cant help hopeing the time is near — God is sertainly fiting me for himself, and when I think it will be soon that I shall be called hence the thought is transporting.

Colonial Colleges: "Nurseries of Piety"

Harvard, 1636

All of this country's colonial colleges arose out of a religious context, nearly all under the sponsorship of a single denomination. This does not imply that the schools were narrowly sectarian; it does imply that religion was the motivating force, the sufficient if not the necessary cause of the colleges' very being. The Puritan commitment to learning manifested itself in the first decade of that "Great Migration" to the Massachusetts Bay Colony. Convinced that they should not "leave an illiterate ministry to the churches, when our present ministers shall lie in the dust," Puritans brought Harvard College into being in 1636. The town where it was situated was promptly renamed "Cambridge," in honor of the English university from which so many of the first generation clergy had graduated. The "College Laws" of 1642 to 1650, excerpted below, reflect the Puritan milieu that nurtured America's first college.

[Source: S. E. Morison, *The Founding of Harvard College* (Cambridge: Harvard University Press, 1935), pp. 333-34.]

1. When any Schollar is able to Read Tully or such like classicall Latine Authour ex tempore, and make and speake true Latin in verse and prose *suo (ut aiunt) Marte,* and decline perfectly the paradigmes of Nounes and verbes in the Greeke toungue, then may hee bee admitted into the Colledge, nor shall any claime admission before such qualifications.

2. Every one shall consider the mayne End of his life and studyes, to know God and Jesus Christ which is Eternall life. Joh. 17. 3.

3. Seeing the Lord giveth wisdome, every one shall seriously by prayer in secret, seeke wisdome of him. prov. 2. 2, 3 etc.

4. Every one shall so exercise himselfe in reading the Scriptures twice a day that they bee ready to give an account of their proficiency theerein, both in theoreticall observations of Language and Logicke, and in practcall and spirituall truthes as their tutour shall require according to their severall abilities respectively, seeing the Entrance of the word giveth light etc. psal. 119. 130.

5. In the publike Church assembly they shall carefully shunne all gestures that shew any contempt or neglect of Gods ordinances and bee ready to give an account to their tutours of their profiting and to use the helpes of Storing themselves with knowledge, as their tutours shall direct them. and all Sophisters and Bachellors (until themselves make common place) shall publiquely repeate Sermons in the Hall whenever they are called forth.

6. they shall eschew all prophanation of Gods holy name, attributes, word, ordinances, and times of worship, and study with Reverence and love carefully to reteine God and his truth in their minds.

7. they shall honour as their parents, Magistrates, Elders, tutours and aged persons, by beeing silent in their presence (except they bee called on to answer) not gainesaying shewing all those laudable expressions of honour and Reverence in their presence, that are in use as bowing before them standing uncovered or the like.

8. they shall bee slow to speake, and eschew not onely oathes, Lies, and uncertaine Rumours, but likewise all Idle, foolish, bitter scoffing, frothy wanton words and offensive gestures.

William & Mary, 1693

Though the first settlers reached Virginia a full generation before colonists formed the Bay Colony, the pleas of the former for a college long went unheeded in London. That appeals had to be made to London at all points to a

[Source: E. W. Knight, ed., *A Documentary History of Education in the South Before 1860* (Chapel Hill: University of North Carolina Press, 1949), I, 509, 511, 513, 521.]

major difference between Virginia and Massachusetts. The latter intended to be as nearly autonomous as possible, the former (a royal colony after 1624) maintained close ties with and dependence upon England's institutions. An Anglican college (as opposed to a Puritan one) could hardly expect to flourish without Church of England blessing and support back home. Thus, the College of William & Mary could not begin until London was ready for it to begin. The Statutes of 1728 set down the purposes of the College as well as the moral, educational, and theological expectations. Blockheads, moreover, were not encouraged.

There are three things which the Founders of this College proposed to themselves, to which all its Statutes should be directed. The First is, That the Youth of Virginia should be well educated to Learning and good Morals. The Second is, That the Churches of America, especially Virginia, should be supplied with good Ministers after the Doctrine and Government of the Church of England; and that the College should be a constant Seminary for this Purpose. The Third is, That the Indians of America should be instructed in the Christian Religion, and that some of the Indian Youth that are well-behaved and well-inclined, being first well prepared in the Divinity School, may be sent out to preach the Gospel to their Countrymen in their own Tongue, after they have duly been put in Orders of Deacons and Priests. . . .

[Concerning Grammar School students,] Special Care likewise must be taken of their Morals, that none of the Scholars presume to tell a Lie, or curse or swear, or talk or do any Thing obscene, or quarrel and fight, or play at Cards or Dice, or set in to Drinking, or do any Thing else that is contrary to good Manners. And that all such Faults may be so much the more easily detected, the Master shall chuse some of the most trusty Scholars for public Observators, to give him an Account of all such Transgressions, and according to the Degrees of Heinousness of the Crime, let the Discipline be used without Respect of Persons.

As to the Method of teaching, and of the Government of the School, let the Usher be obedient to the Master in every Thing, as to his Superior.

On Saturdays and the Eves of Holidays, let a sacred Lesson be prescribed out of Castalio's Dialogues, or Buchanan's Paraphrase of the Psalms, or any other good Book which the President and Master shall approve of, according to the Capacity of the Boys, of which an Account is to be taken on Monday, and the next Day after the Holidays.

The Master shall likewise take Care that all the Scholars learn the Church of England Catechism in the vulgar Tongue; and that they who are further advanced learn it likewise in Latin.

Before they are promoted to the Philosophy School, they who aim at the Privileges and Revenue of a Foundation Scholar, must first undergo an Examination before the President and Masters, and Ministers skilful in the learned Languages; whether they have made due Progress in their Latin and Greek. And let the same Examination be undergone concerning their Progress in the Study of Philosophy, before they are promoted to the Divinity School. And let no Blockhead or lazy Fellow in his Studies be elected. . . .

For avoiding the Danger of Heresy, Schism, and Disloyalty, let the President and Masters, before they enter upon these Offices, give their Assent to the Articles of the Christian Faith, in the same Manner, and in the same Words, as the Ministers in England, by Act of Parliament are obliged to sign the Articles of the Church of England. And in the same Manner too they shall take the Oaths of Allegiance to the King or Queen of England. And further, they shall take an Oath that they will faithfully discharge their Office, according to the College Statutes, before the President and Masters, upon the Holy Evangelists. All this under the Penalty of being deprived of their Office and Salary.

Yale, 1701

The colony of Connecticut, officially launched in 1639, shared with the more populous Bay Colony a commitment to the Puritan or Congregational way. Also like Massachusetts, Connecticut would provide for a continuous ministry both learned and pious. Initially located in Saybrook, Yale in 1716 moved to its permanent home in New Haven. The 1745 student rules, given below, were adopted soon after the Great Awakening had intensified concern throughout the colony for things of the soul. Earlier some Yale students had protested the dead formality at the college, the cool indifference (as they saw it) toward religion. The 1745 rules made such protest less likely in the future.

1. All Scholars Shall Live Religious, Godly and Blameless Lives according to the Rules of Gods Word, diligently Reading the holy Scriptures the Fountain of Light and Truth; and constantly attend upon all the Duties of Religion both in Publick and Secret.

2. That the President, or in his absence One of the Tutors Shall constantly Pray in the College-Hall every morning and Evening: and Shall read a Chapter or Suitable Portion of the Holy Scriptures, unless there be Some other Theological Discourse or Religious Exercise: and Every Member of the College whether Graduates or Undergraduates, whether Residing in the College or in the Town of New-Haven Shall Seasonably Attend upon Penalty that every Undergraduate

[Source: F. B. Dexter, *Biographical Sketches of the Graduates of Yale College . . .* (New York: Henry Holt & Co., 1896), II, 3-5.]

who Shall be absent (without Sufficient Excuse) Shall be Fined one Penny and for comeing Tardy after the Introductory Collect is made Shall be fin'd one half penny.

3. The President is hereby Desired as he hath Time & Opportunity to make and Exhibit in the Hall Such a publick Exposition, Sermon or Discourse as he shall think proper for the Instruction of ye Scholars, and when He Shall See cause So to do and Give public Notice thereof, Every Undergraduate Shall be Obliged to Attend upon the Same Penalty as aforesaid.

4. Every Student of the College Shall diligently attend upon the Duties of Religious Worship, both Private and Publick of the Sabbath Day, and Shall attend upon the Said Public Worship of God in the Meeting-House with the President and Tutors on the Lord's Day and on Days of public Fasting and Thanksgiving appointed by Authority, and all Public Lectures appointed by the Minister of the first Society of New Haven, upon Penalty of Four Pence for absence (without Sufficient reason) on either Part of the Sabbath or any Day of Public Fasting or Thanksgiving and three Pence for Absence on a Lecture, one Penny for comeing Tardy. And if any Student Shall be Detain'd by Sickness or a necessary Occasion He Shall Signifie the Same to the President or any of the Tutors on the morning; or otherwise his Excuse Shall be judged as Groundless unless it otherwise manifestly appear to be Sufficient.

5. No Student of this College Shall attend upon any Religious Meetings either Public or Private on the Sabbath or any other Day but Such as are appointed by Public Authority or Approved by the President upon Penalty of a Fine, Public Admonition, Confession or Otherwise according to the Nature or Demerit of the Offence.

6. That if any Student Shall Prophane the Sabbath by unnecessary Business, Diversion, Walking abroad, or makeing any Indecent Noise or Disorder on the Said Day, or on the Evening before or after, or Shall be Guilty of any Rude, Profane or indecent Behaviour in the Time of Publick Worship, or at Prayer at any Time in the College Hall, He Shall be punished, Admonished or otherwise according to the Nature and Demerit of his Crime.

7. Every Student of this College Shall in Words and Behaviour Shew all Due Honour, Respect and Reverence towards all their Superiours, Such as their natural Parents, Magistrates and Ministers, and Especially to the President, Fellows and Tutors of this College; and Shall in no case use any Reproachful, reviling, Disrespectful or contumacious Language: but on the contrary Shall Shew Them all proper Tokens of Reverence, Obedience and Respect: Such as Uncovering their Heads, Rising up, Bowing and Keeping Silence in their Presence. And particularly all Undergraduates Shall be uncovered in the College Yard when the President or either of the Fellows or Tutors are there: and when They are in their Sight and View in any other Place: and all the Bacchelors of Arts Shall be uncovered in the College Yard when the President is there; and all the Scholars shall Bow when he

Goes in or out of the College Hall, or into the Meeting-House, provided that the Public Worship is not Begun. And Scholars Shall Shew due Respect and Distance to those who are in Senior and Superiour Classes.

Dartmouth, 1769

Eleazar Wheelock (1711-79), a vigorous New Light supporter of the Great Awakening, seized upon the education of the Indian as his great cause. Initially forming an Indian School in 1754 in Lebanon, Connecticut, Wheelock later shifted the location to New Hampshire; there, the school chartered in 1769 took the name of its leading English patron, the Earl of Dartmouth. The college opened its doors to non-Indians as well as to Indians, with the widely known result that the former overwhelmed the latter among the student body. Nevertheless, Wheelock's letter of March 1, 1764 (given below), to the Earl of Dartmouth shows how heavily the concern for the Indian weighed upon this New Light clergyman. The letter also incidentally reveals the utility — one almost says the inevitability — of the name of George Whitefield in anything that pertained to evangelical religion in any of the colonies.

May it please your Lordship,

It must be counted amongst the greatest favors of God, to a wretched world, and that which gives abundant joy to the friends of Zion, that among earthly dignities, there are those who cheerfully espouse the sinking cause of the great Redeemer, and whose hearts and hands are open to minister supplies for the support and enlargement of his kingdom in the world.

As your lordship has been frequently mentioned with pleasure by the lovers of Christ in this wilderness, and having fresh assurance of the truth of that fame of yours, by the Rev. Mr. Whitefield, from his own acquaintance with your person and character, and being encouraged and moved thereto by him, I am now emboldened, without any other apology for myself, than that which the case itself carries in its very front, to solicit your Lordship's favorable notice of, and friendship towards, a feeble attempt to save the swarms of Indian Natives in this land, from final and eternal ruin, which must unavoidably be the issue of those poor miserable creatures, unless God shall mercifully interpose with his blessing upon endeavors to prevent it.

The Indian Charity School, under my care (a narrative of which, herewith transmitted, humbly begs your Lordship's acceptance) has met with such ap-

---

[Source: *Memoirs of the Rev. Eleazar Wheelock, D. D.* . . . (Newburyport: Edward Little & Company, 1811), pp. 238-40.]

probation, and encouragement from gentlemen of character and ability, at home and abroad, and such has been the success of endeavors hitherto used therein, as persuade us more and more, that it is of God, and a device and plan, which, under his blessing, has a greater probability of success, than any that has yet been attempted.

By the blessing and continual care of heaven, it has lived, and does still live and flourish, without any other fund appropriated to its support, than that great One, in the hands of Him, whose the earth is, and the fulness thereof.

And I trust there is no need to mention any other considerations to prove your Lordship's compassions, or invite your liberality on this occasion, than those which their piteous and perishing case does of itself suggest; when once your Lordship shall be well satisfied of a proper and probable way to manifest and express the same with success. Which I do, with the utmost cheerfulness,

Samson Occom
Samson Occom, a Mohegan Indian and a graduate of
Eleazar Wheelock's Indian school in Lebanon, Connecticut,
was ordained a Presbyterian clergyman in 1759.
(National Portrait Gallery, Smithsonian Institution, Washington, D.C.)

submit to your Lordship, believing your determination therein, to be under the direction of him who does all things well. And if the nature and importance of the case be not esteemed sufficient excuse for the freedom and boldness I have assumed, I must rely upon your Lordship's innate goodness to pardon him, who is with the greatest duty and esteem, my Lord,

> Your Lordship's most obedient
> And most humble servant,
> ELEAZAR WHEELOCK

Jonathan Edwards (1703-58)

No one better represents the combination of passion and intellect than Jonathan Edwards. Graduate of Yale College in 1720 and briefly a pastor in New York City, Edwards spent most of his life in Massachusetts: as pastor in Northampton (1726-50) and as missionary to the Indians in Stockbridge (1751-58). In 1757 he accepted the presidency of Princeton, dying soon after taking that office the following year. Author of several major treatises of continuing impact (for example, Religious Affections *in 1746 and* Freedom of the Will *in 1754), Edwards stands above his contemporaries in intellectual acumen and achievement. In a 1733 sermon entitled "A Divine and Supernatural Light," Edwards described how heart and head, passion and intellect, were both involved in real religion. A careful reading of this significant portion of that sermon offers appreciable insight into what the Great Awakening and evangelical religion, at their best, were all about.*

That there is such a thing as a Spiritual and Divine Light, immediately imparted to the soul by God, of a different nature from any that is obtained by natural means.

In what I say on this subject, at this time, I would,

I. Show what this divine light is.

II. How it is given immediately by God, and not obtained by natural means.

III. Show the truth of the doctrine.

And then conclude with a brief improvement.

[Source: *The Works of President Edwards* (New York: Leavitt, Trow & Company, 1844), IV, 439, 440-42, 444, 446, 447-50.]

Jonathan Edwards
Engraving by Amos Doolittle after a painting by Joseph Badger
(National Portrait Gallery, Smithsonian Institution/Art Resource, NY)

I. I would show what this spiritual and divine light is. And in order to it, would show,

First, In a few things what it is not. And here,

1. Those convictions that natural men may have of their sin and misery, is not this spiritual and divine light. Men in a natural condition may have convictions of the guilt that lies upon them, and of the anger of God, and their danger of divine vengeance. . . .

2. This spiritual and divine light does not consist in any impression made upon the imagination. It is no impression upon the mind, as though one saw any thing with the bodily eyes: it is no imagination or idea of an outward light

or glory, or any beauty of form or countenance, or a visible lustre or brightness of any object. The imagination may be strongly impressed with such things; but this is not spiritual light. . . .

3. This spiritual light is not the suggesting of any new truths or propositions not contained in the word of God. This suggesting of new truths or doctrines to the mind, independent of any antecedent revelation of those propositions, either in word or writing, is inspiration; such as the prophets and apostles had, and such as some enthusiasts pretend to. But this spiritual light that I am speaking of, is quite a different thing from inspiration: it reveals no new doctrine, it suggests no new proposition to the mind, it teaches no new thing of God, or Christ, or another world, not taught in the Bible, but only gives a due apprehension of those things that are taught in the word of God.

4. It is not every affecting view that men have of the things of religion that is spiritual and divine light. Men by mere principles of nature are capable of being affected with things that have a special relation to religion as well as other things. A person by mere nature, for instance, may be liable to be affected with the story of Jesus Christ, and the sufferings he underwent, as well as by any other tragical story: he may be the more affected with it from the interest he conceives mankind to have in it: yea, he may be affected with it without believing it; as well as a man may be affected with what he reads in a romance, or sees acted in a stage play. . . . A person therefore may have affecting views of the things of religion, and yet be very destitute of spiritual light. Flesh and blood may be the author of this: one man may give another an affecting view of divine things with but common assistance: but God alone can give a spiritual discovery of them.

But I proceed to show,

Secondly, Positively what this spiritual and divine light is.

And it may be thus described: a true sense of the divine excellency of the things revealed in the word of God, and a conviction of the truth and reality of them thence arising.

This spiritual light primarily consists in the former of these, viz., a real sense and apprehension of the divine excellency of things revealed in the word of God. A spiritual and saving conviction of the truth and reality of these things, arises from such a sight of their divine excellency and glory; so that this conviction of their truth is an effect and natural consequence of this sight of their divine glory. There is therefore in this spiritual light,

1. A true sense of the divine and superlative excellency of the things of religion; a real sense of the excellency of God and Jesus Christ, and of the work of redemption, and the ways and works of God revealed in the gospel. There is a divine and superlative glory in these things; an excellency that is of a vastly higher kind, and more sublime nature than in other things; a glory greatly distinguishing them from all that is earthly and temporal. He that is spiritually enlightened

truly apprehends and sees it, or has a sense of it. He does not merely rationally believe that God is glorious, but he has a sense of the gloriousness of God in his heart. There is not only a rational belief that God is holy, and that holiness is a good thing, but there is a sense of the loveliness of God's holiness. There is not only a speculatively judging that God is gracious, but a sense how amiable God is upon that account, or a sense of the beauty of this divine attribute.

There is a twofold understanding or knowledge of good that God has made the mind of man capable of. The first, that which is merely speculative and notional; as when a person only speculatively judges that any thing is, which, by the agreement of mankind, is called good or excellent, viz., that which is most to general advantage, and between which and a reward there is a suitableness, and the like. And the other is, that which consists in the sense of the heart: as when there is a sense of the beauty, amiableness, or sweetness of a thing; so that the heart is sensible of pleasure and delight in the presence of the idea of it. In the former is exercised merely the speculative faculty, or the understanding, strictly so called, or as spoken of in distinction from the will or disposition of the soul. In the latter, the will, or inclination, or heart, is mainly concerned.

Thus there is a difference between having an opinion, that God is holy and gracious, and having a sense of the loveliness and beauty of that holiness and grace. There is a difference between having a rational judgment that honey is sweet, and having a sense of its sweetness. A man may have the former, that knows not how honey tastes; but a man cannot have the latter unless he has an idea of the taste of honey in his mind. So there is a difference between believing that a person is beautiful, and having a sense of his beauty. The former may be obtained by hearsay, but the latter only by seeing the countenance. There is a wide difference between mere speculative rational judging any thing to be excellent, and having a sense of its sweetness and beauty. The former rests only in the head, speculation only is concerned in it; but the heart is concerned in the latter. When the heart is sensible of the beauty and amiableness of a thing, it necessarily feels pleasure in the apprehension. It is implied in a person's being heartily sensible of the loveliness of a thing, that the idea of it is sweet and pleasant to his soul; which is a far different thing from having a rational opinion that it is excellent. . . .

I come now,

III. To show the truth of the doctrine; that is, to show that there is such a thing as that spiritual light that has been described, thus immediately let into the mind by God. And here I would show briefly, that this doctrine is both *scriptural* and *rational*.

First. It is scriptural. My text is not only full to the purpose, but it is a doctrine that the Scripture abounds in. We are there abundantly taught, that the saints differ from the ungodly in this, that they have the knowledge of God, and a sight of God, and of Jesus Christ. . . .

But this brings me to what was proposed next, viz., to show that,

Secondly, This doctrine is rational.

1. It is rational to suppose, that there is really such an excellency in divine things, that is so transcendent and exceedingly different from what is in other things, that, if it were seen, would most evidently distinguish them. We cannot rationally doubt but that things that are divine, that appertain to the Supreme Being, are vastly different from things that are human; that there is that god-like, high and glorious excellency in them, that does most remarkably difference them from the things that are of men; insomuch that if the difference were but seen, it would have a convincing, satisfying influence upon any one, that they are what they are, viz., divine. What reason can be offered against it? Unless we would argue, that God is not remarkably distinguished in glory from men. . . .

2. If there be such a distinguishing excellency in divine things; it is rational to suppose that there may be such a thing as seeing it. What should hinder but that it may be seen? It is no argument, that there is no such thing as such a distinguishing excellency, or that, if there be, that it cannot be seen, that some do not see it, though they may be discerning men in temporal matters. It is not rational to suppose, if there be any such excellency in divine things, that wicked men should see it. It is not rational to suppose, that those whose minds are full of spiritual pollution, and under the power of filthy lusts, should have any relish or sense of divine beauty or excellency; or that their minds should be susceptive of that light that is in its own nature so pure and heavenly. It need not seem at all strange, that sin should so blind the mind, seeing that men's particular natural tempers and dispositions will so much blind them in secular matters; as when men's natural temper is melancholy, jealous, fearful, proud, or the like.

3. It is rational to suppose, that this knowledge should be given immediately by God, and not be obtained by natural means. Upon what account should it seem unreasonable, that there should be any immediate communication between God and the creature? It is strange that men should make any matter of difficulty of it. Why should not he that made all things, still have something immediately to do with the things that he has made? Where lies the great difficulty, if we own the being of a God, and that he created all things out of nothing, of allowing some immediate influence of God on the creation still? And if it be reasonable to suppose it with respect to any part of the creation, it is especially so with respect to reasonable, intelligent creatures; who are next to God in the gradation of the different orders of beings, and whose business is most immediately with God; who were made on purpose for those exercises that do respect God and wherein they have nextly to do with God: for reason teaches, that man was made to serve and glorify his Creator. And if it be rational to suppose that God immediately communicates himself to man in any affair, it is in this. It is rational to suppose that God would reserve that knowledge and wisdom, that is of such a divine and excellent nature, to be bestowed immediately by himself, and that it

should not be left in the power of second causes. Spiritual wisdom and grace is the highest and most excellent gift that ever God bestows on any creature: in this the highest excellency and perfection of a rational creature consists. It is also immensely the most important of all divine gifts: it is that wherein man's happiness consists, and on which his everlasting welfare depends. How rational is it to suppose that God, however he has left meaner goods and lower gifts to second causes, and in some sort in their power, yet should reserve this most excellent, divine, and important of all divine communications, in his own hands, to be bestowed immediately by himself, as a thing too great for second causes to be concerned in! It is rational to suppose, that this blessing should be immediately from God, for there is no gift or benefit that is in itself so nearly related to the divine nature, there is nothing the creature receives that is so much of God, of his nature, so much a participation of the deity: it is a kind of emanation of God's beauty, and is related to God as the light is to the sun. It is therefore congruous and fit, that when it is given of God, it should be nextly from himself, and by himself, according to his own sovereign will.

It is rational to suppose, that it should be beyond a man's power to obtain this knowledge and light by the mere strength of natural reason; for it is not a thing that belongs to reason, to see the beauty and loveliness of spiritual things; it is not a speculative thing, but depends on the sense of the heart. Reason indeed is necessary in order to it, as it is by reason only that we are become the subjects of the means of it; which means I have already shown to be necessary in order to it, though they have no proper causal in the affair. It is by reason that we become possessed of a notion of those doctrines that are the subject matter of this divine light; and reason may many ways be indirectly and remotely an advantage to it. And reason has also to do in the acts that are immediately consequent on this discovery: a seeing the truth of religion from hence, is by reason; though it be but by one step, and the inference be immediate. So reason has to do in that accepting of, and trusting in Christ, that is consequent on it. But if we take reason strictly, not for the faculty of mental perception in general, but for ratiocination, or a power of inferring by arguments; I say, if we take reason thus, the perceiving of spiritual beauty and excellency no more belongs to reason, than it belongs to the sense of feeling to perceive colors, or to the power of seeing to perceive the sweetness of food. It is out of reason's province to perceive the beauty or loveliness of any thing: such a perception does not belong to that faculty. Reason's work is to perceive truth and not excellency. It is not ratiocination that gives men the perception of the beauty and amiableness of a countenance, though it may be many ways indirectly an advantage to it; yet it is no more reason that immediately perceives it, than it is reason that perceives the sweetness of honey: it depends on the sense of the heart. Reason may determine that a countenance is beautiful to others, it may determine that honey is sweet to others; but it will never give me a perception of its sweetness.

I will conclude with a very brief improvement of what has been said.

First, This doctrine may lead us to reflect on the goodness of God, that has so ordered it, that a saving evidence of the truth of the gospel is such, as is attainable by persons of mean capacities and advantages, as well as those that are of the greatest parts and learning. If the evidence of the gospel depended only on history, and such reasonings as learned men only are capable of, it would be above the reach of far the greatest part of mankind. But persons with but an ordinary degree of knowledge, are capable, without a long and subtile train of reasoning, to see the divine excellency of the things of religion: they are capable of being taught by the Spirit of God, as well as learned men. The evidence that is this way obtained, is vastly better and more satisfying, than all that can be obtained by the arguings of those that are most learned, and greatest masters of reason. And babes are as capable of knowing these things, as the wise and prudent; and they are often hid from these when they are revealed to those. I Cor. i. 26, 27, "For ye see your calling, brethren, how that not many wise men, after the flesh, not many mighty, not many noble are called. But God hath chosen the foolish things of the world."

Secondly. This doctrine may well put us upon examining ourselves, whether we have ever had this divine light, that has been described, let into our souls. If there be such a thing indeed, and it be not only a notion or whimsy of persons of weak and distempered brains, then doubtless it is a thing of great importance, whether we have thus been taught by the Spirit of God; whether the light of the glorious gospel of Christ, who is the image of God, hath shined unto us, giving us the light of the knowledge of the glory of God in the face of Jesus Christ; whether we have seen the Son, and believed on him, or have that faith of gospel doctrines that arises from a spiritual sight of Christ.

Thirdly. All may hence be exhorted earnestly to seek this spiritual light. To influence and move to it, the following things may be considered.

1. This is the most excellent and divine wisdom that any creature is capable of. It is more excellent than any human learning; it is far more excellent than all the knowledge of the greatest philosophers or statesmen. Yea, the least glimpse of the glory of God in the face of Christ doth more exalt and ennoble the soul, than all the knowledge of those that have the greatest speculative understanding in divinity without grace. This knowledge has the most noble object that is or can be, viz., the divine glory or excellency of God and Christ. The knowledge of these objects is that wherein consists the most excellent knowledge of the angels, yea, of God himself.

2. This knowledge is that which is above all others sweet and joyful. Men have a great deal of pleasure in human knowledge, in studies of natural things; but this is nothing to that joy which arises from this divine light shining into the soul. This light gives a view of those things that are immensely the most exquisitely beautiful, and capable of delighting the eye of the understanding. This

spiritual light is the dawning of the light of glory in the heart. There is nothing so powerful as this to support persons in affliction, and to give the mind peace and brightness in this stormy and dark world.

3. This light is such as effectually influences the inclination, and changes the nature of the soul. It assimilates the nature to the divine nature, and changes the soul into an image of the same glory that is beheld. 2 Cor. iii. 18, "But we all with open face, beholding as in a glass the glory of the Lord, are changed into the same image, from glory to glory, even as by the Spirit of the Lord." This knowledge will wean from the world, and raise the inclination to heavenly things. It will turn the heart to God as the fountain of good, and to choose him for the only portion. This light, and this only, will bring the soul to a saving close with Christ. It conforms the heart to the gospel, mortifies its enmity and opposition against the scheme of salvation therein revealed: it causes the heart to embrace the joyful tidings, and entirely to adhere to, and acquiesce in the revelation of Christ as our Saviour: it causes the whole soul to accord and symphonize with it, admitting it with entire credit and respect, cleaving to it with full inclination and affection; and it effectually disposes the soul to give up itself entirely to Christ.

4. This light, and this only, has its fruit in a universal holiness of life. No merely notional or speculative understanding of the doctrines of religion will ever bring to this. But this light, as it reaches the bottom of the heart, and changes the nature, so it will effectually dispose to a universal obedience. It shows God's worthiness to be obeyed and served. It draws forth the heart in a sincere love to God, which is the only principle of a true, gracious, and universal obedience; and it convinces of the reality of those glorious rewards that God has promised to them that obey him.

Suggested Reading (Chapter Two)

Puritan New England has been intensively examined, both in its normative manifestation and its deviations. The classic study of the former remains Perry Miller's two-volume *New England Mind* (1939, 1953), along with his more accessible volume of essays, *Errand into the Wilderness* (1956). How Miller's once dominant vision has been modified is now a frequent scholarly theme; for one clear overview of shifting scholarly fashion, see David D. Hall, "Narrating Puritanism," in *New Directions in American Religious History*, ed. Harry S. Stout and D. G. Hart (1997). A useful anthology that maintains some of Miller's perspective is Alan Heimert and Andrew Delbanco, eds., *The Puritans in America* (1985). The nature of Puritan spiritual life received much needed attention in Charles E. Hambrick-Stowe,

The Practice of Piety (1982), and Charles L. Cohen, *God's Caress: The Psychology of Puritan Religious Experience* (1986). The ordinary Sunday sermon is explicated with equal care in Harry S. Stout, *The New England Soul* (1986).

That New England Puritanism and New England culture were not seamless garments is made fully evident in many fine studies, including David D. Hall, *Worlds of Wonder, Days of Judgment* (1989); Theodore Dwight Bozeman, *To Live Ancient Lives* (1988); Amanda Porterfield, *Female Piety in New England* (1992); Michael W. Kaufmann, *Institutional Individualism: Conversion, Exile, and Nostalgia in Puritan New England* (1998); Laura Henigman, *Coming into Communion: Pastoral Dialogues in Colonial New England* (1999); and Louise A. Breen, *Transgressing the Bounds: Subversive Enterprises Among the Puritan Elite in Massachusetts, 1630-1692* (2001).

The most detailed study of Anne Hutchinson, which examines the dispute over her opinions within an international setting, is Michael P. Winship, *Making Heretics: Militant Protestantism and Free Grace in Massachusetts, 1636-1641* (2002). Documentation for the entire Anne Hutchinson episode may be found in David D. Hall, *The Antinomian Controversy, 1636-1638* (2nd ed., 1990). Witchcraft in Salem has attracted much modern attention from a variety of perspectives, including Paul Boyer and Stephen Nissenbaum's socio-economic *Salem Possessed* (1974), a Freudian interpretation from John P. Demos, *Entertaining Satan: Witchcraft in Colonial New England* (1982), a feminist reading from Carol F. Karlsen, *The Devil in the Shape of a Woman: Witchcraft in Colonial New England* (1987), and an interpretation that stresses the politics of imperial warfare, Mary Beth Norton, *In the Devil's Snare: The Salem Witchcraft Crisis of 1692* (2002). A reminder that New England's history always involved more than just Puritanism is provided by Carla Gardina Pestana, *Quakers and Baptists in Colonial Massachusetts* (1991).

Colonial Anglicanism can be approached through regional studies as well as in the survey noted in Chapter 1: for example, S. Charles Bolton, *Southern Anglicanism: The Church of England in Colonial South Carolina* (1982), or Nelson R. Burr, *The Anglican Church in New Jersey* (1954). The Anglican impact across colonial and denominational boundaries may be drawn from these studies: John Calaam, *Parsons and Pedagogues* (1971); E. S. Gaustad, *George Berkeley in America* (1979); and Joseph Ellis, *The New England Mind in Transition: Samuel Johnson of Connecticut, 1696-1772* (1973). The four-volume collection edited by Herbert Schneider and Carol Schneider, *Samuel Johnson, President of King's College: His Career and Writings* (1929), remains a treasure for colonial Anglicanism. For the Huguenot experience in the colonies, with attention to their rapid absorption in the larger culture, see Jon Butler, *The Huguenots in America* (1983).

Religious diversity was a principal theme for the colonial experience in the middle colonies. Origins of that diversity in the pietist revivals of continental Europe are explored brilliantly in W. R. Ward, *The Protestant Evangelical*

Awakening (1992), a book that provides context for the explicitly American accounts in F. Ernest Stoeffler, *Continental Pietism and Early American Christianity* (1976). Similar themes, with specific reference to German migration, receive insightful attention from A. G. Roeber, *Palatines, Liberty, and Property: German Lutherans in Colonial British America* (1993). Helpful on Pennsylvania with its range of Quaker, German, and sectarian movements are Joseph E. Illick, *Colonial Pennsylvania: A History* (1976), and J. William Frost, *A Perfect Freedom: Religious Liberty in Pennsylvania* (1990). For New York, the outstanding study is Richard W. Pointer, *Protestant Pluralism and the New York Experience* (1988). For the wide-ranging efforts of the patriarch of American Lutheranism, see *The Journals of Henry Melchior Muhlenberg,* ed. Theodore G. Tappert and John W. Doberstein, 2 vols. (1945), and Leonard R. Riforgiato, *Missionary of Moderation: Henry Melchior Muhlenberg and the Lutheran Church in English America* (1980). Other useful studies that as a group suggest the plural pattern that would later characterize the entire nation include Gerald F. DeJong, *The Dutch Reformed Church in the American Colonies* (1978), George Frederick Jones, *The Salzburger Saga: Religious Exiles and Other Germans Along the Savannah* (1984), Ned C. Landsman, *Scotland and Its First American Colony, 1683-1765* (1985), Richard K. MacMaster, *Land, Piety, and Peoplehood: The Establishment of Mennonite Communities in America, 1683-1790* (1985), and Daniel B. Thorp, *The Moravian Community in Colonial North Carolina: Pluralism on the Southern Frontier* (1988).

Study of African Americans and of the slave system that brought so many of them to the new world has reached extraordinary levels of sophistication. Most major studies now stress the international character of slavery — African, South American, Caribbean, and European, as well as North American. And they are more fully alert to how inherited African traditions influenced religious experiences in the new world. An extraordinarily useful survey has been provided by Sylvia R. Frey and Betty Wood, *Come Shouting to Zion: African American Protestantism in the American South and British Caribbean to 1830* (1998). Especially good for other aspects of religious development in slave communities are Mechal Sobel, *The World They Made Together: Black and White Values in Eighteenth-Century Virginia* (1987), and Margaret Washington Creel, *"A Peculiar People": Slave Religion and Community-Culture Among the Gullahs* (1988). For broader treatments that contextualize religious concerns in political, economic, and cultural contexts, see, as samples of a very sophisticated literature, David Brion Davis, *The Problem of Slavery in the Age of Revolution, 1770-1823* (new ed., 1999), Seymour Drescher, *From Slavery to Freedom: Comparative Studies in the Rise and Fall of Atlantic Slavery* (1999), and Ira Berlin, *Generations of Captivity: A History of African-American Slavery* (2003).

The literature on the Great Awakening is large. Good collections of pertinent documents include Alan Heimert and Perry Miller, eds., *The Great Awakening* (1962), and Richard Bushman, ed., *The Great Awakening: Documents on the Revival of Religion, 1740-1745* (new ed., 1989). For stimulating debate on the character of the Awakening, see Jon Butler, "Enthusiasm Described and Decried: The Great Awakening as Interpretive Fiction," *Journal of American History* 69 (Sept. 1982): 305-25; and the full-blown response by Frank Lambert, *Inventing the "Great Awakening"* (1999). The best survey of events in New England remains E. S. Gaustad, *The Great Awakening in New England* (1968 [1957]). For forceful arguments about the importance of Whitefield, see Harry S. Stout, *The Divine Dramatist: George Whitefield and the Rise of Modern Evangelicalism* (1991), and Frank Lambert, *"Pedlar in Divinity": George Whitefield and the Transatlantic Revivals* (1994). For the importance of itineration itself, see Timothy D. Hall, *Contested Boundaries: Itinerancy and the Reshaping of the Colonial American Religious World* (1994). Connections to Britain are well canvassed in Michael Crawford, *Seasons of Grace: Colonial New England's Revival Tradition in Its British Context* (1991), and Marilyn Westerkamp, *Triumph of the Laity: Scots-Irish Piety and the Great Awakening, 1625-1760* (1988). Allen C. Guelzo provides a very helpful summary of recent scholarship in "God's Designs: The Literature of the Colonial Revivals of Religion, 1735-1760," in *New Directions in American Religious History*, ed. Harry S. Stout and D. G. Hart (1997).

Each of the colonial colleges has had its own history told, but several books provide treatment of the whole picture, including Lawrence Cremin, *American Education: The Colonial Experience* (1970); and J. David Hoeveler, *Creating the American Mind: Intellect and Politics in the Colonial Colleges* (2002). Specific studies in which religious concerns are central include Norman Fiering, *Moral Philosophy at Seventeenth-Century Harvard* (1981), and Mark A. Noll, *Princeton and the Republic, 1768-1822* (1989). From the explosion of print on Jonathan Edwards, the place to begin is now George M. Marsden, *Jonathan Edwards: A Life* (2003), which makes full use of the ongoing edition of Edwards's *Works* from Yale University Press under the editorship of Harry S. Stout. For accessible samples from the *Works,* see Wilson H. Kimnach, Kenneth P. Minkema, and Douglas A. Sweeney, eds., *The Sermons of Jonathan Edwards* (1999), and John E. Smith, Harry S. Stout, and Kenneth P. Minkema, eds., *A Jonathan Edwards Reader* (new ed., 2003). For samples of the many fruitful lines of Edwards research currently under way, see the essays collected in Barbara B. Oberg and Harry S. Stout, eds., *Benjamin Franklin, Jonathan Edwards, and the Representation of American Culture* (1993), Stephen J. Stein, ed., *Jonathan Edwards's Writings: Text, Context, Interpretation* (1996), and Sang Hyun Lee and Allen C. Guelzo, eds., *Edwards in Our Time* (1999).

THREE

Revolution: Political and Ecclesiastical

In America, the turbulence of the eighteenth century's final quarter left little untouched. The long War of Independence (seven years of warfare was an American record until Vietnam) gave way to a "critical period" under the Articles of Confederation, then to a daring departure under an entirely new Constitution. Such times surely did try men's souls. They also tried all the old ways of thinking and doing, both institutionally and personally. In succeeding centuries, men and women have searched this period for answers to that hoary question, "What is an American?" We search that period to determine what is "American" about American religion.

Religion and Revolution

War's fury always demands that sides be taken. To cite Thomas Paine again, one cannot endure in time of revolution either the summer soldier or the sunshine patriot. One must choose, must fight, must die. Of course, neither vacillation nor neutrality is the equivalent of treason, but that is a distinction more readily made in times of peace than of war. The American Revolution was hard on those who could not fight on any side (the pacifists), and hard on those who failed to choose the right side (the Loyalists). Pacifism at this time was understood wholly in terms of religious conscience, and even more narrowly in terms of religious affiliation. Conscientious objection to war was more institutional than personal; that is, one found identification in a denomination that had historically and steadily and often painfully renounced the bearing of arms in any cause or for any state. In the Anglo-American world, Quakers achieved the greatest visibility in this regard, and thereby often provoked the greatest irritation. But from the European continent had come Mennonites, Moravians, German Baptists (Dunkers), Brethren, Schwenkfelders, and others who were "persuaded in their consciences to love their enemies, and not to resist Evil. . . ."

While the opinions of these groups united on refusal to bear arms, they divided on subtler points: for example, arranging for a substitute to go to war, or paying taxes to help support the war.

Others, not opposed to war as such, condemned this 1776 war as "one of the most causeless, unprovoked and unnatural [rebellions] that ever disgraced any Country." In the demand to take sides, Loyalists took the "other" side. Some Loyalism arose from quite specific and personal grievances, some from resentments against an entire region or class. Still others felt bound by oaths or pledges, many more by ties of affection for country and king. From a denominational perspective, those who served the Church of England as missionaries experienced the severest strain as both Anglophobia and revolutionary fervor increased. But Anglicans were not alone in the agonies of war's loyalty test, nor did Anglicans en masse oppose the revolution. In the Southern colonies, to cite only one instance, this was manifestly not the case. Patriotism likewise arose from many motives, from the narrowest self-interest to the broadest philosophical defense of mankind's rights. Religion itself also served as provocation and alarm. The 1760s saw an intensified campaign for Anglican bishops, that campaign then being met by an even more intense and anxious determination never to allow such bishops to reach America's shores. Patriots proclaimed their opposition to all tyranny, ecclesiastical or civil. The use of such code words left no doubt as to their meaning: keep all of England's persecuting and imperious lords exactly where they belong — in England.

When the loud demands for liberty echoed from valley to ridge, from farm to town, the rhetoric of revolution began to assume a life of its own. Hanging British customs agents in effigy may have been designed to make only a narrow economic point, but a local quarrel over taxes or tea could swiftly grow into a universal call for all rights and liberties for all Americans. Slogans shouted by the Sons of Liberty were picked up by sons and daughters of oppression: blacks as well as whites, dissenters as well as conformists, doomsayers as well as dreamers. Liberty, once unbottled, followed no fixed or predictable course.

Aftermath of Revolution

After Yorktown and the signing of a highly favorable Treaty of Paris on September 3, 1783, Americans were challenged to give meaning and content to "these United States." In the ecclesiastical realm, the deliberate and bold separation of churches from all agencies of government constituted a most radical, indeed revolutionary step. No western European nation of that eighteenth-century world could conceive of a social and political order maintained apart from an ecclesiastical establishment, an official religion.

But in and among those thirteen independent states, many factors fortu-
itously combined to make the inconceivable happen. For one thing, no single
candidate emerged as the obvious choice for a "Church of the United States"
— certainly not the Church of England. Pietist groups, moreover, vigorously
condemned on principle any linkage between the civil and ecclesiastical realm;
religion was personal, not political, and the redeemed Christian community
was called to live in separation from the world, not in corrupting alliance with
it. Then the founding fathers themselves, largely deist in their orientation and
sympathy, saw the politically powerful church as a liability for the state and a
shackle on those struggling to advance the cause of mankind. Thomas Jefferson and James Madison shaped the course of church-state relationships na-
tionally by directing them so carefully in postrevolutionary Virginia. Documents from their pens transcended time and place to set the United States on a
course which few would have thought possible — or sensible. The Constitution said so little about religion partly because Madison and Jefferson had said
so much.

If Virginia served as the anvil for hammering out religious liberty's guar-
antees, it also served as proving ground for turning principle into practice.
There, moreover, the proving came quickly, unlike New England where the
move toward complete disestablishment of its long-allied church seemed hopelessly bogged down. Early in the seventeenth century, the Church of England
had firmly set its foot on Virginia's soil. And while Anglicanism encountered
difficulty everywhere in the New World, yet its hold in Virginia was firmer than
anywhere else. If after the Revolution, Anglicanism could not maintain its favor
there, then where? But that hold was not maintained in Virginia. Dissenters applied a swift and unrelenting pressure against all vestiges of privilege, all hints
of political patronage. These were deemed totally inappropriate to that new age
into which Americans had entered, that *novus ordo seclorum.*

Of course, rapid change proved unsettling. The nation in 1789, under
"new management" so to speak, loomed as a large question mark over thirteen
sovereign states and nearly three million unsure citizens. What lay in store for
them, and for all churches and sects in this open land? When George Washington was chosen to preside over this untested amalgam, no Bill of Rights had yet
been added to the Constitution. No amendment explicitly fenced in the powers
of government with respect to the churches, some of whom were powerful and
enjoyed respect, many of whom were weak and without favor. Several religious
bodies wrote to the new president, seeking some solace as to their own safety,
some word about the dim path which lay ahead of them. To these groups, as indeed to the nation at large, George Washington offered a calming, steadying assurance. Religion, he said, was essential to the welfare and to the very survival of
the country; and religious persons can expect their nation to be "among the
foremost in examples of justice and liberality."

Religion in the Revolution and the New Republic

As the Republic began its national experiment, institutional religion indeed found itself secure from governmental persecution, immune now to the fine or whip or jail of an earlier day. Such religion was not secure, however, from other sorts of attack: in the name of reason, nature, or relevance. The European Enlightenment appeared first as an exotic import; soon it took root as a sturdy native plant. "Reason," which meant many things, did mean at least one specific thing in the realm of the Christian religion: the rejection of revelation. At the least, revelation was suspect; at the worst, it was mankind's most dangerous delusion, provoking history's bloodiest wars and most merciless persecutions. For some the Bible might remain valuable for its history or morality although certainly not for its theology; for others, however, that ancient book contained only falsehood and fraud, mockery and myth. Universalism, reacting against a dogmatic emphasis on the authoritarian justice of God, argued for a "wideness in God's mercy," a depth in the Creator's boundless benevolence. Unitarianism, rejecting the debilitating notion of humankind's depravity and impotence, stressed the natural prowess and goodness of men and women even more than the oneness of God. And deism, forsaking all denominational labels and biblical categories, embraced the language of creation and the unambiguous decrees of reason, "the only oracle of man."

Thrown against the ropes, institutional religion bounded back into the center of the ring. Much of that rebound is examined in the following chapter. Here, attention is given to two denominations: one a newborn child of Christianity's ever enlarging family, the other Western Christendom's most venerable institution. Methodism, under the leadership of John and Charles Wesley, drew away from a Church of England seen as too staid, too passionless, too bound by form and tradition and bureaucratic sloth. While conceived in England, Methodism grew to its most imposing stature on American prairies and in American forests. As two rapidly growing adolescents, the Methodist Church and the United States got along remarkably well together. Roman Catholicism, unaccustomed to minority status and "free market" competition, also learned to adapt to the Republic's novel ways. Under the perceptive leadership of Maryland's John Carroll, the ancient church did not turn away from the unfamiliar and unnerving. As French priests fled their now anticlerical homeland, as Catholic-inhabited Louisiana Territory passed into United States' hands, and as overwhelming problems seemed to be matched by overwhelming opportunities, Bishop (later Archbishop) Carroll guided a Constantinian church into a Jeffersonian world.

Thus, the newborn nation entered the nineteenth century not with a National Church by its side but with an uneasy partnership of religion and its critics, of churches and their schisms, of youthful visions and mature traditions.

And while the experiences of religion were often intensely personal and private, the challenges were frequently national and public. The nature of private religion is indicated in this chapter by a daughter of the New England Puritans, a peripatetic frontier evangelist, and one of the country's preeminent Catholic women. Such private experiences provided much of the motive power as American religion in all its confounding and stimulating variety was called on to discipline, reform, educate, elevate, and grant spiritual sustenance to the first generation of this new nation.

1. Religion and Revolution

Pacifism

Moravians

Virtually exterminated by Europe's relentless persecution, the Moravians or United Brethren survived only through the patronage and protection of Count Nicholas Ludwig Zinzendorf (1700-60) of Saxony. On his estate remnants of the United Brethren huddled together and, indeed, managed to survive. As their numbers gradually increased, they turned their eyes toward America and toward the challenge of converting the New World's Indians to their own deeply personal evangelical faith. Through the instrumentality of George Whitefield, the Moravians settled in Pennsylvania (Nazareth, later also Bethlehem). Almost immediately, they launched their justly famous missionary effort among the Indians, reaching well beyond the borders of Pennsylvania. The colony of New York soon grew anxious over the Moravian effort in Dutchess, Albany, and Ulster counties, being fearful that the United Brethren would "seduce the Indians from their Allegiance" to the British or, at the very least, infect the Indians with their own pacifist convictions. In 1744 New York's officials ordered the Moravians to stop their preaching and to leave the province. Two years later (May, 1746), officialdom offered a tortured apologia for its intolerant act.

After Whitfield had made an Itinerary or Two through his Majesty's Colonys on this Continent, from Georgia to Boston, & back again . . . and had purchased

---

[Source: Hugh Hastings, ed., *Ecclesiastical Records, State of New York* (Albany, 1902), IV, 2906-8.]

some thousand Acres of Land at the Forks of the River Delaware in Pennsylvania Government, not many miles from the Limitts of this, and there laid the foundation of a large house for a Seminary, where (as given out) Such Youth & Negroes as People would be Fools, or Mad Enough to Entrust to his Management were to be Educated in his New-fangled principles or Tenets whatever they were. Thus Reformation and the True Work of the Lord (as he and his Votaries would have had it supposed) was to go on at a high Rate; & this Scheme was Carryed on by Whitfield 'till he had gull'd a Sufficient Sum out of the deluded people, under Colour of Charity for the Orphan House at Georgia, & this Negro-Academy, but (as most rational to suppose) with real Design under both pretexts to fill his own Pockets; & when he had Carried on the Farce so far as he could well Expect to Profit by, he sells this Estate at Delawarre to Count Zinzendorf a Bishop (as he had been called) or head of a Sect of Germans, called the Moravian Brethren, outwardly professing themselves Protestants, who likewise were Stroling up and down these Colonies, to Vent their Unintelligible Doctrines, & to make proselytes also by Carrying on the same kind of Delusion.

This Count, & his Moravian Brethren, have by many Prudent People been looked upon with a Jealous Eye, ever since his Arrival in these parts, he is called a German Count & as Many of his Countrymen have for several years Successively been imported into, and Settled in Pennsylvania, Roman Catholicks as well as Protestants, Without Distinction, Where it Seems by the Indulgence of the Crown, their Constitution Granted by Charter, all Perswasions Roman Catholicks as well as others are tollerated the free Exercise of their Religion; the Increase of these People in that Colony has been so Great, that they are Computed to be Already much an Overbalance to the English Subjects there. . . .

These Moravians have Compassed Sea & Land to make Proselytes, & have so far succeeded, as to Gain in Pennsylvania, this, and other Colonys, And the house at the Forks before mentioned, is the principal place of Rendezvous & Quarter of the Chiefs of them: 'tis kept according to Whitefields Scheme as a Seminary for Converts, & house of support to their deluded Votaries; & many have Resorted thither; from thence they dispatch their Itenerant Emissarys Teachers or Preachers. . . .

After some of the principal heads of these Moravians had Travelled up & down these Countrys, & made many Converts amongst the Christians, at Length the next Step was, the more difficult part to be Entered upon, the Conversion of the Heathen, by Interspersing Several of the Brethren amongst the Indians in this province, to Reside with them though unqualified as to the knowledge of their Indian Language or any other but their own Mother Tongue; three of them were posted at a Place called Shacomicco in this Province who resided there Some time, and at length intermarried with the Savages, to give them the last Proof of their Affection and good Intentions towards them; this Gave Great Jealousie to the Inhabitants of that County, who made Repre-

Moravian community store, Salem, North Carolina
Moravians, after a brief stay near Savannah, Georgia, settled chiefly in Salem,
North Carolina, as well as in Nazareth and Bethlehem, Pennsylvania.
(Old Salem, Inc.)

sentations to the Judges at the Circuit Court & Afterwards to your Excellency, concerning them, In Order to get them Removed, lest they should Seduce the Indians there from their Fidelity to his Majesty; they were accordingly, by Order in Council Sent for down, & Examined in Council & their behavior & Account of themselves will appear by the Minutes of Council of the ———— day of 174-. It did not appear that they were (nor did they pretend to be) naturalized Subjects of her Majesty, they Came into the Province without your Excellencys Knowledge or Permission; they absolutely refused to take the Oaths to the Government; And when ordered thereupon to Leave the Province and forbid to Reside any more amongst the Indians, one of them impudently, replyed, with a Seeming threatning that perhaps if they left the province, the Indians would follow them and so Artfully were these Emissarys, preachers or Teachers, Stationed through this and some neighboring Colonies, at Convenient Distance, that thereby a Line of Communication seemed to be formed for the Readier Correspondence and Dispatch of Intelligence through the heart of several of these Plantations from one to the other & so to the Fountain head, the house of the Moravian Brethren at the Forks of the Delawarre before mentioned. And, according to Information, messengers were frequently Dispatched backward & forward, which 'twas thought high time to put an Effectual Checque to.

This strange surprizing & audacious Conduct of those people and the foregoing or such like observations and Reflections, 'Twas thought, gave sufficient umbrage for Jealousie Especially in the Time of War; therefore to Guard against the Subtile Devices of Crafty men, Strangers & aliens, & to frustrate all wicked Practices of Designing Persons & Papists in Disguise under any Colour or Appearances whatsoever Calculated to delude the Ignorant Savages, vailed under the Specious Shew of Care for their souls, were, as The Comee. conceive, Inducements to the Passing the act referred to in their Lordships Letter & of the mentioning the Moravians in it, by name.

The Restraints laid by this act upon the Moravian Brethren and such like are conformable to what his Majesty has been pleased to Enjoin your Excellency, by his Royal Instructions, to Observe, within this Province, with Regard to Ministers and Schoolmasters.

Mennonites

Survivors of the radical or Anabaptist wing of the Reformation, the Mennonites migrated to Pennsylvania as early as 1683. Like the Moravians, the Mennonites had known persecution and execution over much of Europe. Both Catholics and Protestants found much to condemn among the Anabaptists so far as their theology and ecclesiastical practices were concerned. Civil authorities, moreover, found their refusal to bear arms particularly intolerable. And that intolerance forced Mennonites to migrate from place to place all over Europe. When revolutionary passions began to build in America, the Mennonites in 1775 petitioned the Pennsylvania Assembly in order to make clear their own theological position and conscientious conviction. And while they could not bear arms, they were prepared in other ways to pay Caesar what was rightfully his. Humbly they added: "we beg the Patience of all those who believe we err. . . ."

[Source: C. H. Smith, *The Mennonite Immigration to Pennsylvania in the Eighteenth Century* (Norristown, Pa.: Norristown Press, 1929), pp. 285-86.]

In the first place we acknowledge us indebted to the most high God, who created Heaven and Earth, the only good Being to thank him for all His great Goodness and Manifold Mercies and Love through our Savior Jesus Christ who is come to save the souls of Men, having all Power in Heaven and on Earth. Further we find ourselves indebted to be thankful to our late worthy assembly for their giving so good an Advice in these troublesome Times to all Ranks of People in Pennsylvania, particularly in allowing those, who, by the Doctrine of our Savior, Jesus Christ, are persuaded in their consciences to love their enemies, and not to resist Evil, to enjoy the Liberty of their Consciences for which, as also for all the good things we enjoy under their Care, we heartily thank that worthy Body of Assembly and all high and low in office who have advised to such a peaceful measure hoping and confiding that they and all others entrusted with Power in this hitherto blessed Province, may be moved by the same spirit of Grace, which animated the first Founder of this province, our late worthy Proprietor William Penn to grant Liberty of Conscience to all its inhabitants that they may in the great and memorable Day of judgment be put on the right Hand of that just judge, who judgeth without Respect of Person and hear these blessed Words, 'Come ye blessed of my Father, inherit the kingdom prepared for you, etc., what ye have done unto one of the least of these my Brethren ye have done unto me,' among which number (i. e. the least of Christ's Brethren) we by his Grace hope to be ranked; and every Lenity and Favor shown to such tender conscience, although weak followers of this our blessed Saviour will not be forgotten by him in that great Day.

The Advice to those who do not find Freedom of Conscience to take up Arm that they ought to be helpful to those who are in Need and distressed Circumstances we receive with Cheerfulness towards all Men of what Station they may be — it being our principle to feed the Hungry and give the Thirsty Drink. We have dedicated ourselves to serve all Men in every Thing that can be helpful to the Preservation of Men's Lives but we find no Freedom in giving or doing, or assisting, in anything by which Men's Lives are destroyed or hurt. We beg the Patience of all those who believe we err on this point. We are always ready, according to Christ's command to Peter, to pay the Tribute, that we may offend no Man, and so we are willing to pay Taxes and so render unto Caesar those Things that are Caesar's, and to God those Things that are God's. Although we think ourselves very weak to give God his due Honour he being a Spirit and Life, and we only Dust and Ashes. We are also willing to be subject to the higher Powers and give in the manner Paul directs us: for he beareth the Sword not in vain, for he is the Minister of God, a Revenger to execute wrath upon him that doeth Evil. This Testimony we lay down before our worthy Assembly and all other Persons in Government, letting them know we are thankful as above mentioned, and that we are not at Liberty in Conscience to take up Arms to conquer our Enemies but rather to pray to God, who has power in Heaven and Earth, for us and Them.

Pacifism in Virginia

The problem posed by conscientious objection appears in vivid clarity in the petition from Dunmore County, to Virginia authorities. Less than three weeks after the Declaration of Independence had been signed, certain Virginia citizens protested that pacifists were being treated too lightly. They viewed it as "extremely impolitic" to allow the burdens of government and military duty to fall unevenly upon the citizenry when the benefits of government were bestowed equally upon all. That there be no ambiguity regarding the general principle being advanced, the Dunmore petitioners explicitly identified the Quakers and the Mennonites as the objects of their concern. (The petition, addressed to the "President and Gentlemen of the Convention of Virginia," is dated July 23, 1776.)

The Humble Petition of the Committee of the County of Dunmore Sheweth

That by an Ordinance passed at a Convention held at the Town of Richmond on the 17th of July 1775, It is ordained that all Quakers and the People called Menonists shall be exempted from serving in the Militia agreeable to the several Acts of the General Assembly of this Colony made for their relief and indulgence in this respect. Your Petitioners have a tender regard for the conscientious scruples of every Religious Society, but at the same time beg leave to represent the Injustice of subjecting one part of the Community to the whole burden of Government, while others equally share the Benefits of it. Your Petitioners consider the above exemption is extremely impolitic as well as unjust in the present unsettled state of the Country. They apprehend it will greatly discourage the People in general from discharging the duties of a Militia and other necessary impositions. Your Petions *(sic)* therefore humbly suggest that in lieu of bearing Arms at General and private Musters, the said Quakers and Menonists may be subjected to the payment of a certain Sum to be annually assessed by the County Courts at laying the Levy on each of them, and in case the Militia shall be called into actual Service that the said exempts be draughted in the same proportion as the Militia of the County and if they refuse to serve or provide able bodied Men to serve in their places respectively, that they be liable to the same Fine as other Militia Men in the like cases are subject to and to render the said Fines and Assessments as little injurious as may be. . . .

[Source: R. K. MacMaster et al., *Conscience in Crisis: Mennonites and Other Peace Churches in America, 1739-1789* (Scottdale, Pa.: Herald Press, 1979), p. 273.]

Schwenkfelders

Also originating in the lush growth of Europe's radical reformation, the tiny Schwenkfelder movement took its name from its founder, Caspar Schwenkfeld (1489-1561), German nobleman and mystic. Befriended by Count Zinzendorf (as the Moravians had been), the Schwenkfelders under his urging migrated to Pennsylvania in 1734. Deliberately nonevangelical and noninstitutional, the group never gained great size (in the mid-1990s, 5 churches with 2,700 members). But in the years of the American Revolution, not even the least among the pacifists could be overlooked or could escape public scorn. A Pennsylvania Militia Act of March 17, 1777, called forth this Schwenkfelder response the following May.

A Candid Declaration of Some So-called Schwenkfelders concerning Present Militia Affairs, May 1, 1777

We who are known by the name Schwenkfelders hereby confess and declare that for conscience' sake it is impossible for us to take up arms and kill our fellowmen; we also believe that so far as knowledge of us goes this fact is well known concerning us.

We have hitherto been allowed by our lawmakers to enjoy this liberty of conscience.

We have felt assured of the same freedom of conscience for the future by virtue of the public resolution of Congress and our Assembly.

We will with our fellow citizens gladly and willingly bear our due share of the common civil taxes and burdens excepting the bearing of arms and weapons.

We can not in consequence of this take part in the existing militia arrangements, though we would not withdraw ourselves from any other demands of the government.

WHEREAS at present through contempt of the manifested divine goodness and through other sins, heavy burdens, extensive disturbances by war and divers military regulations are brought forth and continued.

WHEREAS, we on the first of this month made a candid declaration concerning present military arrangements to the effect that we can not on account of conscience take part in said military affairs and

WHEREAS, it seems indeed probable that military service will be exacted

---

[Source: R. K. MacMaster et al., *Conscience in Crisis: Mennonites and Other Peace Churches in America, 1739-1789* (Scottdale, Pa.: Herald Press, 1979), p. 312.]

from many of our people and that on refusal to render such service heavy fines will be imposed.

Therefore, the undersigned who adhere to the apostolic doctrines of the sainted Casper Schwenkfeld and who seek to maintain the same by public services and by instruction of the young have mutually agreed, and herewith united themselves to this end that they will mutually with each other bear such fines as may be imposed on account of refusal for conscience' sake to render military service in case deadly weapons are carried and used. Those on whom such burdens may fall will render a strict account to the managers of the Charity Fund in order that steps may be taken to a proper adjustment.

Loyalism

Quakers Support the King

That the Quakers were pacifists did not necessarily mean they were neutrals. While sentiment was not unanimous one way or the other, the closer the colonies seemed to come to revolution, the more determined the Quakers (especially in Pennsylvania) became in professing loyalty to George III. They recalled that England's kings, notably Charles II and James II, had rescued them from a persecution-minded Parliament. And these Stuart kings had made possible the very existence of Penn's colony. Thus, the Philadelphia Yearly Meeting in 1774 reminded its constituency that "we are indebted to the King and his royal ancestors for the continued favour of enjoying our religious liberties. . . ."

And as our forefathers were often led to commemorate these and the many instances of Divine Favour conferred on them, thro' the difficulties they encountered in settling in the wilderness, let us be like minded with them — and if after a long time of enjoying the fruits of their labours, and partaking of the blessings of peace and plenty, we should be restrained or deprived of some of our rights and privileges, let us carefully guard against being drawn into the vindication of them, or seeking redress by any measures which are not consistent with our religious profession and principles, nor with the christian patience manifested by your ancestors in such times of trial[.] [A]nd we fervently

---

[Source: *An Epistle from our Yearly-Meeting, Held at Philadelphia* . . . (Philadelphia, 1774), pp. 3-4.]

desire all may impartially consider whether we have manifested that firmness in our love to the cause of Truth, and universal righteousness which is required of us, and that we may unite in holy resolutions to seek the Lord in sincerity, and to wait upon Him daily for wisdom, to order our conduct hereafter in all things to his praise.

And, beloved Friends, we beseech you in brotherly affection to remember, that as under Divine Providence we are indebted to the King and his royal ancestors, for the continued favour of enjoying our religious liberties, we are under deep obligation to manifest our loyalty and fidelity, and that we should discourage every attempt which may be made by any to excite disaffection or disrespect to him, and particularly to manifest our dislike of all such writings as are, or may be published of that tendency.

And as it hath ever been our practice since we were a people, frequently to advise all professing with us to be careful not to defraud the King of his customs or duties, nor to be concerned in dealing in goods unlawfully imported; we find it necessary now most earnestly to exhort that the same care may be continued with faithfulness and diligence, and that Friends keep clear of purchasing any such goods, either for sale or private use; that so we may not be any way instrumental in countenancing or promoting the iniquity, false swearing, and violence, which are common consequences of an unlawful and clandestine trade.

Pennsylvania Anglicans

The widening breach between England and her colonies placed greatest pressure and pain upon the Church of England. In a letter dated June 30, 1775, addressed to the Bishop of London, the Anglican clergy serving in Pennsylvania declare two contrary sentiments: their continuing loyalty to England and their growing sympathy with colonial grievances. Stuck in this awkward posture, "would to God that we could become mediators for the Settlement of the unnatural Controversy that now distracts a once happy Empire."

My Lord,

We now sit down under deep affliction of mind to address your Lordship upon a subject, in which the very existence of our Church in America seems to be interested. It has long been our fervent Prayer to Almighty God, that the unhappy controversy between the Parent Country and these Colonies might be

[Source: W. S. Perry, ed., *Historical Collections Relating to the American Colonial Church* (New York: AMS Press, 1969 [1871]), II, 470-71, 471-72.]

terminated upon Principles honourable and advantageous to both, without proceeding to the extremities of civil war and the horrors of Blood-shed. We have long lamented that such a spirit of Wisdom and Love could not mutually prevail, as might devise some liberal Plan for this benevolent Purpose; and we have spared no means in our power for advancing such a spirit so far as our private Influence and advice could extend. But as to public advice we have hitherto thought it our Duty to keep our Pulpits wholly clear from every thing bordering on this contest, and to pursue that line of Reason and Moderation which became our Characters; equally avoiding whatever might irritate the Tempers of the people, or create a suspicion that we were opposed to the Interest of the Country in which we live.

But the Time is now come, my Lord, when even our silence would be misconstrued, and when we are called upon to take a more public part. The Continental Congress have recommended the 20th of next month as a day of Fasting, Prayer & Humiliation thro' all the Colonies. Our Congregations too of all Ranks have associated themselves, determined never to submit to the Parliamentary claim of taxing them at pleasure; and the Blood already spilt in maintaining this claim is unhappily alienating the affections of many from the Parent Country, and cementing them closer in the most fixed purpose of a Resistance, dreadful even in Contemplation.

Under these Circumstances our People call upon us, and think they have a right to our advice in the most public manner from the Pulpit. Should we refuse, our Principles would be misrepresented, and even our religious usefulness destroyed among our People. And our complying may perhaps be interpreted to our disadvantage in the Parent Country. Under these difficulties (which have been increased by the necessity some of our Brethren have apprehended themselves under of quitting their Charges), and being at a great distance from the advice of our Superiors, we had only our own Consciences and each other to consult, and have accordingly determined on that part, which the general good seem to require. We were the more willing to comply with the request of our Fellow Citizens, as we were sure their Respect for us was so great, that they did not even wish any thing from us inconsistent with our characters as Ministers of the Gospel of Peace. . . .

Tho' it had of late been difficult for us to advise, or even correspond as usual, with our Brethren the Clergy of New York, we find that they have likewise in their Turn officiated to their Provincial Congress now sitting there, as M^{r}. [Jacob] Duche did both this year & the last, at the opening of the Continental Congress.

Upon this fair and candid state of things, we hope your Lordship will think our conduct has been such as became us; and we pray that we may be considered as among His Majesty's most dutiful & loyal subjects in this and every other Transaction of our Lives. Would to God that we could become mediators for the Settlement of the unnatural Controversy that now distracts a once happy Empire. All that we can do is to pray for such a Settlement, and to pursue those Principles of Moderation and Reason which your Lordship has always recommended to us. We have neither Interest nor Consequence sufficient to take any Lead in the Affairs of this great Country. The People will feel and judge for themselves in matters affecting their own civil happiness; and were we capable of any attempt which might have the appearance of drawing them to what they think would be a Slavish Resignation of their Rights, it would be destructive to ourselves, as well as the Church of which we are Ministers. And it is but justice to our Superiors, and your Lordship in particular, to declare that such a Conduct has never been required of us. Indeed, could it possibly be required, we are not backward to say that our Consciences would not permit us to injure the Rights of this Country. We are to leave our families in it, and cannot but consider its Inhabitants intitled, as well as their Brethren in England, to the Right of *granting their own money;* and that every attempt to deprive them of this Right will either be found abortive in the end, or attended with Evils which would infinitely outweigh all the Benefit to be obtained by it.

Personal Clerical Struggles

It is one thing for a convention or even a church to be divided, but quite another to find oneself vilified and threatened externally and wracked by conscience internally. Two Pennsylvania clergymen of the Church of England, both writing in 1776, reveal the revolutionary struggle not in broad political terms but in intimate personal ones. For whom does one now pray? What is conciliation and what is surrender? Where is one's highest loyalty to be placed? (1) The first selection, from SPG missionary Philip Reading (?-?), is dated August 25, 1776, and is sent from Appoquinimy, Delaware. (2) The second, from SPG missionary Thomas Barton (c. 1730-80), comes from Lancaster and is dated November 25, 1776. Both letters are addressed to the Secretary of the Society for the Propagation of the Gospel in Foreign Parts.

1.

The Church of England has now no longer an existence in the United Colonies of America. I humbly beg that this assertion may not be considered as the effect

---

[Source: W. S. Perry, ed., *Historical Collections Relating to the American Colonial Church* (New York: AMS Press, 1969 [1871]), II, 483-84, 485-86, 490.]

of intemperate heat or ungovernable passion. I never was more cool and deliberate than when I make it and therefore will venture to repeat it. The Church of England as by law established has no longer an existence in those parts of America which are denominated "The free and independent States." My reason for speaking in this manner is as follows: I look upon the King's supremacy and the constitution of the Church of England to be so intimately blended together that whenever the supremacy is either suspended or abrogated the fences of the Church are then broken down and its visibility is destroyed. This is actually the case in the present instance. On the second day of July the Congress at Philadelphia were pleased to declare the Colonies which had united in opposition to the measures of Great Britain "Free and independent States." Upon this Declaration it was judged incompatible with the present policy that his Majesty's authority within the new States should any longer be recognized. In this sentiment the generality of our Clergy (as far as has hitherto come to my knowledge) dismissed all those prayers from the public service of the Church wherein the names of the King and the Royal Family are mentioned, and adopted in their stead a prayer for the Congress which is no other if I am rightly informed than the Prayer for the high Court of Parliament altered and suited to the present occasion. "Most gracious God" say they, "we humbly beseech thee as for the States of America in general, so especially for the high Court of Delegates in Congress at this time assembled, &c., &c."

As to myself I was at no loss in determining what part I should bear in this importune juncture. Ever since I entered into the Ministry I had made it a constant rule to read over at proper intervals my ordination vows, the Articles of religion and Canons of our Church; but on the present occasion I read them more attentively than ever. The more I considered them the more I was confirmed in my opinion of the strict obligation I was under to adhere inviolably to what they injoined. To say nothing at present of the oath of allegiance which was evidently framed for securing the subject from joining any foreign power in an attack upon his Sovereign's Crown and dignity, the Canons of the Church have some a direct and others a general tendency to maintain the King's supremacy in Church and State. . . .

Such being my sentiments on this subject I determined for the sake of keeping up the Church in its full visibility agreeably to my obligations to continue reading the public service entire as usual notwithstanding Independence had been declared by the Congress and for one or two Sundays prosecuted my purpose without interruption. But on the twenty-first day of July immediately after the first lesson our senior Churchwarden (out of pure kindness to and friendship for me), coming up to the reading Desk earnestly advised me to omit the prayers for the King and Royal Family as the temper of the prevailing party was such that they would no longer bear the reading if those prayers should be continued. I told him that the present was not a fit season nor the place a proper one for discussing so interesting a subject: that I should for that day at least proceed with the service as usual; because whenever I was compelled to desist from using the prayers for the King and the Royal Family I should desist likewise from using any other part of the public service and that consequently the Church would be shut up.

Being now assured on all hands of the danger with which I was threatened if I persisted in complying with my oaths, vows and subscriptions I thought it high time to consult my own and my family's safety and therefore on the Sunday following (July 28th), when the people were assembled for public worship before I began the service I explained to them the obligations the Clergy of the Church of England are under to assert the King's Supremacy in their public ministrations and acquainted them that as I could not read the Liturgy agreeably to the prescribed form without offending against our Government and incurring the resentment of the people I should on that day declare the Church shut up for six weeks. Accordingly after Nicene Creed I declared in form that as I had no design to resist the authority of the New Government on one hand and as I was determined on the other not to incur the heavy guilt of perjury by a breach of the most solemn promises I should decline attending on the public worship for a short time from that day but that for the benefit of those who were in full and close communion with me, for comforting them in the present distress, for strengthening them in the faith, for encouraging them to persevere in their profession unto the end I would administer the Sacrament of the Lord's Supper on (Septr 8) that day six weeks. I proposed to say more on the subject; but the scene became too affecting for me to bear a farther part in it. Many of the people present were overwhelmed with deep distress and the cheeks of some began to be bathed with tears. My own tongue faultered and my firmness forsook me; beckoning therefore to the Clerk to sing the Psalm, I went up into the pulpit and having exhorted the Members of the Church to hold fast the profession of their faith without wavering and to depend upon the promises of a faithful God for their present comfort and future relief I finished this irksome business, and Apoquiniminck Church from that day has continued shut up.

2.

I have been obliged to shut my Churches to avoid the fury of the populace who would not suffer the Liturgy to be used unless the Collects & Prayers for the King & Royal Family were omitted, which neither by conscience nor the Declaration I made & subscribed when ordained would allow me to comply with; and altho' I used every prudent step to give no offence even to those who usurped authority & Rule & exercised the severest Tyranny over us, yet my life and property have been threatened upon mere *suspicion* of being unfriendly to what is called the American cause. Indeed every Clergyman of the *Church of England* who dared to act upon proper principles was marked out for infamy and insult; in consequence of which the *Missionaries* in particular have suffered greatly. Some of them have been dragged from their horses, assaulted with stones & dirt, ducked in water; obliged to flie for their lives, driven from their habitations & families, laid under arrests & imprisoned! I believe they were all (or at least most of them), reduced to the same necessity with me of shutting up their Churches. It is however a great pleasure to me to assure the Venerable Society that tho' I have been deprived of the satisfaction of discharging my *public* duties to my Congregations, I have endeavored (I trust not unsuccessfully), to be beneficial to them in another way. I have visited them from house to house, regularly instructed their families, baptized & catechized their children; attended their sick and performed such other duties in *private* as aton'd for my suspension from *public preaching*. I think it my duty to inform the Society that these are the principles I acted upon. If I have acted wrong (in not using the Liturgy in that maimed & mangled state, in which it is said some of my reverend brethren used it, rather than shut up my Church *pro Tempore*), I hope the Society will attribute my faults to the strictness of my attachment to what I thought my duty and so forgive me. I should have been very happy to have had their advice and direction on so critical occasion. But that was impossible to be obtained. I now believe the day is near at hand when the Churches will be open & I shall again enter on my *public* duties.

Charles Inglis (1734-1816) of New York

As assistant to the rector of Trinity Church in New York City, Charles Inglis had served in that capacity for about a decade when the American Revolution broke out. Totally opposed to this "unnatural Rebellion," Inglis used his pen both privately and publicly to argue on behalf of England and her Church. Throughout the Revolution, he remained in New York (the city being under British occupation) even as he remained firmly unreconciled to the patriot cause. Early in the War he gloried in the loyalty of the SPG missionaries in all of New York, New Jersey, and New England. He was less sanguine about Anglican ministers in the South, but "I never expected much Good of those Clergy" who had never really joined in the battle to bring a bishop to America. (His letter to the Secretary of the Society for the Propagation of the Gospel is dated October 31, 1776.)

[Source: J. W. Lydekker, *The Life and Letters of Charles Inglis* (London: Society for Promoting Christian Knowledge, 1936), pp. 157, 158-59, 159-60, 161, 170.]

I have the Pleasure to assure you that all the Society's Missionaries, without excepting one, in New Jersey, New York, Connecticut, &, so far as I can learn, in
the other New England Colonies, have proved themselves faithful, loyal Subjects in these trying Times; & have to the utmost of their Power opposed the
Spirit of Disaffection & Rebellion which has involved this Continent in the
greatest Calamities. I must add, that all the other Clergy of our Church in the
above Colonies, tho not in the Society's Service, have observed the same Line of
Conduct; & altho their joint Endeavours could not wholly prevent the Rebellion, yet they checked it considerably for some Time, & prevented many thousands from plunging into it, who otherwise would certainly have done so. . . .

The Clergy, amidst this Scene of Tumult & Disorder, went on steadily
with their Duty; in their Sermons, confirming themselves to the Doctrines of
the Gospel, without touching on politics; using their Influence to allay our
Heats, & cherish a Spirit of Loyalty among their People. This Conduct, however
harmless, gave great offence to our flaming Patriots, who laid it down as a
Maxim — "that those who were not for them, were against them." The Clergy
were everywhere threatened; often reviled with the most approbrious Language; sometimes treated with brutal Violence. Some have been carried Prisoners by armed Mobs into distant Provinces, where they were detained in close
Confinement for several Weeks, & much insulted, without any Crime being
even alleged against them. Some have been flung into jails by Committees, for
frivolous Suspicions of Plots, of which even their Persecutors afterwards acquit-
ted them. Some who were obliged to fly their Own Province to save their Lives,
have been taken Prisoners, sent back, & are threatened to be tried for their Lives
because they fled from Danger. Some have been pulled out of the Reading Desk,
because they prayed for the King, & that before Independency was declared.
Others have been warned to appear at Militia Musters with their Arms — have
been fined for not appearing, & threatened with Imprisonment for not paying
those Fines. Others have had their Houses plundered & their Desks broken
open, under Pretence of their containing treasonable Papers. . . .

The present Rebellion is certainly one of the most causeless, unprovoked
and unnatural that ever disgraced any Country — a Rebellion marked with peculiarly aggravated Circumstances of Guilt & Ingratitude. Yet amidst this general Defection, there are very many who have exhibited Instances of Fortitude
& Adherence to their Duty, which do Honour to Human Nature & Christianity
— many who for Sake of a good Conscience, have incurred Insults, Persecution
& Loss of Property; when a Compliance with the Spirit of the Times had in-
sured them Applause, profit & that Eminence of which the human Heart is naturally so fond. Perhaps such Cases are the most trying to a Man's Fortitude —
much more so, in my Opinion, than those which are sudden, & where Danger,
the more apparent, yet is not more certain or real. . . .

Thus matters continued, the Clergy proceeding regularly in the Discharge of their Duty, where the Hand of Violence did not interfere, untill the Beginning of last July, when the Congress thought proper to make an explicit Declaration of Independency; by which all connection with Great Britain was to be broken off, & the Americans released from any allegiance to our gracious Sovereign. For my part I had long expected this event — it was what the Measures of the Congress from the Beginning uniformly & necessarily led to.

This Declaration increased the Embarrassment of the Clergy. To officiate

Trinity Episcopal Church, Newport, Rhode Island
Erected in 1724, this magnificent structure often served as a meeting place
for those New England Anglicans of whom Inglis writes.
(Trinity Episcopal Church)

publickly, & not pray for the King & Royal Family according to the Liturgy, was against their Duty & Oath, as well as Dictates of their Consciences; & yet to use the Prayers for the King & Royal Family, would have drawn inevitable Destruction on them. The only Course which they could pursue to avoid both evils, was to suspend the public Exercise of their Function, & shut up their Churches. This accordingly was done. . . .

How Matters are circumstanced in the more southerly Colonies, I cannot learn with any Certainty; only that the Provincial Convention of Virginia have taken upon them to publish an Edict by which some Collects for the king are to be wholly omitted in the Liturgy, & others altered, the Word "Commonwealth" being substituted for the King. For my Part I never expected much Good of those Clergy among them who opposed an American Episcopate; if such should now renounce their Allegiance & abandon their Duty, it is no more than what might naturally be looked for. There are however several worthy Clergymen in those Provinces; some of whom, I hear, have taken Sanctuary in England — particularly from Maryland. . . .

Upon the Whole, the Church of England has lost none of its Members by the Rebellion as yet — none, I mean, whose Departure from it can be deemed a Loss. On the contrary, its own Members are more firmly attached to it than ever; & even the sober & more rational among Dissenters — for they are not all equally violent & frantic — look with Reverence & Esteem on the Part which Church People here have acted. I have not a Doubt but, with the Blessing of Providence, His Majesty's Arms will be successful, & finally crush this unnatural Rebellion. In this case, if the Steps are taken which Reason, Prudence & Common Sense dictate, the Church will indubitably increase, & these Confusions will terminate in a large Accession to its Members. Then will be the Time to make that Provision for the American Church which is necessary, & place it on at least an equal Foot with other Denominations, by granting it an Episcopate, & thereby allowing it a full Toleration. If this Opportunity is let slip, I think there is a Moral Certainty that such another will never again offer. . . .

Patriotism: A Matter of Bishops

In the excerpt immediately above, Charles Inglis concluded his letter with an impassioned plea for an episcopate: that is, for a bishop or bishops to come to

[Source: *A Collection of Tracts from the Late News Papers, &c.* . . . (New York: John Holt, 1768), pp. 3-5, 37-39. Punctuation modernized.]

America. Even in the midst of the Revolution, it was not too late, Inglis ar-
gued, for the British government to do what it ought to have done long ago.
Now, the very last opportunity presented itself. This desperate plea came at
the end of a decade or more of passionate public controversy concerning
bishops. So heated was the debate, so bitter the antagonisms, and so sharply
drawn were the opposing sides that this ecclesiastical battle gave strength
and momentum to the political one. In the 1770s patriotism, strangely
enough, could be measured by one's attitude toward bishops. In 1768 New
York's newspapers trumpeted the noise of this war. Leading the Anglican
charge was Thomas Bradbury Chandler (1726-90), New Jersey Anglican and
later Loyalist who, by 1775, found it expedient to leave America for England.
In 1767 Chandler published An Appeal to the Public *in which he made his*
strongest case for an American bishop. The opposing battalion was led by
William Livingston (1723-90), New York lawyer and Presbyterian patriot
who later served the Revolutionary cause with distinction. In the exchange
below, Livingston is the "American whig," Chandler the "Whip for the
American Whig."

The American Whig, March 14, 1768

By this time, I suppose, Dr. Chandler's *Appeal* has safely crossed the Atlantic;
and, if properly introduced, . . . [it promises success] to the cause of Episcopacy
in America; and how by the aid of a Bishop it is like to expand the gentle bosom
of the church so as to receive thousands and ten thousands of Fanatics,
Enthusiastists, Methodists, Deists, Iroquois Indians, and West-India Blacks. . . .
It certainly breathes a noble zeal for the church. Nay, . . . it seems to breathe a
zeal for religion itself. It proves, moreover, what all the Dissenters have always
asserted and what the Doctor and all his brethren have always denied — that
the church of England in America for want of the grand essential (for which the
poor gentleman is now breaking his heart) never was the church of England but
an independent church. It shows farther, what indeed doth not carry with it so
clear a conviction, that though this church hath hitherto been an episcopal
church and always well governed, it hath [in America] nevertheless never been
an episcopal church nor ever governed at all. . . . [Chandler's *Appeal*] assumes
an unusual moderation and so naturally counterfeits the voice of a sheep that it
is not every reader who will discriminate it from that of a wolf. In fine, it be-
moans . . . the numberless souls already perished through the neglect of his all
important plan and congratulates posterity, if not on the hopes of rescuing
them out of purgatory, at least on the prospect of speedily introducing a kind of
millennium by the episcopal triple discharge of *ordination, confirmation* and
government; by virtue of which are to be converted Jews and Infidels, together

with all and singular the Whites, Blacks and Browns, farther than from Dan to Beersheba, even from Lake Superior to Pensacola. . . .

I cannot but think it my duty to administer an antidote to the poison; and to show as well the falsity of the facts as the futility of the reasoning by which the *Appeal* may impose on the weak and credulous. I shall therefore think myself sufficiently authorized, as a friend of truth and society, to prevent to the utmost of my power the fatal, the tremendous mischiefs, which the *Appeal* is so artfully calculated to introduce. . . . I shall . . . fully consider every part of the pamphlet that . . . has the least tendency to introduce an evil more terrible to every man who sets a proper value either on his liberty, property, or conscience than the so greatly and deservedly obnoxious Stamp Act itself. . . .

A Whip for the American Whig, April 4, 1768

When a writer publickly attacks men of good character with virulence, and endeavours by sophistry to set truths (which are held sacred by many sincere Christians) in a disadvantageous light, it may be proper to inquire into his temper and character, and the motives which set him to work. These circumstances, I confess, do not much affect the intrinsic value of any literary composition. But if this latter has a pernicious tendency, either to sow dissentions or raise prejudices among honest men, to unhinge religion, or unsettle any of its principles, [then] the shewing what quarter it comes from will often go a good way to confute it. . . .

Dr. Chandler and his *Appeal* . . . have lately been attacked with great indecency and fury by the American Whig. Now if it happens that this attack comes from an ambitious, disappointed faction, the members of which are well known to have been always enemies to the Church of England, who have wantonly endeavoured to revile it, to ridicule many of those truths which its members hold sacred, and who make religion a political engine to accomplish their designs — the unprejudiced reader, upon knowing this, will treat it with that neglect and contempt it deserves.

To check the insolence of this faction is now become necessary for many reasons. It is high time for the members of the Church of England, whose [leniency] has [been] much and often abused by them, to vindicate themselves from the false aspersions of these enemies to peace and administer some wholesome discipline to the author or authors of the American Whig. . . . [That article] is stuffed with low spurious witticisms, misrepresentations, scurrility, buffoonery, falsehood, abuse, and slander. But to pass by all these, the author deserves flagellation for his blunders, with which this piece is plentifully begrimed. Take the following example. . . . He says the *Appeal* "so naturally counterfeits the voice of a sheep that it is not every reader who will discriminate it from that of a wolf." As much as to say, it sings so like a Nightingale that you can scarce distinguish its voice from that of a hoarse croaking Raven. Or, a thing is so like an egg that you can scarce distinguish it from an oyster. This is the mighty man who is to adjust with precision the limits of religious Liberty and defend it from all encroachment! And great things, no doubt, are to be expected from him!

What were the motives of the present attack on the *Appeal?* Not anything in the Appeal itself, nor the manner in which it is executed. It is written with great moderation and asks nothing but what every denomination of Christians has a right to, and actually enjoys in America, the Church of England only excepted: namely, the liberty of having the institutions of our Church, with its forms of discipline and government, to which a Bishop or Bishops are essentially necessary. . . .

Rhetoric of Revolution

Anthony Benezet (1713-84), 1772

Following the Revocation of the Edict of Nantes (see above, p. 118), the Benezet family, being Huguenots, left Picardy for London. There young Anthony fell under the influence of Quaker teachings, converted to that persuasion, and soon removed to Pennsylvania. Dedicating himself to education and humanitarian reform, Benezet wielded a powerful influence on both sides of the Atlantic, especially in his opposition to the "unnatural and barbarous Traffic" in black slaves. On May 14, 1772, he wrote to a fellow abolitionist in England, Granville Sharp, urging that all means be brought to bear to end "the Iniquity of the Slave Trade." While some were agitating about England's tyranny to America, Benezet (who numbered John Wesley and Benjamin Franklin among his circle) fought against another sort of tyranny.

Philadelphia ye 14th May 1772

Esteemed Friend Granville Sharp I have long been desirous of having an opportunity to communicate & advice with such well minded Persons in England who have a Prospect of the Iniquity of the Slave Trade and are concerned to

---

[Source: Roger Bruns, ed., *Am I Not a Man and a Brother* . . . (New York: Chelsea House, 1977), pp. 193-95.]

prevent its Continuation. And I should have been well pleased to have wrote to thee thereon had I known how to direct particularly as I had taken the freedom to republish but a part of thy acceptable & I trust serviceable Treatise on that interesting Subject, but now finding by a Letter I received from my respected Friend John Wesley that he is acquainted with thee and having a good opportunity by my Friend Captain Falconer Master of the Britannia I make free affectionately to Salute and send thee some copies of a Treatise lately published here on that iniquitous Traffic, giving the best account of its Origine, Progress &c which we have been able to procure. . . .

It is certainly incumbent on every Lover of God & Man to use their best endeavours that a Stop may be put to this unnatural and barbarous Traffic as well on Account of its dreadfull Effect on the poor Negroes in the devastation it occasions in their Country, the destruction & intolerable suffering it entails on those who remain in Bondage & their Offspring, but yet much more so in the Case of their Lordly Oppressors, the People of the West Indies and Southern Colonies, to whom this dreadfull evil will, in its Consequences extend beyond time even in the Regions of Eternity by corrupting their Morals and hard'ning their Hearts to so great a Degree, that they and their offspring become alienated from God, estranged from all good and are hastening to a State of greater far greater and more deeply corrupt Barbarity, than that from whence our Northern Progenitors sprung, before their acquaintance with Christianity. Proof of this is not wanting, it appears even from the wicked Laws, which thou hast quoted in thy Treatise, which bad as they are thro' fear or favour, are seldom put in Execution, and also from the most miserable education of their Youth, who from their Childhood being trained up in willfullness, Pride, Idleness and Tyranny over their Slaves, grow up in Licentiousness and Riot.

My friend John Wesley gives me expectation he will consult with thee, about the expediency of making some weekly publication in the Publick Prints, on the Origine, Nature and dreadfull Effects of the Slave Trade; which appears absolutely necessary, as many well minded People, who may have some Influence are ignorant of the Case; and also, because, way may, thereby, be made for a farther Attempt; towards the removal of this potent Evil, to which we think nothing will so effectually conduce, as a Representation to the King and both Houses of Parliament; this is what we have a right to do and what will, at least, be a Testimony on the behalf of Truth, indeed, we cannot be at the same time Silent and innocent Spectators of the most horrid Scene, if rightly considered, in itself and in its Consequences that was perhaps ever acted upon the Face of the Earth. I have wrote to several of the principal Persons amongst our Friends, the Quakers, on this head, earnestly requesting they would consider whether as they are better acqtd with the prodigious iniquity and dreadfull Consequences attendant on this Practice, and had so publickly in their general yearly Epistle, to their Churches everywhere declared their abhorence of it, it was not their Duty, either as a people, or by their Principal Members, to endeavour the removal of it, by such a Representation. I have also mentioned the matter and sent some of the last and former Treatises to our Agent Benjamin Franklin who, I know, has a due sense of its iniquity and evil consequences; and would, I am persuaded, use his influence, in endeavouring, that an End should be put to the trade.

John Allen (?-?), 1772

The link between pulpit and political liberty in the 1770s has long been recognized as having been a powerful one. The preacher popularized, dramatized, and disseminated notions of liberty which otherwise might have remained the exclusive possession of an intellectual elite. And if so insulated from the masses, such ideas could never have moved an entire populace to revolt. An obscure Baptist minister recently arrived in Boston from England, John Allen in 1772 delivered in the Second Baptist Church of that city "An Oration on the Beauties of Liberty." This pulpit piece proved to be enormously popular, going through rapid reprintings. Allen's oration also demonstrated that freedom from Britain's yoke implied, in the minds of many, freedom from every cruelty, especially that of man's inhumanity to man.

To the Right Honorable the Earl of Dartmouth.[1]

Liberty, my Lord, is the native right of the *Americans;* it is the blood-bought treasure of their Forefathers; and they have the same essential right to their *native laws* as they have to the air they breath in, or to the light of the morning when the sun rises: And therefore they who oppress the *Americans* must be as great enemies to the law of nature, as they who would . . ., if it were in their power, vail the light of the sun from the universe. My Lord, the *Americans* have a privilege [to] boast of above all the world: They never were in bondage to any man, therefore it is more for them to give up their Rights, than it would be for all *Europe* to give up their Liberties into the hands of the *Turks.* Consider what *English* tyranny their Forefathers fled from; what seas of distress they met with; what savages they fought with; what blood-bought treasures, as the dear inheritance of their lives, they have left to their children, and without any aid from the

---

1. The second Earl of Dartmouth, William Legge (1731-1801), served as Secretary of State for the Colonies and President of the Board of Trade.

[Source: Roger Bruns, ed., *Am I Not a Man and a Brother* . . . (New York: Chelsea House, 1977), pp. 258, 259-60.]

King of *England;* and yet after this, these free-born people must be counted Rebels, if they will not loose every right to Liberty, which their venerable Ancestors purchased at so great expence as to lose their lives in accomplishing; and shall not their descendants be strenuous to maintain inviolate those sacred Rights, which God and Nature have given them, to the latest posterity. O *America! America* let it never be said that you have deserted the Grand Cause, and submitted to *English* ministerial *tyranny. . . .*

The Parliament of *England* cannot justly make any laws to tax the *Americans;* for they are not the Representatives of *America;* and therefore they are no legislative power of *America.* The House of Lords cannot do it, for they are Peers of *England,* not of *America;* and if neither King, Lords, nor Commons have any right to oppress or destroy the Liberties of the *Americans,* why is it then that the *Americans* do not stand upon their own strength, and shew their power and importance, when the life of life, and every Liberty that is dear to them is in danger?

Therefore, let me advise you with all the power of affection, with all the pathos of soul, (as one who esteems the full possession of Rights of the *Americans,* as the highest blessing of this life) to stand alarmed. See your danger — death is near — destruction is at the door. — Need I speak? Are not your harbours blockaded from you? Your castle secured by captives — your lives destroyed — revenues imposed upon you — taxation laid — military power oppressing — your Charter violated — your Governor pensioned — your constitution declining — your Liberties departing, and not content with this, they now attack the *life,* the soul and *capitol* of all your Liberties, to create your judges, and make them independent upon you for office or support, and erect new Courts of Admiralty, to take away by violence, the husband from his family, his wife, his home, his friends. Such cruelty and tyranny ought ever to be held in the most hateful contempt, the same as you would *a banditti of slavemakers on the coast of* Africa.

Has not the voice of your Father's blood cried yet loud enough in your ears, "Ye Sons of *America* scorn to be Slaves?" Have you not heard the voice of blood in your streets, louder than that which reached Heaven, that cried for vengeance. That was, faith the Lord to *Cain,* the voice of thy brother's blood, but this is of many brethren. Therefore, if there be any vein, any nerve, any soul, any life, or spirit of Liberty in the Sons of *America,* shew your love for it; guard your freedom, prevent your chains; stand up as one man for your Liberty; for none but those, who set a just value upon this blessing are worthy to enjoy it. . . .

Remarks on the Rights and Liberties of the Africans

Here let me claim your attention. Every tie of nature, every sensation of humanity, every bowel of pity, every compassion as a Christian, engages me to speak for the Personal Liberty and Freedom of those, who are the most distressed of all human beings, the natives of *Africa*. Were they thus distressed by *Indians, Mahometans,* or *Turks* with respect to their Liberty, they would have a right to be redressed and set free; but for mankind to be distressed and kept in Slavery by Christians, by those who love the Gospel of Christ; for such to buy their Brethren (for *of one blood he has made all nations*) and bind them to be Slaves to them and their heirs for life. Be astonished, ye Christians, at this! And what is more shocking even to the tenderness of nature, is to *export them,* for filthy lucre into the hands of Men-tyrants. But what is more alarming yet, and exceeds all bounds, is, for one Christian, and Member of a Church, to export another, and banish her to be a Slave, when in full communion in the Church. Was ever such a thing heard of in the house of God before! Tell it not in *Gath!* Publish it not in the streets of *Boston!* Shall no plea be heard, Shall no argument prevail to *let these oppressed ones* Go Free. Have Christians lost all the tenderness of nature, the feelings of humanity, or the more refined sensations of christianity? Or have the Ministers in silence forgot to shew their people this iniquity? O could they bear to see — to see did I say? nay to feel their children rent from their arms, and see them bound in irons and banished to be *Slaves!* O killing thought! But for Christians to encourage this bloody and inhuman Trade of *Man-stealing,* or *Slave-making,* O how shocking it is! while it may be, their nearer kindred want employment, if not bread to eat. This unlawful, inhuman practice is a sure way for mankind to ruin *America,* and for Christians to bring their children, and their children's children to a morsel of bread. Much has been wrote, and well wrote to dissuade the *Americans* from the practice of so great an Evil; many begin to listen to the laws of humanity and the force of the argument: But surely what the Prophet *Isaiah* says will be sufficient with every true Minister of the Gospel, and with every Christian and Son of Liberty in *America; Isa. lviii. 6. Loose the bands of wickedness, undo the heavy burdens, let the oppressed go free, that ye break every yoke.*

Phillis Wheatley (c. 1753-84), 1774

America's most famous black poet of the eighteenth century, Phillis Wheatley in 1774 wrote to America's most famous ordained Indian of that time, Presbyterian Samson Occom (1723-92). The subject of her letter, not surprisingly, was the "Love of Freedom" — a principle implanted by God in every human breast, male or female, black or white, Indian or European. Like many others

[Source: Roger Bruns, ed., *Am I Not a Man and a Brother* . . . (New York: Chelsea House, 1977), pp. 306, 308.]

Phillis Wheatley
(University of North Carolina Press)

in the era of Revolution, this talented ex-slave saw civil liberty, religious liberty, and human liberty as "inseparably united." (Her letter is dated February 11, 1774.)

Rev'd and honor'd Sir, I have this Day received your obliging kind Epistle, and am greatly satisfied with your Reasons respecting the Negroes, and think highly reasonable what you offer in Vindication of their natural Rights: Those that invade them cannot be insensible that the divine Light is chasing away the thick Darkness which broods over the Land of Africa; and the Chaos which has reign'd so long, is converting into beautiful Order, and reveals more and more clearly, the glorious Dispensation of civil and religious Liberty, which are so inseparably united, that there is little or no Enjoyment of one without the other: Otherwise, perhaps, the Israelites had been less solicitous for their Freedom from Egyptian Slavery; I don't say they would have been contented without it, by no Means, for in every human Breast, God has implanted a Principle, which we call Love of Freedom; it is impatient of Oppression, and pants for Deliverence; and by the

Leave of our modern Egyptians I will assert that the same Principle lives in us. God grant Deliverance in his own Way and Time, and get him honor upon all those whose Avarice impels them to countenance and help forward the Calamities of their fellow Creatures. This I desire not for their Hurt, but to convince them of the strange Absurdity of their Conduct whose Words and Actions are so diametrically opposite. How well the cry for Liberty, and the reverse Disposition for the exercise of oppressive Power over others agree, — I humbly think it does not require the Penetration of a Philosopher to determine.

Isaac Backus (1724-1806), 1774

Far better known than John Allen, the Baptist Isaac Backus organized dissenting religion in New England against tyranny both foreign and domestic. As minister at Middleborough, Massachusetts, Backus saw domestic tyranny in the established Congregational Church which — even in the days of Revolution — continued to tax and fine and jail those who declined to support the state church. When all America is alarmed about a tax on tea, Backus wrote, should not a tax on liberty of conscience be even more an occasion of revulsion and revolt? Should we win independence from England only to surrender it to a privileged and persecuting elite at home? To escape the religious tax imposed upon all, one must apply to the state for a special exemption, for a "certificate." But to do even that implied that politicians have an authority "which we believe in our consciences belongs only to God." Backus made his plea before the Massachusetts legislature on December 2, 1774.

Honored Gentlemen: At a time when all America are alarmed at the open and violent attempts that have been made against their liberties, it affords great cause of joy and thankfulness, to see the colonies so happily united to defend their rights; and particularly that their late Continental Congress have been directed into measures so wise and salutary for obtaining relief and securing our future liberties; and who have wisely extended their regards to the rights and freedom of the poor Africans. Since then the law of equity has prevailed so far, we hope that will move this honorable assembly to pay a just regard to their English neighbors and brethren at home.

It seems that the two main rights which all America are contending for at this day, are — Not to be taxed where they are not represented, and — To have their causes tried by unbiased judges. And the Baptist churches in this province

---

[Source: Alvah Hovey, *A Memoir of the Life and Times of the Rev. Isaac Backus* (New York: Da Capo Press, 1972 [1885]), pp. 215-17, 220-21.]

as heartily unite with their countrymen in this cause, as any denomination in the land; and are as ready to exert all their abilities to defend it. Yet only because they have thought it to be their duty to claim an equal title to these rights with their neighbors, they have repeatedly been accused of evil attempts against the general welfare of the colony; therefore, we have thought it expedient to lay a brief statement of the case before this assembly. . . .

[Massachusetts legislators] never were empowered to lay any taxes but what were of a civil and worldly nature; and to impose religious taxes is as much out of their Jurisdiction, as it can be for Britain to tax America; yet how much of this has been done in this province. Indeed, many try to elude the force of this reasoning by saying that the taxes which our rulers impose for the support of ministers, are of a civil nature. But it is certain that they call themselves ministers of Christ; and the taxes now referred to are to support them under that name; and they either are such, or else they deceive the people. If they are Christ's ministers, he has made laws enough to support them; if they are not, where are the rulers who will dare to compel people to maintain men who call themselves Christ's ministers when they are not? Those who ministered about holy things and at God's altar in the Jewish church, partook of and lived upon the things which were freely offered there; *Even so hath the Lord ordained that they who preach the Gospel, should live of the Gospel*. And such communications are called *sacrifices to God* more than once in the New Testament. And why may not civil rulers appoint and enforce with the sword, any other sacrifice as well as this? . . .

Must we be blamed for not lying still, and thus let our countrymen trample upon our rights, and deny us that very liberty that they are ready to take up arms to defend for themselves? You profess to exempt us from taxes to your worship, and yet tax us every year. Great complaints have been made about a tax which the British Parliament laid upon paper; but you require a paper tax of us annually.

That which has made the greatest noise, is a tax of three pence a pound upon tea; but your law of last June laid a tax of the same sum every year upon the Baptists in each parish, as they would expect to defend themselves against a greater one. And only because the Baptists in Middleboro' have refused to pay that little tax, we hear that the first parish in said town have this fall voted to lay a greater tax upon us. All America are alarmed at the tea tax; though, if they please, they can avoid it by not buying the tea; but we have no such liberty. We must either pay the little tax, or else your people appear even in this time of extremity, determined to lay the great one upon us. But these lines are to let you know, that we are determined not to pay either of them; not only upon your principle of not being taxed where we are not represented, but also because we dare not render that homage to any earthly power, which I and many of my brethren are fully convinced belongs only to God. We cannot give in the certificates you require, without implicitly allowing to men that authority which we believe in our consciences belongs only to God. Here, therefore, we claim charter rights, liberty of conscience. And if any still deny it to us, they must answer it to Him who has said, 'With what measure ye mete, it shall be measured to you again.'

If any ask what we would have, we answer: Only allow us freely to enjoy the religious liberty that they do in Boston, and we ask no more.

We remain hearty friends to our country, and ready to do all in our power for its general welfare.

Isaac Backus,
Agent for the Baptist Churches in this Province.
By advice of their Committee.
Boston, Dec. 2, 1774.

Samuel Sherwood (1730-83), 1776

One bright thread woven through much of America's history glows with millennial expectations. The destiny of the nation is seen in terms of a coming kingdom of God, a direct intervention by God in the affairs of men and nations, a return of Christ to earth to establish and rule over a New Jerusalem. The rhetoric of revolution can exchange its political terminology for a religious one, and that often of a decidedly biblical nature. Babylon (that is, England) "shall fall to rise no more." The "woman in the wilderness" (that is, the bride of Christ, his Church) shall overcome all her adversaries. God will not forsake America because, under providence, "Liberty has been planted here." Nor will he revoke "the grant he has made of this land to his church." So the kingdom will come, wars will cease, and the lion (wolf?) shall lie down by the lamb. Samuel Sherwood, Congregational pastor in Fairfield, Connecticut, and dedicated patriot of the revolutionary cause, here weaves that bright thread most skillfully.

We may, in a peculiar manner, notice the kind dealings of God in his providence towards this branch of his church, that he has planted as a choice vine, in this once howling wilderness. He brought her as on eagles wings from the seat of oppression and persecution "to her own place," has, of his unmerited grace, bestowed liberties and privileges upon her, beyond what are enjoyed in any

---

[Source: Samuel Sherwood, *The Church's Flight into the Wilderness* (New York: S. Loudon, 1776), pp. 45-46, 48-50.]

other part of the world. He has nourished and protected her from being carried away to destruction, when great floods of his wrath and vengeance have been poured forth after her. God has, in this American quarter of the globe, provided for the woman and her seed, a fixed and lasting settlement and habitation, and bestowed it upon her, to be her own property forever. . . .

As there still remains among us, a godly remnant that have not apostatized from God, not departed from the faith of the gospel; and as these prophecies on which we have been treating will, many of them, most probably have their fulfillment in this land; there are yet solid grounds of hope and encouragement for us, in this dark and gloomy day. Tho' we may, in God's righteous providence, be sorely rebuked and chastised for our woeful apostacies, declensions and backslidings, yet we have, I think, good reason to believe, from the prophecies, so far as we are able to understand them, and from the general plan of God's providence, so far as opened to view . . . that we shall not be wholly given up to desolation and ruin. It is not likely nor probable, that God will revoke the grant he made of this land to his church. His gifts as well as calling are without repentance. It does not appear probable that a persecuting, oppressive and tyrannical power will ever be permitted to rear up its head and horns in it, notwithstanding its present violent assaults and struggles. Liberty has been planted here; and the more it is attacked, the more it grows and flourishes. The time is coming and hastening on, when Babylon the great shall fall to rise no more; when all wicked tyrants and oppressors shall be destroyed forever. These violent attacks upon the woman in the wilderness, may possibly be some of the last efforts and dying struggles of the man of sin. These commotions and convulsions in the British empire may be leading to the fulfillment of such prophecies as relate to his downfall and overthrow, and to the future glory and prosperity of Christ's church. It will soon be said and acknowledged, that the kingdoms of this world are become the kingdoms of our Lord, and of his Christ. The vials of God's wrath begin to be poured out on his enemies and adversaries; and there is falling on them a noisome and grievous sore. And to such as have shed the blood of saints and prophets, to them, blood will be given to drink; for they are worthy. And they will gnaw their tongues of falsehood and deceit, for pain; and have the cup of the wine of the fierceness of her wrath; and be rewarded double. The Lamb shall overcome them, for he is Lord of Lords, and King of Kings; and they that are with him are called, and chosen, and faithful. May the Lord shorten the days of tribulation, and appear in his glory, to build up Zion; that his knowledge might cover the earth, as the waters do the seas; that wars and tumults may cease thro' the world, and the wolf and the lamb lie down together, and nothing hurt or destroy throughout his holy mountain.

2. Aftermath of Revolution

Religious Liberty Guaranteed

Thomas Jefferson's Bill for Establishing Religious Freedom, 1779

Virginia was not only the oldest of Britain's Atlantic seaboard colonies, it was in this period also the most populous. Its influence weighed heavily during the Revolution and even more heavily in the early years of the Republic. (In the first thirty-six years of the young nation's existence, every president but one was a Virginian.) In the matter of religious liberty, the path taken by Virginia could prove determinative for the entire country. Two of those early presidents helped Virginia along the untried path toward full liberty of religion. Jefferson (1743-1826), when he died, wished to be remembered for the authorship of two documents: the Declaration of Independence written in 1776, and the Bill given below written three years later (and passed by Virginia's Assembly in 1786). Jefferson argued that if Almighty God refrained from coercing men and women in matters of religion, then it must be "impious presumption" for mere mortals to force the tender consciences of mankind. (Phrases in italics in the text below were omitted from the Bill as ultimately passed.)

Well aware that the opinions and belief of men depend not on their own will, but follow involuntarily the evidence proposed to their minds; that Almighty God hath created the mind free, *and manifested his supreme will that free it shall re-*

[Source: Julian P. Boyd, ed., *The Papers of Thomas Jefferson* (Princeton: Princeton University Press, 1950), II, 545-47.]

main by making it altogether insusceptible of restraint; that all attempts to influence it by temporal punishments, or burthens, or by civil incapacitations, tend only to beget habits of hypocrisy and meanness, and are a departure from the plan of the holy author of our religion, who being lord both of body and mind, yet chose not to propagate it by coercions on either, as was in his Almighty

Thomas Jefferson
Copy of painting by Rembrandt Peale, ca. 1805
(National Archives and Records Administration)

power to do, *but to extend it by its influence on reason alone;* that the impious presumption of legislators and rulers, civil as well as ecclesiastical, who, being themselves but fallible and uninspired men, have assumed dominion over the faith of others, setting up their own opinions and modes of thinking as the only true and infallible, and as such endeavoring to impose them on others, hath established and maintained false religions over the greatest part of the world and through all time: That to compel a man to furnish contributions of money for the propagation of opinions which he disbelieves *and abhors,* is sinful and tyrannical; that even the forcing him to support this or that teacher of his own religious persuasion, is depriving him of the comfortable liberty of giving his contributions to the particular pastor whose morals he would make his pattern, and whose powers he feels most persuasive to righteousness; and is withdrawing from the ministry those temporary rewards, which proceeding from an approbation of their personal conduct, are an additional incitement to earnest and unremitting labours for the instruction of mankind; that our civil rights have no dependance on our religious opinions, any more than our opinions in physics or geometry; that therefore the proscribing any citizen as unworthy the public confidence by laying upon him an incapacity of being called to offices of trust and emolument, unless he profess or renounce this or that religious opinion, is depriving him injuriously of those privileges and advantages to which, in common with his fellow citizens, he has a natural right; that it tends also to corrupt the principles of that *very* religion it is meant to encourage, by bribing, with a monopoly of worldly honours and emoluments, those who will externally profess and conform to it; that though indeed these are criminal who do not withstand such temptation, yet neither are those innocent who lay the bait in their way; *that the opinions of men are not the object of civil government, nor under its jurisdiction;* that to suffer the civil magistrate to intrude his powers into the field of opinion and to restrain the profession or propagation of principles on supposition of their ill tendency is a dangerous falacy, which at once destroys all religious liberty, because he being of course judge of that tendency will make his opinions the rule of judgment, and approve or condemn the sentiments of others only as they shall square with or differ from his own; that it is time enough for the rightful purposes of civil government for its officers to interfere when principles break out into overt acts against peace and good order; and finally, that truth is great and will prevail if left to herself; that she is the proper and sufficient antagonist to error, and has nothing to fear from the conflict unless by human interposition disarmed of her natural weapons, free argument and debate; errors ceasing to be dangerous when it is permitted freely to contradict them.

We the General Assembly of Virginia do enact that no man shall be compelled to frequent or support any religious worship, place, or ministry whatsoever, nor shall be enforced, restrained, molested, or burthened in his body or goods, nor shall otherwise suffer, on account of his religious opinions or belief; but that all men shall be free to profess, and by argument to maintain, their opinions in matters of religion, and that the same shall in no wise diminish, enlarge, or affect their civil capacities.

And though we well know that this Assembly, elected by the people for the ordinary purposes of legislation only, have no power to restrain the acts of succeeding Assemblies, constituted with powers equal to our own, and that therefore to declare this act irrevocable would be of no effect in law; yet we are free to declare, and do declare, that the rights hereby asserted are of the natural rights of mankind, and that if any act shall be hereafter passed to repeal the present or to narrow its operation, such act will be an infringement of natural right.

James Madison's Memorial and Remonstrance, 1785

Since no single denomination emerged as the logical candidate for the "Church of America," then complete separation of church and state was the only alternative — or so it seemed. Actually, another real possibility emerged. For while no single church dominated eighteenth-century America, one single religion did dominate, namely, Christianity. Therefore, reasoned Patrick Henry, Richard Henry Lee, and others, why not establish and support the Christian religion? Henry (1736-99) tried repeatedly to convince Virginia legislators to pass a "General Assessment" bill which would declare that "the Christian Religion shall in all times coming be deemed and held to be the established Religion of this Commonwealth. . . ." James Madison (1751-1836), however, saw an official religion as no more pleasing a prospect than an official church. He wrote his powerful Memorial *against Patrick Henry's plan, bringing those efforts to an end. Madison went on, as Virginia's representative in the First Congress, to push for an amendment to the newly adopted Constitution which would extend the religious liberty won in Virginia to the nation itself. Jefferson and Madison, well before either became president, indeed led the way.*

We the subscribers, citizens of the said Commonwealth, having taken into serious consideration, a Bill printed by order of the last Session of General Assembly, entitled "A Bill establishing a provision for Teachers of the Christian Religion," and conceiving that the same if finally armed with the sanctions of a law,

---

[Source: *The Papers of James Madison* (Chicago: University of Chicago Press, 1973), VIII, 298-304.]

will be a dangerous abuse of power, are bound as faithful members of a free State to remonstrate against it, and to declare the reasons by which we are determined. We remonstrate against the said Bill,

1. Because we hold it for a fundamental and undeniable truth, "that Religion or the duty which we owe to our Creator and the manner of discharging it, can be directed only by reason and conviction, not by force or violence." The Religion then of every man must be left to the conviction and conscience of every man; and it is the right of every man to exercise it as these may dictate. This right is in its nature an unalienable right. It is unalienable, because the opinions of men, depending only on the evidence contemplated by their own minds cannot follow the dictates of other men: It is unalienable also, because what is here a right towards men, is a duty towards the Creator. It is the duty of every man to render to the Creator such homage and such only as he believes to be acceptable to him. This duty is precedent, both in order of time and in degree of obligation, to the claims of Civil Society. Before any man can be considered as a member of Civil Society, he must be considered as a subject of the Governour of the Universe: And if a member of Civil Society, who enters into any subordinate Association, must always do it with a reservation of his duty to the General Authority; much more must every man who becomes a member of any particular Civil Society, do it with a saving of his allegiance to the Universal Sovereign. We maintain therefore that in matters of Religion, no mans right is abridged by the institution of Civil Society and that Religion is wholly exempt from its cognizance. True it is, that no other rule exists, by which any question which may divide a Society, can be ultimately determined, but the will of the majority; but it is also true that the majority may trespass on the rights of the minority.

2. Because if Religion be exempt from the authority of the Society at large, still less can it be subject to that of the Legislative Body. The latter are but the creatures and vicegerents of the former. Their jurisdiction is both derivative and limited: it is limited with regard to the co-ordinate departments, more necessarily is it limited with regard to the constituents. The preservation of a free Government requires not merely, that the metes and bounds which separate each department of power be invariably maintained; but more especially that neither of them be suffered to overleap the great Barrier which defends the rights of the people. The Rulers who are guilty of such an encroachment, exceed the commission from which they derive their authority, and are Tyrants. The People who submit to it are governed by laws made neither by themselves nor by an authority derived from them, and are slaves.

3. Because it is proper to take alarm at the first experiment on our liberties. We hold this prudent jealousy to be the first duty of Citizens, and one of the noblest characteristics of the late Revolution. The free men of America did not wait till usurped power had strengthened itself by exercise, and entangled the question in precedents. They saw all the consequences in the principle, and

they avoided the consequences by denying the principle. We revere this lesson too much soon to forget it. Who does not see that the same authority which can establish Christianity, in exclusion of all other Religions, may establish with the same ease any particular sect of Christians, in exclusion of all other Sects? that the same authority which can force a citizen to contribute three pence only of his property for the support of any one establishment, may force him to conform to any other establishment in all cases whatsoever?

4. Because the Bill violates that equality which ought to be the basis of every law, and which is more indispensible, in proportion as the validity or expediency of any law is more liable to be impeached. If "all men are by nature equally free and independent," all men are to be considered as entering into Society on equal conditions; as relinquishing no more, and therefore retaining no less, one than another, of their natural rights. Above all are they to be considered as retaining an "*equal* title to the free exercise of Religion according to the dictates of Conscience." Whilst we assert for ourselves a freedom to embrace, to profess and to observe the Religion which we believe to be of divine origin, we cannot deny an equal freedom to those whose minds have not yet yielded to the evidence which has convinced us. If this freedom be abused, it is an offence against God, not against man: To God, therefore, not to man, must an account of it be rendered. As the Bill violates equality by subjecting some to peculiar burdens, so it violates the same principle, by granting to others peculiar exemptions. Are the Quakers and Menonists the only sects who think a compulsive support of their Religions unnecessary and unwarrantable? Can their piety alone be entrusted with the care of public worship? Ought their Religions to be endowed above all others with extraordinary privileges by which proselytes may be enticed from all others? We think too favorably of the justice and good sense of these denominations to believe that they either covet pre-eminences over their fellow citizens or that they will be seduced by them from the common opposition to the measure.

5. Because the Bill implies either that the Civil Magistrate is a competent judge of Religious Truth; or that he may employ Religion as an engine of Civil policy. The first is an arrogant pretension falsified by the contradictory opinions of Rulers in all ages, and throughout the world: the second an unhallowed perversion of the means of salvation.

6. Because the establishment proposed by the Bill is not requisite for the support of the Christian Religion. To say that it is, is a contradiction to the Christian Religion itself, for every page of it disavows a dependence on the powers of this world: it is a contradiction to fact; for it is known that this Religion both existed and flourished, not only without the support of human laws, but in spite of every opposition from them, and not only during the period of miraculous aid, but long after it had been left to its own evidence and the ordinary care of Providence. Nay, it is a contradiction in terms; for a Religion not

invented by human policy, must have pre-existed and been supported, before it was established by human policy. It is moreover to weaken in those who profess this Religion a pious confidence in its innate excellence and the patronage of its Author; and to foster in those who still reject it, a suspicion that its friends are too conscious of its fallacies to trust it to its own merits.

7. Because experience witnesseth that ecclesiastical establishments, instead of maintaining the purity and efficacy of Religion, have had a contrary operation. During almost fifteen centuries has the legal establishment of Christianity been on trial. What have been its fruits? More or less in all places, pride and indolence in the Clergy, ignorance and servility in the laity, in both, superstition, bigotry and persecution. Enquire of the Teachers of Christianity for the ages in which it appeared in its greatest lustre; those of every sect, point to the ages prior to its incorporation with Civil policy. Propose a restoration of this primitive State in which its Teachers depended on the voluntary rewards of their flocks, many of them predict its downfall. On which Side ought their testimony to have greatest weight, when for or when against their interest?

8. Because the establishment in question is not necessary for the support of Civil Government. If it be urged as necessary for the support of Civil Government only as it is a means of supporting Religion, and it be not necessary for the latter purpose, it cannot be necessary for the former. If Religion be not within the cognizance of Civil Government how can its legal establishment be necessary to Civil Government? What influence in fact have ecclesiastical establishments had on Civil Society? In some instances they have been seen to erect a spiritual tyranny on the ruins of the Civil authority; in many instances they have been seen upholding the thrones of political tyranny: in no instance have they been seen the guardians of the liberties of the people. Rulers who wished to subvert the public liberty, may have found an established Clergy convenient auxiliaries. A just Government instituted to secure & perpetuate it needs them not. Such a Government will be best supported by protecting every Citizen in the enjoyment of his Religion with the same equal hand which protects his person and his property; by neither invading the equal rights of any Sect, nor suffering any Sect to invade those of another.

9. Because the proposed establishment is a departure from that generous policy, which, offering an Asylum to the persecuted and oppressed of every Nation and Religion, promised a lustre to our country, and an accession to the number of its citizens. What a melancholy mark is the Bill of sudden degeneracy? Instead of holding forth an Asylum to the persecuted, it is itself a signal of persecution. It degrades from the equal rank of Citizens all those whose opinions in Religion do not bend to those of the Legislative authority. Distant as it may be in its present form from the Inquisition, it differs from it only in degree. The one is the first step, the other the last in the career of intolerance. The magnanimous sufferer under this cruel scourge in foreign Regions, must view the

Bill as a Beacon on our Coast, warning him to seek some other haven, where liberty and philanthrophy in their due extent, may offer a more certain repose from his Troubles.

10. Because it will have a like tendency to banish our Citizens. The allurements presented by other situations are every day thinning their number. To superadd a fresh motive to emigration by revoking the liberty which they now enjoy, would be the same species of folly which has dishonoured and depopulated flourishing kingdoms.

11. Because it will destroy that moderation and harmony which the forbearance of our laws to intermeddle with Religion has produced among its several sects. Torrents of blood have been spilt in the old world, by vain attempts of the secular arm, to extinguish Religious discord by proscribing all difference in Religious opinion. Time has at length revealed the true remedy. Every relaxation of narrow and rigorous policy, wherever it has been tried, has been found to assuage the disease. The American Theatre has exhibited proofs that equal and compleat liberty, if it does not wholly eradicate it, sufficiently destroys its malignant influence on the health and prosperity of the State. If with the salutary effects of this system under our own eyes, we begin to contract the bounds of Religious freedom, we know no name that will too severely reproach our folly. At least let warning be taken at the first fruits of the threatened innovation. The very appearance of the Bill has transformed "that Christian forbearance, love and charity," which of late mutually prevailed, into animosities and jealousies, which may not soon be appeased. What mischiefs may not be dreaded, should this enemy to the public quiet be armed with the force of a law?

12. Because the policy of the Bill is adverse to the diffusion of the light of Christianity. The first wish of those who enjoy this precious gift ought to be that it may be imparted to the whole race of mankind. Compare the number of those who have as yet received it with the number still remaining under the dominion of false Religions; and how small is the former! Does the policy of the Bill tend to lessen the disproportion? No; it at once discourages those who are strangers to the light of revelation from coming into the Region of it; and countenances by example the nations who continue in darkness, in shutting out those who might convey it to them. Instead of Levelling as far as possible, every obstacle to the victorious progress of Truth, the Bill with an ignoble and unchristian timidity would circumscribe it with a wall of defence against the encroachments of error.

13. Because attempts to enforce by legal sanctions, acts obnoxious to so great a proportion of Citizens, tend to enervate the laws in general, and to slacken the bands of Society. If it be difficult to execute any law which is not generally deemed necessary or salutary, what must be the case where it is deemed invalid and dangerous? And what may be the effect of so striking an example of impotency in the Government, on its general authority?

14. Because a measure of such singular magnitude and delicacy ought not to be imposed, without the clearest evidence that it is called for by a majority of citizens, and no satisfactory method is yet proposed by which the voice of the majority in this case may be determined, or its influence secured. "The people of the respective counties are indeed requested to signify their opinion respecting the adoption of the Bill to the next Session of Assembly." But the representation must be made equal, before the voice either of the Representatives or of the Counties will be that of the people. Our hope is that neither of the former will, after due consideration, espouse the dangerous principle of the Bill. Should the event disappoint us, it will still leave us in full confidence, that a fair appeal to the latter will reverse the sentence against our liberties.

15. Because finally, "the equal right of every citizen to the free exercise of his Religion according to the dictates of conscience" is held by the same tenure with all our other rights. If we recur to its origin, it is equally the gift of nature; if we weigh its importance, it cannot be less dear to us, if we consult the "Declaration of those rights which pertain to the good people of Virginia, as the basis and foundation of Government," it is enumerated with equal solemnity, or rather studied emphasis. Either then, we must say, that the Will of the Legislature is the only measure of their authority; and that in the plenitude of this authority, they may sweep away all our fundamental rights; or, that they are bound to leave this particular right untouched and sacred: Either we must say, that they may control the freedom of the press, may abolish the Trial by jury, may swallow up the Executive and judiciary Powers of the State; nay that they may despoil us of our very right of suffrage, and erect themselves into an independent and hereditary Assembly or, we must say, that they have no authority to enact into law the Bill under consideration. We the Subscribers say, that the General Assembly of this Commonwealth have no such authority: And that no effort may be omitted on our part against so dangerous an usurpation, we oppose to it, this remonstrance; earnestly praying, as we are in duty bound, that the Supreme Lawgiver of the Universe, by illuminating those to whom it is addressed, may on the one hand, turn their Councils from every act which would affront his holy prerogative, or violate the trust committed to them: and on the other, guide them into every measure which may be worthy of his [blessing, may re]dound to their own praise, and may establish more firmly the liberties, the prosperity and the happiness of the Commonwealth.

Isaac Backus and a Bill of Rights, 1779, 1783

*Just as the deists Jefferson and Madison believed that religion was an affair
solely between the individual and the Creator (an affair which required no
meddlesome political intermediary), so the pietist Backus similarly believed
and argued. Concerned for the dignity and liberty of the state, deists rejected
all notions of a National Church or an established religion. Concerned for
the dignity and purity of Christ's church, pietists rejected all embraces of the
state with respect to religion. Thus a powerful, if accidental, alliance between deist and pietist helped to make the First Amendment an enduring reality: "Congress shall make no law respecting an establishment of religion, or
prohibiting the free exercise thereof. . . ." In 1779 Isaac Backus had been asked
to suggest an appropriate Bill of Rights for the Massachusetts constitution.
His article on religion is given below, together with a more expansive version
of his views set down in his 1783 tract, A Door Opened to Christian Liberty.
Both statements precede Madison's* Memorial *of 1785 and, of course, the national Constitution and its Bill of Rights.*

A Declaration of the Rights, of the Inhabitants of the State of Massachusetts-Bay, in New-England.

1 All men are born equally free and independant, and have certain natural, inherent and unalienable rights, among which are the enjoying and defending life
and liberty, acquiring, possessing, and protecting property, and pursuing and
obtaining happiness and safety.

2 As God is the only worthy object of all religious worship, and nothing
can be true religion but a voluntary obedience unto his revealed will, of which
each rational soul has an equal right to judge for itself, every person has an unalienable right to act in all religious affairs according to the full persuasion of
his own mind, where others are not injured thereby. And civil rulers are so far
from having any right to empower any person or persons, to judge for others in
such affairs, and to enforce their judgments with the sword, that their power
ought to be exerted to protect all persons and societies, within their jurisdiction
from being injured or interrupted in the free enjoyment of this right, under any
pretense whatsoever. . . .

[Source: William G. McLoughlin, ed., *Isaac Backus on Church, State, and Calvinism* (Cambridge: Harvard University Press, 1968), pp. 487-88, 435-38.]

A Door Opened to Christian Liberty

The fathers of this town [Boston] and government mistook the work of civil rulers so much as to imagine that they were to inflict corporal punishments upon men as sinners against God, and not only for crimes against the community. They therefore banished several persons upon pain of death for adultery before they did any for heresy, and some were hanged here for adultery near twenty years before they hanged the Quakers. But the apostle has plainly taught the churches to put away wicked persons out of their communion and says upon it, *Them that are without God judgeth*, 1 *Cor.* v, 13. And in the parable of the tares of the field our Lord has commanded his servants to let the children of his kingdom and the children of the wicked one grow together in the world till the end of it. Which divine laws have ever been violated by all those who have confounded the government of the church and state together. On the one hand they have been deficient about if they have not wholly neglected Gospel discipline in the church, while they have ever invaded their neighbors' rights in the state, under religious pretences. And for twelve or thirteen centuries all colleges and places for superior learning were under the government of men who assumed the power to lay religious bands upon children before they could choose for themselves and to enforce the same by the sword of the magistrate all their days. But I congratulate my countrymen upon the arrival of more agreeable times, and upon the prospect of a much greater reformation before us. For the following reasons convince me that God has now set before us an open door for equal Christian liberty which no man can shut.

1. Not only America but all the kingdoms and states of Europe who have acknowledged the authority of our Congress have set their seal to this truth, that the highest civil rulers derive their power from the consent of the people and cannot stand without their support. And common people know that nothing is more contrary to the rules of honesty than for some to attempt to convey to others things which they have not right to themselves, and no one has any right to judge for others in religious affairs.

2. All former taxes to support worship were imposed in each government by a particular sect who held all others in subordination thereto, which partiality is now expressly excluded from among us.

3. No man can take a seat in our legislature till he solemnly declares, "I believe the Christian religion and have a firm persuasion of its truth." And as surely as it is true Christ is the only HEAD of his Church and she is COMPLETE in him, and is required to do all her acts IN HIS NAME; and all worship of a contrary nature is *will worship* and is only to *satisfy the flesh, Col.* ii, 10, 19-23; iii, 17. And all ministers who were supported by tax and compulsion among us before the late war received that power in the name of the King of Great Britain, and not King Jesus, and they are the only officers in this land that have re-

tained the power over the people which they have received in that name. What-ever gifts and graces any of them have received from Jesus Christ let them faithfully improve the same according to his direction, but, as they would ap-pear loyal to him or friends to their country let them renounce the holding of any earthly head to the church.

4. If this be not done, none can tell who they will have for their head. For the name Protestant is no longer to be a test of our legislators, and to persuade the people to yield thereto the compilers of the constitution said to them, "your dele-gates did not conceive themselves to be vested with power to set up one denomi-nation of Christians above another, for religion must at all times be a matter be-tween God and individuals." This is a great truth, and it proves that no man can become a member of a truly religious society without his own consent and also that no corporation that is not a religious society can have a right to govern in re-ligious matters. Christ said, *who made me a judge, or a divider over you?* And Paul said, *what have I to do to judge them also that are without? Luke* xii, 14; 1 Cor. v, 12. Thus our Divine Lord and the great apostle of the Gentiles explicitly renounced any judicial power over the world by virtue of their religion. And to imagine that *money* can give any *power* in religious matters is the doctrine of Simon the *sor-cerer,* and by such *sorceries* the whore of Babylon hath *deceived all nations, Acts* viii, 18, 19; *Rev.* xviii, 23. It was from thence that the Pope, on May 4, 1493, the year after America was first discovered, presumed to give away the lands of the hea-then therein. And the same power was claimed by the crown of England in grant-ing several charters of this country. From whence some of the states were lately contending in Congress with others, about the western lands on this continent.

5. All the power that the constitution gives our legislature in this respect is to make "suitable provision" for Christian teachers. And according to their dec-laration, divine revelation must determine what is suitable, and that determines that they *shall live of the Gospel, 1 Cor.* ix, 14. Those who under the law collected support for religious teachers *by force* brought complete destruction upon themselves therefor, 1 *Sam.* ii, 16, 25; *Micah* iii, 5-12. Christianity is a voluntary obedience to God's revealed will, and everything of a contrary nature is antichristianism. And all teachers who do not watch for souls as those who must give an account to God, and all people who do not receive and support his faithful ministers as they have opportunity and ability are daily exposed to punishments infinitely worse than men can inflict, *Luke* x, 3-12; *Gal.* vi, 6-9; *Heb.* xiii, 7, 17, 18.

6. Reason and revelation agree in determining that the end of civil gov-ernment is the *good* of the governed by defending them against all such as would work *ill to their neighbors* and in limiting the *power* of rulers there. And those who invade the religious rights of others are *self-condemned,* which of all things is the most opposite to *happiness,* the great end of government, *Rom.* xiii, 3-10; xiv, 10-23.

7. If men will refuse to be happy themselves, yet their power to enslave others is now greatly weakened. And a faithful improvement of our privileges will weaken it more and more till there shall be no more use for *swords* because there shall be *none to hurt or destroy in all God's holy mountain, Isai,* xi, 9; *Micah* iv, 1-4. And who would not be in earnest for that glorious day?

Isaac Backus.
Boston, May 10, 1783.

Religious Liberty Effected

Virginia's Episcopalians, 1785

Just as the state of Virginia set the pattern for legally guaranteeing religious liberty, so it proved the model for swiftly bringing that liberty into actual practice. The Church of England, long the official partner in colonial Virginia's development, found her situation suddenly and radically altered as a result of Jefferson's and Madison's respective bills. Reorganizing under the name of the Protestant Episcopal Church of the United States of America, the old church had to take stock of its new status, assess the damage sustained, and consider the prospects ahead. The document below, dated May 24, 1785, and emanating from the Church's state convention, is addressed "to the Members of the Protestant Episcopal Church in Virginia." After eight years of war and long neglect of her ecclesiastical fortunes, what relief lay ahead for Virginia's "mother church"?

For more than eight years our church hath languished under neglect. We will not, however, believe that her friends have revolted, and therefore trust that a knowledge of her present condition will rekindle their former affections. Religion does not invite by inducements from eternal interest alone; society feels her benignity in remedying the defects of laws. Secret injuries to social rights escape the censures of government. From the constitution of human affairs, human wisdom cannot be certain, that an antidote applied to one evil will not produce another; and many are the duties of imperfect obligation, which no legislative provision can enforce. Nor can society at all times furnish incite-

[Source: F. L. Hawks, *Contributions to the Ecclesiastical History of the United States* (New York: Harper & Brothers, 1836), I, Appendix, 7-8.]

ments to virtuous conduct by rewards; and even if this were practicable, the most enlightened tribunal on earth could not be assured of the purity of the motive which gave birth to the action rewarded. Religion, on the contrary, fixes the eye of conscience on deeds however remote from public view; arrests the hand of vice by holding forth the responsibility of man to his Creator; rescues benevolence from the vortex of self-love; administers self-complacency, that highest prize of merit; and withholds it in spite of partiality when it is not due.

From the earliest day, and in every clime, has the efficacy of religion been acknowledged. Under various forms have her benefits been solicited, and we have enlisted ourselves under the banners of the Protestant Episcopal Church. Let us not then desert this object of our choice, but, conscious of her scriptural authority, devote ourselves to her relief.

Of what is the church now possessed! Nothing but the glebes and your affections. Since the year 1776, she hath been even without regular government, and her ministers have received but little compensation for their services. Their numbers are diminished by death and other causes, and we have as yet no resource within ourselves for a succession of ministers. Churches stand in need of repair, and there is no fund equal to the smallest want.

By the favour of Providence, indeed, the Protestant Episcopal Church is incorporated by law, and under this sanction are we now assembled. We have accepted the invitation of a Convention, lately holden at New-York, to send deputies to another to be holden at Philadelphia in the fall. We shall not enter into a revision of doctrine and worship, until their return and report of the sentiments of those of our communion with whom they may be associated. We have, however, organized the government of the church.

But whither must our labours tend without your assistance, To contempt they cannot; for we have the consciousness of aiming at our common welfare alone. To almost everything under the sun belongs a crisis, which, if embraced, stamps our endeavours with success — if lost, with ruin. In this situation does our church now stand: and why do you hesitate? Are the doctrines of our church less excellent than at any former period? Have you embraced the persuasion of that church, to abandon it in the hour of difficulty? Common justice requires that those who profess themselves to be members of a society, should unite in cherishing it; and let us not be the only example of a religious association withering from the want of support from its own members.

But do not believe that by thus exhorting you to zeal for our church, we mean to provoke an aversion to other Christian societies. It is vain to expect unanimity among mankind; and who can with confidence declare himself infallible? We rather conceive that Christians of every denomination, who are sincere in their opinion, are not less our brethren for maintaining different tenets. It is our duty to be ready to unite upon principles consistent with the gospel, and bring the Christian Church to unity, as nearly as conscience will permit.

We therefore entreat you in the most solemn manner, we conjure you by all the ties of religion to co-operate fervently in the cause of our church. Should these our earnest efforts be abortive, we shall always with truth call the Searcher of hearts to witness, that the downfall of the Protestant Episcopal Church is not to be named among our offences, and to this admonition shall we ever appeal.

Virginia's Baptists, 1786

If Episcopalians asked what lay ahead for their beleaguered church, Virginia's dissenters had no hesitation in offering answers. What lay ahead was the removal of any lingering favoritism or privilege enjoyed by Anglicans before the Revolution. One issue especially troubled the non-Anglicans: that of glebe lands. When an Anglican parish had been laid out in the colonial era by the Virginia legislature, the pattern was to set aside a small amount of land for a church building but also a larger amount of land that could be farmed for the parish's support. This latter grant of land, the "glebes," belonged to all the people now, dissenters argued. To leave them in the hands exclusively of Episcopalians meant that they would continue to enjoy special privilege and favor. The legislature must correct this situation, Baptists and others averred; moreover, the legislature actually passed a law incorporating this new entity called the "Protestant Episcopal Church." What business is that of the state's? Churches, "we humbly conceive, are, or should be, established by the Legislature of Heaven, and not earthly power." Couching their protest in the language of Jefferson and Madison as well as that of the Bible, Baptists meeting in Buckingham County in August, 1786, dispatched the following petition to the Virginia legislature.

When Britain with her cruel Usurpation over her Colonies in America, reduced them to the necessity of taking up Arms, to indicate their Natural Claims. A declaration of Rights . . . was made, by the good People of Virginia. Assembled in full and free Convention, as the Basis and foundation of Government. A constitution so Liberal in Civil, and free in religious concerns, that we readily took the Oath of Fidelity to the State. From this principle we expatiated! for this free government we advanced our property and exposed our lives on the field of battle with our fellow Citizens; being often Stimulated with the harmonious Proclamation of equal Liberty of conscience, and equal claim of property.

As hazardous as the Enterprize appeared, under the interposition of di-

[Source: H. J. Eckenrode, *Separation of Church and State in Virginia* (Richmond: Virginia State Library, 1910), pp. 118-19.]

vine providence, by the prudence of our Ambassadors, the wisdom of our politicians, the skill of our Generals, the bravery of our soldiers and the aid of our Allies; after a seven years Contest, we obtained our liberty, and Independence with a vast empire added to us by the late treaty of peace.

At this happy period, when America emerged from a bloody Obscurity to such a distinguishing figure of importance among the nations of the world; we felicitated our Selves with the enjoyment of every domestic, and Social blessing of human Life: Nor were we willing to harbour a jealous thought of the Legislature, that the bill of Rights, would not be attended to in every particular.

But to our great Surprize, in the Session of 1784, at the request of a few Clergymen, the members of the late established Church of England, were incorporated into a Society, called the "Protestant Episcopal Church," as a body Corporate and politic, and to the ministers & members of that Church, and their Successors were given, all and every Tract, or Tracts of Glebe Land, already purchased, and every other thing the property of the late established Church of England, to the Sole, and only use of the Protestant Episcopal Church.

If Religion or the duty which we owe to our Creator, and the manner of discharging it, can be directed, only by reason and conviction; not by force and violence (so fully expressed in the XVI Art: of the bill of Rights, and the late Act for establishing Religious Liberty) we cannot see with what propriety the General Assembly could incorporate the Protestant Episcopal Church, give her a name, Describe the character of her members, modulate the forms of her government, & apoint the Time and place of her meeting. If this is not done by force, what force can there be in law? and to what lengths this may lead; and what violence it may produce, time only can discover, but we fear the awful consequences. The act appears a Bitumen to Cement Church and State together; the foundation for Ecclesiastical Tyranny, and the first step towards an Inquisition.

New Testament Churches, we humbly conceive, are, or should be, established by the Legislature of Heaven, and not earthly power; by the Law of God and not the Law of the State; by the acts of the Apostles, and not by the Acts of an Assembly. The Incorporating Act then, in the first place appears to cast great contempt upon the divine Author of our Religion, whose Kingdom is not of this world, and Secondly, to give all the property of the State established church to one Society, not more virtuous, nor deserving than other Societies in the Commonwealth, appears contrary to justice, and the express words of the IV Art: of the Bill of Rights, which prohibits rewards or emoluments to any Man, or set of men, except for services rendered the State; and what services that Church has rendered the State, either by her Clergy or Laity, more than other Churches have done, we no not.

If truth is great, and will prevail if left to itself (as declared in the Act Establishing Religious Freedom) we wish it may be so left, which is the only way to convince the gazing world, that Disciples do not follow Christ for Loaves, and that Preachers do not preach for Benefices.

Virginia's Presbyterians, 1787

Almost exactly a year after the Baptist petition, Presbyterians offered their own argument for the sale of the glebe lands. The ancestors of Virginia's present-day Presbyterians, Baptists, and Methodists, they declared, had been taxed for the purchase of these lands; therefore, to take what is common property and bestow it upon a single newly created denomination "is too glaring a piece of injustice to pass unnoticed, or be suffered to continue in a free country."

That your petitioners are sorry to be under the necessity of calling the attention of our political guardians to matters which may in some respects be considered of a peculiar nature, at a time when probably objects of great magnitude, and of general influence, not only to this state; but to the whole continent, may call for their deliberations. But actuated by the same principles which engaged us in, and carried us through the late glorious contest, a love of liberty and political equality, we think it a part of that duty which as freemen and citizens we owe to ourselves and posterity, again to address your honourable house: and whilst we acknowledge with all that gratitude which becomes good citizens, the attention given by your honourable body to the grievances which we formerly complained of, we cannot but express our sorrow to see how slowly and with what seeming reluctance, equal justice is done, and all denominations of christians in the state put in possession of their constitutional rights.

We cannot enjoy that happiness, nor place that confidence in our government which we would wish, whilst we see our legislature in the face of human justice, and the inalienable rights of all the citizens, hold up a particular sect, or denomination of christians, as the objects of political favour. This we suppose is undenyably the case, in the exclusive appropriation of the glebes and churches to the protestant episcopal church, to the possession of which she has not the least shadow of a claim. As she differs from the Church of England, in the articles of her faith, the plan of her discipline, and the ceremonies of her worship; she is no more the same than the church of England is the same with the church of Rome; and has no pretext for identity, unless it be that the same persons compose her members, which composed the members of that ancient

---

[Source: H. J. Eckenrode, *Separation of Church and State in Virginia* (Richmond: Virginia State Library, 1910), pp. 131-32.]

church, which is now no more in America. And therefore has no better right, than a great number of the Methodist, Baptist and Presbyterian churches, who can all plead the same; being once members of that Church. These glebes and churches, were purchased with the common property of all the citizens of all denominations; and so far as there was any thing laudable in the institution which extorted this money it was that convenient places of worship might be provided for the people at large. Then to take what is common property, and designed for common benefit, and bestow upon this infant church, to the exclusion of a great majority of the community, is too glaring a piece of injustice to pass unnoticed, or be suffered to continue in a free country.

We therefore pray the honourable house, to take the matter under their serious consideration, and adopt those measures which common justice must dictate. That the glebes be sold, and the money thence arising be divided, amongst the different denominations of Christians in each parish, in proportion to their number of tithes; to be by them applied to the religious uses of their respective communities. And that the churches with their furniture be so disposed of, that the people at whose expence they were procured, may enjoy the benefit of them in common for religious worship.

This will give more general satisfaction, and be a better means of promoting Virtue & happiness, than any mode which a civil legislature, who have temporal things as their sole and immediate object, would by leaving the line of their duty devise.

Religious Liberty Tested:
The Administration of George Washington (1789-97)

By 1789 the nation had a new civil structure which, among other things, gave greater authority to the central government. Would that authority turn into tyranny? Would "president" simply be a disguised form of "king"? How safe were the liberties of individual citizens under this unproven government, and specifically, how secure was one to worship, or not worship, as he or she chose? These questions had special force when the first president took office, for Washington — consciously or otherwise — would by every official action define the meaning of the presidency and the direction of the nation. The is-

[Source: Norman Cousins, *"In God We Trust": The Religious Beliefs and Ideas of the American Founding Fathers* (New York: Harper & Brothers, 1958), pp. 58-59, 60, 61, 63. All letters abridged.]

sue was not so much George Washington's personal religious position *(though there was interest in that too), but the policies of the chief executive with respect to America's already pluralistic people. Thus, (1) Baptists, (2) Presbyterians, (3) Quakers, (4) Roman Catholics, (5) Jews, and (6) others all wrote to President Washington, first to offer congratulations on his election, but second usually also to express anxious hopes concerning the safety of their own liberties in the realm of religion. To each group, Washington replied with even-handed respect, giving assurance to all, even those previously persecuted and disdained, that the new government of the United States would give to "bigotry no sanction, to persecution no assistance...."*

1.

Reply to an Address Sent by the General Committee of the United Baptist Churches in Virginia, May, 1789

If I could have entertained the slightest apprehension, that the constitution framed in the convention, where I had the honor to preside, might possibly endanger the religious rights of any ecclesiastical society, certainly I would never have placed my signature to it; and if I could now conceive that the general government might ever be so administered as to render the liberty of conscience insecure, I beg you will be persuaded, that no one would be more zealous than myself to establish effectual barriers against the horrors of spiritual tyranny, and every species of religious persecution. For you doubtless remember, that I have often expressed my sentiments that every man, conducting himself as a good citizen, and being accountable to God alone for his religious opinions, ought to be protected in worshipping the Deity according to the dictates of his own conscience.

2.

Reply to an Address Sent by the General Assembly of Presbyterian Churches in the United States (Address Dated May 26, 1789; Washington's Reply Undated)

While I reiterate the professions of my dependence upon Heaven as the source of all public and private blessings; I will observe that the general prevalence of piety, philanthropy, honesty, industry and economy seems, in the ordinary course of human affairs, particularly necessary for advancing and confirming the happiness of our country. While all men within our territories are protected in worshipping the Deity according to the dictates of their consciences; it is rationally to be expected from them in return, that they will be emulous of evinc-

Apotheosis of Washington
David Edwin (after R. Peale)
(© National Portrait Gallery, Smithsonian Institution/Art Resource, NY)

ing the sanctity of their professions by the innocence of their lives and the beneficence of their actions; for no man, who is profligate in his morals, or a bad member of the civil community, can possibly be a true Christian, or a credit to his own religious society.

I desire you to accept my acknowledgments for your laudable endeavors to render men sober, honest, and good Citizens, and the obedient subjects of a lawful government.

3.
Reply to an Address Sent by the Religious Society Called Quakers from Their Yearly Meeting for Pennsylvania, New Jersey, Delaware, and the Western Parts of Maryland and Virginia, September 28, 1789 (Reply Undated)

Government being, among other purposes, instituted to protect the persons and consciences of men from oppression, it certainly is the duty of rulers, not only to abstain from it themselves, but according to their stations, to prevent it in others.

The liberty enjoyed by the people of these States, of worshipping Almighty God agreeably to their consciences, is not only among the choicest of their *blessings*, but also of their *rights*. While men perform their social duties faithfully, they do all that society or the state can with propriety demand or expect; and remain responsible only to their Maker for the religion, or modes of faith, which they may prefer or profess.

Your principles and conduct are well known to me; and it is doing the people called Quakers no more than justice to say, that (except their declining to share with others the burthen of the common defense) there is no denomination among us, who are more exemplary and useful citizens.

I assure you very explicitly, that in my opinion the conscientious scruples of all men should be treated with great delicacy and tenderness; and it is my wish and desire, that the laws may always be as extensively accommodated to them, as a due regard to the protection and essential interests of the nation may justify and permit.

4.
Reply to a Congratulatory Address by a Committee of Roman Catholics Waiting Upon the President, March 15, 1790, according to the Maryland *Journal* and Baltimore *Advertiser*

I feel that my conduct in War and in Peace has met with more general approbation than could reasonably have been expected; and I find myself disposed to consider that fortunate circumstance, in a great degree, resulting from the able support and extraordinary candor of my fellow-citizens of all denominations.

As mankind become more liberal, they will be more apt to allow, that all those who conduct themselves as worthy members of the community are equally entitled to the protection of civil government. I hope ever to see America among the foremost nations in examples of justice and liberality. And I presume, that your fellow-citizens will not forget the patriotic part which you took in the accomplishment of their revolution, and the establishment of their government; or the important assistance, which they received, from a Nation in which the Roman Catholic religion is professed. . . . May the members of your Society in America, animated alone by the pure spirit of Christianity, and still conducting themselves as the faithful subjects of our free government, enjoy every temporal and spiritual felicity.

5.
Reply to Moses Seixas, Sexton of the Hebrew Congregation of Newport, Who Sent Washington a Letter of Welcome on His Visit to the Town of Newport, August 17, 1790

The citizens of the United States of America have a right to applaud themselves for having given to Mankind examples of an enlarged and liberal policy, a policy worthy of imitation. All possess alike liberty of conscience and immunities of citizenship. It is now no more that toleration is spoken of, as if it was by the indulgence of one class of people that another enjoyed the exercise, of their inherent natural rights. For happily the Government of the United States, which gives bigotry no sanction, to persecution no assistance requires only that they who live under its protection should demean themselves as good citizens, in giving it on all occasions their effectual support.

It would be inconsistent with the frankness of my character not to avow that I am pleased with your favorable opinion of my administration, and fervent wishes for my felicity. May the Children of the Stock of Abraham, who dwell in this land, continue to merit and enjoy the good will of the other Inhabitants, while every one shall sit in safety under his own vine and fig-tree, and there shall be none to make him afraid. May the father of all mercies scatter light and not darkness in our paths, and make us all in our several vocations useful here, and in his own due time and way everlastingly happy.

6.

Letter to the Clergy of Different Denominations Residing in and near the City of Philadelphia, March 3, 1797

Believing, as I do, that *Religion* and *Morality* are the essential pillars of Civil society, I view, with unspeakable pleasure, that harmony and brotherly love which characterizes the Clergy of different denominations, as well in this, as in other parts of the United States; exhibiting to the world a new and interesting spectacle, at once the pride of our Country and the surest basis of Universal Harmony.

That your labours for the good of Mankind may be crowned with success; that your temporal enjoyments may be commensurate with your merits; and that the future reward of good and faithful Servants may be yours, I shall not cease to supplicate the Divine Author of life and felicity.

3. Religion in the Revolution and the New Republic

Religion, Rational and Natural

Universalism

To the extent that colonial Americans had a dominant theological orienta-
tion, Calvinism emerged as the early favorite. Congregationalists, Presby-
terians, Dutch and German Reformed, Baptists, and even large numbers of
Anglicans thought in terms of God's choice of his elect, those called out and
saved for all eternity. If some were chosen, many were not. And by the second
half of the eighteenth century, some theologians and popular preachers
turned away from what seemed a rigid exclusivism to a more merciful and
encompassing universalism. If Calvinism emphasized the justice of God, Uni-
versalism extolled his benevolence, explaining that God loved all, Christ died
for all, and ultimately all would be saved. (1) So Boston Congregationalist
Charles Chauncy (1705-87) wrote, and circulated at first quite privately, The
Salvation of All Men, the Grand Thing aimed at in the Scheme of God . . .
(1784). (2) So a former Baptist, Elhanan Winchester (1751-97), moved in his
late twenties toward the conviction that a moral and loving God would seek
— and at last attain — the good of all his creatures. In the excerpts below,
Chauncy offers formal "proofs of universal salvation," while Winchester pro-
vides a more personal or existential account of his theological pilgrimage.

[Source: (1) Charles Chauncy, *The Salvation of All Men* . . . (London: Charles Dilly, 1784),
pp. 1-3; punctuation modernized. (2) Edwin M. Stone, *Biography of Rev. Elhanan Winches-*
ter (New York: Arno Press, 1972 [1836]), pp. 42-44.]

1.

As the First Cause of all things is infinitely benevolent, 'tis not easy to conceive that he should bring mankind into existence, unless he intended to make them finally happy. And if this was his intention, it cannot well be supposed, as he is infinitely intelligent and wise, that he should be unable to project, or carry into execution, a scheme that would be effectual to secure, sooner or later, the certain accomplishment of it. Should it be suggested, Free agents, as men are allowed to be, must be left to their own choices, in consequence whereof blame can be reflected justly no where but upon themselves . . . the answer is perfectly obvious. Their Creator, being perfectly benevolent, would be disposed to prevent their making, or at least, their finally persisting in such wrong choices; and, being infinitely intelligent and wise, would use suitable and yet effectual methods in order to attain this end. Should it be said further, Such free agents as men are may oppose all the methods that can be used with them, in consistency with liberty, and persist in wrong pursuits . . . the reply is, This is sooner said than proved. Who will undertake to make it evident that infinite wisdom, excited by infinite benevolence, is incapable of devising expedients whereby moral agents, without any violence offered to their liberty, may certainly be led, if not at first, yet after various repeated trials, into such determinations and consequent actions as would finally prepare them for happiness? It would be hard to suppose that infinite wisdom should finally be outdone by the obstinacy and folly of any free agents whatsoever. If this might really be the case, how can it be thought, with respect to such free agents, that they should ever have been produced by an infinitely benevolent cause? If the only good God knew . . . that some free agents would make themselves unhappy, notwithstanding the utmost efforts of his wisdom to prevent it, why did he create them?

2.

In the house where I lodged, when I first came to [Philadelphia], I had, in the freedom of conversation, and with some appearance of joy, expressed myself in general terms upon the subject, but always in the exact words of Scripture, or in such a manner as this, viz: — That I could not help hoping that God would finally bring *every knee to bow* and *every tongue to swear;* and that *at the name of Jesus every knee should bow, of things in heaven,* and *things in earth;* and *things under the earth;* and *that every tongue* should *confess* JESUS CHRIST to be *Lord to the glory of God the Father.* And that I hoped, *that in the dispensation of the fulness of times, he might gather together in one all things in* CHRIST, *both which are in heaven, and which are on earth,* &c.

Such passages as these I mentioned in this manner, hoping that they would be fulfilled. The people of the house seemed surprised, and asked me if I believed so; I answered, "That sometimes I could not help hoping that it might be so." I could hardly have imagined among friends that any danger could have arisen from my expressing a hope that the Scriptures were true.

However these false friends told a minister, whom for a number of years I had esteemed as my best and most intimate friend, that I was turned heretic, and believed in the doctrine of the *Universal Restoration,* and desired him to convince me. Some time after he met with me in the street, and in a very abrupt manner told me, that he had wanted to see me for some time, that he might give me a piece of his mind; that he had been informed by such a person, that I was inclined to the doctrine of the *Universal Restoration,* and then, instead of using any argument to convince me, or taking any method for my recovery, added this *laconic speech,* "If you embrace this sentiment, I shall no longer own you for a brother." And he has hitherto been as good as his word, having never written nor spoken to me from that day to this, and when I have since offered to shake hands with him, he refused; and yet he was one whom I esteemed above any other on earth, as a hearty, sincere, long-tried, and faithful friend. If my intimate friend treated me in such a manner, what had I not to expect from my open and avowed enemies?

I now foresaw the storm, and I determined to prepare for it, not by denying what I had said, but by examining and determining for myself, whether the sentiment was according to scripture or not. If I found that it was not, I was determined to retract, but if it was, to hold it fast, let the consequences be what they might. I had now no time to lose. I expected in a short time to be called to an account, and examined respecting this doctrine, and obliged either to *defend or deny it;* I was already too well persuaded that it was true, to do the latter without hesitation, and yet not sufficiently for the former. For this purpose, I shut myself up chiefly in my chamber, read the Scriptures, and prayed to God to lead me into all truth, and not suffer me to embrace any error; and I think that with an upright mind, I laid myself open to believe whatever the Lord had revealed. It would be too long to tell all the teachings I had on this head; let it suffice, in short, to say, that I became so well persuaded of the truth of the *Universal Restoration,* that I was determined never to deny it, let it cost ever so much, though all my numerous friends should forsake me, as I expected they would, and though I should be driven from men, and obliged to dwell in caves or dens of the earth, and feed on wild roots and vegetables, and suffer the loss of all things, friends, wealth, fame, health, character, and even life itself. The truth appeared to me more valuable than all things, and as I had found it, I was determined never to part with it, let what would be offered in exchange.

Unitarianism

If Universalism concerned itself chiefly with the nature and benevolence of
God, Unitarianism (despite its anti-Trinitarian tag) concerned itself more
with the nature and rationality of man. Men and women were not the de-
praved sinners which Calvinism had made them out to be; on the contrary,
they were God's noblest creation, possessed of keen moral sense and reliable
powers of reason. Unitarianism had its American base chiefly in New En-
gland, in fact virtually around Boston, where the movement arose first as a
theological (later as an ecclesiastical) faction within the prevailing Congre-
gationalism. By 1825, Unitarianism had become a distinctly separate de-
nomination. (1) William Ellery Channing (1780-1842) was its leading
preacher, apologist, theologian, and social reformer. In a famous ordination
sermon delivered in Baltimore in 1819, Channing set forth the essentials of
"Unitarian Christianity." (2) Ralph Waldo Emerson (1803-82) was ordained
a Unitarian minister in Boston's Second Church; he turned eventually to
Transcendentalism (see Chapter Four, below). Around 1832, Emerson signals
his departure from orthodoxy by rejecting the formal necessity of adminis-
tering the Lord's Supper in worship.

1.
William Ellery Channing

There are two natural divisions under which my thoughts will be arranged. I
shall endeavour to unfold, 1st, The principles which we adopt in interpreting
the Scriptures. And 2dly, Some of the doctrines, which the Scriptures, so interpreted, seem to us clearly to express.

I. We regard the Scriptures as the records of God's successive revelations
to mankind, and particularly of the last and most perfect revelation of his will
by Jesus Christ. Whatever doctrines seem to us to be clearly taught in the Scriptures, we receive without reserve or exception. We do not, however, attach equal
importance to all the books in this collection. Our religion, we believe, lies
chiefly in the New Testament. . . .

Our leading principle in interpreting Scripture is this, that the Bible is a
book written for men, in the language of men, and that its meaning is to be
sought in the same manner as that of other books. We believe that God, when

---

[Source: (1) *The Works of William E. Channing*, 6th ed. (Boston: James Munroe & Co.,
1846), pp. 60-63, 69-70, 71, 75, 77-78, 82-83, 85-86, 87-88, 90-92, 93-94, 99-100. (2) Ralph
Waldo Emerson, *Miscellanies* (Boston: Houghton, Mifflin & Co., 1878), pp. 21-26, 28-29.]

he speaks to the human race, conforms, if we may so say, to the established rules of speaking and writing. How else would the Scriptures avail us more, than if communicated in an unknown tongue?

Now all books, and all conversation, require in the reader or hearer the constant exercise of reason; or their true import is only to be obtained by continual comparison and inference. Human language, you well know, admits various interpretations; and every word and every sentence must be modified and explained according to the subject which is discussed, according to the purposes, feelings, circumstances, and principles of the writer, and according to the genius and idioms of the language which he uses. . . .

We profess not to know a book, which demands a more frequent exercise of reason than the Bible. In addition to the remarks now made on its infinite connexions, we may observe, that its style nowhere affects the precision of science, or the accuracy of definition. Its language is singularly glowing, bold, and figurative, demanding more frequent departures from the literal sense, than that of our own age and country, and consequently demanding more continual exercise of judgment. — We find, too, that the different portions of this book, instead of being confined to general truths, refer perpetually to the times when they were written, to states of society, to modes of thinking, to controversies in the church, to feelings and usages which have passed away, and without the knowledge of which we are constantly in danger of extending to all times, and places, what was of temporary and local application. — We find, too, that some of these books are strongly marked by the genius and character of their respective writers, that the Holy Spirit did not so guide the Apostles as to suspend the peculiarities of their minds, and that a knowledge of their feelings, and of the influences under which they were placed, is one of the preparations for understanding their writings. With these views of the Bible, we feel it our bounden duty to exercise our reason upon it perpetually, to compare, to infer, to look beyond the letter to the spirit, to seek in the nature of the subject, and the aim of the writer, his true meaning; and, in general, to make use of what is known, for explaining what is difficult, and for discovering new truths. . . .

II. Having thus stated the principles according to which we interpret Scripture, I now proceed to the second great head of this discourse, which is, to state some of the views which we derive from that sacred book, particularly those which distinguish us from other Christians.

1. In the first place, we believe in the doctrine of God's UNITY, or that there is one God, and one only. To this truth we give infinite importance, and we feel ourselves bound to take heed, lest any man spoil us of it by vain philosophy. The proposition, that there is one God, seems to us exceedingly plain. We understand by it, that there is one being, one mind, one person, one intelligent agent, and one only, to whom underived and infinite perfection and dominion

belong. We conceive, that these words could have conveyed no other meaning to the simple and uncultivated people, who were set apart to be the depositaries of this great truth, and who were utterly incapable of understanding those hairbreadth distinctions between being and person, which the sagacity of later ages has discovered. We find no intimation, that this language was to be taken in an unusual sense, or that God's unity was a quite different thing from the oneness of other intelligent beings.

We object to the doctrine of the Trinity, that, whilst acknowledging in words, it subverts in effect, the unity of God. According to this doctrine, there are three infinite and equal persons, possessing supreme divinity, called the Father, Son, and Holy Ghost. Each of these persons, as described by theologians, has his own particular consciousness, will, and perceptions. They love each other, converse with each other, and delight in each other's society. They perform different parts in man's redemption, each having his appropriate office, and neither doing the work of the other. The Son is mediator and not the Father. The Father sends the Son, and is not himself sent; nor is he conscious, like the Son, of taking flesh. Here, then, we have three intelligent agents, possessed of different consciousnesses, different wills, and different perceptions, performing different acts, and sustaining different relations; and if these things do not imply and constitute three minds or beings, we are utterly at a loss to know how three minds or beings are to be formed. . . .

We do, then, with all earnestness, though without reproaching our brethren, protest against the irrational and unscriptural doctrine of the Trinity. . . .

2. Having thus given our views of the unity of God, I proceed in the second place to observe, that we believe in the unity of Jesus Christ. We believe that Jesus is one mind, one soul, one being, as truly one as we are, and equally distinct from the one God. We complain of the doctrine of the Trinity, that, not satisfied with making God three beings, it makes Jesus Christ two beings, and thus introduces infinite confusion into our conceptions of his character. This corruption of Christianity, alike repugnant to common sense and to the general strain of Scripture, is a remarkable proof of the power of a false philosophy in disfiguring the simple truth of Jesus. . . .

Surely, if Jesus Christ felt that he consisted of two minds, and that this was a leading feature of his religion, his phraseology respecting himself would have been colored by this peculiarity. The universal language of men is framed upon the idea, that one person is one person, is one mind, and one soul; and when the multitude heard this language from the lips of Jesus, they must have taken it in its usual sense, and must have referred to a single soul all which he spoke, unless expressly instructed to interpret it differently. But where do we find this instruction? Where do you meet, in the New Testament, the phraseology which abounds in Trinitarian books, and which necessarily grows from the doctrine of two natures in Jesus? Where does this divine teacher say, "This I speak as

God, and this as man; this is true only of my human mind, this only of my divine"? Where do we find in the Epistles a trace of this strange phraseology? Nowhere. It was not needed in that day. It was demanded by the errors of a later age.

We believe, then, that Christ is one mind, one being, and, I add, a being distinct from the one God. That Christ is not the one God, not the same being with the Father, is a necessary inference from our former head, in which we saw that the doctrine of three persons in God is a fiction. But on so important a subject, I would add a few remarks. We wish, that those from whom we differ, would weigh one striking fact. Jesus, in his preaching, continually spoke of God. The word was always in his mouth. We ask, does he, by this word, ever mean himself? We say, never. On the contrary, he most plainly distinguishes between God and himself, and so do his disciples. How this is to be reconciled with the idea, that the manifestation of Christ, as God, was a primary object of Christianity, our adversaries must determine. . . .

3. Having thus given our belief on two great points, namely, that there is one God, and that Jesus Christ is a being distinct from, and inferior to, God, I now proceed to another point, on which we lay still greater stress. We believe in the *moral perfection of God*. We consider no part of theology so important as that which treats of God's moral character; and we value our views of Christianity chiefly as they assert his amiable and venerable attributes.

It may be said, that, in regard to this subject, all Christians agree, that all ascribe to the Supreme Being infinite justice, goodness, and holiness. We reply, that it is very possible to speak of God magnificently, and to think of him meanly; to apply to his person high-sounding epithets, and to his government, principles which make him odious. The Heathens called Jupiter the greatest and the best; but his history was black with cruelty and lust. We cannot judge of men's real ideas of God by their general language, for in all ages they have hoped to soothe the Deity by adulation. We must inquire into their particular views of his purposes, of the principles of his administration, and of his disposition towards his creatures.

We conceive that Christians have generally leaned towards a very injurious view of the Supreme Being. They have too often felt, as if he were raised, by his greatness and sovereignty, above the principles of morality, above those eternal laws of equity and rectitude, to which all other beings are subjected. We believe, that in no being is the sense of right so strong, so omnipotent, as in God. We believe that his almighty power is entirely submitted to his perceptions of rectitude; and this is the ground of our piety. It is not because he is our Creator merely, but because he created us for good and holy purposes; it is not because his will is irresistible, but because his will is the perfection of virtue, that we pay him allegiance. We cannot bow before a being, however great and powerful, who governs tyrannically. We respect nothing but excellence, whether on earth or in heaven. We venerate not the loftiness of God's throne, but the equity and goodness in which it is established.

We believe that God is infinitely good, kind, benevolent, in the proper sense of these words; good in disposition, as well as in act; good, not to a few, but to all; good to every individual, as well as to the general system. . . .

Now, we object to the systems of religion, which prevail among us, that they are adverse, in a greater or less degree, to these purifying, comforting, and honorable views of God; that they take from us our Father in heaven, and substitute for him a being, whom we cannot love if we would, and whom we ought not to love if we could. We object, particularly on this ground, to that system, which arrogates to itself the name of Orthodoxy, and which is now industriously propagated through our country. This system indeed takes various shapes, but in all it casts dishonor on the Creator. According to its old and genuine form, it teaches, that God brings us into life wholly depraved, so that under the innocent features of our childhood is hidden a nature averse to all good and propense to all evil, a nature which exposes us to God's displeasure and wrath, even before we have acquired power to understand our duties, or to reflect upon our actions. According to a more modern exposition, it teaches, that we came from the hands of our Maker with such a constitution, and are placed under such influences and circumstances, as to render certain and infallible the total depravity of every human being, from the first moment of his moral agency; and it also teaches, that the offence of the child, who brings into life this ceaseless tendency to unmingled crime, exposes him to the sentence of everlasting damnation. Now, according to the plainest principles of morality, we maintain, that a natural constitution of the mind, unfailingly disposing it to evil and to evil alone, would absolve it from guilt; that to give existence under this condition would argue unspeakable cruelty; and that to punish the sin of this unhappily constituted child with endless ruin, would be a wrong unparalleled by the most merciless despotism. . . .

4. Having thus spoken of the unity of God; of the unity of Jesus, and his inferiority to God; and of the perfections of the Divine character; I now proceed to give our views of the mediation of Christ, and of the purposes of his mission. With regard to the great object which Jesus came to accomplish, there seems to be no possibility of mistake. We believe that he was sent by the Father to effect a moral, or spiritual deliverance of mankind; that is, to rescue men from sin and its consequences, and to bring them to a state of everlasting purity and happiness. We believe, too, that he accomplishes this sublime purpose by a variety of methods; by his instructions respecting God's unity, parental character, and moral government, which are admirably fitted to reclaim the world from idolatry and impiety, to the knowledge, love, and obedience of the Creator; by his promises of pardon to the penitent, and of divine assistance to those who labor for progress in moral excellence; by the light which he has thrown on the path of duty; by his own spotless example, in which the loveliness and sub-

limity of virtue shine forth to warm and quicken, as well as guide us to perfection; by his threatenings against incorrigible guilt; by his glorious discoveries of immortality; by his sufferings and death; by that signal event, the resurrection, which powerfully bore witness to his divine mission, and brought down to men's senses a future life; by his continual intercession, which obtains for us spiritual aid and blessings; and by the power with which he is invested of raising the dead, judging the world, and conferring the everlasting rewards promised to the faithful. . . .

We farther agree in rejecting, as unscriptural and absurd, the explanation given by the popular system, of the manner in which Christ's death procures forgiveness for men. This system used to teach as its fundamental principle, that man, having sinned against an infinite Being, has contracted infinite guilt, and is consequently exposed to an infinite penalty. We believe, however, that this reasoning, if reasoning it may be called, which overlooks the obvious maxim, that the guilt of a being must be proportioned to his nature and powers, has fallen into disuse. Still the system teaches, that sin, of whatever degree, exposes to endless punishment, and that the whole human race, being infallibly involved by their nature in sin, owe this awful penalty to the justice of their Creator. It teaches, that this penalty cannot be remitted, in consistency with the honor of the divine law, unless a substitute be found to endure it or to suffer an equivalent. It also teaches, that, from the nature of the case, no substitute is adequate to this work, save the infinite God himself; and accordingly, God, in his second person, took on him human nature, that he might pay to his own justice the debt of punishment incurred by men, and might thus reconcile forgiveness with the claims and threatenings of his law. Such is the prevalent system. Now, to us, this doctrine seems to carry on its front strong marks of absurdity; and we maintain that Christianity ought not to be encumbered with it, unless it be laid down in the New Testament fully and expressly. We ask our adversaries, then, to point to some plain passages where it is taught. We ask for one text, in which we are told, that God took human nature that he might make an infinite satisfaction to his own justice, for one text, which tells us, that human guilt requires an infinite substitute; that Christ's sufferings owe their efficacy to their being borne by an infinite being; or that his divine nature gives infinite value to the sufferings of the human. Not *one word* of this description can we find in the Scriptures; not a text, which even hints at these strange doctrines. They are altogether, we believe, the fictions of theologians. Christianity is in no degree responsible for them. We are astonished at their prevalence. What can be plainer, than that God cannot, in any sense, be a sufferer, or bear a penalty in the room of his creatures? How dishonorable to him is the supposition, that his justice is now so severe, as to exact infinite punishment for the sins of frail and feeble men, and now so easy and yielding, as to accept the limited pains of Christ's human soul, as a full equivalent for the endless woes due from the world? . . .

5. Having thus stated our views of the highest object of Christ's mission, that it is the recovery of men to virtue, or holiness, I shall now, in the last place, give our views of the nature of Christian virtue, or true holiness. We believe that all virtue has its foundation in the moral nature of man, that is, in conscience, or his sense of duty, and in the power of forming his temper and life according to conscience. We believe that these moral faculties are the grounds of responsibility, and the highest distinctions of human nature, and that no act is praiseworthy, any farther than it springs from their exertion. We believe, that no dispositions infused into us without our own moral activity, are of the nature of virtue, and therefore, we reject the doctrine of irresistible divine influence on the human mind, moulding it into goodness, as marble is hewn into a statue. Such goodness, if this word may be used, would not be the object of moral approbation, any more than the instinctive affections of inferior animals, or the constitutional amiableness of human beings.

By these remarks, we do not mean to deny the importance of God's aid or Spirit; but by his Spirit, we mean a moral, illuminating, and persuasive influence, not physical, not compulsory, not involving a necessity of virtue. We object, strongly, to the idea of many Christians respecting man's impotence and God's irresistible agency on the heart, believing that they subvert our responsibility and the laws of our moral nature, that they make men machines, that they cast on God the blame of all evil deeds, that they discourage good minds, and inflate the fanatical with wild conceits of immediate and sensible inspiration. . . .

We are accustomed to think much of the difficulties attending religious inquiries; difficulties springing from the slow developement of our minds, from the power of early impressions, from the state of society, from human authority, from the general neglect of the reasoning powers, from the want of just principles of criticism and of important helps in interpreting Scripture, and from various other causes. We find, that on no subject have men, and even good men, ingrafted so many strange conceits, wild theories, and fictions of fancy, as on religion; and remembering, as we do, that we ourselves are sharers of the common frailty, we dare not assume infallibility in the treatment of our fellow-Christians, or encourage in common Christians, who have little time for investigation, the habit of denouncing and condemning other denominations, perhaps more enlightened and virtuous than their own. Charity, forbearance, a delight in the virtues of different sects, a backwardness to censure and condemn, these are virtues, which, however poorly practised by us, we admire and recommend; and we would rather join ourselves to the church in which they abound, than to any other communion, however elated with the belief of its own orthodoxy, however strict in guarding its creed, however burning with zeal against imagined error.

I have thus given the distinguishing views of those Christians in whose names I have spoken. We have embraced this system, not hastily or lightly, but after much deliberation; and we hold it fast, not merely because we believe it to be true, but because we regard it as purifying truth, as a doctrine according to godliness, as able to "work mightily" and to "bring forth fruit" in them who believe. That we wish to spread it, we have no desire to conceal; but we think, that we wish its diffusion, because we regard it as more friendly to practical piety and pure morals than the opposite doctrines, because it gives clearer and nobler views of duty, and stronger motives to its performance, because it recommends religion at once to the understanding and the heart, because it asserts the lovely and venerable attributes of God, because it tends to restore the benevolent spirit of Jesus to his divided and afflicted church, and because it cuts off every hope of God's favor, except that which springs from practical conformity to the life and precepts of Christ. We see nothing in our views to give offence, save their purity, and it is their purity, which makes us seek and hope their extension through the world.

2.
"The Lord's Supper," Ralph Waldo Emerson

I proceed to state a few objections that in my judgment lie against its use in its present form.

1. If the view which I have taken of the history of the institution be correct, then the claim of authority should be dropped in administering it. You say, every time you celebrate the rite, that Jesus enjoined it; and the whole language you use conveys that impression. But if you read the New Testament as I do, you do not believe he did.

2. It has seemed to me that the use of this ordinance tends to produce confusion in our views of the relation of the soul to God. It is the old objection to the doctrine of the Trinity, — that the true worship was transferred from God to Christ, or that such confusion was introduced into the soul that an undivided worship was given nowhere. Is not that the effect of the Lord's Supper? I appeal now to the convictions of communicants, and ask such persons whether they have not been occasionally conscious of a painful confusion of thought between the worship due to God and the commemoration due to Christ. For the service does not stand upon the basis of a voluntary act, but is imposed by authority. It is an expression of gratitude to Christ, enjoined by Christ. There is an endeavor to keep Jesus in mind, whilst yet the prayers are addressed to God. I fear it is the effect of this ordinance to clothe Jesus with an authority which he never claimed and which distracts the mind of the worshipper. I know our opinions differ much respecting the nature and offices of Christ, and the degree of veneration to which he is entitled. I am so much a Unitarian

as this: that I believe the human mind can admit but one God, and that every effort to pay religious homage to more than one being, goes to take away all right ideas. I appeal, brethren, to your individual experience. In the moment when you make the least petition to God, though it be but a silent wish that he may approve you, or add one moment to your life, — do you not, in the very act, necessarily exclude all other beings from your thought? In that act, the soul stands alone with God, and Jesus is no more present to your mind than your brother or your child.

But is not Jesus called in Scripture the Mediator? He is the mediator in that only sense in which possibly any being can mediate between God and man, — that is, an instructor of man. He teaches us how to become like God. And a true disciple of Jesus will receive the light he gives most thankfully; but the thanks he offers, and which an exalted being will accept, are not compliments, commemorations, but the use of that instruction.

3. Passing other objections, I come to this, that the use of the elements, however suitable to the people and the modes of thought in the East, where it originated, is foreign and unsuited to affect us. Whatever long usage and strong association may have done in some individuals to deaden this repulsion, I apprehend that their use is rather tolerated than loved by any of us. We are not accustomed to express our thoughts or emotions by symbolical actions. Most men find the bread and wine no aid to devotion, and to some it is a painful impediment. To eat bread is one thing; to love the precepts of Christ and resolve to obey them is quite another.

The statement of this objection leads me to say that I think this difficulty, wherever it is felt, to be entitled to the greatest weight. It is alone a sufficient objection to the ordinance. It is my own objection. This mode of commemorating Christ is not suitable to me. That is reason enough why I should abandon it. If I believed it was enjoined by Jesus on his disciples, and that he even contemplated making permanent this mode of commemoration, every way agreeable to an Eastern mind, and yet on trial it was disagreeable to my own feelings, I should not adopt it. I should choose other ways which, as more effectual upon me, he would approve more. For I choose that my remembrances of him should be pleasing, affecting, religious. I will love him as a glorified friend, after the free way of friendship, and not pay him a stiff sign of respect, as men do those whom they fear. A passage read from his discourses, a moving provocation to works like his, any act or meeting which tends to awaken a pure thought, a flow of love, an original design of virtue, I call a worthy, a true commemoration.

4. The importance ascribed to this particular ordinance is not consistent with the spirit of Christianity. The general object and effect of the ordinance is unexceptionable. It has been, and is, I doubt not, the occasion of indefinite good; but an importance is given by Christians to it which never can belong to any form. My friends, the apostle well assures us that "the kingdom of God is

Ralph Waldo Emerson
(Art Resource, NY)

not meat and drink, but righteousness and peace and joy in the Holy Ghost." I am not so foolish as to declaim against forms. Forms are as essential as bodies; but to exalt particular forms, to adhere to one form a moment after it is outgrown, is unreasonable, and it is alien to the spirit of Christ. If I understand the distinction of Christianity, the reason why it is to be preferred over all other systems and is divine is this, that it is a moral system; that it presents men with truths which are their own reason, and enjoins practices that are their own justification; that if miracles may be said to have been its evidence to the first Christians, they are not its evidence to us, but the doctrines themselves; that every practice is Christian which praises itself, and every practice unchristian which condemns itself. I am not engaged to Christianity by decent forms, or saving ordinances; it is not usage, it is not what I do not understand, that binds me to it, — let these be the sandy foundations of falsehoods. What I revere and obey in it is its reality, its boundless charity, its deep interior life, the rest it gives to mind, the echo it returns to my thoughts, the perfect accord it makes with my reason through all its representation of God and His Providence; and the persuasion and courage that come out thence to lead me upward and onward. Freedom is the essence of this faith. It has for its object simply to make men good and wise. Its institutions then should be as flexible as the wants of men. That form out of which the life, and suitableness have departed, should be as worthless in its eyes as the dead leaves that are falling around us. . . .

. . . I have proposed to the brethren of the Church to drop the use of the elements and the claim of authority in the administration of this ordinance, and have suggested a mode in which a meeting for the same purpose might be held, free of objection.

My brethren have considered my views with patience and candor, and have recommended, unanimously, an adherence to the present form. I have therefore been compelled to consider whether it becomes me to administer it. I am clearly of opinion I ought not. This discourse has already been so far extended that I can only say that the reason of my determination is shortly this: — It is my desire, in the office of a Christian minister, to do nothing which I cannot do with my whole heart. Having said this, I have said all. I have no hostility to this institution; I am only stating my want of sympathy with it. Neither should I ever have obtruded this opinion upon other people, had I not been called by my office to administer it. That is the end of my opposition, that I am not interested in it. I am content that it stand to the end of the world, if it please men and please Heaven, and I shall rejoice in all the good it produces.

As it is the prevailing opinion and feeling in our religious community, that it is an indispensable part of the pastoral office to administer this ordinance, I am about to resign into your hands that office which you have confided to me. It has many duties for which I am feebly qualified. It has some which it will always be my delight to discharge according to my ability, wherever I exist.

And whilst the recollection of its claims oppresses me with a sense of my unworthiness, I am consoled by the hope that no time and no change can deprive me of the satisfaction of pursuing and exercising its highest functions.

Deism

Rejecting all special revelation and all institutional religion, deism moved well beyond either Universalism or Unitarianism in its abandonment of traditional Christianity. Since it opposed all churches, deism naturally had none of its own. And since it rejected all revelation, it naturally appealed to no scripture. Without priest or institution or dogma, it naturally did not survive — at least not as an identifiable "school" or movement. But many deist attitudes or concerns did survive, particularly since so many of the founding fathers were themselves deists. The deist contribution to the First Amendment has already been noted. Deist suspicion of speculative thought as well as the deist readiness to identify religion with morality characterizes much of American religion in subsequent years. (1) Thomas Paine (1737-1809) in his strident Age of Reason *(1794, 1796) represents deism in its most uncompromising, blunt, and unsophisticated form. (2) Thomas Jefferson and John Adams, reconciled in their post-presidential retirements, carried on a brilliant correspondence which dealt with religion among many other subjects. In their views, reason is honored, state support of religion scorned, and institutional religion eyed with grave suspicion.*

1.

Thomas Paine, from *The Age of Reason*

In the former part of *The Age of Reason* I have spoken of the three frauds, *mystery, miracle,* and *prophecy;* and as I have seen nothing in any of the answers to that work that in the least affects what I have there said upon those subjects, I shall not encumber this Second Part with additions that are not necessary.

I have spoken also in the same work upon what is called *revelation,* and have shewn the absurd misapplication of that term to the books of the Old Testament and the New, for certainly revelation is out of the question in reciting any thing of which man has been the actor or the witness. That which man has

---

[Source: (1) Moncure D. Conway, ed., *The Writings of Thomas Paine* (New York: AMS Press, 1967 [1896]), IV, 183-86. (2) Lester J. Cappon, ed., *The Adams-Jefferson Letters* (Chapel Hill: University of North Carolina Press, 1959), II, 372-75, 512.]

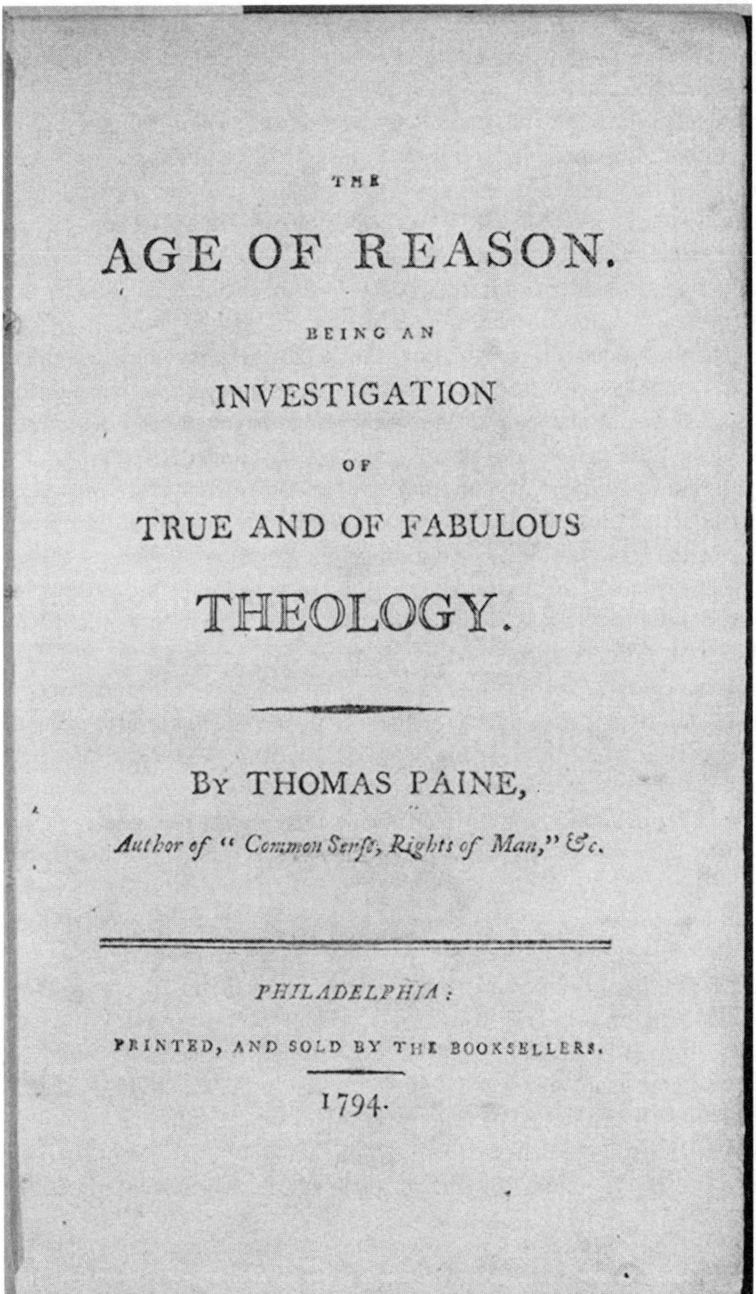

THE

AGE OF REASON.

BEING AN

INVESTIGATION

OF

TRUE AND OF FABULOUS

THEOLOGY.

By THOMAS PAINE,

Author of " Common Sense, Rights of Man," &c.

PHILADELPHIA:

PRINTED, AND SOLD BY THE BOOKSELLERS.

1794.

Cover, *Age of Reason*
(Library of Congress)

done or seen, needs no revelation to tell him he has done it, or seen it — for he knows it already — nor to enable him to tell it or to write it. It is ignorance, or imposition, to apply the term revelation in such cases; yet the Bible and Testament are classed under this fraudulent description of being all *revelation.* . . .

But though, speaking for myself, I thus admit the possibility of revelation, I totally disbelieve that the Almighty ever did communicate any thing to man, by any mode of speech, in any language, or by any kind of vision, or appearance, or by any means which our senses are capable of receiving, otherwise than by the universal display of himself in the works of the creation, and by that repugnance we feel in ourselves to bad actions, and disposition to good ones.

The most detestable wickedness, the most horrid cruelties, and the greatest miseries, that have afflicted the human race, have had their origin in this thing called revelation, or revealed religion. It has been the most dishonourable belief against the character of the divinity, the most destructive to morality and the peace and happiness of man, that ever was propagated since man began to exist. It is better, far better, that we admitted, if it were possible, a thousand devils to roam at large, and to preach publicly the doctrine of devils, if there were any such, than that we permitted one such impostor and monster as Moses, Joshua, Samuel and the Bible prophets, to come with the pretended word of God in his mouth, and have credit among us.

Whence arose all the horrid assassinations of whole nations of men, women, and infants, with which the Bible is filled; and the bloody persecutions, and tortures unto death and religious wars, that since that time have laid Europe in blood and ashes; whence arose they, but from this impious thing called revealed religion, and this monstrous belief that God has spoken to man? The lies of the Bible have been the cause of the one, and the lies of the Testament [of] the other. . . .

It is incumbent on every man who reverences the character of the Creator, and who wishes to lessen the catalogue of artificial miseries, and remove the cause that has sown persecutions thick among mankind, to expel all ideas of a revealed religion as a dangerous heresy, and an impious fraud. What is it that we have learned from this pretended thing called revealed religion? Nothing that is useful to man, and everything that is dishonourable to his Maker. What is it the Bible teaches us? — rapine, cruelty, and murder. What is it the Testament teaches us? — to believe that the Almighty committed debauchery with a woman engaged to be married; and the belief of this debauchery is called faith.

2.
Jefferson-Adams Correspondence

Adams to Jefferson

Quincy Sept. 14. 1813

Dear Sir

. . . The human Understanding is a revelation from its Maker which can never be disputed or doubted. There can be no Scepticism, Pyrrhonism or Incredulity or Infidelity here. No Prophecies, no Miracles are necessary to prove this celestial communication. This revelation has made it certain that two and one make three; and that one is not three; nor can three be one. We can never be so certain of any Prophecy, or the fullfillment of any Prophecy; or of any miracle, or the design of any miracle as We are, from the revelation of nature i.e. natures God that two and two are equal to four. Miracles or Prophecies might frighten Us out of our Witts; might scare us to death; might induce Us to lie; to say that We believe that 2 and 2 make 5. But We should not believe it. We should know the contrary.

Had you and I been forty days with Moses on Mount Sinai and admitted to behold, the divine Shekinah, and there told that one was three and three, one: We might not have had courage to deny it, but We could not have believed it. The thunders and Lightenings and Earthqu[ak]es and the transcendant Splendors and Glories, might have overwhelmed Us with terror and Amazement: but We could not have believed the doctrine. We should be more likely to say in our hearts, whatever We might say with our Lips, This is Chance. There is no God! No Truth. This is all delusion, fiction and a lie: or it is all Chance. But what is Chance? It is motion; it is Action; it is Event; it is Phenomenon, without Cause. Chance is no cause at all. It is nothing. And Nothing has produced all this Pomp and Splendor; and Nothing may produce Our eternal damnation in the flames of Hell fire and Brimstone for what We know, as well as this tremendous Exhibition of Terror and Falshood.

God has infinite Wisdom, goodness and power. He created the Universe. His duration is eternal, a parte Ante, and a parte post. His presence is as extensive as Space. What is Space? an infinite, spherical Vaccuum. He created this Speck of Dirt and the human Species for his glory: and with the deliberate design of making, nine tenths of our Species miserable forever, for his glory. This is the doctrine of Christian Theologians in general: ten to one.

Now, my Friend, can Prophecies, or miracles convince You, or Me, that infinite Benevolence, Wisdom and Power, created and preserves, for a time, innumerable millions to make them miserable, forever; for his own Glory? Wretch! What is his Glory? Is he ambitious? does he want promotion? Is he vain, tickled with Adulation? Exulting and tryumphing in his Power and the Sweetness of his

Vengeance? Pardon me, my Maker, for these Aweful Questions. My Answer to them is always ready: I believe no such Things. My Adoration of the Author of the Universe is too profound and too sincere. The Love of God and his Creation; delight, Joy, Tryumph, Exultation in my own existence, 'tho but an Atom, a Molecule Organique, in the Universe; are my religion. Howl, Snarl, bite, Ye Calvinistick! Ye Athanasian Divines, if You will. Ye will say, I am no Christian: I say Ye are no Christians: and there the Account is ballanced. Yet I believe all the honest men among you, are Christians in my Sense of the Word. . . .

When I was in England from 1785, to 1788 I may say, I was intimate with Dr. [Richard] Price. I had much conversation with him at his own House, at my houses, and at the houses and Tables of many Friends. In some of our most unreserved Conversations, when We have been alone, he has repeatedly said to me "I am inclined to believe that the Universe, is eternal and infinite. It seems to me that an eternal and infinite Effect, must necessarily flow from an eternal infinite Cause; and an infinite Wisdom Goodness and Power, that could have been induced to produce a Universe in time, must have produced it from eternity." "It seems to me, the Effect must flow from the Cause."

Now, my Friend Jefferson, suppose an eternal self existent Being existing from Eternity, possessed of infinite Wisdom, Goodness and Power, in absolute total Solitude, Six thousand Years ago, conceiving the benevolent project of creating a Universe! I have no more to say, at present.

It has been long, very long a settled opinion in my Mind that there is now, never will be, and never was but one being who can Understand the Universe. And that it is not only vain but wicked for insects to pretend to comprehend it.

JOHN ADAMS

Jefferson to Adams

Monticello. May 5. 17.

Dear Sir

. . . Your recommendations are always welcome, for indeed the subjects of them always merit that welcome, and some of them in an extraordinary degree. They make us acquainted with what there is of excellent in our ancient sister state of Massachusets, once venerated and beloved, and still hanging on our hopes, for what need we despair of after the resurrection of Connecticut to light and liberality. I had believed that, the last retreat of Monkish darkness, bigotry, and abhorrence of those advances of the mind which had carried the other states a century ahead of them. They seemed still to be exactly where their forefathers were when they schismatised from the Covenant of works, and to consider, as dangerous heresies, all innovations good or bad. I join you therefore in sincere congratulations that this den of the priesthood is at length broken up, and that a protestant popedom is no longer to disgrace the American history and character. If, by *religion,* we are to understand *Sectarian dogmas,* in which no two of them agree, then your exclamation on that hypothesis is just, 'that this would be the best of all possible worlds, if there were no religion in it.' But if the moral precepts, innate in man, and made a part of his physical constitution, as necessary for a social being, if the sublime doctrines of philanthropism, and deism taught us by Jesus of Nazareth in which all agree, constitute true religion, then, without it, this would be, as you again say, 'something not fit to be named, even indeed a Hell.'

TH: JEFFERSON

Religion, Evangelical and Hierarchical

Methodism (White)

American Methodism, initially a mere appendage to the Wesleyan societies formed within the Church of England, gained its ecclesiastical independence shortly after the United States had won its political independence. In the famous "Christmas Conference" gathered in Baltimore in 1784, the Methodist Episcopal Church was born. Tending that birth was Dr. Thomas Coke (1747-1813), who presided as John Wesley's personal representative. The infant was soon delivered, however, into the hands of Francis Asbury (1745-1816), who emerged as the father of American Methodism. Coke and Asbury served for a time jointly as superintendents or bishops, but Coke grew increasingly involved in Methodist matters back in England. Asbury remained steadfastly American and steadfastly in America, setting the pattern for the kind of itinerant ministry which chiefly characterized Methodism throughout the nineteenth century. The Christmas Conference had much to do — and do quickly. For the rapidly growing Methodist movement needed direction, organization, encouragement, and leadership, all at once. Symptomatic of the rush was the ordination of Francis Asbury one day as deacon, the next day as elder, and the day after that as superintendent (or bishop, as he preferred to say). This was only one of the actions taken in "great haste, and . . . in a little time."

[Source: *The Journals and Letters of Francis Asbury* (Nashville: Abingdon Press, 1958), I, 474, 476.]

We then rode to Baltimore, where we met a few preachers: it was agreed to form ourselves into an Episcopal Church, and to have superintendents, elders, and deacons. When the conference was seated, Dr. Coke and myself were unanimously elected to the superintendency of the Church, and my ordination followed, after being previously ordained deacon and elder, as by the following certificate may be seen.

Know all men by these presents, That I, Thomas Coke, Doctor of Civil Law; late of Jesus College, in the University of Oxford, Presbyter of the Church of England, and Superintendent of the Methodist Episcopal Church in America; un-

"Cradle of Methodism," Barrett's Chapel near Frederick, Maryland
Entering Maryland before 1770, Methodists soon dominated the state.
Robert Strawbridge formed this first society on Pipe Creek as other
lay leaders introduced Methodism into New York.
(Keystone-Mast Collection, University of California, Riverside)

der the protection of Almighty God, and with a single eye to his glory; by the imposition of my hands, and prayer, (being assisted by two ordained elders,) did on the twenty-fifth day of this month, December, set apart Francis Asbury for the office of a deacon in the aforesaid Methodist Episcopal Church. And also on the twenty-sixth day of the said month, did by the imposition of my hands, and prayer, (being assisted by the said elders,) set apart the said Francis Asbury for the office of elder in the said Methodist Episcopal Church. And on this twenty-seventh day of the said month, being the day of the date hereof, have, by the imposition of my hands, and prayer, (being assisted by the said elders,) set apart the said Francis Asbury for the office of a superintendent in the said Methodist Episcopal Church, a man whom I judge to be well qualified for that great work. And I do hereby recommend him to all whom it may concern, as a fit person to preside over the flock of Christ. In testimony whereof I have hereunto set my hand and seal this twenty-seventh day of December, in the year of our Lord 1784.

Thomas Coke.

Twelve elders were elected, and solemnly set apart to serve our societies in the United States, one for Antigua, and two for Nova Scotia. We spent the whole week in conference, debating freely, and determining all things by a majority of votes. The Doctor preached every day at noon, and some one of the other preachers morning and evening. We were in great haste, and did much business in a little time.

Methodism (Black)

From the seventeenth century into the eighteenth and beyond, the general pattern of religious worship was for blacks and whites to attend the same services (though seating might be separate). Not long after the Christmas Conference, however, black Methodists began to seek their own ecclesiastical fellowship. Under the leadership of ex-slave Richard Allen (1760-1831), the African Methodist Episcopal Church emerged in 1816 as the nation's first denomination specifically for blacks. In the excerpt below, Allen tells of the early struggles (beginning in 1787), the initial opposition to the forming of a separate denomination, and of his biding loyalty — despite this opposition — to Methodism. Methodism, he explained, had done much for him and his people and he would not forsake it. Its "plain and simple gospel," moreover, had wide appeal, and its discipline possessed much merit.

[Source: *The Life Experience and Gospel Labors of the Rt. Rev. Richard Allen* (New York: Abingdon Press, 1960 [1793]), pp. 28-30.]

Richard Allen
(National Portrait Gallery, Smithsonian Institution, Washington, D.C.)

We bore much persecution from many of the Methodist connection; but we have reason to be thankful to Almighty God, who was our deliverer. The day was appointed to go and dig the cellar. I arose early in the morning and addressed the throne of grace, praying that the Lord would bless our endeavors. Having by this time two or three teams of my own — as I was the first proposer of the African church, I put the first spade in the ground to dig a cellar for the same. This was the first African Church or meetinghouse that was erected in the United States of America. We intended it for the African preaching house or church; but finding that the elder stationed in this city was such an opposer to our proceedings of erecting a place of worship, though the principal part of the directors of this church belonged to the Methodist connection, the elder stationed here would neither preach for us, nor have anything to do with us. We then held an election, to know what religious denomination we should unite with. At the election it was determined — there were two in favor of the Methodist, the Rev. Absalom Jones and myself, and a large majority in favor of the Church of England. The majority carried. Notwithstanding we had been so violently persecuted by the elder, we were in favor of being attached to the Methodist connection; for I was confident that there was no religious sect or denom-ination would suit the capacity of the colored people as well as the Methodist; for the plain and simple gospel suits best for any people; for the unlearned can understand, and the learned are sure to understand; and the reason that the Methodist is so successful in the awakening and conversion of the colored peo-ple, the plain doctrine and having a good discipline. But in many cases the preachers would act to please their own fancy, without discipline, till some of them became such tyrants, and more especially to the colored people. They would turn them out of society, giving them no trial, for the smallest offense, perhaps only hearsay. They would frequently, in meeting the class, impeach some of the members of whom they had heard an ill report, and turn them out,

Absalom Jones
Ordained by Bishop William White of the Protestant
Episcopal Church, Absalom Jones was chosen in 1796
to lead the African Episcopal Church
of St. Thomas in Philadelphia.
(National Portrait Gallery, Smithsonian Institution, Washington, D.C.
On indefinite loan from the Wilmington Society of Fine Arts, Delaware Art Museum)

saying, "I have heard thus and thus of you, and you are no more a member of society" — without witnesses on either side. This has been frequently done, notwithstanding in the first rise and progress in Delaware state, and elsewhere, the colored people were their greatest support; for there were but few of us free; but the slaves would toil in their little patches many a night until midnight to raise their little truck and sell to get something to support them more than what their masters gave them, but we used often to divide our little support among the white preachers of the Gospel. This was once a quarter. It was in the time of the old Revolutionary War between Great Britain and the United States. The Methodists were the first people that brought glad tidings to the colored people. I feel thankful that ever I heard a Methodist preach. We are beholden to the Methodists, under God, for the light of the Gospel we enjoy; for all other denominations preached so high-flown that we were not able to comprehend their doctrine; Sure am I that reading sermons will never prove so beneficial to the colored people as spiritual or extempore preaching. I am well convinced that the Methodist has proved beneficial to thousands and ten times thousands. It is to be awfully feared that the simplicity of the Gospel that was among them fifty years ago, and that they conform more to the world and the fashions thereof, they would fare very little better than the people of the world. The discipline is altered considerably from what it was. We would ask for the good old way, and desire to walk therein.

In 1793 a committee was appointed from the African Church to solicit me to be their minister, for there was no colored preacher in Philadelphia but myself. I told them I could not accept of their offer, as I was a Methodist. I was indebted to the Methodists, under God, for what little religion I had; being convinced that they were the people of God, I informed them that I could not be anything else but a Methodist, as I was born and awakened under them, and I could go no further with them, for I was a Methodist, and would leave you in peace and love.

Roman Catholicism

As noted many times in earlier chapters, Roman Catholicism found scant favor in British North America, especially anywhere outside of Maryland. And in the New Republic Catholics, despite the generous assurances of George Washington, still had good reason to be wary of their neighbors. They also had to be wary of Europe's Catholics (and the Vatican) who generally saw

[Source: Peter Guilday, *The Life and Times of John Carroll* (Westminster, Md.: The Newman Press, 1954 [1922]), pp. 225-27.]

democracy as a form of radicalism and religious liberty as encouragement of error. The young American Church had much going against it, but it had John Carroll (1735-1815) going for it. A native of Maryland who went abroad to receive Jesuit training for the priesthood, Carroll returned home in 1774 to tend to the scattered Catholic missions as best he could. In 1784 he was named Vicar Apostolic for the United States (later bishop, then archbishop of Baltimore). The Vatican sought a report on the condition of the Roman Catholic Church in America, requesting a Relation from Carroll. By correspondence, Carroll gathered as much information as possible from his fellow clergy over a period of three or four months. Then on March 1, 1785, he sent to Leonardo Cardinal Antonelli the following account.

1. On the Number of Catholics in the United States.

There are in Maryland about 15,800 Catholics; of these there are about 9,000 freemen, adults or over twelve years of age; children under that age, about 3,000; and about that number of slaves of all ages of African origin, called negroes. There are in Pennsylvania about 7,000, very few of whom are negroes, and the Catholics are less scattered and live nearer to each other. There are not more than 200 in Virginia who are visited four or five times a year by a priest. Many other Catholics are said to be scattered in that and other states, who are utterly deprived of all religious ministry. In the State of New York I hear there are at least 1,500. (Would that some spiritual succor could be afforded them!) They have recently, at their own expense, sent for a Franciscan Father from Ireland, and he is said to have the best testimonials as to his learning and life; he had arrived a little before I received the letters in which faculties were transmitted to me, communicable to my fellow-priests. I was for a time in doubt whether I could properly approve this priest for the administration of the sacraments. I have now, however, decided, especially as the feast of Easter is so near, to consider him as one of my fellow-priests, and to grant him faculties, and I trust that my decision will meet your approbation. As to the Catholics who are in the territory bordering on the river called Mississippi and in all that region which following that river extends to the Atlantic Ocean, and from it extends to the limits of Carolina, Virginia, and Pennsylvania — this tract of country contains, I hear, many Catholics, formerly Canadians, who speak French, and I fear that they are destitute of priests. Before I received your Eminence's letters there went to them a priest, German by birth, but who came last from France; he professes to belong to the Carmelite order; he was furnished with no sufficient testimonials that he was sent by his lawful superior. What he is doing and what is the condition of the Church in those parts, I expect soon to learn. The jurisdiction of the Bishop of Quebec formerly extended to some part of

John Carroll
(National Portrait Gallery, Smithsonian Institution, Washington, D.C.)

that region; but I do not know whether he wishes to exercise any authority there, now that all these parts are subject to the United States.

2. On the Condition, Piety, and Defects, etc., of Catholics:

In Maryland a few of the leading more wealthy families still profess the Catholic faith introduced at the very foundation of the province by their ancestors. The greater part of them are planters and in Pennsylvania almost all are farmers, except the merchants and mechanics living in Philadelphia. As for piety, they are for the most part sufficiently assiduous in the exercises of religion and in frequenting the sacraments, but they lack that fervor, which frequent appeals to the sentiment of piety usually produce, as many congregations hear the word of God only once a month, and sometimes only once in two months. We are reduced to this by want of priests, by the distance of congregations from each other and by difficulty of travelling. This refers to Catholics born here, for the condition of the Catholics who in great numbers are flowing in here from different countries of Europe, is very different. For while there are few of our na-

tive Catholics who do not approach the sacraments of Penance and the Holy
Eucharist, at least once a year, especially in Easter time, you can scarcely find
any among the newcomers who discharge this duty to religion, and there is reason to fear that the example will be very pernicious especially in commercial
towns. The abuses that have grown among Catholics are chiefly those, which result from unavoidable intercourse with non-Catholics, and the examples
thence derived: namely more free intercourse between young people of opposite sexes than is compatible with chastity in mind and body; too great fondness
for dances and similar amusements; and an incredible eagerness, especially in
girls, for reading love stories which are brought over in great quantities from
Europe. Then among other things, a general lack of care in instructing their
children and especially the negro slaves in their religion, as these people are
kept constantly at work, so that they rarely hear any instructions from the
priest, unless they can spend a short time with one; and most of them are consequently very dull in faith and depraved in morals. It can scarcely be believed
how much trouble and care they give the pastors of souls.

3. On the Number of the Priests, Their Qualifications, Character and Means of Support.

There are nineteen priests in Maryland and five in Pennsylvania. Of these two
are more than seventy years old, and three others very near that age: and they
are consequently almost entirely unfit to undergo the hardships, without which
this Vineyard of the Lord cannot be cultivated. Of the remaining priests, some
are in very bad health, and there is one recently approved by me for a few
months only, that in the extreme want of priests I may give him a trial; for some
doings were reported of him which made me averse to employing him. I will
watch him carefully, and if anything occurs unworthy of priestly gravity I will
recall the faculties granted, whatever inconvenience this may bring to many
Catholics: for I am convinced that the Catholic faith will suffer less harm, if for
a short time there is no priest at a place, than if living as we do among fellow-
citizens of another religion, we admit to the discharge of the sacred ministry, I
do not say bad priests, but incautious and imprudent priests. All the other clergymen lead a life full of labour, as each one attends congregations far apart, and
has to be riding constantly and with great fatigue, especially to sick calls. Priests
are maintained chiefly from the proceeds of the estates; elsewhere by the liberality of the Catholics. There is properly no ecclesiastical property here: for the
property by which the priests are supported, is held in the names of individuals
and transferred by will to devisees. This course was rendered necessary when
the Catholic religion was cramped here by laws, and no remedy has yet been
found for this difficulty, although we made an earnest effort last year. There is a

college in Philadelphia, and it is proposed to establish two in Maryland, in which Catholics can be admitted, as well as others, as presidents, professors and pupils. We hope that some educated there will embrace the ecclesiastical state. We think accordingly of establishing a Seminary, in which they can be trained to the life and learning suited to that state.

The Practice of Piety

Susanna Anthony of Newport

Samuel Hopkins (1721-1803) was a student of Jonathan Edwards who pastored the First Congregational Church in Newport, Rhode Island, where he offered special encouragement to those in his congregation who sought to live according to the highest standards of awakened piety. One such woman was Susanna Anthony (1726-1791) who had been converted in 1741 just as the fervor of the First Great Awakening was rising to its peak. After Hopkins moved to Newport in 1770, Anthony began exchanging letters with her pastor, who arranged to have some of these letters and extensive extracts from her journal published after her death. These writings reveal a precise Christian along historic Puritan lines who battled throughout a long life against herself, her environment, and her sense of sin. Anthony's religious life was noteworthy (1) for its remarkable sense of personal struggle, which is illustrated here in journal entries from the mid-1750s. But it was also often marked by (2) a strong sense of spiritual exaltation, as illustrated in letters she wrote to her pastor. Anthony was the sixth child in a family of seven daughters; she never married, but was noteworthy for many years in attending Newport's sick and dying.

January 31st, 1755 — I have been all this week trying to spend a day, or part of a day, with God in secret; but every day has had its necessary incumbrances, clog and hindrance. Last night had some glimpse of light, peace, joy and confidence in God; but it was soon gone. This day I have set myself to prayer, and reviewing my various experiences, if possible to give a turn to my mind; but I

[Source: *The Life and Character of Miss Susanna Anthony, who died, in Newport (R.I.) (June 23, MDCCXCI, in the sixty fifth year of her age. Consisting chiefly in Extracts from her Writings . . . Compiled by Samuel Hopkins* (Worcester, Mass.: Leonard Worcester, 1796), pp. 130-31, 178-79.]

scarce know what I am about. My head is pained, confused and bewildered, so that I get lost. My heart, I know not what it is. I always found it wicked; but I have little humbling sense of it now. I tell God, I am as vile a wretch as ever lived; but I am not affected with it. I tell him, I want none but him; that he is the only real good; but I feel no realizing sense of his divine, infinite excellence. I believe these things, because I once felt the power of them; and not because I now see. My eyes run down with tears, while I express these things, before my more flapid [?] heart is affected. O what a soul have I! The members and organs of my body are more affected than that: My tongue to complain, my eyes to weep.

Feb. 1st. I was forced from those duties yesterday; my bodily illness increasing so that I was scarce able to hold up my head. And this day I find myself to disordered, that I can attend on no duty with any fixed engagedness. Well, my God, I am thine. Let me not repine; but quietly bear they hand.

Feb. 1st. At night. Blessed by God for nearer access, and enlargement in prayer, with two or three christian friends, this afternoon; and some freedom this night, though attended with bodily disorders. O when will the happy day of release arrive!

July 3rd, 1755. Fast day. Much incumbered last night; unfit for preparation for the exercises of this day: And so awaked this morning, unsettled as to the particular duties of the day. Yet God graciously afforded some near and lively access to him, in prayer for Zion, both in secret, public and private. My soul reached after God, and laid hold on the truth, faithfulness, and almighty power of Jehovah, and head of the church. Sure I am, without a scruple, that I prefer Jerusalem to my chief joy. I almost forget my own private and spiritual concerns, only as they stand in relation to, and are included in, the prosperity of Zion. If Christ has a church in the world, and they are all united together, as members in the body, and united to Christ, as their head, I surely feel the inseparable union, beyond all the ties of nature, or law of common friendship. Strong influence, powerful efficacy! But weary and spent in family and secret duties at night. O frail and faultering [?] flesh! When shall I get free!

April 21, 1774.

Reverend and dear Sir,

GOD has of late been calling up my attention to solemn and tender scenes. I have felt the ties of nature, and I hope the tender bonds of christian affection [?], to one of the best of mothers, a member of Christ, in pain and distress, under great infirmities, to a very sensible degree: Under which the infinitely condescending Jehovah has set himself before me, as so infinitely fit to govern, and worthy to be submitted to, yea, rejoiced in, in every dispensation, that I have been constrained to say, Surely there needs no more to make all heaven and earth rejoice, than to know that this God reigns. O where can there be any true pleasure, but in a heart wholly disposed to close in with every exhibition that Jehovah makes of himself, as well in the judgments of his hands, as the laws of his mouth? O what a fountain of inexpressible pleasure overflows and sweetens the bitterest waters of Marah, in that single sentence, It is the Lord, THE LORD!

But, here I pause — while tears of admiration and joy are my highest expression! Fain would I lisp his praises! Fain would I speak of his glories! But O! I find I do not feel what I ought; nor can I express what I feel. When shall my soul be unfettered! When shall the heart of the rash understand! When shall the stammerer speak plain! O when shall my whole soul unite in the most perfect manner, strongest degree and universal extent, to every exhibition of the unbounded, infinite, glorious rectitude and perfection of Jehovah's nature and government! But, instead of this, is it possible that I shall again take back what I have said? God has of late made me repeatedly confess that he doth all things well, and, as it were, crowd all things into his hands, professing my hearty subjection to him, and his government. I have been calling him Lord and King; owning his infinite right and fitness to govern; recounting his mighty deeds; proclaiming his sovereign authority; exclaiming against every degree of opposition to him, and his government; judging and condemning to utter destruction all his implacable enemies. And O, now, how infinitely aggravated must my guilt be, if, on trial, I do in the least degree retract, or take back what I have said! But such an heart I know I have in me: And, therefore, if after all I should perish, out of my own mouth I am condemned: And if saved, sovereign grace shall have all the glory. O how infinitely wise and good this constitution! How rich, how free the grace that comes to sinners through Jesus Christ!

John Leland of New England and Virginia

John Leland, who is introduced below (pp. 301-3) as a strong advocate of Jeffersonian freedom, was also an earnest and life-long preacher of traditional evangelical faith. He was also a notable hymn-writer who tried to capture in verse what he preached in a long career that took him from his native Massachusetts through a long sojourn in Virginia and then back to his native ground. The hymns communicate much of what people were hearing from such itinerants as Leland, but also much of what such preachers were trying to say.

[Source: L. F. Greene, ed., *The Writings of the Late Elder John Leland* . . . (New York: Arno Press, 1969 [1845]), pp. 322-24, 325-26.]

Invitation to Pilgrims.

Wand'ring pilgrims, mourning Christians,
　　Weak and tempted lambs of Christ,
Who endure great tribulation,
　　And with sin are much distressed;
Christ hath sent me to invite you,
　　To a rich and costly feast;
Let not shame nor pride prevent you, —
　　Come, — the rich provision taste.

If you have a heart lamenting,
　　And bemoan your wretched case,
Come to Jesus Christ repenting;
　　He will give you gospel grace;
If you want a heart to fear him,
　　Love and serve him all your days;
Come to Jesus Christ and ask him;
　　He will guide you in his ways.

If your heart is unbelieving,
　　Doubting Jesus' pard'ning love,
Lie hard by Bethesda waiting
　　Till the troubled waters move.
If no man appear to help you,
　　All their efforts prove but talk,
Jesus, Jesus, he can heal you,
　　Rise, take up your bed and walk.

If, like Peter, you are sinking
　　In the sea of unbelief,
Wait with patience, constant praying,
　　Christ will send you sweet relief;
He will give you grace and glory,
　　All your wants shall be supplied;
Canaan, Canaan, lies before you,
　　Rise and cross the swelling tide.

Death shall not destroy your comfort,
　　Christ will guard you thro' the gloom;
Down he'll send a heavenly envoy,
　　To convey your spirit home;

There, you'll spend your days in pleasure,
    Free from every want and care;
Come, oh come, my blessed Saviour,
    Fain my spirit would be there.

The Intercession of Christ.

Now the Saviour stands a pleading,
    At the sinner's bolted heart;
Now in heaven he's interceding,
    Undertaking sinner's part;
Now he pleads his sweat and blood-shed,
    Shows his wounded hands and feet;
Father, save them, though they're blood-red,
    Raise them to a heavenly seat.

Sinners, hear your God and Saviour,
    Hear his gracious voice to-day;
Turn from all your vain behaviour,
    O repent, return, and pray;
Open now your hearts before him,
    Bid the Saviour welcome in,
O receive and glad adore him,
    Take a full discharge from sin.

Now he's waiting to be gracious,
    Now he stands and looks at thee;
See, what kindness, love and pity,
    Shine around to you and me;
Sinners, can you hate that Saviour?
    Can you thrust him from your arms?
Once he died for your behaviour,
    Now he calls you by his charms.

O be wise, before you languish
    On a bed of dying strife;
Endless joy or endless anguish,
    Turn upon th' events of life;
Come, for all things now are ready,
    Yet there's room for many more;
O ye blind, ye lame and needy,
    Come to grace's boundless store.

The Preacher's Life.

How arduous is the preacher's fight!
　　What pangs his vitals feel!
To preach the gospel day and night,
　　To hearts as hard as steel.

While some blaspheme and show their spite,
　　And mock at all they hear,
Others, in chase of vain delight,
　　Like adders, stop the ear.

To heaven he turns his weeping eyes,
　　To antidote despair,
With broken heart, and longing eyes,
　　He tries the effect of prayer.

If God, propitious, hear his cry,
　　And some small fruit he see,
How soon the hopeful prospects die,
　　How short the jubilee.

When sinners hear the Saviour's voice,
　　And feel the power divine,
The preacher's heart and soul rejoice,
　　To see the gospel shine.

What courage, faith, and holy zeal,
　　Transport his ravished breast,
What inward joy his spirits feel,
　　To see his labors blessed.

But ah! how short the shining day;
　　How soon the night appears!
All those of Asia turn away,
　　How gloomy then his fears!

Good God! he cries, with anxious breast,
　　Are all my labors vain?
Must all the lambs and sheep of Christ,
　　Turn goats and wolves again?

Elizabeth Ann Seton of Baltimore

Elizabeth Ann Bayley Seton (1774-1821) grew up in New York as the daughter of a noted physician, and as an Episcopalian. In 1794 she married the son of a well-to-do New York merchant. The couple had five children before business reverses led to bankruptcy; William Seton died soon thereafter in Italy where the family had gone for reasons of his health. In Italy Elizabeth Seton found herself drawn to the Catholic Church, where she was instructed by, among others, Antonio Filicchi, to whom the letter that follows was addressed. After she returned to the United States, Elizabeth was admonished by Episcopal leaders, including John Henry Hobart (the "Mr. H." of the letter), but she persevered in her new course and became a Catholic on March 15, 1805. Soon she opened a school for girls in Baltimore, which led on to the founding in 1809 of the Sisters of Charity, one of the first Catholic religious orders in America. She gave the rest of her short life to promoting education for girls and providing needed care for the sick. In 1975 she was named the first American-born saint in the Catholic church. The letter below portrays some of the intense internal deliberation that led her to enter the Church of Rome.

27th September 1804

Most dear friend and Brother

It is necessary to lay the restraint of Discretion on my pen while I thank you for your letter of the 20th which though but two hours ago recieved has been already read over many times — the pen is restrained, but the heart which is before God blesses and adores him in unbounded thanksgiving for such a friend — your goodness to me he only can reward. —

to answer you fully now would not be proper in any way, especially as you see my poor Soul is still more unsettled and perplexed from day to day, not from any failure in its prayers or intreaties to God which are rather redoubled than neglected, but like a Bird struggling in a net it cannot escape its fears and tremblings —

This afternoon after dismissing the children to play, I went to my knees in my little closet to consider what I should do, and how my Sacred duty would direct — Should I again read those Books I first recieved from Mr. H.? my heart revolted, for I know there are all the *black accusations* and the Sum of them too sensibly torment my Soul — Should I again go over those of the Catholick Doctrine though every page I read is familiar to me and my memory represents in

---

[Source: Ellin Kelly and Annabelle Melville, eds., *Elizabeth Seton: Selected Writings*, Sources of American Spirituality (New York: Paulist, 1987), pp. 147-49.]

rotation, the different instructions and replies? — since your absence I have read the book your Brother first gave me and the one you also gave, with the most careful attention — not only with attention but always with Prayer — and now must look up to that as my only refuge, Prayer at all times, in all places —

really Antonio my most dear Brother to whom I can speak every secret of my Soul, I *have* and *do* pray so much that it seems every thought is Prayer, and when I awake from my short sleeps my mind seems to have been praying — and the poor eyes are really almost blind with incessant tears — for can I pray for such a favor without a beating heart and torrents of tears — my children say "poor Mamma," continually and really are better than they were that they may not add to my Sorrow — Yet sweet are these tears, and sweet are the sorrows, great is my comfort that though the Almighty source of Light does not visit me with his blessed light, yet he does not leave me contented and insensible in my darkness —

29th　　This day has been a feast day to the children and a holiday from school that I might give the greatest portion of the hours to God — you would have been pleased to hear their questions about *St. Michael* and how eagerly they listened to the history of the good offices done to us by the Blessed angels, and of St. Michael driving Lucifer out of heaven etc. they always wait on their knees after prayers till I bless them each with the Sign of the Cross and I look up to God with a humble hope that he will not forsake us —

I could tell you many things my Brother but must wait for the much wished for hour when we shall be seated with our big book at the table — *I* could cry out now as my poor Seton used to Antonio Antonio Antonio, but call back the thought and my Soul cries out Jesus Jesus Jesus — there it finds rest, and heavenly Peace, and is hushed by that dear Sound as my little Babe is quieted by my cradle song —

The Jesus Psalter in the little Book you gave me is my favourite office because it so often repeats that name — and when thought goes to you Antonio and imagines you in the promiscuous company you must meet, without any solid gratification — fatigued by your excursions, *wandering in your fancy* etc. etc. etc. etc. Oh how I pray that the Holy Spirit may not leave you and that your dear Angel may even *pinch* you at *the* hour of Prayers rather than suffer you to neglect them.

you charge me not to neglect the lives of the Saints — which I could not if I would, for they interest me so much that the little time I can catch for reading is all given to them, indeed they are a relaxation to my mind, for they lessen all my troubles and make them as nothing by comparison — when I read that St. Austin was long in a fluctuating state of mind between error and truth, I say to myself be Patient, God will bring you Home at last — and as for the lessons of self denial and Poverty if St. Francis De Sales and the Life of our dear Master had not before pointed out to me the many virtues and graces that accompany them I should even wish for them to be like these dear dear Saints in any respect —

Antonio Antonio why cannot my poor Soul be satisfied that your religion is now the same that theirs then was — how can it hesitate — why must it struggle — the Almighty only can decide —

do my Brother tell me something about yourself you certainly must know how grateful even the smallest particular is to an absent friend always anxious for your happiness and wellfare — I am ashamed of my own letters they are all Egotism but my Soul is so intirely engrossed by one subject that it cannot speak with freedom on any other — day after day passes and I see no one, indeed I can say with perfect truth at all times I prefer my Solitude to the company of any human being except that of my most dear A. you know my heart you know my thoughts, my pains and sorrows hopes and fears — Johnathan loved David as his own Soul and if I was your Brother, Antonio I would never leave you for one hour — but as it is I try rather to turn every affection to God, well knowing that there alone their utmost exercise cannot be misapplied and most ardent hopes can never be disappointed —

Religion in the Young Republic

While the first federal census was taken in 1790, no attempt was then made to gather any data about religion. For a profile of religion in the new nation, one is therefore dependent upon less systematic observing and reporting. The "father of American geography," Congregational clergyman Jedidiah Morse (1761-1826), first published his American Geography *in 1789. In this and many succeeding editions be gave considerable attention to religion. In the excerpts below, taken from his second edition, one may get acquainted with Morse (for example, his views on slavery and the Protestant work ethic) at the same time that one learns more about the distribution of denominations in the America of the 1790s.*

[United States]. From the best accounts that can at present be obtained, there are, within the limits of the United States, three millions, eighty three thousand, and six hundred souls. This number, which is rapidly increasing both by emigrations from Europe, and by natural population, is composed of people of almost all nations, languages, characters and religions.

[Source: Jedidiah Morse, *The American Geography* . . . , 2nd ed. (London: John Stockdale, 1792), pp. 63, 65, 146-47, 268-70, 387, 451.]

[Slavery]. Much has been written of late to shew the injustice and iniquity of enslaving the African; so much as to render it unnecessary here to say any thing on that part of the subject. We cannot, however, forbear introducing a few observations respecting the influence of slavery upon policy, morals and manners. From repeated and accurate calculations, it has been found that the expence of maintaining a slave, especially if we include the purchase-money, is much greater than that of maintaining a free man; and the labour of the free man, influenced by the powerful motive of gain, is at least twice as profitable to the employer as that of the slave. Besides, slavery is the bane of industry. It renders labour, among the whites, not only unfashionable, but disreputable. Industry is the off-spring of necessity rather than of choice. Slavery precludes this necessity; and indolence, which strikes at the root of all social and political happiness, is the unhappy consequence.

[New England]. Before the late war, which introduced into New-England a flood of corruptions, with many improvements, the sabbath was observed with great strictness; no unnecessary travelling, no secular business, no visiting, no diversions were permitted on that sacred day. They considered it as consecrated to divine worship, and were generally punctual and serious in their attendance upon it. Their laws were strict in guarding the sabbath against every innovation. The supposed severity with which these laws were composed and exe-

Congregational Church, Lincoln County, Maine
(National Archives)

cuted, together with some other traits in their religious [i.e., Congregational] character, have acquired for the New-Englanders the name of a superstitious, bigotted people. But superstition and bigotry are so indefinite in their signification, and so variously applied by persons of different principles and educations, that it is not easy to determine whether they ever deserved that character. . . . [W]e will only observe that, since the war, a catholic, tolerant spirit . . . has greatly increased and is becoming universal; and if they do not break the proper bound, and liberalize away all true religion, of which there is much danger, they will counteract that strong propensity in human nature, which leads men to vibrate from one extreme to its opposite.

[New York]. The various denominations in this state, with the number of their respective congregations, are as follows:

English Presbyterian	87
Dutch Reformed	66
(including six of the German language)	
Baptists	30
Episcopalians	26
Friends, or Quakers	20
German Lutheran	12
Moravians	2
Methodists	1
Roman Catholic	1
Jews	1
Shakers	unknown

. . . The Methodist interest, though small in this state, has greatly increased in the southern states since the revolution. They have estimated their number at 37,800. But their numbers are so various in different places, at different times, that it would be a matter of no small difficulty to find out their exact amount. The late famous Mr. John Wesley has been called the Father of this religious sect. They warmly oppose the Calvinistic doctrines of election and final perseverance, and maintain that sinless perfection is attainable in this life. Their mode of preaching is entirely extemporaneous, very loud and animated, bordering on enthusiasm. They appear studiously to avoid connection in their discourses, and are fond of introducing pathetic stories, which are calculated to affect the tender passions. Their manner is very solemn, and their preaching is frequently attended with a surprising effect upon their audiences. Their churches are supplied by their preachers in rotation.

The Shakers are a sect who sprung up in Europe. A part of them came from England to New-York in 1774, and being joined by others, they settled at

Nisqueaunia, above Albany, whence they spread their doctrines, and increased to a considerable number; but their interest is now fast declining. . . . Their worship, if such extravagant conduct may be so called, consists principally in dancing, singing, leaping, clapping their hands, falling on their knees, and uttering themselves in groans and sighs, in a sound resembling that of the roaring of water; turning around on their heels with astonishing swiftness, to shew, as they say, the power of God. All these gesticulations are performed in the most violent and boisterous manner, and occasion, at intervals, a shuddering not unlike that of a person in a strong fit of the ague. Hence they are called, not improperly, *Shakers.*

[Virginia]. The present denomination of christians in Virginia are Presbyterians, who are the most numerous and inhabit the western parts of the state; Episcopalians, who are the most ancient settlers, and occupy the eastern and first settled parts of the state. Intermingled with these are great numbers of Baptists and Methodists. The proportional numbers of these several denominations have not been ascertained. The Episcopalians, or as Mr. Jefferson calls them, the "Anglicans," have comparatively but few ministers among them; and these few, when they preach, which is seldom more than once a week, preach to very thin congregations. The Presbyterians, in proportion to their numbers, have more ministers, who preach oftener and to larger audiences. The Baptists and Methodists are generally supplied by itinerant preachers, who have large and promiscuous audiences, and preach almost every day, and often several times a day.

The bulk of these religious sects are of the poorer sort of people, and many of them very ignorant (as is indeed the case with the other denominations), but they are generally a moral, well-meaning set of people. They exhibit much zeal in their worship, which appears to be composed of the mingled effusions of piety, enthusiasm, and superstition.

[Georgia]. In regard to religion, politics and literature, this state is yet in its infancy. In Savannah is an Episcopal church, a Presbyterian church, a Synagogue, where the Jews pay their weekly worship, and a German Lutheran church supplied occasionally by a German minister from Ebenezer, where there is a large convenient stone church and a settlement of sober industrious Germans of the Lutheran religion. In Augusta they have an Episcopal church. In Midway is a society of Christians, established on the [C]ongregational plan. . . . Their ancestors emigrated in a colony from Dorchester, near Boston, about the year 1700. . . . They, as a people, retain in a great measure, that simplicity of manner, that unaffected piety and brotherly love which characterized their ancestors, the first settlers of New England. The upper counties are supplied, pretty generally, by Baptist and Methodist ministers. But the greater part of the state is not supplied by ministers of any denomination.

Suggested Reading (Chapter Three)

Scholarship on religion in the era of the Revolution continues to benefit from modern debates over the place of religion in contemporary public life. Yet academic studies that work harder at getting the history right than at shaping modern public opinion usually have a longer shelf life. Among the best overviews are Patricia U. Bonomi, *Under the Cope of Heaven: Religion, Society and Politics in Colonial America* (1986), Ronald Hoffman, ed., *Religion in a Revolutionary Age* (1994), and James H. Hutson, *Religion and the Founding of the American Republic* (1998). Also helpful with a full range of sources from the era is Ellis Sandoz, ed., *Political Sermons of the American Founding Era, 1730-1805* (2nd ed., 1998). The bicentennial of the American Revolution had earlier called forth a number of relevant works, including Jerald Brauer, ed., *Religion and the American Revolution* (1976), Mark A. Noll, *Christians in the American Revolution* (1977), and John F. Berens, *Providence and Patriotism in Early America, 1640-1815* (1978). Several important studies have explored the cultural transformations accelerated or created by the Revolution, including Alan Heimert, *Religion and the American Mind from the Great Awakening to the Revolution* (1966), Stephen A. Marini, *Radical Sects of Revolutionary New England* (1982), Susan Juster, *Disorderly Women: Sexual Politics and Evangelicalism in Revolutionary New England* (1994), Christopher Grasso, *A Speaking Aristocracy: Transforming Public Discourse in Eighteenth-Century Connecticut* (1999), and with particular attention to Roman Catholics in the United States and Canada, Charles B. Hanson, *Necessary Virtue: The Pragmatic Origins of Religious Liberty in New England* (1998).

Pacifism is thoroughly explored in Peter Brock, *Pacifism in the United States from the Colonial Era to the First World War* (1968), and for one important non-resistant group, Richard K. MacMaster, et al., *Conscience in Crisis: Mennonites and Other Peace Churches in America, 1730-1789* (1979). The difficulties of pacifist Moravians in eastern Pennsylvania is a tale told well by Francis S. Fox, *Sweet Land of Liberty: The Ordeal of the American Revolution in Northampton County, Pennsylvania* (2000). Insights into Anglican Loyalism may be derived from the autobiography of Jonathan Boucher, *Reminiscences of an American Loyalist* (1925), as well as from Bruce E. Steiner's biography, *Samuel Seabury* (1971). Treatment that goes beyond just Anglicans is found in Robert M. Calhoon, Timothy M. Barnes, and George A. Rawlyk, eds., *Loyalists and Community in North America* (1994). Intense controversy over whether to install Anglican bishops in the colonies can be followed in full detail in A. L. Cross, *The Anglican Episcopate and the American Colonies* (1964 [1902]), as well as in Carl Bridenbaugh, *Mitre and Sceptre* (1962). Frederick V. Mills examines the bishop question after the Revolution from the standpoint of the denomination's internal operations, *Bishops by Ballots* (1978). On slavery in this period, Sylvia R. Frey is effective on actions by blacks themselves, *Water from the Rock: Black Resistance in a Revolutionary Age* (1991), and James D. Essig explores white anti-slavery efforts, *The Bonds of Wickedness: American Evangelicals Against Slavery, 1770-1808* (1982). Mysteries of millennialism, which received a great stimulus in this period, are unfolded in Ernest L. Tuveson, *Redeemer Nation* (1968), James T. Davidson, *The Logic of Millennial Thought in Eighteenth-Century New England* (1977), Nathan O. Hatch, *The Sacred Cause of Liberty: Republican Thought and the Millennium in Revolutionary New England* (1977), and Ruth H. Bloch, *Visionary Republic: Millennial Themes in American Thought, 1756-1800* (1985).

For the unique American experiment in church-state matters, orientation is provided by E. S. Gaustad, *Church and State in America* (1999). A useful selection of documents has been provided by John F. Wilson and Donald L. Drakeman, eds., *Church and State in American History* (2nd ed., 1987). For the founding period itself, the five volumes of sources in *The Founders' Constitution*, ed. Philip B. Kurland and Ralph Lerner (1987) are indispensable. Important studies on the strategically important precedents of this founding era include William Lee Miller, *The First Liberty: Religion and the American Republic* (1986), Thomas J. Curry, *The First Freedoms: Church and State in America to the Passage of the First Amendment* (1986), Merrill D. Peterson and Robert C. Vaughan, eds., *The Virginia Statute for Religious Freedom* (1988), John Witte, Jr., *Religion and the American Constitutional Experiment* (2000), and Derek H. Davis, *Religion and the Continental Congress, 1774-1789* (2000). For the religious views of Washington, Jefferson, Madison, Franklin, and John Adams, one may turn to E. S. Gaustad, *Faith of Our Fathers* (1987), and John G. West, Jr., *The Politics of Revelation and Reason: Religion and Civil Life in the New Nation* (1996).

The rational religion of the early Republic reflected much of the entire Enlightenment spreading across Europe. For studies sensitive to how American uses of the Enlightenment could sometimes make common cause with traditional religion, see Henry F. May, *The Enlightenment in America* (1976); and Donald H. Meyer, *The Democratic Enlightenment* (1976). The early history of Unitarianism is well explained in Conrad Wright, *The Beginnings of Unitarianism in America* (1955), and nicely supplemented by a solid collection of documents edited by Sydney E. Ahlstrom and Jonathan S. Cary, *An American Reformation: A Documentary History of Unitarian Christianity* (1985). Useful biographies of early liberal thinkers have been provided by Charles W. Akers, *Called Unto Liberty: A Life of Jonathan Mayhew, 1720-1766* (1964), Edward M. Griffin, *Old Brick: Charles Chauncy of Boston, 1705-1787* (1980), Robert J. Wilson III, *The Benevolent Deity: Ebenezer Gay and the Rise of Rational Religion in New England, 1696-1787* (1984), and John Corrigan, *The Hidden Balance: Religion and the Social Theories of Charles Chauncy and Jonathan Mayhew* (1987).

Deism is nicely situated in its trans-Atlantic milieu by Kerry Walters, *The American Deists* (1992), and by Edward H. Davidson and William J. Scheick, eds., *Paine, Scripture, and Authority* (1994).

For the specific denominational traditions in the founding period and immediately thereafter, the Methodists have been the subject of some of the best recent scholarship, including Russell E. Richey, *Early American Methodism* (1991), A. Gregory Schneider, *The Way of the Cross Leads Home: The Domestication of American Methodism* (1993), Christine Leigh Heyrman, *Southern Cross: The Beginnings of the Bible Belt* (1997), Cynthia Lynn Lyerly, *Methodism and the Southern Mind, 1770-1810* (1998), John H. Wigger, *Taking Heaven by Storm: Methodism and the Rise of Popular Christianity in America* (1998), Dee E. Andrews, *The Methodists and Revolutionary America, 1760-1800* (2000), and Nathan O. Hatch and John H. Wigger, eds., *Methodism and the Shaping of American Culture* (2001). The socially significant role of evangelicals in the Revolutionary period is explored carefully for a single colony in Rhys Isaac, *The Transformation of Virginia, 1740-1790* (1982). Jay Dolan's single-volume history of American Catholicism gives full attention to the career of John Carroll and its consequences, *American Catholic Experience* (1987).

To place the random samples selected from Jedidiah Morse into a more comprehensive context, consult Lester J. Cappon, ed., *Atlas of Early American History: The Revolutionary Era, 1760-1790* (1976), and E. S. Gaustad and Philip L. Barlow, *New Historical Atlas of Religion in America* (2000).

FOUR

Liberty Unleashed

The opening decades of the nineteenth century found American religion in remarkably good health. Despite the attacks of rationalists and deists, despite the
vulnerability of a militarily weak nation, despite the deliberate divorce of the
federal government from the institutions of faith, the churches and religiously
motivated individuals prepared themselves to Christianize a continent. Liberty
seemed not so much a principle to be defended as an experience to be enjoyed
— with exuberance and exhilaration. Clearly much needed to be done, and, after the Louisiana Purchase in 1803 (virtually doubling the territory of the
United States), the "much" took an enormous geographical leap. By mid-
century, as a result of the 1845 annexation of Texas, the Mexican-American War
of 1846-47, and the Oregon Treaty concluded with Britain in 1846, the territorial
challenge extended from shore to shore. Would the religious forces of a new nation be equal to the task of resisting barbarism and immorality, of promoting
civilization and Christian virtue?

The Voluntary Principle

That this task rested upon action entirely voluntary only added to its heavy burden. To some, depending altogether upon good will and free choice seemed an
unnecessary risk. In Chapter Three, Patrick Henry's alternative to taking that
risk has been noted — an alternative quickly and firmly set aside by the state of
Virginia. The states of Connecticut and Massachusetts, however, moved neither
quickly nor firmly to eradicate all lingering traces of official support for religion. After all, the Congregational Church was not to be compared with the
Church of England; no war had been fought against Congregationalism, nor
did any stigma of Loyalism mark New England's established church. And Congregationalists did, in fact, still predominate in that area, this despite the intrusion of Anglicans, Baptists, Methodists, and Quakers. A total embrace of the

"voluntary principle" came to New England, therefore, only tardily and painfully. From the year of the Constitution's adoption in 1789, a full generation passed before Connecticut in 1818 finally abandoned all legal favoritism toward the Congregational Church; in Massachusetts, yet another decade and a half went by before a similar definitive separation occurred. Congregationalists, then, tested the roiling waters of religious liberty with due deliberation; once wet by those waters, however, Congregationalists took a leading role in the assertion and application of voluntarism in America's religious life.

That new principle of voluntarism enjoyed its most conspicuous expression, not in denominational institutions or agencies, but in "societies" and "unions" and "associations" dedicated to the application of Christian doctrine and Christian ethic to a rapidly expanding — and diversifying — population. These several societies were interdenominational (though exclusively Protestant), personal (individuals, not churches, became members), and infused with a common vision of what America and its people ought to be. Through voluntary effort and voluntary financing, the societies published tracts and Bibles, supported schools and missions, fought intemperance and war, assisted widows and orphans, ministered to the halt and the blind, promoted the rights of black slaves and white women, and in general launched a moral crusade of mighty power and enduring effect. Of course, problems outran solutions, especially in the realm of slavery; nonetheless, much social reform (and some social control) emanated from these concerned individuals seeking new mechanisms for old human problems as well as for some fresh political and geographical ones.

Revivalism in this period evolved into a familiar and apparently permanent feature of American religion. Prominent along the frontier, it found its way powerfully into the cities as well; strongly supported by many Protestant groups, it reached into Catholicism with similar effect. It was promoted by notable women preachers like Harriet Livermore. Revivalism's theoretician, apologist, and practitioner par excellence in this half-century was Charles G. Finney, professor at and sometime president of Oberlin College. Finney's leadership is such that he clearly deserves the wide attention which he has received in American history; yet, as later portions of the chapter illustrate, revivalism moved far beyond the ministrations of even so influential a figure as this Presbyterian college president.

Progress and the Perfect Society

More conspicuous even than revivalism, certainly more controversial, were the varied utopian experiments spawned (some to an early death) in the pre–Civil War period. In the Western world generally, a firm belief in progress characterized the nineteenth century. But in America particularly, that conviction inspired countless attempts to give cosmic progress a helping human hand. Since the opening of the West afforded ample room for such experimentation and since few Americans in that day doubted that society could be made more nearly perfect, nothing daunted the dreamers and the zealots. From the East Coast all the way to the Pacific, men and women reached for a heaven that could be brought down to earth. If heaven never quite descended intact, the face of American religion and of American history was never quite the same again.

Restorations and Expectations

While some social planners explored new economic modes and startling marital relationships, other religious visionaries knew that perfection lay not ahead, but behind. What America needed and what Christian conscience demanded was not the creation of something new, but a return to something old: to the age of the apostles in the time of Christ, to the sacred writings set down in that first century of the Christian era. There and only there could one discover the pattern for the good life, the proper social order, the pure New Testament church. Restorationism thus emerged as another major motif of American religion in the first half of the nineteenth century. To arrive at a higher level of perfection, one must only remove eighteen hundred years of error, corruption, and the barnacled accumulation of misdeeds. To bring about the kingdom of God on earth, the clock of history must be turned back.

Paradoxically, however, other Americans in these same decades proclaimed that history had nothing at all to do with the kingdom of God. That reign of Christ on earth, that New Jerusalem lay beyond history. God, not man, would bring the kingdom about; God would intervene directly, would take charge immediately, interrupting the mundane chain of cause and effect, of historical change and development. In the 1830s and 40s many saw the millennium (or thousand years of peace foretold in the Book of Revelation) as virtually at hand. Christ will come again, and soon — possibly in this generation, in this decade, in this very year! Others saw the Second Coming as an event having already occurred, Christ reappearing this time in the form of a woman. Still others found their fondest hopes met in establishing communication with departed loved ones, speaking from beyond the grave; for these persons, such direct contact with the spiritual world gave the best answer (as Horace Greeley noted) to the ancient query: "If a man die, shall he live again?"

Denominations and Winning the West

For most of the denominations in nineteenth-century America, the beckoning West presented the most obvious challenge, the most tantalizing opportunity. Along a sprawling, shifting, lawless frontier, some denominations proved better able than others to meet the challenge or make the most of the opportunity. None could wholly ignore, however, the thousands who migrated, the hundreds of villages that mushroomed, the innumerable needs that multiplied. And while those voluntary societies discussed above met many of the needs, the denominations themselves also gave monies and personnel and anxious concern. For those moving beyond the Alleghenies, it was sometimes enough to know that the churches they left behind still cared. But generally the ecclesiastical role was far more active than that: teaching, preaching, reforming, sustaining, healing. As the Atlantic seaboard population advanced steadily westward, the native American population retreated or resisted or perished. What was for many a challenging opportunity was for others a chilling tragedy.

Voluntarism Revisited

In these decades American religion exhibited so much bustle, inventiveness, optimism, and robust health as to make it — and the nation — appear almost invincible. The voluntary principle accounted for so many achievements and promised so many more. Revivalism, especially in a concentrated burst of power in 1858, saved souls, awakened sleepy sinners, and spoke, or so it seemed, to an entire people. Once its mighty engines roared to their full power, could revivalism save even a nation? Could it roll away the injustices of slavery and solve the economic and social complexities associated with that "peculiar institution"? Or was this too much to ask of revivalism, or of voluntarism, or of utopian optimism, or even of religion as a whole? Liberty unleashed opened up before the American people a plethora of possibilities — some bright with promise, some dark with foreboding.

1. The Voluntary Principle

Disestablishment

Connecticut

Lyman Beecher (1775-1863), one of Connecticut's most famous clerical sons, served as the Congregational minister in the Litchfield parish of that state from 1810 to 1826. During this time, Connecticut's still-official church clung to its favored position as long as possible. But in 1818 the state with great hesitation and under even greater pressure from other religious groups took that final step of severing all remaining ties between state and church. Convinced that such a disestablishment of "the standing order" would bring ruin upon the church and eventually upon the state, Beecher fought vigorously against such a move. But once it happened, he dramatically reversed his opinion, embracing that which he had so vigorously resisted: the voluntary principle.

The efforts we made to execute the laws and secure a reformation of morals reached the men of piety, and waked up the energies of the whole state, so far as the members of our churches, and the intelligent and moral portion of our congregations were concerned. These, however, proved to be a minority of the suffrage of the state. Originally all were obliged to support the standing order. Every body paid without kicking. . . .

When, however, other denominations began to rise, and complained of their consciences, the laws were modified. There never was a more noble regard to the rights of conscience than was shown in Connecticut. Never was there a

---

[Source: Barbara M. Cross, ed., *The Autobiography of Lyman Beecher* (Cambridge, Mass.: Harvard University Press, 1961), I, 251-53.]

body of men that held the whole power that yielded to the rights of conscience more honorably.

The habit of legislation from the beginning had been to favor the Congregational order and provide for it. Congregationalism was the established religion. All others were dissenters, and complained of favoritism. The ambitious minority early began to make use of the minor sects on the ground of invidious distinctions, thus making them restive. So the democracy, as it rose, included nearly all the minor sects, besides the Sabbath-breakers, rum-selling tippling folk, infidels, and ruff-scuff generally, and made a dead set at us of the standing order.

It was a long time, however, before they could accomplish any thing, so small were the sects and so united the Federal phalanx. After defeat upon defeat, and while other state delegations in Congress divided, ours, for twenty years a unit, Pierrepont Edwards, a leader of the Democrats, exclaimed, "As well attempt to revolutionize the kingdom of heaven as the State of Connecticut!"

But throwing Treadwell[1] over in 1811 broke the charm and divided the party; persons of third-rate ability, on our side, who wanted to be somebody, deserted; all the infidels in the state had long been leading on that side; the minor sects had swollen, and complained of having to get a certificate to pay their tax where they liked; our efforts to enforce reformation of morals by law made us unpopular; they attacked the clergy unceasingly, and myself in particular, in season and out of season, with all sorts of misrepresentation, ridicule, and abuse; and finally, the Episcopalians, who had always been stanch Federalists, were disappointed of an appropriation for the Bishop's Fund, which they asked for, and went over to the Democrats.

That overset us. They slung us out like a stone from a sling. . . . It was a time of great depression and suffering. It was the worst attack I ever met in my life. . . . I worked as hard as mortal man could, and at the same time preached for revivals with all my might, and with success, till at last, what with domestic afflictions and all, my health and spirits began to fail. It was as dark a day as ever I saw. The odium thrown upon the ministry was inconceivable. The injury done to the cause of Christ, as we then supposed, was irreparable. For several days I suffered what no tongue can tell *for the best thing that ever happened to the State of Connecticut.* It cut the churches loose from dependence on state support. It threw them wholly on their own resources and on God.

They say ministers have lost their influence; the fact is, they have gained. By voluntary efforts, societies, missions, and revivals, they exert a deeper influence than ever they could by queues, and shoe-buckles, and cocked hats, and gold-headed canes.

---

1. John Treadwell, governor of Connecticut from 1809 to 1811.

Massachusetts

In Massachusetts the overthrow of the "standing order" took even longer and grew even more complicated. Not until 1833 was the separation between church and state finally accomplished. Legal complications arose from disputes internal to Congregationalism itself: the sharp quarrels between Trinitarians and Unitarians that started in a disagreement over theology and ended in a fight about property. Well before that tangle was thrown to the courts to unravel, John Leland, whose hymns were presented in the previous chapter, called for the complete disestablishment of the long-favored church. A Jeffersonian Republican (and later a Jacksonian Democrat), Leland saw no consistency whatsoever between the nation's First Amendment and the state's continued insistence on playing favorites among the several denominations. In a "fashionable fast-day sermon" delivered in 1801, Leland declared that all religious oppression, whether in the Old World or the New, derived from that single "rotten nest-egg, which is always hatching vipers: I mean the principle of intruding the laws of men into the kingdom of Christ. . . ." Like the deist Jefferson, the pietist Leland would gladly trade that vile principle for a far superior voluntary one.

How just is this remark, that "Religious opinions are not the objects of civil government, nor in any way under its control." If that part of the world which is become Christian, (so called,) had attended to this remark, what infinite evils would have been avoided? Had Spain hearkened thereto, two hundred thousand South Americans would not have been slaughtered as they were. For want of this, in France, in the reign of Charles IX, A.D. 1751, a persecution began, which in thirty years destroyed thirty-nine Princes, one hundred and forty-eight Counts, two hundred and thirty-four Barons, one hundred and forty-seven thousand five hundred and eighteen gentlemen, and seven hundred and sixty thousand of the common people; and in Ireland, in the days of Charles I. of England, above two hundred thousand Protestants were cruelly murdered in a few days.

I suppose that all Protestants, will unite in condemning this cruelty in Papists, because Papists are such blood-thirsty bigots; but pray have not Protestants done the same, whenever they have established their religion by law, and supported their preachers by a tax?

In the reign of the two Charleses, in England, two thousand preachers, and six thousand privates lost their livings, and the chief of them their lives, for

---

[Source: L. F. Greene, ed., *The Writings of the Late Elder John Leland . . .* (New York: Arno Press, 1969 [1845]), pp. 240-42, 251-52.]

non-conformity. But leaving these distant nations, let us turn our eyes on our own country.

The first settlers of Massachusetts had left the rod of oppression in England, and fled to America for freedom; but not fully understanding that religious opinions were not under the control of civil government, in 1635, they passed a sentence of banishment against Roger Williams, because he opposed the interference of law in matters of religion; and three months afterwards, they made an attempt to seize him, and send him back to England; but he fled to Providence, and obtained a grant of land from the Narraganset Indians. . . .

About sixty years past, a very general revival of religion took place in New England; soon afterwards, a very considerable separation from the established religion followed, which occasioned abundance of distraints and imprisonments. For about forty of the last years, the Baptists have chiefly borne the lash; for no other society has arisen to any considerable importance. The point in debate is this: the law of the state says that, where the majority of a town, parish or precinct, choose a preacher, and contract with him for his hire, it shall be levied upon all within the limits of said town, parish or precinct, according to poll and property; and that it shall be collected in legal form, and distrained for, if not paid without. It also makes the same provision for building and repairing meeting-houses. It has hitherto been the case, that in most of the towns the Baptists have been the minority; consequently, they have been distrained upon, and imprisoned, because they would not pay their money voluntarily to preachers in whom they did not place confidence, nor approve of their sentiments; and to build meeting-houses where they did not choose to worship. He must be a poor logician, who does not trace this oppression back to its origin, to that rotten nest-egg, which is always hatching vipers: I mean the principle of intruding the laws of men into the kingdom of Christ, which kingdom is not of this world.

But all the art and force that is used, neither effect uniformity nor stop the increase of the Baptists. In the beginning of the last century, there were but four Baptist churches in Massachusetts; but now there are one hundred and thirty-six churches, in which are eight thousand four hundred and sixty-three members, besides all their adherents; and in which churches there are one hundred and five ministers.

The religious laws of Massachusetts are frequently varying, but the stump is always preserved with a band of iron. Legal force is always used in directing the worship of God, as if human law was the mainspring of the gospel. . . .

I shall now proceed to offer a number of reasons why religious laws and test oaths should never be woven into constitutions, or mixed with the laws of state.

First. It makes a constitution, or statute law book, look more like a catechism than a rule of political life. Some have placed Apocrypha in the Bible, where it should not be; but, in this case, religion becomes prostitute among the laws of state.

Second. It makes the opinions of fallible men, the test of orthodoxy for all the people. View such laws in the most favorable light, they are but the opinions of their makers; and shall the judgment of one man in a thousand, be the rule for the faith and worship of the whole thousand?

Third. A religious establishment, reduces religion to a level with the principles of state policy, and turns officers of the church into ministers of state.

Fourth. It holds forth a tempting bait to men to embrace *that* religion which is pampered by the law, without searching after truth conscientiously.

Fifth. It checks all rational conviction of the errors in the national creed; for if those errors are arrested and condemned by a man, he must be proscribed and legally persecuted.

Sixth. It raises the uniformists to arrogance and superiority, and sinks the non-conformists into disgrace and depression; and, thereby, destroys that confidence and friendly equality, which is essential to the happiness of any state.

Seventh. It creates and upholds a power, which Jesus Christ has never ordained, either for the civil or ecclesiastical department.

Eighth. It tends to keep people in ignorance. By implicitly believing what the ruler and the priest says, they give up their own judgments, and suppose it is a crime to think and speak for themselves.

Ninth. It is the parent of all the legal persecution, for conscience sake, that has been on earth, and has drenched the world in blood.

Tenth. It is every way calculated to destroy those peaceable, harmless, amiable qualities among men, which religion, in its simplicity, inculcates.

Eleventh. It tends to make Deists, and support infidelity, more than any one cause. Nothing tends so much to convince candid spectators, that there is nothing in a religion, as to see the disciples of that religion inattentive to its rules. I will here confine myself to the Christian religion. It is confessed by all, in our land, that the precepts of the New Testament exceed everything that ever appeared among men, of the kind. The common failings of the professed followers of Christ, greatly weaken the faith of serious inquirers; but, when those who profess to be his greatest friends, break over all the bounds of justice, humanity and pity; and, because they have the power in their hands, will proscribe, imprison, banish, rob, hang, and burn all those who differ with them in judgment; and all this under pretence of serving the meek, harmless, just, holy and compassionate *Prince of Peace;* what strong arguments these are to convince men, who are not void of all humanity, that the religion of Jesus is only a mask to cover the most atrocious crimes that ever were committed.

Voluntary Societies and Society's Reform

Lyman Beecher on Dueling and Temperance

Beecher's battle on behalf of the "standing order" represented a genuine and active concern for the moral health of the new nation in general as well as Connecticut in particular. When, long after that battle was done, Beecher moved west to Cincinnati, his national concern intensified. Even in Connecticut (that land of "steady habits"), however, Beecher organized, preached, and agitated for society's sound moral health. (1) In a sermon delivered on Long Island, April 16, 1806, Lyman Beecher reviewed all the theoretical arguments against dueling (this was two years after the scandalous and tragic duel between Aaron Burr and Alexander Hamilton); then, in the excerpt below, he turned to the disastrous practical consequences. (2) In his Autobiography Beecher, alarmed at the sharp increase in ministerial consumption of intoxicating liquors, moved that a committee or a society be formed to do something about the problem. Such action was wholly characteristic of Lyman Beecher: don't just bemoan or wring hands, but get moving and fight back for sound social reform.

1.

If the despotic principles of duelling, however, terminated in theory, they might excite our compassion as mere distempers of the brain; but their practical influence is powerful and fatal, as inimical to our rights in *fact* as it is in theory, tending directly and powerfully to the destruction of civil liberty. These tendencies in a few particulars permit me to notice — and,

1. Equal laws are essential to civil liberty, but equal laws are far from satisfying the elevated claims of duellists. That protection which the law affords to them in common with others, they despise. They must have more — a right to decide upon and to redress their own grievances. When we please, (say they) we will avail ourselves of the law; and when we please we will legislate for ourselves. For the plodding vulgar the full forms of law may suffice, but for a reputation so sacred as ours, and for feelings so refined, they are vastly inadequate. Nor shall they restrain our hand from the vindication of our honor, or protect

---

[Source: (1) *Lyman Beecher and the Reform of Society: Four Sermons, 1804-1828* (New York: Arno Press, 1972), pp. 16-21. (2) Barbara M. Cross, ed., *The Autobiography of Lyman Beecher* (Cambridge, Mass.: Harvard University Press, 1961), I, 179-82.]

the wretch who shall presume to impeach it. Is this liberty and equality? Are these gentlemen, indeed, so greatly superior to the people? Is their reputation so much more important? Are their feelings so much more sacred? — Is pain more painful to them? Must we bear all injuries which the law cannot redress? Must we stifle our resentments, or if we vent them in acts of murder, swing upon the gallows, while they with impunity express their indignation and satiate with blood their revengeful spirits? . . .

2. The administration of justice ought, above all things to be impartial. The rich and the honorable to be equally liable to punishment for their crimes with the poor, and, according to their desert, punished with equal severity. But while duellists bear sway, this can never be. It is a fact in this state, at the present moment, that the man who steals a shilling is more liable to detection, and more sure to be punished, and to experience a heavy penalty, than the man who in a duel murders his neighbor. Is this equal? Shall petty thefts excite our indignation, and be punished with exemplary severity, while murderers with bold impunity walk on every side?

3. A sacred regard to law is indispensable to the existence of a mild government. In proportion as obedience ceases to be voluntary, and the contempt of law becomes common, must the nerves of government be strengthened, until it approach in essence, if not in name, to a monarchy. We must have protection; and the more numerous and daring the enemy, the more power must be delegated to subdue and control them. That contempt of law, therefore, which is manifested by the duellist, is a blow at the vitals of liberty. It is the more deadly because, from the genius of our government, the example has a peculiar influence. In despotic governments the example of the legislator may not be so efficacious. Chains, dungeons, racks and gibbets. may keep the people in their place, altho' their rulers should give themselves a license to sin. Viewed at such an abject distance, the example loses also much of its influence. But under the mild government of a republic there is no such immense distance between the rulers and the ruled, and no such terrific restraints to deter from the imitation of their example. To elevate to office, therefore, duellists, those deliberate contemners of law, is to place their example in the most conspicuous point of view, and to clothe it with most woful efficacy to destroy public virtue. Select for your rulers men of profligate example, who contemn the religion and despise the laws of their country, and they need not conspire to introduce despotism; you will yourselves introduce it — you will flee to it as the damned will to rocks and mountains, to shield you from the operation of more intolerable evils.

4. The tendency of duelling to restrain liberty of speech and of the press, is certainly direct and powerful. The people have a right to investigate the conduct of rulers, and to scrutinise the character of candidates for office; and as the private moral character of a man is the truest index, it becomes them to be particular on this point. But who will speak on this subject? Who will publish,

Lyman Beecher
(National Portrait Gallery, Smithsonian Institution, Washington, D.C.
Gift of Mrs. Fredson Bowers)

when the duellist stands before him with pistol at the breast? If a few, duellists themselves and mad with ambition, will brave the danger, how many are there who will not? And what aggravates the restraint, the more unprincipled and vile the man, and the greater the need of speaking, the greater the danger of unveiling his enormity; While bent upon promotion, and desperate in his course, he is prepared to seal in death the lip that shall publish his infamy. What should we think of a law that forbad to publish the immoralities of candidates for office — which made death the penalty of transgression, and which produced annually as many deaths as this nefarious system of duelling? We should not endure it a moment. If Congress were to sanction by a law the maxims of duelling, it would produce a revolution. And will you bear encroachments upon liberty from lawless individuals which you would not bear a moment from the government itself? Would you spurn from your confidence legislators who should make such laws, and will you by your votes clothe with legislative power individuals who, in contempt of law do the same thing?

Nor let any imagine that the influence of this engine of despotism is small; it is powerful already, and is every year becoming more so, as duelling increases; and God only knows where its influence will end. The actual encroachments of Britain, when we first began to resist them, were not one half so alarming as the encroachments of duellists. To have been parallel she must have executed wantonly, without judge or jury, as many as have fallen in duels. What sensations would such conduct have excited? Had it depended on our votes merely, would England have continued to legislate? And shall lawless despots at this day perform what all the fleets and armies of England could not.

5. Duelling in its operation exposes to additional risque and danger those who would rise to usefulness and fame in civil life. With what views can a christian parent look to the law as a profession for his son, where, if he rise to fame, he must join the phalanx of murder — or if he refuse, experience their united influence against him? If the road to Albany or to Washington was beset with robbers — if they sacrificed yearly as many as are now slain in duels, could the wretches live unmolested? Their crimes notorious, could they mingle in society? — Could they boast of their prowess and glory in their shame? Could they enjoy your confidence, receive your suffrage, and be elected the guardians of civil liberty?

6. The inconsistency of voting for duellists is most glaring.

To profess attachment to liberty and vote for men whose principles and whose practice are alike hostile to liberty — to contend for equal laws and clothe with legislative power those who despise them — to enact laws, and intrust their execution to men who are the first to break them, is a farce too ridiculous to be acted by freemen. In voting for the duellist you patronise a criminal whom, in your law, you have doomed to die. With one hand you erect the gallows, and with the other rescue the victim. At one breath declare him unfit to live, and the next constitute him the guardian of your rights. Cancel, I beseech you, the law against duelling — annihilate your criminal code — level to the ground your prisons, and restore to the sweets of society, and embraces of charity, their more innocent victims. Be consistent. If you tolerate one set of villains, tolerate them all. If murder does not stagger your confidence, let it not waver at inferior crimes.

In your prayers, also, you entreat that God would bestow upon you good rulers; and you always pray, in reference to their *moral character,* that they may be *just men, ruling in the fear of God.* But by voting for duellists you demonstrate the hypocrisy of these prayers — for when, by the providence of God, it is left to your choice whom you will have, you vote for murderers. Unless, therefore, you would continue to mock God, you must cease praying for good men, or you must cease to patronise men of blood.

2.

Soon after my arrival at Litchfield I was called to attend the ordination at Plymouth of Mr. Heart, ever after that my very special friend. I loved him as he did me. He said to me one day, "Beecher, if you had made the least effort to govern us young men, you would have had a swarm of bees about you; but, as you have come and mixed among us, you can do with us what you will."

Well, at the ordination at Plymouth, the preparation for our creature comforts, in the sitting-room of Mr. Heart's house, besides food, was a broad sideboard covered with decanters and bottles, and sugar, and pitchers of water. There we found all the various kinds of liquors then in vogue. The drinking was apparently universal. This preparation was made by the society as a matter of course. When the Consociation arrived, they always took something to drink round; also before public services, and always on their return. As they could not all drink at once, they were obliged to stand and wait as people do when they go to mill.

There was a decanter of spirits also on the dinner-table, to help digestion, and gentlemen partook of it through the afternoon and evening as they felt the need, some more and some less; and the sideboard, with the spillings of water, and sugar, and liquor, looked and smelled like the bar of a very active grog-shop. None of the Consociation were drunk; but that there was not, at times, a considerable amount of exhilaration, I can not affirm.

When they had all done drinking, and had taken pipes and tobacco, in less than fifteen minutes there was such a smoke you couldn't see. And the noise I can not describe; it was the maximum of hilarity. They told their stories, and were at the height of jocose talk. They were not old-fashioned Puritans. They had been run down. Great deal of spirituality on Sabbath, and not much when they got where there was something good to drink.

I think I recollect some animadversions were made at that time by the people on the amount of liquor drank, for the tide was swelling in the drinking habits of society.

The next ordination was of Mr. Harvey, in Goshen, and there was the same preparation, and the same scenes acted over, and then afterward still louder murmurs from the society at the quantity and expense of liquor consumed.

These two meetings were near together, and in both my alarm, and shame, and indignation were intense. 'Twas that that woke me up for the war. And silently I took an oath before God that I would never attend another ordination of that kind. I was full. My heart kindles up at the thoughts of it now.

There had been already so much alarm on the subject, that at the General Association at Fairfield in 1811, a committee of three had been appointed to make inquiries and report measures to remedy the evil. A committee was also appointed by the General Association of Massachusetts for the same purpose that same month, and to confer with other bodies.

I was a member of General Association which met in the year following at Sharon, June, 1812, when said committee reported. They said they had attended to the subject committed to their care; that intemperance had been for some time increasing in a most alarming manner; but that, after the most faithful and prayerful inquiry, they were obliged to confess they did not perceive that any thing could be done.

The blood started through my heart when I heard this, and I rose instanter, and moved that a committee of three be appointed immediately, to report at this meeting the ways and means of arresting the tide of intemperance.

The committee was named and appointed. I was chairman, and on the following day brought in a report, the most important paper that ever I wrote.

Abstract of Report.

The General Association of Connecticut, taking into consideration the undue consumption of ardent spirits, the enormous sacrifice of property resulting, the alarming increase of intemperance, the deadly effect on health, intellect, the family, society, civil and religious institutions, and especially in nullifying the means of grace and destroying souls, recommend,

1. Appropriate discourses on the subject by all ministers of Association.

2. That District Associations abstain from the use of ardent spirits at ecclesiastical meetings.

3. That members of Churches abstain from the unlawful vending, or purchase and use of ardent spirits where unlawfully sold; exercise vigilant discipline, and cease to consider the production of ardent spirits a part of hospitable entertainment in social visits.

4. That parents cease from the ordinary use of ardent spirits in the family, and warn their children of the evils and dangers of intemperance.

5. That farmers, mechanics, and manufacturers substitute palatable and nutritious drinks, and give additional compensation, if necessary, to those in their employ. . . .

And that these practical measures may not be rendered ineffectual, the Association do most earnestly entreat their brethren in the ministry, the members of our churches, and the persons who lament and desire to check the progress of this evil, that they neither express nor indulge the melancholy apprehension that nothing can be done on this subject; a prediction eminently calculated to paralyze exertion, and become the disastrous cause of its own fulfillment. For what if the reformation of drunkards be hopeless, may we not stand between the living and the dead, and pray and labor with effect to stay the spreading plague, And what if some will perish after all that can be done, shall we make no effort to save any from destruction, because we may not be able to turn away every one from the path of ruin? . . .

Immense evils, we are persuaded, afflict communities, not because they are incurable, but because they are tolerated; and great good remains often unaccomplished merely because it is not attempted.

American Bible Society (1816)

A heavily Protestant America implied a Bible-reading America. As the young Republic faced the unknowns of the Louisiana and other Territories, many Protestants believed it urgent that Bibles ("well printed and accurate") be supplied to frontier settlers as rapidly as possible. To assist further, "well executed Stereotype plates" could be sent to larger towns in the West, enabling Bibles to be printed and distributed at minimum expense or delay. No government agency stood ready to perform such a task; no single church had the means to perform such a task. What then? Voluntarism, once more, was the answer. A voluntary association of like-minded individuals could do what could not be done "by insulated zeal." If Americans would only practice organization and cooperation, then we shall "perform achievements astonishing to ourselves. . . ."

To the People of the United States.

Every person of observation has remarked that the times are pregnant with great events. The political world has undergone changes stupendous, unexpected, and calculated to inspire thoughtful men with the most boding anticipations.

That there are in reserve, occurrences of deep, of lasting, and of general interest, appears to be the common sentiment. Such a sentiment has not been excited without a cause, and does not exist without an object. The cause is to be sought in that Providence which adapts, with wonderful exactitude, means to ends; and the object is too plain to be mistaken by those who carry a sense of religion into their speculations upon the present and the future condition of our afflicted race.

[Source: *Constitution of the American Bible Society . . . May, 1816 . . .* (New York: G. F. Hopkins, 1816), pp. 13-18.]

An excitement, as extraordinary as it is powerful, has roused the nations to the importance of spreading the knowledge of the one living and true God, as revealed in his Son, the Mediator between God and men, Christ Jesus. This excitement is the more worthy of notice, as it has followed a period of philosophy, falsely so called, and has gone in the track of those very schemes which, under the imposing names of reason and liberality, were attempting to seduce mankind from all which can bless the life that is, or shed a cheering radiance on the life that is to come.

We hail the re-action, as auspicious to whatever is exquisite in human enjoyment, or precious to human hope. We would fly to the aid of all that is holy, against all that is profane; of the purest interest of the community, the family, and the individual, against the conspiracy of darkness, disaster, and death — to help on the mighty work of Christian charity — to claim our place in the age of Bibles.

We have, indeed, the secondary praise, but still the praise, of treading in the footsteps of those who have set an example without a parallel — an example of the most unbounded benevolence and beneficence: and it cannot be to us a source of any pain, that it has been set by those who are of one blood with the most of ourselves; and has been embodied in a form so noble and so Catholick, as *"The British and Foreign Bible Society."*

The impulse which that institution, ten thousand times more glorious than all the exploits of the sword, has given to the conscience of Europe, and to the slumbering hope of millions in the region and shadow of death, demonstrates to Christians of every country what they cannot do by insulated zeal, and what they can do by co-operation.

In the United States we want nothing but concert to perform achievements astonishing to ourselves, dismaying to the adversaries of truth and piety; and most encouraging to every evangelical effort, on the surface of the globe.

No spectacle can be so illustrious in itself, so touching to man, or so grateful to God, as a nation pouring forth its devotion, its talent, and its treasures, for that kingdom of the Saviour which is righteousness and peace.

If there be a single measure which can overrule objection, subdue opposition, and command exertion, this is the measure. That all our voices, all our affections, all our hands, should be joined in the grand design of promoting "peace on earth and good will toward man" — that they should resist the advance of misery — should carry the light of instruction into the dominions of ignorance; and the balm of joy to the soul of anguish; and all this by diffusing the oracles of God — addresses to the understanding an argument which cannot be encountered; and to the heart an appeal which its holiest emotions rise up to second.

Under such impressions, and with such views, fathers, brethren, fellow-citizens, the *American Bible Society* has been formed. Local feelings, party prejudices, sectarian jealousies, are excluded by its very nature. Its members are leagued in that, and in that alone, which calls up every hallowed, and puts down every unhallowed, principle — the dissemination of the Scriptures in the received versions where they exist, and in the most faithful where they may be required. In such a work, whatever is dignified, kind, venerable, true, has ample scope: while sectarian littleness and rivalries can find no avenue of admission. . . .

It is true, that the prodigious territory of the United States — the increase of their population, which is gaining every day upon their moral cultivation — and the dreadful consequences which will ensue from a people's outgrowing the knowledge of eternal life; and reverting to a species of heathenism, which shall have all the address and profligacy of civilized society, without any religious control, present a sphere of action, which may for a long time employ and engross the cares of this Society, and of all the local Bible Societies of the land.

In the distinct anticipation of such an urgency, one of the main objects of the *American Bible Society,* is, not merely to provide a sufficiency of well printed and accurate editions of the Scriptures; but also to furnish great districts of the American continent with well executed Stereotype plates, for their cheap and extensive diffusion throughout regions which are now scantily supplied, at a discouraging expense; and which, nevertheless, open a wide and prepared field for the reception of revealed truth.

Yet, let it not be supposed, that geographical or political limits are to be the limits of the *American Bible Society.* That designation is meant to indicate, not the restriction of their labour, but the source of its emanation. They will embrace, with thankfulness and pleasure, every opportunity of raying out, by means of the Bible, according to their ability, the light of life and immortality, to such parts of the world, as are destitute of the blessing, and are within their reach. In this high vocation, their ambition is to be fellow-workers with them who are fellow-workers with God.

American Sunday School Union (1824)

The American Sunday School Union, organized in 1824, constituted another instance of that rush toward a voluntary Christianizing and civilizing of the American continent. Vastly underrated as both a cultural and an educational institution, the Sunday School actually brought literacy — and then literature — to thousands on the frontier who otherwise would have been denied both. Sunday Schools, moreover, did not require the presence of or-

[Source: *The American Sunday School Magazine,* July 1824, pp. 4-6.]

*dained clergymen in order to function effectively. They therefore often pre-
ceded the establishment of a church or substituted entirely for the church
that never came. As a lay institution, the Sunday School utilized the human
resources at hand; more often than not, these resources were female. Thus
able and dedicated women found here a significant outlet for their talents
and energies. But Sunday Schools, scattered haphazardly in the nation's
sparsely settled lands, could be made even more effective if gathered together
in a national unit. Or at least, so goes the argument presented below.*

The well known axiom, "Union is power," will apply to every thing. There is no
efficiency, physical, intellectual, or moral, but may be traced to this principle. It
is a "principle in the kingdom of Christ; and no man can oppose it without a
direct attack upon that fundamental law of his kingdom, by which the saints of
God are made co-workers with him. This principle then may be applied in all
its force to the union of Sabbath schools; and the various considerations which
may be urged in support of this position are too numerous, and embrace too
large a body of facts, to find a place in a single article, or in one number of our
Magazine. We will, however, notice some of them. The improvements in
Sunday school education can be only partially known and adopted, and the intelligence which might animate wavering exertion, direct inquiring benevolence, and promote more energetic and extensive plans of instruction, cannot
be communicated for the benefit of all, through any existing medium than one
general society.

That zeal which is now private and retired, will be likely to languish, while
the teachers pursue their kind employment in separate situations, without that
communication which would stimulate each other's efforts. Hence arises the
necessity of a General Union. The beneficial effects of such a Christian union
and co-operation would soon be experienced, and the cause of Sunday schools
become more successful, and their influence more extensive. Except perhaps in
some of our larger towns and cities, the Sunday school teachers resemble "scattered warriors in an enemy's country; individually they have been valiant and
victorious in their separate stations;" but a combination of talent, of energy,
and of means, and the most approved plans of instruction are needed. Under
the banner of such a union as is now organized, the Sunday school teachers in
every city, and town, and village, and neighbourhood in our extensive country,
may pursue their delightful employments, with the fullest assurance of complete success. . . .

Through the various publications which the Union will circulate, "information will be extended, useful plans and pleasing facts reported, the general
experience rendered available to individuals, mutual encouragements will excite each other's zeal, and mutual prayers ascending to the throne of grace,
would bring down blessings from the God of love."

In the union of the friends of Sunday schools in a National Institution, there will be "no sacrifice of principle, no compromise of duty, no interference with the internal management of smaller associations; all discordant elements must be banished, and union with Christ and union with each other" form the basis of the American Sunday School Union.

"Union, to be effective, must be something more than the mere name; the feelings must be deeply excited, the whole soul interested, and we must sincerely sympathise with each other in our joys and sorrows, and thus fulfil the law of Christ. We must blend the harmlessness of the dove, with the wisdom of the serpent, and evince our love to Jesus, to his cause, and to his people, by the ardour of our feelings, the energy of our conduct, and the amplitude of our benevolence."

American Tract Society (1825) and the Colporteur System

(1) The American Tract Society, organized in New York City in 1825, reflects still another facet of voluntarism in American religion. Protestants of several denominations joined together "to diffuse a knowledge of our Lord Jesus Christ as the Redeemer of sinners." Such diffusion was to be accomplished by a wide distribution of inexpensive religious tracts. Since 1825, many religious groups have discovered the virtues and the force of the printing presses; the Tract Society pointed the way. (2) Convinced that the Protestant Reformation itself had succeeded only through the use of the colporteur — a traveling peddler or distributor of religious literature — the Tract Society enthusiastically endorsed this system as peculiarly adapted to America. The Society's reasons for such an endorsement are given below.

1.

The Executive Committee of the AMERICAN TRACT SOCIETY, by this document, beg the privilege of addressing the Christian community upon one of the most interesting subjects which has ever attracted the notice of those whose stations or whose character give them influence over the destiny of their fellow men. In the month of March last [1824], incipient measures were adopted in the city of

---

[Source: *The American Tract Society Documents, 1824-1925* (New York: Arno Press, 1972): (1) "Address of the Executive Committee," pp. 3, 4-6; (2) "The American Colporteur System," pp. 6-7, 8-9.]

New-York, with the view of forming a Society, to be denominated the AMERI-
CAN TRACT SOCIETY; the object of which should be, "to diffuse a knowledge of
our Lord Jesus Christ as the Redeemer of sinners, and to promote the interests
of vital godliness and sound morality, by the circulation of Religious Tracts, calculated to receive the approbation of all Evangelical Christians." . . .

In making this early presentation of their object to the friends of the Redeemer in the United States, and in venturing most respectfully to urge the
claims of this institution to general patronage, the Committee feel that it is
needless to exhibit, to any considerable extent, the superior advantages of that
method of moral and religious instruction which is pursued by the distribution
of Tracts. Though men are fallen by their iniquity, and are to be recovered from
their apostacy and condemnation only through the redemption that is in Christ
Jesus, and by the renewing of the Holy Ghost, yet does this method of mercy
most distinctly recognize the use of means in the business of their salvation.
Next to the Bible and the living Ministry, one of these means of light and salvation will be found to be, short, plain, striking, entertaining, and instructive
Tracts, exhibiting in writing some of the great and glorious truths of the Gospel. "The Word of Truth" is the great instrument of moral renovation. He who
scatters it scatters the seed of the Kingdom, and many look for the harvest in
God's own good time and way. A Tract may be perused at leisure; it may be consulted in the hour of retirement and solitude; it can be read in a little time; and
though it may contain instruction important and weighty enough for the consideration of the sage, and yet simple enough to be accommodated to the taste
and intelligence of a child, may be easily weighed and deposited in the memory.
This method of instruction is peculiarly calculated for the poor, and is especially demanded by the poor of an extended population. It is a method by
which the blessings of a religious education may, to no inconsiderable degree,
be extended to the lower ranks of society with peculiar facility, and which, as a
practical system, is already entitled to the claims of successful experiment. It is a
means of doing good which is level to every capacity, and adapted to every condition. The man of low attainment in science, the mother, the child, the obscure
in the meanest condition, can give away a Tract, and, perhaps, accompany it
with a word of advice or admonition, with as much promise of success as a Missionary or an Apostle. A Minister may distribute Tracts among his people, and
thus impress and extend his public instructions where the impressions of his
official duty would otherwise be lost, or never extended; and in this way he may
double his usefulness, and devote two lives to his Master's glory instead of one.
The teacher and the pupil, the parent and the child, the master and the servant,
may become to each other the most effectual preachers, by the distribution of
Tracts. The traveller may scatter them along the roads and throughout the inns
and cottages; and in return, the inns and cottages may spread them before the
eye of the thoughtless traveller. Merchants may distribute them to ship-masters,

and ship-masters to seamen; men of business may transmit them, with every bale of goods, to the remote corners of the land and globe; and thus the infinitely important truths of the Gospel — truths by which it is the purpose of the God of Heaven to make men "wise to salvation" — like the diffusive light, may be emitted from numberless sources, and in every direction. All this may be done in the most inoffensive and inobtrusive way; with no magisterial authority; no claims of superior wisdom or goodness; and no alarm to human pride or frowardness. All this may be done, too, with no loss of time. "A Tract can be given away and God's blessing asked upon it in a moment." Aside from the influence of those institutions which involve no expense at all, in no way can so much probable good be effected at so little expense, as by the distribution of Tracts. A Tract which contains *ten pages* can be published for a *single cent!* And when we recollect how long a single Tract may be preserved, by how many individuals and families it may be read, and when read by them, to how many others it may be lent, it is difficult to conceive of a way in which more good can be accomplished by a very small amount of means.

2.

The United States furnish a field of unequalled interest for the employment of the colporteur system, to which it has a peculiar adaptation, whether we regard the vastness of our territory and the sparseness of our population, the rapidity of our growth, the peculiarity of our institutions, the inadequacy of present means of instruction, the extent and nature of prevailing errors, the concentration of motives to the immediate evangelization of the country, or the ease and rapidity with which the system may be indefinitely extended and applied to all classes.

(1.) *Vast and sparsely populated territory.*

Such is *the vastness of the country* as to require, especially in the newer States, an itinerant system of evangelization. The territory of the United States spreads over a surface of 2,000,000 square miles, and approaches in superficial extent that of the kingdom of Great Britain, including all its colonies and dependencies in Europe, Asia, Africa and America. How difficult in the early history of such a country to supply its entire scattered population with the *stated* means of grace! If we estimate the number of evangelical preachers at 10,000, and they were equally distributed over this territory, it would furnish but one for every 200 square miles; but with such a disproportionate number located east of the Alleghanies, how much greater must be the destitution of ministers of the Gospel at the West. Unlike the early settlement of New England, where

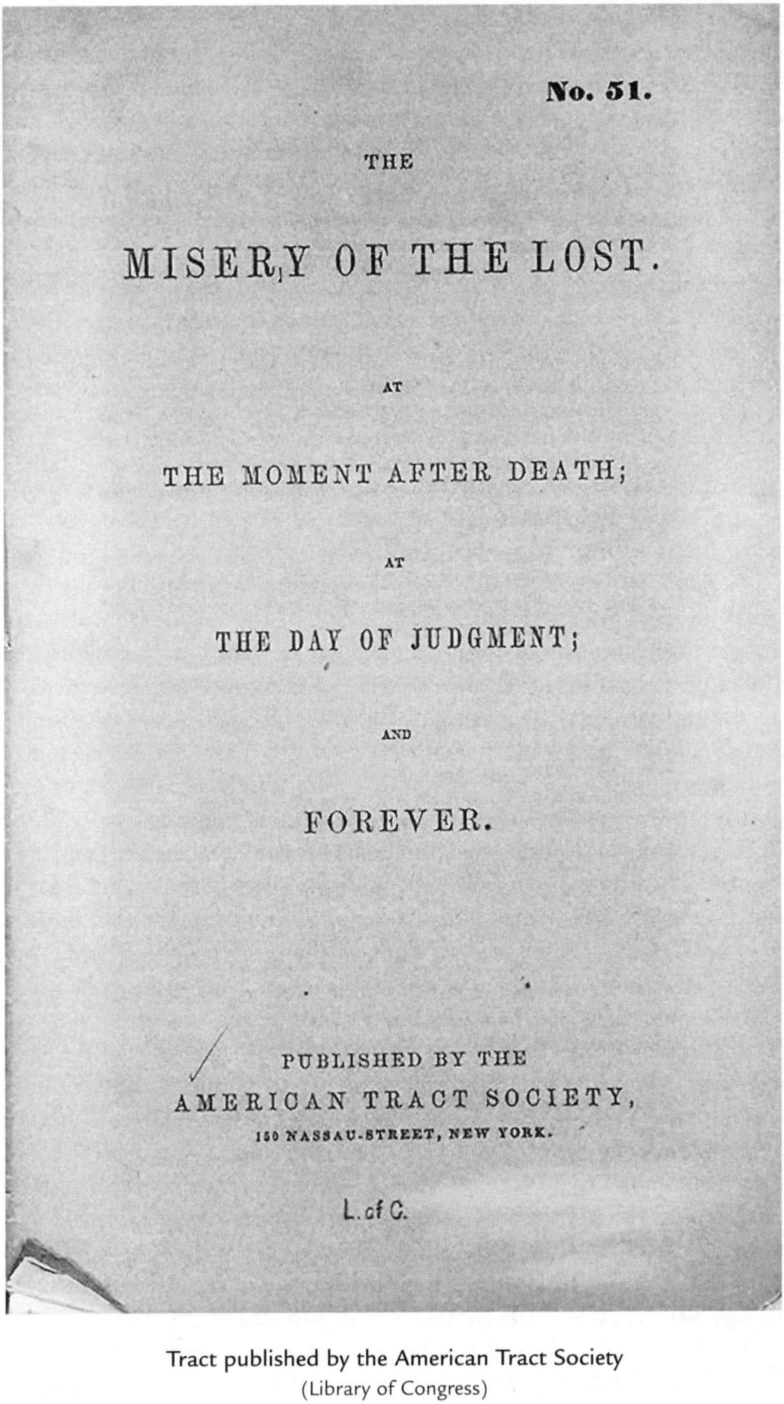

No. 51.

THE

MISERY OF THE LOST.

AT

THE MOMENT AFTER DEATH;

AT

THE DAY OF JUDGMENT;

AND

FOREVER.

PUBLISHED BY THE

AMERICAN TRACT SOCIETY,

150 NASSAU-STREET, NEW YORK.

L. of C.

Tract published by the American Tract Society
(Library of Congress)

motives of piety and safety led the colonists to cluster together in *villages*, —
having by law a school for every fifty householders, — the settlers in our western forests and prairies plant their families wherever the land is most productive, irrespective of all considerations of social, educational or religious advantages. Instead of being of one faith, the same new township may possess single
representatives of all the creeds of christendom; or the majority may have no
faith, being indifferent or neglectful of all religion. There is no homogeneous-
ness, and no possibility of sustaining the ministry of a particular order in the
midst of prejudice or carelessness. Thousands and tens of thousands of families
are thus circumstanced; and so long as millions of acres of cheap government-
lands tempt the hardy pioneer to a western home, such must be the condition
of multitudes of our fellow-countrymen. . . .

(2.) Peculiarity of our institutions — necessity and facilities for universal evangelization.

The *peculiarity of our institutions* illustrates the adaptation of the colporteur system to our country, and furnishes one of the strongest motives to its
employment. Republican institutions like ours are based on the theory of the
ability of the people to govern themselves, and presuppose the existence of intelligence and virtue. Their perpetuity is only secure as this theory is realized,
and the mass of the people possess the requisite means of intellectual and
moral improvement. It is not enough that a portion of the people, or even a
majority, are enlightened; for ignorant and factious minorities have a power
under a government of universal suffrage possessed no where else, and are increasingly dangerous with the growing violence of party spirit and unscrupu-
lous demagogueism. In confederated States, too, we must share a common destiny, so that neglect of any part endangers the safety of the whole. We are
embarked in a noble vessel; but the starting of a single plank, the shifting of the
ballast, the parting of a shroud may engulf us all.

In this view the accumulation of means of instruction in a few favored
States to the neglect of the million is sheer folly and madness; and the effects of
this policy have led an ultra-royalist historian of England and an ultra-
democratic reviewer in America to sneer at the idea of a people attempting to
govern themselves, and to pronounce our government in this respect a failure.
That such must be the issue with such a mass of ignorance as is indicated by our
last census, (700,000 white persons over the age of twenty who cannot read,)
and with the accumulation of foreign immigrants and the increasing power of
Rome, we have reason to fear, unless speedy and well adapted means are employed to carry light to the hitherto neglected classes. Primary schools must be
every where established; colleges, academies and seminaries of learning must

pour out knowledge; ministers must be multiplied; but all these require time — too much time, we fear, to be seasonable; and even if they were in operation, it would by no means supersede the necessity and desirableness of an agency that is truly republican — going as the colporteur does to *all the people*, and first of all to those to whom no one else goes with means of light and salvation. If we would ignite a mass of anthracite, we must place the kindling at the bottom: if we would kindle the fire of knowledge and piety, we must commence at the lowest point of social being.

But there is another view of this matter. Under our institutions all religious systems are tolerated — none are patronised. Truth and error are left alike to their own resources. Perfect impunity is secured even to the man who chooses to propagate principles destructive of all virtue and liberty; and on the other hand, every christian is free to promote his own plans of usefulness, and to influence every individual for good whom he can reach. Shall this feature of our government be made the occasion of poisoning the public mind through the thousand channels of error? And shall the defence and propagation of the Gospel be considered a matter of professional duty, when on all other subjects men are accustomed to influence the opinions and conduct of their fellow-men? Or does not the obligation rest with mountain weight on individual christians to put forth their utmost endeavors to spread abroad the truth as it is in Jesus, and to give all needed aid to such agencies as contemplate the evangelization of the whole people?

Revivalism

Harriet Livermore before Congress

Harriet Livermore (1788-1868) was one of a surprisingly large number of women who, in the first decades of the nineteenth century, took an active part in the intense revival preaching of the era. These women were primarily Methodists or participants in anti-denominational "Christian" movements, and many of them were African Americans. Long before "women's rights" became a public issue, they pushed back the boundaries of traditional religious practice. Most, however, were not much concerned with "rights" as such, but rather with the pressing need they felt to proclaim the Christian

---

[Source: *Daily National Intelligencer*, 12 Jan. 1827, p. 1. This document was kindly supplied by Professor Catherine Brekus.]

gospel that had touched their own lives. Harriet Livermore, the daughter and grand-daughter of Congressmen, was among the best known of these itinerants, as indicated by the invitation she received to preach before the assembled houses of Congress on January 8, 1827. The account that follows was printed as a letter in a Washington, D.C. newspaper a few days after this memorable event.

WASHINGTON, *9th Jan. 1827.*

MY BELOVED CHILD: I witnessed a scene yesterday, so novel and impressive, that I cannot forbear attempting a description of it. I say attempting, for the sensibilities were more strongly affected than the senses, consequently a just delineation is very difficult. It had been rumored for some weeks, that a woman of considerable pretensions had solicited in vain for permission to preach in the Representatives Hall at the Capitol. So you see, after all the professions of veneration for our sex, made by mankind, when tested by their acts, they say "What good thing can come out of Nazareth?"

Thanks to the Christian Pastors of Georgetown: they invited her to their Churches, from whence the fame of her eloquence spread through the City — curiosity prevailed over illiberal prejudice, and she was invited to preach at the Capitol. We attended at an early hour, and found the hall lobby, and gallery, so completely filled that it was almost impossible to get admission. And I am told the Avenue itself was full of persons excluded.

When I looked round and saw the numerous audience, greater than I had ever seen on any former occasion, I trembled for the yet unseen female who was to address them. At length she appeared, attended by a friend. Her figure is good, her height somewhat above mediocrity, her face pale, perhaps some would say plain, but pleasing, and indicative of great serenity and goodness. They were both dressed in a style so simple and neat, you would have taken them for Quakers. She ascended the Speaker's Chair, and her friend seated herself by her. She commenced, in the usual manner, by prayer and singing. She then read the 112th psalm in a voice somewhat hurried and tremulous, and selected her text from 2d Samuel, 23rd chap. part of the 3d and all of the 4th verses — "He that ruleth over men must be just, ruling in the fear of God. And he shall be as the light of the morning, when the sun riseth, even a morning without clouds, as the tender grass springing out of the earth by clear shining after rain."

The President, and many members of Congress, were present. From her text, you will readily perceive her address was intended principally for the rulers of the nation. But she embraced the whole multitude — the rulers of schools — the rulers of families: and, as individuals, the rulers of our passions.

Her language was correct, persuasive, and, judging by my own feelings, the profound attention and sympathy of the audience, extremely eloquent. Many wept even to sobbing. C first yielded to the general impression, and even

I, although unused to the [?] mood, I, who thought my heart was scarred by affliction, and my eyes dried by weeping, found that heart relenting, and those eyes dissolving in a trickling thaw.

Judging, as I said, by my own feelings, and I have no other test, I should say she is the most eloquent preacher I have listened to since the days of Mr. WADDELL.

But no language can do justice to the pathos of her singing. For when she closed by singing a hymn, that might with propriety be termed a prayer, in which she asks the divine perfections of each sacred character recorded in Scripture, her voice was so melodious, and her face beamed with such heavenly goodness, as to resemble a transfiguration and you were compelled to accord them all to her. I could have listened from morn till noon, and from noon till dewy eve of a Summer's day. It savoured more of inspiration than any thing I ever witnessed; and to enjoy the frame of mind which I think she does, I would relinquish the world. Call this rhapsody if you will: but would to God you had heard her! I think you would have felt as I did, and I may add, as I now do.

C. G. Finney

Charles Grandison Finney (1792-1875) was more than merely a preacher at revivals. He promoted and defended revivalism, analyzed and systematized it to the point that it would ever after be a fixed feature of American religion. Lawyer, minister, theological professor, and college president (of Oberlin), Finney understood revivalism to be an essential part of an evangelical religion that would reform both the person and the social order. He turned Oberlin into a major stop along the underground railroad which spirited enslaved blacks toward Canada; he also proclaimed a perfectionism that challenged the new convert to greater heights of ethical achievement; and he modified a Calvinism that appeared to restrict human freedom and minimize the significance of free choice. Above all else, however, Finney prepared a lawyer-like brief in defense of the revival. In the excerpt below, he explains what a revival is — and what it is not.

I shall now proceed with the main design, to show,
    I. What a revival of religion is not;
   II. What it is; and,
  III. The agencies employed in promoting it.

[Source: William G. McLoughlin, ed., *Lectures on Revivals of Religion* . . . (Cambridge, Mass.: Harvard University Press, 1960), pp. 12-17.]

I. A Revival of Religion Is Not a Miracle.

1. A miracle has been generally defined to be, a Divine interference, setting aside or suspending the laws of nature. It is not a miracle, in this sense. All the laws of matter and mind remain in force. They are neither suspended nor set aside in a revival.

2. It is not a miracle according to another definition of the term miracle — *something above the powers of nature*. There is nothing in religion beyond the ordinary powers of nature. It consists entirely in the *right exercise* of the powers of nature. It is just that, and nothing else. When mankind become religious, they are not *enabled* to put forth exertions which they were unable before to put forth. They only exert the powers they had before in a different way, and use them for the glory of God.

3. It is not a miracle, or dependent on a miracle, in any sense. It is a purely philosophical result of the right use of the constituted means — as much so as any other effect produced by the application of means. There may be a miracle among its antecedent causes, or there may not. The apostles employed miracles, simply as a means by which they arrested attention to their message, and established its Divine authority. But the miracle was not the revival. The miracle was one thing; the revival that followed it was quite another thing. The revivals in the apostles' days were connected with miracles, but they were not miracles.

I said that a revival is the result of the *right* use of the appropriate means. The means which God has enjoyed for the production of a revival, doubtless have a natural tendency to produce a revival. Otherwise God would not have enjoined them. But means will not produce a revival, we all know, without the blessing of God. No more will grain, when it is sowed, produce a crop without the blessing of God. It is impossible for us to say that there is not as direct an influence or agency from God, to produce a crop of grain, as there is to produce a revival. What are the laws of nature, according to which, it is supposed, that grain yields a crop? They are nothing but the constituted manner of the operations of God. In the Bible, the word of God is compared to grain, and preaching is compared to sowing seed, and the results to the springing up and growth of the crop. And the result is just as philosophical in the one case, as in the other, and is as naturally connected with the cause.

I wish this idea to be impressed on all your minds, for there has long been an idea prevalent that promoting religion has something very peculiar in it, not to be judged of by the ordinary rules of cause and effect; in short, that there is no connection of the means with the result, and no tendency in the means to produce the effect. No doctrine is more dangerous than this to the prosperity of the church, and nothing more absurd.

Suppose a man were to go and preach this doctrine among farmers, about their sowing grain. Let him tell them that God is a sovereign, and will give them a crop only when it pleases him, and that for them to plow and plant and labor as if they expected to raise a crop is very wrong, and taking the work out of the hands of God, that it interferes with his sovereignty, and is going on in their own strength; and that there is no connection between the means and the result on which they can depend. And now, suppose the farmers should believe such doctrine. Why, they would starve the world to death.

Just such results will follow from the church's being persuaded that promoting religion is somehow so mysteriously a subject of Divine sovereignty, that there is no natural connection between the means and the end. What *are* the results? Why, generation after generation have gone down to hell. No doubt more than five thousand millions have gone down to hell, while the church has been dreaming, and waiting for God to save them without the use of means. It has been the devil's most successful means of destroying souls. The connection is as clear in religion as it is when the farmer sows his grain.

There is one fact under the government of God, worthy of universal notice, and of everlasting remembrance; which is, that the most useful and important things are most easily and certainly obtained by the use of the appropriate means. This is evidently a principle in the Divine administration. Hence, all the *necessaries* of life are obtained with great *certainty* by the use of the simplest means. The luxuries are more difficult to obtain; the means to procure them are more intricate and less certain in their results; while things absolutely hurtful and poisonous, such as alcohol and the like, are often obtained only by torturing nature, and making use of a kind of infernal sorcery to procure the death-dealing abomination. This principle holds true in moral government, and as spiritual blessings are of surpassing importance, we should expect their attainment to be connected with *great certainty* with the use of the appropriate means; and such we find to be the fact; and I fully believe that could facts be known it would be found that when the appointed means have been *rightly* used, spiritual blessings have been obtained with greater uniformity than temporal ones.

II. I Aim to Show What a Revival Is.

It presupposes that the church is sunk down in a backslidden state, and a revival consists in the return of the church from her backslidings, and in the conversion of sinners.

1. A revival always includes conviction of sin on the part of the church. Backslidden professors cannot wake up and begin right away in the service of God, without deep searchings of heart. The fountains of sin need to be broken up. In a true revival, Christians are always brought under such convictions; they see their sins in such a light, that often they find it impossible to maintain a

hope of their acceptance with God. It does not always go to that extent; but there are always, in a genuine revival, deep convictions of sin, and often cases of abandoning all hope.

2. Backslidden Christians will be brought to repentance. A revival is nothing else than a new beginning of obedience to God. Just as in the case of a converted sinner, the first step is a deep repentance, a breaking down of heart, a getting down into the dust before God, with deep humility, and forsaking of sin.

3. Christians will have their faith renewed. While they are in their backslidden state they are blind to the state of sinners. Their hearts are as hard as marble. The truths of the Bible only appear like a dream. They admit it to be all true; their conscience and their judgment assent to it; but their faith does not see it standing out in bold relief, in all the burning realities of eternity. But when they enter into a revival, they no longer see men as trees walking, but they see things in that strong light which will renew the love of God in their hearts. This will lead them to labor zealously to bring others to him. They will feel grieved that others do not love God, when they love him so much. And they will set themselves feelingly to persuade their neighbors to give him their hearts. So their love to men will be renewed. They will be filled with a tender and burning love for souls. They will have a longing desire for the salvation of the whole world. They will be in agony for individuals whom they want to have saved; their friends, relations, enemies. They will not only be urging them to give their hearts to God, but they will carry them to God in the arms of faith, and with strong crying and tears beseech God to have mercy on them, and save their souls from endless burnings.

4. A revival breaks the power of the world and of sin over Christians. It brings them to such vantage ground that they get a fresh impulse towards heaven. They have a new foretaste of heaven, and new desires after union to God; and the charm of the world is broken, and the power of sin overcome.

5. When the churches are thus awakened and reformed, the reformation and salvation of sinners will follow, going through the same stages of conviction, repentance, and reformation. Their hearts will be broken down and changed. Very often the most abandoned profligates are among the subjects. Harlots, and drunkards, and infidels, and all sorts of abandoned characters, are awakened and converted. The worst part of human society are softened, and reclaimed, and made to appear as lovely specimens of the beauty of holiness.

The New Lebanon Convention

Preaching such as Finney's, and also Harriet Livermore's, gave a consider-
able shock to traditional church life in America. One of the responses to the
success of revival preaching was that leaders in the older, more formal
churches began to edge around toward revivalist practices themselves. But
another response was to oppose mightily the drift toward revivalism. Pre-
cisely in the attempt to deal with the pros and cons of revival, a notable gath-
ering of clergy took place at New Lebanon, New York, during the week of July
18-26, 1827. The group included Finney, Lyman Beecher (see above, pp. 304-
5), Asahel Nettleton (1783-1844, a major revivalist who yet opposed many of
the "new measures" associated with Charles Finney), and many other dis-
tinguished Congregationalist and Presbyterian clergy from New England
and New York state. The minutes reproduced below of what was decided on
July 24 show how carefully the ministers were trying to respond to the new
practices. What these minutes cannot reveal, however, is that the tide of re-
vival had swept far beyond the point where any self-selected group of Eastern
ministers could contain its workings or effects.

Tuesday, July 24

Met according to adjournment, and opened with prayer.

Present the same as yesterday, except Mr. Nettleton. The minutes of yesterday were read.

Mr. Edwards introduced the following proposition:

"The existence in the churches of evangelists, in such numbers as to constitute an influence in the community, separate from that of the settled pastors, and the introduction, by evangelists, of measures, without consulting
the pastors, or contrary to their judgment and wishes, by an excitement of
popular feeling which may seem to render acquiescence unavoidable, is to
be carefully guarded against, as an evil which is calculated, or at least liable,
to destroy the institution of a settled ministry, and fill the churches with
confusion and disorder."

The Motion was seconded, and after some discussion, the Convention
united in a season of prayer.

After further discussion, the question was taken, and all voted in favor of
the proposition, except Mr. Churchill, who was absent.

Mr. Edwards introduced the following proposition:

[Source: *New York Observer and Religious Chronicle,* Aug. 4, 1827, p. 123.]

"Language adapted to irritate, on account of its manifest personality, such as describing the character, designating the place, or any thing which will point out an individual or individuals before the assembly, as the subjects of invidious remark, is, in public prayer and preaching, to be avoided."

The motion was seconded, and after some discussion Mr. Lansing moved to amend the proposition, by striking out the words, "on account of its manifest personality, such as" — which motion was seconded, and after discussion, was lost.

After further discussion, the question was taken, and twelve voted in favor of the proposition, and five declined voting, as follows: *For the proposition,* Messrs. Norton, Beecher, Churchill, Gillet, Tenney, Humphrey, Frost, Hawes, Weeks, Weed, Edwards, and Smith. *Declined voting,* Messrs. Beman, Lansing, Gale, Aikin, and Finney.

Messrs. Lansing and Aikin entered the following, as their reason: "The undersigned do decline voting on the foregoing particular, not because they do not most unequivocally condemn such personality in preaching as makes an invidious exposure of individuals, but because they suppose that the article in question may be liable to such construction, as to lead many to say, that such *characteristic* preaching is condemned by this Convention, as is adapted to make sinners suppose that their individual case is intended.

D. C. Lansing, S. C. Aikin.

On the motion of Mr. Edwards, the following propositions were agreed to:

"All irreverent familiarity with God, such as men use towards their equals, or which would not be proper for an affectionate child to use towards a worthy parent, is to be avoided."   *Voted unanimously.*

"From the temporary success of uneducated and ardent young men, to make invidious comparisons between them and settled pastors; to depreciate the value of education, or introduce young men as preachers without the usual qualifications, is incorrect and unsafe."   *Voted unanimously.*

"To state things which are not true, or not supported by evidence, for the purpose of awakening sinners, or to represent their condition as more hopeless than it really is, is wrong."   *Voted unanimously.*

"Unkindness and disrespect to superiors in age or station, is to be carefully avoided."   *Voted unanimously.*

"In promoting and conducting revivals of religion, it is unsafe, and of dangerous tendency, to connive at acknowledged errors, through fear that enemies will take advantage from our attempt to correct them."   *Voted unanimously.*

"The immediate success of any measure, without regard to its scriptural character, or its future and permanent consequences, does not justify that measure, or prove it to be right."   *Voted unanimously.*

"Great care should be taken to discriminate between holy and unholy affections, and to exhibit with clearness the scriptural evidences of true religion."
                                                                    Voted unanimously.

"No measures are to be adopted in promoting and conducting revivals of religion, which those who adopt them are unwilling to have published, or which are not proper to be published to the world."   *Voted unanimously.*

Adjourned to meet at half-past 2 o'clock. Concluded with prayer.

2. Progress and the Perfect Society

Transcendentalism and Brook Farm

Emerson as Transcendentalist

Transcendentalism, a "sort of mid-summer madness that overtook a few intellectuals in or around Boston about the year 1840" (as Perry Miller wrote), emphasized the personal religious search more than the corporate one. Men and women must be self-reliant, Emerson noted, adding that a sect is merely a convenient incognito to excuse a man from the necessity of thinking. And in his famous "Address at Harvard Divinity School" delivered in 1838, the Concord sage bemoaned the current tendency to flock to this saint or that poet, "avoiding the God who seeth in secret." Men and women persist in thinking "society wiser than their own soul," not knowing, not believing that their souls are "wiser than the whole world." In transcendentalism's own journal, The Dial, Emerson addressed himself to the nature of this movement designated "by no very good luck" as transcendentalism. "The more liberal thought of intelligent persons acquires a new name in each period or community . . ." (The Dial, January 1842) and this name, for better or worse, is ours. In January of 1843 Emerson explained in more detail the transcendentalist revolt against materialism.

The first thing we have to say respecting what are called *new views* here in New England, at the present time, is, that they are not new, but the very oldest of thoughts cast into the mould of these new times. The light is always identi-

---

[Source: *The Dial*, January 1843, reprinted by Russell & Russell (New York, 1961), pp. 297-99, 303.]

cal in its composition, but it falls on a great variety of objects, and by so falling is first revealed to us, not in its own form, for it is formless, but in theirs; in like manner, thought only appears in the objects it classifies. What is popularly called Transcendentalism among us, is Idealism; Idealism as it appears in 1842. As thinkers, mankind have ever divided into two sects, Materialists and Idealists; the first class founding on experience, the second on consciousness; the first class beginning to think from the data of the senses, the second class perceive that, the senses are not final, and say, the senses give us representations of things, but what are the things themselves, they cannot tell. The materialist insists on facts, on history, on the force of circumstances, and the animal wants of man; the idealist on the power of Thought and of Will, on inspiration, on miracle, on individual culture. These two modes of thinking are both natural, but the idealist contends that his way of thinking is in higher nature. He concedes all that the other affirms, admits the impression of sense, admits their coherency, their use and beauty, and then asks the materialist for his grounds of assurance that things are as his senses represent them, But I, he says, affirm facts not affected by the illusions of senses, facts which are of the same nature as the faculty which reports them, and not liable to doubt; facts which in their first appearance to us assume a native superiority to material facts, degrading these into a language by which the first are to be spoken; facts which it only needs a retirement from the senses to discern. Every materialist will be an idealist; but an idealist can never go backward to be a materialist.

The idealist, in speaking of events, sees them as spirits. He does not deny the sensuous fact; by no means; but he will not see that alone. He does not deny the presence of this table, this chair, and the walls of this room, but he looks at these things as the reverse side of the tapestry, as the *other end,* each being a sequel or completion of a spiritual fact which nearly concerns him. This manner of looking at things, transfers every object in nature from an independent and anomalous position without there, into the consciousness. Even the materialist Condillac, perhaps the most logical expounder of materialism, was constrained to say, "Though we should soar into the heavens, though we should sink into the abyss, we never go out of ourselves; it is always our own thought that we perceive." What more could an idealist say?

The materialist, secure in the certainty of sensation, mocks at fine-spun theories, at star-gazers and dreamers, and believes that his life is solid, that he at least takes nothing for granted, but knows where he stands, and what he does. Yet how easy it is to show him, that he also is a phantom walking and working amid phantoms, and that he need only ask a question or two beyond his daily questions, to find his solid universe growing dim and impalpable before his sense. The sturdy capitalist, no matter how deep and square on blocks of Quincy granite he lays the foundations of his banking-house or Exchange, must set it, at last, not on a cube corresponding to the angles of his structure, but on a mass of unknown materials, and solidity, red-hot or white-hot, perhaps at the core, which rounds off to an almost perfect sphericity, and lies floating in soft air, and goes spinning away, dragging bank and banker with it at a rate of thousands of miles the hour, he knows not whither, — a bit of bullet, now glimmering, now darkling through a small cubic space on the edge of an unimaginable pit of emptiness. And this wild baloon, in which his whole venture is embarked, is a just symbol of his whole state and faculty. One thing, at least, he says is certain, and does not give me the headache, that figures do not lie; the multiplication table has been hitherto found unimpeachable truth; and, moreover, if I put a gold eagle in my safe, I find it again to-morrow; — but for these thoughts, I know not whence they are. They change and pass away. But ask him why he believes that an uniform experience will continue uniform, or on what grounds he founds his faith in his figures, and he will perceive that his mental fabric is built up on just as strange and quaking foundations as his proud edifice of stone.

In the order of thought, the materialist takes his departure from the external world, and esteems a man as one product of that. The idealist takes his departure from his consciousness, and reckons the world as an appearance. The materialist respects sensible masses, Society, Government, social art, and luxury, every establishment, every mass, whether majority of numbers, or extent of space, or amount of objects, every social action. The idealist has another measure, which is metaphysical, namely, the *rank* which things themselves take in his consciousness; not at all, the size or appearance. Mind is the only reality, of which men and all other natures are better or worse reflectors. Nature, literature, history, are only subjective phenomena. Although in his action overpowered by the laws of action, and so, warmly coöperating with men, even preferring them to himself, yet when he speaks scientifically, or after the order of thought, he is constrained to degrade persons into representatives of truths. He does not respect labor, or the products of labor, namely, property, otherwise than as a manifold symbol, illustrating with wonderful fidelity of details the laws of being; he does not respect government, except as far as it reiterates the law of his mind; nor the church; nor charities; nor arts, for themselves; but hears, as at a vast distance, what they say, as if his consciousness would speak to him through a pantomimic scene. His thought, — that is the Universe. His experience inclines him to behold the procession of facts you call the world, as flowing perpetually outward from an invisible, unsounded centre in himself, centre alike of him and of them, and necessitating him to regard all things as having a subjective or relative existence, relative to that aforesaid Unknown Centre of him. . . .

Although, as we have said, there is no pure transcendentalist, yet the tendency to respect the intuitions, and to give them, at least in our creed, all authority over our experience, has deeply colored the conversation and poetry of the present day; and the history of genius and of religion in these times, though impure, and as yet not incarnated in any powerful individual, will be the history of this tendency.

Peabody on Brook Farm

Despite the highly personal, highly "self-reliant" character of transcendentalism, one of that movement's early members, George Ripley (1802-80), determined in 1841 to establish near Boston a cooperative dedicated to "a more wholesome and Simple life." Even before this community located in West Roxbury came to be called Brook Farm, one strong Ripley supporter praised this utopian effort "to live a religious and moral life worthy the name." This partisan, Elizabeth P. Peabody (1804-94), is best known for her advocacy of the kindergarten, but her causes were many and her enthusiasms inexhaustible. An intimate of Margaret Fuller, Emerson, Ripley, Channing, and others within transcendentalism, Peabody here in an 1842 article unfolds the "Plan of the West Roxbury Community."

In the last number of the Dial [October 1841] were some remarks, under the perhaps ambitious title, of "A Glimpse of Christ's Idea of Society;" in a note to which, it was intimated, that in this number, would be given an account of an attempt to realize in some degree this great Ideal, by a little company in the midst of us, as yet without name or visible existence. The attempt is made on a very small scale. A few individuals, who, unknown to each other, under different disciplines of life, reacting from different social evils, but aiming at the same object, — of being wholly true to their natures as men and women; have been made acquainted with one another, and have determined to become the Faculty of the Embryo University.

In order to live a religious and moral life worthy the name, they feel it is necessary to come out in some degree from the world, and to form themselves into a community of property, so far as to exclude competition and the ordinary rules of trade; — while they reserve sufficient private property, or the means of obtaining it, for all purposes of independence, and isolation at will. They have bought a farm, in order to make agriculture the basis of their life, it being the most direct and simple in relation to nature.

A true life, although it aims beyond the highest star, is redolent of the

[Source: *The Dial*, January 1842, reprinted by Russell & Russell (New York, 1961), pp. 361-63.]

healthy earth. The perfume of clover lingers about it. The lowing of cattle is the natural bass to the melody of human voices.

On the other hand, what absurdity can be imagined greater than the institution of cities? They originated not in love, but in war. It was war that drove men together in multitudes, and compelled them to stand so close, and build walls around them. This crowded condition produces wants of an unnatural character, which resulted in occupations that regenerated the evil, by creating artificial wants. Even when that thought of grief,

> "I know, where'er I go
> That there hath passed away a glory from the Earth,"

came to our first parents, as they saw the angel, with the flaming sword of self-consciousness, standing between them and the recovery of spontaneous Life and joy, we cannot believe they could have anticipated a time would come, when the sensuous apprehension of Creation — the great symbol of God — would be taken away from their unfortunate children, — crowded together in such a manner as to shut out the free breath and the Universal Dome of Heaven, some opening their eyes in the dark cellars of the narrow, crowded streets of walled cities. How could they have believed in such a conspiracy against the soul, as to deprive it of the sun and sky, and glorious apparelled Earth! — The growth of cities, which were the embryo of nations hostile to each other, is a subject worthy the thoughts and pen of the philosophic historian. Perhaps nothing would stimulate courage to seek, and hope to attain social good, so much, as a profound history of the origin, in the mixed nature of man, and the exasperation by society, of the various organized Evils under which humanity groans. Is there anything, which exists in social or political life, contrary to the soul's Ideal? That thing is not eternal, but finite, saith the Pure Reason. It has a beginning, and so a history. What man has done, man may *undo*. "By man came death; by man also cometh the resurrection from the dead."

The plan of the Community, as an Economy, is in brief this; for all who have property to take stock, and receive a fixed interest thereon; then to keep house or board in commons, as they shall severally desire, at the cost of provisions purchased at wholesale, or raised on the farm; and for all to labor in community, and be paid at a certain rate an hour, choosing their own number of hours, and their own kind of work. With the results of this labor, and their interest, they are to pay their board, and also purchase whatever else they require at cost, at the warehouses of the Community, which are to be filled by the Community as such. To perfect this economy, in the course of time they must have all trades, and all modes of business carried on among themselves, from the lowest mechanical trade, which contributes to the health and comfort of life, to the finest art which adorns it with food or drapery for the mind.

All labor, whether bodily or intellectual, is to be paid at the same rate of wages; on the principle, that as the labor becomes merely bodily, it is a greater sacrifice to the individual laborer, to give his time to it; because time is desirable for the cultivation of the intellect, in exact proportion to ignorance. Besides, intellectual labor involves in itself higher pleasures, and is more its own reward, than bodily labor.

Another reason, for setting the same pecuniary value on every kind of labor, is, to give outward expression to the great truth, that all labor is sacred, when done for a common interest. Saints and philosophers already know this, but the childish world does not; and very decided measures must be taken to equalize labors, in the eyes of the young of the community, who are not beyond the moral influences of the world without them. The community will have nothing done within its precincts, but what is done by its own members, who stand all in social equality; — that the children may not "learn to expect one kind of service from Love and Goodwill, and another from the obligation of others to render it," — a grievance of the common society stated, by one of the associated mothers, as destructive of the soul's simplicity. Consequently, as the Universal Education will involve all kinds of operation, necessary to the comforts and elegances of life, every associate, even if he be the digger of a ditch as his highest accomplishment, will be an instructer in that to the young members. Nor will this elevation of bodily labor be liable to lower the tone of manners and refinement in the community. The "children of light" are not altogether unwise in their generation. They have an invisible but all-powerful guard of principles. Minds incapable of refinement, will not be attracted into this association. It is an Ideal community, and only to the ideally inclined will it be attractive; but these are to be found in every rank of life, under every shadow of circumstance. Even among the diggers in the ditch are to be found some, who through religious cultivation, can look down, in meek superiority, upon the outwardly refined, and the book-learned.

Oneida Community and Bible Communism

Complex Marriage

Whatever the premises upon which a "perfect" society was planned and built, the hardest questions concerned sex and marriage. Private family life

[Source: *Bible Communism* . . . (New York: AMS Press, 1973 [1853]), pp. 82-85.]

narrowed the circle of benevolence and love, while unlimited sexual inter-
course led to an indulgent and vicious society. The Shaker "solution" of for-
bidding sexual intercourse entirely sacrificed "the vitality of society in secur-
ing its peace." The author of those words, John Humphrey Noyes (1811-86),
thought that in his Oneida Community he had found the ideal middle path
between profligacy and celibacy. Moving his small group in 1847 from Put-
ney, Vermont to Oneida in western New York, Noyes opted for what he called
complex marriage. In this system, neither monogamy nor polygamy pre-
vailed, but a community-directed plan for union between the sexes that
viewed all men as Potential (if temporary) husbands, all women as potential
(if temporary) wives, all offspring as children of the entire community.
Noyes based his communitarianism (or "communism") on the Bible; in the
document below, he argues that the more familiar marital arrangements do
not have an explicit scriptural endorsement.

So much as this is perfectly clear: that they [New Testament writers] were not in favor of *freedom of divorce,* as a means of mitigating the difficulties connected with marriage. There cannot be any mistake about the fact that Christ, instead of being in favor of freedom of divorce, as it had existed under the Mosaic dispensation, restored the law to Its simplicity and rigor, allowing no divorce except in cases of adultery. (Mark 10.) And Paul stood substantially on the same ground; that is, he forbade believers for any cause to sunder the external marriage tie. (1 Cor. 7.) It is true he supposed the case of separation brought about by the departure of an unbelieving partner, and said that the other was not in bondage in such cases. — Whether this in his mind amounted to the privilege of divorce and marrying again, we cannot perhaps determine; but at all events, it was his will that the whole movement and responsibility of separation should be laid on the unbeliever. He did not allow *the gospel* to introduce separation between husband and wife, or to relax at all the marriage code.

The Bible view of divorce may be illustrated thus: Suppose a commercial system which brings people into a general condition of debt, one to another. Now one way to mitigate this fact and release people from such a state of things, would be by enacting a general Bankrupt law, which would make an end of all obligations by legal repudiation. The Bankrupt law operates to release a man from his promises; and this is just the nature of any legal increase of freedom of divorce. — Christ and Paul, however, were clearly opposed to any Bankrupt law in relation to marriage, as being a mode of discharge not contemplated in the original contract, and as dishonestly rescinding unlimited obligations.

Sympathizing with them in this respect, we as Bible Communists . . . will loyally abide by the view of Christ and of Paul on that subject. If there is to be any alleviation of the miseries of marriage, it is not to come by freedom of divorce.

Again, we are clear that the teachings of the New Testament were sufficiently distinct against *polygamy*. We do not recollect any thing very positive and decisive on this point that can be quoted; but there is a strong intimation of Paul's opinion in the passage where he says, 'a bishop must be the husband of one wife.' (1 Tim. 3:2.)

We do not think it is fair at all to infer any thing against polygamy from the saying that 'what God hath joined together men must not put asunder' — the original doctrine of the inviolability of contracts on which Christ insisted in regard to marriage — because it is not a matter of course that a man shall abandon his first wife by taking a second. No such thing did happen, under the polygamic economy of the patriarchs; on the contrary it was well understood that the contract with the first wife could be fulfilled consistently with taking a second. Christ in that saying is pointing his artillery against putting away. If polygamy were understood to be a nullification of any previous marriage, then that saying would operate against it. But there is no intimation of any such thing in the New Testament, and hence the objection to polygamy must be placed on other grounds. . . .

Here we may dwell for a moment on the identity in principle of monogamy with polygamy. And it will then be seen, that in following Christ we are further from the position of polygamists than ordinary society. It is plain that the fundamental principle of monogamy and polygamy is the same; to wit, the ownership of woman by man. The monogamist claims one woman as his wife — the polygamists, two or a dozen; but the essential thing, the bond of relationship constituting marriage, in both cases is the same, namely, a claim of ownership.

The similarity and the difference between monogamy and polygamy, may be illustrated thus: Suppose slavery to be introduced into Pennsylvania, but limited by law, so that no man can own more than *one* slave. That might be taken to represent monogamy, or the single wife system. In another State suppose men are allowed to own any number they please. That corresponds to polygamy. Now what would be the difference between these two States, in respect to slavery? There would be a difference in the details, and external limitations of the system, but identity in principle. The State that allowed a man to have but one slave, would be on the same general basis of principle with the State that allowed him to have a hundred. Such, we conceive, is the relation between monogamy and polygamy; and as we understand the New Testament, the state which Jesus Christ and Paul were in favor of was neither, but a state of entire freedom from both.

Scientific Propagation

Noyes's rationale for "complex marriage" included a conviction that this system enhanced the prospects for a finer species of humanity in succeeding generations. Properly suited males and females mated (under the supervision of the community) to create the very best progeny, whereas monogamy "leaves mating to be determined by a general scramble, without attempt at scientific direction." This experiment in eugenics, "the noble art of breeding from the best," ended when the religious community itself collapsed by 1880. Thus, no long-term results emerged from John Humphrey Noyes's vigorously denounced program of scientific breeding.

1. Undoubtedly the institution of marriage is an absolute bar to scientific propagation. It distributes the business of procreation in a manner similar to that of animals which pair in a wild state; that is, it leaves mating to be determined by a general scramble, without attempt at scientific direction. Even if the phrenologists and scientific experts had full power to rearrange the pairs from time to time according to their adaptations, there would still be nothing like the systematic selection of the best and suppression of the poorest, which is perfecting the lower animals. How much progress would the horse-breeders expect to make if they were only at liberty to bring their animals together in exclusive pairs?

As we have already intimated, marriage ignores the great difference between the reproductive powers of the sexes, and restricts each man, whatever may be his potency and his value, to the amount of production of which one woman, chosen blindly, may be capable. And while this unnatural and unscientific restriction is theoretically equal for all, practically it discriminates against the best and in favor of the worst; for while the good man will be limited by his conscience to what the law allows, the bad man, free from moral check, will distribute his seed beyond the legal limits as widely as he dares. . . .

2. As the general law of marriage forbids breeding from the best, so the special law and public opinion against consanguineous marriages forbids breeding in and in. And as there is no sure line of demarcation between incest and the allowable degrees of consanguinity in marriage, the tendency of high-toned moralists is generally to extend the domain of the law of incest, and so make all approach to scientific propagation as difficult as possible. Thus there have been movements in various quarters within a few years to place marrying a deceased wife's sister under the ban of law; and the State of New Hampshire

---

[Source: J. H. Noyes, *Essay on Scientific Propagation* (Oneida: Oneida Community, n.d.), pp. 18, 19-20, 21-22.]

has quite recently forbidden the marriage of first cousins as incestuous. At the same time it must be acknowledged that an opposite tendency has manifested itself among scientific men in Europe and in this country. The pressure of analogy from animal-breeding has led physiologists and ethnologists to reexamine the old doctrines in regard to consanguineous connections, and venture on some resistance to the prevailing ideas of incest. This is done very carefully, of course, so as not to give shocks. The most that has been attempted has been to defend the marriages of cousins, dropping an occasional hint in extenuation of the pairing of uncles with nieces. . . .

3. Besides the general difficulties which science has to contend with in the laws of marriage and incest, defended by the whole mass of religionists and moralists, there are particular sects which sin against the law of scientific propagation in special ways, and with a high hand. Let us look at some of them.

The Catholic Church forbids its priests to marry. But its priests are its best men. Therefore the Catholic Church discriminates directly and outrageously *against* the laws of scientific propagation. In effect it castrates the finest animals in its flocks. It encourages the lowest scavenger to breed *ab libitum,* and forbids Father Hyacinthe to leave a single copy of himself behind him. . . .

The Shakers are in the same position with the Catholics. They claim to be the noblest and purest people in the world, a sacred generation, raised by grace high above the rest of mankind; and yet, with full powers to propagate their kind, they virtually castrate themselves, and expend their labors and wealth on their own comfort and on misbegotten adopted children, leaving the production of future generations to common sinners. Doubtless they excuse themselves by appealing to the examples of Jesus and Paul; but they wrong those martyrs of the past. Jesus and Paul were soldiers who had not where to lay their heads, and well they might refrain from taking women and children into their terrible warfare. But the Shakers live in peace and plenty, having the best of houses, farms and barns, and actually breed the best of horses and cattle. So that they have no such excuse as the early Christians had for refusing to breed men. We doubt not that they are sinning in ignorance; but that only makes it the more our duty to tell them that, with their large communistic conservatories, and their material and spiritual wealth, they are just the people to take hold of scientific propagation in earnest, and in advance of the rest of the world; and they could not do a better thing for themselves or for mankind than to expend the vast fund of self-denial and cross-bearing purity which they have accumulated in celibacy on a conscientious and persevering effort to institute among themselves the noble art of breeding from the best.

Latter-Day Saints and New Revelation

If the Oneida Community was the most radical of the religious utopias, Mormonism was the most successful. Stemming from the visions of the young Joseph Smith (1805-44), secured by the revelations in the Book of Mormon (first published in 1830), and graced with the gifts of organization, discipline, and sacrifice, the Church of Jesus Christ of Latter-Day Saints wrote a dramatic chapter into America's history. Smith's 1843 revelation regarding polygamy or plural marriage aggravated the outsiders' suspicions of and hostility toward this distinctly different, stubbornly separate group. That hostility led in 1844 to the assassination of Joseph Smith. That crime led in turn, first, to the elevation of Brigham Young to leadership over the largest body of Mormons and, second, to that group's exodus from a still-hostile Illinois to an empty desert in the far west: the Great Salt Lake Basin. This was only the last in a series of moves — from New York to Ohio, Ohio to Missouri, Missouri to Illinois. In nineteenth-century America, no utopian adventure escaped scorn; few escaped violence. The history of early Mormonism is a history of vigilantes and armies, of mobs and massacres. Eight excerpts follow, without further introduction, illustrating the turbulent years of the utopian experiment that stayed.

1.

Joseph Smith Recounts His First Vision (1820)

My mind at times was greatly excited, the cry and tumult were so great and incessant. The Presbyterians were most decided against the Baptists and Methodists, and used all the powers of both reason and sophistry to prove their errors, or, at least, to make the people think they were in error. On the other hand, the Baptists and Methodists in their turn were equally zealous in endeavoring to establish their own tenets and disprove all others.

[Sources: (1) B. H. Roberts, ed., *History of the Church of Jesus Christ of Latter-Day Saints* (Salt Lake City: Deseret Book Co., 2nd ed. rev., 1964), I, 4-6. (2) Lucy Mack Smith, *Biographical Sketches of Joseph Smith the Prophet . . .* (New York: Arno Press, 1969 [1853]), pp. 143-45, 145-46. The author was Joseph Smith's mother. (3) *Deseret News Extra*, September 14, 1852; as printed in Lawrence Foster, *Religion and Sexuality: Three American Communal Experiments of the Nineteenth Century* (New York: Oxford University Press, 1981), pp. 313, 315-16, 318. (4) Smith, *Biographical Sketches of Joseph Smith the Prophet . . .* , pp. 278-79. (5) Roberts, ed., *History of the Church of Jesus Christ of Latter-Day Saints*, VII, 230. (6) Roberts, ed., *History of the Church of Jesus Christ of Latter-Day Saints*, VII, 478-79, 480. (7) Roberts, ed., *History of the Church of Jesus Christ of Latter-Day Saints*, VII, 454-55. (8) Roberts, ed., *History of the Church of Jesus Christ of Latter-Day Saints*, VII, 601.]

Joseph Smith
(National Portrait Gallery, Smithsonian Institution, Washington, D.C.)

In the midst of this war of words and tumult of opinions, I often said to myself, what is to be done? Who of all these parties are right; or, are they all wrong together? If any one of them be right, which is it, and how shall I know it? While I was laboring under the extreme difficulties caused by the contests of these parties of religionists, I was one day reading the Epistle of James, first chapter and fifth verse, which reads:

> If any of you lack wisdom, let him ask of God, that giveth to all men liberally, and upbraideth not; and it shall be given him.

Never did any passage of Scripture come with more power to the heart of man than this did at this time to mine. It seemed to enter with great force into every feeling of my heart. I reflected on it again and again, knowing that if any person needed wisdom from God, I did; for how to act I did not know and unless I could get more wisdom than I then had, I would never know; for the teachers of religion of the different sects understood the same passage of Scripture so differently as to destroy all confidence in settling the question by an appeal to the Bible. At length I came to the conclusion that I must either remain in darkness and confusion, or else I must do as James directs, that is, ask of God. I at length came to the determination to "ask of God," concluding that if He gave wisdom to them that lacked wisdom, and would give liberally, and not upbraid, I might venture. So, in accordance with this, my determination to ask God, I retired to the woods to make the attempt. It was on the morning of a beautiful, clear day, early in the spring of eighteen hundred and twenty. It was the first time in my life that I had made such an attempt, for amidst all my anxieties I had never as yet made the attempt to pray vocally.

After I had retired to the place where I had previously designed to go, having looked around me, and finding myself alone, I kneeled down and began to offer up the desires of my heart to God. I had scarcely done so, when immediately I was seized upon by some power which entirely overcame me, and had such an astonishing influence over me as to bind my tongue so that I could not speak. Thick darkness gathered around me, and it seemed to me for a time as if I were doomed to sudden destruction. But, exerting all my powers to call upon God to deliver me out of the power of this enemy which had seized upon me, and at the very moment when I was ready to sink into despair and abandon myself to destruction — not to an imaginary ruin, but to the power of some actual being from the unseen world, who had such marvelous power as I had never before felt in any being — just at this moment of great alarm, I saw a pillar of light exactly over my head, above the brightness of the sun, which descended gradually until it fell upon me.

It no sooner appeared than I found myself delivered from the enemy which held me bound. When the light rested upon me I saw two personages, whose brightness and glory defy all description, standing above me in the air. One of them spoke unto me, calling me by name, and said — pointing to the other —

"This Is My Beloved Son, Hear Him."

My object in going to inquire of the Lord was to know which of all the sects was right, that I might know which to join. No sooner, therefore, did I get possession of myself, so as to be able to speak, than I asked the personages who stood above me in the light, which of all the sects was right — and which I should join. I was answered that I must join none of them, for they were all wrong, and the personage who addressed me said that all their creeds were an abomination in His sight: that those professors were all corrupt; that "they draw near to me with their lips, but their hearts are far from me; they teach for doctrines the commandments of men: having a form of godliness, but they deny the power thereof." He again forbade me to join with any of them: and many other things did he say unto me, which I cannot write at this time. When I came to myself again, I found myself lying on my back, looking up into heaven. When the light had departed, I had no strength; but soon recovering in some degree, I went home. And as I leaned up to the fireplace, mother inquired what the matter was. I replied, "Never mind, all is well — I am well enough off." I then said to my mother, "I have learned for myself that Presbyterianism is not true."

2.
Printing of the Book of Mormon in 1830

Oliver Cowdery[2] commenced the work immediately after Joseph left, and the printing went on very well for a season, but the clouds of persecution again began to gather. The rabble, and a party of restless religionists, began to counsel together, as to the most efficient means of putting a stop to our proceedings.

About the first council of this kind was held in a room adjoining that in which Oliver and a young man by the name of Robinson were printing. Mr. Robinson, being curious to know what they were doing in the next room, applied his ear to a hole in the partition wall, and by this means overheard several persons expressing their fears in reference to the Book of Mormon. One said, "it was destined to break down every thing before it, if not put a stop to," and, "that it was likely to injure the prospects of their ministers," and then inquired, whether they should endure it. "No, no," was the unanimous reply. It was then asked, "how shall we prevent the printing of this book?" Upon which it was resolved by the meeting, that three of their company should be appointed to go to the house of Mr. Smith, on the following Tuesday or Wednesday, while the men were gone to their work, and request Mrs. Smith to read the manuscript to them; that, after she had done reading it, two of the company should endeavour to divert her attention from it to some other object, while the third, seizing the opportunity, should snatch it from the drawer, or wherever it should be kept, and commit it immediately to the flames.

"Again," said the speaker, "suppose we fall in this, and the book is printed in defiance of all that we can do to the contrary, what means shall we then adopt? Shall we buy their books and allow our families to read them?" They all responded, "No." They then entered into a solemn covenant, never to purchase

2. An early associate of Joseph Smith's, Cowdery actively aided in the preparation of the Book of Mormon and, in the "Testimony of Three Witnesses" published with the book, vouched for its authenticity.

even a single copy of the work, or permit one member of their families to buy or read one, that they might thus avert the awful calamity which threatened them.

Olivery Cowdery came home that evening, and, after relating the whole affair with much solemnity, he said, "Mother, what shall I do with the manuscript? where shall I put it to keep it away from them?"

Kirtland Temple in Ohio, c. 1904
Ohio, the site of the first Latter-Day Saint temple, did not long endure
as a major Mormon center, with migrations quite early to Missouri
and Illinois, followed by the great exodus to Utah.
(Keystone-Mast Collection, University of California, Riverside)

"Oliver," said I, "I do not think the matter so serious after all, for there is a watch kept constantly about the house, and I need not take out the manuscript to read it to them unless I choose, and for its present safety I can have it deposited in a chest, under the head of my bed, in such a way that it never will be disturbed." I then placed it in a chest, which was so high, that when placed under the bed, the whole weight of the bedstead rested upon the lid. Having made this arrangement, we felt quite at rest, and that night, the family retired to rest at the usual hour, all save Peter Whitmer,[3] who spent the night on guard. . . .

On the fourth day subsequent to the afore-mentioned council, soon after my husband left the house to go to his work, those three delegates appointed by the council, came to accomplish the work assigned them. Soon after they entered, one of them began thus: —

"Mrs. Smith, we hear that you have a gold bible; we have come to see if you will be so kind as to show it to us?"

"No, gentlemen," said I, "we have no gold bible, but we have a translation of some gold plates, which have been brought forth for the purpose of making known to the world the plainness of the Gospel, and also to give a history of the people which formerly inhabited this continent." I then proceeded to relate the substance of what is contained in the Book of Mormon, dwelling particularly upon the principles of religion therein contained. I endeavoured to show them the similarity between these principles, and the simplicity of the Gospel taught by Jesus Christ in the New Testament. "Notwithstanding all this," said I, "the different denominations are very much opposed to us. The Universalists are alarmed lest their religion should suffer loss, the Presbyterians tremble for their salaries, the Methodists also come, and they rage, for they worship a God without body or parts, and they know that our faith comes in contact with this principle."

After hearing me through, the gentlemen said, "can we see the manuscript, then?"

"No, sir," replied I, "you cannot see it. I have told you what it contains, and that must suffice."

He made no reply to this, but said, "Mrs. Smith, you and the most your children have belonged to our church for some length of time, and we respect you very highly. You say a great deal about the Book of Mormon, which your son has found, and you believe much of what he tells you, yet we cannot bear the thoughts of losing you, and they do wish — I wish, that if you do believe those things, you would not say anything more upon the subject — I do wish you would not."

---

3. Peter Whitmer, Jr., like Cowdery, asserted the genuineness of the Book of Mormon, Whitmer doing so in the "Testimony of Eight Witnesses" which is regularly published in the book.

"Deacon Beckwith," said I, "if you should stick my flesh full of faggots, and even burn me at the stake, I would declare, as long as God should give me breath, that Joseph has got that Record, and that I know it to be true."

At this, he observed to his companions, "You see it is of no use to say anything more to her, for we cannot change her mind." Then, turning to me, he said, "Mrs. Smith, I see that it is not possible to persuade you out of your belief, therefore I deem it unnecessary to say anything more upon the subject."

"No, sir," said I, "it is not worth your while."

3.
Joseph Smith's Revelation on Plural Marriage, 1843

Revelation,

Given to Joseph Smith, Nauvoo, July 12th, 1843.

Verily thus saith the Lord, unto you my servant Joseph, that inasmuch as you have enquired of my hand, to know and understand wherein I the Lord justified my servants, Abraham, Isaac, and Jacob; as also Moses, David, and Solomon, my servants, as touching the principle and doctrine of their having many wives, and concubines: Behold! and lo, I am the Lord thy God, and will answer thee as touching this matter: Therefore, prepare thy heart to receive and obey the instructions which I am about to give unto you; for all those, who have this law revealed unto them, must obey the same; for behold! I reveal unto you a new and an everlasting covenant. . . .

I am the Lord thy God, and will give unto thee the law of my Holy Priesthood, as was ordained by me, and my Father, before the world was. Abraham received all things, whatsoever he received, by revelation and commandment, by my word, saith the Lord, and hath entered into this exaltation, and sitteth upon his throne.

Abraham received promises concerning his seed, and of the fruit of his loins, — from whose loins ye are, viz., my servant Joseph, — which were to continue, so long as they were in the world; and as touching Abraham and his seed, out of the world, they should continue; both in the world and out of the world should they continue as innumerable as the stars, or, if ye were to count the sand upon the sea-shore, ye could not number them. This promise is yours, also, because ye are of Abraham, and the promise was made unto Abraham, and by this law are the continuation of the works of my Father, wherein he glorifieth himself. Go ye, therefore, and do the works of Abraham, — enter ye into my law, and ye shall be saved. But if ye enter not into my law, ye cannot receive the promises of my Father, which he made unto Abraham.

God commanded Abraham, and Sarah gave Hagar to Abraham, to wife. And why did she do it? Because this was the law, and from Hagar sprang many people. This, therefore, was fulfilling, among other things, the promises. Was Abraham, therefore, under condemnation? Verily, I say unto you, *Nay;* for I the Lord commanded it. Abraham was commanded to offer his son Isaac; nevertheless, it was written, thou shalt not kill. Abraham, however, did not refuse, and it was accounted unto him for righteousness.

Abraham received concubines, and they bare him children, and it was accounted unto him for righteousness, because they were given unto him, and he abode in my law: as Isaac also, and Jacob did none other things [than] that which they were commanded; and because they did none other things than that which they were commanded, they have entered into their exaltation, according to the promises, and sit upon thrones; and are not angels, but are Gods. David also received many wives and concubines, as also Solomon, and Moses my servant; as also many others of my servants from the beginning of creation until this time; and in nothing did they sin, save in those things which they received not of me. . . .

Now as touching the law of the priesthood, there are many things pertaining thereunto. Verily, if a man be called of my Father, as was Aaron, by mine own voice, and by the voice of him that sent me, and I have endowed him with the keys of the power of this priesthood, if he do anything in my name, and according to my law, and by my word, he will not commit sin, and I will justify him. Let no one, therefore, set on my servant Joseph; for I will justify him; for he shall do the sacrifice which I require at his hands for his transgressions, saith the Lord your God.

And again, as pertaining to the law of the Priesthood; — if any man espouse a virgin, and desire to espouse another, and the first give her consent; and if he espouses the second, and they are virgins, and have vowed to no other man, then is he justified; he cannot commit adultery, for they are given unto him; for he cannot commit adultery with that, that belongeth unto him, and to none else: and if he have ten virgins given unto him by this law, he cannot commit adultery; for they belong to him; and they are given unto him; — therefore is he justified. But if one, or either of the ten virgins, after she is espoused, shall be with another man, she has committed adultery, and shall be destroyed; for they are given unto him to multiply and replenish the earth, according to my commandment, and to fulfil the promise which was given by my Father before the foundation of the world; and for their exaltation in the eternal worlds, that they may bear the souls of men; for herein is the work of my Father continued, that he may be glorified.

4.
Joseph Smith's Martyrdom, June 27, 1844

My sons [Joseph and his brother Hyrum] were thrown into jail [in Carthage, Illinois, June 25, 1844], where they remained three days, in company with brothers Richards, Taylor, and Markham. At the end of this time, the Governor disbanded most of the men, but left a guard of eight of our bitterest enemies over the jail, and sixty more of the same character about a hundred yards distant. He then came into Nauvoo with a guard of fifty or sixty men, made a short speech, and returned immediately. During his absence from Carthage, the guard rushed brother Markham out of the place at the point of the bayonet. Soon after this, two hundred of those discharged in the morning rushed into Carthage, armed, and painted black, red, and yellow, and in ten minutes fled again, leaving my sons murdered and mangled corpses!!

In leaving the place, a few of them found Samuel coming into Carthage, alone, on horseback, and, finding that he was one of our family, they attempted to shoot him, but he escaped out of their hands, although they pursued him at the top of their speed for more than two hours. He succeeded the next day in getting to Nauvoo, in season to go out and meet the procession with the bodies of Hyrum and Joseph, as the mob had the *kindness* to allow us the privilege of bringing them home, and burying them in Nauvoo, notwithstanding the immense reward which was offered by the Missourians for Joseph's head.

Their bodies were attended home by only two persons, save those that went from this place. These were brother Willard Richards, and a Mr. Hamilton; brother John Taylor having been shot in prison, and nearly killed, he could not be moved until some time afterwards.

After the corpses were washed, and dressed in their burial clothes, we were allowed to see them. I had for a long time braced every nerve, roused every energy of my soul, and called upon God to strengthen me; but when I entered the room, and saw my murdered sons extended both at once before my eyes, and heard the sobs and groans of my family, and the cries of "Father! Husband! Brothers!" from the lips of their wives, children, brother, and sisters, it was too much, I sank back, crying to the Lord, in the agony of my soul, "My God, my God, why hast thou forsaken this family!" A voice replied, "I have taken them to myself, that they might have rest." Emma [wife of Joseph] was carried back to her room almost in a state of insensibility. Her oldest son approached the corpse, and dropped upon his knees, and laying his cheek against his father's, and kissing him, exclaimed, "Oh, my father! my father!" As for myself, I was swallowed up in the depth of my afflictions; and though my soul was filled with horror past imagination, yet I was dumb, until I arose again to contemplate the

Courthouse in Carthage, Illinois,
scene of the assassination of Joseph and Hyrum Smith
(Keystone-Mast Collection, University of California, Riverside)

spectacle before me. Oh! at that moment how my mind flew through every scene of sorrow and distress which we had passed together, in which they had shown the innocence and sympathy which filled their guileless hearts. As I looked upon their peaceful, smiling countenances, I seemed almost to hear them say — "Mother, weep not for us, we have overcome the world by love; we carried to them the Gospel, that their souls might be saved; they slew us for our testimony, and thus placed us beyond their power; their ascendancy is for a moment, ours is an eternal triumph."

5.
Brigham Young Assumes Leadership, 1844

I do not care who leads the church, even though it were Ann Lee [of the Shakers]; but one thing I must know, and that is what God says about it. I have the keys and the means of obtaining the mind of God on the subject.

I know there are those in our midst who will seek the lives of the Twelve as they did the lives of Joseph and Hyrum. We shall ordain others and give the fulness of the priesthood, so that if we are killed the fulness of the priesthood may remain.

Joseph conferred upon our heads all the keys and powers belonging to the Apostleship which he himself held before he was taken away, and no man or set of men can get between Joseph and the Twelve in this world or in the world to come.

How often has Joseph said to the Twelve, 'I have laid the foundation and you must build thereon, for upon your shoulders the kingdom rests.'

The Twelve, as a quorum, will not be permitted to tarry here long; they will go abroad and bear off the kingdom to the nations of the earth, and baptize the people faster than mobs can kill them off. I would like, were it my privilege, to take my valise and travel and preach till we had a people gathered who would be true.

My private feelings would be to let the affairs of men and women alone, only go and preach and baptize them into the kingdom of God: yet, whatever duty God places upon me, in his strength I intend to fulfill it.

6.
Exodus Announced, October 8, 1845

The exodus of the nation of the only true Israel from these United States to a far distant region of the west, where bigotry, intolerance and insatiable oppression lose their power over them — forms a new epoch, not only in the history of the church, but of this nation. And we hereby timely advise you to consider well, as the spirit may give you understanding, the various and momentous bearings of this great movement, and hear what the spirit saith unto you by this our epistle.

Jesus Christ was delivered up into the hands of the Jewish nation to save or condemn them, to be well or maltreated by them according to the determinate counsel and foreknowledge of God. And regard not that even in the light of a catastrophe wholly unlooked for. The spirit of prophecy has long since portrayed in the *Book of Mormon* what might be the conduct of this nation towards the Israel of the last days. The same spirit of prophecy that dwelt richly in the bosom of Joseph has time and again notified the counselors of this church of emergencies that might arise, of which this removal is one; and one too in which all the Latter-day Saints throughout the length and breadth of all the United States should have a thrilling and deliberate interest. The same evil that premeditated against Mordecai awaited equally all the families of his nation. If the authorities of this church cannot abide in peace within the pale of this nation, neither can those who implicitly hearken to their wholesome counsel. A word to the wise is sufficient. You all know and have doubtless felt for years the necessity of a removal provided the government [U. S.] should not be sufficiently protective to allow us to worship God according to the dictates of our own consciences, and of the omnipotent voice of eternal truth. . . . Wake up, wake up, dear brethren, we exhort you, from the Mississippi to the Atlantic, and from Canada to Florida, to the present glorious emergency in which the God of heaven has placed you to prove your faith by your works, preparatory to a rich endowment in the Temple of the Lord, and the obtaining of promises and deliverances, and glories for yourselves and your children and your dead. And we are well persuaded you will do these things, though we thus stir up your pure minds to remembrance. In so doing, the blessings of many, ready to perish like silent dew upon the grass, and the approbation of generations to come, and the hallowed joys of eternal life will rest upon you. And we can not but assure you in conclusion of our most joyful confidence, touching your union and implicit obedience to the counsel of the Great God through the Presidency of the saints. With these assurances and hopes concerning you, we bless you and supplicate the wisdom and furtherance of the Great Head of the Church upon your designs and efforts.

[Signed] BRIGHAM YOUNG, President.
Willard Richards, Clerk.

7.
Requirements for the Journey, 1845

Requirements of Each Family of Five
for the Journey across the Plains

Each family consisting of five adults, will require 1 good strong wagon, well covered. 3 good yokes of oxen between the ages of four and ten. Two or more cows. One or more good beeves, some sheep if they have them.

One thousand pounds of flour or other bread stuff and good sacks to put it in.

One bushel of beans.

One hundred pounds of sugar.

One good musket or rifle to each man.

One pound of powder and three lbs. lead (or perhaps more).

Two lbs. tea, 5 lbs. coffee.

Twenty-five pounds of salt.

A few pounds of dried beef, or bacon, as they choose.

A good tent and furniture to each two families.

From ten to fifty pounds of seed to a family.

And from twenty-five to one hundred pounds of farming or other tools.

Clothing and bedding to each family of five persons not to exceed five hundred pounds.

One or more sets of saw and gristmill irons to each company of one hundred families.

Cooking utensils to consist of a bake-kettle, frying-pan, coffee pot, tin cups, plates, and forks, spoons, pans, etc., etc., as few as will do.

A few goods to trade with the Indians.

A little iron and steel, a few pounds of nails.

Each wagon supposed to be loaded on the start with one ton without the persons or twenty-eight hundred including them.

If going to the coast it is not necessary to carry seed wheat, oats or grass. Nor are cattle and sheep absolutely necessary except to live on while upon the journey, as the country abounds in both cattle and sheep. A few horses will be necessary for each company. Also a few cannon and ammunition for the same. The journey to the coast will require some four or five months, being upwards of two thousand miles.

There was also added two sets of pulley blocks and rope for crossing rivers to each company.

Two ferry boats to each company.

One keg of alcohol of five gallons for each two families.

Ten pounds of dried apples for each family.

Five pounds of dried peaches.

Twenty pounds of dried pumpkin.

Two pounds of black pepper.

One pound of cayenne.

One-half pound mustard.

Twelve nutmegs. One fish seine for each company. Hooks and lines for each family.

8.

Church Authorities Appeal to Iowa Governor, February 28, 1846

To His Excellency,
Governor of the Territory of Iowa,

Honored Sir: The time is at hand, in which several thousand free citizens of this great Republic, are to be driven from their peaceful homes and firesides, their property and farms, and their dearest constitutional rights — to wander in the barren plains, and sterile mountains of western wilds, and linger out their lives in wretched exile far beyond the pale of professed civilization; or else be exterminated upon their own lands by the people, and authorities of the state of Illinois. As life is sweet we have chosen *banishment* rather than death. But Sir, the terms of our banishment are so rigid that we have not sufficient time allotted us to make the necessary preparations to encounter the hardships and difficulties of those dreary and uninhabited regions. We have not time allowed us to dispose of our property, dwellings, and farms, consequently, many of us will have to leave them unsold, without the means of procuring the necessary provisions, clothing, teams, etc. to sustain us but a short distance beyond the settlements: hence our persecutors have placed us in very unpleasant circumstances.

To stay, is death by 'fire and sword', to go into banishment unprepared, is death by starvation. But yet under these heart-rending circumstances, several hundreds of us have started upon our dreary journey, and are now encamped in Lee county, Iowa, suffering much from the intensity of the cold. Some of us are already without food, and others barely sufficient to last a few weeks: hundreds of others must shortly follow us in the same unhappy condition.

Therefore, we, the Presiding Authorities of the Church of Jesus Christ of Latter-day Saints, as a committee in behalf of several thousand suffering exiles, humbly ask your Excellency to shield and protect us in our constitutional rights, while we are passing through the territory over which you have jurisdiction. And should any of the exiles be under the necessity of stopping in this territory for a time, either in the settled or unsettled parts, for the purpose of raising crops, by renting farms or upon the public lands, or to make the necessary preparations for their exile in any lawful way, we humbly petition your Excellency to use an influence and power in our behalf; and thus preserve thousands of American citizens, together with their wives and children from intense sufferings, starvation and death.

And your petitioners will ever pray.

3. Restorations and Expectations

Restorationism: Disciples of Christ

Barton Stone (1772-1844)

America's best-known restorationist movement is that associated with the names of Barton Stone and Alexander Campbell. Initially separate, the groups led by each man merged into one early in the 1830s. A Presbyterian associated with Kentucky's famous Cane Ridge revival, Barton Stone along with some associates enunciated in 1804 the characteristic principles of restorationism: returning to the Bible for all authority and direction, rejecting sectarian or denominational labels, and bringing the primitive church of first-century Palestine to the expanding frontier of nineteenth-century America. Stone was the acknowledged leader of Kentucky revivalism no less than of Kentucky restorationism.

The Last Will and Testament of the Springfield Presbytery

The Presbytery of Springfield, sitting at Cane-ridge, in the county of Bourbon, being, through a gracious Providence, in more than ordinary bodily health, growing in strength and size daily; and in perfect soundness and composure of mind; but knowing that it is appointed for all delegated bodies once to die; and considering that the life of every such body is very uncertain, do make, and ordain this our last Will and Testament, in manner and form following, viz.:

[Source: W. E. Tucker and L. G. McAllister, *Journey into Faith* (St. Louis: Bethany Press, 1975), pp. 77-79.]

Imprimis. We *will,* that this body die, be dissolved, and sink into union with the Body of Christ at large; for there is but one Body, and one Spirit, even as we are called in one hope of our calling.

Item. We *will,* that our name of distinction, with its *Reverend* title, be forgotten, that there be but one Lord over God's heritage and his name One.

Item. We *will,* that our power of making laws for the government of the church and executing them by delegated authority, forever cease; that the people may have free course to the Bible, and adopt *the law of the Spirit of life in Christ Jesus.*

Item. We *will,* that candidates for the Gospel ministry henceforth study the Holy Scriptures with fervent prayer, and obtain license from God to preach the simple Gospel, *with the Holy Ghost sent down from heaven,* without any mixture of philosophy, vain deceit, traditions of men, or the rudiments of the world. And let none henceforth take *this honor to himself, but he that is called of God, as was Aaron.*

Item. We *will,* that the church of Christ resume her native right of internal government — try her candidates for the ministry, as to their soundness in the faith, acquaintance with experimental religion, gravity and aptness to teach; and admit no other proof of their authority but Christ speaking in them. We will, that the church of Christ look to the Lord of the harvest to send forth laborers into his harvest; and that she resume her primitive right of trying those *who say they are apostles, and are not.*

Item. We *will,* that each particular church, as a body, actuated by the same spirit, choose her own preacher, and support him by a free will offering, without a written *call or subscription* — admit members — remove offences; and never henceforth *delegate* her right of government to any man or set of men whatever.

Item. We *will,* that the people henceforth take the Bible as the only sure guide to heaven; and as many as are offended with other books, which stand in competition with it, may cast them into the fire if they choose; for it is better to enter into life having one book, than having many to be cast into hell.

Item. We *will,* that preachers and people, cultivate a spirit of mutual forbearance; pray more and dispute less; and while they behold the signs of the times, look up, and confidently expect that redemption draweth nigh.

Item. We *will,* that our weak brethren, who may have been wishing to make the Presbytery of Springfield their king, and wot not what is now become of it, betake themselves to the Rock of Ages, and follow Jesus for the future.

Alexander Campbell (1788-1866)

In western Pennsylvania, meanwhile, Alexander Campbell (together with his father, Thomas) reached similar conclusions about the necessity of finding a common Christian unity by means of a common loyalty to the New Testament. Five years after the Cane Ridge statement, the Campbells issued a "Declaration and Address" that also called for promoting a "simple evangelical christianity." Then in 1835, Campbell in a more definitive statement of restorationist theology laid down the principles of Christian union. While Campbell hoped that his movement would bring an end to denominationalism and to sectarian bickering, he instead brought into being a new denomination: the Disciples of Christ. Even more ironically, that frontier denomination managed, through schism and separation, to spin off a couple more denominations within a century of Campbell's death. On the American frontier, restoring the primitive church of the apostolic age seemed so alluring; it proved so difficult.

"I pray — for those who shall believe on me through their teaching, *that all may be one;* that as thou, Father, art in me, and I in thee, *they also may be one in us, that the world may believe* that thou hast sent me, and that thou gavest me the glory, which I have given them, that *they may be one,* as we are one; I in them, and thou in me, *that their union may be perfected:* and that *the world may know* that thou hast sent me, and that thou lovest them as thou lovest me." Thus Messiah prayed; and well might he pray thus, seeing he was wise enough to teach that, "If a kingdom be torn by factions, that kingdom cannot subsist. And if a family be torn by factions, that family cannot subsist. By civil dissensions any kingdom may be desolated; and no city or family, where such dissensions are, can subsist."

If this be true, — and true it is, if Jesus be the Messiah, — in what moral desolation is the kingdom of Jesus Christ! Was there at any time, or is there now, in all the earth, a kingdom more convulsed by internal broils and dissensions, than what is commonly called the church of Jesus Christ? Should any one think it lawful to paganize both the Greek and Latin churches — to eject one hundred millions of members of the Greek and Roman communions from the visible and invisible precincts of the Christian family or kingdom of Jesus Christ, and regard the Protestant faith and people as the only true faith and the only true citizens of the kingdom of Jesus; what then shall we say of them, con-

---

[Source: Alexander Campbell, *The Christian System, in Reference to the Union of Christians, and the Restoration of Primitive Christianity* . . . 4th ed. (New York: Arno Press, 1969 [1866]), pp. 105-8.]

Alexander and Margaret Campbell
(Library of Congress)

templated as the visible kingdom over which Jesus presides as Prophet, Priest, and King? Of forty millions of Protestants shall we constitute the visible kingdom of the Prince of Peace? Be it so for the sake of argument; and what then? The Christian army is forty millions strong; but how do they muster? Under forty ensigns? Under forty antagonist leaders? Would to God there were but forty! In the Geneva detachment alone there is almost that number of petty chiefs. My soul sickens at the details!

Take the English branch of the Protestant faith — I mean England and the United States and all the islands where the English Bible is read; and how many broils, dissensions, and anathemas may we compute? I will not attempt to name the antagonizing creeds, feuds, and parties, that are in eternal war, under the banners of the Prince of Peace. And yet they talk of love and charity, and of the conversion of the Jews, the Turks, and Pagans!!!

Shall we turn from the picture, lay down our pen, and languish in despair? No: for Jesus has said, "Happy the *peace-makers,* for they shall be called *sons of God."* But who can make peace when all the elements are at war? Who so enthusiastic as to fancy that he can stem the torrent of strife or quench the violence of sectarian fire? But the page of universal history whispers in our ears, "If you tarry till all the belligerent armies lay down their arms and make one spontaneous and simultaneous effort to unite, you will be as very a simpleton as he that sat by the Euphrates waiting till all its waters ran into the sea." . . .

From Messiah's intercession above quoted, it is incontrovertible that union is strength, and disunion weakness; that there is a plan founded in infinite wisdom and love, by which, and by which alone, the world may both *believe* and *know* that God has sent his Son to be the Saviour of the world; and, like all the schemes of Heaven, it is simple to admiration. No mortal need fancy that he shall have the honor of devising either the plan of uniting Christians in one holy band of zealous co-operation, or of converting Jews and Gentiles to the faith that Jesus is that *seed* in whom all the families of the earth are yet to be blessed. The plan is divine. It is ordained by God; and, better still, it is already revealed. Is any one impatient to hear it? Let him again read the intercessions of the Lord Messiah, which we have chosen for our motto. Let him then examine the two following propositions, and say whether these do not express Heaven's own scheme of augmenting and conserving the body of Christ.

1st. *Nothing is essential to the conversion of the world but the union and co-operation of Christians.*

2d. *Nothing is essential to the union of Christians but the Apostles' teaching or testimony.*

Or does he choose to express the plan of the Self-Existent in other words? Then he may change the order, and say —

1st. *The testimony of the Apostles is the only and all-sufficient means of uniting all Christians.*

2d. *The union of Christians with the Apostles' testimony is all-sufficient and alone sufficient to the conversion of the world.*

Neither truth alone nor union alone is sufficient to subdue the unbelieving nations; but truth and union combined are omnipotent. They are *omnipotent,* for God is in them and with them, and has consecrated and blessed them for this very purpose.

These two propositions have been stated, illustrated, developed, (and shall I say proved?) in the "Christian Baptist," and "Millennial Harbinger," to the conviction of thousands. Indeed, one of them is as universally conceded as it has been proposed, viz.: *That the union of Christians is essential to the conversion of the world;* and though, perhaps, some might be found who would question whether, if all Christians were united, the whole world could be converted to God; there is no person, of whom we have heard, who admits a general or universal prevalence of the gospel in what is usually called the millennial age of the world, and who admits that moral means will have anything to do with its introduction, who does not also admit that the union of Christians is essential to that state of things. Indeed, to suppose that all Christians will form one communion in that happy age of the world, and not before it, is to suppose a moral effect without a cause.

The second proposition, viz.: *That the word or testimony of the Apostles is itself all-sufficient and alone sufficient to the union of all Christians,* cannot be rationally doubted by any person acquainted with that testimony, or who admits the competency of their inspiration to make them infallible teachers of the Christian institution. And, indeed, all who contend for those human institutions called creeds contend for them as necessary only to the existence of a party, or while the present schisms, contentions, and dissensions exist. Therefore, all the defences of creeds, ancient and modern, while they assert that the Bible alone is the only perfect and infallible rule of faith and morals, not only concede that these symbols called *creeds* are imperfect and fallible, but also that these creeds never can achieve what the Bible, without them, can accomplish.

Millennialism

Shakers

Remembered more for the simplicity of their communal life, or for their celibacy, or for their lively forms of worship, the Shakers themselves emphasized the Second Coming of Christ. The group's official name so testifies: the United Society of Believers in Christ's Second Coming (the Millennial Church). For Shakers, moreover, that Second Coming was not some distant, dimly perceived event to be ushered in by war and great tribulation. Rather, it was an event of this age, Christ having already appeared — and as a woman! Christ came first through a male, Jesus of Nazareth; Christ now appears or is made manifest in a female, "Mother" Ann Lee (1736-84). A

[Source: Frederick W. Evans, *Compendium of the Origin, History, Principles, Rule and Regulations, Government and Doctrine of the* [*Shakers*] (New York: AMS Press, 1975 [1867]), pp. 65-70.]

native of England, Ann came to America in 1774 where she taught that pro-creation was unnecessary since the kingdom of God was at hand. Further-more, she argued, the "Church in Jesus" was a celibate church; to enter into this church and therefore into the millennium, one must live a life of purity and strict devotion. Shakerism had its greatest growth in nineteenth-century America where it benefited from widespread revivalism. The lead-ing Shaker writer of that period, Frederick W. Evans (1808-93), describes below the "Character of the Primitive Christian Church" — a character which the simple, celibate Shaker communities would re-create, as nearly as it lay in their power to do.

1. Jesus Christ foretold two things of great importance. *One* was, that the Chris-tian Church, which he originated, would not continue, but would be utterly de-stroyed. He said that himself and his disciples were "the light of the world;" and he counselled souls to walk in the light while they had it, because "the night cometh wherein no man can work." That is, there would come a time when "in-iquity would abound, and the love of many would wax cold," and when there would be no true Church on the earth. The same was confirmed by his Apos-tles, who said there would be a "falling away," and that "that man of sin would be *revealed*," in place of a revelation of Christ.

2. The *other* was, that another appearing on earth of the same Christ (or second Adam and Eve) as had been manifested to him (Jesus) would take place, to establish a second and more perfect Christian Church, precisely according to the Pattern of the Christian Church *in himself;* for then Christ would come, not in *one* individual only, but "in the clouds of [the fourth] heaven, with power and great glory;" that is, in *numbers* of persons, or "clouds of witnesses," in and among whom Christ would make his "second appearing without sin unto sal-vation." "Behold the Lord cometh in ten thousand of his saints."

3. For the Shaker idea is, that in Jesus alone were all the characteristics of a perfect Christian; that the Apostles stood upon a *lower* plane, and were children of God by "adoption" only, *not really.* This point is conclusively proved from the conjoint testimony of themselves and Jesus.

4. Jesus said he had "many things to say unto them that they were not able to bear," and exclaimed of them, "O ye of little faith!" These expressions, with the mistaken conceptions the Apostles had formed of the nature of his king-dom and of the resurrection, demonstrate that they only "knew in part, proph-esied in part, and saw as through a glass darkly" and imperfectly.

5. The Apostles were "only a *kind* of first-fruits;" not the kingdom itself. But they had the spirit of promise and of hope, that in the second appearing, when Christ should be manifested in the order of *Mother*, through a *female*, as he had been in the order of *Father*, through *Jesus*, they should sit down with Je-sus on his throne — rise to the same plane.

6. This was the condition and expectation of the Apostolic Church, whose members were all Hebrews. For, as Maria Childs remarks, "Christianity was somewhat exclusive and national in its character, being preached only by Jesus, and addressed only to Hebrews."

7. The Church professed to live a virgin life; and those in it who "waxed wanton against Christ," and *married,* had "damnation, because they had cast off their first faith" of *celibacy.* "They had all things common." The 8,000 who were converted in two days "sold all their possessions" of houses and land, and formed a perfect community. They did not call the least thing their *"own."* They took no part in the heathen governments, either in being officers or electing officers. They would not swear, or take oaths. They would not fight, or engage in war; and they suffered much persecution because they would not enlist in the armies of the Roman empire.

8. They bore a testimony against sin, saying, "He who sinneth hath not seen Christ, neither known him." They had the gift of healing the sick. "Is any sick among you? let him send for the elders of the Church," etc.; and often their shadow or their clothes imparted a healing power to the invalid. They "looked for the second appearing of Christ, and hasted unto the coming of the day of the Lord."

9. This was the *Jewish* Christian Church, the temple of God, and was founded by the Apostles one degree below the Church in Jesus. And when Peter preached Christianity to the Gentiles, he founded the *Gentile* Christian Church on a plane still lower than that of the *Jewish* Christian Church.

10. The *Gentile* Christian Church did not introduce war or slavery, but it did introduce *marriage* and *private property;* yet both these institutions were under restrictions drawn from the Mosaic laws, to which the Gentiles had never been accustomed. They were restricted to *one* wife, and subjected to self-denial in many respects; that was all they were able to bear. But they were not saved from sin; and they looked for the second coming of Christ, when, as the Apostle told them, those who had wives would be just the same as if they were not married; and those who owned property, as though they possessed nothing; as then they would rise into the order of the Church above them.

11. The Shaker writers say that unless this distinction between the *Jewish* Christian Church and the *Gentile* Christian Church be observed, the various writings of the New Testament can not be understood, as all the Epistles to the Gentile Christian Churches contain very different doctrines to those addressed to the Hebrews, and as contained in the four Gospels. The Gentile Christians were fed with "milk, and not with meat, because they were not able to bear it." They were written to "as unto carnal, and not as unto spiritual."

12. The five most prominent practical principles of the Pentecost Church were, first, *common property;* second, *a life of celibacy;* third, *nonresistance;* fourth, a *separate* and *distinct government;* and, fifth, *power over physical disease.*

Millerites

More readily identified with millennialism than the Shakers are the follow-ers of William Miller (1782-1849). Farmer, preacher, and biblical interpreter in upstate New York, Miller saw the Second Coming as both literal and im-minent. Christ would return as a physical, visible being; he would return with the spiritual forces of heaven on his side; he would return soon. After many years of study and calculation, William Miller concluded that this grand cataclysmic event would occur in 1843. Using the Bible as a book of history as well as of prophecy, Miller reasoned that the words of Daniel 8:14 concerning "two thousand and three hundred evenings and mornings" really meant a period of 2,300 years. Furthermore, this 2,300-year period began in 457 B.C. when Artaxerxes gave the commandment to restore and rebuild Je-rusalem (Ezra 7:11-13). Now, the restoration of the New Jerusalem (coinci-dent with Christ's Second Coming) will occur precisely 2,300 years after 457 B.C. Mathematically, that inescapably pointed to the year 1843 when the present world would come to an end. (So much of America was caught up in these calculations and predictions that Horace Greeley's New York Tribune *published an extra edition on March 2, 1843, to refute Miller's mathematics!) The excerpt below, first published by Miller in 1836 (seven years before the end), assumes a readership thoroughly familiar with biblical material and fully prepared to accept biblical authority. In the America of the 1830s and 40s, that audience was large.*

The time or length of the vision — the 2,300 days. What must we understand by days? In the prophecy of Daniel it is invariably to be reckoned years; for God hath so ordered the prophets to reckon days. Numb. xiv. 34, "After the number of days in which ye searched the land, even forty days, each day for a year, shall you bear your iniquities, even forty years." Ezek. iv. 5, 6, "For I have laid upon thee the years of their iniquity, according to the number of the days, three hun-dred and ninety days; so shalt thou bear the iniquity of the house of Israel. And when thou hast accomplished them, lie again on thy right side, and thou shalt bear the iniquity of the house of Judah forty days; I have appointed thee each day for a year." In these passages we prove the command of God. We will also show that it was so called in the days of Jacob, when he served for Rachel, Gen. xxix. 27: "Fulfil her week (seven days) and we will give thee this also, for the ser-vice which thou shalt serve with me yet other seven years."

Nothing now remains to make it certain that our vision is to be so under-

---

[Source: William Miller, *Evidence from Scripture and History of the Second Coming of Christ about the Year 1843* (Boston: Moses A. Dow, 1841), pp. 51, 53-54.]

New York Herald Tribune on William Miller, March 2, 1843

stood, but to prove that Daniel has followed this rule. This we will do, if your patience will hold out, and God permit. . . .

We shall again turn your attention to the Bible. Look at Ezra vii, 11-13: "Now this is the copy of the letter that the king, Artaxerxes, gave unto Ezra, the priest, the scribe, a scribe of the law of God: perfect peace, and at such a time. I make a decree that all they of the people of Israel, and of his priests and Levites in my realm, which are minded of their own free will to go up to Jerusalem, go with thee." This is the decree given when the walls of Jerusalem were built in troublous times. See, also, Neh. iv. 17-23. Ezra and Nehemiah being contemporary, see Neh. viii. 1. The decree to Ezra was given in the seventh year of Artaxerxes' reign, Ezra vii. 7, and that to Nehemiah in the twentieth year, Neh. ii, 1. Let any one examine the chronology, as given by Rollin or Josephus, from the seventh year of Artaxerxes to the twenty-second year of Tiberius Caesar, which was the year our Lord was crucified, and he will find it was four hundred and ninety years. The Bible chronology says that Ezra started to go up to Jerusalem on the 12th day of the first month, (see Ezra viii. 31,) 457 years before the birth of Christ; he being 33 when he died, added to 457, will make 490 years. Three of the evangelists tell us he was betrayed two days before the feast of the passover, and of course was the same day crucified. The passover was always kept on the 14th day of the first month forever, and Christ being crucified two days before, would make it on the 12th day, 490 years from the time Ezra left the river Ahava to go unto Jerusalem.

If this calculation is correct, — and I think no one can doubt it — then the seventy weeks was fulfilled to a day when our Savior suffered on the cross. Is not the seventy weeks fairly proved to have been fulfilled by years? And does not this prove that our vision and the 2300 days ought to be so reckoned? Yes, if these seventy weeks are a part of *the vision.* Does not the angel say plainly, I have come to show thee; therefore understand the matter, and consider the vision? Yes. Well, what can a man ask for more than plain positive testimony, and a cloud of circumstances agreeing with it?

But one thing still remains to be proved. When did the 2300 years begin? Did it begin with Nebuchadnezzar's dream? No. For if it had, it must have been fulfilled in the year A.D. 1697. Well, then, did it begin when the angel Gabriel came to instruct Daniel into the 70 weeks? No, for if then, it would have been finished in the year A.D. 1762. Let us begin it where the angel told us, from the going forth of the decree to build the walls of Jerusalem in troublous times, 457 years before Christ; take 457 from 2300, and it will leave A.D. 1843; or take 70 weeks of years, being 490 years, from 2300 years, and it will leave 1810 after Christ's death. Add his life, (because we begin to reckon our time at his birth,) which is 33 years, and we come to the same A.D. 1843.

Adventists (Seventh-day)

When the world did not end in 1843 or even, as a quick recalculation sug-
gested it might, in 1844, followers of William Miller suffered what is called in
Adventist history "the Great Disappointment." Many of those disappointed
watchers for the Second Coming turned away from millennialism altogether,
some even from biblical religion altogether. One group led by Ellen G. White
(1827-1915) gathered the scattered and uncertain remnant who still looked
for that Advent, who still clung to the biblical prophecies. (Those prophecies
were revised, however, to explain that Christ did in 1843 enter the heavenly
sanctuary; this step was a necessary prelude to his return to earth where he
would then establish the New Jerusalem and cleanse the earthly sanctuary.)
Following the Bible as the authoritative guide in prophecy, these Adventists
also followed it in history: specifically, the history of the Jewish Sabbath. God
had commanded that one day in seven be kept holy; that commandment had
never been modified or abrogated; that one day was unmistakably the sev-
enth day of the week, and not the first day. In the context in which these be-
lievers moved, millennialism was already assumed and understood. What
was necessary, therefore, was a more sustained defense and explanation of
their sabbatarianism. In the first issue of Seventh-day Adventism's first jour-
nal, the argument for Saturday is made with the same biblical intensity that
characterized Miller's predictions.

What Day of the Week do the Scriptures designate as the Sabbath?

To this question, it might be supposed that every person who has any acquaintance with the subject would readily reply — *The Seventh*. We are aware, however, that efforts are made to render this a difficult point to determine. We shall,
therefore, make a few remarks upon it.

It is plainly recorded that the Creator, after laboring the first six days, in
which he completed the work of creation, rested the following day, which was
the seventh in the order of creation. This particular day God therefore sanctified and blessed. "And God blessed the *seventh* day." When the law was given at
Mount Sinai, the observance of the seventh day was commanded; and the manner in which the fourth commandment is expressed shows beyond a doubt that
one particular and definite day was known to Israel by this name. Consequently, they needed no instruction as to what day was intended. This is observable in Exodus 16:22 where the sixth and seventh days of the week are men-

---

[Source: *Second Advent Review and Sabbath Herald*, November 1850, pp. 1-2.]

tioned by their ordinal names, as a subject with which the people were familiarly acquainted. In this place also, the seventh day is declared to be the Sabbath. There can be no reasonable doubt but that the day which in the time of Moses was known as the seventh day was the same in its weekly succession with that which is called the *seventh day* in Genesis 2:3. . . . But what removes all obscurity from the subject is that God has positively declared that the day which he commanded to be observed in Exodus 20 is the same on which he rested at the close of creation. "Remember the Sabbath day to keep it holy." "The seventh day is the Sabbath of the Lord thy God." "For in six days the Lord made heaven and earth, the sea and all that in them is, and rested on the seventh day; wherefore the Lord blessed the Sabbath day and hallowed it." This language is definite. . . .

In this connection, we would remark that the sabbatical law does not appoint *a* seventh day, but *the* seventh day. It is but a flimsy subterfuge to pretend that the fourth commandment enjoins only a seventh part of our time to be kept holy. The people of Israel never so understood the law of the Sabbath; and their uniform conduct ever since shows that they understood it to mean the last day of the week, and that only. . . .

Is it necessary to change the Sabbath in order to commemorate the completion of the work of redemption? It is said the work of redemption is greater than that of creation; hence, the necessity for a change of the day of the Sabbath. In reply to this we remark, the Scriptures are entirely silent respecting the comparative greatness of the two works; and while they give us no information on this point, we are not warranted in making our own suppositions the ground of practice, to the neglect of a positive injunction. But supposing the work of redemption to be greater than that of creation, is it therefore necessary to celebrate it on a different day? Both these works were conceived by the same mind and wrought by the same hand. And since God has seen fit to make the seventh day a time to commemorate his creative work, why not gather together all his merciful works for us, and celebrate them on one and the same day? The greatness of redemption, therefore, instead of being a reason for a change, is a reason why the Sabbath as originally given should be doubly dear to us.

Spiritualism

Margaret Fox (1833-93)

*Utopians, transcendentalists, millennialists — all believed in the immediacy
of the spiritual world. The world of ordinary sight and sound was not all in
the world there was. Nor was a life of a mere threescore and ten years all the
life there was. In trying to verify and locate that other world and the bountiful life lived therein, nothing raised expectations more, nothing confirmed
hopes more surely than the "scientific" evidences which spiritualism provided. Spiritualism, or the contact established between persons living in this
world and spirits inhabiting that other world, had its sedate and sober side
— as well as its P. T. Barnum carnival side. One side or another of this
nineteenth-century phenomenon managed to touch the lives of millions of
Americans. For some, it was only a curiosity, a parlor game; for others, however, it was the truest religion, the last best hope. Once again, upstate New
York provided the stage where the drama was set. Margaret Fox as a young
girl first heard strange rappings and stranger voices; as a mature woman, she
conducted seances, made converts, and annoyed skeptics. The following report, issued by her mother, is aimed at the skeptics.*

Certificate of Mrs. Margaret Fox, Wife of John D. Fox, the Present Occupant of the House.

We moved into this house on the 11th December, 1847, and have resided here
ever since. We formerly resided in the city of Rochester. We first heard this noise
about a fortnight ago. It sounded like some one knocking in the east bedroom,
on the floor; sometimes it sounded as if the chair moved on the floor; we could
hardly tell where it was. This was in the evening, just after we had gone to bed.
The whole family slept in that room together, and all heard the noise. There was
four of our family, and sometimes five. The first night that we heard the rapping, we all got up and lit a candle; and searched all over the house. The noise
continued while we were hunting, and was heard near the same place all the
time. It was not very loud, yet it produced a jar of the bedsteads and chairs, that
could be felt by placing our hands on the chair, or while we were in bed. It was a
feeling of a tremulous motion, more than a sudden jar. It seemed as if we could

---

[Source: *A Report of the Mysterious Noises Heard in the House of Mr. John D. Fox in . . .
Wayne County* [New York] (Rochester: E. E. Lewis, 1848), pp. 5-9.]

feel it jar while we were standing on the floor. It continued this night until we went to sleep. I did not go to sleep until nearly 12 o'clock. The noise continued to be heard every night.

On Friday night, the 31st of March, it was heard as usual, and, we then for the first time called in the neighbors. Up to this time we had never heard it in the day time, or at least did not notice it at all.

On Friday night we concluded to go to bed early, and not let it disturb us; if it came, we thought we would not mind it, but try and get a good night's rest. My husband was here on all these occasions, heard the noise and helped search. It was very early when we went to bed on this night; hardly dark. We went to bed so early, because we had been broken so much of our rest that I was almost sick.

My husband had not gone to bed when we first heard the noise on this evening. I had just laid down. It commenced as usual. I knew it from all other noises I had ever heard in the house. The girls, who slept in the other bed in the room, heard the noise, and tried to make a similar noise by snapping their fingers. The youngest girl is about 12 years old; she is the one who made her hand go. As fast as she made the noise with her hands or fingers, the sound was followed up in the room. It did not sound any different at that time, only it made the same number of noises that the girl did. When she stopped, the sound itself stopped for a short time.

The other girl [Margaret], who is in her 15th year, then spoke in sport and said, "Now do this just as I do. Count one, two, three, four," &c., striking one hand in the other at the same time. The blows which she made were repeated as before. It appeared to answer her by repeating every blow that she made. She only did so once. She then began to be startled; and then I spoke and said to the noise, "Count ten," and it made ten strokes or noises. Then I asked the ages of my different children successively, and it gave a number of raps, corresponding to the ages of my children.

I then asked if it was a human being that was making the noise? and if it was, to manifest it by the same noise. There was no noise. I then asked if it was a spirit? and if it was, to manifest it by two sounds. I heard two sounds as soon as the words were spoken. . . .

Many called in that night, who were out fishing in the creek, and they all heard the same noise. The same questions were frequently repeated as others came in, and the same answers were obtained. Some of them staid here all night. I and my family all left the house but my husband. I went to Mrs. Redfield's and staid all night: my children staid at some of the other neighbors. My husband and Mr. Redfield staid in the house all that night.

On the next day the house was filled to overflow all day. This was on Saturday. There was no sound heard through the day; but in the evening the noise commenced again. Some said that there were three hundred people present at this time. They appointed a committee, and many questions were asked. . . .

I am not a believer in haunted houses or supernatural appearances. I am very sorry that there has been so much excitement about it. It has been a great deal of trouble to us. It was our misfortune to live here at this time; but I am willing and anxious that the truth should be known, and that a true statement should be made. I cannot account for these noises; all that I know is, that they have been heard repeatedly, as I have stated. I have heard this rapping again this (Tuesday) morning, April 4. My children also heard it.

I certify that the above statement has been read to me, and that the same is true; and that I should be willing to take my oath that it was so, if necessary.

(Signed,)
MARGARET FOX
[The Mother]
April 11th, 1848

Horace Greeley (1811-72)

The politically active journalist, Horace Greeley, not only reported on American religion, he plunged into it. A man of great energies and often uncritical enthusiasms, Greeley found himself attracted to the "Rochester knockings" of the Fox family. As a good reporter, he sought much more information and even personal experience with spiritualism. His reflective conclusions about the movement show that in this instance his skepticism tempered his enthusiasm.

I believe I heard vaguely of what were called "The Rochester Knockings" soon after they were first proclaimed, or testified to, in the Spring of 1848; but they did not attract my attention till, during a brief absence from New York, — perhaps while in Congress, — I perused a connected circumstantial account of the alleged phenomena, signed by several prominent citizens of Rochester, and communicated by them to The Tribune, wherein I read it. It made little impression on my mind, though I never had that repugnance to, or stubborn incredulity regarding, occurrences called supernatural which is evinced by many. My consciousness of ignorance of the extent or limitations of the natural is so vivid, that I never could realize that difficulty in crediting what are termed miracles, which many affirm. Doubtless, the first person who observed the attraction of iron by the magnet supposed he had stumbled upon a contradiction to, or violation of, the laws of nature, when he had merely enlarged his own ac-

---

[Source: Horace Greeley, *Recollections of a Busy Life* . . . (New York: J. B. Ford and Co., 1868), pp. 234-35, 239-41.]

quaintance with natural phenomena. The fly that sees a rock lifted from its bed may fancy himself witness of a miracle, when what he sees is merely the interposition of a power, the action of a force, which transcends his narrow conceptions, his ephemeral experience. I know so very little of nature, that I cannot determine at a glance what is or is not supernatural; but I know that things do occur which are decidedly superusual, and I rest in the fact without being able, or feeling required, to explain it.

I believe that it was early in 1850 that the Fox family, in which the so-called Knockings had first occurred or been noted, — first at the little hamlet known as Hydesville, near Newark, Wayne Co., N.Y., — came to New York, and stopped at a hotel, where I called upon them, and heard the so-called "raps," but was neither edified nor enlightened thereby. Nothing transpired beyond the "rappings"; which, even if deemed inexplicable, did not much interest me. In fact, I should have regretted that any of my departed ones had been impelled to address me in the presence and hearing of the motley throng of strangers gathered around the table on which the "raps" were general made. . . .

The failures of the "mediums" were more convincing to my mind than their successes. A juggler can do nearly as well at one time as another; but I have known the most eminent "mediums" spend a long evening in trying to evoke the "spiritual phenomena," without a gleam of success. I have known this to occur when they were particularly anxious — and for obviously good reasons — to astound and convince those who were present and expectant; yet not even the faintest "rap" could they scare up. Had they been jugglers, they could not have failed so utterly, ignominiously.

But, while the sterile "sittings" contributed quite as much as the other sort to convince me that the "rappings" were not all imposture and fraud, they served decidedly to disincline me to devote my time to what is called "investigation." To sit for two dreary, mortal hours in a darkened room, in a mixed company, waiting for some one's disembodied grandfather or aunt to tip a table or rap on a door, is dull music at best; but so to sit in vain is disgusting.

I close with a few general deductions from all I have seen or known of "spirit-rapping."

I. Those who discharge promptly and faithfully all their duties to those who "still live" in the flesh can have little time for poking and peering into the life beyond the grave. Better attend to each world in its proper order.

II. Those who claim, through the "mediums," to be Shakespeare, Milton, Byron, &c., and try to prove it by writing poetry, invariably come to grief. I cannot recall a line of "spiritual" poetry that is not weak, if not execrable, save that of Rev. Thomas L. Harris, who is a poet still in the flesh. After he dies, I predict that the poetry sent us as his will be much worse than he ever wrote while in the body. Even Tupper, appalling as is the prospect, will be dribbling worse rhymes upon us after death than even he perpetrated while on earth.

III. As a general rule, the so-called "Spiritual communications" are vague, unreal, shadowy, trivial. They are not what we should expect our departed friends to say to us. I never could feel that the lost relative or friend who professed to be addressing me was actually present. I do not doubt that foolish, trifling people remain so (measurably) after they have passed the dark river; I perceive that trivial questions must necessarily invite trivial answers; but, after making all due allowance, I insist that the "spiritual" literature of the day, in so far as it purports to consist of communications or revelations from the future life, is more inane and trashy than it could be if the sages and heroes, the saints and poets, of by-gone days were really speaking to us through these pretended revelations.

IV. Not only is it true (as we should in any case presume) that nearly all attempts of the so-called "mediums" to guide speculators as to events yet future have proved melancholy failures, but it is demonstrated that the so-called "spirits" are often ignorant of events which have already transpired. They did not help fish up the broken Atlantic Cable, nor find Sir John Franklin, nor dispel the mystery which still shrouds the fate of the crew and passengers of the doomed steamship President, — and so of a thousand instances wherein their presumed knowledge might have been of use to us darkly seeing mortals. All that we have learned of them has added little or nothing to our knowledge, unless it be in enabling us to answer with more confidence that old, momentous question, "If a man die, shall he live again?"

V. On the whole (though I say it with regret) it seems to me that the great body of the "Spiritualists" have not been rendered better men and women — better husbands, wives, parents, children — by their new faith. I think some have been improved by it, — while many who were previously good are good still, — and some have morally deteriorated. I judge that laxer notions respecting Marriage, Divorce, Chastity, and stern Morality generally, have advanced in the wake of "Spiritualism." And, while I am fully aware that religious mania so-called has usually a purely material origin, so that revivals have often been charged with making persons insane whose insanity took its hue from the topic of the hour, but owed its existence to purely physical causes, I still judge that the aggregate of both Insanity and Suicide has been increased by "Spiritualism."

VI. I do not know that these "communications" made through "mediums" proceed from those who are said to be their authors, nor from the spirits of the departed at all. Certain developments strongly indicate that they do; others, that they do not. We know that they say they do, which is evidence so far as it goes, and is not directly contradicted or rebutted. That some of them are the result of juggle, collusion, or trick, I am confident; that others are not, I decidedly believe. The only certain conclusion in the premises to which my mind has been led is forcibly set forth by Shakespeare in the words of the Danish prince: —

"There are more things in heaven and earth, Horatio,
Than are dreamt of in your philosophy."

VII. I find my "spiritual" friends nowise less bigoted, less intolerant, than the devotees at other shrines. They do not allow me to see through my own eyes, but insist that I shall see through theirs. If my conclusion from certain data differs from theirs, they will not allow my stupidity to account for our difference, but insist on attributing it to hypocrisy, or some other form of rascality. I cannot reconcile this harsh judgment with their professions of liberality, their talk of philosophy. But, if I speak at all, I must report what I see and hear.

4. Denominations and Winning the West

Plan of Union: Congregationalists and Presbyterians

The Plan Adopted, 1801

Because an entire continent required evangelization and reform, Presbyterians and Congregationalists agreed to pool their resources in order to accomplish that task in "union and harmony." Such agreement was possible because theological differences between these two Calvinist denominations were minimal. Differences in church government — a tighter organization prevailed among Presbyterians — did eventually give some advantage to that denomination. The four regulations below, however, attempted a genuine even-handedness in this early ecumenical venture.

Plan of Union

Regulations adopted by the General Assembly of the Presbyterian Church in America, and by the General Association of the State of Connecticut, (provided said Association agree to them,) with a view to prevent alienation, and to promote union and harmony in those new settlements which are composed of inhabitants from these bodies.

1. It is strictly enjoined on all their missionaries to the new settlements, to endeavour, by all proper means, to promote mutual forbearance, and a spirit of accommodation between those inhabitants of the new settlements who hold

---

[Source: Williston Walker, *The Creeds and Platforms of Congregationalism* (Boston: Pilgrim Press, 1960 [1893]), pp. 530-31.]

the Presbyterian, and those who hold the Congregational form of church government.

2. If in the new settlements any church of the Congregational order shall settle a minister of the Presbyterian order, that church may, if they choose, still conduct their discipline according to Congregational principles, settling their difficulties among themselves, or by a council mutually agreed upon for that purpose. But if any difficulty shall exist between the minister and the church, or any member of it, it shall be referred to the Presbytery to which the minister shall belong, provided both parties agree to it; if not, to a council consisting of an equal number of Presbyterians and Congregationalists, agreed upon by both parties.

3. If a Presbyterian church shall settle a minister of Congregational principles, that church may still conduct their discipline according to Presbyterian principles, excepting that if a difficulty arise between him and his church, or any member of it, the cause shall be tried by the Association to which the said minister shall belong, provided both parties agree to it; otherwise by a council, one-half Congregationalists and the other Presbyterians, mutually agreed upon by the parties.

4. If any congregation consist partly of those who hold the Congregational form of discipline, and partly of those who hold the Presbyterian form, we recommend to both parties that this be no obstruction to their uniting in one church and settling a minister; and that in this case the church choose a standing committee from the communicants of said church, whose business it shall be to call to account every member of the church who shall conduct himself inconsistently with the laws of Christianity, and to give judgment on such conduct. That if the person condemned by their judgment be a Presbyterian, he shall have liberty to appeal to the Presbytery; if he be a Congregationalist, he shall have liberty to appeal to the body of the male communicants of the church. In the former case, the determination of the Presbytery shall be final, unless the church shall consent to a farther appeal to the Synod, or to the General Assembly; and in the latter case, if the party condemned shall wish for a trial by a mutual council, the cause shall be referred to such a council. And provided the said standing committee of any church shall depute one of themselves to attend the Presbytery, he may have the same right to sit and act in the Presbytery as a ruling elder of the Presbyterian church.

The Plan Implemented

Higher education in the Midwest is the most obvious monument to the Plan of Union or "Presbygational" cooperation. Such institutions as Western Reserve (1826), Knox (1837), Grinnell (1847), and Ripon (1851) are among those given life and nurture in the course of the Plan's operation. In the excerpt provided here, Congregationalist Julian M. Sturtevant argues against a rigid denominational control of the colleges, even when no one doubted that without the denomination the college would never have come into being. Sturtevant is explicit: "The very spirit and principle of Denominationalism must be abjured in our Colleges." Christian yes, but sectarian no, argues the author who looks to Harvard and Yale as appropriate models to follow. The very notion of "denomination," moreover, is a peculiarly American one, and a notion not conducive to a magnanimous and cooperative Christianity. Nor is it a notion likely to do anything but divide the West and defeat the entire missionary and evangelical effort.

Denominational Colleges

We owe our readers an apology for the phrase which we have placed at the head of this Article. We confess it is not exactly classical. The word "denominational" is of recent American origin; and we remember the time when the combination of this word with Colleges would have seemed harsh, if not quite unintelligible. But changes in ideas and institutions compel changes in words; and Americans are not necessarily to be charged with relapsing into barbarism, if they do make changes in the English language, corresponding to the novel ideas and social combinations, which have originated on this side of the Atlantic.

Diversity of religious denomination has increased so rapidly within the last quarter of a century, and has become so important an element in American society, that there is an imperative necessity of an adjective expressive of it. The word "sectarian" might be supposed to meet this want; but it always implies more or less of censure, and for that reason men are not fond of applying it to themselves and their party. They are apt to flatter themselves that though much attached to the religious denomination to which they belong, they are still not sectarians. They feel, therefore, the need of a word which will describe zeal for a denomination, as they like to call it, without any implication of a narrow and sectarian spirit. For this purpose, evidently, the word "denominational" was

[Source: *The New Englander,* February 1860, pp. 68-69, 87-88.]

coined, and has obtained currency; and we shall profit nothing by protesting against its use, for it meets a widely felt want.

The phrase, "Denominational Colleges," is also the product of comparatively recent changes in the minds of the American people. It is within the memory of men yet not far from the meridian of life, that the thought had scarcely been entertained by any mind that a College should be in any sense the representative of a sect, or that such Colleges as Princeton, and Columbia, and Yale, were not suitable for the education of any American youth, whatever might be the religious views of his parents.

But it is supposed the world is growing wiser. Many now regard it as an established law of society, that no College can flourish unless its very life is intertwined with that of some religious denomination; and that conversely no denomination, or, as persons entertaining such views would generally prefer to say, no church, can be expected to prosper without a system of Colleges forming a part of its organic life.

The process by which these ideas have taken possession of the popular mind is quite marvelous. They are not the result of any new light which has been thrown upon the subject by discussion, or by discovery, or by the experience of educators. They are the direct products of that multiplication of sects, and that vast increase of the sectarian spirit which have so strangely characterized the last half century of our history. Men full of zeal for their religious denomination, and ambitious of its aggrandizement, have discovered that Colleges are instruments of power, and have therefore eagerly seized upon them, and sought to wield them with as much efficiency as possible, for denominational purposes. . . .

There is but one remedy for all this. The very spirit and principle of Denominationalism must be abjured in our Colleges. We must found them upon a broad and comprehensive platform of Evangelic Faith. We must cooperate in sustaining them as Christians, and not as Sectarians. We must cherish them not as belonging to our sect; but to Christ and the Church universal. We must esteem them precious, not as the instruments of aggrandizing our Denomination, but as blessings to our country, to mankind, and to the distant future. We think it requires no prophetic power to predict, that if any truly noble Institutions of liberal learning are to be reared up in the West, and stand there in strength and beauty in distant generations and ages, this only is the foundation on which they are to be reared. The spirit of sect, if it is to be consulted in the premises, will only multiply feeble and starving enterprises, to destroy one another by their mutual rivalships. If any man believes that any one of our Western States can thoroughly found and efficiently sustain all the Colleges, which sect originates, supply them with the requisite endowments and instruments of instruction, and sustain in them Faculties composed of men who by vigorous and varied talent, large and generous culture, are qualified for their high position, especially that it can furnish to each of them a respectable number of students, affording fit employment for men of such talents and attainments; if any man, we say, believes this, or does not see that such multiplication of Colleges renders it nearly impossible to raise any one of all the number to this truly dignified position for generations to come, that man has, it seems to us, studied the subject to very little purpose. And he who does not see that the spirit of sect, in all its influence on our College building enterprises, increases and aggravates this evil to an unlimited extent, has been still more unsuccessful in his observations. If we are ever to succeed in founding Colleges in the West worthy of the name, we must first learn that the spirit of sect, though followed by thousands as an infallible oracle, is in truth the most dangerous adviser we can consult.

Frontier Religion: Baptists and Methodists

Baptist Conversion

The strength of the Baptist appeal on the frontier lay in the accessibility of its theology to those of little education or sophistication. The farmer-preacher was a commonplace among frontier Baptists: that is, a man who — like his neighbors — earned his living as a farmer but who — in addition — took the lead in organizing a church and proclaiming a simple gospel. He could be understood; moreover, he could be found, in great numbers, along the sparsely settled frontier. Other denominations might have to wait until friends in the East could dispatch a college-educated, properly ordained minister to the interior, but not the Baptists. The theology was accessible, and the minister as well. The Bible was also accessible, along with rivers or creeks for the ritual of baptism. Not much more than that was needed, as the following account of Jacob Bower attests. Born of German Baptist parents in Lancaster County, Pennsylvania, Bower (1786-1857+) moved with his family to Kentucky when he was in his teens. After his marriage and conversion, he moved his own family to Illinois to avoid raising his children in a slave state. There, he too became a frontier preacher.

About this time [1812] I had a great desire to be united with some society of christians. And in those days there were no societies in that part of Kentucky

[Source: W. W. Sweet, ed., *Religion on the American Frontier: The Baptists, 1783-1830* (New York: Cooper Square Publishers, 1964 [1931]), pp. 197-99.]

but Baptists, Tunkars,[4] and some Methodists, and for a time I could not decide which of them to offer myself to for membership. I felt quite unworthy to be united with any, for I verily thought with myself, that if I was a child of grace at all, I was less than the least of all saints, and unworthy the name of a christian. I first thought of Uniting with the Tunkars. And if Mr. Hendrix (their preacher) had come into the vicinity, I would have been baptized by him. (by trine immersion) I thought that it must be the right way, or Father would not have been baptized that way. But I could not arrive at any decission on the subject. I therfore resolved to read the new Testament, and go the way it pointed out to me, and unite with that church which practised, and walked nearest to the divine rule. I commenced at the first chapter of Mathew, determined to read the Testament through and through again & again till I could be able to decide. I had a German Testament, and when I could not well understand the English, the German would explain it to me. It was just three weeks from the time I obtained a hope in the saviour, till Hazle Creek Baptist Church Meeting; of an eavning I would gather dry brush (sticks) to make a fire, light enough to see to read by. I read on and soon came to the conclusion that according to the book Baptism must be received by immersion. I could not tell what Baptism ment. But the German Testament said *Taufen,* and this I knew was to dip, Diping &c. But here arose another difficulty, to know whether this Taufen ment once, or thrice. When I read to Rom. 6-4. Being buried with Christ in Baptism &c. I supposed that baptism, must in some way resemble a burial. When I read Colos. 2-12 the words repeeted, I paused, and began to reason on this point — Lord teach me that I may understand thy word aright. Lead me in the path thou wilt have me to walk. I thought that Baptism was a sign of a death — a burial and a resorection. And as the dead are buried only once, so baptism is to be performed only once, one immersion only to represent a deth to sin, a planting, or buri-ing with Christ, and rise to walk in newness of life.

I became perfectly satisfied in relation to Baptism. But I could not be satisfied as to myself being a proper subject. I resolved, however, that I would go to meeting, and I would tell the Church exactly, or as near as I could recollect, all how I had been exercised in my mind, and ask them to give me council, but I did not believe that they would receive me, for if they thought of me, as I did of mysel, they would be sure not to receive me. Council was what I wanted. I went to meeting, and after a sermon by their pastor, Eld. Benjamin Talbert. The fellowship of the church was enquired for: a door was opened for to hear expeariences. I had not heard an experience related at that place for four years. But I ventured forward — told my tale, then asked for council. The moderator said, "Can any person forbid water?" In a moment I was threwn into the strongest kind of temptation. He extended to me the hand of fellowship for the water,

4. Also known as German Baptists or, at present, Church of the Brethren.

I first thought of refusing my hand. Thinking that he was jesting — making sport of me. But old Brother David Rhoads gathered me into his arms, and all the members rushed forward to give me their hands, som wept aloud for joy, my jealously was removed — singing and shaking of hands all through the crowd. That afternoon 16 persons were received for Baptism, and two came who wer rejected. The next day, being the first Lords day in March, 1812, I, with fifteen others were Baptized. And like one of old, for a time, I went on my way rejoicing. During that revival, 76 persons were aded to Hazle Creek Church, by baptism.

Methodist Circuit

Methodists achieved accessibility through the instrument of the itinerant preacher, the circuit rider. Even before a hamlet or village was formed, the Methodist traveling preacher (an inevitable feature of American folklore) would be on hand to instruct, baptize, convert, marry the betrothed, bury the dead. Such ministrations made life on the frontier more bearable, though life for the circuit rider himself often seemed scarcely so. James Gilruth (1793-1873), born on the Virginia side of the Ohio River, moved with his family as a young boy to Scioto County, Ohio. He grew up in a region that knew neither school nor church. By means of other itinerants, however, Gilruth heard the gospel, was converted when he was about twenty-five years of age, and determined soon thereafter to enter the ministry himself. Later, he traveled not only all across Ohio but into Iowa and Michigan as well. From 1832 to 1836, he served as Presiding Elder of the Detroit District within the Ohio Methodist Conference. The record below would scarcely encourage great hordes of young men to follow in his steps.

Tusd July 29. [1834] Rose at sunup — Spent the forepart of the day in sundry small matters — In the afternoon went to Wm Collens to git some hay — Taking My wife 2 smallest children suped at Br Mainards & returned home a little before sundown Day clear & pleasant to bed about 9.

    Wed July 30. Rose about sun rise — spent the morning till 10 in sundry small chores — tended the funeral of Mr Welshs infant — halled wood in the afternoon Day as yesterday — to bed about 10

    Thursd July 31. Rose about 6 — Spent the day in aranging my papers money etc for Conferance (Giting my horse shod and making the necessary preparations) — counting tracts till ½ past 10 — Day as yesterday — to bed at 11 — ...

[Source: W. W. Sweet, ed., *Religion on the American Frontier: The Methodists, 1783-1840* (New York: Cooper Square Publishers, 1964 [1946]), pp. 370-71, 375-76.]

Methodist circuit preacher
(Library of Congress)

Frid Aug 8 . . . Made arangement to set out on horseback for Ft Finley —
Br Bibbins hors having become lame I set off alone about 9 uncouth like
enough having 3 bed quilts & 5 lb cotten to carry beside great coat etc — I fed at
Mr Sergants at the Big Spring — And in the afternoon rode to Finley & found
My children well My daughter had been delivered of a child on the 4th of July
but by the ignorent & bruital conduct of the Midwife the child was killed I
spent the evening conversing with them on these & other matters till near 10 —

Sat Aug 9 . . . spent ½ an hour assisting Frederik to catch a Raccoon that
had come into his corn — And the rest of the morning in looking at his improvements & in conversation till about 8 A.M. when we all set off for
campmeeting 2½ miles distent — I preached with great liberty at 11 from John
iii 5 & then called for Mourners a nomber presented themselves for the prayers
of the righteous & it was said that two of them experienced peace. I preached

again at 4. from Ps. cxix. 1 with clearness and some power. — & again at candle-
light from Matt xxii 39. with some power — In all my labour to day I was fa-
voured with the attention of the people & the comfort of the spirit. At this I
again called for Mourners some came and Prayer meeting continued for some
time. Day hot with some thunder showers passing about — one of whom fill
[fell] on us; accompanied by a pretty severe wind that broke down some timber
very near the camp ground. To bed about 9. pretty tired.

Retreats and Revivals: Roman Catholicism

Retreats in Maryland

*Bishop John Carroll, as already noted, found his responsibilities and his dio-
cese growing by enormous increments, but without any corresponding increase in personnel. Grateful, therefore, for the arrival in 1792 of a French
Sulpician father, John Baptist David, Carroll dispatched this priest to lower
Maryland for an evangelistic effort. (Father David was but one of many cler-
ics who fled from the violent anticlericalism of the French Revolution of
1789.) Father David employed in his evangelism the technique of the spiritual "retreat": a period and place set aside for several days of intensive
prayer, instruction, and exhortation. In the excerpt below, one sees the Catholic retreat producing a piety and zeal similar to that of the Protestant revival. And David's technique worked well in the West.*

Very soon after his [David's] arrival in the United States, Bishop Carroll ascertained that he knew enough of English to be of service on the missions, and he
accordingly sent him to attend to some Catholic congregations in the lower
part of Maryland. M. David had been but four months in America, when he
preached his first sermon in English; and he had the consolation to find, that he
was not only well understood, but that his discourse made a deep impression
on his hearers. For twelve years he laboured with indefatigable zeal on this mission, in which he attended to the spiritual wants of three numerous congregations. He was cheered by the abundant fruits with which God every where
blessed his labours.

Feeling that mere transient preaching is generally of but little permanent

[Source: M. J. Spalding, *Sketches of the Early Catholic Missions of Kentucky* . . . (New York:
Arno Press, 1972 [1844]), pp. 219-20.]

utility, he resolved to commence regular courses of instruction in the form of Retreats; and so great was his zeal and industry, that he gave four Retreats every year to each of his congregations. The first was for the benefit of the married men; the second, for that of the married women; the third and fourth, for that of the boys and girls. To each of these classes he gave separate sets of instructions, adapted to their respective capacities and wants.

His discourses were plain in their manner, and solid and thorough in their matter. He seldom began to treat, without exhausting a subject. At first, but few attended his Retreats: but gradually the number increased, so as to embrace almost all the members of his congregations. But he appeared to preach with as much zeal and earnestness to the few, as to the many. He was often heard to say, that the conversion or spiritual profit of even *one* soul, was sufficient to enlist all the zeal, and to call forth all the energies of the preacher.

Great were the effects, and most abundant the fruits, of M. David's labours on the missions of Maryland. On his arrival among them, he found his congregations cold and neglectful of their Christian duties; he left them fervent and exemplary. Piety every where revived; the children and servants made their first communion; the older members of the congregations became regular communicants. Few that were instructed by him could soon forget their duty: so great was the impression he left, and so thorough was the course of instruction he gave. To the portion of Maryland, in which he thus signalized his zeal, he bequeathed a rich and abundant legacy of spiritual blessings, which was destined to descend from generation to generation: and the good people of those parts still exhibit traces of his zeal, and still pronounce his name with reverence and gratitude.

Bishop Flaget's Jubilee of 1826-27

Benedict Joseph Flaget (1763-1850), another Sulpician father fleeing the French Revolution, arrived in the United States in 1791. In 1808 he reluctantly agreed to serve as frontier bishop of a diocese whose See was in Bardstown, Kentucky. For the remaining thirty-two years of his life (except for a visit to Europe, 1835-39), Flaget made Bardstown and, after 1841, Louisville the center of vigorous missionary activity in the West. In 1825-26 a Jubilee Year opened the second quarter of the century, even as it marked the beginning of the pontificate of Leo XII. Because of the enormous size of Flaget's diocese, the Jubilee had to be extended over a two-year period. The account

[Source: M. J. Spalding, *Sketches of the Early Catholic Missions of Kentucky . . .* (New York: Arno Press, 1972 [1844]), pp. 293-96.]

> *below, describing the effect of the Jubilee, reads at some points as though it were a Methodist camp meeting.*

The promulgation of the Jubilee has been for the Diocess of Bardstown an epoch of the most abundant benedictions. The zeal with which the faithful every where performed the exercises; the modesty and recollection they exhibited; and, above all, the eagerness they manifested to approach the Tribunal of Penance and the Holy Table; all prove, that, while the Vicar of Jesus Christ opened on earth the treasures of the church, God was pleased, from high heaven, to cast an eye of mercy on this portion of the New World, and to prepare, beforehand, so to speak, the graces which he was to scatter over it with a sort of profusion.

Under circumstances so favourable to the spiritual good of the flock confided to his care, Bishop Flaget did not think that he ought to spare himself. He hesitated not to put himself at the head of his missionaries; and, despite the fatigue inseparable from long journeys, he wished to share with them in all the labours, as well as in all the consolations, of a ministry as august as it is painful.

Two years had been allowed him by the Pontiff for the promulgation of the Jubilee in all the parts of his vast Diocess. He himself granted six months to each congregation, for the same purpose, in order that all might be the more easily enabled to gather its fruits. The conditions prescribed for gaining the Indulgence were: to visit, at four, or at least at three, different times the church of the congregation; to assist at all the public exercises as far as practicable; to recite the Litany of the Saints, with some other stated prayers; and finally, to say five *Our Fathers* and five *Hail Marys,* according to the intentions of the Sovereign Pontiff.

As to the order and nature of the exercises, they were not every where the same: it was necessary to adapt them to places and circumstances. At the Cathedral, they commenced with the celebration of the Holy Sacrifice of the Mass. This was immediately followed by the sermon, after which the Prayers above indicated were recited. At three o'clock, P.M., a conference took place between two priests, on some dogmatical point. At half past six o'clock in the evening, another sermon was delivered for the convenience of the citizens of Bardstown, both Catholic and Protestant, who might not have been able during the day to attend the meetings. These exercises continued for eight days; and this was likewise observed in all the other congregations, except in those where the number of Catholics was very inconsiderable. In the latter, however, but two instructions were given on each day.

Although the churches were crowded, yet the slightest disorder never occurred. The attention to the word of God was constantly kept up, and what was yet more consoling, the effects of the sermons were admirable. It would have been difficult to behold a greater concourse of persons at the tribunal of penance. At four o'clock in the morning, and even at two o'clock, in the congregation of St. Charles, although it was the month of December, in the middle of winter, a large crowd of persons, of whom many had travelled several miles, pressed for admission at the door of the church. Scarcely had it been opened, when the places destined for hearing confessions were thronged, and they did not cease to be so until late in the evening. Among the faithful, many remained the whole day without taking nourishment, and even without changing their places, for fear of being deprived of the consolations after which they so ardently sighed: yet, notwithstanding all the care they thus took, many were compelled to wait till after the conclusion of the exercises, before they could share in the graces flowing from the Sacrament of Penance.

All hearts appeared to be truly moved. This was seen in the vividness of the sorrow and in the abundance of tears, which accompanied the confession of their sins. Sinners of the most inveterate habits were seen weeping over their past wanderings, and prepared to make the greatest sacrifices to amend their lives. Many, too, profitted by this happy season to renew marriages contracted before Protestant ministers, and rendered null by the impediment of infidelity. Others, surmounting all false shame, repaired previous sacrilegious confessions. All, in fine, gave extraordinary evidence of repentance, and showed a firm resolution to lead for the future, lives more Christian, or more perfect.

During the week of the Jubilee, all temporal affairs seemed forgotten; only those of the soul were attended to: and as the greater part of the Catholics came from a distance of eight, ten, or twelve miles, they remained during the whole day in the church. They did not leave it, for a moment, except to take a frugal repast on the grass, or in the adjoining wood. Not only did the labourers and farmers, who constituted the majority of the Catholics, give these beautiful examples of fervour and zeal, but persons of every condition — merchants, physicians, magistrates, legislators — showed themselves equally eager to profit by the graces of heaven. Human respect, so powerful under other circumstances, had given way to more noble sentiments: and all thought of nothing else but of giving open and public evidences of their strong attachment to a religion, which was the only source of their consolation and happiness.

Missions vs. Revivals

Revivals, whether on the frontier or not, received much criticism on the grounds of their frothy emotion, simplified theology, and temporary effect. Critics of Protestant revivalism were both numerous and articulate. Partly to avoid the unsavory associations with which these critics had tarnished the

[Source: *Brownson's Quarterly Review*, July 1858, pp. 306-8.]

"revival," Catholics generally preferred to speak of the "mission." Orestes Brownson, a Catholic editor who will be more fully introduced in the next chapter, wrote in 1858 that Catholic missions shared some traits with Protestant revivals: for example, the creation of emotional excitement. The mission, however, "judiciously directed and moderated" such excitement, insuring also that it was "made subservient to a good end." The Roman Catholic Church was also careful, Brownson wrote, not to "overdo the matter." Under such limits and with such watchful supervision, the mission could do great good both on the western frontier and in the eastern city.

Revivals are attended with excitement, and so are missions. In this they are alike. But this is no objection against missions, unless it be proved that revivals are to be condemned, precisely because of the excitement they produce, and that all use of excitement in religious doings is noxious. This, we think, cannot be done. We believe, with Cardinal Wiseman, that sometimes, for the purpose of "arousing the slumbering energies of congregations," "*stronger excitement is required* than the voice of ordinary admonition." We admit that a mission is likely to produce, and is intended to produce, this stronger excitement in a congregation where one is given. But we maintain that in the Catholic Church this excitement is judiciously directed and moderated, and made subservient to a good end, that end being the preparation of the soul for the supernatural gifts of divine grace. In the natural world perpetual calm and quiet are noxious. A thunderstorm, or a brisk shower of rain, is very useful for clearing the atmosphere and refreshing the earth, So it is in religion. Too great and long-continued quiet subsides into stupor and death. An occasional excitement is like a little mental electricity. The ordinary character of the services of the Church is calm and quiet. But in Lent and Advent of each year, she seeks to make them more solemn and arousing in their character, and bids her priests excite the people to penance and prayer in a special manner. By her missions she arouses them more powerfully still. But these are occasional. In stationary and well-ordered congregations, it is only about once in from five to seven years that a mission can be given with salutary effect. Thus, the Church is careful not to overdo the matter, knowing that too frequent an administration of tonics and stimulants, is as hurtful in the spiritual as in the natural order. But, in their proper place, she is not afraid to use them. Excitement is necessary for a large class who are so far gone in spiritual lethargy, that nothing short of a powerful stimulant will have any effect upon them. The missionaries of the Catholic Church intend and expect to get hold of the worst, the most negligent, and the most vicious part of the population. Souls stupefied by drunkenness, or obdurate through long impenitence, and sunk in sensuality, must be brought to reflect seriously to do penance, and to renounce their evil courses. How is it possible to make the smallest impression on them, without something startling, interesting, exciting, which shall act as a counter-stimulant to the influence of vice and passion. Numbers, everywhere, have ceased to receive the Sacrament, to attend Church, to say their prayers even; are profoundly ignorant of their religion, and completely indifferent to it, and are bringing up their families without any religion, except a remembrance that they have been baptized and call themselves Catholic. How are such people to be drawn to the Church, instructed, and made good and attentive Christians, unless there is some powerful attraction to stimulate their curiosity, to work on their senses and feelings, and thus to prepare them to receive truth and to be brought to their duty? For such, missions are the necessary and almost the only means of salvation. And even for the well-instructed and exemplary portion of a congregation, it is very salutary to listen to a series of sermons on the eternal truths, and a complete course of instructions, and to pass a few days in extraordinary exercises of devotion. For a small class habituated to meditation, no doubt, a calm, quiet retreat spent in solitude and silence, is more agreeable and more salutary. But these are few; the majority, even of the higher and more educated class, can only take part in, and be benefited by, what are called *popular devotions,* and the only way of giving them the benefit of the spiritual exercises is by means of a mission.

Frontier Fate: Winning, Losing

A Survivor's "Cup of Sorrow"

The "conquest" of the West represented more than victory over nature and irreligion; it meant, ultimately, a conquest of the Native American as well. In the course of the long and tragic process of conquest, the Indian often fought back, vigorously and violently. Farmers, hunters, trappers, travelers, missionaries (men, women, and children) fell before the tomahawk and the arrow. A Kentucky frontiersman and sometime companion of Daniel Boone, Thomas Baldwin (1748-1835+) escaped that fate himself, but all members of his family (wife, two sons, one daughter) died at the hands of the Indians. What follows from this "Christian Philosopher" — as he came to be called — is the doleful consolation of his religion. As he lived the remainder of his life in utter isolation in western Kentucky, he meditated on the dark ways of Providence.

[Source: *Narrative of the Massacre . . . of the Wife & Children of Thomas Baldwin . . .* (New York: Garland Publishing Co., 1977 [1836]), pp. 17-19.]

It is the blessed religion which I would recommend as worthy to be cherished by all, that prepares their minds for all the events of this inconstant state, and instructs them in the nature of true happiness — afflictions will not then attack them by surprize, and will not therefore overwhelm them — they are not then overcome by disappointment, when that which is mortal dies; — they meet the changes in their lot without unmanly dejection — in the multitude of our sorrows in this world of misery, what but Religion can afford us consolation? It assures us that thro' all our disappointment and wo, there is a friend present with us, on whose affection, wisdom, power, and goodness, we can perfectly rely; and that an infinitely merciful and powerful Protector sustains us, guiding our erring footsteps, and strengthening our feeble spirits. He permits no afflictions to approach us but for some gracious and merciful purpose; to excite in us an earnest solicitude for our salvation, to reclaim us from error, or to subdue some favorite passion — subject to the control of this Almighty Guardian, all the trials of life are designed to establish our faith, to increase our humble dependence, to perfect our love and fortify our patience, and to make us meet for the inheritance of glory. So long as our Heavenly father is possessed of infinite wisdom to understand perfectly what is best for his children, and of infinite mercy to will all that he sees to be best for them, shall we not choose to have him do what he pleases? Dark are the ways of Providence while we are wrapt up in mortality — but, convinced there is a God, we must hope and believe, that all is right.

Although it has been my lot to drink deep of the cup of sorrow, yet I have never found my heart inclined to charge God foolishly — a gracious heart elevates nearer and nearer to God in affliction, and can justify him in his severest strokes, acknowledging them to be all just and holy — and hereby the soul may comfortably evidence to itself its own uprightness and sincere love to Him; yea, it hath been of singular use to some souls, to take right measures of their love to God in such trials; He that appointed the seasons of the year, appointed the seasons of our comfort in our relations; and as those seasons cannot be altered, no more can these; — all the course of Providence is guided by an unalterable decree; what falls out casually to our apprehension, yet falls out necessarily in respect to God's appointment — admit that he hath sorely afflicted us for our sins, by bereaving us by a sudden stroke of death of our nearest and dearest friends, yet there is no reason that we should be too much cast down under our severe afflictions, for it may be the fruits of his love to, and care of our souls, for to the afflicted he says, "whom I love, I rebuke and chasten."

That our greatest afflictions, so considered, many times prove our greatest blessings, is probably known by experience to many. It was my heavy afflictions, in being so suddenly and lamentably deprived of my family, that led me to prefer a life of retirement; and in that retirement from the busy scenes of the world, I was led to engage more seriously and earnestly in the perusal of the

Holy Scriptures, whereby I was taught to seek a balm in that blessed RELI-
GION, that has never failed to sustain me in my most solitary moments; and by
my own experience, I can assure all, the rich and the poor, the happy and the
miserable, the healthy and the sick, in short, all descriptions of persons, whatever may be their station or their circumstances in this life, that they will experience infinite advantage in a religious retirement from the world; and while
thus situated, whatever their troubles and afflictions may be, they ought to bear
them without a murmur. A good man can never be miserable, who cheerfully
submits to the will of Providence. To be truly happy in this world, we must
manifest a quiet resignation to the will of an impartial God. If while we remain
inhabitants of this "miserable world," we quietly submit to the will of, and exercise a true love to Him, we have great reason to believe that we shall hereafter be
permitted to taste higher delights, and experience a degree of happiness that
this frail world does not afford. As our prospects close not with this life, but are
extended to the future, it is necessary that we should make provision for that
also; none ought therefore to postpone the business of Religion, till night over-
takes them — the night of death — when no man can work. Religion consoles
the aching heart of the afflicted, and reconciles the unhappy to their misfor-
tunes — the grieved parent who has buried his earthly comfort, his beloved
partner and darling children, in the bosom of the valley, is comforted and
cheered by the flattering persuasions of Religion — he is assured by it that if he
lives faithful to Christ, he shall revisit his beloved friends in that blessed place
where dwells every felicity, and an antidote for every care and painful sensation.
To you, sir, and to all, I would then say, whatever may be your or their rank in
life, if you wish to be happy in this world, and to secure a certainty of being infinitely more so in the world to come, I pray thee cherish RELIGION. That this
may be the happy and final choice of all, is and ever shall be the prayer of their
aged friend and well wisher,

THOMAS BALDWIN.

A Victim's Valley of Death

*Not only did churches accompany the settlers along the frontier, but those in-
stitutions often served as advance scouts well ahead of that frontier. Missionaries at distant outposts welcomed new arrivals from the East even as they
reached out, sometimes successfully and sometimes not, to the Indian tribes*

[Source: C. M. Drury, ed., *First White Women over the Rockies* (Glendale, Calif.: Arthur H. Clark Co., 1963), I, 123-24, 125-26.]

*in their immediate area. At the age of twenty-eight, Narcissa Whitman
(1808-47) made the overland trek with her husband all the way from the
East Coast to the Oregon Territory. There this Presbyterian missionary couple worked among the Cayuse, Nez Percé, and Flatheads. In the excerpt below, Narcissa Whitman provides some early impressions of the Indians as
well as a glimpse into the nature of her duties. She also happily recounts the
birth of their first child, a daughter who tragically drowned two years later.
But even harsher tragedy lay ahead. As the white population increased in the
Territory, Indian resistance and resentment grew correspondingly. Late in
1847, a band of Cayuse Indians attacked the mission station, slaying both of
the Whitmans as well as twelve other whites temporarily housed at the station. Narcissa Whitman had not yet reached her fortieth year.*

Wieletpoo [Waiilatpul] Jan 2 1837. Universal fast day. Through the kind Providence of God we are permitted to celebrate this day in heathen lands. It has
been one of peculiar interest to us, so widely separated from kindred souls,
alone, in the thick darkness of heathenism. We have just finished a seperate
room for ourselves with a stove in it, lent by Mr P for our use this winter. Thus I
am spending my winter as comfortably as heart could wish, & have suffered less
from excessive cold than in many winters previous in New York. Winters are
not very severe here. Usually they have but little snow say there is more this
winter now on the ground than they have had for many years previous & that
the winter is nearly over. After a season of worship during which I felt great
depressure of spirits, we visited the lodges. All seemed well pleased as I had not
been to any of them before.

We are on the lands of the Old Chief Umtippe who with a lodge or two
are now absent for a few days hunting deer. But a few of the Cayuses winter
here. They appear to seperate in small companies, makes their cashes of provision in the fall & remain for the winter, & besides they are not well united. The
young Chief Towerlooe is of another family & is more properly the ruling chief.
He is Uncle to the Young Cayuse Halket now at Red River Mission whom we expect to return this fall & to whom the chieftainship belongs by inheritance. The
Old Chief Umtippe has been a savage creature in his day. His heart is still the
same, full of all manner of hypocracy deceit and guile. He is a mortal beggar as
all Indians are. If you ask a favour of him, sometimes it is granted or not just as
he feels, if granted it must be well paid for. A few days ago he took it into his
head to require pay for teaching us the language & forbid his people from coming & talking with us for fear we should learn a few words of them. The Cayuses
as well as the Nez Perces are very strict in attending to their worship which they
have regularly every morning at day break & eve at twilight and once on the
Sab. They sing & repeat a form of prayers very devoutly after which the Chief
gives them a talk. The tunes & prayers were taught them by a Roman Catholic

trader. Indeed their worship was commenced by him. As soon as we became settled we established a meeting among them on the Sab in our own house. Did not think it best to interfere with their worship but during the time had a family bible class & prayer meeting. Many are usually in to our family worship especially evenings, when we spend considerable time in teaching them to sing. About 12 or 14 boys come regularly every night & are delighted with it.

Sab Jan 29 Our meeting to day with the Indians was more interesting than usual. I find that as we succeed in their language in communicating the truth to them so as to obtain a knowledge of their views & feelings, my heart becomes more & more interested in them. They appear to have a partial knowledge of the leading truths of the Bible; of sin, so far as it extends to outward actions, but know [no] knowledge of the heart.

Feb 1st Husband has gone to Walla W to day & is not expected to return untill tomorrow eve, & I am alone for the first time to sustain the family altar, in the midst of a room full of native youth & boys, who have come in to sing as usual. After worship several gathered close arround me as if anxious I should tell them some thing about the Bible. I had been reading the 12th chap of Acts, & with Richards help endeavoured to give them an account of Peter imprisonment &c, as well as I could. O that I had full possession of their language so that I could converse with them freely. . . .

March 6th Sab eve. To day our congregation has increased very considerably in consequence of the arrival of a party of Indians during the past week. A strong desire is manifest in them all to understand the truth & to be taught. Last

Whitman mission in Oregon, 1843
(Presbyterian Historical Society)

Narcissa Whitman
(Presbyterian Historical Society)

eve our room was full of men & boys, who came every eve to learn to sing. The whole tribe both men women & children would like the same privaledge if our room was larger & my health would admit so much singing. Indeed I should not attempt to sing with them, were it not for the assistance my Husband renders. You will recollect when he was in Angelica he could not sing a single tune. Now he is able to sing several tunes & lead the school in them. This saves me a great deal hard singing. I have thought many times if the singers in my Fathers family could have the same priviledge or were here to assist me in this work how much good they could do. I was not aware that singing was a qualification of so much importance to a missionary. While I was at Vancouver one Indian woman came a great distance with her daughter as she said to hear me sing with the children. The boys have introduced all the tunes they can sing alone, into their morning & eve worship, which they sing very well. To be at a distance & hear them singing them, one would almost forget he was in a savage land.

March 30th Again I can speak of the goodness & mercy of the Lord to us in an especial manner. On the evening of my birthday March 14th we received the gift of a little Daughter a treasure invaluable. During the winter my health was very good, so as to be able to do my work. About a week before her birth I was afflicted with an inflamatory rash which confined me mostly to my room. After repeated bleeding it abated very considerably. I was sick but about two hours. She was born half past eight, so early in the evening that we all had time to get considerable rest that night.

5. Voluntarism Revisited

The Principle Observed, 1851

Alexis de Tocqueville's famous book Democracy in America *(published first in France in two parts, 1835, 1840) has long been considered one of the most perceptive studies of American character and society. In this book, de Tocqueville (1805-1859) sought to define the ways in which American life had developed differently from Europe. Significantly, de Tocqueville held that religion was one of the most salient features of the American democracy, because, in contrast to Europe, active religious faith worked harmoniously with a populist or democratic politics. Several years after returning to France, de Tocqueville wrote a major study of France's own revolution. Even when writing about his native land de Tocqueville still had other interesting things to say about America. In particular, his argument in this later work (1) reiterated the message of* Democracy in America *by underscoring how closely traditional religion worked with liberal political ideas. It also (2) contrasted the organization of society in French Canada (Quebec) and the United States by noting how important the principle of voluntary organization was for all aspects of American life, including religion. In that section, "Canada" means French Quebec, rather than English-speaking Canada.*

1.

I stop the first American whom I meet, whether in his country or elsewhere, and I ask him if he thinks religion is useful for the stability of law and the good

[Source: Alexis de Tocqueville, *The Old Regime and the Revolution*, ed. François Furet and Françoise Mélonio, trans. Alan S. Kahan (Chicago: University of Chicago Press, 1998), pp. 206, 280-281.]

order of society; he immediately responds that a civilized society, but above all a free society, cannot subsist without religion. Respect for religion, in his eyes, is the greatest guarantee of the stability of the state and the security of individuals. Those least versed in the science of government know this much. However, in political matters, there was not a country in the world where the boldest doctrines of the philosophes of the eighteenth century were more applied than in America; only the antireligious doctrines of the French were never able to make headway there, even with the advantage of unlimited freedom of the press.

2.

20. How It Is in Canada That One Can best Judge The Administrative Centralization of the Old Regime

It is in colonies that one can best judge the form of the metropolitan government, because there all its characteristic traits are usually enlarged, and become more visible. When I want to judge the spirit of the government of Louis XIV and its vices, it is to Canada that I must go. There one can perceive the object's deformities as if under a microscope.

In Canada, a crowd of obstacles that past facts or the former social state presented, openly or secretly, to the free development of the government's ideas did not exist. The nobility was almost nonexistent, or at least it had lost almost all its roots; the Church no longer had its dominant position; feudal traditions were lost or obscured; the judiciary was no better rooted in old institutions and old mores. There nothing prevented the central power from abandoning itself to all its natural inclinations and from making all laws in accordance with the views which inspired it. In Canada, therefore, not the shadow of municipal or provincial institutions was permitted, no authorized collective power, no individual initiative. An intendant who had a position much differently preponderant than his colleagues had in France; a government that meddled in still more things than in the metropolis, and even wanted to do everything from Paris, despite the eighteen hundred leagues which separated them. In Canada the government never adopted the great principles which can render a colony populous and prosperous, but, on the contrary, employed all kinds of petty artificial procedures and little regulatory tyrannies to increase and spread the population: forced cultivation, all lawsuits arising from land concessions taken away from the courts and returned to the judgment of the government alone, requirements to farm in a certain way, obligations to live in certain places rather than others, etc. — this happened under Louis XIV; these edicts are countersigned by Colbert. One would think oneself in Algeria, in the fall bloom of modern centralization. Canada is in fact the faithful picture of what we have always seen in Algeria. On both sides one is in the presence of this government that is almost as numerous as the population, dominant, active, regulatory, constraining, wanting to foresee everything, taking everything over, always more familiar with the interests of the governed than they are themselves, constantly active and sterile.

In the United States, on the contrary, the English system of decentralization is exaggerated: the towns become almost independent municipalities, kinds of democratic republics. The republican element which is the base of English mores and the English constitution displays itself without opposition and develops. Government, properly speaking, does little in England, and individuals do much; in America, the government is no longer involved in anything, so to speak, and individuals uniting together do everything. The absence of upper classes, which made the inhabitant of Canada still more submissive to the government than the inhabitant of France was at that time, made the inhabitant of the English colonies more and more independent of authority.

In both colonies one ended up with the foundation of an entirely democratic society; but in Canada, at least as long as Canada remained French, equality was joined with absolute government; in the United States it was combined with freedom. And as for the material consequences of these two methods of colonization, we know that in 1763, the time of the English conquest of Canada, its population was 60,000, and the population of the English colonies 3 million.

The Principle Defined, 1856

This chapter began with examples of the voluntary genius of American religion hard at work: reforming society, promoting religious liberty, zealously pursuing evangelical aims across a continent. The first historian of these abundant religious energies in America, Presbyterian Robert Baird (1798-1863), spent some twenty-eight years in Europe on behalf of the Protestant cause. He found Europeans eager for information and perspective on America's proliferating, exciting religions. In 1843, therefore, Baird provided the first systematic attempt to explain this rapidly changing picture to friends abroad. In his Religion in America, *he succinctly described that principle which, in his view, distinguished the religion found in America from that found almost anywhere else in the world. And that principle promised much, he argued, for the future of Christianity everywhere.*

[Source: Robert Baird, *Religion in America,* rev. ed. (New York: Harper & Brothers, 1856), pp. 365-67.]

We here close our notice of the development of the Voluntary Principle in the United States; the results will appear more appropriately in another part of this work. If it is thought that I have dealt too much in details, I can only say that these seemed necessary for obvious reasons. There being no longer a union of Church and State in any part of the country, so that religion must depend, under God, for its temporal support wholly upon the voluntary principle: it seemed of much consequence to show how vigorously, and how extensively, that principle has brought the influence of the Gospel to bear in every direction upon the objects within its legitimate sphere. In doing this, I have aimed at answering a multitude of questions proposed to me during a residence and travels in Europe.

I have shown how, and by what means, funds are raised for the erection of church edifices, for the support of pastors, and for providing destitute places with the preaching of the Gospel — this last involving the whole subject of our home missionary efforts. And as ministers must be provided for the settlements forming apace in the West, as well as for the constantly increasing population to be found in the villages, towns, and cities of the East, I entered somewhat at length into the subject of education, from the primary schools up to the theological seminaries and faculties.

It was next of importance to show how the press is made subservient to the cause of the Gospel and the extension of the kingdom of God; then, how the voluntary principle can grapple with existing evils in society, such as intemperance, Sabbath breaking, slavery, and war, by means of diverse associations formed for their repression or removal; and, finally, I have reviewed the beneficent and humane institutions of the country, and illustrated the energy of the voluntary principle in their origin and progress.

The reader who has had the patience to follow me thus far, must have been struck with the vast versatility, if I may so speak, of this principle. Not an exigency occurs in which its application is called for, but forthwith those who have the heart, the hand, and the purse to meet the case, combine their efforts. Thus the principle seems to extend itself in every direction with an all-powerful influence. Adapting itself to every variety of circumstances, it acts wherever the Gospel is to be preached, wherever vice is to be attacked, wherever suffering humanity is to be relieved.

Nor is this principle less beneficial to those whom it enlists in the various enterprises of Christian philanthropy, than to those who are its express objects. The very activity, energy, and self-reliance it calls forth, are great blessings to the individual who exercises these qualities, as well as to those for whose sake they are put forth, and to the community at large. Men are so constituted as to derive happiness from the cultivation of an independent, energetic, and benevolent spirit, in being co-workers with God in promoting His glory, and the true welfare of their fellow-men.

We now take leave of this part of our subject, to enter upon that for which all that has hitherto been said must be considered preparatory — I mean the direct work of bringing men to the knowledge and possession of salvation.

The Principle Demonstrated, 1858

Revivalism has already been discussed, but the subject must be returned to once again — now not on the frontier, but in the cities. For 1858 was a year of miracle and wonder. The renewed religious interest of that time revealed itself first, mildly enough, in a series of noon-day prayer meetings initiated in Boston and New York. Meetings in downtown churches became so crowded and intense that rules had to be posted in an effort to give all a chance to pray and exhort. (1) That old hand at revivals, Charles Finney, reported that the 1858 movement "swept over the land with such power" as to bring about some 50,000 conversions in a single week. (2) Harriet Beecher Stowe (1811-96), daughter of Lyman Beecher and of course author of Uncle Tom's Cabin, *hoped that "the great revival of 1858" might become "the great reformation of 1858." (3) And even from England they came to observe and quickly report the goings on in America. What made American preaching so powerful? And if powerful, did it have sufficient force, even in 1858, to overcome the divisions of race, region, and political conviction?*

1.

This winter of 1857-58 will be remembered as the time when a great revival prevailed throughout all the Northern states. It swept over the land with such power, that for a time it was estimated that not less than fifty thousand conversions occurred in a single week. This revival had some very peculiarly interesting features. It was carried on to a large extent through lay influence, so much so as almost to throw the ministers into the shade. There had been a daily prayer-meeting observed in Boston for several years; and in the autumn previous to the great outburst, the daily prayer-meeting had been established in Fulton street, New York, which has been continued to this day. Indeed, daily prayer-meetings were established throughout the length and breadth of the Northern states. I recollect in one of our prayer-meetings in Boston that winter, a gentleman arose and said, "I am from Omaha, in Nebraska. On my journey

[Sources: (1) C. G. Finney, *Memoirs* . . . (New York: A. S. Barnes & Co., 1876), pp. 442-44. (2) H. B. Stowe, "The Revival," *The Independent*, March 11, 1858, pp. 1-2. (3) Isabella Lucy Bird Bishop, *The Aspects of Religion in the U. S. A.* (New York: Arno Press, 1972 [1859]), pp. 1-2, 156-60.]

> **Brethren are earnestly requested to adhere to the 5 minute rule.**

> PRAYERS & EXHORTATIONS
> Not to exceed 5 minutes,
> *in order to give all an opportunity.*
>
> *NOT MORE than 2 CONSECUTIVE*
> PRAYERS OR EXHORTATIONS.
>
> NO CONTROVERTED POINTS
> — *DISCUSSED.* —

The Noon-Day Prayer Meetings, 1858
The revival of 1858 first found its voice and
its spiritual propellant in the downtown
weekday prayer meeting — held
at noon and open to all.
(T. W. Chambers, *The Noon Prayer Meeting
of the North Dutch Church, New York* [1858])

East I have found a continuous prayer-meeting all the way. We call it," said he, "about two thousand miles from Omaha to Boston; and here was a prayer-meeting about two thousand miles in extent."

In Boston we had to struggle, as I have intimated, against this divisive influence, which set the religious interest a good deal back from where we had left it the spring before. However, the work continued steadily to increase, in the midst of these unfavorable conditions. It was evident that the Lord intended to make a general sweep in Boston. Finally it was suggested that a business-men's prayer-meeting should be established, at twelve o'clock, in the chapel of the Old South church, which was very central for business men. The Christian friend, whose guests we were, secured the use of the room, and advertised the meeting. But whether such a meeting would succeed in Boston at that time, was considered doubtful. However, this brother called the meeting; and to the surprise of almost everybody the place was not only crowded, but multitudes could not get in at all. This meeting was continued, day after day, with wonderful results. The place was, from the first, too strait for them, and other daily meetings were established in other parts of the city.

Mrs. Finney held ladies' meetings daily at the large vestry of Park street. These meetings became so crowded, that the ladies would fill the room, and then stand about the door on the outside, as far as they could hear on every side.

One of our daily prayer-meetings was held at Park street church, which would be full whenever it was open for prayer; and this was the case with many other meetings in different parts of the city. The population, large as it was, seemed to be moved throughout. The revival became too general to keep any account at all of the number of conversions, or to allow of any estimate being made that would approximate the truth. All classes of people were inquiring everywhere. Many of the Unitarians became greatly interested, and attended our meetings in large numbers.

This revival is of so recent date that I need not enlarge upon it, because it became almost universal throughout the Northern states. A divine influence seemed to pervade the whole land. Slavery seemed to shut it out from the South. The people there were in such a state of irritation, of vexation, and of committal to their peculiar institution, which had come to be assailed on every side, that the Spirit of God seemed to be grieved away from them. There seemed to be no place found for him in the hearts of the Southern people at that time. It was estimated that during this revival not less than five hundred thousand souls were converted in this country.

As I have said, it was carried on very much through the instrumentality of prayer-meetings, personal visitation and conversation, by the distribution of tracts, and by the energetic efforts of the laity, men and women. Ministers nowhere opposed it that I am aware of. I believe they universally sympathized with it. But there was such a general confidence in the prevalence of prayer, that the people very extensively seemed to prefer meetings for prayer to meetings for preaching. The general impression seemed to be, "We have had instruction until we are hardened; it is time for us to pray." The answers to prayer were constant, and so striking as to arrest the attention of the people generally throughout the land. It was evident that in answer to prayer the windows of heaven were opened and the Spirit of God poured out like a flood. The New York Tribune at that time published several extras, filled with accounts of the progress of the revival in different parts of the United States.

2.
"The Revival"

The great turning of the public mind to religion forms so marked an event in our present times that even secular papers are noticing it. For the most part, too, their notices are not scoffing or disrespectful, but tentative, serious, and suggestive. They seem to say, "There is need enough among us of a revival of religion, heaven knows — pray God only that it be real, and of the right kind."

They say, we hope it will do some good to men in a political and business capacity — that it will make them honest, and true, and upright, and magnanimous. "No revival has ever done anything for Wall street yet," says one — "we hope this may." "We hope," says another, "that prayer for the slave may not be considered an intrusion in these frequent prayer-meetings, and that some penitence may be felt and expressed for the share which Northern churches have had in aiding and abetting a system of robbery and oppression." So speaks the outside world as she looks gravely, sadly, not scoffingly, on the spectacle of thronging churches and opening prayer-meetings, — and her demand is just.

There is something in a right name. The term "revival" seems by general consent to have been adopted into our language as expressive of these seasons; but we should much prefer a term formerly much employed among certain re-

Harriet Beecher Stowe
(National Portrait Gallery, Smithsonian Institution, Washington, D.C.)

ligious denominations — "reformation." Instead of the great revival of 1858, we should be happy to read the great reformation of 1858.

Many worldly people, and some very Christian people, have a prejudice against anything like periodicity in religious impulse. They dislike revivals. Why should the Divine One, who is always love, say they, be considered as operating impulsively and periodically on the human soul, sometimes shining and sometimes withdrawing? It is urged furthermore, that the expectation of such seasons becomes in the end a motive for sloth and inaction and a neglect of an even and constant culture of the religious nature.

All this may have some truth in it; but, nevertheless, it is a fact that religious impulses, like all other impulses, have always come over the world in waves. — To begin with the day of Pentecost, in which three thousand were converted in one day, we find all along the line of the History of the Church that there were seasons when religious impulses were more than usually fervent, and religious labors successful. . . .

We believe in no raptures, in no ecstacies, in no experiences that do not bring the soul into communion with Him who declared He came to set at liberty them that are bound and bruised. Revivals of religion have not been confined to Christian countries. Old heathenism had them. Popish Rome has them. Modern heathenism has them. One and all of these have had turns of unusual fervor in their way. One and all have had their trances, illuminations, and mysterious ecstacies. But those only are Christian revivals which make men like Christ; or, if they do not make them like Him, at least set them on the road of trying to be like Him. We say, therefore, to our friends, that the period of a great religious impulse has come; that there will be revival all over the land, either false or true — either of a Christian or a heathen type; and by their fruits shall ye know them. We are glad to hear that some of the most effective revival preachers confine their attention very much to preaching to the church. We are glad to hear that. It is quite necessary that those who profess to be the exponents of religion before the community, should have some deeper and higher ideas of what religion is.

So that when they go forth with the Apostolic message, "Repent and be converted every one of you," they need not be met with the scornful reply, "Converted, sir, converted to what? Converted into a man who defends slavery — converted into one who dares not testify against a profitable wickedness — converted into a man whose religion never goes into his counting-house — converted into a man who has no conscience in his politics, and who scoffs at the higher law of God? No, sir; I desire no such conversion. Whatever your raptures may be, I desire no part with them."

And let the solemn question go out to every Christian, to every parent, "Do you want your neighbors, friends, and children converted into such Christians as you have been?" If not, is there not a deeper conversion necessary for you?

3.

The "great revival" in America is now admitted as a fact by men of all parties. After making every due allowance for "exaggerations," and the warm colouring of "enthusiasm," it is recognized, as among the most noteworthy phenomena of the day, that the influence of the Holy Spirit has been felt during the past eighteen months in the United States to an extent unprecedented in any other country or period. To deny it would be blindly to reject the concurrent testimony of some of the most enlightened and sober-minded men in America. This revival still attracts deep interest among Christians of all denominations who desire the triumph of the gospel, and who recognize in the spread of Protestant Christianity the true germ of universal brotherhood; and it naturally leads to an inquiry into the state of the Transatlantic Churches, and of religion generally, in a country whose characteristics differ so widely from our own. These questions present themselves to many minds: What is the external influence of religion in the States? What is the attitude of the Churches with respect to slavery? What is the general style of preaching? . . .

In the South the preaching is still the same, more polished perhaps in its language than in the West, but earnest and Evangelical. There, as elsewhere, the pulpit seeks to convince men of sin, and that the Gospel is blessed in the South I do not doubt any more than that its progress is hindered by one important omission. The Southern ministers denounce drunkenness and other vices; dishonest dealing, worldliness, the love of display, &c; but the sin of Slavery, and the sins which arise out of it, pass unrebuked. We hear of other sins as elsewhere; but the one terrible system which denies to 4,000,000 human beings the right of indissoluble marriage, and the sacredness of the parental tie, which sustains an iniquitous internal Slave-trade, which vitiates alike public and private morals, this the pulpit protects and fosters, and denounces as "sceptics" or "abolitionists" all who assert on the broad basis of moral right the equality of the human race. With this exception no aspersion can be cast on the Southern pulpit, for no country possesses a more compact mass of orthodox preaching. The Slaves in very many localities participate in the privileges of a pure Gospel preached in a manner which accords with their simplicity and ignorance, Evangelical in its sentiments, though often, to our ideas, painfully grotesque in its language.

The first great characteristic of American preaching is its serious earnestness. Men preach as if they felt the responsibility of the ministry and the value of souls. "We believe and therefore speak," appears to give the directness which their preaching certainly has. They preach as if the lost state of man and salvation through Christ were the grandest and most outstanding realities in the universe, and strive to prepare dying men for death, judgment, and eternity. A second characteristic is its faithfulness. The ministers are not intimidated, as some persons in England suppose, by the rich and influential in their congregations who dislike the truth. They faithfully preach Christ crucified; they urge upon their hearers to repent and denounce the sins of every class and profession and of professing Christians with a boldness and plainness which I have never heard equalled. A third, is its simplicity. The preachers generally take plain texts and prefer to give their natural and obvious meaning rather than anything far-fetched or philosophical. Familiar, vigorous, and perspicuous language is generally preferred to the ornate and rhetorical. Men preach to educated hearers in language which is perfectly intelligible to the uneducated. A fourth and very marked characteristic is that American preaching dwells much on immediate reconciliation with God. The becoming reconciled to God "today" is continually urged upon sinners. The call to repent and believe the Gospel immediately is for ever sounding in the ears of those who are recognized as "unconverted," and no delay is excused, and no excuse is accepted. Christ is preached, not Christianity; and the immediate acceptance of his atonement is constantly urged. A fifth characteristic is that it is systematic. That is, that the highest style of Evangelical preaching strives to maintain a proper connection between the discourses successively delivered from the same pulpit, and to make every statement and argument bear upon and strengthen that which precedes it, so as to tend to the final results of demonstration and clearness rather than to present separated and isolated statements of truth. A sixth characteristic is that it is eminently practical. The unconverted are urged to repentance and faith, and Christians are incessantly directed to "walk worthy of the vocation whereunto they are called," to live for the glory of God, and the salvation of men. Of late years this idea has had an ever-increasing prominence given to it in preaching, that every Christian in every sphere of life is under an obligation so to live, that by his influence, conversation, and example, he may promote the welfare of men. The line which separates the Church from the world is also drawn so distinctly, that none can doubt on which side of it they are to be found. A seventh characteristic is that it dwells much on the work of the Holy Spirit. The idea of the importance of his work and office is a dominant one in American preaching, and the need of his work of conversion, the necessity of his co-operation with the setting forth of the Gospel, and the promise of the Spirit as the great and permanent ascension gift of Christ, are among the most prominent of pulpit themes, and have been so for a hundred years. In addition to these seven characteristics, it may be stated that American preaching is very doctrinal and very philosophical in the highest sense of the word, and consequently contains all the elements of power.

Suggested Reading (Chapter Four)

Winthrop Hudson's *The Great Tradition of the American Churches* (1953) remains a classic account of how voluntarism was understood and how it operated in the nineteenth century. Europe's interest in the operation of that peculiarly American principle is revealed through the selections in Milton B. Powell's anthology, *The Voluntary Church: American Religious Life (1740-1865) Seen Through the Eyes of European Visitors* (1967). This volume contains comments by celebrated foreign visitors like Frances Trollope, Harriet Martineau, and Alexis de Tocqueville (whose seminal *Democracy in America* has recently been retranslated and re-edited by Harvey C. Mansfield and Delba Winthrop [2000]). For showing how the early decades of the nineteenth century radically altered the face of religion in America, two works are essential, Nathan O. Hatch, *The Democratization of American Christianity* (1989), and Jon Butler, *Awash in a Sea of Faith: Christianizing the American People* (1990). Both sharpen themes that are strikingly exemplified in Michael C. Kenny, *The Perfect Law of Liberty: Elias Smith and the Providential History of America* (1994), and brilliantly generalized in Gordon S. Wood, *The Radicalism of the American Revolution* (1992). Timothy L. Smith's important book, *Revivalism and Social Reform* (1957), tracks the results of voluntary religious organization to the time of the Civil War.

For the complex interactions between religion and American national culture in the republican era, three books by Daniel Walker Howe offer unusually perceptive analysis: *The Unitarian Conscience: Harvard Moral Philosophy, 1805-1861* (1970), *The Political Culture of the American Whigs* (1979), and *Making the American Self: Jonathan Edwards to Abraham Lincoln* (1997). A fine survey for this era has been provided by Curtis D. Johnson, *Redeeming America: Evangelicals and the Road to Civil War* (1993). Also outstanding, but on narrower themes, are Donald Mathews, *Religion in the Old South* (1977), Lewis O. Saum, *The Popular Mood of Pre–Civil War America* (1980), and Robert M. Calhoon, *Evangelicals and Conservatives in the Early South, 1740-1861* (1988).

Voluntarism in action is displayed in Charles I. Foster's *An Errand of Mercy: The Evangelical United Front, 1790-1837* (1960), a book that emphasizes the Anglo-American cooperation that is also a major theme in Richard Carwardine, *Transatlantic Revivalism: Popular Evangelicalism in Britain and America, 1790-1865* (1978). What Perry Miller called the "Evangelical Basis" covers some of the same territory in his suggestive *Life of the Mind in America from the Revolution to the Civil War* (1965). More comprehensive on the same era is Jean V. Matthews, *Toward a New Society: American Thought and Culture, 1800-1830* (1991). The importance of the newly developed Sunday school receives excellent analysis in Anne M. Boylan's *Sunday School: The Formation of an American Institution, 1790-1880* (1988). What some historians label the "Second Great

Awakening" also points to this same burst of voluntary religious energies, as documented in these important studies: Bruce D. Dickinson, *And They All Sang Hallelujah: Plain-folk Camp-meeting Religion, 1800-1845* (1981), Terry D. Bilhartz, *Urban Religion and the Second Great Awakening: Church and Society in Early National Baltimore* (1986), Charles Hambrick-Stowe, *Charles G. Finney and the Spirit of American Evangelicalism* (1996), and Catherine Brekus, *Strangers and Pilgrims: Female Preaching in America, 1740-1865* (1998).

Perry Miller's anthology, *The Transcendentalists* (1950), remains an important collection of documents with interpretation. A participant in as well as observer of that "mid-summer madness," Octavius Brooks Frothingham in 1876 wrote *Transcendentalism in New England*, an excellent insider's account that is available in a modern format (1972). Orientation for the ever-fascinating but elusive Emerson can be found in *The Cambridge Companion to Ralph Waldo Emerson* (1999). For ties of the various transcendentalists to more traditional religious movements, see Anne C. Rose, *Transcendentalism as a Social Movement, 1830-1850* (1981). Roger Lundin has provided an informative study of one of the most important New England writers not recruited by the transcendentalists, *Emily Dickinson and the Art of Belief* (1998).

Utopian movements are well treated by Mark Holloway, *Heavens on Earth: Utopian Communities in America, 1680-1880* (rev. ed., 1966); Robert S. Fogarty, *American Utopianism* (1972); and Fogarty, *Dictionary of American Communal and Utopian History* (1980). On Oneida itself, see Constance Noyes Robertson's two books: *Oneida Community: An Autobiography, 1851-1876* (1970), and *Oneida Community: The Breakup, 1876-1881* (1972). Mormon history has been an increasingly fruitful subject for both insiders and outsiders to the movement, including Leonard Arrington and Davis Britton, *The Mormon Experience* (1980), Jan Shipps, *Mormonism: The Story of a New Tradition* (1985), Richard L. Bushman, *Joseph Smith and the Beginnings of Mormonism* (1984), John L. Brooke, *The Refiner's Fire: The Making of Mormon Cosmology, 1644-1844* (1994), and Richard N. Ostling and Joan K. Ostling, *Mormon America: The Power and the Promise* (1999). The Shakers have received magisterial treatment from Stephen J. Stein, *The Shaker Experience in America* (1992). Outstanding recent treatments of the Millerites and associated movements include Ronald L. Numbers and Jonathan M. Butler, eds., *The Disappointed: Millerism and Millenarianism in the Nineteenth Century* (1987), and Ruth Alden Doan, *The Miller Heresy, Millennialism, and American Culture* (1987). Ira Rosenwaike examines American Jewry in the early decades of the nineteenth century in his study *On the Edge of Greatness* (1985), and there is much of interest on nineteenth-century Jewish organization in Jonathan D. Sarna, *The American Jewish Experience* (1986). For minorities and utopian communities, R. Laurence Moore offers a brilliant interpretation in *Religious Outsiders and the Making of Americans* (1986).

The theme of Restorationism is broader than the history of a single movement such as the groups associated with the names of Alexander Campbell and Barton W. Stone. This reality is evident in Richard T. Hughes and C. Leonard Allen, *Illusions of Innocence: Protestant Primitivism in America, 1639-1875* (1988), and Richard T. Hughes, ed., *The American Quest for the Primitive Church* (1988). Yet those looking particularly for solid work on the Campbellite traditions have been well served by David Edwin Harrell, *Quest for a Christian America: The Disciples of Christ and American Society to 1866* (1966).

The broad popularity of Spiritualism is the subject of R. Laurence Moore, *In Search of White Crows: Spiritualism, Parapsychology, and American Culture* (1977). In much of the experimentation in the nineteenth century, non-traditional marital arrangements were proposed and sometimes adopted, as documented, for example, by Louis J. Kern, *An Ordered Love: Sex Roles and Sexuality in Victorian Utopians* (1980), and Lawrence Foster, *Religion and Sexuality* (1981). One can learn much from the reminiscences of leading Baptist and Methodist clergy, for example, with respect to the Baptists, *The Memoirs of John Mason Peck* (1965 [1854]), and for the Methodists, the oft-reprinted *Autobiography of Peter Cartwright* (1956 [1856]). A scholarly effort to set such early-national movements in context is Gregory A. Wills, *Democratic Religion: Freedom, Authority, and Church Discipline in the Baptist South, 1785-1900* (1997). On the adaptation of Roman Catholics to American ways, a particularly informative study is Jay P. Dolan, *Catholic Revivalism: The American Experience, 1830-1900* (1978). Outstanding on the relatively unsuccessful efforts of Congregationalists to adjust to the frontier is James R. Rohrer, *Keepers of the Covenant: Frontier Missions and the Decline of Congregationalism, 1774-1818* (1995). A large view of a perennially problematic relationship is provided by R. Pierce Beaver, *Church, State and the American Indians* (1966).

For background on Robert Baird, consult the modern abridgment of his *Religion in America* (1970), with an excellent introduction by Henry W. Bowden. Baird's contemporary, Philip Schaff, who was also concerned about explaining America's religions to Europeans, is well served by Perry Miller's modern edition of his *America: A Sketch of Its Political, Social, and Religious Character* (1961).

FIVE

Evangelical Empire: Rise and Fall

In the concluding section of Chapter Four, Robert Baird spoke positively of the voluntary principle that could grapple with every evil, conquer every vice, relieve every suffering. This grand principle, he added, extended "itself in every direction with an all-powerful influence." The present chapter opens with Baird once more, but here he speaks in more muted tones. Surveying the widening spectrum of theological opinion in America, he finds it necessary to distinguish between "evangelical" and "unevangelical" forces in America, between those who shared basic Calvinist assumptions (or at least Protestant ones) and those who did not. The Evangelical Empire was, in other words, showing signs of division and strain. Other voices — dissonant, dissenting — spoke out, doing so with a force and a frequency that ensured their being heard. In the generation before the Civil War, the Evangelical Empire still stood, but its foundations trembled.

Theology

Theologically, a Protestant hue colored most of the land. Biblical imagery and biblical ideology still permeated the culture: salvation was a common concern, repentance a familiar event, conversion an ordinary occurrence, theological argot a recognized medium of exchange. Alexander Campbell, leader of the Restorationists, spelled out his contemporaries' objections to Roman Catholicism. Princeton's Charles Hodge saw evangelical Christianity as threatened not so much by the presence of Catholics or Mormons or Jews as by the faithless within the besieged Empire. Some mistook morality for piety, or reason for revelation, or respectability for redemption. And if those widespread misperceptions were not corrected, Hodge declared, the Empire was indeed doomed and deserved to be. Methodist Phoebe Palmer, by contrast, looked to inward holiness for what was needed. Congregationalist Horace Bushnell, keenly conscious of deep fissures developing within Protestantism, gave himself to buttressing and bridging. His theological effort, however, was more than a simple repair of older structures. With originality and comprehensiveness, he moved beyond the tired disputes (revivalist versus antirevivalist, unitarian versus trinitarian, literalist versus rationalist, Calvinist versus transcendentalist) to new theological understandings and appreciations. And for a time, Bushnellian synthesizing held real promise. John W. Nevin's creativity was different, since he rejected so much of the standard American approach to theology. Still others, like Charles Porterfield Krauth, would hold the weakening Empire together by keeping faith with secure and stable European traditions, contending that New World ways need not require the retheologizing of all truths formerly deemed immutable. Whatever its successes or failure, theology at mid-century was no backwater, brackish pool; tides rolled and fresh currents moved, as configurations below the surface slowly began to shift.

Pluralism

The early nineteenth century saw the first numerically significant influx of Jews, the immigration coming chiefly from Germany. Well-educated and culturally sophisticated Jewish leaders, impressed by an America open both geographically and religiously, tended to embrace their new environment with eager enthusiasm. In these United States Jews need not crouch behind ghettoed walls, need not be left behind in the Western world's undaunted march toward Progress, need not be insular or foreign or unchanged. In short, the west European Jew could not only migrate to America; he or she could become American. It followed, therefore, that ancient Hebrew writings should be presented in modern American idiom, that ancient liturgical patterns should yield to a contemporary mode of obeisance to God. Before the Civil War an Americanizing excitement largely obscured the inevitable differences concerning the rate or extent of modernizing appropriate to Judaism. Later, leaders would sharply divide over sabbath schools, food laws, synagogue seating, and a host of other issues. But in this generation of immigrants there was much to do and so little time. Both the Lord (Yahweh) and the Law (Torah) required much of thee, O Israel: to travel, translate, preach, teach, all the while faithfully interpreting America to the Jew and the Jew to America.

Because Jews were few and their recent past one of suffering and oppression, the Evangelical Empire did not see itself in the 1840s as especially threatened by the sons and daughters of Abraham and Sarah. It was not so with respect to Roman Catholics who arrived, not by the dozens, but by the thousands and tens of thousands. Ireland, suffering from severe poverty and failed potato harvests, provided the greatest number of emigrants. By 1850 Roman Catholicism had become a major American denomination; within a few more years it was the largest American denomination. So Roman Catholicism, clearly, could not be ignored: not by the Bairds, Bushnells, Hodges, or Campbells, nor by the ordinary mortals weaned on a steady diet of papal persecution, papal bigotry, and papal intrigue. Roman Catholics themselves, like many of the Jews of this period, saw the Americanization of their church as an opportunity not to be missed. Exactly what "Americanization" meant was, to be sure, subject to debate and disagreement. At least to a few Catholics it meant that church members choose their own pastors, control their own parish property, settle their disputes more by majority vote than by episcopal fiat. Others who did not argue for a democratic church polity did argue for a Roman Catholic Church congenial with a democratic state. Catholicism did not demand monarchy, did not abhor liberty, need not ally itself with political forces of reaction and repression. Two Americans, both converted as adults to Catholicism — Orestes Brownson and Isaac Hecker — saw their special charge to be keeping lines of communication open between Catholics and non-Catholics. Together (as was said of Brownson) they would prove to Catholics their right to be Americans, to Americans their right to be Catholics. Hispanic Catholics were, of course, even more suspect: foreign in language, foreign in religion ("unevangelical," said Baird), foreign in ethnicity (not Anglo-Saxon, said a dominant culture). As a result Hispanic Catholicism suffered long-lasting neglect, both from its own hierarchy and its nation's history.

The Protestant hegemony or Empire might indeed be slipping away. To some Americans this meant more than a threat to Protestantism; the nation itself faced gravest danger. New immigrants not only failed so regularly to be both evangelical and Protestant; they failed also, it was argued, to understand or appreciate or embrace constitutional liberties and Anglo-Saxon niceties. Nativists — those who would keep America for the native-born, white Protestants — trusted few outside their own tight circle. Those least trusted and most feared, the rapidly expanding number of Roman Catholics, bore the brunt of nativist suspicion and wrath. Only angry words can be offered as documents here, but angry deeds erupted too: a convent near Boston burned to the ground in 1834, a seminary and two churches in Philadelphia deliberately set ablaze in 1844, homes of Irish immigrants wrecked, and in New York similar violence prevented only by the vigilance of Bishop John Hughes. For a time ugly Americans in both politics and religion threatened to wrest control from those of saner mind and larger spirit.

As new arrivals from Europe added to the meaning of religious pluralism, so also did revival among Native Americans. As European civilization spread over more of North America, Native Americans throughout the continent were forced to deal with a loss of tribal tradition and identity. Whether through trading with white colonists, forced removal from lands of origin, or partial assimilation into white society, indigenous North Americans could not avoid cultural reorientation. Starting in the mid-eighteenth century, indigenous peoples eschewed, in varying degrees, tribal distinctives in order to embrace the common "Indian" identity they shared in relation to whites. In 1762, the "Delaware Prophet" Neolin received a revelation and took it to those tribes located around Lake Erie. He urged a severing of all ties with European culture, a message that inspired a brief flurry of efforts to throw off the yoke of European societies. Though perhaps not directly influenced by Neolin, the theme of preserving Indian identity over against the encroaching white culture would be frequently repeated among Native Americans in following years. That theme added even more diversity to a religious landscape that by mid-century was beginning to strain.

Human Rights

Fortunately, the country plunged into no religious war; unfortunately, that potential conflict yielded to a stronger one of black and white, slave and free, north and south. The issue above all issues that neither diminished nor disappeared: how long could a nation endure half-slave and half-free? American religion, even if it so chose, could not remain aloof from that question. Many churches chose, on the contrary, to enter fully into the fray — but by no means all on the same side. Blacks, whose interest in the issue was as inescapable as it was personal, could hardly be charged with indifference, though great numbers of them lacked both platform and articulate voice. Christianity among the slaves helped some to endure their suffering, others to revolt against it. Thus religion, as Willie Lee Rose has written, "brought forth both Nat Turners and Uncle Toms [but] in either case it caused slaves to *think*. . . ." So black spokesmen and spokeswomen did find their voices, did rouse their audiences, did point accusing fingers at a religion in league with a system of intolerable oppression.

Just as revolutionary rhetoric refused to stay confined to a quarrel about stamps and tea, so human rights rhetoric spread from slaves to other subjugated elements of the population: for example, women. Abolitionist Angelina Grimké in 1837 wrote to her future husband: ". . . we are placed very unexpectedly in a very trying situation, in the foreground of an entirely new contest — a contest for the *rights of woman* as a moral, intelligent and responsible being." It might have been better to keep the two struggles (one for black rights and one for female rights) separate, but their conjunction has "been brought about by a concatenation of circumstances over which we had no control." Yet another battle for human rights loomed in the 1830s over which apparently no one had control, certainly not the losers: the American Indians. The oft-told tale of the betrayal and expulsion of the Cherokees gave little comfort then or now to the witnesses to the continuing struggle for human rights.

1. Theology in the New Nation

Robert Baird's "General Remarks"

Robert Baird, introduced above (p. 393), found diversity not limited to ecclesiastical institutions; it extended as well to theological convictions. Baird sought, however, to rescue the Evangelical Empire from hopeless relativism by sharply distinguishing between the "evangelical denominations" and the "unevangelical sects." The former, who agreed on "the vital or essential points," were in Baird's view the clear hope of the growing nation. The latter, beginning with the Roman Catholics (who have "buried the Truth amid a heap of corruptions of heathenish origin") and dropping all the way "down to the Mormons" ("the grossest of all the delusions"), are in contrast the nation's despair.

Having concluded these notices of the various denominations — evangelical and non-evangelical — in the United States, I would now offer a few remarks on the history and present state of theological opinion in this country. Fully and philosophically treated, this could not fail to interest sincere inquirers after truth in all countries, but it would require not a chapter, but a volume, and would hardly be consistent with the nature of this work. We must leave such a discussion to another time, and, probably, to other hands, and shall now merely touch on a few general topics.

I. Let us first mark some of the causes and influences to which the diversity of religious doctrines may be traced. The chief of these are,

1. Differences of origin and ancestry. This we have already noticed, but must refer to it again.

[Source: Robert Baird, *Religion in America*, rev. ed. (New York: Harper & Brothers, 1856), pp. 577-79.]

Had the whole territory of the United States been originally settled by one class of men, holding the same system of religious opinions, more uniformity of doctrine might reasonably have been looked for. But what philosophical inquirer, knowing the different origins of New England, Pennsylvania, Virginia, and New York, would expect that the mere federal union of States that differ so much in their original inhabitants, could ever bring them all to complete religious uniformity? Let us but look at the number of different religious bodies — different, I mean, in their origin — to be found in these and the other States of the Union. (1.) The New England Congregational churches, formed by emigrant Puritans, and, down to the epoch of our Revolution, sympathizing strongly with all the changes of opinion among the English dissenters. (2.) The Presbyterian Church, in its larger and smaller branches, very much of Scotch and Irish origin, and still aiming at an imitation of the Church of Scotland as its pattern. (3.) The Episcopal Church, an off-shoot from the Church of England, dreading and almost scorning to borrow ideas from any quarter save its Mother Church. (4.) The Dutch Reformed Church, which long received its ministers from Holland, and still glories in the Heidelberg Catechism and the decrees of the Synod of Dort. (5.) The Lutherans, the Reformed, and other German churches, who preserve their old nationality, both by being still organized as distinct communions, and by the constant emigration of ministers and people from their original fatherland. Now, why should we expect to see all these fused and amalgamated in the United States more than in Europe?

2. Mark, too, that none of their ministers can extend any such *direct* influence over other churches than their own, as might make the exercise of brotherly love pass into close intimacy and final amalgamation. Each denomination has its own colleges and theological seminaries; each its own weekly, monthly, or quarterly periodicals; and some of them may almost be said to have an independent religious literature, edited and published by their own responsible agents. All this is counterbalanced only by many ministers of different denominations receiving their classical and scientific education at the same institutions, preparatory to their more strictly professional studies.

3. The freedom allowed in the United States to all sorts of inquiry and discussion necessarily leads to a diversity of opinion, which is seen not only in there being different denominations, but different opinions also in the same denomination. Perhaps there is not a single ecclesiastical convention in which there are not two parties at least, whose different views lead sometimes to discussions keenly maintained, yet turning generally upon points which, however interesting, are confessedly not of fundamental importance. On what may be called vital or essential points there is little disputation, just because there is much harmony in all the Evangelical Communions. Nor could it be well otherwise, seeing that in doctrine and practice they all take the Bible as their inspired and sole authoritative guide.

4. Nor must we forget that what may be called provincial peculiarities necessarily lead so far to diversities of religious sentiment. A true Eastern man from Connecticut, and a true Western man, born and brought up on the banks of the Ohio, can hardly be expected to speculate alike on dubious points in theology, any more than on many other subjects. So, also, are the inhabitants of the North and South distinguished from each other by peculiarities fully as marked as those that distinguish the northern from the southern inhabitants of Great Britain.

II. Yet it is not difficult to draw a line between the various unevangelical sects on the one hand, and those that may be classed together as evangelical denominations on the other. The chief of the former, as we have said, are the Roman Catholics, Unitarians, Christians, Universalists, Hicksite Quakers, Swedenborgians, Jews, Shakers, and so on down to the Mormons, beginning with the sect that has buried the Truth amid a heap of corruptions of heathenish origin, and ending with the grossest of all the delusions that Satanic malignity or human ambition ever sought to propagate. Now it will be observed that, with the exception of the first two, these sects have few elements of stability. Their ministers are almost all men of little learning, and that little is almost all concentrated in specious endeavors to maintain their tenets, by perverting the Scriptures, by appealing to the prejudices of their hearers, and by misrepresenting and ridiculing the doctrines of opponents who meet their subtle arguments with the plain declarations of Scripture, as well as with unanswerable arguments drawn from sound reason.

Alexander Campbell

Alexander Campbell, introduced above (p. 354), was untypical for his age because of the militancy with which he fought against traditional denominationalism. But he was typical for many American Protestants in thinking that the growing American strength of the Catholic church posed a problem both religiously and politically. Unlike some of the nativists whose activities are featured later in this chapter, Campbell always stated his objections to Rome peacefully. As one of the great public debaters in an era of great public debate, Campbell was especially pleased when John Purcell, the Catholic Bishop of Cincinnati, agreed to debate him on the merits of

[Source: *A Debate on the Roman Catholic Religion: held in the Sycamore-Street Meeting House, Cincinnati, from the 13th to the 21st of January, 1837. Between Alexander Campbell of Bethany, Virginia, and the Rt. Rev. John B. Purcell, Bishop of Cincinnati* (Cincinnati: James, 1851), pp. vii-viii.]

Purcell's church. The ensuing public addresses, with rebuttals, took place over more than a week in Cincinnati in 1837. Campbell, however, got to draw up the agenda, which reveals the rough road that Bishop Purcell was forced to climb.

Points at Issue.

1. The Roman Catholic Institution, sometimes called the 'Holy, Apostolic, Catholic, Church,' is not now, nor was she ever, catholic, apostolic, or holy; but is a *sect* in the fair import of that word, older than any other sect now existing, not the 'Mother and Mistress of all Churches,' but an apostacy from the only true, holy, apostolic, and catholic church of Christ.[1]

2. Her notion of apostolic succession is without any foundation in the Bible, in reason, or in fact; an imposition of the most injurious consequences, built upon unscriptural and anti-scriptural traditions, resting wholly upon the opinions of interested and fallible men.

3. She is not uniform in her faith, or united in her members; but mutable and fallible, as any other sect of philosophy or religion — Jewish, Turkish, or Christian — a confederation of sects, under a politico-ecclesiastic head.

4. She is the "Babylon" of John, the "Man of Sin" of Paul, and the Empire of the "Youngest Horn" of Daniel's Sea Monster.

5. Her notions of purgatory, indulgences, auricular confession, remission of sins, transubstantiation, supererogation, &c., essential elements of her system, are immoral in their tendency, and injurious to the well-being of society, religious and political.

6. Notwithstanding her pretensions to have given us the Bible, and faith in it, we are perfectly independent of her for our knowledge of that book, and its evidences of a divine original.

7. The Roman Catholic religion, if infallible and unsusceptible of reformation, as alleged, is essentially anti-American, being opposed to the genius of all free institutions, and positively subversive of them, opposing the general reading of the scriptures, and the diffusion of useful knowledge among the whole community, so essential to liberty and the permanency of good government.

A. CAMPBELL.

CINCINNATI, 12th January, 1837.

---

1. The Restorationist movement; see above, pp. 352-57.

Charles Hodge (1797-1878)

Educated at Princeton and for over half a century professor at that Presbyte-
rian institution, Hodge fought for the theology which he (and Baird) saw as
the supporting columns of the Evangelical Empire. Such theology must be
biblical, confessional, traditional, and more concerned about the sovereignty
of God than the dignity of man. In the excerpt below, Hodge contrasts this
true evangelical Calvinist theology with the rationalizing, moralizing, tem-
porizing, non-Calvinist sort. This selection is taken from the journal which
Hodge himself dominated and directed from 1825 to 1871.

From an early period in the history of the Church, there have been two great
systems of doctrine in perpetual conflict. The one begins with God, the other
with man. The one has for its object the vindication of the Divine supremacy
and sovereignty in the salvation of men; the other has for its characteristic aim
the assertion of the rights of human nature. It is specially solicitous that nothing should be held to be true, which cannot be philosophically reconciled with
the liberty and ability of man. It starts with a theory of free agency and of the
nature of sin, to which all the anthropological doctrines of the Bible must be
made to conform. . . . Every man, according to this system, stands his probation
for himself, and is not under condemnation until he voluntarily transgresses
some known law, for it is only such transgression that falls under the category
of sin. In regeneration, according to the principles above stated, there cannot be
the production of a new moral nature, principle or disposition, as the source of
holy exercises. That change must consist in some act of the soul, something
which lies within the sphere of its own power, some act of the will or some
change subject to the will. The influence by which regeneration is effected must
be something which can be effectually resisted in the utmost energy of its operation. This being the case, the sovereignty of God in the salvation of men must
of necessity be given up. . . .

From these theoretical views, others of a practical nature necessarily follow. Conviction of sin must accommodate itself to the theory that there is no
sin but in the voluntary transgression of known law; a sense of helplessness
must be modified by the conviction of ability to repent and believe, to change
our own heart and keep all God's commands. . . . The view which this system
presents of the plan of salvation, of the relation of the soul to Christ, of the nature and office of faith, modifies and determines the whole character of experimental religion.

[Source: Charles Hodge, *Biblical Repository and Princeton Review,* 23 (1851), 308-19, without Hodge's extensive notes.]

The system antagonistic to the one just described has for its object the vindication of the supremacy of God in the whole work of man's salvation, both because [he] is in fact supreme, and because man being in fact utterly ruined and helpless, no method of recovery which does not so regard him is suited to his relation to God, or can be made to satisfy the necessities of his nature. This system does not exalt a theory of morals or of liberty over the Scriptures as a rule by which they are to be interpreted. It accommodates its philosophy to the fact revealed in the divine word. As the Bible plainly teaches that man was created holy, that he is now born in sin, that when renewed by the Holy Ghost he receives a new nature, it admits the doctrine of created holiness, innate sin, and of infused or inherent grace. It acknowledges Adam as the head and representative of his posterity, in whom we had our probation, in whom we sinned and fell, so that we come into the world under condemnation, being born the children of wrath. . . . It admits that by this innate, hereditary, moral depravity men are altogether indisposed, disabled and made opposite to all good; so that their ability to do good works is not at all of themselves, but wholly from the Spirit of Christ. It recognizes justice as distinguished from benevolence, to be an essential attribute of God, an attribute which renders the punishment of sin necessary, not merely as a means of moral impression, but for its own sake. It, therefore, regards the work of Christ as designed to satisfy justice and to fulfill the demands of the law by his perfect obedience to its precepts, and by enduring its penalty in the room and stead of sinners. . . .

There are three leading characteristics of this system, by which it is distinguished from that to which it stands opposed. The latter is characteristically rational. It seeks to explain every thing so as to be intelligible to the speculative understanding. The former is confessedly mysterious. The Apostle pronounces the judgment of God to be unsearchable and his ways past finding out. . . . The system which Paul taught was not a system of common sense, but of profound and awful mystery. The second distinguishing characteristic of this system is that its whole tendency is to exalt God and to humble men. It does not make the latter feel that he is the great end of all things, or that he has his destiny in his own hands. . . . It is not the wise, the great, or the noble whom God calls, but the foolish, the base, and those that are not [great], that they who glory should glory in the Lord. Thirdly, this system represents God as himself the end of all his works both in creation and in redemption. It is not the universe, but God; not the happiness of creatures, but the infinitely higher end of divine glory, which is contemplated in all these revelations and dispensations. For of him, through him, and to him are all things: to whom be glory for ever. Amen.

Phoebe Palmer (1807-1874)

In contrast to the theology promoted by Charles Hodge and many other leading men of the period, Phoebe Worrall Palmer thought that practical piety was more important than any right ordering of doctrine. This daughter of Methodists and wife of a prominent New York City physician underwent an experience of religious recommitment and deepening when she began taking part in a "Tuesday Meeting for the Promotion of Holiness" hosted by her sister Sarah Worrall Lankford. When Phoebe Palmer began to speak and then write about her experience, she found that many others were longing, as she had longed, for a deeper understanding of Christian life than could be supplied by any dogmatic formula. Through her book The Way of Holiness, *first published in 1845, and then through many other volumes, her periodical* Guide to Holiness, *and a very popular career of public speaking, Phoebe Palmer became the leading American advocate of "Holiness" theology, an emphasis that remains strong to this day in Methodist, Pentecostal, and other denominational traditions. The selection that follows contains part of Phoebe Palmer's third-person narration of her own experience that marked a pathway followed by a host of others in later American life.*

From the preceding views she discerned clearly, that *one* more step must be taken ere she could fully test the faithfulness of God. "Faithful is he who hath called you, who also *will do* it," was now no longer a matter of opinion, but a truth confidently believed, and she saw that she must relinquish the confident expression before indulged in, as promising something in the *future,* "Thou *wilt* receive me," for the yet more confident expression, implying *present* assurance, "Thou *dost* receive!" It is, perhaps, almost needless to say, that the enemy who had heretofore endeavored to withstand every step of the Spirit's leadings, now confronted her, with much greater energy. The suggestion that it was strangely presumptuous to believe in such a way, was presented to her mind with a plausibility which only Satanic subtilty could invent. But the resolution to believe was fixed; and then the Spirit most inspiringly said to her heart, "The kingdom of heaven suffereth violence, and the violent take it by force."

And now, realizing that she was engaged in a transaction eternal in its consequences, she here, in the strength, and as in the presence of the Father, Son, and Holy Spirit, and those spirits that minister to the heirs of salvation, said, "O, Lord, I call heaven and earth to witness that I *now lay body, soul,* and

---

[Source: Phoebe Palmer, *The Way of Holiness, with notes by the way; being a narrative of religious experience resulting from a determination to be a Bible Christian* (New York: Lane & Scott, 1851), pp. 40-44.]

spirit, with *all these redeemed powers, upon thine altar, to be for ever* THINE! 'TIS DONE! *Thou hast promised to receive me! Thou canst not be unfaithful! Thou dost receive me now!* From this time henceforth I *am thine — wholly thine!*"

The enemy suggested, "'Tis but the work of your own understanding — the effort of your own will." But the Spirit of the Lord raised up a standard which Satan, with his combined forces, could not overthrow. It was by the following presentation of truth that the Spirit helped her infirmities: "Do not your perceptions of right — even your *own understanding* — assure you that it is matter of *thanksgiving to God* that you have been thus enabled to present your all to him?" "Yes," responded her whole heart, "it has all been the work of the Spirit. I will praise him! Glory be to God in the highest! Worthy is the Lamb to receive glory, honor, and blessing! Hallelujah! the Lord God Omnipotent reigneth! Yes, thou dost reign unrivaled in my heart! Thou hast subdued all things to thyself, and now thou dost reign throughout the empire of my soul, the Lord God of every motion!" The SPIRIT now bore full testimony to her spirit, of the TRUTH *of* THE WORD! She felt in experimental verity that it was not in vain she had believed; her very existence seemed lost and swallowed up in God; she plunged, as it were into an immeasurable ocean of love, light, and power, and realized that she was encompassed with the "favor of the Almighty as with a shield: and felt assured, while she continued thus, to rest her entire being on the faithfulness of God, she might confidently stand rejoicing in hope," and exultingly sing with the poet —

> "My steadfast soul from falling free,
>   Shall now no longer rove,
> But Christ be all in all to me,
>   And *all my soul be* LOVE."

She now saw infinite propriety, comprehensiveness, and beauty, in those words of DIVINE origin, from which she had before shrunk, as implying a state too high and sacred for ordinary attainment or expectation.

HOLINESS, SANCTIFICATION, *perfect love,* were words no longer so incomprehensible, or indefinite in nature or bearing, in relation to the individual experience of the Lord's redeemed ones. She wondered not that it should be said, in reference to the "WAY OF HOLINESS," "The *ransomed of the Lord shall walk there!*" She perceived that these terms were most significantly expressive of a state of soul in which *every* believer should live, and felt that no words of mere earthly origin could imbody to her own perceptions, or convey to the understanding of others, half the comprehensiveness of meaning contained in them, and which stand forth so prominently in the word of God, thereby assuring men that they are given by the express dictation of the Holy Spirit.

Horace Bushnell (1802-76)

While Presbyterian Hodge drew sharply a line between "us" and "them,"
Congregationalist Bushnell tried to build bridges between a Calvinism un-
der siege and newer grounds of understanding in Christian thought and
practice. In the first half of the nineteenth century, especially in New En-
gland, no subject threatened to divide Christians more deeply or more irrep-
arably than the doctrine of the Trinity: God's unique nature as Three in
One. Abstract, abstruse, mystery wrapped in paradox — the Christian affir-
mation of God the Father, the Son, and the Spirit was all of this and more.
To a growing number of Americans, the doctrine seemed an unnecessary im-
pediment, an ancient relic, a burdensome bit of baggage still being dragged
along as it had been for centuries and centuries. Bushnell, the Connecticut
pastor and subtle theologian, met this challenge head on. He defended the
doctrine of the Trinity, but not in terms of biblical assertions or creedal prop-
ositions (as Hodge might have done); rather, he saw it as a "practical truth"
necessary for the religious life, as an excellent means "to keep alive the pro-
foundest, most adequate sense of God's infinity. . . ."

That the Christian trinity is in any sense a practical truth appears in our day to
be very generally unsuspected.

Thus among the outsiders, the light-minded critics and worldly cavilers
of profane literature, the trinity . . . is taken for a standing example of the utterly
barren futilities preached and contended for as articles of religion.

The class of Unitarian believers handle the subject more seriously, and
arrive at the conclusion, which they assert with peremptory confidence, that
it is a stupendous theologic fiction, a plain absurdity in itself and in its effects, one of the worst practical hindrances to the power of the gospel; for
how can it be less when it annihilates the simplicity of God, confuses the
mind of the worshiper, and even makes the faith of God an impossible subject to the unbeliever?

Meantime how many of the formally professed believers of the doctrine
are free to acknowledge that they see no practical value in it, and will even
blame the preacher who maintains it, for spending his time and breath in a
matter so far out of the way of the practical life, a merely curious article or rid-
dle of the faith. And how many others, even of the more serious class of believers, would say, if they were to speak out what is in their feeling, that they take

---

[Source: Horace Bushnell, "The Christian Trinity, a Practical Truth," *New Englander,* 12
(1854), taken from H. Shelton Smith, ed., *Horace Bushnell* (New York: Oxford University
Press, 1965), pp. 199-200, 204-6, 207, 209-10, 211-12.]

the trinity as a considerable drawback on the idea of God. They would recoil indeed from the thought, as being even a blamable irreverence, of imagining any improvement of God; but if they could think of him as a simple unit of personality, in the manner of the Unitarians, he would consciously be just so much more to their mind, and their practical relations towards him would be proportionally cleared and comforted. . . .

We come now to the question itself, What is the practical import of the

Horace Bushnell
(General Theological Seminary)

trinity? Wherein consists its value? It is needed, we answer, to serve two main purposes:

1. To save the dimensions or the practical infinity of God, consistently with his personality. God is never fully presented to the mind, or adequately conceived, except when he is conceived under these two conditions together; viz., as a being really infinite, and also as existing in terms of society and personal mutuality with us. Accordingly we shall find, on the right and left of the Christian trinity, two distinct views which are both fatally defective and mutually opposite to each other.

First, the view of the pantheists, who are instigated by a desire to establish, or adequately conceive, the infinity of God. Struggling after this they spread themselves over all space and time and substance, and looking at *the All,* as an eternal going on of spiritual development under laws of eternal necessity, they call it God. Their God is the largest thought they can raise — largest, that is, in extent and containing boundary, but he is no person. Personality has been lost in the struggle after magnitude, or rather it has been actually dismissed as untenable; because the word, logically treated and literally taken, presents God under conditions of time and date, waking up to create worlds, exercised by thoughts, remembrances, reasonings, attentions, and affections personal — all which is contrary to the rational infinity of God. The doctrine of God's personality is therefore deliberately cast away as being a logical and necessary limit on his perfection; for it is not perceived that though the word *person* is finite, it may yet have an application, figurative, that is legitimate, and leaves all finite implications behind, availing only to set the infinite in terms of society with us. The result is that God, in this rejection of his personality, becomes a vast platitude; or, if not this, a dreary, all-containing abyss; a being, unconscious, a fate, a stupendous IT, without meaning or value to our religious nature; a theme of barren rhapsody and vaporing declamation, not a friend, not a redeemer, not an object of personal affinity, love or truth.

Over against these pantheistic aberrations we have the doctrine of Unitarianism, which represents God, in opposition to pantheism, as being personal, and because of the supposed absurdities, or rational impossibilities of trinity, one person. Clearing thus at once the dearth of pantheism and the contradictions of trinity, it presents a universal Father, one person; who, being a strict undivisible unity, is therefore no offense or stumbling block to reason.

The result is that the personality or relational state of God is saved in the completest manner; God is a person, a simple unit of reason, a Father eternal, creating and ruling the worlds and doing all things for the benefit of his children. But the difficulty now is that the dimensions are lost, the infinite magnitude is practically taken away. And precisely here, as was just now intimated, is one of the grand practical uses of trinity. The Unitarians supposed that when they had carried out their doctrine and shown that God is a simple unit of fatherhood, they had gained a great point, cleared the confusion, reduced the absurdity, and presented to the world a being so lovely in his character and so rational in his evidence that all intelligent worshipers must rejoice, and the world itself must shortly turn itself to him in love. But alas! there was a fatal difficulty which they did not suspect, and which time only could reveal; viz., that in going on to assert the one God, always under the same figure of personality, till that figure became a well-nigh literal affirmation, the dimensions of God would be reduced to the measures of the human figure, and their one God, their Great Father, would be a name without magnitude, or any genuine power of impression. . . .

Setting now these two failures against one another, the failure of pantheism and the failure of Unitarianism, we perceive exactly what is the problem answered by the Christian trinity. By asserting three persons instead of one, and also instead of none, it secures at once the practical infinity of God and the practical personality of God. By these cross relations of a threefold grammatic personality, the mind is thrown into a maze of sublimity, and made to feel at once the vastness, and with that the close society, also, of God. He is not less personal than he would be under the one personality of Unitarianism, and is kept meantime, by the threefold personality, from any possible diminution under the literal measures of the figure; for God cannot become either one person or three, in any literal sense, when steadfastly held as both.

In this respect the trinity, Father, Son, and Holy Ghost, practically accepted and freely used, with never a question about the speculative nature of the mystery, with never a doubt of God's rigid and perfect unity, will be found to answer exactly the great problem of the practical life of religion; viz., how to keep alive the profoundest, most adequate sense of God's infinity, and at the same time the most vivid and intensest sense of his social and mutual relationship as a person. And this, if I am right, is more to say than could be said of any other known or possible denomination for God. Regarded simply as a literary exploit, if that were all, it is at once the profoundest practical expedient ever adopted, and the highest wonder ever accomplished in human language. . . .

II. To another view of the Christian trinity, in which it is seen to have a practical relation to our character and our state as sinners. Here it is the instrument and co-efficient of a supernatural grace or redemptive economy. Not, as we sometimes hear, that an infinite atonement is wanted, which none but an infinite and divine person could execute — that is only a very crude and distant approximation to the truth. The need we are here to discover is broader and more comprehensive, resting in the fact that God's universal economy is, in its very conception, twofold; comprising at one pole an economy of nature, and at the other an economy of supernatural grace; requiring, in order to an easy practical adjustment of our life under it, a twofold conception of God that corresponds; for which reason the Scripture three are sometimes spoken of by Calvin and others as composing an economic trinity. . . .

Now there is, we have already intimated, a higher and more comprehensive view of God's universal kingdom, in which it includes and harmonizes these two economies, viz., nature and the supernatural, and by these two factors, like the contending forces of astronomy, settles and adjusts its orbit. And the Christian trinity gives us a conception of God which exactly meets such a truth, leveling it always to the practical uses of our life. Using the term God sometimes in a sense broad enough to comprehend all the complexities of his kingdom, we are able, when we need such aid for the practical accommodation of our faith, to lay hold of relational terms that exactly represent the two economies in their action with and upon each other. First we have the term Father, which sets him before us as the king of nature, the author and ground of all existent things and causes. Next we have the Son and the Spirit, which represent the supernatural; the Son coming into nature from above nature, incarnate in the person of Jesus, by a method not in the compass of nature, erecting a kingdom in the world that is not of the world: the Spirit coming in the power of the Son, to complete, by an inward supernatural working, what the Son began by the address he made without to human thought, and the forces he imported into nature by his doctrine, his works, his life, and his death.

Having now these terms or denominations provided, we use them freely in their cross relations, as a machinery accommodated to our sin and the struggles of our faith; putting our trust in the Son as coming down from God, offering himself before God, going up to God, interceding before God, reigning with God, by him accepted, honored, glorified, and allowed to put all things under his feet; invoking also God and Christ to send down the Spirit, and let him be the power of a real indwelling life, coursing through our nature, breathing health into its diseases, and so rolling back the penal currents of justice to set us free. Having these for the instruments of our thought and feeling and faith towards God, and suffering no foolish quibbles of speculative logic to intervene and plague us, asking never how many Gods there are, or how it is possible for one to come out from another, act before another, take us from or to another; but assured of this, at every moment, that God is one and only one forever, however multiform in his vehicle; how lively, and full, and blessed, and easy too, is the converse we receive through these living personations, so pliant to our use as finite men, so gloriously accommodated to our state as sinners.

J. W. Nevin (1803-1886)

John Williamson Nevin was unusual for a theologian in his own day because he found almost nothing positive in America's common religious practices. Although he had attended Charles Hodge's Princeton Theological Seminary, his later duties at the Seminary of the German Reformed Church in Mercersburg, Pennsylvania, brought him into contact with religious writers from the Continent. That experience alienated him from common American patterns of thought and common habits of American religious practice. In particular, he came to reject revivalism; he regretted the impact of what he called "Puritanism" on religion; he held out strongly for a more philosophical approach to religious thought; and he looked with favor on the traditional confessions of the German Reformed Church (especially the Heidelberg Catechism). Sometime after 1860, Nevin wrote a short summary of "the Mercersburg Theology" for one of his students. It refers to the major books in which he outlined his own convictions as well as to the work of Philip Schaff, the Swiss-born theologian and historian, who worked with Nevin at Mercersburg from the early 1840s to the mid 1860s (on Schaff, see below, pp. 566-68).

What is called the "Mercersburg System of Theology" grew into shape without calculation or plan. It owes its existence properly not to any spirit of philosophical speculation as has been sometimes imagined, but to an active interest in practical Christianity. Questions of religious life have governed in succession the course of its history. Still those have moved, with more or less insight always, round a common centre; and the system is found to be accordingly in the end sufficiently scientific, and in full harmony with itself throughout.

Historically it may be said to have commenced with the publication in 1843 of the *Anxious Bench* — a tract, which found wide favor, but drew upon its author at the same time in certain quarters a perfect hurricane of reproach. Then came the sermon on *Church Unity* preached by Dr. Nevin at the opening of the Triennial Convention of the Reformed Dutch and German Reformed Churches held at Harrisburg in the year 1844; a discourse sanctioned by the full approbation of the worthy representatives of both Churches at the time, the positions of which, however, on the subject of the Mystical Union and in opposition to the sect system, were felt by many afterwards to involve a dangerous tendency. Dr. Schaff's memorable *Principle of Protestantism*, published in 1845,

---

[Source: John W. Nevin, "Letter to Dr. Henry Harbaugh," in *Catholic and Reformed: Selected Theological Writings of John Williamson Nevin*, ed. Charles Yrigoyen, Jr., and George H. Bricker (Pittsburgh: Pickwick, 1978), pp. 407-11.]

brought out the tendency, in the apprehension of such persons, under still more alarming proportions. This was followed, the next year, by the *Mystical Presence,* with a translation of Dr. Ullmann's most masterly tract on *The Distinctive Character of Christianity* prefixed in the form of a Preliminary Essay. The work was a vindication at large of the old Calvinistic Doctrine of the Lord's Supper, conveying against the general Protestantism of the present time a charge of wholesale defection from the Protestant sacramental faith of the sixteenth century. The tract *Antichrist* was a regular assault upon the sect system, as being in full antagonism to the true idea of the Church, and such a heresy as draws after it virtually in the end a Gnostic denial of the proper mystery of the Incarnation itself. As the occasions of Theological discussion were multiplied, it was felt necessary to establish a special organ for carrying it forward, the more so as it seemed altogether impractical to gain a fair hearing in any other quarter. Hence, the *Mercersburg Review,* the pages of which for some years form a sort of progressive picture of the system to whose exposition and defence it has been all along devoted. So much for the general history of the movement. We come now to what is more important[:] the organization of inward structure of the Mercersburg System regarded as a whole.

Its cardinal principle is the fact of the Incarnation. This viewed not as a doctrine or speculation but as a real transaction of God in the world, is regarded as being necessarily itself the essence of Christianity, the sum and substance of the whole Christian redemption. Christ saves the world, not ultimately by what he teaches or by what he does, but by what he *is* in the constitution of his own person. His person in its relations to the world carries in it the power of victory over sin, death, and hell, the force thus of a real atonement or reconciliation between God and man, the triumph of a glorious resurrection from the dead, and all the consequences for faith which are attributed to this in the grand old symbol called the Apostles' Creed. In the most literal sense accordingly Christ is here held to be the "way, the truth and the life," the "resurrection and the life," the principle of "life and immortality" — the "light" of the world, its "righteousness," and its "peace." The "grace which brings salvation" in this view is of course always a real affluence from the new order of existence, which has been thus made to be by the exaltation of the Word made flesh at the right hand of God. It must be supernatural as well as natural, and the organs and agencies by which it works must in the nature of the case carry with them objectively some thing of the same character and force. To resolve all into the opinions and feelings of those who call themselves believers, is to do away with the proper objects of faith altogether; for these must be apprehended as actually at hand under a supernatural form. They are all mysteries, holding in them objectively some measure of what belongs to the mystery of Christ's glorification. In this way the Church is an object of faith — the presence of a new creation in the old world of nature — the body of Christ through which as a medium and organ he reveals himself and works till the end of time. Its ministers hold a divine power from him by apostolic succession. Its sacraments are not signs merely, but goals of the grace they represent. Baptism is for the remission of sins. The Eucharist includes the real presence of Christ's whole glorified life, in a mystery, by the power of the Holy Ghost. The idea of the Church, so sound, [which] is made to be in this way an object of faith, involves necessarily the attributes which were always ascribed to it in the beginning, unity, sanctity, catholicity, and apostolicity. The spirit of sect, as it cleaves to Protestantism at the present time, is a very great evil, which is of itself sufficient to show that if Protestantism had any historical justification in the beginning, its mission thus far has been only half fulfilled, and that it can be rationally approved only as it is taken to be an interimistic preparation for some higher and better form of Christianity hereafter.

The distinguishing character of the Mercersburg Theology, in one word, is its Christological interest, its way of looking at all things through the Person of the crucified and risen Saviour. This, as the world now stands, embraces necessarily all that enters into the conception of the Church Question — the problem of problems for the Christianity of the present time. That the system has been able to solve in full the difficulties belonging to this great subject, its friends have never pretended for one moment to imagine. On the contrary, they have always confessed their sense of vast practical embarrassment confronting their views. But they have not considered this a sufficient reason for refusing to affirm what has appeared to them to be biblically or historically true, in spite of such inconvenience. Facts and principles have a right to challenge attention at times, even if no satisfactory scheme can be offered for their application. The Mercersburg Theology claim the advantage of standing here, in its main positions, on the same ground with the faith of the early Church. Its Christology is that of the ancient Creeds. It insists on casting the Christian belief of the world still in the same primitive mould; and the burden of its controversy with those who stand opposed to it is that they either ignore the Apostles' Creed altogether or else make no earnest with its proper historical sense, but vainly imagine that it may be superseded or mended by other modern forms of confession, more suited to their own unchurchly sense.

In thus agreeing with the Creed, the system of course holds itself to be to the same extent in full agreement with the proper sense of the Scriptures; where in truth all stress is laid on the Person of Christ, on his resurrection from the dead, on his glorification at the right hand of God, on the sending of the Holy Ghost, and on his presence and working through all time in the Church which is his body, the fulness of Him that filleth all in all.

Charles Porterfield Krauth (1823-83)

While Bushnell struggled to hold a culture together, other theologians labored to hold a denomination together. Many emigrating Europeans left behind a cohesive, stable, taken-for-granted church establishment — only to find in America's expansive lands no theological or ecclesiastical cohesion at all. Lutherans, for example, came from nations where (more often than not) their religion was the only genuine option. But in America such were the confusion and complexity that Lutherans many times found more identity as Swedes or Danes or Finns than they did as Lutherans. C. P. Krauth, professor in the Lutheran Seminary in Philadelphia, wanted these Americans to find their identity as Lutherans, as faithful followers of Martin Luther's reform. In 1856 Krauth directed the Synod of Pittsburgh in the reaffirmation of its historic loyalty to the confession of faith "framed by" Philipp Melanchthon in 1530 "with the advice, aid, and concurrence of Luther and the other great theologians . . . at the Diet of Augsburg."

Whereas, Our Church has been agitated by proposed changes in the Augsburg Confession — changes whose necessity has been predicated upon alleged errors in that Confession;

And *Whereas,* the changes and the charges connected with them, though set forth by individual authority, have been endorsed by some synods of the Lutheran Church and urged upon others for approval, and have been noticed by most of the synods which have met since they have been brought before the Church;

And *Whereas,* amid conflicting statements, many who are sincerely desirous of knowing the truth are distracted, knowing not what to believe, and the danger of internal conflict and schism is incurred;

And *Whereas,* our synods are the source whence an official declaration in regard to things disputed in the Church may naturally and justly be looked for;

We, therefore, in Synod assembled, in the presence of the Searcher of Hearts, desire to declare to our churches, and before the world, our judgment in regard to these changes and these charges, and the alienation among brethren which may arise from them:

I. *Resolved,* That by the Augsburg Confession we mean that document which was framed by Melanchthon, with the advice, aid, and concurrence of Luther and the other great theologians, and presented by the

---

[Source: Adolph Spaeth, *Charles Porterfield Krauth* (New York: Arno Press, 1969 [1898]), pp. 377-79.]

Protestant princes and Free Cities of Germany at the Diet of Augsburg, in 1530.

II. *Resolved,* That while the basis of our General Synod has allowed of diversity in regard to some parts of the Augsburg Confession, that basis never was designed to imply the right to alter, amend, or curtail the Confession itself.

III. *Resolved,* That while this Synod, resting on the Word of God as the sole authority in matters of faith, on its infallible warrant rejects the Romish doctrine of the real presence or Transubstantiation, and with it the doctrine of Consubstantiation; rejects the Mass, and all ceremonies distinctive of the Mass; denies any power in the Sacraments as an *opus operatum,*[2] or that the blessings of baptism and the Lord's Supper can be received without faith; rejects Auricular Confession, and priestly absolution; holds that there is no priesthood on earth except that of all believers, and that God only can forgive sins; and maintains the sacred obligation of the Lord's day; and while we would with our whole heart reject any part of any confession which taught doctrines in conflict with this our testimony, nevertheless, before God and His Church, we declare that in our judgment the Augsburg Confession, properly interpreted, is in perfect consistence with this our testimony and with holy Scripture as regards the errors specified.

IV. *Resolved,* That while we do not wish to conceal the fact that some parts of the doctrine of our Confession in regard to the Sacraments are received in different degrees by different brethren, yet that even in these points, wherein we as brethren in Christ agree to differ, till the Holy Ghost shall make us see eye to eye, the differences are not such as to destroy the foundation of faith, our unity in labor, our mutual confidence, and our tender love.

V. *Resolved,* That now, as we have ever done, we regard the Augsburg Confession lovingly and reverently as the "good confession" of our fathers, witnessed before heaven, earth, and hell.

VI. *Resolved,* That if we have indulged harsh thoughts and groundless suspicions, if we have without reason criminated and recriminated, we here humbly confess our fault before our adorable Redeemer, beseeching pardon of Him and of each other, and covenant anew with Him and with each other to know nothing among men but Jesus Christ and Him crucified — acknowledging Him as our only Master, and regarding all who are in the living unity of faith with Him as brethren.

VII. *Resolved,* That we will *resist* all efforts to sow dissensions among us on the ground of minor differences, all efforts on the one hand to restrict

2. Automatic benefit.

the liberty which Christ has given us, or on the other to impair the purity of the "faith once delivered to the saints," and that with new ardor we will devote ourselves to the work of the Gospel, to repairing the waste places of Zion, to building up one another in holiness, and in pointing a lost world to the "Lamb of God" — and that this our covenant with Christ and with each other is made in singleness of heart, without personal implication, duplicity of meaning, or mental reservation, we appeal to Him before whose judgment bar we shall stand, and through whose grace alone we have hope of heaven.

2. Pluralism or Protestantism

Judaism

Isaac Leeser as Catechist

Born in Prussia in 1806, Leeser came to the United States (Virginia) when he was eighteen years of age. By the time he was twenty-three, he had been named rabbi of Philadelphia's Mikveh Israel Congregation. For the remainder of his sixty-two years, Leeser involved himself totally in Judaism's organizational, educational, and theological life. Education remained a leading concern, one evidence being Leeser's founding of Maimonides College in Philadelphia one year before his death. Another evidence was his composition in 1839 of a catechism for Jewish youth. The preface to that teaching instrument is excerpted below.

The present is one of the series of books for the promotion of religious knowledge among the Israelites, whose vernacular is the English language, which I announced in my first publication about nine years ago. Although as yet the sale of my works has been scarcely adequate to defray the expenses: I have never given up the pleasing idea of supplying at convenient intervals, according to the best of my limited abilities, the lamentable deficiency of devotional works, which is on all sides admitted to exist among us. I would, however, do injustice to my feelings were I to let the present opportunity pass without acknowledging the kindness which has been extended to my various efforts, even in distant parts, by persons entirely unknown to me. Such indul-

---

[Source: J. L. Blau and S. W. Baron, eds., *The Jews of the United States, 1790-1840: A Documentary History*, 3 vols. (New York: Columbia University Press, 1963), II, 451-52, 453-54.]

gence, to the many defects discoverable in my writings, whilst it encourages me to persevere amidst many difficulties which need not be made public, claims my sincere thanks, and demands of me greater care and unremitting labour for the future, to prove that I have not been altogether unworthy of the kindness extended to me. But to Him above, who has not withheld from me his light and his manifold blessings, my heartfelt gratitude is justly due in a high degree, for having permitted me to accomplish what I have done, without much human assistance. . . .

It has been my endeavour to make myself understood by children of from eight to fourteen years old; yet I fear that I may have failed, oftener than I should do, of rendering the subject-matter sufficiently clear. I trust, however, that teachers and parents will not put the book into the hands of their pupils and children, without giving at least a cursory explanation, which, it is confidently hoped, will be enough to assist the learner.

Occasionally a subject has been introduced more than once, which originated in the idea that it is better to have all the points connected together exhibited at one view; for children are but too apt to forget what they have learned some weeks back. So likewise were several Bible-texts quoted more than once, when it was thought that the same text would be the best applicable to explain or elucidate different subjects. This quoting twice may in a few instances have arisen from inadvertence, which is very likely to occur in a work so difficult to compose, on account of the youth of the persons for whose instruction it is intended; but generally it was done designedly for the reason given. I trust that some allowance will be made, if I have not succeeded in imparting all the interest, variety, and polish, such a work might have received by others better acquainted than I can pretend to be with the operation of the youthful mind; but the reader may be assured of one thing, that not a passage or a word even was allowed to pass without much care and anxious reflection; it was my endeavour to teach the truth, and the truth only.

Believing that as the scholar advances in a work, the matter may with advantage be a little more elaborately given, in order to require always a sufficient degree of application and study: I have not hesitated to use language a little more complicated and rather longer paragraphs in the latter than in the first chapters. Still, if thought too difficult, the chapters on the Moral Law, the Messiah, and the Life after Death and other portions, may be advantageously deferred till a second reading, as they are not absolutely necessary to an understanding of the whole subject.

With the confident hope that this unpretending work may have its useful effects, to awaken in the young a spirit of devotion and piety, I commit it to the care of the Great Teacher, who bestowed on us his law, as a guide to our souls, unto the haven of that happiness which He has destined for those who fear his name and lay hold of his covenant, to obey his will all the days that they live on the earth.

Philadelphia,
Iyar 23d, 5599
May 7th, 1839

Isaac Mayer Wise in Albany

Leader of the movement eventually known as Reform Judaism, Wise (1819-1900) left his native Bohemia in 1845 for America. A man of great energies and exalted vision of Judaism's future in his newly adopted land, Rabbi Wise exercised a broad and powerful influence. In his delightful Reminiscences, *he tells of his call in 1846 to the Beth-El Congregation of Albany, New York. In recounting that story with typical candor, Wise reveals much of himself as well as the formative status of Judaism in America at that time.*

A large congregation had assembled in the synagogue in the evening. They listened to the old *Rosh Hashanah*[3] melodies, which appealed none the less strongly to me, and brought back the sounds I had learned to love in my youth. Therefore I did not notice that I was the object of curious attention, and when I did notice this at last, I became so embarrassed that I was happy when the last note of the *Yigdal*[4] sounded, and the people wished one another all that was good. When somewhat later I thought of the faces that I had seen in my audience, I imagined that I was still in Syracuse. Everything passed off well in the morning. There was much speaking and singing, blessing and promising. The *shacharith chazan*,[5] it is true, could not sing well. His breathing was too labored; but he read Hebrew so poorly that he would have been able to conduct the service successfully in the most orthodox congregation. It is well known that poor Hebrew reading and indecorum were as necessary an accompaniment of Jewish orthodoxy as was dog Latin of Catholic orthodoxy, and the poorest imaginable translation of the Psalms, of Scotch Presbyterianism. And not an iota of this necessary accompaniment could be omitted.

When my turn came I stepped to the improvised pulpit (there were no

3. High holy days inaugurating the New Year and culminating in *Yom Kippur,* Day of Atonement.
4. Prayer composed by Maimonides.
5. The cantor (or chief singer), in this case for the morning synagogue service.

[Source: David Philipson, ed., *Reminiscences by Isaac M. Wise* (New York: Central Synagogue of New York, 2nd ed., 1945 [1901]), pp. 42-46. Notes provided by the editor.]

Isaac Mayer Wise
(National Portrait Gallery, Smithsonian Institution, Washington, D.C.)

pulpits in American synagogues in those days, since the congregations gave no thought to employing preachers) with the firm determination to move the hearts of the assembled multitude, and I spoke like an old pastor whose flock threatened to dissolve. Hagar and Ishmael served as symbols for body and soul. I characterized culture and religion as bread and water, and likened the wandering in the wilderness to the course of human life. "And she went and lost her way," was the first knotty point. Here I was able to bring all my weapons into play. I passed in review all the faults and mistakes of all the centuries, and the listening auditory which had never heard such a flood of words was completely overwhelmed and dumbfounded. Thereupon followed the second phrase, "And she threw the child under the terebinth." This I applied to the inner remorse of the sinner, and expatiated upon this until the sobbing in the gallery became so audible that I felt compelled to stop. Finally I spoke of the angel and the spring. These I called the voice of conscience and the perennial fount of religion, etc., which unite mother and child at last in comfort and hope, and lead to a beautiful future. I concluded with an expression of the hoped-for reconciliation and brotherhood of mankind. As I left the pulpit and glanced at the congregation I felt triumphant, for it seemed to me that I had struck the right note this time. At the close of the service the people crowded about me, overwhelmed me with congratulations and compliments, accompanied me as a procession from the synagogue to Stern's hostelry, and well-nigh crushed me beneath the weight of South German Jewish phrases, until Moses Schloss finally took pity on me and carried me home to dinner. Upon arriving there, I was about to breathe easier when the noble housewife, the amiable and kind-hearted Madame Amelia Schloss, came, and thereupon another woman, and still another, and still another, all of whom sang the same tune, which ended with the agreeable cadenza of a fine *yom tob*[6] dinner at two o'clock. Immediately after dinner, Messrs. Minster and Newwitter, the presiding officers of the second Jewish congregation of Albany, came, and requested me to preach in their synagogue on the morrow. Since Schloss agreed to the proposition, I accepted the invitation, and on the following day policemen had to be placed before the doors of the synagogue for fear lest the great mass of people would break down the old house, the synagogue being on the second floor of a building that was not very strong. My fortune was made as far as Albany was concerned. . . .

There was an antipathy at that time in America to rabbis and preachers in general, just as there was a prejudice against cultured people of any kind, because they were looked upon as unpractical and helpless. The peddler's pack was too heavy for them, work too hard, and their learning profited naught. There was no room in the synagogue for preachers and rabbis. The *chazan* was the Reverend. He was all that was wanted. The congregations desired nothing further. The *chazan* was reader, cantor, and blessed everybody for *chai pasch*,[7] which amounted to 41/2 cents. He was teacher, butcher, circumciser, blower, gravedigger, secretary. He wrote the amulets with the names of all the angels and demons on them for women in confinement, read *shiur*[8] for the departed sinners, and played cards or dominoes with the living; in short, he was a *kol-bo*,[9] an encyclopedia, accepted bread, turnips, cabbage, potatoes as a gift, and peddled in case his salary was not sufficient. He was *sui generis*, half priest, half beggar, half oracle, half fool, as the occasion demanded. The congregations were satisfied, and there was no room for preacher or rabbi. Among all the *chazanim*[10] whom I learned to know at that time, there was not one who had a common-school education or possessed any Hebrew learning.

6. Holiday.
7. Eighteen droppings; i. e., a small or negligible amount.
8. Prayer for the dead.
9. Literally, a garbage can; a collector of everything.
10. Plural of *chazan*.

Leeser's Missionary Journeys

Besides teaching, editing, translating, and organizing schools and seminar-
ies, Isaac Leeser also somehow found time to travel extensively all across
America. As an itinerant rabbi, Leeser encouraged loyalty to orthodox Juda-
ism in the context of American opportunity and the English language. In his
wide-ranging travels, Leeser was sometimes called upon to comment on or
deal with purely local matters; all the while, however, he kept his eye on the
larger question of Judaism's future role in America. He was, as Jacob Rader
Marcus notes, "America's most gifted Jewish religious leader and organizer
before the Civil War."

From the Great Lakes to the Gulf of Mexico
We set out on the ninth of November [1851] and returned on the twenty-
seventh of February [1852], after an absence of nearly sixteen weeks, during
which we travelled upwards of 5,200 miles, and visited at least twenty-five settlements or congregations of Israelites, from the shores of Lake Erie to the Gulf
of Mexico, and were about forty-one entire or parts of days actually in motion.
Hence it will be readily understood that we did not spend much idle time, although we were so much longer absent than we calculated on, especially if it is
taken in consideration that we were detained by ice at St. Louis during fifteen
days, when we only calculated on staying but four. In this manner, too, we were
prevented from visiting many points which we might have touched at, and in
fact we were compelled to leave much undone which was in our original plan
when we first left home. . . .

Cleveland

During our recent journey we paid a visit of a few days to this beautiful city on
the shore of Lake Erie. We found there two congregations, the eldest organized
under the charge of Rev. B. L. Fould, and the other under that of the Rev.
Isidore Kalisch. We delivered, by invitation, a lecture in the synagogue of the
latter, on Wednesday evening, the nineteenth of November [1851]. This place of
worship is a large room in the Seneca Block, situated on Superior Street, and is
handsomely fitted up. . . .

We had no time to visit the other synagogue, but several of its members

---

[Source: J. R. Marcus, *Memoirs of American Jews, 1775-1865,* 3 vols. (Philadelphia: Jewish
Publication Society of America, 1955), II, 70-74, 78-79. The words of Marcus are from
p. 59.]

were present at the lecture. We would merely state in this connexion, without any desire to reopen the question, and [without] leading to a controversy, that notwithstanding the slurs cast upon the transaction in the public press and the Jewish paper of New York, the divorce granted by Mr. Joseph Levy was, to our apprehension, entirely conformable to the Jewish law. . . . The reason which induced Mr. Levy to lend his aid in merely granting the husband a *religious* divorce, leaving it to the courts of the land to decide on the merits of the application on merely legal grounds, appeared to us sufficiently weighty to justify his course.

It must not be forgotten, that though we Israelites go on the principle, . . . "The laws of the country are binding," it does not say that therefore we may dispense with the observance of our own laws. So in regard to divorces. It would be wrong here, when both parties live in America, to let a divorce take place without a final action on the part of the courts or legislatures, as the case may be. But, as Jews, we cannot recognise any separation so obtained, as by the law of Moses no marriage tie, if once legally entered into, can be dissolved, except by the death of the husband, or by his absolving the wife in the legal form from her obligation to him. . . . Anything short of this would expose the wife, if she marries again, to the sin of adultery, and her children would be excluded from the congregation of Israel *forever.* Now, as we understand the case, there was danger to fear that should a divorce be pronounced by the court, it might happen that the parties could not then be brought together to consummate the separation by our [Jewish religious] laws. Wherefore, if the facts are as represented to us — and thus far we have had no reason to doubt them — the preliminary divorce on Jewish grounds was not alone proper, but highly praiseworthy.

Mr. Levy, it is true, occupies in the synagogue no salaried position. He is practically, like we are, a man of the people; but he, like us, also teaches when called on, and, we believe, lectures in the good old fashion, perhaps, every Sabbath, and is well-supplied with books of the highest authority, and has, probably, the best rabbinical library in the country. It is, therefore, nothing to the subject that he is engaged in business. Judaism knows nothing of idlers, of men who merely teach for money, and though it is perfectly consonant both with common sense and our practices to support from the public purse those who devote themselves to the public service as rabbis, teachers, ministers, schochatim,[11] and synagogue servants of whatever kind, it does not say that rabbinical functions appertain alone to those who hold office, or that none but those elected by especial congregations for particular purposes are to teach in public, for no other reason than that they have to support themselves by commerce or labour. Rabbi Joshua, the celebrated antagonist of Rabban Gamliel,

---

11. Or shohetim, ritual slaughterers of animals and poultry.

was a smith, and still this great chief of our [ancient] Sanhedrin disdained not to seek the humble roof of the mechanic, to ask his forgiveness for the, perhaps, unintentional wrong done him.

We hope that day may never come when we shall have privileged classes among us, other than those owing their claims to superior knowledge of the law. This is the standard, and beyond this nothing is required to render a man's acts valid and recognisable in Israel. In saying the above we do not wish to interfere in any congregational business of Cleveland or elsewhere, but merely to express our opinion in regard to the impropriety of the question, "Who is authorized in Cleveland to grant a divorce?" as though all the rights of the Jewish Church were inherent in New York, Baltimore, and Philadelphia only. Away with such arrogance; wherever our Torah has pitched her tent, *there* is authority, and we would respect the decision of a wayfarer in the western wilds, the moment he has produced his certificate of qualification, and is known to be in possession of an unblemished character. And as regards the matter at issue, Cleveland may well be proud that both congregations can boast of men fit to represent Judaism and its interests anywhere all over the land. Mr. Levy has sent us a long communication written in pure Hebrew, which we would have spread before the public had our magazine appeared at the usual periods. But so much time has since then elapsed, that it would be, perhaps, exciting a long debate, which would be practically useless. . . .

Cincinnati

We reached Cincinnati on the twenty-first of November [1851], and found here four congregations: the first, having Polish *minhag* ["rite"], worshipping in Broadway; the second, German, in Lodge Street; the third, also German, in Race Street, we think, over the Canal; and the fourth, again, is Polish, whose place of worship we did not visit. . . .

We learn, however, that in addition to the day school of the B'nai Jeshurun, a Sunday school has lately been started, in January, under the general superintendence of the Rev. J. Rosenfeld; and five weeks after commencing they had assembled already nearly 200 scholars. . . .

We regret to learn from our correspondent that some pious persons have opposed this movement of diffusing religious information on the first day of the week, which is from many reasons a day of compulsory leisure, and when those who attend general schools are disengaged, and hence can devote some time to religious studies, for which they have no leisure during the other days in the week. Now we perfectly agree with those who object to the movement, that religious instruction should not be confined to one day out of seven, but should be a daily exercise; and our endeavours to effect this should be an evidence of our sincerity. But if we cannot obtain all of what we need, it strikes us that it would not be the part of wisdom to refuse accepting what is really attainable. It is indeed true that Jewish children do not attend, as a rule, Jewish schools, even where such are established. At another time we may have to say more on this topic. The fact cannot be disputed. We therefore ask our friends: "Will you place a hindrance in the way of this enterprise, by which, should you succeed in breaking it up, you could to a surety deprive many of the only chances they will probably ever have to obtain the least knowledge of religion?"

The case may be deplorable. It in fact *is* so; but let us not reject the only remedy we have at hand, in the hope that, if children have once tasted the waters of life, they will thirst for more. At the same time, we would urge on the projectors and supporters of the Sunday school not to rest satisfied with this fragment of religious education, but to do all in their power. And if this is done, they must succeed to establish regular schools, under proper teachers, to instruct all in the language of the Hebrews, "the speech of Canaan," and to give them a thorough knowledge of their religion, and its principles and belief, so that no itinerant speaker shall ever after have even the shadow of a cause to tell them, "that they and their children are entirely ignorant of their faith." Without saying aught of the bad taste which such a declaration involves, we would merely state that happy indeed would we be, if people observed *all* they know, imperfectly as they have been educated. But this much is necessary, that religion should be so impressed on the mind that all of Israel should cheerfully practise the duties which flow from an acknowledgement of their faith. This a Sunday school can but improperly effect; hence the necessity for more ample instruction. . . .

California

While at St. Louis, we spoke with a gentleman, one of our new subscribers, who had just returned from California. We learned from him that Judaism was awakening in that distant land from its slumbers, and that now people can be supplied with [Kosher] meat, wherefore the excuse, which the absence of this made for trangression, has been removed. He also told us that at Sacramento City, where he was during the autumnal holydays, these were celebrated with proper spirit, and that their synagogue was filled with worshippers.

It strikes us that if the people were only settled once in the respective towns, and that they purposed ending their days there, and not regard themselves as mere roving sojourners and homeless adventurers, we should soon hear of many and permanent communities being formed at all the prominent points in California and Oregon. But our misfortune is that many seek the distant West for no other reason than to acquire all the wealth possible in the least imaginable space of time. Hence the idea of making any spot their home there does not enter their imagination; and hence they are not willing to contribute a large amount of funds towards erecting suitable houses of prayer and engaging ministers of the mental capacity and moral qualifications, such as are most needed in a new country, to act as missionaries, and, to use an expressive word, as apostles of our faith. Still, this evil will correct itself every day more, as the country becomes more settled; and we yet look forward, in a short time, to the joyful news that many synagogues will be consecrated, and that they will have ample room to accommodate the many thousands now there, on every Sabbath and festival. We occasionally meet, in the public papers, with some evidence of the kind, which proves that the Jewish heart is true, though so many display not the spirit of ready obedience which the law demands of Israelites; and no matter who the pioneers are, it is not to be doubted but that others will follow to complete what the first have begun, though these be the uneducated, and, it may be, the unworthy.

Roman Catholicism

Trusteeism

In the first half of the nineteenth century, Roman Catholicism moved from a nearly invisible minority to the largest single church in America. Such explosive growth brought vexing problems both internal and external. Among the Catholic laity, surrounded as they were by Protestant men and women who seemed to "own and operate" their own churches, sentiment grew for a greater voice in their own parish affairs. "Trusteeism," as the resulting controversy came to be called, was formally denounced in 1822 by Pius VII. The pope bemoaned the tendency of "trustees or administrators of the temporal properties of the churches" to act independently of their bishops, or to "arrogate to themselves" the choosing or dismissing of their pastors. Four years before that papal judgment, the archbishop of Baltimore, Ambrose Maréchal (1764-1828), had reported to the Vatican on the state of Roman Catholicism in America. Generally optimistic ("There is no region in the world where the Catholic religion can be propagated more quickly or widely and where it exists more securely than in the United States of America"), Maréchal nonetheless saw trusteeism as a serious matter and potential cause of widespread schism.

[Source: J. T. Ellis, ed., *Documents of American Catholic History* (Milwaukee: Bruce Publishing Co., 1956), pp. 219-21.]

It should therefore be noted: — 1. that the American people pursue with a most ardent love the civil liberty which they enjoy. For the principle of civil liberty is paramount with them, so that absolutely all the magistrates, from the highest to the lowest, are elected by popular vote at determined times in the year. Likewise all the Protestant sects, who constitute the greater part of the people, are governed by these same principles, and as a result they elect and dismiss their pastors at will. Catholics in turn, living in their midst, are evidently exposed to the danger of admitting the same principles of ecclesiastical government. Clever and impious priests, who flatter them and appeal to their pride, easily lead them to believe that they also possess the right of choosing their pastors and dismissing them as they please. 2. When the Catholics in some part of my diocese become numerous enough to think that they can build a church, first of all each contributes a few coins to the common fund; and since the amount is seldom sufficient, then they select two or three men, whom they depute as their representatives to solicit contributions in the cities and villages from their fellow citizens, both Catholics and Protestants. When they have once collected enough money, then they buy a large enough tract of land upon which to build a church and priest house and to have a cemetery. However, when they have once decided to buy this tract, sometimes they hand over to the bishop the title of possession, so that he is the true possessor of this ecclesiastical property and is considered as such by the civil tribunals. But it often happens that the legislators of the province approach and obtain from them the title of possession, upon the condition that they transmit it to four or five Catholic men, who are elected annually by the congregation. In this case, these men are not only the temporal administrators of the temporalities of the church *(marguilliers)* as they are in Europe, but they have possession and are considered the true possessors of all the temporal goods of the church in the eyes of the civil tribunals and they can with impunity exercise over them the same authority as they do over their own homes and lands. However, a schism has never taken place in those churches, of which the bishop holds the civil title; in fact, it is impossible for it to happen there. For if the priest, who is constituted the pastor of this church, is addicted to drunkenness or impurity or other scandalous vices, and will not correct his life, then the bishop, by reason of the title he possesses, can at once remove him, just as any citizen has the right of expelling those who presume to occupy his home against his will. For he could easily obtain an order of eviction from the magistrates. But if the title of possession is in the hands of the temporal administrators *(marguilliers)*, then they can easily raise the flag of rebellion against the bishop. If indeed the greater part of them do not fear God and conceive a hatred for their pastor, they will continually remove him from the church, no matter how great the sanctity of his life and customs; besides they deprive the entire Catholic congregation of the use of the church. This is the state of affairs at Norfolk, where the impious Doctor Oliver Fernandez and two Irish drunkards, destitute of all religion, removed from their church a most holy man, the pastor, Mr. Lucas,[12] and all his Catholic fellow citizens. Likewise when a priest is leading a scandalous life and, instead of nourishing, is rather devastating the flock of the Lord by his bad example, if the bishop takes measures against him, or also threatens to punish him, it often happens that the temporal administrators come to his defense with cunning and impious theories, whether by maintaining that the bishop is proceeding unjustly against him, or by declaring that he has appealed to Rome, or by arguing that they, and they alone, have the natural right of selecting and removing their pastors. And if he has once been able to convince them of these wicked principles, then the impious priest, protected by the temporal administrators, publicly withstands the authority of his bishop, calumniates him, sacrilegiously performs his sacred ministry, and lays waste the flock of Christ. Nor do the civil laws of the American republic offer any remedy for this great evil. Over and above, if such a priest is even more brazen and skilled in deceit, he gathers false testimony everywhere from the offscourings of the people. Then he busies himself in strengthening this testimony, by obtaining upon it the seal of Protestant magistrates, who secretly rejoice in dissensions of this kind among Catholics. After this, having collected money here and there, he sends to Rome a messenger, who knows well how to assume a semblance of piety and to speak in a reverential manner.

Orestes A. Brownson (1803-76)

Though briefly introduced in the previous chapter, O. A. Brownson requires a more formal presentation. Brownson's life constitutes nineteenth-century America's most fascinating religious pilgrimage: from Presbyterianism to Universalism to skepticism to Unitarianism to transcendentalism and — finally — to Roman Catholicism. As lay editor and writer, Brownson addressed himself to both politics and religion, seeking the most fruitful interaction between the two. Following his own embrace of Catholicism in 1844, Brownson tried to set aside those Protestant anxieties and hostilities toward Catholicism which he knew to be widespread. Far from being a threat to America's liberties, only Catholicism (Brownson argued) could sustain democracy. (1) The first excerpt is from an essay entitled "Protestantism Ends in Transcendentalism" (1846). (2) The second document carries the title "Catholicity Necessary to Sustain Popular Liberty" (1845).

---

12. James Lucas, a French-born priest, had been appointed in December, 1815, to serve the congregation at Norfolk, Virginia, by Archbishop Leonard Neale. [Ellis's note.]

[Sources: Orestes A. Brownson, *Essays and Reviews, Chiefly on Theology, Politics, and Socialism* (New York: Arno Press, 1972 [1852]), (1) pp. 230-32; (2) pp. 372-73, 375-76, 378-81.]

1.

The "No Popery" cry which our *Evangelicals* are raising, and which rings in our ears from every quarter, does not in the least discompose us. In this very cry we hear an additional proof of what we are maintaining. We understand the full significance of this cry. The Protestant masses are escaping from their leaders. The sectarian ministers, especially of the species *Evangelical,* are losing their hold on their flocks, and finding that their old petrified forms, retained from Luther, or Calvin, or Knox, will no longer satisfy them, — have no longer vitality for them. Their craft is in danger; their power and influence are departing, and *Ichabod* is beginning to be written on their foreheads. They see the handwriting on the wall, and feel that something must be done to avert the terrible doom that awaits them. Fearfulness and trembling seize them, and, like the drowning man, they catch at the first straw, and hope, and yet with the mere hope of despair, that it will prove a plank of safety. They have no resource in their old, dried-up, dead forms. They must look abroad, call in some extrinsic aid, and by means of some foreign power, delay the execution of the judgment they feel in their hearts has already been pronounced against them. They must get up some excitement which will captivate the people and blind their reason. No excitement seems to them more likely to answer their purpose than a "No Popery" excitement, which they fancy will find a firm support in the hereditary passions and prejudices of their flocks. Here is the significance of this "No Popery" excitement.

But this excitement will prove suicidal. Times have changed, and matters do not stand as they did in the days of Luther, and Zwingli, and Henry, and Calvin, and Knox. The temper of men's minds is different, and there is a new order of questions up for solution. The old watchwords no longer answer the purpose. What avails it to prove the Pope to be Antichrist, to populations that do not even believe in Christ? What avails it to thunder at Catholicity with texts which are no longer believed to have a divine authority? Protestantism must now fall back on her own principles, and fight her battles with her own weapons. She must throw out her own banner to the breeze, and call upon men to gather and arm and fight for progress, for liberty, for the unrestricted right of private judgment, or she will not rally a corporal's guard against Catholicity. But the moment she does this, she is, as the French say, *enfoncée;* for she has subsisted and can subsist only by professing one thing and doing another. Let our Evangelical doctors, in their madness, rally, in the name of progress, of liberty, of private judgment, an army to put down the Pope, and the matter will not end there. Their forces, furnished with arms against Catholicity, will turn upon themselves, and in a hoarse voice, and if need be, from brazen throats and tongues of flame, exclaim, "No more sham, gentlemen. We go for principle. We do not unpope the Pope to find a new pope in each petty presbyter, and a spy and informer in each brother or sister communicant. You are nothing to us. Freedom, gentlemen; doff your gowns, abrogate all your creeds and confessions, break up all your religious organizations, abolish all forms of worship except such as each individual may choose and exercise for himself, and acknowledge in fact, as well as in name, that every man is free to worship one God or twenty Gods, or no God at all, as seems to him good, unlicensed, unquestioned, or take the consequences. We will no more submit to your authority than you will to that of the Pope."

This is the tone and these the terms in which these "No Popery" doctors will find, one of these days, their flocks addressing them; for we have only given words to what they know as well as we is the predominant feeling of the great majority of the Protestant people. The very means, in the present temper of the Protestant public, they must use to insure their success, cannot fail to prove their ruin. They will only hasten the issue they would evade. Deprived, as they now are, for the most part, of all *direct* aid from the civil power, the force of things is against them, and it matters little whether they attempt to move or sit still. They were mad enough in the beginning to take their stand on a movable foundation, and they must move on with it, or be left to balance themselves in vacuity; and if they do move on with it, they will simply arrive — nowhither. They are doomed, and they cannot escape. Hence it is all their motions affect us only as the writhings and death-throes of the serpent whose head is crushed.

Orestes A. Brownson
(Library of Congress)

2.

There is no foundation for virtue but in religion, and it is only religion that can command the degree of popular virtue and intelligence requisite to insure to popular government the right direction and a wise and just administration. A people without religion, however successful they may be in throwing off old institutions, or in introducing new ones, have no power to secure the free, orderly, and wholesome working of any institutions. For the people can bring to the support of institutions only the degree of virtue and intelligence they have; and we need not stop to prove that an infidel people can have very little either of virtue or intelligence, since, in this professedly Christian country, this will and must be conceded us. We shall, therefore, assume, without stopping to defend our assumption, that religion is the power or influence we need to take care of the people, and secure the degree of virtue and intelligence necessary to sustain popular liberty. We say, then, if democracy commits the government to the people to be taken care of, religion is to take care that they take proper care of the government, rightly direct and wisely administer it.

But what religion? It must be a religion which is above the people and controls them, or it will not answer the purpose. If it depends on the people, if the people are to take care of it, to say what it shall be, what it shall teach, what it shall command, what worship or discipline it shall insist on being observed, we are back in our old difficulty. The people take care of religion; but who or what is to take care of the people? We repeat, then, what religion? It cannot be Protestantism, in all or any of its forms; for Protestantism assumes as its point of departure that Almighty God has indeed given us a religion, but *has given it to us not to take care of us, but to be taken care of by us.* It makes religion the ward of the people; assumes it to be sent on earth a lone and helpless orphan, to be taken in by the people, who are to serve as its nurse. . . .

It is evident, from these considerations, that Protestantism is not and cannot be the religion to sustain democracy; because, take it in which stage you will, it, like democracy itself, is subject to the control of the people, and must command and teach what they say, and of course must follow, instead of controlling, their passions, interests, and caprices.

Nor do we obtain this conclusion merely by reasoning. It is sustained by facts. The Protestant religion is everywhere either an expression of the government or of the people, and must obey either the government or public opinion. The grand reform, if reform it was, effected by the Protestant chiefs, consisted in bringing religious questions before the public, and subjecting faith and worship to the decision of public opinion, — public on a larger or smaller scale, that is, of the nation, the province, or the sect. Protestant faith and worship tremble as readily before the slightest breath of public sentiment, as the aspen leaf before the gentle zephyr. The faith and discipline of a sect take any and every direction the public opinion of that sect demands. All is loose, floating, — is here to-day, is there to-morrow, and, next day, may be nowhere. The holding of slaves is compatible with Christian character south of a geographical line, and incompatible north; and Christian morals change according to the prejudices, interests, or habits of the people, — as evinced by the recent divisions in our own country among the Baptists and Methodists. The Unitarians of Savannah refuse to hear a preacher accredited by Unitarians of Boston. . . .

Protestantism is insufficient to restrain these, for it does not do it, and is itself carried away by them. The Protestant sect governs its religion, instead of being governed by it. If one sect pursues, by the influence of its chiefs, a policy in opposition to the passions and interests of its members, or any portion of them, the disaffected, if a majority, change its policy; if too few or too weak to do that, they leave it and join some other sect, or form a new sect. If the minister attempts to do his duty, reproves a practice by which his parishioners "get gain," or insists on their practising some real self-denial not compensated by some self-indulgence, a few leading members will tell him very gravely, that they hired him to preach and pray for them, not to interfere with their business concerns and relations; and if he does not mind his own business, they will no longer need his services. The minister feels, perhaps, the insult; he would be faithful; but he looks at his lovely wife, at his little ones. These to be reduced to poverty, perhaps to beggary, — no, it must not be; one struggle, one pang, and it is over. He will do the bidding of his masters. A zealous minister in Boston ventured, one Sunday, to denounce the modern spirit of trade. The next day, he was waited on by a committee of wealthy merchants belonging to his parish, who told him he was wrong. The Sunday following, the meek and humble minister publicly retracted, and made the *amende honorable.*

Here, then, is the reason why Protestantism, though it may institute, cannot sustain popular liberty. It is itself subject to popular control, and must follow in all things the popular will, passion, interest, ignorance, prejudice, or caprice. This, in reality, is its boasted virtue, and we find it commended because under it the people have a voice in its management. . . . Protestantism is not the religion wanted; for it is precisely a religion that can and will govern the people, be their master, that we need.

If Protestantism will not answer the purpose, what religion will? The Roman Catholic, or none. The Roman Catholic religion assumes, as its point of departure, that it is instituted not to be taken care of by the people, but to take care of the people; not to be governed by them, but to govern them. The word is harsh in democratic ears, we admit; but it is not the office of religion to say soft or pleasing words. It must speak the truth even in unwilling ears, and it has few truths that are not harsh and grating to the worldly mind or the depraved heart. The people need governing, and must be governed, or nothing but anarchy and destruction await them. They must have a master. The word must be spoken.

But it is not our word. We have demonstrated its necessity in showing that we have no security for popular government, unless we have some security that the people will administer it wisely and justly; and we have no security that they will do this, unless we have some security that their passions will be restrained, and their attachments to worldly interests so moderated that they will never seek, through the government, to support them at the expense of justice; and this security we can have only in a religion that is above the people, exempt from their control, which they cannot command, but must, on peril of condemnation OBEY. Declaim as you will; quote our expression — THE PEOPLE MUST HAVE A MASTER, — as you doubtless will; hold it up in glaring capitals, to excite the unthinking and unreasoning multitude, and to doubly fortify their prejudices against Catholicity; be mortally scandalized at the assertion that religion ought to govern the people, and then go to work and seek to bring the people into subjection to your banks or moneyed corporations through their passions, ignorance, and worldly interests, and in doing so, prove what candid men, what lovers of truth, what noble defenders of liberty, and what ardent patriots you are. We care not. You see we understand you, and, understanding you, we repeat, the religion which is to answer our purpose must be *above* the people, and able to COMMAND them. We know the force of the word, and we mean it. The first lesson to the child is, *obey;* the first and last lesson to the people, individually or collectively, is, OBEY; — and there is no obedience where there is no authority to enjoin it.

The Roman Catholic religion, then, is necessary to sustain popular liberty, because popular liberty can be sustained only by a religion free from popular control, above the people, speaking from above and able to command them, — and such a religion is the Roman Catholic. It acknowledges no master but God, and depends only on the divine will in respect to what it shall teach, what it shall ordain, what it shall insist upon as truth, piety, moral and social virtue. It was made not by the people, but for them; is administered not by the people, but for them; is accountable not to the people, but to God. Not dependent on the people, it will not follow their passions; not subject to their control, it will not be their accomplice in iniquity; and speaking from God, it will teach them the truth, and command them to practise justice.

Isaac T. Hecker (1819-88)

Friend and correspondent of Brownson's, Hecker too converted to Roman Catholicism in his maturity — and in the same year, 1844. Under Brownson's urging, Hecker had earlier tried transcendentalism and even Brook Farm to see if these met his spiritual longings. They did not. Nor did Bronson Alcott's utopian effort known as Fruitlands offer any more satisfying solace. When Hecker turned at last to Roman Catholicism, he — unlike Brownson — entered a monastic order. Later (1858), he even founded his own: the Paulist Fathers. Seeing this group's special mission to be the conversion of Protestants to Catholicism, Hecker also wished to demonstrate the fundamental compatibility between Catholic theology and American liberty. (1) A brief excerpt, dated 1855, shows Hecker's stance vis-à-vis the Protestantism he had left behind. (2) A portion of the remarkable correspondence between Hecker and Brownson treats problems of the soul, the church, the nation.

1.

The supremacy of private judgment was, and still continues to be, the generative and distinctive principle of Protestantism; to deny it would be to condemn the reformation from its incipient step. It was on this principle that the great reformer, Luther, took his stand at Worms, when he appealed to God and his own conscience in justification of his opinions and conduct.

Protestantism points with pride to the attitude of Dr. Martin Luther, and makes it her glory and boast to have disenthralled man from all authority in religion, except his own private judgment.

We do not wish to rob it of its glory. It is properly the glory of Protestantism. But it is on this ground we take it up, find fault with it, and condemn it.

We condemn Protestantism, as insufficient to meet the wants of man's heart, as unable to satisfy the demands of man's intelligence, and as faithless in representing the authority of Christ.

The heart condemns it, because the supreme want of the heart is peace. But this can only be gained by an unerring and divine authority upon which the heart can repose with feelings of perfect security. Protestantism denies all such authority, the heart therefore condemns it.

[Source: (1) Isaac T. Hecker, *Questions of the Soul* (New York: Arno Press, 1978 [1855]), pp. 129-31. (2) J. F. Gower and R. M. Leliaert, eds., *The Brownson-Hecker Correspondence* (Notre Dame: University of Notre Dame Press, 1979), pp. 175-77, 182-83, 199-200, 279-81.]

Reason condemns it, because religion is not a system of opinions resting upon man's private judgment, but a body of revealed truths, adapted and necessary to the full development and perfection of man's intelligence and heart, and depending upon an unerring and divine authority. Luther's appeal, therefore, to his own private judgment at Worms, was a great mistake; he played the part of the angel of darkness in the garb of light, fit only

> "To fool a crowd with glorious lies,
> To cleave a creed in sects and cries." (Tennyson)

2.
Hecker to Brownson, March 27, 1855

My Dear friend,

. . . You cannot imagine how much I was interested in your analysis of the true elements of the American character. There is no doubt that if we hope for the conversion of our country we must aim at the conversion of the class of minds you describe. What you say of myself modesty forbids me to say that I believe even one half, on the other hand, you have given to me such a lesson of practical humility that you have only excited envy in my breast.

It seems to me from what I have already seen & heard this book has made the call for another necessary, and that to meet the same class of persons. To show the adaptation of the Church to these wants or requirements of the Intellect. Ripley, Bancroft and several others do not deny the adaptation of the Church to the wants of the heart but refuse to yield on the score of the intellect. These men need to be shown that the first demand of the Church is that man should follow the guide of Reason; that faith, authority, etc are demanded by reason to its full growth & perfection. This would give an occassion [sic] to show the beautiful logical unity in the mysteries & dogmas of the Church, and how great a respect & reverence the Church shows to man's reason in demanding his faith & obedience. *We* know that it is *only* the Church that pays the respect & that true deference to reason which this divine gift to man ought to have. We should have to show how reason was made to know the truth. How the Church supposes this. Exemplify it by her different treatment of infants & adults. And that the supposition she acts upon, that Truth has been revealed, is in harmony with the attributes of God & the dictates of reason etc. *To show how the dogmas of the Church answer in a way, to the demands of the intellect, as the sacraments do to the wants of the heart.* Having made this class of mind interested, they will become now willing listeners to *"The Claims of Reason."*

Of course I do not intend to make an attempt at this, but merely throw out these hints as they arise in my mind.

Brownson to Hecker, [c. June 1, 1855]

Rev. & very dear Father,

. . . With regard to the other matters you speak of I think as you do. The simple truth is our old controversialists have their method, and they will look with distrust on our new method, & fancy it full of danger. Very few of them have any suspicion that times have changed and that old errors are to be refuted under new forms & from a different stand-point, yet I do not despair.

Our great difficulty in getting our religion fairly presented to the American mind is the real dislike of the American people and character felt by a large portion of our bishops & clergy, and their settled conviction that nothing can be done for their conversion. They are not missionaries, but have the characteristics of an old national clergy, but of a nation not ours. There is the great difficulty. We cannot appeal to our own countrymen, and use those forms of expression necessary to render ourselves intelligible to them without seeming to them to attack either the Irish clergy or the Irish people. But God in his good Providence will enable us to surmount in due time this obstacle. The Irish people, the laity, are far less unamerican than their clergy, and if permitted to follow their own sympathies will very soon be prepared to second us. They are a noble people when not misled.

Brownson to Hecker, September 29, 1857

Rev. & dear Father,

. . . There is not a more loyal people on earth than the American, or more ready to obey the law; but they of course cannot be made submissive to the arbitrary will of any man. They will obey cheerfully and scrupulously the law, or the man who governs in the name of the law or as the vicar of our Lord, but they will not obey arbitrary power, & never can be made to submit to a centralized despotism, whether exerted in the name of religion or politics. They must be governed as free men, not as slaves, as men endowed with reason and free will, not as machines. Whoever would exert a favorable influence on them must prove to them that the Church leaves them their autonomy.

The things cited abroad which cast so much discredit upon us are[,] you and I both know, to a great [e]xtent the work of Europeans and of Europeans not infrequently born in the bosom of the Church, who have migrated hither, and who never understand liberty in the American sense. The licentiousness of the country we owe in great part to the rebels, revolutionists, & apostates that Europe annually casts upon our shores. Let the responsibility rest where it belongs. For much has been made of the Know Nothing movement at home and abroad.[13] And I am sorry to find that it has had a serious effect on the minds of many Catholics here who ought to have seen in it nothing more than one of those devices of the enemy which are sure to turn to his own disgrace. A few acts of violence have [been] committed, but nothing here has occurred like what is constantly occurring in countries governed by nominally Catholic princes. . . . There is no Catholic country in the world where the laws are so favorable to Catholicity as with us, even in the matter of Church property. The difficulties on the subject we experience grow out of the neglect on the part of our Catholic authorities to study and take advantage of them. We might with perfect ease, without any sacrifice of anything the Church holds essential[,] have the whole force of the law in our favor. The Church here stands legally on a par with the most favored sect and is freer than any where else on earth. Yet these silly Know Nothing movements have created a distrust in many minds of republican institutions, and the influence of the clergy in France is felt by our own bishops & clergy.

There is the great difficulty. France not Rome governs the Catholic mind in this country, and while French Catholics remain Imperial, the great body of Catholics in this country, at least of those who are in authority[,] will be openly or secretly anti republican in their tendencies. American born Catholics are generally republican, attached from feeling & conviction as well as from policy to their country and her institutions, alike opposed to despotism and to radicalism. Hence they are distrusted by the European party amongst us, who feel every action and reaction in the Catholic populations of the Old World.

The question to be decided at Rome is whether we who love our country and wish her to be converted to the Church without being brought under the political system of Europe, are to be sustained, or are to be discouraged, and only those protected or countenanced who insist that Catholicity and Europeanism shall stand or fall on our soil together! Can our people become Catholics without ceasing to be Americans, or without becoming foreigners in this our native land, won from the wilderness by their labor, & defended by their arms?

You and I, my reverend Father, have maintained that our institutions[,] our civilization in a word, are perfectly compatible with Catholicity, and we have labored to prove it. We have contended that nothing is needed by our people to be thoroughly a Catholic people but their conversion to the Catholic faith, that our institutions are good, and are as well fitted to Catholics as to non-Catholics, indeed far better. Are we to be in this sustained or are we to be censured at Rome? This is the question. If the Vicar of Christ says we are wrong, he may rely on our submission without a murmur. But I do not believe he will ever say that.

13. See section on "Nativism," below, pp. 463-67.

Hecker to Brownson, January 30, 1870

My Dear Dr.

Nothing is more surprising to an American, than the increased interest and appreciation of men of all schools and parties in Europe, of the principles of our free institutions & the state of things existing in our country. They are becoming aware of the fact, that the light to be derived from our experience, would remove serious difficulties existing in their own and many other minds in Europe. At this moment, no greater service can be rendered, than to give to Europe, the explanation of the relations of the Church to our free institutions. . . .

The present condition of things in Europe is not unlike that of the 16th century. The discoveries and other important events at that epoch created a desire for amelioration and reforms in society & the Church. The impatience for reforms in the Church was the occasion of a deplorable separation and heresy. Recent discoveries and a more general education has given rise in different populations in our day to the demand for changes in matters both political & religious.

In political matters

It is evident that among other causes, the existing success in political self-government in the U.S., exerts a great influence on the entire populations of Europe. From this has arisen the demand on their part, of a larger share of action in the direction of the interests and destiny of their own countries. If concessions of this kind be not granted, the nations of Europe run a great risk as in 1789 and 1848 and 9, to be overthrown by revolutions.

England has taken the lead in this direction, & has prudently enlarged the basis of political suffrage; Napoleon has followed suit, and retained his imperial crown by changing the government of France from absoluteism [*sic*] to constitutional monarchy. Italy and Spain have made changes but too sudden and too sweepingly to last; Austria has acted with her wonted caution, & Prussia, despotic as she is, cannot maintain herself against the inevitable. If she pushes repression too far, a Republic will be proclaimed as in 1849, over her head.

It is therefore the dictate of political wisdom in the present crisis in Europe, to prevent revolutions by a wise concession of greater political power to the people. If capable, why should not the people have a larger share in the direction of the destiny of their own country?

This extension of political power to the people, is in no way hostile to the spirit and dogmas of the Catholic Religion. For the more the responsibility in the direction of a nation is shared by those who compose it, provided they rightly fulfill its duties, the greater their dignity and merit, & the greater the glory of God. And if Kings derive their right to govern from God through the people, which is the common opinion of Catholic theologians, why should not the people exercise that right in proportion to their ability of self-government?

This concession of greater political power to the people, will call forth fresh zeal in the Church to educate and direct the people in order properly to fulfill their new responsibilities. This will extend her influence, and a new title of gratitude for her services, and show in a new light the absolute necessity of Religion to sustain civil society and good government. For nowhere is the directing or restraining influence of Religion felt to be so necessary as there w[h]ere the people and the Govt. under the external restraints of political power — as in a free government.

Regarding therefore from this point of view the changes which are now taking place in the political governments of Europe, Religion has nothing to fear. If rightly understood, and met on the part of religion with a friendly eye, they may be the providential means of her regaining the good will and the affections of the populations of Europe and renewing her ancient glories on their soil.

In religious matters

It is also evident that a change between the Church and State in Europe is impending. The union that had existed has been undergoing a change for some time past, and to meet these changes concordats were invented and adopted. As long as the political power was in the hand of the King or a few individuals, and stationary, such arrangements served their purposes. The present changes render them almost a nullity. What the King or Kaiser thinks is no longer the standard of right or wrong for the people; their decisions serve no longer for the basis of political action. Public opinion and the vote of the people is now the practical rule of all political action. The concordats made with [the] Emperor of Austria, the King of Italy and the Queen of Spain are set aside by a power greater than that of the throne. The one made with France needs only a change in the ministry, & which may take place at any moment, to render it of no more value than so much waste paper.

The changes in those relations which have existed in many states in Europe, between the Church and State, whatever may be our opinion, whether we deplore or desire them, are taking place, and further ones are pending. These changes will eventually necessitate the Church to assume her own independance [*sic*], and throw herself upon the offerings of her children for support.

These changes will be consummated only by overcoming great difficulties and by great sacrifices. But by a willingness to foresee them, and to prepare for them, they may be greatly lessened.

It will demand on the part of the Episcopate and the priesthood a closer following of the Apostolic example of living; a more earnest and direct manner in preaching the Gospel; and this will produce a closer union of sympathy and interests between the priesthood and the people. It will tend to place the foundations of Religion where our Maker intended they should be, on the convictions of each individual soul and on personal sacrifices.

The loss sustained by the Church by the withdrawal of state support, will not be without its compensation. It will leave her her national freedom so necessary to her true existance [*sic*] and advancement. The freedom to choose her own ministers, freed from the control of state dictation. Is not this exemption of state control in a matter of such vital importance to the Church sufficient to compensate for the many great sacrifices which she will have to make?

Who knows but that the Church[,] no longer confiding in princes, and trusting to Him who alone is her great strength and support, her life will be renewed, her influence extended over all Europe, and in a near future, Europe will be reconstructed on a basis more in harmony with the principles of Christianity.

John England (1786-1842)

Bishop of Charleston, South Carolina, from 1820 until his death twenty-two years later, John England founded the first Catholic newspaper in America in 1822. And like Hecker and Brownson who came after him, England was interested in reaching a wider audience in order to make Catholicism's case more effectively. In the course of his preaching, pleading, contending, and writing, this southern bishop left very few issues of the day as he had found them. (1) In 1838, Bishop England used his paper to defend his Church against the charges of ignorance or obscurantism, that defense revealing some deftness in humor and style. (2) In 1841, in a more formal address delivered in Boston, England took up the old challenge of "the Catholic religion as being incompatible with civil and religious liberty."

1.
Education — Insanity

It is, our readers will say, a very curious juxtaposition, yet it is not that we are about to say, as was said of St. Paul, that too much learning made him mad.

One of the most insolent and most unfounded assertions of some of the modest gentlemen, who are filled with spurious pity for the delusion of Papists, is, that the Protestant religion, is now, and always has been, the friend of science, and that Popery has been allied to ignorance. Hence, the old and young boys who, in these states, are selected to make public orations, or to spout at college commencements, seldom allow an opportunity of the kind to pass with-

---

[Source: *The Works of the Right Reverend John England, First Bishop of Charleston* (Cleveland: Arthur H. Clark Co., 1908), (1) V, 70-71; (2) VII, 73-75.]

out rounding off a few periods with the light shed by Luther, and the Reformation, the mariner's compass, gas, and the blow-pipe; steam-engines and safety valves, have not yet been superadded to Doctor Faustus and the printing press. We could bear all this with Christian patience, and be sufficiently just to reciprocate the pity so generously bestowed, where it was neither needed nor desired; — but when the Catholics are parcelled out into classes, and those accounted most happy and enlightened, who dwell amongst Protestants, and their literature, their civilization, and their freedom, are asserted to be in the direct ratio of their proximity to Protestantism, we get somewhat discontented and impatient; for we perceive a great deterioration of our powers of perception, and detect a wonderful delusion of our mind.

We have lived chiefly in the midst of Protestants, and can feel happy at knowing that several most respectable men and women of their persuasion, are amongst our most worthy and most intimate friends; — but in good sooth, we never found that they were beings of a superior race, elevated midway between Papists and the heavenly intelligences. We found them to be like all other kinds of men and women, some with good clear heads, and some a little thick and muddy, just like Papists.

We also found that some of them had good information and others were just so so. If then the assertion to which we have alluded be true, our powers of perception are greatly at fault.

But moreover we have laboured under a great delusion, and what is worse, it is likely to continue. We do verily believe, perhaps it is only imagination, that the best-informed Catholics we ever met with, were men who lived at a great distance from Protestants, and who never had the advantages of their tuition, proximity, or example. We therefore were led to believe that it was possible to have learning, education, civilization, and liberty, though Protestantism had never existed, and that Catholics could uphold and preserve these, even though religion should have been left unaltered, and that persons may enjoy just as much civil liberty in San Marino, as in Hanover, or in Prussia, and that children could be as well and as universally educated in Austria, as they are in England.

2.

In a large portion of the civilized world, charges are prevalent against the Catholic religion as being incompatible with civil and religious liberty. On what are these charges founded? From the pages of history it is said that the Roman Catholic religion is at war with the spirit of republicanism. But allow me to ask in what way? The principle of republicanism is the equality of men. We teach that all Christians have a common Parent — that all are equally redeemed by the blood of the Saviour — that all must appear before a common God who knows no distinction of persons — where, then, is the inconsistency? Look through the records of the world, and see where the principles of true republicanism are first to be found. They had their origin in Christianity, and their earliest instance is in the church of which we are members. Her institutions are eminently republican. Her rulers are chosen by the common consent — her officers are obliged to account strictly to those over whom they preside — her guide is a written constitution of higher force than the will of any individual. What call you this? Aristocracy? Monarchy? It is republicanism. Look again. Where were the bulwarks found that stayed the ravages of the barbarians of the North, when they devastated the south of Europe? In the republican Catholic States of Italy. Go to a nation still more familiar to you — search the pages of English history. One strain pervades them all — a perpetual assault upon the memory of the prelates of the Catholic Church. Charges are brought that they were overbearing, haughty and tyrannical. Where are the proofs, There are none. Go to the Records of Parliament, and you will find the same thing there. Look at Britain in more ancient times, before the Norman conquest. One of her kings sent to Rome — he addressed the Pope, and requested of him a code of laws for the government of his realm. What was the answer of this haughty, tyrannical, all-grasping potentate, who is represented as having his foot upon the necks of kings and emperors? It may even now be found in her archives. "I can give you principles, but not laws. Your duty as a monarch is to consult your men of wisdom, acquainted with the wishes and necessities of your people; regulate your conduct by their advice, but govern your land in your own way. Nations differ widely, and that which is proper for one might be highly injurious to another." The principles of the common law, that mighty fabric in which English liberty is said to reside, have been traced back to the Catholic Church. In this, then, is the germ of liberty to be found. After the Norman conquests then it was that the conqueror dictated to his captives his own laws. But who refused to bow down in tame submission to his usurpation? The bishops of England were the men. They rested their claims upon the ancient compact; they took the laws of Alfred and of Edward, and from these demanded of the conqueror himself an acknowledgment of the rights secured to the people by Edward. And when the base hypocrite, John, endeavoured still more closely than before, to fetter the people, it was the Archbishop of Canterbury, and the bishops of England, that resisted his power. At the field Runnymede they wrung from his reluctant hand the Magna Charta, which is regarded as the English constitution, but which is only a part of what the people enjoyed under the laws of Alfred.

These are the men who have been stigmatized as proud, as haughty, as ambitious. They were ambitious — just as your Hancocks were ambitious — just as your Warrens were ambitious — just as your Montgomerys were ambitious — just as those other men were ambitious who pledged their lives, their fortunes, and their sacred honour, to the support of that declaration whose successful maintenance wrested from the monarch of England the political rights which we now enjoy. But the historians of England, even while the word of liberty was upon their lips, filled their pages with misrepresentations of the principles of the Catholic prelates, and calumnies upon their characters. Why was this? Because the Catholic religion was prescribed law. Hence it is, that the pages of history have been garbled and distorted by the British historian, because the Catholic prelates resisted to the utmost, the unjust encroachments of the British kings. The history of the American colonies, before they became an independent nation, more especially during the earlier years of their settlement, exhibits marked indications of the same spirit of intolerance towards the Catholic religion; and this, too, on the part of those who themselves fled to this continent as a refuge from religious persecution. In this we find the explanation why, for generation after generation, the same charges against Catholicism have been made — because the same dynasties have been set up, and its opposition has been the same to all. But if we endeavour to correct this source of evil, if we say — "let history be divested of its prejudices and misrepresentations — let education be separated from sectarianism — let the truth alone be recorded and taught" — then are we told — we have been told — that we are turbulent and discontented. Even in this country attempts have been made to divide the republic on account of religious differences — but, thank Heaven! the public mind is becoming more and more enlightened on this point, and men are beginning to perceive that the greatest curse which could befall our country, would be the encouragement of any spirit of sectarian persecution. Let us beseech God, in his infinite mercy to avert from us all such spirit of uncharitableness and unkindness. Before Heaven, let us always avoid it. Let us be a band of brothers as to our common rights — as to our religious differences, let us bury them. Would to God that we may always act in this manner — that we may overcome the spirit of our nature, and imbibe only the spirit of Christian charity. Oh! that we all may, with reference to our opponents, enter into the blessed spirit of that prayer — "Father, forgive them, for they know not what they do." Let us, then, endeavour with all our might to reduce these principles to practice, and in the discharge of our duty to the republic, regard it as a duty to God. Thus shall we achieve the great object of our constitution — thus shall we obtain of God his blessing. If we are assailed from abroad, let us join together as a band of brothers to repel the assault. Thus shall peace, and happiness, and prosperity reign among us — thus shall we be contented with the things and the liberty given to us in this transitory scene, having our eyes fixed on the better things and the true liberty, promised to us in Heaven, as the children of God.

Hispanic Catholicism

Despite most textbook accounts, Roman Catholicism in nineteenth-century America cannot be comprehended alone in terms of eastern expansion into the West. For there already was a "West" so far as this universal church was concerned, a West whose population was rooted in both the North American continent and the Roman Catholic Church. By 1850, the Catholicism of first Spain, then Mexico, had become the Catholicism of the western United States. Into that domain of Hispanic Catholicism, Anglo-Saxon Protestantism was a late intruder. One keen observer, commenting on the "two occupations of California," left no doubt regarding his preference for the first, Hispanic one. The English Catholic Herbert Vaughan (1832-1903), later (1893) cardinal and primate of England, visited California in 1864. The report excerpted below is based on his observations made during that visit.

Let us now proceed with the subject before us, and draw out briefly two contrasts: one between the Spanish or Catholic and the Anglo-Saxon or non-Catholic conduct and policy towards the original lords of the soil, the Indians; the other as between the names they gave to the localities which were the scenes of their respective labours. It will indicate a difference of tone and spirit sufficiently remarkable.

Of course all Californians are not to be held responsible for the acts of a low and heartless section of ruffians, any more than all Englishmen are accountable for the atrocities which we have perpetrated in times past in India or Oceanica. But as we would not pass over the crimes committed by the Anglo-Saxon race in India, were India our topic, so neither will we be silent here on deeds of equal atrocity with any of which we were guilty, committed in these latter days by some of the new occupiers of California.

The love of souls and the love of wealth do not indeed, grow in the same heart. We have already faintly sketched the result of the Church's love of souls on the temporal and spiritual well-being of the indigenous population of California. Under her gentle care was realized for its inhabitants the happiness, peace, and plenty of Paraguay. The Anglo-Saxon and the thirst for gold ushered in, alas! on these poor creatures — made in the divine image, and called equally with ourselves to an eternal share in the love of the Sacred Heart — not a miserable existence, but absolute destruction. The love of Mammon has been the murderer of the native owners of the soil. The iron heart and the iron arm of the Anglo-Saxon invaders have cleared all before them. . . .

[Source: F. J. Weber, ed., *Documents of Catholic California History, 1784-1963* (Los Angeles: Dawson's Book Shop, 1965), pp. 102-7.]

We have been ourselves assured by eye-witnesses that such incidents as the following have frequently happened in the gold diggings. A man would be quietly cleaning his gun or rifle on a Sunday morning, when he would spy an Indian in the distance, and, without the least hesitation, would fire at him as a mark. The Indians were fair game, just as bear or elk were, and men would shoot them by way of pastime, not caring whether the mark was a "buck" or a "squaw," as they call them — that is, a man or a woman. Murder became thus a relaxation. And we must add, that not only American citizens, but also men who pride themselves on the greater civilization and virtue of their country, nearer home, thus imbrued their hands with reprobate levity in the blood of their fellow creatures. Men have been heard seriously to argue that the Indians and Chinese have no immortal souls, and that we have no duty to them as to fellow-men. "What! help to civilize them! What! they have souls! They have no business with civilization, and have no souls." And another person argued, as he thought, in a way which showed a more pious and spiritual nature, and was more commendable. He said he did not wish to promote civilization and Christianity among the Indians; they did not take to it, and always remained the devil's vineyard. "Let us serve the cause of the Lord by destroying this vineyard; I am always ready to assist in the destruction of those red devils." . . .

The other contrast is quickly drawn. It shall be the contrast of names. We do not wish to found any strong argument upon it. Names are not actions and yet to call a man hard names is the next thing to giving him hard blows; and we

San Xavier del Bac mission, Tucson, Arizona
Associated with the missionary efforts of Jesuit Eusebio Kino (1645-1711),
this striking mission still serves a largely Indian congregation.
(Keystone-Mast Collection, University of California, Riverside)

Mission San Luis Rey, Oceanside, California
Franciscan Junipero Serra (1713-84) began his famous "chain of missions"
in California with a mission in San Diego in 1760; ultimately the chain
reached north to San Francisco de Solano (Sonoma) by 1823.
(Franciscan Fathers)

know that, "out of the abundance of the heart the mouth speaketh." Let the two
lists go down in parallel columns, and illustrate the old times and the new.

Spanish baptisms of localities or settlements —	*Yankee baptisms of localities or settlements —*
San Francisco	Jackass Gulch
Sacramento	Jim Crow Cañon
La Purisima Concepcion	Loafer Hill
Trinidad	Whiskey Diggings
Jesus Maria	Slap Jack Bar
Santa Cruz	Yankee Doodle
Nuestra Señora de Soledad	Skunk Gulch
Los Angeles	Chicken Thief Flat
San Jose	Ground Hog's Glory

San Pedro	Hell's Delight
San Miguel	Devil's Wood
San Rafael	Sweet Revenge
Santa Clara	Shirt-tail Cañon
Santa Barbara	Rough and Ready
San Luis Obispo	Rag Town
San Pablo	Git up and Git
Buena Vista	Bob Ridley Flat
Mariposa	Humpback Slide
San Fernando	Swell-head Diggings
Alcatraz	Bloody Run
Contra Costa	Murderers' Bar
San Mateo	Rat-trap Slide
Plumas	Hang Town

We may now dismiss these contrasts, which we have only insisted on in order to bring into greater relief the spirit of God and the spirit of Mammon. The Spaniard went with the tenderest devotedness to serve and save the Indian, recognized him from the first as a brother. The Yankee came, straining every nerve and energy in the pursuit of wealth; the Indian was in his way; he recognized no spiritual ties of brotherhood; his soul presented to him no divine image deserving of his love and service — rather it was said, let him be trodden into the mire, or perish from the face of the land. The former cast over their humble settlements, on the coast and inland, the sacred association of the names of mysteries and holy saints, so that men from all generations might be reminded that they are of the race of all the people of God; whereas the latter have named many of the places where they have dug for gold with the names of their hideous crimes, and with terms compared to which the nomenclature of savage and uncivilized tribes is Christian and refined.

This sketch of the principal features of the two occupations of California, as they have borne upon the native population, may be sufficient for our present purpose. We shall presently dwell upon the better qualities in the American character — the natural foundations upon which religion has to be built. Our object is not to write a political or commercial essay; all we attempt is to note the action of the Church at the present day upon the heterogeneous elements which compose the population of California, and to record as briefly as may be the several influences observable as making up that action.

It has long been a favourite theme with the anti-Catholic philosophers of the day to descant upon the feebleness of the Catholic Church. They judge her as a purely human institution, good in her day; but her day is gone. She was a good nurse, who held the leading-strings which mankind needed in early childhood. But we have grown to the ripeness of perfection; and the good nurse has grown old and past work; she may be allowed therefore to potter about the world, as an old servant round her master's hall and grounds, till she dies and is buried away. We may render some little service if we point to one more instance of her present vigour and vitality in our own day, — if we can show that she is stamping her impress upon the lettered horde that has overrun the western shore as she did formerly upon the unlettered hordes that possessed themselves of the plains of Italy, or of the wolds of England. We believe that she is by degrees assimilating into herself the strange mass of the Californian population; she is standing out in the midst of them as the only representative of religious unity, order and revelation. She is executing her commission in California today as faithfully as she did when Peter entered Rome, or Augustine Kent, or Xavier Asia, or Solano the wilds of South America.

Nativism

Samuel F. B. Morse (1791-1872)

Son of Jedidiah Morse (see above, p. 288), Samuel Morse is best known for his invention of the telegraph in 1837 and of the code which bears his name. He is less widely known as a painter of some distinction and, perhaps, least widely known as a vehement foe of Roman Catholicism. That opposition, he pointed out, was not to Catholicism as a religion but as a political system in league with unfriendly European powers. Yet every action of the Church, every missionary effort, every papal pronouncement, Morse understood in wholly political terms. In his summation below, nativism's basic distrust of all that is foreign leaps forth from the text. Indeed, the whole point of Morse's 1835 diatribe was to halt "foreign immigration."

I have set forth in a very brief and imperfect manner the evil, the great and increasing evil, that threatens our free institutions from *foreign interference.* Have I not shown that there is real cause for alarm? Let me recapitulate the facts in the case, and see if any one of them can be denied; and if not, I submit it to the calm decision of every American, whether he can still sleep in fancied security, while incendiaries are at work; and whether he is ready quietly to surrender his liberty, civil and religious, into the hands of foreign powers.

[Source: Samuel F. B. Morse, *Imminent Dangers to the Free Institutions of the United States Through Foreign Immigration* (New York: Arno Press, 1969 [1835]), pp. 15-16.]

1. It is a fact, that in this age the subject of civil and religious liberty agitates in the most intense manner the various European governments.

2. It is a fact, that the influence of American free institutions in subverting European despotic institutions is greater now than it has ever been, from the fact of the greater maturity, and long-tried character, of the American form of government.

3. It is a fact, that Popery is opposed in its very nature to Democratic Republicanism; and it is, therefore, as a political system, as well as religious, opposed to civil and religious liberty, and consequently to our form of government.

4. It is a fact, that this truth, respecting the intrinsic character of Popery, has lately been clearly and demonstratively proved in public lectures, by one of the Austrian Cabinet, a devoted Roman Catholic, and with the evident design (as subsequent events show) of exciting the Austrian government to a great enterprise in support of absolute power.

5. It is a fact, that this Member of the Austrian Cabinet, in his lectures, designated and proscribed this country by name, as the *"great nursery of destructive principles; as the Revolutionary school for France and the rest of Europe,"* whose contagious example of Democratic liberty had given, and would still give, trouble to the rest of the world, unless the evil were abated.

6. It is a fact, that very shortly after the delivery of these lectures, a Society was organized in the Austrian capital, called the St. Leopold Foundation, for the purpose "of promoting the greater activity of Catholic Missions in America."

7. It is a fact, that this Society is under the patronage of the Emperor of Austria, — has its central direction at Vienna, — is under the supervision of Prince Metternich, — that it is an extensive combination, embodying the civil, as well as ecclesiastical *officers,* not only of the *whole Austrian Empire,* but of the neighbouring Despotic States, — that it is actively at work, collecting moneys, and sending agents to this country, to carry into effect its designs.

8. It is a fact, that the agents of these foreign despots, are, for the most part, *Jesuits.*

9. It is a fact, that the effects of this society are already apparent in the otherwise unaccountable increase of Roman Catholic cathedrals, churches, colleges, convents, nunneries, &c., in every part of the country; in the sudden increase of Catholic emigration; in the increased clanishness of the Roman Catholics, and the boldness with which their leaders are experimenting on the character of the American people.

10. It is a fact, that an unaccountable disposition to riotous conduct has manifested itself within a few years, when exciting topics are publicly discussed, wholly at variance with the former peaceful, deliberative character of our people.

11. It is a fact, that a species of police, unknown to our laws, has repeatedly been put in requisition to keep the peace among a certain class of foreigners, who are Roman Catholics, viz., Priest-police.

12. It is a fact, that Roman Catholic Priests have interfered to influence our elections.

13. It is a fact, that politicians on both sides have propitiated these priests, to obtain the votes of their people.

14. It is a fact, that numerous Societies of Roman Catholics, particularly among the Irish foreigners, are organized in various parts of the country, under various names, and ostensibly for certain benevolent objects; that these societies are united together by correspondence, all which may be innocent and praiseworthy, but, viewed in connexion with the recent aspect of affairs, are at least suspicious.

15. It is a fact, that an attempt has been made to organize a military corps of Irishmen in New-York, to be called the O'Connel Guards; thus commencing a military organization of foreigners.

16. It is a fact, that the greater part of the foreigners in our population is composed of Roman Catholics.

Facts like these I have enumerated might be multiplied, but these are the most important, and quite sufficient to make every American settle the question with himself, whether there is, or is not, danger to the country from the present state of our Naturalization Laws. I have stated what I believe to be facts. If they are *not* facts, they will easily be disproved, and I most sincerely hope they will be disproved. If they are facts, and my inferences from them are wrong, I can be shown where I have erred, and an inference more rational, and more probable, involving less, or perhaps no, danger to the country, can be deduced from them, which deduction, when I see it, I will most cheerfully accept, as a full explanation of these most suspicious doings of Foreign Powers.

I have spoken in these numbers freely of a particular religious sect, the Roman Catholics, because from the nature of the case it was unavoidable; because the foreign political conspiracy is identified with that creed. With the *religious tenets* properly so called, of the Roman Catholic, I have not meddled. If foreign powers, hostile to the principles of this government, have combined to spread any religious creed, no matter of what denomination, that creed does by that very act become a subject of political interest to all citizens, and must and will be thoroughly scrutinized. We are compelled to examine it. We have no choice about it. If instead of combining to spread with the greatest activity the Catholic Religion throughout our country, the Monarchs of Europe had united to spread Presbyterianism, or Methodism, I presume, there are few who would not see at once the propriety and the necessity of looking most narrowly at the political bearings of the peculiar principles of these Sects, or of any other Protestant Sects: and members of any Protestant Sects too, would be the last to complain of the examination. I know not why the Roman Catholics in this land of scrutiny are to plead exclusive exemption from the same trial.

Awful Disclosures

One year after Morse sounded his nativist alarm, the most popular as well as the most scandalous anti-Catholic book fell into the hands of an eager Protestant public prepared to believe the worst. If only someone on the inside of the Catholic Church would be kind enough to tell them the worst. A small volume entitled Awful Disclosures of Maria Monk, *purporting to give the "true confessions" of a young woman who had lived in a nunnery in Montreal, seemed to do the trick. Most Americans, having never been inside a nunnery, often wondered — or worried — about what went on in there. "Maria Monk" was only too glad to tell, not in explicit salacious detail (that would become the fashion of the next century), but in suggestion and intimation. The facts were hair-raising, the only problem being that they weren't facts at all, only nativist fancy.*

1.

She gave me another piece of information which excited other feelings in me, scarcely less dreadful. Infants were sometimes born in the convent: but they were always baptized and immediately strangled! This secured their everlasting happiness; for the baptism purified them from all sinfulness, and being sent out of the world before they had time to do any thing wrong, they were at once admitted into heaven. How happy, she exclaimed, are those who secure immortal happiness to such little beings! Their little souls would thank those who kill their bodies, if they had it in their power!

Into what a place and among what society had I been admitted! How differently did a Convent now appear from what I had supposed it to be! The holy women I had always fancied the nuns to be, the venerable Lady Superior, what were they? And the priests of the Seminary adjoining, some of whom indeed I had had reason to think were base and profligate men, what were they all? I now learnt they were often admitted into the nunnery, and allowed to indulge in the greatest crimes, which they and others called virtues.

After having listened for some time to the Superior alone, a number of the nuns were admitted, and took a free part in the conversation. They concurred in every thing which she had told me, and repeated, without any signs of shame or compunction, things which criminated themselves. I must acknowledge the truth, and declare that all this had an effect upon my mind. I ques-

---

[Source: *Awful Disclosures of Maria Monk* (New York: Howe & Bates, 1836), (1) pp. 58-59; (2) pp. 124-25.]

tioned whether I might not be in the wrong, and felt as if their reasoning might have some just foundation. I had been several years under the tuition of Catholics, and was ignorant of the Scriptures, and unaccustomed to the society, example, and conversation of Protestants; had not heard any appeal to the Bible as authority, but had been taught, both by precept and example, to receive as truth every thing said by the priests. I had not heard their authority questioned, nor any thing said of any other standard of faith but their declarations. I had long been familiar with the corrupt and licentious expressions which some of them use at confessions, and believed that other women were also. I had no standard of duty to refer to, and no judgment of my own which I knew how to use, or thought of using.

All around me insisted that my doubts proved only my own ignorance and sinfulness; that they knew by experience they would soon give place to true knowledge, and an advance in religion; and I felt something like indecision.

2.

A number of nuns usually confessed on the same day, but only one could be admitted into the room at a time. They took their places just without the door, on their knees, and went through the preparation prescribed by the rules of confession; repeating certain prayers, which always occupy a considerable time. When one was ready, she rose from her knees, entered, and closed the door behind her; and no other one even dare touch the latch until she came out.

I shall not tell what was transacted at such times, under the pretence of confessing, and receiving absolution from sin: far more guilt was often incurred than pardoned; and crimes of a deep die were committed, while trifling irregularities, in childish ceremonies, were treated as serious offences. I cannot persuade myself to speak plainly on such a subject, as I must offend the virtuous ear. I can only say, that suspicion cannot do any injustice to the priests, because their sins cannot be exaggerated.

Religious Know-Nothings

In the 1850s political nativism had its most dramatic expression in the emergence of the American or Know-Nothing Party. A decade or more before that time religious nativism organized itself into a variety of societies, associa-

---

[Source: Ray Allen Billington, *The Protestant Crusade, 1800-1860: A Study of the Origins of American Nativism* (New York: Macmillan Co., 1938), pp. 437-38.]

tions, and unions, most of them managing to publish periodicals whose re-
petitive purpose was to resist the encroachments of "popery" and call atten-
tion to potential subversions of American liberty. One such organization,
"The American Society to Promote the Principles of the Protestant Reforma-
tion," published its constitution on June 24, 1840, in the American Protestant Vindicator.

Whereas, the principles of the court of Rome are totally irreconcilable with the
gospel of Christ; liberty of conscience; the rights of man; and with the constitution and laws of the United States of America. — And whereas, the influence of
Romanism is rapidly extending throughout this Republic, endangering the
peace and freedom of our country — Therefore, being anxious to preserve the
ascendancy of "pure religion and undefiled," and to maintain and perpetuate
the genuine truths of Protestantism unadulterated; with devout confidence in
the sanction of the Great Head of the Church to aid our efforts in withstanding
the "power and great authority of the Beast, and the strong delusion of the False
Prophet," we do hereby agree to be governed by the following Constitution:

I. This Society shall be called "The American Society, to promote principles of the Protestant Reformation."

II. To act as a Home Missionary society — to diffuse correct information
concerning the distinctions between Protestantism and Popery — to arouse
Protestants to a proper sense of their duty in reference to the Romanists — and
to use all evangelical methods to convert the Papists to Christianity by Lectures,
and the dissemination of suitable Tracts and standard books upon the Romish
controversy.

III. Any person who subscribes to the principles of this Constitution, and
who contributes in any way to the funds of this Society, may be a member, and
shall be entitled to a vote at all public meetings.

IV. The officers of this Society shall be a President, Vice-Presidents, a
Treasurer, a Foreign Secretary, a Corresponding, and a Recording Secretary, —
all to be elected by members of this Society.

V. This Society shall annually elect an Executive Committee of twenty
gentlemen residing in New York city, and its vicinity, five of whom shall be a
quorum, to do business, provided the President, or some one of the officers be
one of them present. They shall enact their own bye [*sic*] laws, fill vacancies in
their body, employ agents, and fix their compensation, appropriate the funds,
call special meetings of the Society, and zealously endeavor to accomplish the
object of the institution.

VI. Any Society or Association founded on the same principles, may become auxiliary to this Society; and the officers of each auxiliary Association
shall, ex-officio, be entitled to deliberate at all meetings of the Society, for the
transaction of its affairs.

THE AIM OF POPE PIUS IX.

"BEWARE! THERE IS DANGER IN THE DARK!"

Protestant nativism, 1855
(Library of Congress)

VII. This constitution may be amended by a vote of two-thirds of all the members present at any annual meeting of the Society, which shall be held on the second Tuesday of May, and should it be prevented from taking place at that time, all the officers elected at the former annual meeting shall hold over until such meeting shall be duly called and held.

VIII. Any person contributing the sum of twenty dollars, or more, to the funds of the Society, shall be constituted a life member; and those who have made donations, or otherwise rendered eminent service in the cause, shall be entitled to honorary membership.

Native American Revivals

Handsome Lake

In 1799, Handsome Lake, a Seneca prophet, survived a near-death experience and subsequently received a revelation. Rather than promote resistance to the sweep of European civilization, Handsome Lake urged his followers in the Iroquois nation to return to moral standards of living, to retain as much as they could of traditional practices, but also to allow for the adoption of some elements of white culture. In doing so, Handsome Lake introduced Gaiwiiyo or the "Good Word," which served as a distinct tradition practiced by many Iroquois to this date. In the following excerpt from The Revelation of Handsome Lake, *as recounted by Chief Edward Cornplanter, one can see certain similarities with the drive toward Christian "holiness" that would later inspire Phoebe Palmer.*

Now This Is Gaiwiio

The beginning was in Yai''kni [May], early in the moon, in the year 1800.
It commences now.

A Time of Trouble

The place is[14] Ohi'io' [on the Allegany river], in Diono'sade'gĭ [Cornplanter village].
Now it is the harvest time, so he[15] said.

---

14. The present tense is always used by Chief Cornplanter.
15. The narrator, Handsome Lake.

[Source: Arthur C. Parker, "The Code of Handsome Lake, Seneca Prophet," in William N. Fenton, ed., *Parker on the Iroquois* (Syracuse, NY: Syracuse University Press, 1968), pp. 20-22.]

Now a party of people move. They go down in canoes the Allegany river. They plan to hunt throughout the autumn and the winter seasons.

Now they land at Ganowoñ'go[n] [Warren, Pa.] and set up camp.

The weather changes and they move again. They go farther down the river. The ice melts opening up the stream and so they go still farther down. They land at Diondēgǎ [Pittsburgh]. It is a little village of white people [literally, "our younger brethren"[16]]. Here they barter their skins, dried meat and fresh game for strong drink. They put a barrel of it in their canoes. Now all the canoes are lashed together like a raft.

Now all the men become filled with strong drink (gonigä'nongi). They yell and sing like demented people. Those who are in the middle canoes do this.[17]

Now they are homeward bound.

Now when they come to where they had left their wives and children these embark to return home. They go up Cornplanter creek, Awe'gäo[n].

Now that the party is home the men revel in strong drink and are very quarrelsome. Because of this the families become frightened, and move away for safety. So from many places in the bushlands camp fires send up their smoke.

Now the drunken men run yelling through the village and there is no one there except the drunken men. Now they are beastlike and run about without clothing and all have weapons to injure those whom they meet.

Now there are no doors left in the houses for they have all been kicked off. So, also, there are no fires in the village and have not been for many days. Now the men full of strong drink have trodden in the fireplaces. They alone track there and there are no fires and their footprints are in all the fireplaces.

Now the dogs yelp and cry in all the houses for they are hungry.

So this is what happens.

The Sick Man

And now furthermore a man becomes sick. Some strong power holds him.

Now as he lies in sickness he meditates and longs that he might rise again and walk upon the earth. So he implores the Great Ruler to give him strength that he may walk upon this earth again. And then he thinks how evil and loathsome he is before the Great Ruler. He thinks how he has been evil ever since he

---

16. The Seneca term is Honio''o[n], meaning "our younger brother."

17. The intoxicated men were put in the middle canoes to prevent their jumping into the water. The more sober men paddled from the outer canoes. This debauchery was common among the Six Nations at the beginning of the 19th century.

had strength in this world and done evil ever since he had been able to work. But notwithstanding, he asks that he may again walk.

So now this is what he sang: O'gi'we [the Death chant], Ye'ondǎ'thǎ [the Women's song], and Gone'owoⁿ [the Harvest song]. Now while he sings he has strong drink with him.

Now it comes to his mind that perchance evil has arisen because of strong drink and he resolves to use it nevermore. Now he continually thinks of this every day and every hour. Yea, he continually thinks of this. Then a time comes and he craves drink again for he thinks that he can not recover his strength without it.

Now two ways he thinks: what once he did and whether he will ever recover.

The Two Ways He Thinks

Now he thinks of the things he sees in the daylight.

The sunlight comes in and he sees it and he says, "The Creator made this sunshine." So he thinks. Now when he thinks of the sunshine and of the Creator who made it he feels a new hope within him and he feels that he may again be on his feet in this world.

Now he had previously given up hope of life but now he begs to see the light of another day. He thinks thus for night is coming. So now, he makes an invocation that he may be able to endure the night.

Now he lives through the night and sees another day. So then he prays that he may see the night and it is so. Because of these things he now believes that the Great Ruler has heard him and he gives him thanks.

Now the sick man's bed is beside the fire. At night he looks up through the chimney hole and sees the stars and he thanks the Great Ruler that he can see them for he knows that he, the Creator, has made them.

Now it comes to him that because of these new thoughts he may obtain help to arise from his bed and walk again in this world. Then again he despairs that he will ever see the new day because of his great weakness. Then again he has confidence that he will see the new day, and so he lives and sees it.

For everything he sees he is thankful. He thinks of the Creator and thanks him for the things he sees. Now he hears the birds singing and he thanks the Great Ruler for their music.

So then he thinks that a thankful heart will help him.

Now this man has been sick four years but he feels that he will now recover.

And the name of the sick man is Ganio'dai'io [Handsome Lake] a council chief [Hoya'ne].

Tenskwatawa

In 1804, a Shawnee prophet, Tenskwatawa, "The Open Door," also came close to death and emerged with a message. Like previous Native American prophets, Tenskwatawa fiercely rejected white influence over Indian life and encouraged virtuous behavior. He exhorted his followers to give up inter-tribal warfare, polygamy, and promiscuity. Inspired by this message, Tenskwatawa's brother Tecumseh organized numerous tribes for the purpose of self-betterment, including the forcible removal of whites from native lands. Tecumseh's death at the Battle of Thames in 1813 signaled also the death of their movement. Before that took place, however, Tenskwatawa in 1808 made a speech to then-General William H. Harrison, part of which is reproduced below. The Prophet employed an accommodating tone, yet re-mained firm in his opinion that only by rejecting what the whites had brought, including alcohol, could their culture be preserved.

"Father: — It is three years since I first began with that system of religion which I now practice. The white people and some of the Indians were against me; but I had no other intention but to introduce among the Indians, those good princi-ples of religion which the white people profess. I was spoken badly of by the white people, who reproached me with misleading the Indians; but I defy them to say that I did any thing amiss.

"Father, I was told that you intended to hang me. When I heard this, I in-tended to remember it, and tell my father, when I went to see him, and relate to him the truth.

"I heard, when I settled on the Wabash, that my father the governor, had declared that all the land between Vincennes and fort Wayne, was the property of the Seventeen Fires. I also heard that you wanted to know, my father, whether I was God or man; and that you said if I was the former, I should not steal horses. I heard this from Mr. Wells, but I believed it originated with himself.

"The Great Spirit told me to tell the Indians that he had made them, and made the world — that he had placed them on it to do good, and not evil.

"I told all the red skins, that the way they were in was not good, and that they ought to abandon it.

"That we ought to consider ourselves as one man; but we ought to live agreeably to our several customs, the red people after their mode, and the white people after theirs; particularly, that they should not drink whiskey; that it was not made for them, but the white people, who alone knew how to use it; and

---

[Source: Benjamin Drake, *Life of Tecumseh, and his brother the prophet* (Cincinnati: Ander-son, Gates & Wright, 1858), pp. 107-109.]

that it is the cause of all the mischiefs which the Indians suffer; and that they must always follow the directions of the Great Spirit, and we must listen to him, as it was he that made us: determine to listen to nothing that is bad: do not take up the tomahawk, should it be offered by the British or by the long knives: do not meddle with any thing that does not belong to you, but mind your own business, and cultivate the ground, that your women and your children may have enough to live on.

"I now inform you, that it is our intention to live in peace with our father and his people forever.

"My father, I have informed you what we mean to do, and I call the Great Spirit to witness the truth of my declaration. The religion which I have established for the last three years, has been attended to by the different tribes of Indians in this part of the world. Those Indians were once different people; they are now but one: they are all determined to practice what I have communicated to them, that has come immediately from the Great Spirit through me.

"Brother, I speak to you as a warrior. You are one. But let us lay aside this character, and attend to the care of our children, that they may live in comfort and peace. We desire that you will join us for the preservation of both red and white people. Formerly, when we lived in ignorance, we were foolish; but now, since we listen to the voice of the Great Spirit we are happy.

"I have listened to what you have said to us. You have promised to assist us: I now request you, in behalf of all the red people, to use your exertions to prevent the sale of liquor to us. We are all well pleased to hear you say that you will endeavor to promote our happiness. We give you every assurance that we will follow the dictates of the Great Spirit.

"We are all well pleased with the attention that you have showed us; also with the good intentions of our father, the President. If you give us a few articles, such as needles, flints, hoes, powder, &c., we will take the animals that afford us meat, with powder and ball."

3. Human Rights and American Religion

Black Religion and Slavery

Lemuel Haynes

One of the first articulate and published African Americans to make a mark on the world of American publishing was Lemuel Haynes (1753-1833). After being raised as an indentured servant in Massachusetts and serving as a soldier in the American Revolution, Haynes was drawn into the orbit of the "New Divinity" theology and gained a theological education by apprenticeship to Rev. Daniel Ferrand in Canaan, Connecticut. Haynes then taught school briefly before being called as a minister to a Congregational church in Rutland, Vermont. Through long and distinguished service as a minister, Haynes worked hard to promote the ideals of New Divinity Calvinism, the values of American republican politics, and the cause of abolition for slaves. His Fourth of July Sermon in 1801, which is excerpted below, dealt with the subject of "True Republicanism." Haynes held that this ideal could be obtained only by careful attention to God's law, and especially by acting with justice toward "the poor Africans, among us."

"But ye shall not so: but he that is greatest among you, let him be as the younger; and he that is chief, as he that doth serve."

Luke 22:26

[Source: Richard Newman, ed., *Black Preacher to White America: The Collected Writings of Lemuel Haynes, 1774-1833* (Brooklyn: Carlson, 1990), pp. 77-78, 80-82.]

The occasion of these words was a dispute among the disciples of Christ about superiority, as may be seen by attending to ver. 24th; And there was also a strife among them, which of them should be accounted the greatest. They had imbibed a strange notion that the Saviour was about to emancipate the Jews from the Roman yoke, and to restore their civil rights. Elated with the delusive prospect, they began to contend for posts of honor, and who should have the pre-eminence in the new establishment. The insatiable thirst in mankind for preference has appeared in every age, and been a fruitful source of many evils. Our blessed Lord, to manifest his detestation against such haughty ambition, points his disciples to the gentile world, ver. 25th: "And he said unto them, The Kings of the Gentiles exercise lordship over them; and they that exercise authority upon them arc called benefactors." Plainly suggesting, that for them to seek for posts of honor under the specious garb of sanctity, was symbolizing with the heathen, and acting perfectly inconsistent with the nature of that kingdom, he came to introduce; the lineaments of which are concisely drawn in my text: "But ye shall not be so: but he that is greatest among you let him be as the younger, and he that is chief as he that doth serve."

In which words we have the nature, and design of a free government, epitomised, by the unerring hand of wisdom. Liberty and equality are words very familiar at the present day, and may possibly be abused. That there ought to be a kind of subordination among men, none will dispute; and that it is beneficial to society, is equally obvious. A veneration for parents, difference [deference] to the aged, and respect to officers both in church and state, are matters taught us in the word of God. The idea is implied in my text; a proud ambitious aspiring temper was what Christ went to discard. To be greatest was the design of the disciples, without a generous regard to the community at large; to get into office was the great object: blind to the interest of the commonwealth, the importance of the matter did not come up to view; but in a heedless manner they would thrust themselves forward, only to be called great. If from such selfish motives men crowd themselves into office, a similar administration may well be expected. It is of singular importance to ascertain the true criterion of greatness. When a man distinguishes himself by a proper regard for the general good, he is then worthy the name; he rises to eminence, and commands a kind of veneration from all around him. — This is that true dignity the blessed Jesus taught among men, and that shone conspicuous in his life. *He that is greatest among you let him be as the younger; and he that is chief, as he that doth serve.* Plainly suggesting, that it is the design of the appointment to office, to serve the public, and is the only test of true greatness. . . .

It may further be observed, that a free republican government has the preference to all others, in that it tends to destroy those distinctions among men that ought never to exist. "All men are born equally free and independent & have certain inherent and unalienable rights" to use the language of our own constitution, which coincides with the holy oracles, Acts 17:26. The more this can be maintained the nearer it answers the original perfect draught. If God saw such a state of society was most favorable to men, it ought still to be maintained. The distinctions only to be reprobated are such as have no true merit in them, but are merely nominal, such as birth, riches, empty titles, etc. — These were the things contended for by the disciples of Jesus, which he discards in the text; they would be great without goodness or without serving the public. Palm upon an aspiring mortal the flattering titles of King, Prince, Lord, etc. merely because he was born under a more splendid roof or lay in a softer cradle, than his neighbor, has more gold in his chest, and his farm is wider at both ends, or what thro' mistake has a higher parentage, he will at once forget the only test of true greatness, and only value himself on his being able to tyrannize over others, and can look down on his own species with contempt. This at once throws the balance of power into the wrong scale and enervates the bands of society. This has been the fruitful source of domination and blood-shed which has denominated this world an aceldama; this has kept Europe at war with little cessation for more than nine centuries; and its influence has been felt in the happy climes of North America. — Blessed be God! the bloody flag could not be established on our shores; and while others are falling victims to the hard and cruel hand of tyranny, we enjoy peace, far from the din of war, and the hideous habitations of cruel oppressors.

There cannot be a greater source of evil to mankind than to imbibe wrong sentiments about true greatness. — In a land like ours, where the people are free and view each other as brethren engaged in one common cause, virtue and philanthropy will be considered as the true criterions of distinction. — He will be esteemed great who is servant of all, who is willing to devote his talents to the public good. These are the prominent features of a free, republican government, and should attach us to our present constitution.

Again, A free, independent administration, like ours, is very friendly to knowledge and instruction; it expands the human mind, and gives it a thirst after improvement. The amazing progress that these states have made in useful arts and science, of almost every kind, during the twenty five years of our independence, will justify the present remark; perhaps no history will be read to better advantage. — When men are made to believe that true dignity consists in outward parade and pompous titles, they forget the thing itself, and the greater part of the community view the other as unattainable, they look up to others as above them, and forget to think for themselves, nor retain their own importance in the scale of being. Hence, under a monarchal government, people are commonly ignorant; they know but little more than to bow to despots, and crouch to them for a piece of bread.

The propriety of this idea will appear strikingly evident by pointing you to the poor Africans, among us. What has reduced them to their present pitiful,

abject state? Is it any distinction that the God of nature hath made in their formation? Nay — but being subjected to slavery, by the cruel hands of oppressors,
they have been taught to view themselves as a rank of beings far below others,
which has suppressed, in a degree, every principle of manhood, and so they become despised, ignorant, and licentious. This shews the effects of despotism,
and should fill us with the utmost detestation against every attack on the rights
of men: while we cherish and diffuse, with a laudable ambition, that heaven-
born liberty wherewith Christ hath made us free. Should we compare those
countries, where tyrants are gorged with human blood, to the far more peaceful
regions of North America, the contrast would appear striking.

On the whole, does it not appear that a land of liberty is favourable to
peace, happiness, virtue and religion, and should be held sacred by mankind?

Slave Religion

*Often the religion of the American slave gained ground more in spite of the
whites than through their active aid. (1) In the first account below, a former
Kentucky slave, Henry Bibb, recounts in his 1849 autobiography the great
difficulty blacks had in learning to trust a loving God while they suffered
"unjustly under the lash, without friends, without protection of law or gospel. . . ." (2) Yet, somehow, blacks did find refuge in the Christian religion,
large numbers being especially drawn to the Baptists. A Scottish weaver,
William Thomson, describes below "the imposing and solemn effect" of a
baptism in a South Carolina river (on St. Helena Island) in 1840. That ritual washing was followed by a service of worship where, within limits, a new
fellowship prevailed.*

1.

In 1833, I had some very serious religious impressions, and there was quite a
number of slaves in that neighborhood, who felt very desirous to be taught to
read the Bible. There was a Miss Davis, a poor white girl, who offered to teach a
Sabbath School for the slaves, notwithstanding public opinion and the law was
opposed to it. Books were furnished and she commenced the school; but the
news soon got to our owners that she was teaching us to read. This caused quite
an excitement in the neighborhood. Patrols were appointed to go and break it

---

[Source: Willie Lee Rose, *A Documentary History of Slavery in America* (New York: Oxford
University Press, 1976), (1) pp. 458-59; (2) pp. 463-65.]

up the next Sabbath. They were determined that we should not have a Sabbath School in operation. For slaves this was called an incendiary movement.

The Sabbath is not regarded by a large number of the slaves as a day of rest. They have no schools to go to; no moral nor religious instruction at all in many localities where there are hundreds of slaves. Hence they resort to some kind of amusement. Those who make no profession of religion, resort to the woods in large numbers on that day to gamble, fight, get drunk, and break the Sabbath. This is often encouraged by slaveholders. When they wish to have a little sport of that kind, they go among the slaves and give them whiskey, to see them dance, "pat juber," sing and play on the banjo. Then get them to wrestling, fighting, jumping, running foot races, and butting each other like sheep. This is urged on by giving them whiskey; making bets on them; laying chips on one slave's head, and daring another to tip it off with his hand; and if he tipped it off, it would be called an insult, and cause a fight. Before fighting, the parties choose their seconds to stand by them while fighting; a ring or a circle is formed to fight in, and no one is allowed to enter the ring while they are fighting, but their seconds and the white gentlemen. They are not allowed to fight a duel, nor to use weapons of any kind. The blows are made by kicking, knocking, and butting with their heads; they grab each other by their ears, and jam their heads together like sheep. If they are likely to hurt each other very bad, their masters would rap them with their walking canes, and make them stop. After fighting, they make friends, shake hands, and take a dram together, and there is no more of it.

But this is all principally for want of moral instruction. This is where they have no Sabbath Schools; no one to read the Bible to them; no one to preach the gospel who is competent to expound the Scriptures, except slaveholders. And the slaves, with but few exceptions, have no confidence at all in their preaching, because they preach a pro-slavery doctrine. They say, "Servants be obedient to your masters; — and he that knoweth his master's will and doeth it not, shall be beaten with many stripes; — " means that God will send them to hell, if they disobey their masters. This kind of preaching has driven thousands into infidelity. They view themselves as suffering unjustly under the lash, without friends, without protection of law or gospel, and the green eyed monster tyranny staring them in the face. They know that they are destined to die in that wretched condition, unless they are delivered by the arm of Omnipotence. And they cannot believe or trust in such a religion, as above named.

2.

On my arrival in South Carolina, the first thing that particularly attracted my attention was negro slavery. Two days after my arrival in Beaufort, the quarterly meeting of the Baptist Church occurred, being Sunday the 11th October 1840; and, as I understood that some sixteen or eighteen negro slaves were to be baptized, I went to the river in the morning at seven o'clock, and found the banks crowded with some hundreds of black faces, and few white people.

It was a beautiful morning, with a clearer sky than is often seen in Scotland. I almost expected to see something ridiculous, but, in reality, the whole affair had rather an imposing and solemn effect. The black people behaved themselves decently, and with great propriety, much more so than a parcel of young gentlemen who were, looking on, enjoying the scene in their own way, but not much to their credit, as men of sense or good feeling. The parson, who was dressed in a white gown, went into the river, till the water came up to his waist. A very large fat negro man, named Jacob, one of the deacons of the church, led the people into the river, and stood by, while the parson immersed them, I suppose, to see that none of them were carried off by the stream; and sure enough, it would have taken a pretty strong tide to carry *him* off. They went into the river one by one, the men first, and then the women. The effect was really solemn, as the clear voice of the pastor resounded through the crowd, and along the banks of the river, with the words — "I baptize thee in the name of the Father, and of the Son, and of the Holy Ghost — Amen;" and when all was done, they came up from the river, in a body, singing the beautiful hymn —

> "I'm not ashamed to own my Lord,
> Or to defend his cause:
> Maintain the glory of his cross,
> And honour all his laws."

At eleven o'clock we went to church, which was very crowded. I believe there are about twelve or fourteen hundred negro members belonging to it, partly house servants, but mostly slaves from the cotton plantations in the neighbourhood. In the church, the negroes (with the exception of those who were baptized in the morning), were seated in the gallery, the men on the one side, and the women on the other. They had a very strange appearance to me. It was a novel sight to see so many blacks. They appeared all very much alike, as much so as a flock of sheep does to a stranger. In their outward appearance, they were the most serious and attentive congregation I have seen. After prayer and praise, the negroes who were baptized in the morning, were requested by the pastor to stand up, when he addressed himself to them; telling them particularly their duty to God and to their master, and to hold fast by the profession of Christianity they had that day made. Then the pastor, the Rev. Mr. Fuller, who was standing, surrounded by his elders, immediately before the pulpit, told them to come forward, and receive the right hand of fellowship. As they came forward, he took them by the hand, and bade them welcome as brethren in Christ. I took particular notice of the shaking of hands. It was a real transaction; and in the act, the women made a curtsey, and the men a bow; with a better grace than many of the servant lads and lasses in this country would have done. All, except one, were new members; and on this one they had been exercising church discipline; I believe, for incontinence; but, after a reprimand before the congregation, he was bid "Go in peace, and sin no more." All churches admit them members, after instructing them in the great features of Christianity and some of the most practical and useful dogmas. I frequently conversed with them on this subject, and they generally had a tolerable scriptural idea of Hell and the Devil, of God and Heaven, and of Jesus Christ, who died for their sins; or, with the ideas of a little schoolboy, they would tell me that Heaven is good and that Hell is bad, — that the wicked will be punished in the one, and the good enjoy the other. Yet some of them are learned in the Scriptures. I have heard them praying and exhorting in their own homely way; but, as with their white brethren, this does not appear to have any practical effect on their conduct.

In the afternoon the Sacrament of the Supper was administered. There were black deacons, who handed round the bread and wine to the negroes. They all used the same wine and bread. The white people did not use any of the cups that the slaves drank out of, but the cups that the whites had used were then used by some of the slaves. The negroes have generally fine voices, and they joined in the psalmody of the church. They, of course, do not use any books; for it is contrary to law to teach a negro to read or write; but the pastor gives out the hymn in two lines at a time. They appeared to pay great attention to the service; but I was sorry to observe that the minister never turned his eye to the galleries, nor addressed himself to the limited capacities of the slaves. Judging from the discourse, and the manner of the minister, one would not have known there was an ignorant negro in the house, although there were five or six times as many black skins as white.

Nat Turner

The slave insurrection in 1831 that was led by Nat Turner of Virginia struck fear into hearts throughout the entire South. Turner, who was thirty years old when the revolt began on August 22, 1831, succeeded in mobilizing a small band of African Americans who killed about 60 white Virginians before the revolt was put down. When he was in prison, Turner was visited by

---

[Source: *The Confessions of Nat Turner* (1831), as found in *William Styron's Nat Turner,* ed. John Henrik Clarke (Boston: Beacon, 1968), pp. 99-103.]

*Thomas R. Gray, to whom he spoke a considerable "confession," part of
which is presented below. Of special note in that confession are the many elements it contained of the era's standard Methodist practices, including visions, dreams, and a radical absorption of the Scripture. Six days after making this "confession," Nat Turner was executed for his leadership of the
rebellion. His memory, however, lingered powerfully as an inspiration to
many blacks and as consternation to many in white society.*

SIR, — You have asked me to give a history of the motives which induced me to
undertake the late insurrection, as you call it — To do so I must go back to the
days of my infancy, and even before I was born. I was thirty-one years of age the
2nd of October last, and born the property of Benj. Turner, of this county. In
my childhood a circumstance occurred which made an indelible impression on
my mind, and laid the ground work of that enthusiasm, which has terminated
so fatally to many, both white and black, and for which I am about to atone at
the gallows. It is here necessary to relate this circumstance — trifling as it may
seem, it was the commencement of that belief which has grown with time, and
even now, sir, in this dungeon, helpless and forsaken as I am, I cannot divest
myself of. Being at play with other children, when three or four years old, I was
telling them something, which my mother overhearing, said it had happened
before I was born — I stuck to my story, however, and related somethings
which went, in her opinion, to confirm it — others being called on were greatly
astonished, knowing that these things had happened, and caused them to say in
my hearing, I surely would be a prophet, as the Lord had shewn me things that
had happened before my birth. And my father and mother strengthened me in
this my first impression, saying in my presence, I was intended for some great
purpose, which they had always thought from certain marks on my head and
breast — [a parcel of excrescences which I believe are not at all uncommon,
particularly among negroes, as I have seen several with the same. In this case he
has either cut them off or they have nearly disappeared] — My grandmother,
who was very religious, and to whom I was much attached — my master, who
belonged to the church, and other religious persons who visited the house, and
whom I often saw at prayers, noticing the singularity of my manners, I suppose,
and my uncommon intelligence for a child, remarked I had too much sense to
be raised, and if I was, I would never be of any service to any one as a slave — To
a mind like mine, restless, inquisitive and observant of every thing that was
passing, it is easy to suppose that religion was the subject to which it would be
directed, and although this subject principally occupied my thoughts — there
was nothing that I saw or heard of to which my attention was not directed —
The manner in which I learned to read and write, not only had great influence
on my own mind, as I acquired it with the most perfect ease, so much so, that I
have no recollection whatever of learning the alphabet — but to the astonish-

ment of the family, one day, when a book was shewn to me to keep me from crying, I began spelling the names of different objects — this was a source of wonder to all in the neighborhood, particularly the blacks — and this learning was constantly improved at all opportunities — when I got large enough to go to work, while employed, I was reflecting on many things that would present themselves to my imagination, and whenever an opportunity occurred of look-ing at a book, when the school children were getting their lessons, I would find many things that the fertility of my own imagination had depicted to me be-fore; all my time, not devoted to my master's service, was spent either in prayer, or in making experiments in casting different things in moulds made of earth, in attempting to make paper, gun-powder, and many other experiments, that although I could not perfect, yet convinced me of its practicability if I had the means. I was not addicted to stealing in my youth, nor have ever been — Yet such was the confidence of the negroes in the neighborhood, even at this early period of my life, in my superior judgment, that they would often carry me with them when they were going on any roguery, to plan for them. Growing up among them, with this confidence in my superior judgment, and when this, in their opinions, was perfected by Divine inspiration, from the circumstances al-ready alluded to in my infancy, and which belief was ever afterwards zealously inculcated by the austerity of my life and manners, which became the subject of remark by white and black. — Having soon discovered to be great, I must ap-pear so, and therefore studiously avoided mixing in society, and wrapped my-self in mystery, devoting my time to fasting and prayer — By this time, having arrived to man's estate, and hearing the scriptures commented on at meetings, I was struck with that particular passage which says: "Seek ye the kingdom of Heaven and all things shall be added unto you." I reflected much on this pas-sage, and prayed daily for light on this subject — As I was praying one day at my plough, the spirit spoke to me, saying "Seek ye the kingdom of Heaven and all things shall be added unto you." *Question* — what do you mean by the Spirit. *Ans.* The Spirit that spoke to the prophets in former days — and I was greatly astonished, and for two years prayed continually, whenever my duty would per-mit — and then again I had the same revelation, which fully confirmed me in the impression that I was ordained for some great purpose in the hands of the Almighty. Several years rolled round, in which many events occurred to strengthen me in this my belief. At this time I reverted in my mind to the re-marks made of me in my childhood, and the things that had been shewn me — and as it had been said of me in my childhood by those by whom I had been taught to pray, both white and black, and in whom I had the greatest confi-dence, that I had too much sense to be raised, and if I was, I would never be of any use to any one as a slave. Now finding I had arrived to man's estate, and was a slave, and these revelations being made known to me, I began to direct my at-tention to this great object, to fulfil the purpose for which, by this time, I felt assured I was intended. Knowing the influence I had obtained over the minds of my fellow servants, (not by the means of conjuring and such like tricks — for to them I always spoke of such things with contempt) but by the communion of the Spirit whose revelations I often communicated to them, and they believed and said my wisdom came from God. I now began to prepare them for my purpose, by telling them something was about to happen that would terminate in fulfilling the great promise that had been made to me — About this time I was placed under an overseer, from whom I ranaway — and after remaining in the woods thirty days, I returned, to the astonishment of the negroes on the plantation, who thought I had made my escape to some other part of the country, as my father had done before. But the reason of my return was, that the Spirit appeared to me and said I had my wishes directed to the things of this world, and not to the kingdom of Heaven, and that I should return to the service of my earthly master — "For he who knowetb his Master's will, and doeth it not, shall be beaten with many stripes, and thus have I chastened you." And the negroes found fault, and murmured against me, saying that if they had my sense they would not serve any master in the world. And about this time I had a vision — and I saw white spirits and black spirits engaged in battle, and the sun was darkened — the thunder rolled in the Heavens, and blood flowed in streams — and I heard a voice saying, "Such is your luck, such you are called to see, and let it come rough or smooth, you must surely bare it." I now withdrew myself as much as my situation would permit, from the intercourse of my fellow servants, for the avowed purpose of serving the Spirit more fully — and it appeared to me, and reminded me of the things it had already shown me, and that it would then reveal to me the knowledge of the elements, the revolution of the planets, the operation of tides, and changes of the seasons. After this revelation in the year of 1825, and the knowledge of the elements being made known to me, I sought more than ever to obtain true holiness before the great day of judgment should appear, and then I began to receive the true knowledge of faith. And from the first steps of righteousness until the last, was I made perfect; and the Holy Ghost was with me, and said, "Behold me as I stand in the Heavens" — and I looked and saw the forms of men in different attitudes — and there were lights in the sky to which the children of darkness gave other names than what they really were — for they were the lights of the Savior's hands, stretched forth from east to west, even as they were extended on the cross on Calvary for the redemption of sinners. And I wondered greatly at these miracles, and prayed to be informed of a certainty of the meaning thereof — and shortly afterwards, while laboring in the field, I discovered drops of blood on the corn as though it were dew from heaven — and I communicated it to many, both white and black, in the neighborhood — and I then found on the leaves in the woods hieroglyphic characters, and numbers, with the forms of men in different attitudes, portrayed in blood, and representing the figures I had seen before in the heavens. And now the Holy Ghost had revealed itself to me, and made plain the miracles it had shown me — For as the blood of Christ had been shed on this earth, and had ascended to heaven for the salvation of sinners, and was now returning to earth again in the form of dew — and as the leaves on the trees bore the impression of the figures I had seen in the heavens, it was plain to me that the Savior was about to lay down the yoke he had borne for the sins of men, and the great day of judgment was at hand.

Daniel A. Payne (1811-93)

Payne, who speaks below as a Lutheran minister, later became a leading Methodist preacher, educator, and bishop. Ordained at a Lutheran synod gathered in 1839 in Fordsboro, New York, Payne seized the occasion to protest powerfully against slavery's dehumanizing of mankind and womankind. The twenty-eight-year-old black native of South Carolina, compelled by God, condemned the "diabolical design" of slavery, but in so doing he consciously spoke for all oppressed.

Sir — I am opposed to slavery, not because it enslaves the black man, but because it enslaves *man*. And were all the slaveholders in this land men of color, and the slaves white men, I would be as thorough and uncompromising an abolitionist as I now am; for whatever and whenever I may see a being in the form of a man, enslaved by his fellow man, without respect to his complexion, I shall lift up my voice to plead his cause, against all the claims of his proud oppressor; and I shall do it not merely from the sympathy which man feels towards suffering man, but because *God, the living God,* whom I dare not disobey, has commanded me to open my mouth for the dumb, and to plead the cause of the oppressed. . . .

The very moment that a man conceives the diabolic design of enslaving his brother's body, that very moment does he also conceive the still more heinous design of fettering his will, for well does he know that in order to make his dominion supreme over the body, he must fetter the living spring of all its motions. Hence, the first lesson the slave is taught is to yield his will unreservedly and exclusively to the dictates of his master. And if a slave desire to educate himself or his children, in obedience to the dictates of reason, or the laws of God, he does not, he cannot do it without the consent of his master. Does reason and circumstances and the Bible command a slave to preach the gospel to his brethren? Slavery arises, and with a frown, an oath and a whip, fetters or ob-

[Source: *Journal of Negro History,* 52 (1967), 60-61.]

structs the holy volition of his soul! I knew a pious slave in Charleston, who was a licensed exhorter in the Methodist Episcopal Church; this good man was in the habit of spending his Saturday nights on the surrounding plantations, preaching to the slaves. One night, as usual, he got into a canoe, sailed upon James' Island. While in the very act of preaching the unsearchable riches of Christ to dying men, the patroles seized him and whipped him in the most cruel manner, and compelled him to promise that he would never return to preach again to those slaves. In the year 1834, several colored brethren, who were also exhorters in the Methodist Episcopal Church commenced preaching to several *destitute white families,* who gained a subsistence by cultivating some poor lands about three or four miles from Charleston. The first Sunday I was present; the house was nearly filled with these poor white farmers. The master of the house was awakened to a sense of his lost condition. During the following week he was converted. On the third Sunday from the day he was convinced of sin he died in the triumphs of faith, and went to heaven. On the fourth Sunday from the time the dear brethren began to preach, the patroles scented their track, and put them to chase. Thus, an end was put to their labors. Their willing souls were fettered, and the poor whites constrained to go without the preaching of the gospel. In a word, it is in view of man's moral agency that God commands him to shun vice, and practice virtue. But what female slave can do this? I lived 24 years in the midst of slavery, and never knew but six female slaves who were reputedly virtuous! What profit is to the female slave that she is disposed to be virtuous? Her will, like her body, is not her own; they are both at the pleasure of her master; and he brands them at his will. *So it subverts the moral government of God.*

Frederick Douglass (c. 1817-95)

The black voice most powerfully raised against slavery was that of a Maryland slave who early escaped to freedom and soon joined the forces of abolition. Even as Douglass denounced slavery, he denounced with equal force a Christianity that appeared to tolerate if it did not actually condone that brutal bondage. An effective speaker, Douglass addressed audiences across America and in the British Isles as well. Asked why he labored also in England, he responded that slavery was "a system of such gigantic evil, so strong, so overwhelming in its power, that no one nation is equal to its removal. It requires the humanity of Christianity, the morality of the world, to

---

[Source: John W. Blassingame, ed., *The Frederick Douglass Papers,* 1st ser. (New Haven: Yale University Press, 1979), I, (1) 16-17; (2) 281-83. Quotation above is taken from pp. 292-93.]

remove it." Portions of two speeches (and audience reactions thereto) are
presented below: (1) in Boston, January 28, 1842, where Douglass spoke to
some 4,000 persons crowded into Faneuil Hall; and (2) in London, May 22,
1846, where great numbers pressed together in Finsbury Chapel to hear this
black abolitionist.

1.

I rejoice to be permitted, as well as to be able to speak upon this subject in
Faneuil Hall. I will not detain you long, for I stand here a slave. (No! no! from
the meeting.) A slave at least in the eye of the Constitution. (No! no! *with em-*
phasis from the meeting.) It is a slave by the laws of the South, who now addresses you. (That's it! *from the meeting.*) My back is scarred by the lash — that
I could show you. I would, I could make visible the wounds of this system upon
my soul. I merely rose to return you thanks for this cheering sight, representing
as I do, the two and a half millions remaining in that bondage from which I
have escaped. I thank God that I have the opportunity to do it. Those bondmen,
whose cause you are called to espouse, are entirely deprived of the privilege of
speaking for themselves. They are goods and chattels, not men. They are denied
the privileges of the Christian — they are denied the rights of citizens. They are
refused the claims of the man. They are not allowed the rights of the husband
and the father. They may not name the name of Liberty. It is to save them from
all this, that you are called. Do it! — and they who are ready to perish shall bless
you! Do it! and all good men will cheer you onward! Do it! and God will reward
you for the deed; and your own consciences will testify that you have been true
to the demands of the religion of Christ. (Applause.)

But what a mockery of His religion is preached at the South! I have been
called upon to describe the style in which it is set forth. And I find our ministers
there learn to do it at the northern colleges. I used to know they went away
somewhere I did not know where, and came back ministers; and this is the way
they would preach. They would take a text — say this: — "Do unto others as
you would have others do unto you." And this is the way they would apply it.
They would explain it to mean, "slaveholders, do unto *slave-holders* what you
would have them do unto you:" — and then looking impudently up to the
slaves' gallery, (for they have a place set apart for us, though it is said they have
no prejudice, just as is done here in the northern churches;) looking high up to
the poor colored drivers, and the rest, and spreading his hands gracefully
abroad, he says, (mimicking,) "And you too, my friends, have souls of infinite
value — souls that will live through endless happiness or misery in eternity. Oh,
labor diligently to make your calling and election sure. Oh, receive into your
souls these words of the holy apostle — 'Servants, be obedient unto your mas-

Frederick Douglass
(National Archives and Records Administration)

ters.' (Shouts of laughter and applause.) Oh, consider the wonderful goodness of God! Look at your hard, horny hands, your strong muscular frames, and see how mercifully he has adapted you to the duties you are to fulfil! (continued laughter and applause) while to your masters, who have slender frames and long delicate fingers, he has given brilliant intellects, that they may do the *think-*

ing, while you do the *working.*" (Shouts of applause.) It has been said here at the North, that the slaves have the gospel preached to them. But you will see what sort of a gospel it is: — a gospel which, more than chains, or whips, or thumb-screws, gives perpetuity to this horrible system.

2.

There are many of these crimes which if the white man did not commit, he would be regarded as a scoundrel and a coward. In South Maryland, there is a law to this effect: — that if a slave shall strike his master, he may be hanged, his head severed from his body, his body quartered, and his head and quarters set up in the most prominent place in the neighbourhood. (Sensation.) If a col-oured woman, in the defence of her own virtue, in defence of her own person, should shield herself from the brutal attacks of her tyrannical master, or make the slightest resistance, she may be killed on the spot. (Loud cries of "Shame!") No law whatever will bring the guilty man to justice for the crime.

But you will ask me, can these things be possible in a land professing Christianity? Yes, they are so; and this is not the worst. No, a darker feature is yet to be presented than the mere existence of these facts. I have to inform you that the religion of the southern states, at this time, is the great supporter, the greater sanctioner of the bloody atrocities to which I have referred. (Deep sen-sation). While America is printing tracts and Bibles; sending missionaries abroad to convert the heathen; expending her money in various ways for the promotion of the Gospel in foreign lands, the slave not only lies forgotten — uncared for, but is trampled under foot by the very churches of the land. What have we in America? Why we have slavery made part of the religion of the land. Yes, the pulpit there stands up as the great defender of this cursed *institution,* as it is called. Ministers of religion come forward, and torture the hallowed pages of inspired wisdom to sanction the bloody deed. (Loud cries of "Shame!") They stand forth as the foremost, the strongest defenders of this "institution." As a proof of this, I need not do more than state the general fact, that slavery has ex-isted under the droppings of the sanctuary of the south, for the last 200 years, and there has not been any war between the *religion* and the *slavery* of the south.

Whips, chains, gags, and thumb-screws have all lain under the droppings of the sanctuary, and instead of rusting from off the limbs of the bondman, these droppings have served to preserve them in all their strength. Instead of preaching the Gospel against this tyranny, rebuke, and wrong, ministers of reli-gion have sought, by all and every means, to throw in the background whatever in the Bible could be construed into opposition to slavery, and to bring forward that which they could torture into its support. (Cries of "Shame!") This I conceive to be the darkest feature of slavery, and the most difficult to attack, because it is identified with religion, and exposes those who denounce it to the charge of infidelity. Yes, those with whom I have been labouring, namely, the old organization Anti-Slavery Society of America, have been again and again stigmatized as infidels, and for what reason? Why, solely in consequence of the faithfulness of their attacks upon the slaveholding religion of the southern states, and the northern religion that sympathizes with it. (Hear, hear.)

I have found it difficult to speak on this matter without persons coming forward and saying, "Douglass, are you not afraid of injuring the cause of Christ? You do not desire to do so, we know; but are you not undermining religion?" This has been said to me again and again, even since I came to this country, but I cannot be induced to leave off these exposures. (Loud cheers.)

I love the religion of our blessed Saviour, I love that religion that comes from above, in the "wisdom of God, which is first pure, then peaceable, gentle, and easy to be entreated, full of mercy and good fruits, without partiality and without hypocrisy." I love that religion that sends its votaries to bind up the wounds of him that has fallen among thieves. I love that religion that makes it the duty of its disciples to visit the fatherless and widow in their affliction. I love that religion that is based upon the glorious principle, of love to God and love to man (cheers); which makes its followers do unto others as they themselves would be done by. If you demand liberty to yourself, it says, grant it to your neighbours. If you claim a right to think for yourselves, it says, allow your neighbours the same right. If you claim to act for yourselves, it says, allow your neighbours the same right. It is because I love this religion that I hate the slaveholding, the woman-whipping, the mind-darkening, the soul-destroying religion that exists in the southern states of America. (Immense cheering.) It is because I regard the one as good, and pure, and holy, that I cannot but regard the other as bad, corrupt, and wicked. Loving the one I must hate the other, holding to the one I must reject the other, and I, therefore, proclaim myself an infidel to the slave-holding religion of America. (Reiterated cheers.)

Why, as I said in another place, to a smaller audience the other day, in answer to the question, "Mr. Douglass, are there not Methodist churches, Baptist churches, Congregational churches, Episcopal churches, Roman Catholic churches, Presbyterian churches in the United States, and in the southern states of America, and do they not have revivals of religion, accessions to their ranks from day to day, and will you tell me that these men are not followers of the meek and lowly Saviour?" Most unhesitatingly I do. Revivals in religion, and revivals in the slave trade, go hand in hand together. (Cheers.) The church and the slave prison stand next to each other, the groans and cries of the heartbroken slave are often drowned in the pious devotions of his religious master. (Hear, hear.) The church-going bell and the auctioneer's bell chime in with each other; the pulpit and the auctioneer's block stand in the same neighbourhood; while the blood-stained gold goes to support the pulpit, the pulpit covers the infernal business with the garb of Christianity. We have men sold to build churches, women sold to support missionaries, and babies sold to buy Bibles and communion services for the churches. (Loud cheers.)

Sojourner Truth (c. 1797-1883)

Female and black and abolitionist, Sojourner Truth on each of those grounds aroused deep animosity and on occasion provoked violent resistance. Speaking throughout the Northeast and Midwest, the New York native began as a curiosity but ended as a force. That force was directed against slavery and in behalf of human rights, all human rights. Two observers describe encounters along the speaking trail: (1) in Indiana in 1858 where Sojourner Truth is charged with the ultimate fraud; and (2) in Iowa in 1863 where her simple oratory persuades and forewarns.

1.

Sojourner Truth, an elderly colored woman, well known throughout the Eastern States, is now holding a series of anti-slavery meetings in Northern Indiana. Sojourner comes well recommended by H. B. Stowe, yourself, and others, and was gladly received and welcomed by the friends of the slave in this locality. Her progress in knowledge, truth, and righteousness is very remarkable, especially when we consider her former low estate as a slave. The border-ruffian Democracy of Indiana, however, appear to be jealous and suspicious of every anti-slavery movement. A rumor was immediately circulated that Sojourner was an impostor; that she was, indeed, a man disguised in women's clothing. It appears, too, from what has since transpired, that they suspected her to be a mercenary hireling of the Republican party.

At her third appointed meeting in this vicinity, which was held in the meeting-house of the United Brethren, a large number of democrats and other pro-slavery persons were present. At the close of the meeting, Dr. T. W. Strain, the mouthpiece of the slave Democracy, requested the large congregation to "hold on," and stated that a doubt existed in the minds of many persons present respecting the sex of the speaker, and that it was his impression that a majority of them believed the speaker to be a man. The doctor also affirmed (which was

[Source: *Narrative of Sojourner Truth* . . . (Battle Creek, Mich.: published for the author, 1878), (1) pp. 137-39; (2) pp. 146-48.]

not believed by the friends of the slave) that it was for the speaker's special benefit that he now demanded that Sojourner submit her breast to the inspection of some of the ladies present, that the doubt might be removed by their testimony. There were a large number of ladies present, who appeared to be ashamed and indignant at such a proposition. Sojourner's friends, some of whom had not heard the rumor, were surprised and indignant at such ruffianly surmises and treatment.

Confusion and uproar ensued, which was soon suppressed by Sojourner, who, immediately rising, asked them why they suspected her to be a man. The Democracy answered, "Your voice is not the voice of a woman, it is the voice of a man, and we believe you are a man." Dr. Strain called for a vote, and a boisterous "Aye," was the result. A negative vote was not called for. Sojourner told them that her breasts had suckled many a white babe, to the exclusion of her own offspring; that some of those white babies had grown to man's estate; that, although they had sucked her colored breasts, they were, in her estimation, far more manly than they (her persecutors) appeared to be; and she quietly asked them, as she disrobed her bosom, if they, too, wished to suck! In vindication of her truthfulness, she told them that she would show her breast to the whole congregation; that it was not to her shame that she uncovered her breast before them, but to their shame.

2.

The graphic sketch of her by the author of "Uncle Tom's Cabin" has doubtless been read with interest by thousands. No pen, however, can give an adequate idea of Sojourner Truth. This unlearned African woman, with her deep religious and trustful nature burning in her soul like fire, has a magnetic power over an audience perfectly astounding. I was once present in a religious meeting where some speaker had alluded to the government of the United States, and had uttered sentiments in favor of its Constitution. Sojourner stood, erect and tall, with her white turban on her head, and in a low and subdued tone of voice began by saying: "Children, I talks to God and God talks to me. I goes out and talks to God in de fields and de woods. [The weevil had destroyed thousands of acres of wheat in the West that year.] Dis morning I was walking out, and I got over de fence. I saw de wheat a holding up its head, looking very big. I goes up and takes holt ob it. You b'lieve it, dere was *no* wheat dare? I says, God [speaking the name in a voice of reverence peculiar to herself], what *is* de matter wid *dis* wheat? and he says to me, 'Sojourner, dere is a little weasel in it.' Now I hears talkin' about de Constitution and de rights of man. I comes up and I takes hold of dis Constitution. It looks *mighty big,* and I feels for *my* rights, but der aint any dare. Den I says, God, what *ails* dis Constitution? He says to me, "Sojourner, dere is a little *weasel* in it." The effect upon the multitude was irresistible.

On a dark, cloudy morning, while she was our guest, she was sitting, as she often was wont to do, with her cheeks upon her palms, her elbows on her knees; she lifted up her head as though she had just wakened from a dream, and said, "Friend Dugdale, poor old Sojourner can't read a word, will you git me de Bible and read me a little of de Scripter?" Oh, yes, Sojourner, gladly, said I. I opened to Isaiah, the 59th chapter. She listened as though an oracle was speaking. When I came to the words, None calleth for justice, nor any pleadeth for truth; your hands are defiled with blood, and your fingers with iniquity; they conceive mischief, and bring forth iniquity; they hatch cockatrice's eggs, and weave the spider's web; he that eateth of their eggs dieth, and that which is crushed breaketh out into a viper, she could restrain herself no longer, and, bringing her great palms together with an emphasis that I shall never forget, she exclaimed, "*Is dat thare?* 'It shall break out into a viper.' *Yes, God told me dat.* I never heard it read afore, *now* I know it *double!*" Of course her mind was directed to the heinous institution of American slavery, and she regarded these terrible words of the seer as prophetic concerning its fearful consequences.

Schism over Slavery

The Methodists

Neither the Catholics nor the Dutch Reformed suffered schism over the slavery issue, but three other denominations did break apart. The first to do so, the Methodists, severed their national fellowship in 1844, creating two new, largely white organizations: the Methodist Episcopal Church and the Methodist Episcopal Church, South. (Nearly a century later, in 1939, the southern and northern branches came back together.) In the year of separation itself, with all of its attendant agony and torment of spirit, a northern editor argues vainly against breaking up a denomination only two generations old. The large issue, of course, was slavery; the narrow issue was whether the Methodists could or should appoint a slaveholder to the high office of bishop.

[Source: *Christian Advocate and Journal*, June 26, 1844, p. 182.]

The True Grounds upon Which the Southern Portion of the M. E. Church Must Rest, If the Contemplated Separation from their Present Connection Should Be Effected

In the present crisis it is important that our brethren of the ministry, and of the laity, should examine carefully the causes which have led the General Conference to make provision for a division of the Church, at the earnest request of the delegates from the southern annual conferences. . . .

The question of separation or continued union is therefore to be settled by the south; and may our fathers' God direct them in their determination. But we earnestly beseech our brethren of the south not to suffer passion or feeling to mislead them in the all-important matter which is submitted to their decision. They are to decide, not only for themselves, but for posterity. Their action will influence, for good or for evil, the destinies of their children and their children's children . . . perhaps in eternity. We know that God can overrule all to his glory — even our mistakes and misjudgments; but as agents undergoing probation before him, endowed with reason, and furnished with revelation to guide them, they are bound by every consideration, moral and religious, to act cautiously, prudently, and with a single eye to duty, under the best lights which their circumstances afford. . . .

Let us, then, calmly and dispassionately inquire, what are the causes or considerations which impel the Southern to separate from the Northern portion of the Methodist Episcopal Church?

It cannot be denied that the Church has, from time to time, accommodated her disciplinary regulations to the necessities of her ministry and membership in the slaveholding states. Originally, slaveholding was not tolerated at all; but at that time the civil legislation of none of the states forebade the emancipation of slaves. This state of things was soon changed, and it became impracticable to make them free in some states. The history of our Church action on the subject of slavery will show that the General Conference has been compelled, by the force of these circumstances, gradually to relax her Discipline; not to favor slaveholding, but in mercy to the slaves; not to withdraw her opposition to the system, which she still declared to be "a great evil," but to avoid the greater evil of enforcing upon Methodist masters, on pain of expulsion from the Church, what the obligations of humanity forbid. The Church, however, retreated from her original position with evident reluctance, and step by step. . . .

What, then, has been done to force the South to separation? What new grievance or injury has been inflicted by Church action upon our brethren of the South? We are compelled to answer, None — absolutely none! . . .

We know of nothing which can be urged but the historical fact that the ministry, acting by their delegates in General Conference, have uniformly selected the Bishops, or General Superintendents, from among the non-slaveholding Elders; thus, virtually excluding such as held slaves from the highest dignity in the Church. No rule of Discipline has been enacted which excludes slaveholders from the Episcopate; but the uniform practice of the Conference, when a new incumbent of the office was to be selected, was as decisive in this regard . . . as if it had been based on the most positive enactment. [A]nd in every instance, since any considerable portion of the ministry became slaveholders, the objection to the admission of slavery into the Episcopate has been unreservedly urged during the canvass which preceded the election of a Bishop.

For a long time the practice of the General Conference, as above stated, was not only acquiesced in by the Southern delegation, but generally concurred with as the dictate of sound prudence. So late as 1832, when Bishop Andrew was elected, he was nominated by a Southern delegate who would himself have had the preference, if he had not been inextricably connected with slavery. It could not have been satisfactory to all, that slaveholding should be considered a disqualification for the Episcopate, but no serious difficulty was occasioned by it at that time.

At the next General Conference, held in Cincinnati in 1836, a more formidable opposition was made to the exclusion of slaveholders from the Episcopate. Three Bishops were to be elected; and while it was admitted by the delegates from the non-slaveholding conferences that it would be proper that one of them should be taken from the South, . . . they refused to vote for any candidate who held slaves. The Southern delegates refused to nominate a candidate on this condition, vehemently urging it as a necessary qualification, for at least one of the Bishops to be elected, that he should be a slave-holder. The resistance to this claim excited, for the first time, manifest dissatisfaction among the Southern delegates, and the feeling has been kept alive to the present time.

In 1840 no Bishop was elected, and therefore no occasion occurred for controversy on the subject; but during the interval between the session of 1840 and the late session in New York, strong intimations were given . . . that the claim for a slaveholding Bishop was to be urged with zeal and pertinacity at the General Conference of 1844. Indeed, it was fairly stated that a refusal on the part of the North to grant this claim would lead to a separation of the Church.

Upon the whole, it will be seen, that the admission of slavery into the Episcopate is as impracticable as it would be unwise and disastrous; and if it has become a *sine qua non* with our Southern brethren, separation is inevitable. But we insist that there is no other real cause for such a calamity; and we cannot but hope "the sober second thought" of the Southern Churches will determine them to abandon this new ground of dissension, and adhere to the union.

The Baptists

In 1845 the Baptists separated along northern and southern lines, with no reconciliation having yet taken place. Again the issue was unmistakably slavery, with the precise focus upon the question of the appropriateness of a Baptist missionary being a slaveholder. National organization among the Baptists was still fairly recent (the first Triennial Convention had met in Philadelphia in 1814) when only a generation later schism struck. From the contrasting views presented below, one sees issues galloping at such a pace that neither compromise nor conciliation is able to catch up. Both the (1) northern and the (2) southern perspectives are presented anonymously.

1.

Though some months have elapsed since the southern churches, by a concerted movement, separated themselves in a body from the General Convention of the Baptist denomination of the United States, that event has not lost its interest or importance. It is an event which belongs to the history of Baptists and of Baptist missions; and correct opinions should now be formed of the just responsibilities of those, by whose influence and agency this separation has been produced. The South makes loud complaints and serious accusations against the Acting Board established at Boston; whether these complaints and accusations are well founded and just, or unfounded and unjust, however it may be to others, surely cannot be a matter of indifference to the party accused. Though the course of the Board has been already much discussed, and various and conflicting opinions have been formed and expressed in regard to it, yet we are not aware that the specific charges made by the Southern Convention against the Board have been particularly examined. We propose to examine those charges, and the grounds on which they rest, in the hope that now, when the excitement produced by the withdrawal of the South has in some degree subsided, a correct and just judgment may be formed of the conduct of the Board.

The history of the proceedings, which led to the separation of the South from the General Convention, may be given in few words. In November, 1844, "The Baptist State Convention of Alabama" adopted a preamble and certain resolutions, which they forwarded to the Acting Board, at Boston, by one of which resolutions the Board understood the Convention of Alabama as intending to demand of the Board distinctly to avow, whether they would or would

---

[Source: *The Christian Review*, (1) 40 (1845), 481-82, 496-97; (2) 41 (1846), 114-15, 124-25, 135.]

not appoint a slaveholder a missionary. To this demand, after expressing regret that it had been made, as unnecessary, and stating that in thirty years in which the Board had existed, no slaveholder, to their knowledge, had applied to be appointed a missionary, and that such an event as a slaveholder's taking slaves with him, could not, for reasons expressed, possibly occur, the Board frankly and plainly answered in the following words: "If, however, any one should offer himself as a missionary, having slaves, and insist on retaining them as his property, we could not appoint him. One thing is certain, we never can be a party to any arrangement which would imply approbation of slavery."

The publication of this answer of the Board was immediately followed by the manifestation of excited feeling on the part of the South. Agitation and discussion were kept up till May, in the present year, when a Southern Baptist Convention was held at Augusta, in Georgia. This Convention resolved to withdraw from the General Convention, and to form a separate organization for supporting missions. . . .

How was it possible for the Board to act otherwise than they did act? They were asked, not by strangers, but by persons directly interested in the question, and to whom the Board stood in the fiduciary relation of agents or trustees, whether they would appoint a slaveholder a missionary. The question was in the most general form, and of course, importing a slaveholder under the common and ordinary circumstances of slaveholding. The Board could not say it was a matter of doubt or uncertainty in their minds how they should act in such case. They had a clear and decided opinion. The only alternative was, to express, or conceal their opinion. If any man thinks that the members of the Board, as upright men and Christians, might have concealed their opinions on this subject, with a view to obtain money from the South, which might not be obtained if their opinions were expressed, we have no argument to offer to that man, and must decline all discussion with him. His standard of morals, and of upright and honorable conduct must be such as to preclude the possibility of his appreciating the motives which actuated the Board. The members of the Board, at the time of accepting their appointment, had no reason to believe that, with their known views and feelings on the subject of slavery, the South would expect that they could, according to their sense of duty, appoint slaveholders as missionaries. The opinions of the members of the Board on the subject of slavery being well known, the course of action which would naturally follow, under the influence of those opinions, was properly supposed to be understood and acquiesced in by all interested, and it could not be necessary to make, uncalled for, any particular declaration as to that course of action. It was enough that the general opinions and feelings of the Board were well understood, if nothing more specific was desired. But when the Board is distinctly asked if they would appoint a slaveholder a missionary, and a distinct avowal of the opinion of the Board on this subject is desired by a party in interest, it seems to us clear, beyond doubt, that the Board could do nothing but the precise thing they in fact did.

2.

The leading article in the Christian Review for December, 1845, is a review of the Minutes of the Southern Baptist Convention, held at Augusta, Ga., May, 1845. The design of the article is to vindicate the decision of the Acting Board of the Baptist General Convention, touching the resolutions of the Alabama Convention, and to cast the responsibility of the recent division of the Baptist denomination, in the missionary enterprise, on the South. This is the first vigorous attempt which we have noticed, to justify the proceeding of the Board. The defence was tardy in making its appearance. It has, no doubt, been carefully prepared. Every thing which legal knowledge and ingenuity can do, has been done, to make good the defence. The article merits a respectful notice. It is a grave and ingenious discussion of a deeply interesting subject, published in a permanent form, and likely to produce an impression, very unfavorable to the Southern Convention, on those who have not an opportunity of seeing the other side. We had hoped that the subject would be permitted to sleep, not because we felt unprepared to vindicate the course of the Southern Convention, but because the discussion is likely to arouse and perpetuate feelings which all good men desire to see allayed. The Board, or their friends, however, have deemed it proper to pursue a different course. They had a perfect right to do so. We feel imperatively called on to buckle on our armor for the defence of our course; and we will solemnly endeavor to be governed in the combat by the principles of fairness and generosity.

The reviewer maintains, that the action of the Boston Board was constitutional, but if it were otherwise, that the South did not seek the proper remedy for the evil. We join issue with him, on both these points. We assert that the decision of the Acting Board was unconstitutional; but even if it were not, that the South adopted the only prudent and feasible course. . . .

The Reviewer is apprized that the unconstitutionality of the decision was not our only, nor indeed our chief objection to it. We considered it glaringly unjust to the South. It excludes the South, either directly or by fair inference, from all participation in the Foreign Mission enterprise, except in contributing funds, a privilege granted to the ungodly. If a slaveholder cannot be appointed a missionary, lest the appointment should imply, on the part of the Board, approbation of slavery, neither can he be appointed an agent, or to any office, for the same reason. Nor does the consequence stop here. If a slaveholder is unfit to be appointed to office, then those persons who own no slaves, but countenance slavery, are connected with slaveholding churches, and derive their authority to preach the gospel from them, are equally unfit; and these two classes embrace all the ministers in the South. We now ask — we put it to the common sense and candor of every man, Is it fair, is it equal — that the South shall participate in all the burdens of the Convention, and be excluded from all its privileges? Our lot has been cast in a land where slavery prevails. We did not originate it. Many of us lament most sincerely its existence. We did not choose the place of our birth. Many of us had slavery entailed on us by laws which we did not enact, and which we could not, even if it were politic to do so, repeal. We must, in many cases, retain possession of our slaves, or disregard the laws of the land, and the principles of humanity and religion. We claim for ourselves the right of acting in regard to this delicate and embarrassing subject, according to the dictates of our own consciences, without foreign control or interference. And we ask again, Is it just that we should be summarily excluded, by the mere action of the Board, from all participation in the work of sending the gospel to the heathen, save that of contributing money to the treasury? . . .

The separation has taken place. Posterity will judge of the matter, and lay the responsibility where it ought to be laid. At any rate, we must all soon appear at a tribunal where no sophistry can deceive, and no partiality pervert judgment. In view of this solemn reckoning, the best of us have great cause to exclaim, "Lord, enter not into judgment with thy servants." Henceforward, let there be no strife between the North and South. We are brethren. Our interest is one and indivisible. Entertaining similar views of the kingdom of Christ, we should vie with each other in labors and sacrifices to extend and perpetuate it.

The Presbyterians

The last major separation, that of the Presbyterians, came in 1857. In that year, two major treatises reveal the depth of the divergence on an issue both moral and political. (1) Albert Barnes (1789-1870), graduate of Princeton Seminary and pastor of the First Presbyterian Church in Philadelphia, argued that the time for defense of slavery had passed; furthermore, he declared, to continue such a defense — and especially to base that defense on the Bible — was to bring calamity and ridicule down upon the entire Christian enterprise. (2) Frederick A. Ross (1796-1883), pioneer preacher in East Tennessee and then pastor of the Presbyterian Church in Huntsville, Alabama, took a sharply opposing view; addressing his brother minister directly,

---

[Sources: (1) Albert Barnes, *The Church and Slavery* (Philadelphia: Parry & McMillan, 1857), pp. 34-39. (2) Frederick A. Ross, *Slavery Ordained of God* (Philadelphia: J. B. Lippincott & Co., 1857), pp. 94, 95-97, 98-100, 101-2.]

Ross condemned that abolitionism which had tortured the Bible into an antislavery tract and into an automatic endorsement of everything that Thomas Jefferson might have thought or said.

1.

It is now impossible to convince the world that slavery is *right*, or is in accordance with the will of God. No decisions of councils or synods, and no teachings of a hierarchy, will change the onward course of opinion on this subject. No alleged authority of the Bible will satisfy men at large that the system is not always a violation of the laws that God has enstamped on the human soul. No apologies for it will take it out of the category of crime in the estimation of mankind at large, and place it in the category of virtues. The sentiment that it is wrong, — always wrong, — that it is a violation of the great laws of our being, — that it is contrary to the benevolent arrangements of the Maker of the race, — is becoming as fixed as the everlasting hills; and nothing can eradicate this sentiment from the hearts of mankind. This sentiment is becoming deeper and deeper in the convictions of the world every year; and, whatever may change, this is destined to remain unchangeably fixed. There is nothing more certain than that the world will *not* be brought to approve of slavery, and that the malediction of all good men will rest upon the system. No matter on what this sentiment impinges, it will be held; and nothing will be long held that is opposed to this deep conviction of the essential evil of the system. Men that are not otherwise disposed to be infidels *will* be infidels if, as the price of faith, they are required to abjure this conviction, and to hold that slavery is from God.

What, then, in this state of things, will be the effect of teaching that slavery is authorized by the Bible, — a professed revelation from God? That *in* that revelation slavery is contemplated as a permanent institution? That, according to the received interpretation, and the views of those who hold it to be a revelation from God, it is plainly implied that slavery is on the same basis as the relation of parent and child, guardian and ward, and as such is to be tolerated in the church, and to be among the things that are to be perpetuated and extended wherever the Bible controls human belief and conduct? That, according to the fair and received teachings of that book, it implies no more criminality to be a slaveholder than to be a father, a brother, or a neighbour? That the object of the Bible, so far as this is concerned, is to legislate *for* the system, and not to *remove* it; and that they who attempt to secure the emancipation of those held in bondage, and to impart to others the blessings of freedom, are 'radicals' and 'fanatics'? That to attempt to carry out practically the statement in the Declaration of Independence, that "*all* men are created equal," and "that they are endowed by their Creator with certain inalienable rights; that among these are life, LIB-

ERTY, and the pursuit of happiness," is a violation of all the teachings of God's revealed will to mankind? That men who seek to transfuse into their own bosoms, in behalf of the African race, the sentiments which made Samuel Adams and John Hancock what they were, cherish feelings at war with revealed religion? And that men who seek to carry out practically what the world has been struggling for in the great battles of liberty, are 'fanatics' and 'disorganizers,' — are enemies of the plain teaching of the Bible, and rejecters of the word of God?

On many minds there *can* be but one result of such views. It will be, so far as these are regarded as the teachings of the Bible, to lead men to reject the Bible; to confirm skeptics in infidelity; and to furnish an argument to the rejecter of revelation which it will not be possible to answer. Such views impinge on great principles of human nature, and are at war with the teachings of God in the human soul, and with the lessons drawn from his dealings with the nations of the earth. All that is great and noble in man; all the instinctive aspirations for freedom in his own bosom; all his desires for liberty for himself and for his children; all the deep convictions in the soul in regard to human rights and the inestimable value of liberty, is at war with such teachings; and all the struggles for freedom in the world — all the lessons of history — go to confirm the impression that a book which contains such views of human bondage — which would place it among the lawful relations of life, and make provision for its being perpetual — CANNOT be from God. Men will say, and say in a form which cannot be met, 'If such are the teachings of the Bible, it is impossible that that book should be a revelation given to mankind from the true God. He has written, as if "graven with an iron pen and lead in the rock forever," other lessons than these on the souls of men; and both cannot be true. Nothing can be more certain than that man was formed by his Maker for freedom, and that all men have a right to be free. Nothing can be more true than the declaration in the immortal instrument which asserts our national independence, that "all men are created equal; that they are endowed by their Creator with certain inalienable rights; and that among these are life and LIBERTY." Nothing can be more certain than that God has implanted in the human soul a desire of liberty which is a fair expression of what he intends shall be the settled condition of things in the world. We want no book,' such men will go on to say, 'which proclaims other doctrines than these; we can embrace no book as a revelation from God which does not coincide with the great laws of our nature, — those laws which proclaim that all men have a right to be free. No book which departs in its teachings from those great laws CAN POSSIBLY BE FROM God.'

It is easy to see what would be the effect of similar teachings in any parallel case. Suppose it were alleged to be true that the Bible sanctioned polygamy, and that polygamy was regarded there as on the same basis as the original relation of marriage, or as any other lawful relation of life. Suppose that this was affirmed, by a large class of the best interpreters, to be the teaching of the Bible, and that it was so regarded by the church at large. And suppose that constant apologies were made for the institution of polygamy, and that it was maintained that men in this relation were responsible only for the abuses of the system, — for the quarrels, brawls, strifes, and jealousies that grow out of it. And suppose that the terms 'fanatics' and 'enemies of the Bible' were freely applied in the church to all who should call in question the lawfulness of polygamy, and seek to restore marriage to what seems to be an obvious law of nature, — the connection with one wife. What would be the effect of this doctrine in regard to the reception of the Bible as a revelation from God? In Pagan, Mohammedan, and Mormon regions it might not operate extensively in preventing the belief that it might be a divine revelation: but what would be the effect in a civilized land? Millions there are who could not, and would not, receive a book with such teachings as containing a revelation from God; and, whatever pretended external evidences such a book might have in its favour, they would say, 'We cannot receive it as containing the teachings of divine wisdom. God has organized society on a different basis; and a book containing such teachings cannot be from heaven.'

2.

Rev. A. Barnes: —

Dear Sir: — You have recently published a tract: — "The Church and Slavery." . . .

I agree, and I disagree, with you. I harmonize in your words, — "The present is eminently a time when the views of every man on the subject of slavery should be uttered in unambiguous tones." I agree with you in this affirmation; because the subject has yet to be fully understood; because, when understood, if THE BIBLE does *not* sanction the system, the MASTER must cease to be the master. The SLAVE must cease to be the slave. He must be *free*, AND EQUAL IN POLITICAL AND SOCIAL LIFE. *That* is your *"unambiguous tone."* Let it be heard, if *that* is the word of God.

But if THE BIBLE *does* sanction the system, then *that* "unambiguous tone" will silence abolitionists who admit the Scriptures; it will satisfy all good men, and give peace to the country. That is the *"tone"* I want men to hear. Listen to it in the past and present speech of providence. The time was when *you* had the very *public sentiment* you are now trying to form. From Maine to Louisiana, the American mind was softly yielding to the impress of emancipation, in some hope, however vague and imaginary. Southern as well as Northern men, in the church and out of it, not having sufficiently studied the word of God, and, under our own and French revolutionary excitement, looking only at the evils of slavery, wished it away from the land. It was a *mistaken* public sentiment. Yet, such as it was, you had it, and it was doing your work. It was Quaker-like, mild and affectionate. It did not, however, work fast enough for you. You thought that the negro, with his superior attributes of body and mind and higher advantages of the nineteenth century, might reach, in a day, the liberty and equality which the Anglo-American had attained after the struggle of his ancestors during a thousand years! You got up the agitation. You got it up in the Church and State. You got it up over the length and breadth of this whole land. Let me show you some things you have secured, as the results of your work.

First Result of Agitation.

1. The most consistent abolitionists, affirming the sin of slavery, on the maxim of created equality and unalienable right, after torturing the Bible for a while, to make it give the same testimony, felt they could get nothing from the book. They felt that the God of the Bible disregarded the thumb-screw, the boot, and the wheel; that he would not speak for them, but against them. These consistent men have now turned away from the word, in despondency; and are seeking, somewhere, an abolition Bible, an abolition Constitution for the United States, and an abolition God.

This, sir, is the *first result* of your agitation: — the very van of your attack repulsed, and driven into infidelity.

A Second Result of Agitation.

2. Many others, and you among them, are trying in exactly the same way just mentioned to make the Bible speak against slave-holding. You get nothing by torturing the English version. People understand English. Nay, you get little by applying the rack to the Hebrew and Greek; even before a tribunal of men like you, who proclaim beforehand that Moses, in Hebrew, and Paul, in Greek, must condemn slavery because *"it is a violation of the first sentiments of the Declaration of Independence."* You find it difficult to persuade men that Moses and Paul were moved by the Holy Ghost to sanction the philosophy of Thomas Jefferson! You find it hard to make men believe that Moses saw in the mount, and Paul had vision in heaven, that this future *apostle of Liberty* was inspired by Jesus Christ. . . .

A Third Result of Agitation.

3. Meanwhile, many of your most pious men, soundest scholars, and sagacious observers of providence, have been led to study the Bible more faithfully in the

light of the times. And they are reading it more and more in harmony with the views which have been reached by the highest Southern minds, to wit: — That the relation of master and slave is sanctioned by the Bible; — that it is a relation belonging to the same category as those of husband and wife, parent and child, master and apprentice, master and hireling; — that the relations of husband and wife, parent and child, *were ordained in Eden for man, as man,* and *modified after the fall,* while the relation of slavery, as a system of labor, is *only one form of the government ordained of God over fallen and degraded man;* — that the *evils* in the system are *the same evils* of OPPRESSION we see in the relation of husband and wife, and all other forms of government; — that slavery, as a relation, suited to the more degraded or the more ignorant and helpless types of a sunken humanity, is, like all government, intended *as the proof of the curse of such degradation, and at the same time to elevate and bless;* — that the relation of husband and wife, being for man, as man, *will ever be over him,* while slavery will remain so long as God sees it best, as a controlling power over the ignorant, the more degraded and helpless; — and that, when he sees it for the good of the country, he will cause it to pass away, if the slave can be elevated to liberty and equality, political and social, with his master, *in* that country; or *out of* that country, if such elevation cannot be given therein, but may be realized in some other land: all which result must be left to the unfoldings of the divine will, *in harmony with the Bible,* and not to a newly-discovered dispensation. . . .

Another Result of Agitation.

4. The Southern slave-holder is now satisfied, as never before, that the relation of master and slave is sanctioned by the Bible; and he feels, as never before, the obligations of the word of God. He no longer, in his ignorance of the Scriptures, and afraid of its teachings, will seek to defend his common-sense opinions of slavery by arguments drawn from "Types of Mankind," and other infidel theories; but he will look, in the light of the Bible, on all the good and evil in the system. And when the North, as it will, shall regard him holding from God this high power for great good, — when the North shall no more curse, but bid him God-speed, — then he will bless himself and his slave, in nobler benevolence. With no false ideas of created equality and unalienable right, but with the Bible in his heart and hand, he will do justice and love mercy in higher and higher rule. Every evil will be removed, and the negro will be elevated to the highest attainments he can make, and be prepared for whatever destiny God intends. This, sir, is the *fourth result* of your agitation: — to make the Southern master *know,* from the Bible, his right to be a master, and his duty to his slave.

Women's Rights:
The Grimké Sisters and Theodore Weld

As the arguments over black rights grew vehement and vigorous, the notion of a corollary set of rights began to occur to many: the rights of women. Sojourner Truth had joined black rights and female rights together, even as Pastor Ross (in the excerpt above) had joined together the subjugation of both slaves and women. A major convert of Finney's revival preaching, Theodore Weld (1803-95) had turned all the weaponry of evangelical Protestantism against slavery, and had done so with telling effect. In 1838 Weld married another antislavery agitator, Angelina Grimké (1805-76). Together with her sister Sarah Grimké (1792-1873), Angelina spoke powerfully — and therefore threateningly — on behalf of abolition and the rights of women. For the two South Carolina sisters (Episcopalians who turned Quaker) soon found feminism and abolitionism to be indissolubly linked. (1) In 1836, Angelina Grimké, daring to present abolitionism to a most unlikely audience in a most unlikely region of the country, appealed to "the Christian women of the South" to join the battle for the slave's freedom. (2) In an exchange of letters between Weld and Angelina Grimké (this is prior to their marriage), the burning issue of women's rights, and all rights, are addressed; it seems, wrote Theodore Weld, that "Human rights are sex'd."

1.

Respected Friends,

It is because I feel a deep and tender interest in your present and eternal welfare that I am willing thus publicly to address you. Some of you have loved me as a relative, and some have felt bound to me in Christian sympathy, and Gospel fellowship; and even when compelled by a strong sense of duty, to break those outward bonds of union which bound us together as members of the same community, and members of the same religious denomination, you were generous enough to give me credit, for sincerity as a Christian, though you believed I had been most strangely deceived. I thanked you then for your kindness, and I ask you *now*, for the sake of former confidence, and former friend-

[Sources: (1) A. E. Grimké, *Appeal to the Christian Women of the South* (New York: Arno Press, 1969 [1836], pp. 1-3. (2) G. H. Barnes and D. L. Dumond, *Letters of Theodore Dwight Weld, Angelina Grimké Weld and Sarah Grimké, 1822-1844* (New York: D. Appleton-Century, 1934), I, 411-12, 414-16.]

ship, to read the following pages in the spirit of calm investigation and fervent prayer. . . . Solomon says, "faithful are the *wounds* of a friend." I do not believe the time has yet come when *Christian women* "will not endure sound doctrine," even on the subject of Slavery, if it is spoken to them in tenderness and love, therefore I now address *you.*

To all of you then, known or unknown, relatives or strangers, (for you are all *one* in Christ,) I would speak. I have felt for you at this time, when unwelcome light is pouring in upon the world on the subject of slavery; light which even Christians would exclude, if they could, from our country, or at any rate from the southern portion of it, saying, as its rays strike the rock bound coasts of New England and scatter their warmth and radiance over her hills and valleys, and from thence travel onward over the Palisades of the Hudson, and down the soft flowing waters of the Delaware and gild the waves of the Potomac, "hitherto shalt thou come and no farther;" I know that even professors of His name who has been emphatically called the "Light of the world" would, if they could, build a wall of adamant around the Southern States whose top might reach unto heaven, in order to shut out the light which is bounding from mountain to mountain and from the hills to the plains and valleys beneath, through the vast extent of our Northern States. But believe me, when I tell you, their attempts will be as utterly fruitless as were the efforts of the builders of Babel; and why? Because moral, like natural light, is so extremely subtle in its nature as to overleap all human barriers, and laugh at the puny efforts of man to control it. All the excuses and palliations of this system must inevitably be swept away, just as other "refuges of lies" have been, by the irresistible torrent of a rectified public opinion. "The *supporters* of the slave system," says Jonathan Dymond in his admirable work on the Principles of Morality, "will *hereafter* be regarded with the *same* public feeling, as he who was an advocate for the slave trade *now is.*" It will be, and that very soon, clearly perceived and fully acknowledged by all the virtuous and the candid, that in *principle* it is as sinful to hold a human being in bondage who has been born in Carolina, as one who has been born in Africa. All that sophistry of argument which has been employed to prove, that although it is sinful to send to Africa to procure men and women as slaves, who have never been in slavery, that still, it is not sinful to keep those in bondage who have come down by inheritance, will be utterly overthrown. We must come back to the good old doctrine of our forefathers who declared to the world, "this self evident truth that all men are created equal, and that they have certain *inalienable* rights among which are life, *liberty,* and the pursuit of happiness." It is even a greater absurdity to suppose a man can be legally born a slave under *our free Republican* Government, than under the petty despotisms of barbarian Africa. If then, we have no right to enslave an African, surely we can have none to enslave an American; if it is a self evident truth that *all* men, every where and of every color are born equal, and have an *inalienable right to liberty,* then it is equally true that *no* man can be born a slave, and no man can ever *rightfully* be reduced to *involuntary* bondage and held as a slave, however fair may be the claim of his master or mistress through wills and title-deeds.

2.

New York, N. Y. July 22. 37.
Saturday evening

My dear Sister Angelina

I have been in receipt of your letter five or six days. Should have answered it by return mail, but the most important members of the Executive Committee were out of town, and I have not been able to get a sight at the individual whom I wished most to see on the subject of your letter until nine o'clock tonight. *Seeing* them however has been with me a mere matter of course, in compliance with your request, and to relieve you of all anxiety, and not because I had the least doubt as to their feelings on the subject referred. Your relation to the Executive Committee seems rather a relation of Christian kindness — a sort of *co-operative* relation recognizing harmony of views and feelings, with common labors, joys and trials in a common cause, rather than *authority* on the one hand and a *representative* agency on the other. In short the relation which you sustain to the Ex. Com. no more attaches their *sanction* to your public holdings-forth to promiscuous assemblies than it does to your "theeing and thouing" or to your tight crimped caps, seven by nine bonnets, or that impenetrable drab that defieth utterly all amalgamation of colors! If any gainsay your speaking in public and to *men,* they gainsay the *Quakers* and not the *abolitionists.* They fly in the face of a *denominational* tenet, not an *anti slavery* doctrine or *measure.* I mean *distinctively:* I would to God that every anti slavery woman in this land had heart and head and womanhood enough and leisure withal to preach as did the captive woman in the second century to the warriors of a vandal army and to a barbarian monarch and his court till savage royalty laid off its robes at the foot of the cross and a fierce soldiery relaxed and wept under the preaching of a woman. God give thee a mouth and wisdom to prophesy like the daughters of Philip, like Huldah and Deborah.

If the men wish to come, it is downright *slaveholding* to shut them out. *Slaveholders* undertake to say that *one* class of human beings shall not be profited by public ministrations. I pray you leave slaveholders "alone in their glory". If I should ever be in the vicinity of your meetings I shall act on the principle that he that hath ears to hear hath a right to *use* them; and if you undertake to stuff them with cotton or to barricade them with brick and mortar, we'll have just as much of a breeze about it as can be made at all consistent with "peace principles".

Why! folks talk about women's preaching as tho' it was next to highway robbery — eyes astare and mouth agape. Pity women were not born with a split stick on their tongues! Ghostly dictums have fairly beaten it into the heads of the whole world save a fraction, that *mind* is *sexed,* and *Human rights* are *sex'd, moral obligation sex'd;* and to carry out the farce they'll probably beat up for a general match making and all turn in to pairing off in couples matrimonial, *consciences,* accountabilities, arguments, duties, philosophy, facts, and theories in the abstract. So much for the "March of mind", i.e. proxy-thinking, India rubber consciences, expediency, tom fooleries, with "whatsoever defileth and worketh abomination and maketh a lie". But enough of *this.*

Groton [Mass.] 8th Month 12. [1837]

My Dear Brother

No doubt thou hast heard by this time of all the fuss that is now making in this region about our stepping so far out of the bounds of female propriety as to lecture to promiscuous assemblies. My auditors literally sit some times with "mouths agape and eyes astare", so that I cannot help smiling in the midst of "rhetorical flourishes" to witness their perfect amazement at hearing a woman speak in the churches. I wish thou couldst see Brother Phelp's letter to us on this subject and sisters admirable reply. I suppose he will soon come out with a conscientious protest against us. I am waiting in some anxiety to see what the Executive Committee mean to do in these troublous times, whether to renounce us or not. But seriously speaking, we are placed very unexpectedly in a very trying situation, in the forefront of an entirely new contest — a contest for the *rights* of *woman* as a moral, intelligent and responsible being. Harriet Martineau[18] says "God and man know that the time has not come for women to make their injuries even heard of": but it seems as tho' it had come *now* and that the exigency must be met with the firmness and faith of woman in by gone ages. I cannot help feeling some regret that this sh'ld have come up *before* the Anti Slavery question was settled, so fearful am I that it may injure that blessed cause, and then again I think this must be the Lord's time and therefore the *best* time, for it seems to have been brought about by a concatenation of circumstances over which we had no control. The fact is it involves the interests of every minister in our land and therefore they will stand almost in a solid phalanx against woman's rights and I am afraid the discussion of this question will divide in Jacob and scatter in Israel; it will also touch every man's interests at

---

18. Harriet Martineau (1802-1876), noted British author, traveled throughout the United States in 1834-1836, met many of the abolitionists, and eulogized them in *The Martyr Age in America* (London, 1838). The complete account of her experiences in this country is contained in *Society in America,* 3 vols. (London, 1837), and *Retrospect of Western Travel,* 3 vols. (London, 1838).

home, in the tenderest relation of life; it will go down into the very depths of his soul and cause great searchings of heart. I am glad H. Winslow[19] of Boston has come out so boldly and told us just what I believe is in the hearts of thousands of men in our land. I must confess my womanhood is insulted, my moral feelings outraged when I reflect on these things, and I am sure *I know just* how the free colored people feel towards the whites when they pay them more than common attention; it is *not paid as a* RIGHT, but *given as a* BOUNTY on a *little* more than *ordinary* sense. There is not one man in 500 who really understands what kind of attention is alone acceptable to a woman of pure and exalted moral and intellectual worth. Hast thou read Sisters letters in the Spectator?[20] I want thee to read them and let us know what thou thinkest of them. That a wife is *not* to be subject to her husband in any other sense than I am to her or she to me, seems to be strange and *alarming* doctrine indeed, but how can it be otherwise unless *she surrenders her moral responsibility,* which *no woman has a right* to do? . . . WHO will stand by woman in the great struggle? As to our being Quakers being an *excuse* for our speaking in public, we do *not* stand on this ground at all; we ask *no* favors for ourselves, but *claim* rights for our *sex.* If it is wrong for woman to lecture or preach then let the Quakers give up their false views, and let other sects refuse to hear their women, but if it is *right* then let *all* women who have gifts, "mind their calling" and enjoy "the liberty wherewith Christ hath made them free", in that declaration of Paul, "In Christ Jesus there is neither male nor female." O! if in our intercourse with each other we realized this great truth, how delightful, ennobling and dignified it would be, but as I told the Moral Reform Society of Boston in my address, *this* reformation *must begin with ourselves.*

19. Hubbard Winslow (1799-1864), graduate of Yale, studied theology for two years at Andover and completed his theological course at Yale. At this time he was preaching in the Bowdoin Street Congregational Church at Boston, Lyman Beecher's old charge. His sermon on the divine limitations upon woman's activities was later expanded into the treatise, *The Appropriate Sphere of Woman* (Boston, 1840). He was more widely known for his numerous books and tracts than for his preaching.

20. Sarah Grimké's letters were first published in the *New England Spectator,* and then printed under the title, *Letters on the Condition of Woman and the Equality of the Sexes* (Boston, 1838).

[All notes are those of editors Barnes and Dumond.]

Indian Rights: The Cherokees

U.S. House of Representatives

If blacks and women were slowly making a few gains in nineteenth-century America, Indians were not. When Indian-fighter Andrew Jackson became the seventh president of the United States in 1828, the policy of Indian removal proved irresistible. That such policy should be exercised against the Cherokees of northwest Georgia only magnified the irony and the agony. For these Indians were the most civilized, the most Christianized of all. If whites could not live beside such Indians as these in peace and harmony, then what Indians? And where? For the moral dimensions of this decision to remove, portions of a long speech delivered to the House of Representatives in 1831 will serve. The speaker, Unitarian clergyman and Massachusetts congressman Edward Everett (1794-1865), found little to commend in the whole sorry record of federal policy regarding the Indians.

I cannot disguise my impression, that it is the greatest question which ever came before Congress, short of the question of peace and war. It concerns not an individual, but entire communities of men, whose fate is wholly in our hands, and concerns them — not to the extent of affecting their interests, more or less favorably, within narrow limits. As I regard it, it is a question of inflicting the pains of banishment from their native land on seventy or eighty thousand human beings, the greater part of whom are fixed and attached to their homes in the same way that we are. We have lately seen this House in attendance, week after week, at the bar of the other House, while engaged in solemn trial of one of our own functionaries, for having issued an order to deprive a citizen of his liberty for twenty-four hours. It is a most extraordinary and astonishing fact, that the policy of the United States toward the Indians — a policy coeval with the revolution, and sanctioned in the most solemn manner on innumerable occasions — is undergoing a radical change, which, I am persuaded, will prove as destructive to the welfare and lives of its subjects, as it will to their rights; and that neither this House, nor the other House, has ever, even by resolution, passed directly upon the question.

But it is not merely a question of the welfare of these dependent beings, nor yet of the honor and faith of the country which are pledged to them — it is a question of the Union itself. What is the Union? Not a mere abstraction; not a

---

[Source: W. E. Washburn, ed., *The American Indian and the United States: A Documentary History* (New York: Random House, 1973), II, 1128-29, 1164-67.]

word; not a form of Government; it is the undisputed paramount operation, through all the States, of those functions with which the Government is clothed by the constitution. When that operation is resisted, the Union is in fact dissolved. I will not now dwell on this idea; but the recent transactions in Georgia have been already hailed in the neighboring British provinces as the commencement of that convulsion of these United States, to which the friends of liberty throughout the world look forward with apprehension, as a fatal blow to their cause. . . .

The President has, with his annual message, sent us a letter from the superintendent of the Bureau of Indian Affairs, in which that officer states that the law of 1802 "is the principal one which governs all our relations with the Indian tribes," and recommends its revisal and modification, to suit the changes produced by subsequent treaties, and other causes. The same message is accompanied by the letter from the Secretary of War, to which I have already referred; telling us that the provisions of that law are unconstitutional, and the President neglects to enforce them in favor of those tribes over which the States have extended their laws.

Let us, then, the Congress of the United States, if we think this law is constitutional, make provision to execute it; if we think it is defective, let us amend it. If we think it is unconstitutional, let us repeal it. That law, by which all our Indian relations are regulated, ought not surely to remain in its present state.

If the treaties are constitutional, let us enforce them. If they are unconstitutional, let us abrogate them; let us repeal the proviso of the last session; declare them null and void, and make what compensation we can to the deluded beings who, relying upon our faith, have, at different periods, ceded to us mighty and fertile regions, as a consideration for the guaranty contained in these compacts. . . .

Sir, I will not believe that Georgia will persevere. She will not, for this poor corner, scarcely visible on the map of her broad and fertile domains, permit a reproach to be cast upon her and the whole Union to the end of time.

As for the character of the country to which it is proposed to remove the Indians, I want only light. It was all we asked last session; all I ask now. I quoted then all the authorities, favorable as well as unfavorable, with which I was acquainted. The friends of the policy refused us the only means of getting authentic information on the subject — a commission of respectable citizens of the United States, sent out for the purpose. Since the subject was discussed last session, two more witnesses, not then heard, have spoken. Dr. James, who was appointed to accompany Colonel Long on his tour of exploration in this region, has thus expressed himself: "The region to which Mr. McCoy proposes to remove the Indians would, such is its naked and inhospitable character, soon reduce civilized men who should be confined to it to barbarism."

In 1827, before this question was controverted, a report was made by the commissioners appointed to lay out a road from the western boundary of Missouri to Santa Fe, in New Mexico. These commissioners report, that, in the whole line of their march, extending seven hundred miles, if all the wood which they passed were collected into one forest, it would not exceed a belt of trees three miles in width!

But all this does not change the question. It merely suggests the possibility of an alternative of evil. If all the land were as fertile as some small part of it probably is; if it were as safe from the wild tribes of the desert, as it is notoriously exposed; if wood and water were as abundant as they are confessedly scarce; if it were the paradise which it is not; so much the worse for the Indians — the miserable victims whom we are going to delude into it. The idea that they can there be safe is perfectly chimerical; and every argument to show that the land is good, is an argument of demonstration that they will soon be driven from it. If all these treaties cannot save them, nothing can. What pledges can we give stronger than we have given?

It is partly for this reason that I urge the House to settle the question; and the more plainly we meet it, if we settle it against the Indians, the more humane will be our conduct. If we intend to be faithless to all these compacts, let our want of faith be made as signal and manifest as it can be.

Here, at the centre of the nation, beneath the portals of the capitol, let us solemnly auspicate the new era of violated promises, and tarnished faith. Let us kindle a grand council-fire, not of treaties made and ratified, but of treaties annulled and broken. Let us send to our archives for the worthless parchments, and burn them in the face of day. There will be some yearnings of humanity as we perform the solemn act. They were negotiated for valuable considerations; we keep the consideration, and break the bond. One gave peace to our afflicted frontier; another protected our infant settlements. Many were made when we were weak; nearly all at our earnest request. Many of them were negotiated under the instructions of Washington, of Adams, and of Jefferson — the fathers of our liberty. They are gone, and will not witness the spectacle; but our present Chief Magistrate, as he lays them, one by one, on the fire, will see his own name subscribed to a goodly number of them.

Sir, they ought to be destroyed, as a warning to the Indians to make no more compacts with us. The President tells us that the Choctaw treaty is probably the last which we shall make with them. This is well; though, if they remain on our soil, I do not see how future treaties are to be avoided. But I trust it is the last we shall make with them; that they will place themselves beyond the reach of our treaties and our laws; of our promises. . . .

Sir, it is for this Congress to say whether such is the futurity we will entail on these dependent tribes. If they must go, let it not be to any spot within the United States. They are not safe; they cannot bind us — they cannot trust us. We shall solemnly promise, but we shall break our word. We shall sign and seal, but we shall not perform. Let them go to Texas; let them join the Camanches, for their sakes, and for ours; for theirs, to escape the disasters of another removal — for ours, that we may be spared its shame.

Cherokee Nation v. *State of Georgia* (1831)

In 1831 the issue of human rights came to the Supreme Court of the United States, and it came in the form of the rights of Cherokees as a treaty-making nation. In violation of all previous agreements and understandings with this small nation, the state of Georgia had moved to evict, to destroy the national and cultural integrity of the Cherokee people. President Jackson took no step in their defense. Congress formed no wall of opposition. The Indians' last hope lay with the Supreme Court, and that hope was soon dashed. The Cherokee nation was not really a foreign power with a right to sue, the Court concluded, but a "domestic dependent nation" with no standing before the Court. "If it be true that the Cherokee nation have rights, this is not the tribunal in which those rights are to be asserted. If it be true that wrongs have been inflicted . . . this is not the tribunal which can redress the past or prevent the future." That bleak decision was not unanimous, and the vigorous dissent of Justice Smith Thompson is excerpted below. It was not enough, however, to "prevent the future."

Mr. Justice Thompson, dissenting. — Entertaining different views of the questions now before us in this case, and having arrived at a conclusion different from that of a majority of the court, and considering the importance of the case and the constitutional principle involved in it; I shall proceed, with all due respect for the opinion of others, to assign the reasons upon which my own has been formed.

In the opinion pronounced by the court, the merits of the controversy between the state of Georgia and the Cherokee Indians have not been taken into consideration. The denial of the application for an injunction has been placed solely on the ground of want of jurisdiction in this court to grant the relief prayed for. It became, therefore, unnecessary to inquire into the merits of the case. But thinking as I do that the court has jurisdiction of the case, and may grant relief, at least in part; it may become necessary for me, in the course of my opinion, to glance at the merits of the controversy; which I shall, however, do very briefly, as it is important so far as relates to the present application. . . .

[Source: W. E. Washburn, ed., *The American Indian and the United States: A Documentary History* (New York: Random House, 1973), IV, 2580-81, 2583-84, 2598-99. Quotation above is taken from p. 2558.]

Whether the Cherokee Indians are to be considered a foreign state or not, is a point on which we cannot expect to discover much light from the law of nations. We must derive this knowledge chiefly from the practice of our own government, and the light in which the nation has been viewed and treated by it.

That numerous tribes of Indians, and among others the Cherokee nation, occupied many parts of this country long before the discovery by Europeans, is abundantly established by history; and it is not denied but that the Cherokee nation occupied the territory now claimed by them long before that period. It does not fall within the scope and object of the present inquiry to go into a critical examination of the nature and extent of the rights growing out of such occupancy, or the justice and humanity with which the Indians have been treated, or their rights respected.

That they are entitled to such occupancy, so long as they choose quietly and peaceably to remain upon the land, cannot be questioned. The circumstance of their original occupancy is here referred to, merely for the purpose of showing, that if these Indian communities were then, as they certainly were, nations, they must have been foreign nations, to all the world; not having any connexion, or alliance of any description, with any other power on earth. And if the Cherokees were then a foreign nation; when or how have they lost that character, and ceased to be a distinct people, and become incorporated with any other community?

They have never been, by conquest, reduced to the situation of subjects to any conqueror, and thereby lost their separate national existence, and the rights of self government, and become subject to the laws of the conqueror. When ever wars have taken place, they have been followed by regular treaties of peace, containing stipulations on each side according to existing circumstances; the Indian nation always preserving its distinct and separate national character. And notwithstanding we do not recognize the right of the Indians to transfer the absolute title of their lands to any other than ourselves; the right of occupancy is still admitted to remain in them, accompanied with the right of self government, according to their own usages and customs; and with the competency to act in a national capacity, although placed under the protection of the whites, and owing a qualified subjection so far as is requisite for public safety. But the principle is universally admitted, that this occupancy belongs to them as matter of right, and not by mere indulgence. They cannot be disturbed in the enjoyment of it, or deprived of it, without their free consent; or unless a just and necessary war should sanction their dispossession. . . .

That the Cherokee nation of Indians have, by virtue of these treaties, an exclusive right of occupancy of the lands in question, and that the United States are bound under their guarantee, to protect the nation in the enjoyment of such occupancy; cannot, in my judgment, admit of a doubt; and that some of the laws of Georgia set out in the bill are in violation of, and in conflict with those treaties and the act of 1802, is to my mind equally clear. But a majority of the court having refused the injunction, so that no relief whatever can be granted, it would be a fruitless inquiry for me to go at large into an examination of the extent to which relief might be granted by this court, according to my own view of the case.

I certainly, as before observed, do not claim, as belonging to the judiciary, the exercise of political power. That belongs to another branch of the government. The protection and enforcement of many rights, secured by treaties, most certainly do not belong to the judiciary. It is only where the rights of persons or property are involved, and when such rights can be presented under some judicial form of proceedings, that courts of justice can interpose relief.

This court can have no right to pronounce an abstract opinion upon the constitutionality of a state law. Such law must be brought into actual or threatened operation, upon rights properly falling under judicial cognizance, or a remedy is not to be had here.

The laws of Georgia set out in the bill, if carried fully into operation, go the length of abrogating all the laws of the Cherokees, abolishing their government, and entirely subverting their national character. Although the whole of these laws may be in violation of the treaties made with this nation, it is probable this court cannot grant relief to the full extent of the complaint. Some of them, however, are so directly at variance with these treaties and the laws of the United States touching the rights of property secured to them, that I can perceive no objection to the application of judicial relief. The state of Georgia certainly could not have intended these laws as declarations of hostility, or wish their execution of them to be viewed in any manner whatever as acts of war; but merely as an assertion of what is claimed as a legal right: and in this light ought they to be considered by this court.

Worcester v. State of Georgia (1832)

A Congregational missionary to the Cherokees, Samuel A. Worcester (1798-1859) resisted the systematic effort to undermine if not destroy the Cherokee nation. Taking advantage of the Cherokee alphabet developed by the brilliant Sequoyah (c. 1770-1843), Worcester had translated a portion of the Bible into Cherokee and encouraged the Indians in the publication of their own newspaper. For opposing the state of Georgia and refusing to acknowledge its authority with respect to the Cherokees, Worcester received a sen-

[Source: W. E. Washburn, ed., *The American Indian and the United States: A Documentary History* (New York: Random House, 1973), IV, 2621-22, 2623.]

tence of four years at hard labor in the penitentiary. The missionary ap-
pealed to the Supreme Court, was upheld, and was eventually released. None
of this did much for the Cherokees, however, who were forced to follow "the
trail of tears" from their native homeland to Oklahoma.

The Indian nations had always been considered as distinct, independent political communities, retaining their original natural rights, as the undisputed possessors of the soil, from time immemorial, with the single exception of that imposed by irresistible power, which excluded them from intercourse with any
other European potentate than the first discoverer of the coast of the particular
region claimed: and this was a restriction which those European potentates imposed on themselves, as well as on the Indians. The very term "nation," so generally applied to them, means "a people distinct from others." The constitution,
by declaring treaties already made, as well as those to be made, to be the supreme law of the land, has adopted and sanctioned the previous treaties with
the Indian nations, and consequently admits their rank among those powers
who are capable of making treaties. The words "treaty" and "nation" are words
of our own language, selected in our diplomatic and legislative proceedings, by
ourselves, having each a definite and well understood meaning. We have applied them to Indians, as we have applied them to the other nations of the earth.
They are applied to all in the same sense.

   Georgia, herself, has furnished conclusive evidence that her former opinions on this subject concurred with those entertained by her sister states, and by
the government of the United States. Various acts of her legislature have been
cited in the argument, including the contract of cession made in the year 1802,
all tending to prove her acquiescence in the universal conviction that the Indian
nations possessed a full right to the lands they occupied, until that right should
be extinguished by the United States, with their consent: that their territory was
separated from that of any state within whose chartered limits they might reside, by a boundary line, established by treaties: that, within their boundary,
they possessed rights with which no state could interfere: and that the whole
power of regulating the intercourse with them, was vested in the United States.
A review of these acts, on the part of Georgia, would occupy too much time,
and is the less necessary, because they have been accurately detailed in the argument at the bar. Her new series of laws, manifesting her abandonment of these
opinions, appears to have commenced in December 1828.

   In opposition to this original right, possessed by the undisputed occu-
pants of every country; to this recognition of that right, which is evidenced by
our history, in every change through which we have passed; is placed the
charters granted by the monarch of a distant and distinct region, parcelling out
a territory in possession of others whom he could not remove and did not attempt to remove, and the cession made of his claims by the treaty of peace.

Sequoyah of the Cherokees
Sequoyah's Indian alphabet helped make the Cherokees among the most
literate of the American Indian tribes; their degree of assimilation
heightened the tragic irony of the abuse they suffered.
(National Portrait Gallery, Smithsonian Institution, Washington, D.C.)

The actual state of things at the time, and all history since, explain these charters; and the king of Great Britain, at the treaty of peace, could cede only what belonged to his crown. These newly asserted titles can derive no aid from the articles so often repeated in Indian treaties; extending to them, first, the protection of Great Britain, and afterwards that of the United States. These articles are associated with others, recognizing their title to self government. The very fact of repeated treaties with them recognizes it; and the settled doctrine of the law of nations is, that a weaker power does not surrender its independence — its right to self government, by associating with a stronger, and taking its protection. A weak state, in order to provide for its safety, may place itself under the protection of one more powerful, without stripping itself of the right of government, and ceasing to be a state. Examples of this kind are not wanting in Europe. "Tributary and feudatory states," says Vattel, "do not thereby cease to be sovereign and independent states, so long as self government and sovereign and independent authority are left in the administration of the state." At the present day, more than one state may be considered as holding its right of self government under the guarantee and protection of one or more allies.

The Cherokee nation, then, is a distinct community, occupying its own territory, with boundaries accurately described, in which the laws of Georgia can have no force, and which the citizens of Georgia have no right to enter, but with the assent of the Cherokees themselves, or in conformity with treaties, and with the acts of congress. The whole intercourse between the United States and this nation, is, by our constitution and laws, vested in the government of the United States.

The act of the state of Georgia, under which the plaintiff in error was prosecuted, is consequently void, and the judgment a nullity. . . .

It is the opinion of this court that the judgment of the superior court for the county of Gwinnett, in the state of Georgia, condemning Samuel A. Worcester to hard labour, in the penitentiary of the state of Georgia, for four years, was pronounced by that court under colour of a law which is void, as being repugnant to the constitution, treaties, and laws of the United States, and ought, therefore, to be reversed and annulled.

Suggested Reading (Chapter Five)

The antebellum period marked the high-water mark in America for theology that was both carefully wrought from internal church sources and publicly influential through sermons, journal articles, and books. Four works that feature authors from this period, though with coverage for American history as a whole, are Sydney E. Ahlstrom, ed., *Theology in America* (1967), Patrick W. Carey, ed., *American Catholic Religious Thought* (1987), Mark G. Toulouse and James O. Duke, eds., *Makers of Christian Theology in America* (1997), and Toulouse and Duke, eds., *Sources of Christian Theology in America* (1999). A magisterial overview of theology treated in its internal development is provided by E. Brooks Holifield, *Theology in America: Christian Thought from the Age of the Puritans to the Civil War* (2003), a volume complemented by the externally oriented treatment in Mark A. Noll, *America's God, from Jonathan Edwards to Abraham Lincoln* (2002). On the individual theologians excerpted in this chapter, see Henry Bowden's edition of Baird's *Religion in America* (chapter four); for Alexander Campbell, the early chapters of Richard T. Hughes, *Reviving the Ancient Faith: The Story of Churches of Christ in America* (1996); John W. Stewart and James H. Moorhead, eds., *Charles Hodge Revisited* (2002); for Phoebe Palmer, Melvin Easterday Dieter, *The Holiness Revival of the Nineteenth Century* (1980); Robert Bruce Mullin, *The Puritan as Yankee: A Life of Horace Bushnell* (2002); William DiPuccio, *The Interior Sense of Scripture: The Sacred Hermeneutics of John W. Nevin* (1998); and for Charles Porterfield Krauth, Theodore G. Tappert, ed., *Lutheran Confessional Theology in America, 1840-1880* (1972).

The emigration of German Jews to nineteenth-century America is briefly but clearly described in Nathan Glazer's survey, *American Judaism* (rev. ed., 1972), but sharper focus on Isaac Leeser is found in Lance Jonathan Sussman, *Isaac Leeser and the Making of American Judaism* (1995). For Isaac Mayer Wise, the sources are more plentiful, including J. G. Heller, *Isaac M. Wise: His Life, Work, and Thought* (1965), and Sefton D. Temkin, *Isaac Mayer Wise: Shaping American Judaism* (1992). For problems encountered by Jews in the nineteenth century, see Morton Borden's *Jews, Turks, and Infidels* (1984), and for the same history in even broader context, Naomi Cohen, *Jews in Christian America* (1992). For Roman Catholicism before the Civil War, the best avenue of access to issues confronting the country, this church, and the relationship between the two is through the lives of Orestes Brownson and Isaac Hecker. On Brownson, a portion of whose momentous output is available in twenty published volumes, see Hugh Marshall, *Orestes Brownson and the American Republic* (1972), and the helpful anthology edited by Patrick W. Carey, *Orestes Brownson* (1991). One story of Hecker's life became itself part of the controversy between Roman Catholicism from a European perspective and from an American one, namely, Walter Elliot's *Life of Father Hecker* (1972 [1891]), with a controversial introduction by Bishop John Ireland. Solid studies of Hecker include John Farina, *An American Experience of God: The Spirituality of Isaac Hecker* (1981), and David J. O'Brien, *Isaac Hecker: An American Catholic* (1992). The classic treatment of the first bishop of Charleston, South Carolina, is that of Peter Guilday, *The Life and Times of John England, 1786-1842*, 2 vols. (1969 [1927]). For the attraction of Catholicism to an elite group of New England savants, see Jenny Franchot, *Roads to Rome: The Antebellum Protestant Encounter with Catholicism* (1994), and for the Catholic story in a major American city, Dale B. Light, *Rome and the New Republic: Conflict and Community in Philadelphia Catholicism between the Revolution and the Civil War* (1996). Kenneth J. Zanca provides a useful set of documents in *American Catholics and Slavery, 1789-1866* (1994).

The unhappy story of American nativism does not end with the Civil War. For the earlier episodes, see Ray Allen Billington's enduring *The Protestant Crusade, 1800-1860* (1938), and for later, John Higham, *Strangers in the Land: Patterns of American Nativism* (1955). Several of the essays in Robert N. Bellah and Frederick E. Greenspahn, *Uncivil Religion: Interreligious Hostility in America* (1987), treat similar themes.

For revivals of Native American religion, the classic account is Anthony F. C. Wallace, *The Death and Rebirth of the Seneca* (1969). But see also Michael Hittman, *Wovoka and the Ghost Dance* (1990), David Aberle, *The Peyote Religion Among the Navaho* (1991), and Gregory Evans Dowd, *A Spirited Resistance: The North American Struggle for Unity, 1745-1815* (1992).

Studies of slavery, including slave religion, have reached a level of great sophistication. Paving the way for a number of important studies were a classic overview by Albert J. Raboteau, *Slave Religion: The "Invisible Institution" in the Antebellum South* (1978), and an equally impressive reconstruction of slave existence by Eugene D. Genovese, *Roll, Jordan Roll: The World the Slaves Made* (1974). A volume edited by David W. Wills and Richard Newman, *Black Apostles at Home and Abroad: Afro-Americans and the Christian's Mission from the Revolution to Reconstruction* (1982), sheds much light on a neglected theme. The role of African Americans in emancipation is demonstrated, with focus on the United States, by Benjamin Quarles, *Black Abolitionists* (1969), and for the broader Atlantic world in Lamin O. Sanneh, *Abolitionists Abroad: American Blacks and the Making of Modern West Africa* (2000). An indispensable autobiography for this period was provided by Daniel A. Payne's *Recollection of Seventy Years* (1968 [1888]). Important biographical studies of important African Americans now include John Saillant, *Black Puritan, Black Republican: The Life and Thought of Lemuel Haynes, 1753-1833* (2003), David W. Blight, *Frederick Douglass's Civil War: Keeping Faith in Jubilee* (1989), and Nell Irvin Painter, *Sojourner Truth: A Life, a Symbol* (1996).

The denominational divisions over slavery that foreshadowed the political divisions of the Civil War is the subject of C. C. Goen, *Broken Churches, Broken Nation* (1985). The sisters Angelina and Sarah Grimké have been very well served by Gerda Lerner's excellent *The Grimké Sisters from South Carolina* (1967). Several books from William G. McLoughlin offer particularly astute treatment of Cherokee life, missionary attention, and community building and destruction, before, during, and after the Cherokee's forced exit from northern Georgia, including *Cherokees and Missionaries, 1783-1839* (1984), *Cherokee Renaissance in the New Republic* (1986), *Champions of the Cherokees: Evans and John B. Jones* (1990), and *After the Trail of Tears: The Cherokee's Struggle for Sovereignty, 1839-1880* (1993).

SIX

Sectional Crisis and Reconstruction

The Civil War has been called "the second American Revolution" for at least two reasons. For the South, it represented an effort to break away from what was considered a tyrannical central government, and so reprised the themes of America's War for Independence. For the North, it represented a determination to preserve the Union at all costs, and so reshaped the tasks of government along with the scope of national power. For both regions, religious questions were everywhere predominant in what took place. Religious convictions loomed large in contentions that led to the war, religious activities and religious thought were prominent during the war, and religious hopes with disappointments were very much a part of Reconstruction and its aftermath. Even by comparison with the conflict to break with Great Britain, the Civil War was preeminently a war of religion.

Debate over Slavery

When war finally came in 1861, the narrow issue was the right of states to secede. But everyone knew that the issue over which some states were willing to secede, while others were resisting secession, was slavery — or more particularly, the question of whether slavery would be extended into the new territories of the United States. When Americans took up the question of slavery, reactions varied widely. Some found religion pointedly relevant to the question of slavery's retention or abolition; others found it irrelevant, since to them the issue was primarily political or economic not moral or theological. Among those who looked at the peculiar institution from the perspective of Christianity, the Bible was offered as a sure friend of slavery — and as its bitter foe. The Golden Rule was, to some, only another way of demanding emancipation now, while for others it was a call to paternal protection of the helpless and weak, of those yet in a child-like stage of development. Years before the nation itself took up arms in civil strife, churches had drawn themselves up into warring camps, challenging each other's motives, doctrines, honor, and loyalty to flag, faith, and God. Anyone closely observing the nation's religious opinion-makers in the 1840s and 1850s could not be surprised by the decision of the nation's states in the 1860s.

Americans who took up religious arguments for and against slavery came from all walks of life, and they developed almost every possible approach to the issue. Some were all-out champions of the existing system as directly ordained by God. Others defended slavery in principle while calling upon slave-holders to act with greater humanity to the slaves. Still others favored gradual emancipation, and of that number some wanted to see slave-owners paid for giving up their "property" while others considered it just for liberated slaves to be staked with "forty acres and a mule." Still others appealed for the immediate abolition of the system. For all of these views there were forceful religious arguments to hand, often backed by appeals to the "spirit" or the "letter" of the Scriptures.

The Civil War as a Religious Event

Whatever the arguments and however strenuously they were prosecuted, in the end, as Abraham Lincoln put it with laconic simplicity in his Second Inaugural Address, "And the war came." Once the conflict was under way, the attention of the churches shifted to the needs of troops in the field and to the privations of families left behind. Agencies like the Sanitary Commission, the Christian Commission, and the YMCA mobilized to provide practical help as well as religious assistance to military units. Corps of chaplains were recruited for both North and South. And religious perspectives informed much of the reporting on the war as well.

During the mid-nineteenth century and through the time of the Civil War, religious periodicals still dominated the landscape of popular and learned journalism. There was, as a consequence, an immense amount of commentary on the war and all of its related issues from religious angles of vision. The nature of theological reflection depended considerably on where it came from. Trust in providence was common, for example, but providence appeared to be acting differently depending upon where you stood in relation to the Mason-Dixon line. Theological commentary on the war ranged widely, but it was a central feature at all stages of the conflict.

Meditations on the Nation under God

Beyond explicitly theological commentary about the Civil War's events and circumstances, there were also a number of individuals who tried to step back in the effort to say what it all meant. The quality of such meditation was high, whether it came from professional churchmen like Philip Schaff and Charles Hodge, or from lay religious thinkers like John Brown and Abraham Lincoln. Their words focused attention at the time. In the case of some of the utterances of Abraham Lincoln, words from the era of the Civil War have remained alive as defining statements about the national purpose as a whole.

After the War

For one important body of Americans, the Civil War wrought a momentous as well as a beautiful creation: namely, freedom. The Emancipation Proclamation, which took effect in Confederate states on January 1, 1863, though far from having an immediate effect everywhere and far from curing all the ills of the black experience, nonetheless gave to freed men and women a great new hope. To realize the opportunities and aspirations of liberated slaves, the Constitution needed to be amended and national conscience needed to be reconstructed. The latter has taken longer than the former. But even in the midst of war and in the heart of the nation's capital, black Methodist Daniel Payne could celebrate the Emancipation, "yea, rather the *Redemption* of the enslaved people of the District of Columbia." To Payne, it was time to say, "Welcome to the Ransomed."

While emancipation could be seen as the end of one long road, most understood it as the beginning of another. Northern churches called for helpers to hurry to their side; for every thousand freed slaves, we require "at least one able, experienced, faithful missionary to preach to them, to teach, to organize and counsel them." Each missionary, moreover, required several teachers as assistants. And if a million should be emancipated, then a thousand missionaries will be required, with thousands more to be recruited as assistants. Schools did spring up, churches did gather money and deploy personnel, African Americans did join existing churches or set about creating their own. Not all was achieved that had been hoped, since the end of federally sponsored Reconstruction in 1876 led to a resurgence of whites-only power in the South. But for blacks and whites alike, the days after the Civil War were days of new beginnings that began to chart the shape of the country's religious life as it has existed to this day.

1. Debate over Slavery

Varieties of Abolitionism

Elijah Lovejoy (1802-37)

A Presbyterian minister and newspaper editor, Elijah Lovejoy published an abolitionist newspaper in St. Louis from 1833 to 1836. So great was the opposition to his antislavery stance that he moved across the Mississippi River to Alton, Illinois, where he vowed to publish the Alton Observer. *But opposition to abolitionism was no less in Illinois than it had been in Missouri. On Lovejoy's arrival in Alton in July 1836 his printing press was destroyed. A year later, in August 1837, an angry mob destroyed a second press and, in September, a third. In November of that same year, Lovejoy, determined that yet another press was not going to be dumped into the river, stood guard over his property. On November 7, 1837, he was shot and killed, a martyr to two causes: freedom of the press and freedom for blacks. (1) His sentiments with respect to slavery are given as of July 1837; (2) his futile plea, shortly before his death, for some assistance in the protection of his life and his property.*

1.
What Are the Doctrines of Anti-Slavery Men?

A young man had become exceedingly angry with an ancient philosopher, and had raised his cane to strike him. "Strike," said the philosopher — "strike, but

---

[Source: Joseph C. and Owen Lovejoy, *Memoir of the Rev. Elijah P. Lovejoy* . . . (New York: Arno Press, 1969 [1838]), (1) pp. 234-37; (2) pp. 278-81.]

hear me." He listened, and was convinced. There is not, probably, an individual, who reads this, that cannot recollect some instance in his life, in which his strong opposition to certain measures and principles, he now sees, was entirely owing to groundless and unreasonable prejudices; and he is a fortunate man who can recollect but one such instance.

In respect to the subject now to be discussed, the writer frankly confesses no one of his readers can possibly be more prejudiced, or more hostile to anti-slavery measures or men, than he once was. And his, too, were honest, though, alas! how mistaken, prejudices. They arose partly from the fact that the "new measures" came directly in contact with his former habits of thought and action, and partly, and chiefly, from the strange and astonishingly perverted representations given of leading men and their principles, in this new movement. We recollect no instance of parallel misrepresentation, except the charge brought against Christ of casting out devils by Beelzebub, the prince of devils. These misrepresentations were started by a few, and honestly believed by the many. They still prevail to a very great extent. Very probably some of our readers may be under their influence more or less. We ask them to be candid with themselves, and if they find this to be the case, to make an effort to throw them off, and come to the perusal of what follows, ready to embrace the truth wherever it is found. For truth is eternal, unchanging, though circumstances may, and do operate to give a different colour to it, in our view, at different times. And truth will prevail, and those who do not yield to it must be destroyed by it. What then are the doctrines of Anti-Slavery men?

First Principles.

1. Abolitionists hold that "all men are born free and equal, endowed by their Creator with certain inalienable rights, among which are life, LIBERTY, and the pursuit of happiness." They do not believe that these rights are abrogated, or at all modified by the colour of the skin, but that they extend alike to every individual of the human family.

2. As the above-mentioned rights are in their nature inalienable, it is not possible that one man can convert another into a piece of property, thus at once annihilating all his personal rights, without the most flagrant injustice and usurpation. But American Slavery does this — it declares a slave to be a "THING," a "CHATTEL," an article of personal "PROPERTY," a piece of "MERCHANDISE," and now actually holds TWO AND A HALF MILLIONS of our fellow-men in this precise condition.

3. Abolitionists, therefore, hold American Slavery to be a *wrong*, a legalized system of inconceivable injustice, and a SIN. That it is a sin against God, whose prerogative as the rightful owner of all human beings is usurped, and

against the slave himself, who is deprived of the power to dispose of his services as conscience may dictate, or his Maker require. And as whatever is morally wrong can never be politically right, and as the Bible teaches, and as Abolitionists believe, that "righteousness exalteth a nation, while sin is a reproach to any people," they also hold that Slavery is a political evil of unspeakable magnitude, and one which, if not removed, will speedily work the downfall of our free institutions, both civil and religious.

4. As the Bible inculcates upon man but one duty in respect to sin, and that is, immediate repentance; Abolitionists believe that all who hold slaves, or who approve the practice in others, should *immediately* cease to do so.

5. Lastly, Abolitionists believe, that as all men are *born* free, so all who are now held as slaves in this country were BORN FREE, and that they are slaves now is the sin, not of those who introduced the race into this country, but of those, and those alone, who now hold them, and have held them in Slavery from their birth. Let it be admitted, for argument's sake, that A or B has justly forfeited his title to freedom, and that he is now the rightful slave of C, bought with his money, how does this give C a claim to the posterity of A down to the latest generation? And does not the guilt of enslaving the successive generations of A's posterity belong to their respective masters, whoever they be? No where are the true principles of freedom and personal rights better understood than at the South, though their practice corresponds so wretchedly with their theory. Abolitionists adopt, as their own, the following sentiments, expressed by Mr. [John] Calhoun in a speech on the tariff question, delivered in the Senate of the United States, in 1833: — "He who *earns* the money — *who digs it out of the earth* with the sweat of his brow, has a *just title* to it against the Universe. *No* one has a right to touch it, *without his consent*, except his government, and *it only* to the extent of its legitimate wants: to take more is *robbery.*" Now, this is precisely what slave-holders do, and Abolitionists do but echo back their own language, when they pronounce it *"robbery."*

2.

"Mr. chairman — it is not true, as has been charged upon me, that I hold in contempt the feelings and sentiments of this community, in reference to the question which is now agitating it. I respect and appreciate the feelings and opinions of my fellow-citizens, and is one of the most painful and unpleasant duties of my life, that I am called upon to act in opposition to them. If you suppose, sir, that I have published sentiments contrary to those generally held in this community, because I delighted in differing from them, or in occasioning a disturbance, you have entirely misapprehended me. But, sir, while I value the good opinion of my fellow-citizens, as highly as any one, I may be permitted to

Elijah P. Lovejoy
(Library of Congress)

say, that I am governed by higher considerations than either the favour or the fear of man. I am impelled to the course I have taken, because I fear God. As I shall answer it to my God in the great day, I dare not abandon my sentiments, or cease in all proper ways to propagate them.

"I, Mr. Chairman, have not desired, or asked any *compromise.* I have asked for nothing but to be protected in my rights as a citizen — rights which God has given me, and which are guaranteed to me by the constitution of my country. Have I, sir, been guilty of any infraction of the laws? Whose good name have I injured? When and where have I published any thing injurious to the reputation of Alton? Have I not, on the other hand, laboured, in common, with the rest of my fellow-citizens, to promote the reputation and interests of this city? What, sir, I ask, has been my offence? Put your finger upon it — define it — and I stand ready to answer for it. If I have committed any crime, you can easily convict me. You have public sentiment in your favour. You have your juries, and you have your attorney, (looking at the Attorney-General,) and I have *no doubt* you can *convict* me. But if I have been guilty of no violation of law, why am I hunted up and down continually like a partridge upon the mountains? Why am I threatened with the *tar-barrel?* Why am I waylaid every day, and from night to night, and my life in jeopardy every hour?

"You have, sir, made up, as the lawyers say, a false issue; there are not two parties between whom there can be a *compromise.* I plant myself, sir, down on my unquestionable *rights,* and the question to be decided is, whether I shall be protected in the exercise, and enjoyment of those rights — *that is the question, sir;* — whether my property shall be protected, whether I shall be suffered to go home to my family at night without being assailed, and threatened with tar and feathers, and assassination — , whether my afflicted wife, whose life has been in jeopardy, from continued alarm and excitement, shall night after night be driven from a sick bed into the garret to save her life from the brickbats and violence of the mobs; *that sir, is the question.*" Here, much affected and overcome by his feelings, he burst into tears. Many, not excepting even his enemies, wept — several sobbed aloud, and the sympathies of the whole meeting were deeply excited. He continued. "Forgive me, sir, that I have thus betrayed my weakness. It was the allusion to my family that overcame my feelings. Not, sir, I assure you, from any fears on my part. I have no personal fears. Not that I feel able to contest the matter with the whole community, I know perfectly well I am not. I know, sir, that you can tar and feather me, hang me up, or put me into the Mississippi, without the least difficulty. But what then? Where shall I go? I have been made to feel that if I am not safe at Alton, I shall not be safe any where. I recently visited St. Charles to bring home my family, and was torn from their frantic embrace by a mob. I have been beset night and day at Alton. And now if I leave here and go elsewhere, violence may overtake me in my retreat, and I have no more claim upon the protection of any other community than I have upon this; and I have concluded, after consultation with my friends, and earnestly seeking counsel of God, to *remain at Alton,* and here to insist on protection in the exercise of my rights. If the civil authorities refuse to protect me, I must look to God; and if I die, I have determined to make my grave in Alton."

William Lloyd Garrison (1805-1879)

Immediately after he first began to publish The Liberator *in 1831, William Lloyd Garrison became famous (and also infamous) as the North's most ar-*

[Source: *The Liberator,* vol. 15, as printed in *William Lloyd Garrison, 1805-1879: The Story of His Life Told by His Children,* vol. 3 (New York: Century, 1889), pp. 145-47.]

dent proponent of abolitionism. Garrison, who was New England born and bred, had early been apprenticed as a printer, and then as a young man was influenced by contact with Quakers to move against slavery. What distinguished Garrison from many of his fellow abolitionists, however, was his willingness to give up certain aspects of traditional Christianity if they were thought to encourage slavery. The column reproduced below from 1845 details Garrison's arguments about the relative weight of traditional views concerning Scripture and what he took to be the moral mandates of the hour.

Of the millions who profess to believe in the Bible as the inspired word of God, how few there are who have had the wish or the courage to know on what ground they have formed their opinion! They have been taught that, to allow a doubt to arise in their minds on this point, would be sacrilegious, and to put in peril their salvation. They must believe in the plenary inspiration of the "sacred volume," or they are "infidels," who will justly deserve to be "cast into the lake of fire and brimstone." Imposture may always be suspected when reason is commanded to abdicate the throne; when investigation is made a criminal act; when the bodies or spirits of men are threatened with pains and penalties if they do not subscribe to the popular belief; when appeals are made to human credulity, and not to the understanding.

Now, nothing can be more consonant to reason than that the more valuable a thing is, the more it will bear to be examined. If the Bible be, from Genesis to Revelation, divinely inspired, its warmest partisans need not be concerned as to its fate. It is to be examined with the same freedom as any other book, and taken precisely for what it is worth. It must stand or fall on its own inherent qualities, like any other volume. To know what it teaches, men must not stultify themselves, nor be made irrational by a blind homage. Their reason must be absolute in judgment, and act freely, or they cannot know the truth. They are not to object to what is simply incomprehensible — because no man can comprehend how it is that the sun gives light, or the acorn produces the oak; but what is clearly monstrous, or absurd, or impossible, cannot be endorsed by reason, and can never properly be made a test of religious faith, or an evidence of moral character.

To say that everything contained within the lids of the Bible is divinely inspired, and to insist upon the dogma, as fundamentally important, is to give utterance to a bold fiction, and to require the suspension of the reasoning faculties. To say that everything in the Bible is to be believed, simply because it is found in that volume, is equally absurd and pernicious. It is the province of reason to "search the scriptures," and determine what in them is true, and what false — what is probable, and what incredible — what is historically true, and what fabulous — what is compatible with the happiness of mankind, and what ought to be rejected as an example or rule of action — what is the letter that killeth, and what the spirit that maketh alive. When the various books of the Bible were written, or by whom they were written, no man living can tell. This is purely a matter of conjecture; and as conjecture is not certainty, it ceases to be authoritative. Nor is it of vast consequence, in the eye of reason, whether they to whom the Bible is ascribed wrote it or not; whether Paul was the author of the Epistle to the Hebrews, or of any other Epistle which is attributed to him; whether Moses wrote the Pentateuch, or Joshua the history of his own exploits, or David the Psalms, or Solomon the Proverbs; or whether the real authors were some unknown persons. "What is writ, is writ," and it must stand or fall by the test of just criticism, by its reasonableness and utility, by the probabilities of the case, by historical confirmation, by human experience and observation, by the facts of science, by the intuition of the spirit. Truth is older than any parchment, and would still exist though a universal conflagration should consume all the books in the world. To discard a portion of scripture is not necessarily to reject the truth, but may be the highest evidence that one can give of his love of truth.

Harriet Beecher Stowe

Stowe, who is introduced above (p. 395), subscribed to a variety of abolitionism that was not as radical as William Lloyd Garrison's. Yet, especially as displayed in her landmark novel, Uncle Tom's Cabin *(1852), Stowe argued consistently against slavery. Because of the great popularity of that novel, she became one of the most important forces against slavery, both in the United States and through her many readers abroad. In the extract that follows, Stowe parodies the contention that slavery was supported by the Bible, a contention that enjoyed a great deal of support, as later selections in this chapter will demonstrate.*

"Well, ladies," said St. Clare, as they were comfortably seated at the dinner-table, "and what was the bill of fare at church to-day?"

"O, Dr. G — preached a splendid sermon," said Marie. "It was just such a sermon as you ought to hear; it expressed all my views exactly."

"It must have been very improving," said St. Clare. "The subject must have been an extensive one."

"Well, I mean all my views about society, and such things," said Marie. "The text was, 'He hath made everything beautiful in its season;' and he showed how all the orders and distinctions in society came from God; and that it was so

---

[Source: Harriet Beecher Stowe, *Uncle Tom's Cabin, or Life Among the Lowly* (Garden City, NY: Nelson Doubleday, ca. 1900), pp. 197-200.]

appropriate, you know, and beautiful, that some should be high and some low, and that some were born to rule and some to serve, and all that, you know; and he applied it so well to all this ridiculous fuss that is made about slavery, and he proved distinctly that the Bible was on our side, and supported all our institutions so convincingly. I only wish you'd heard him."

"O, I didn't need it," said St. Clare. "I can learn what does me as much good as that from the Picayune, any time, and smoke a cigar besides; which I can't do, you know, in a church."

"Why," said Miss Ophelia, "don't you believe in these views?"

"Who, — I? You know I'm such a graceless dog that these religious aspects of such subjects don't edify me much. If I was to say anything on this slavery matter, I would say out, fair and square, 'We're in for it; we've got 'em, and mean to keep 'em, — it's for our convenience and our interest;' for that's the long and short of it, — that's just the whole of what all this sanctified stuff amounts to, after all; and I think that will be intelligible to everybody, everywhere."

"I do think, Augustine, you are so irreverent!" said Marie. "I think it's shocking to hear you talk."

"Shocking! it's the truth. This religious talk on such matters, — why don't they carry it a little further, and show the beauty, in its season, of a fellow's taking a glass too much, and sitting a little too late over his cards, and various providential arrangements of that sort, which are pretty frequent among us young men; — we'd like to hear that those are right and godly, too."

"Well," said Miss Ophelia, "do you think slavery right or wrong?"

"I'm not going to have any of your horrid New England directness, cousin," said St. Clare, gayly. "If I answer that question, I know you'll be at me with half a dozen others, each one harder than the last; and I'm not a going to define my position. I am one of the sort that lives by throwing stones at other people's glass houses, but I never mean to put up one for them to stone."

"That's just the way he's always talking," said Marie; "you can't get any satisfaction out of him. I believe it's just because he don't like religion, that he's always running out in this way he's been doing."

"Religion!" said St. Clare, in a tone that made both ladies look at him. "Religion! Is what you hear at church religion? Is that which can bend and turn, and descend and ascend, to fit every crooked phase of selfish, worldly society, religion? Is that religion which is less scrupulous, less generous, less just, less considerate for man, than even my own ungodly, worldly, blinded nature? No! When I look for a religion, I must look for something above me, and not something beneath."

"Then you don't believe that the Bible justifies slavery," said Miss Ophelia.

"The Bible was my *mother's* book," said St. Clare. "By it she lived and died, and I would be very sorry to think it did. I'd as soon desire to have it proved that my mother could drink brandy, chew tobacco, and swear, by way of satisfying me that I did right in doing the same. It wouldn't make me at all more satisfied with these things in myself, and it would take from me the comfort of respecting her; and it really is a comfort, in this world, to have anything one can respect. In short, you see," said he, suddenly resuming his gay tone, "all I want is that different things be kept in different boxes. The whole frame-work of society, both in Europe and America, is made up of various things which will not stand the scrutiny of any very ideal standard of morality. It's pretty generally understood that men don't aspire after the absolute right, but only to do about as well as the rest of the world. Now, when any one speaks up, like a man, and says slavery is necessary to us, we can't get along without it, we should be beggared if we give it up, and, of course, we mean to hold on to it, — this is strong, clear, well-defined language; it has the respectability of truth to it; and, if we may judge by their practice, the majority of the world will bear us out in it. But when he begins to put on a long face, and snuffle, and quote Scripture, I incline to think he isn't much better than he should be."

"You are very uncharitable," said Marie.

"Well," said St. Clare, "suppose that something should bring down the price of cotton once and forever, and make the whole slave property a drug in the market, don't you think we should soon have another version of the Scripture doctrine? What a flood of light would pour into the church, all at once, and how immediately it would be discovered that everything in the Bible and reason went the other way!"

"Well, at any rate," said Marie, as she reclined herself on a lounge, "I'm thankful I'm born where slavery exists; and I believe it's right, — indeed, I feel it must be; and, at any rate, I'm sure I couldn't get along without it."

"I say, what do you think, Pussy?" said her father to Eva, who came in at this moment, with a flower in her hand.

"What about, papa?"

"Why, which do you like the best, — to live as they do at your uncle's, up in Vermont, or to have a house-full of servants, as we do?"

"O, of course, our way is the pleasantest," said Eva.

"Why so?" said St. Clare, stroking her head.

"Why, it makes so many more round you to love, you know," said Eva, looking up earnestly.

"Now, that's just like Eva," said Marie; "just one of her odd speeches."

"Is it an odd speech, papa?" said Eva, whisperingly, as she got upon his knee.

"Rather, as this world goes, Pussy," said St. Clare. "But where has my little Eva been, all dinner-time?"

"O, I've been up in Tom's room, hearing him sing, and Aunt Dinah gave me my dinner."

"Hearing Tom sing, hey?"

"O, yes! he sings such beautiful things about the New Jerusalem, and bright angels, and the land of Canaan."

"I dare say; it's better than the opera, isn't it?"

"Yes, and he's going to teach them to me."

"Singing lessons, hey? — you *are* coming on."

"Yes, he sings for me, and I read to him in my Bible; and he explains what it means, you know."

"On my word," said Marie, laughing, "that is the latest joke of the season."

"Tom isn't a bad hand, now, at explaining Scripture, I'll dare swear," said St. Clare. "Tom has a natural genius for religion. I wanted the horses out early, this morning, and I stole up to Tom's cubiculum there, over the stables, and there I heard him holding a meeting by himself; and, in fact, I haven't heard anything quite so savory as Tom's prayer, this some time. He put in for me, with a zeal that was quite apostolic."

"Perhaps he guessed you were listening. I've heard of that trick before."

"If he did, he wasn't very politic; for he gave the Lord his opinion of me, pretty freely. Tom seemed to think there was decidedly room for improvement in me, and seemed very earnest that I should be converted."

"I hope you'll lay it to heart," said Miss Ophelia.

"I suppose you are much of the same opinion," said St. Clare. "Well, we shall see, — shan't we, Eva?"

Frederick Douglass

To Frederick Douglass (see introduction above, pp. 482-83), the power of traditional religion loomed as one of the most important obstacles to abolition. In this column from his newspaper in March 1861, Douglass attacks the notion that the Scriptures offer unambiguous support for the slave system. Although the column appeared in March 1861, Douglass cannot yet sense that the Civil War would soon work a fundamental alteration with respect to slavery. The theologians to whom he refers were among those who defended slavery as a biblical institution.

The Pro-Slavery Mob and the Pro-Slavery Ministry.

These two Powers have been harmoniously and simultaneously active, since the second of December, in the service of the American slave system. The union

[Source: *Douglass' Monthly,* March 1861, pp. 1-2.]

and concert between them is as admirable as their work is hateful and diabolical. The causes that have moved the one to pelt us with brickbats, have equally
moved the other to pester us with sermons. — The weapons of the one are brutal, and those of the other spiritual; but they amount to about the same thing in
the end. Both aim to guard, defend and perpetuate, in all its fiendish rigor, the
thrice-accursed system of Human Slavery. The piety of the Church, and the
profanity and obscenity of the Mob, are morally the same, and express, in their
characteristic ways, the same demoniacal idea. That idea is the righteousness of
robbery where the victim is black, and the robber is white — for nobody at the
North, we think, would defend Slavery, even from the Bible, but for this color
distinction. What it would be a State's Prison offense to do to a white man, is
quite innocent and praiseworthy to perpetrate as against a human being of a
different complexion. Color makes all the difference in the application of our
American Christianity. To the whites it is full of love and tenderness. To the
blacks it is full of hate and bitterness. The same Book which is full of the Gospel
of Liberty to one race, is crowded with arguments in justification of the slavery
of another. Those who shout and rejoice over the progress of Liberty in Italy,
would mob down, pray and preach down Liberty at home as an unholy and
hateful thing.

The aspect of the times must be admitted to be somewhat gloomy and
dark for the Abolition cause. During a period of more than thirty years have the
Abolitionists, with zeal and ability unsurpassed by those exhibited in any other
great moral movement, plied the National heart and conscience with sound
doctrine, and have endeavored to bring this guilty nation to repentance, and to
deliver the slave, and now to human seeming they are as far from the accomplishment of their work, as during the pro-slavery mobs of twenty-five years
ago. . . .

Pro-Slavery Mobs are evidently contagious. Boston set the example, on
the third of December, by breaking up a lawful meeting in Tremont Temple.
Since then, the disorder has traveled like the Cholera from East to West, until it
has nearly reached the States west of the Mississippi. The mobocrats generally
profess to act for the Government, for "the Union, the constitution and the
Laws," and fall upon unarmed men and women with arms and insults, and disperse them as the enemies of the Government. The same brave gentlemen know
how to keep out of the way of the real enemies of the Government. The men
who rob the National Treasury, steal powder, balls and shells, capture mints and
muskets, take possession of forts, arsenals and other property belonging to the
United States, and openly defy the Government, are called friends; while we,
whose only sin is a desire to put an end to the real disturbing force in American
Civilization, are set down and treated as enemies. Towns like Syracuse, which
have enjoyed the largest advantages for learning the principles of Self-
Government and the sacredness of Free Speech, have displayed the greatest

amount of baseness and brutality in trampling upon those principles, and the greatest contempt for that right. The very liberality and enlightenment, formerly characteristic of that community, seems to have been a motive for setting at defiance all decency in the exhibition of its homage to Slavery. The Mob, in burning Mr. MAY and Miss ANTHONY in effigy, acted as though mothers, wives and sisters were held in brutal contempt in that community. The contemplation of the disgusting scene on that occasion must evermore mantle with the blush of shame over man and woman dwelling in that hitherto decent and respectable community.

But the rowdies have been scarcely more active in their devotion to our National Barbarism than the Reverends. The higher we go up in the scale of ecclesiastical gradation, the more heartless and cruel do we find the enemies of our cause. In our number for last month, we took occasion to hold up to deserved reprobation, Rev. Dr. SHAW's apology for Slavery, and his cowardly denunciation of Abolitionists. Sermons worse than his have been lately preached by other eminent Doctors of Divinity. We have been called upon to answer some of these with arguments instead of denunciation. But what arguments can we use towards men who, like Bishop HOPKINS, bring Christ and his Apostles, Moses and the Prophets, with whole columns of Bible quotations, to prove that another man has a better right to our body and soul than we have, and quotes the Bible to show that the race to which we belong are deemed by the Almighty to be only fit to be the property of the white race? We argue with no such disputants. It would be insulting to Common Sense, an outrage upon all right feeling, for us, who have worn the heavy chain, and felt the biting lash, to consent to argue with Ecclesiastical Sneaks who are thus prostituting their Religion and Bible to the base uses of popular and profitable iniquity. They don't need light, but the sting of honest rebuke. They are of their father the Devil, and his works they do, not because they are ignorant, but because they are base. On the side of the Oppressor there is power, and the crafty creatures know just where they belong.

The Sermons of Drs. VANDYKE, HOPKINS, THORNWELL, and others, to prove that God is well pleased with slaveholding and slave-catching, and that those are the chief of sinners who oppose the slave system and seeks its abolition, may well give inaffable joy to the hearts of Atheists, and of all who wish to see the Bible sink beneath the waves of universal contempt. What reverence can men have for a Book that authorizes one race to make beasts of burden of another? What love can a man have for a God who plunges him in the hell of Slavery? A thousand times over, give us the Religion or no Religion of the Infidel, with its Justice and Humanity, than the Religion of Slavery as taught by these crafty and cruel Doctors of Divinity. — We are at the end of argument with such persons. If they press the Bible into the service of Slavery, so much the worse for the Bible. We are quite tired of quoting text against text, not because

we cannot find as many on our side, the side of Liberty, as these Doctors find on
the side of Slavery, but because we have had enough of these arguments. The
man that will go to God, or to the Bible, to look for arguments in support of a
desire to work his brother man without wages, is a hypocrite as well as a scoundrel, and is below the level of argument. Some things are too evidently wrong to
admit of argument or apology. Humanity instinctively turns from Slavery with
a shudder. We have here the utterance of the voice of God in man, and to its
high and instantaneous teaching we may listen in preference to any voice for
Slavery drawn from the Bible.

Orestes A. Brownson

*Not an abolitionist properly speaking, Brownson by 1861 concluded that
emancipation must be granted to the slaves. He further concluded that this
could only come about if Abraham Lincoln forthrightly took the lead in this
matter. Two years before the Emancipation Proclamation was at last issued,
Brownson in marvelous prose argued that the time had now come for such a
step to be taken. The nation was at war, the world was watching, civilization
hung in the balance. If America does not now take a stand for the human
rights of all persons ("whether white or black, yellow or copper-colored"),
then we shall "deserve, as we shall receive, the scorn and derision of the
whole world."*

The question of the abolition of slavery is becoming with us a practical question in a sense it has never before been. The Rebellion of the Slave States, which
has for its object, not so much the dissolution of the Union, or the separation of
the South from the North, as the reconstruction of the Union on the basis of
slavery, or, as the Vice-President of the Confederate States has it, with "slavery
as its cornerstone," and therefore the extension of slavery over the whole country, cannot fail to force this question upon the grave attention of every citizen
of the loyal States, who loves his country, and believes in the practicability of
freedom. The Slave States, by their rebellion and war on the Union, are compelling us to regard this question as one which must soon be practically met, and
are forcing all loyal citizens to make their election between the preservation of
the Union and the preservation of slavery. This, whatever the Federal administration, whatever individuals or parties in the Free States, with, or without
Southern or pro-slavery proclivities, may wish or desire, is pretty soon to be the
inevitable issue of the terrible struggle in which our glorious, and hitherto

[Source: *Brownson's Quarterly Review*, 2 (1861), 511, 512-13, 516-17, 520, 521-22.]

peaceful Republic is now engaged. Perhaps, at the moment we write, the last of August, a majority of the people of the Free States may not only shrink from this issue, but even honestly believe it possible to avert it altogether. The bare suggestion of the abolition of slavery may shock, perhaps, enrage them; but events march, and men who mean to be successful, or not to be left behind, must march with them. . . .

We need not say, for the fact is well known to our readers, that no man, according to his ability and opportunity, has, since April, 1838, more strenuously opposed the abolition movement in the Free States than we have; not because we loved slavery, or had any sympathy with that hateful institution, but because we loved the Constitution of the Union, and because we believed that liberty at home and throughout the world was far more interested in preserving the union of these States under the Federal constitution, than in abolishing slavery as it existed in the Southern section of our common country. But we believe, and always have believed, that liberty, the cause of free institutions, the hopes of philanthropists and Christians, both at home and abroad, are more interested in preserving the Union and the integrity of the nation, than they are or can be in maintaining negro-slavery. If we have opposed abolition heretofore because we would preserve the Union, we must, *a fortiori,* oppose slavery whenever, in our judgment, its continuance becomes incompatible with the maintenance of the Union, or of our nation as a free republican state. . . .

The real question now before the loyal States is not, whether the Rebellion shall be suppressed by force of arms, or a peaceful division of the country into two separate and independent Republics submitted to. Any one who has any knowledge of the plans and purposes of the Rebels, knows well, that the division of the territory of the Union into two independent Republics is far short of what they are aiming at. The leaders of the Rebellion, they who planned it, they who have stirred it up, and armed it against the Union, have worked themselves into the conviction, that slavery is not to be looked upon as an evil, under certain circumstances to be tolerated, but as a good to be desired, which religion and humanity require not only to be perpetuated, but extended the farthest possible. Their doctrine is, that liberty is not practicable for a whole people, that it is practicable only for a class or a race; and that republicanism can subsist and be practically beneficial, only where the laboring class is deprived of all political and civil rights, and reduced to slavery. . . .

You must give them another battle-cry than that of "Law and Order," or you will not stir their heart, that mighty American heart which conquered this country from the savage and the forest, proclaimed and won its independence, constituted the Union, and made the American nation one of the great nations of the earth. It is not for us, even if we were able, to give that battle-cry; it must be given by genius in authority, and fall either from the lips of the President, or the Commander-in-Chief of our armies. Neither may as yet be prepared to utter it; but, if this nation has a future, if its destiny is, as we have hitherto boasted, to prove what man may be when and where he has the liberty to be himself, uttered by one or the other it ere long will be, and in tones that will ring out through the whole Union, and through the whole civilized world now anxiously listening to hear it. The Union is and must be sacred to liberty. Here man must be man, nothing more, and nothing less. Slaves must not breathe our atmosphere; and we must be able to adopt the proud boast of our Mother Country, "The slave that touches our soil is free." This is the destiny of this New World, if destiny it have, — the destiny our fathers toiled for, fought for, bled for, and to this we their children must swear to be faithful, or die to the last man.

White Apologists

American Colonization Society

Before the lines hopelessly hardened between those who would extend slavery and those who would eradicate it, some sought a compromise of sorts in the form of exporting blacks "back" to Africa. (The reason for the quotation marks around "back" is that most of America's blacks at this point had never seen Africa.) While the proposal was directed only toward free blacks, proponents saw the colonization effort as the best solution for all blacks when general emancipation should come. And some could even argue that emancipation would come sooner if everyone realized that colonization would follow immediately thereafter. Coming into existence in 1817, the American Colonization Society, with mixed motives and mixed results, did manage to send about 6,000 blacks to Liberia between 1821 and 1867. In the throes of organizing the Society, many contrasting voices were heard. Here, Kentucky's Henry Clay (1777-1852) is willing to talk about colonization for "the free people of color in the United States," but the "delicate question" of slavery is strictly off limits. A reporter at the meeting summarized his remarks.

Mr. Clay (on taking the chair) . . . understood the object of the present meeting to be to consider of the propriety and practicability of colonizing the free people of color in the United States, and of forming an association in relation to

---

[Source: *A View of the Exertions Lately Made for the Purpose of Colonizing the Free People of Colour* . . . (Washington: Jonathan Elliot, 1817), pp. 4-6.]

that object. That class of the mixt population of our country was, [he said], peculiarly situated. They neither enjoyed the immunities of freemen, nor were they subject to the incapacities of slaves, but partook in some degree of the qualities of both. From their condition, and the unconquerable prejudices resulting from their color, they never could amalgamate with the free whites of this country. It was desirable, therefore, both as it respected them and the residue of the population of the country, to drain them off. Various schemes of colonization had been thought of, and a part of our own continent, it was thought by some, might furnish a suitable establishment for them. But for his part, Mr. C[lay] said, he had a decided preference for some part of the coast of Africa. There ample provision might be made for the colony itself, and it might be rendered instrumental to the introduction, into that extensive quarter of the globe, of the arts, civilization and christianity. There was a peculiar, a moral fitness in restoring them to the land of their fathers. And if, instead of the evils and sufferings which we have been the innocent cause of inflicting upon the inhabitants of Africa, we can transmit to her the blessings of our arts, our civilization and our religion, may we not hope that America will extinguish a great portion of that moral debt which she has contracted to that unfortunate continent? We should derive much encouragement in the prosecution of the object which had assembled us together by the success which had attended the colony of Sierra Leone. That establishment had commenced 20 or 25 years ago, under the patronage of private individuals in Gt. Britain. . . . We have their example before us; and can there be a nobler cause than that which, while it proposed to rid our own country of a useless and pernicious, if not a dangerous portion of its population, contemplates the spreading of the arts of civilized life, and the possible redemption from ignorance and barbarism of a benighted quarter of the globe!

It was proper and necessary distinctly to state, [Mr. Clay added], that he understood it constituted no part of the object of this meeting to touch or agitate; in the slightest degree, a delicate question connected with another portion of the coloured population of our country. It was not proposed to deliberate on, or consider at all, any question of emancipation, or that was connected with the abolition of slavery. It was upon that condition alone, he was sure, that many gentlemen from the south and the west, whom he saw present, had attended or could be expected to co-operate. It was upon that condition, only, that he himself had attended. He would only further add that he hoped, in their deliberations, they would be guided by that moderation, politeness and deference for the opinions of each other, which were essential to any useful result. But when he looked around and saw the respectable assemblage, and recollected the humane and benevolent purpose which had produced it, he felt it unnecessary to insist farther on this topic.

John England

South Carolina's Bishop England, in a series of letters to the nation's Secretary of State, defended slavery as found in the South. "Domestic slavery," to use England's term, must be distinguished from the "compulsory slavery of an invaded people" as well as from the slave trade which had indeed been condemned by Pope Gregory XVI in 1839. But neither natural law nor papal decree precluded Catholics in the American South from being slave-holders. Slavery, "the result of sin by divine dispensation," when "established by human legislation" and "when the dominion of the slave is justly acquired by the master," is lawful "not only in the sight of the human tribunal, but also in the eye of Heaven. . . ." The letter excerpted below is dated October 13, 1840.

Respecting domestic slavery, we distinguish it from the compulsory slavery of an invaded people in its several degrees. I shall touch upon the varieties separately. The first is "voluntary;" that which exists amongst us is not of that description, though I know very many instances where I have found it to be so; but I regard not the cases of individuals, I look to the class. In examining the lawfulness of voluntary slavery, we shall test a principle against which abolitionists contend. They assert, generally, that slavery is contrary to the natural law. The soundness of their position will be tried by inquiring into the lawfulness of holding in slavery a person, who has voluntarily sold himself. Our theological authors lay down a principle, that man in his natural state is master of his own liberty, and may dispose of it as he sees proper; as in the case of a Hebrew, (*Exodus* xxi. 5,) who preferred remaining with his wife and children as a slave, to going into that freedom to which he had a right; and as in the case of the Hebrew, (*Levit.* xxv. 47,) who, by reason of his poverty, would sell himself to a sojourner or to a stranger. Life and its preservation are more valuable than liberty, and hence when Esther addresses Assuerus, (vii. 4,) she lays down the principle very plainly and naturally. "For we are sold, I and my people, to be destroyed and slain, and to perish. But if we had been sold for bondsmen and bondswomen, I had held my tongue." The natural law then does not prohibit a man from bartering his liberty and his services to save his life, to provide for his sustenance, to secure other enjoyments which he prefers to that freedom and to that right to his own labour, which he gives in exchange for life and protection. Nor does the natural law prohibit another man from procuring and bestowing upon him those advantages, in return for which he has agreed to bind himself

---

[Source: *The Works of the Right Reverend John England, First Bishop of Charleston* (Cleveland: Arthur H. Clark Co., 1908), V, 192-94. Quotation above is from p. 195.]

to that other man's service, provided he takes no unjust advantage in the bargain. Thus a state of voluntary slavery is not prohibited by the law of nature; that is, a state in which one man has the dominion over the labour and the ingenuity of another to the end of his life, and consequently in which that labour and ingenuity are the property of him who has the dominion, and are justly applicable to the benefit of the master and not of the slave. All our theologians have from the earliest epoch sustained, that though in a state of pure nature all men are equal, yet the natural law does not prohibit one man from having dominion over the useful action of another as his slave; provided this dominion be obtained by a just title. That one man may voluntarily give this title to another, is plain from the principle exhibited, and from the divine sanction to which I have alluded.

In one point of view, indeed, we may say that the natural law does not establish slavery, but it does not forbid it — and I doubt how far any of the advocates of abolition would consent to take up for refutation, the following passage of St. Thomas of Aquin, —

> "The common possession of all things is said to be of the natural law, because the distinction of possessions and slavery were not introduced by nature, but by the reason of man, for the benefit of human life: and thus the law of nature is not changed by their introduction, but an addition is made thereto."

As well may the wealthy merchant then assert, that it is against the law of nature that one man should possess a larger share of the common fund belonging to the human family for his exclusive benefit, as that it is against the law of nature for one man to be the slave of another. The existence of slavery is considered by our theologians to be as little incompatible with the natural law as is the existence of property. The sole question will be in each case, whether the title on which the dominion is claimed be valid.

I know many slaves who would not accept their freedom; I know some who have refused it; and though our domestic slavery must upon the whole be regarded as involuntary, still the exceptions are not so few as are imagined by strangers.

It may be asked why any one should prefer slavery to freedom. I know many instances where the advantages to the individual are very great; and so, sir, I am confident do you, yet I am not in love with the existence of slavery. I would never aid in establishing it where it did not exist. . . .

The situation of a slave, under a human master, insures to him food, raiment, and dwelling, together with a variety of little comforts; it relieves him from the apprehensions of neglect in sickness, from all solicitude for the support of his family, and in return, all that is required is fidelity and moderate labour. I do not deny that slavery has its evils, but the above are no despicable benefits. Hence I have known many freedmen who regretted their manumission.

James Henley Thornwell (1812-1862)

James Henley Thornwell of South Carolina was one of the South's leading public theologians in the 1850s and early 1860s. As a much-respected pastor and theological professor in Columbia, South Carolina, Thornwell defended conservative Presbyterian theology as well as the biblical basis for slavery. Unlike some of his Southern contemporaries, Thornwell had traveled and studied (Andover, Harvard) in the North. He did not like what he saw there, particularly of the beginnings of the new industrial society, which he felt degraded workers much more than the slave system did its workers. In his view, set forth in many painstaking tracts, sermons, and articles, the slave system provided for more wholesome social relations because it rested on what Thornwell considered to be divine mandates. Thornwell was distinctive among Southern slave advocates, however, for insisting on the humanity of African Americans and on the need of slave-owners to instruct their slaves in the rudiments of Christian faith. Such arguments did not appease abolitionists; rather, the energy that Thornwell put into his arguments made him one of their most visible opponents. The extracts that follow are from a sermon first delivered in 1850.

The Rights and Duties of Masters

Masters, give unto your Servants that which is just and equal, knowing that ye also have a master in Heaven.

Colossians IV, 1

God has not permitted such a remarkable phenomenon as the unanimity of the civilized world, in its execration of slavery, to take place without design. This great battle with the Abolitionists, has not been fought in vain. The muster of such immense forces — the fury and bitterness of the conflict — the disparity in resources of the parties in the war — the conspicuousness — the unexampled conspicuousness of the event, have all been ordered for wise and benefi-

---

[Source: David B. Chesebrough, ed., *"God Ordained This War": Sermons on the Sectional Crisis, 1830-1865* (Columbia: University of South Carolina Press, 1991), pp. 177-78, 181, 182-83, 186-87.]

cient results; and when the smoke shall have rolled away, it will be seen that a real progress has been made in the practical solution of the problems which produced the collision. . . .

Truth must triumph, God will vindicate the appointments of His Providence — and if our institutions are indeed consistent with righteousness and truth, we can calmly afford to bide our time — we can watch the storm which is beating furiously against us, without terror or dismay — we can receive the assault of the civilized world — trusting in Him who has all the elements at His command, and can save as easily by one as a thousand. . . . It is not the narrow question of abolitionism or of slavery — not simply whether we shall emancipate our negroes or not; the real question is the relations of man to society — of States to the individual, and of the individual to States; a question as broad as the interests of the human race.

These are the mighty questions which are shaking thrones to their centres — upheaving the masses like an earthquake, and rocking the solid pillars of this Union. The parties in this conflict are not merely abolitionists and slaveholders — they are atheists, socialists, communists, red republicans, jacobins, on the one side, and friends of order and regulated freedom on the other. In one word, the world is the battle ground — Christianity and Atheism the combatants; and the progress of humanity the stake. One party seems to regard Society, with all its complicated interests, its divisions and subdivisions, as the machinery of man — which, as it has been invented and arranged by his ingenuity and skill, may be taken to pieces, re-constructed, altered or repaired, as experience shall indicate defects or confusion in the original plan. The other party beholds in it the ordinance of God; and contemplates "this little scene of human life," as placed in the middle of a scheme, whose beginnings must be traced to the unfathomable depths of the past, and whose development and completion must be sought in the still more unfathomable depths of the future — a scheme, as Butler expresses it, "not fixed, but progressive — every way incomprehensible" — in which, consequently, irregularity is the confession of our ignorance — disorder the proof of our blindness, and with which it is as awful temerity to tamper as to sport with the name of God. . . .

The apostle not merely recognizes the moral agency of slaves, in the phraseology which he uses, but treats them as possessed of conscience, reason and will — by the motives which he presses. He says to them in effect that their services to their masters are duties which they owe to God — that a moral character attaches to their works, and that they are the subjects of praise or blame according to the principles upon which their obedience is rendered. . . .

If, then, slavery is not inconsistent with the existence of personal rights and of moral obligation, it may be asked in what does its peculiarity consist? What is it that makes a man a slave? We answer, the obligation to labour for another, determined by the Providence of God, independently of the provisions of a contract. The right which the master has is a right, not to the *man,* but to his *labour;* the duty which the slave owes is the service which, in conformity with this right, the master exacts. The essential difference betwixt free and slave-labour is, that one is rendered in consequence of a contract; the other is rendered in the consequence of a command. The labourers in each case are equally moral, equally responsible, equally men. But they work upon different principles. . . .

The Providence of God marks out for the slave the precise services, in the lawful commands of the master, which it is the Divine will that he should render; the painful necessities of his case are often as stringent upon the free labourer, and determine, with as stern a mandate, what contracts he shall make. Neither can he be said to select his employments. God allots to each his position — places one immediately under command — and leaves the other not unfrequently a petitioner for a master.

Whatever control the master has over the person of the slave, is subsidiary to this right to his labour; what he sells is not the man, but the property in his services — true he chastises the man, but the punishments inflicted for disobedience are no more inconsistent with personal responsibilities than the punishments inflicted by the law for breaches of contract. On the contrary, punishment in contradistinction from suffering, always implies responsibility, and a right which cannot be enforced, is a right, which society, as an organized community, has not yet acknowledged. The chastisements of slaves are accordingly no more entitled to awaken the indignation of loyal and faithful citizens — however pretended philanthropists may describe the horrors of the scourge and the lash — than the penalties of disgrace, imprisonment, or death, which all nations have inflicted upon crimes against the State. All that is necessary in any case, is that the punishment should be *just.* . . . It is not part of the essence of slavery, however, that the rights of the slave should be left to the caprice or to the interest of the master; and in the Southern States, provisions are actually made — whether adequate or inadequate it is useless here to discuss — to protect him from want, cruelty, and unlawful domination. Provisions are made which recognize the doctrine of the Apostle, that he is a subject of rights, and that justice must be rendered to his claims. . . .

This view of the subject exposes the confusion, which obtains in most popular treatises of morals, of slavery with involuntary servitude. The service, in so far as it consists in the motions of the limbs or organs of the body, must be voluntary, or it could not exist at all. If by voluntary be meant, however, that which results from hearty consent, and is accordingly rendered with cheerfulness, it is precisely the service which the law of God enjoins. Servants are exhorted to obey from considerations of duty; to make conscience of their tasks, with good will doing service, as to the Lord, and not to men. Whether, in point of fact, their service, in this sense, shall be voluntary, will depend upon their

moral character. But the same may be said of free labour. There are other motives beside the lash that may drive men to toil, when they are far from toiling
with cheerfulness or good will. . . .

The fundamental mistake of those who affirm slavery to be essentially
sinful, is that the duties of all men are specifically the same. . . . The argument,
fully and legitimately carried out, would condemn every arrangement of society, which did not secure to all its members an absolute equality of position; it
is the very spirit of socialism and communism.

The doctrine of the Bible, on the other hand, is that the specifick duties
— the things actually required to be done, are as various as the circumstances
in which men are placed. . . . The circumstances in which men are placed in this
sublunary state are exceedingly diversified, but there is probably no external
condition in which the actual discipline to which men are subjected may not
terminate in the temper of universal holiness. Some are tried in one way, some
in another — some are required to do one set of things, some another — but
the spirit of true obedience is universally the same — and the result of an effectual probation is, in every case, a moral sympathy with the moral perfections of
God. The lesson is the same, however different the textbooks from which it has
been taught.

Now, unless slavery is incompatible with the habitudes of holiness — unless it is inconsistent with the spirit of philanthropy or the spirit of piety — unless it furnishes no opportunities for obedience of the law, it is not inconsistent
with the pursuit or attainment of the highest excellence. It is no abridgement of
moral freedom; the slave may come from the probation of *his* circumstances as
fully stamped with the image of God, as those who have enjoyed an easier lot —
he may be as completely in unison with the spirit of universal rectitude, as if he
had been trained on flowery beds of ease. Let him discharge his *whole* duty in
the actual circumstances of his case, and he is entitled to the praise of a perfect
and an upright man. The question with God is — not *what* he has done — but
how; — man looketh at the outward circumstances, but God looketh at the
heart. . . . The slave is to show his reverence for God — the freedom of his inward man — by a cheerful obedience to the lawful commands of his master; —
the master, his regard for one who is his master in heaven, by rendering to the
slave that which is just and equal. The character of both is determined, in the
sight of God, by the spirit which pervades their single acts, however the acts
may differ in themselves.

Thornton Stringfellow (1788-1869)

Unlike the well-known figure of James Henley Thornwell, Thornton Stringfellow occupied a humbler station as pastor of the Stevensburg Baptist Church in Culpeper County, Virginia. Precisely because of his ordinary status, however, Stringfellow's arguments on behalf of slavery seemed to carry extra weight. To those so inclined, they seemed to convey the verdict of common sense rather than the unusual reasoning of an elite intellectual. One of Stringfellow's earlier works on the subject was given a much wider audience when in 1860 it appeared as a key essay in a major compilation that pulled together many of the most important pro-slavery arguments of the preceding two decades. The extract printed here appears at the end of a long discussion of the biblical texts that Stringfellow thought showed the divine sanction for slavery as it existed in the South.

My reader will remember that the subject in dispute is, whether involuntary and hereditary slavery was ever lawful in the sight of God, the Bible being judge.

1. I have shown by the Bible, that God decreed this relation between the posterity of Canaan, and the posterity of Shem and Japheth.

2. I have shown that God executed this decree by aiding the posterity of Shem, (at a time when "they were holiness to the Lord,") to enslave the posterity of Canaan in the days of Joshua.

3. I have shown that when God ratified the covenant of promise with Abraham, he recognized Abraham as the owner of slaves he had bought with his money of the stranger, and recorded his approbation of the relation, by commanding Abraham to circumcise them.

4. I have shown that when he took Abraham's posterity by the hand in Egypt, five hundred years afterward, he publicly approbated the same relation, by permitting every slave they had bought with their money to eat the Passover, while he refused the same privilege to their *hired servants.*

5. I have shown that God, as their national law-giver, ordained by express statute, that they should buy slaves of the nations around them, (the seven devoted nations excepted,) and that these slaves and their increase should be a perpetual inheritance to their children.

6. I have shown that God ordained slavery by law for their captives taken

---

[Source: Thornton Stringfellow, "The Bible Argument; or, Slavery in the Light of Divine Revelation," in *Cotton Is King, and Pro-Slavery Arguments*, ed. E. N. Elliott (Augusta, Ga.: Pritchard, Abbot & Loomis, 1860), pp. 506-07.]

in war, while he guaranteed a successful issue to their wars, so long as they obeyed him.

7. I have shown that when Jesus ordered his gospel to be published through the world, the relation of master and slave existed by law in every province and family of the Roman Empire, as it had done in the Jewish commonwealth for fifteen hundred years.

8. I have shown that Jesus ordained, that the legislative authority which created this relation in that empire, should be obeyed and honored as an ordinance of God, as all government is declared to be.

9. I have shown that Jesus has prescribed the mutual duties of this relation in his kingdom.

10. And lastly, I have shown, that in an attempt by his professed followers to disturb this relation in the Apostolic churches, Jesus orders that fellowship shall be disclaimed with all such disciples, as seditious persons — whose conduct was not only dangerous to the State, but destructive to the true character of his gospel dispensation.

2. The Civil War as a Religious Event

The Scene

An Outcry against War

When the Civil War began in April 1861, most religious commentary dealt with arguments for or against slavery, or contended for the ultimate righteousness of either the North or the South. Yet there were also a few who, while not belonging to the historic pacifist churches, nonetheless spoke out against the recourse to arms as a simple mistake. One of the most forceful of these voices appeared in Alexander Campbell's newspaper, the Millennial Harbinger, *in July 1861. Just as the military campaigns were getting underway, this Restorationist writer (identified only as "W.K.P.") offered a strong testimony against the warfare that would soon engulf the nation. The article was entitled "A Plea for Peace."*

It seems that, so far, very few are found pleading for peace. The rage for shedding human blood is running madly through the land. — Nearly all the religious papers have caught the epidemic, and are breathing forth the most terrible exhortations to the soldiery to strike boldly and well in the work of carnage. The pulpit rings with the clarion notes of war-sermons, and the ministers of the Prince of Peace have, in many cases, become the panders to the bloody Moloch of war. What must we think of this? The soldier of the cross lays down the weapons that are not carnal for those that are: — the man who would shudder at the thought of inflicting a deliberate private injury upon his fellow-being, is

---

[Source: W.K.P., "A Plea for Peace," *The Millennial Harbinger*, new ser., 4, July 1861, pp. 405-7, 408-9.]

going forth, in studied and artful preparation, to perpetrate the widest public ruin that fire and sword can execute; he who has taught others to weep with those that weep, is marching eagerly to wake in many a quiet home the voice of wailing and woe, and to spread the pall of a gloomy desolation over wide regions of unoffending people. Fire and sword — desolation and death — carnage and bloodshed — inhuman, brutal, bloody, barbarous war — these are summoning their furies to rally in the dread work of social sin and human murder, and what shall be the cry of the people of Christ? Shall we render a blind and implicit obedience to the madness that riots in death? Shall we give up our right to reason, throw conscience prostrate at the feet of power — abandon the right to think — forget that we are Christians — obey man rather than God — beat our plowshares into swords and our pruning-hooks into spears — study war instead of peace — labor to send men violently and prematurely to hell, rather than to snatch them as brands from the burning! Shall the spirit of Christ or the spirit of Satan rule in our hearts! How can we hesitate — what can bewilder our judgment — who shall absolve us from our duty?

What answer do our feelings give to the call to war? Can the heart of the Christian be in the work? Does he sympathize with its revenge? Has he a taste for its cruelty? Does he enjoy the cries of the distressed — exult in the agonies of the wounded — take delight in the carnage of the battlefield — or gloat, like a demon, on the marred and mangled forms of the brutally murdered victims of contending fury? Can he rise from the earnest prayer that his whole nature may be adorned with all the graces of the Spirit — go from the tranquil pleasures of the family altar, or the peaceful communion of the public sanctuary, and *feel* that the fierce strife and struggle of grappling foes, thirsting for each other's blood, is a work fit for his calling, or congenial to his heart? O, my brethren! let us sit down upon the plains of Bethlehem with the watching shepherds, under its quiet and cloudless sky, and listen to the cry of the angel, who came with the proclamation of "good tidings of great joy for all people," till we catch the spirit of the Prince of Peace, and fill our souls with the power of his divine compassion; — and then let us look upon the warring elements of the field of mortal strife, and ask the heart, subdued by the love of God, and reconciled by the suffering and sacrifice of Christ, if it can take pleasure in the cruel spectacle, or part in the bloody work. Is it not horrible to think, that we have been at great pains and expense and peril to make a widow and an orphan! to leave a happy home desolate! — To send tender Christian hearts mourning about the streets, wailing for *their* dead — *our* victims! To look behind us and to see the green meadows trampled into dust — the waving harvest-fields, ripe for the sickle, crushed beneath the feet of infantry, the hoof of cavalry, or the heavy wheels of rolling artillery — the cottage and its happy flowers a desolation; hamlet and village and town smoking ruins; the magnificence and wealth of cities sacked and in ashes; and all hearts — poor, loving, suffering human hearts, like our own — bleeding with the unutterable woe, and none to comfort them! Christian Brother, can you lend your heart to a work like this! No. A nobler calling is ours:

> "The goodness of the heart is shown in deeds
> Of peacefulness and kindness. Hand and heart
> Are one thing, with the good, as thou shouldst be.
> Do my words trouble thee? then treasure them:
> Pain overgot gives peace, as death doth Heaven.
> All things that speak of Heaven, speak of peace."

But we are fascinated by the glory of war. "Grim-visaged" as it is, it comes bedecked with trappings so gaudy, that we are caught by its glitter and show. The flashing of arms, the blast of the trumpet, the martial tread, measured to stately music, and the rustling of banners over brave hearts — these things set the ambitious soul on fire, and make it burn for glory. Thus the shame of war is covered over with fig leaves, and its nakedness is concealed; for when we ask, *Whence come wars and fightings amongst us?* the answer must be now, as of old — *Come they not even of our lusts?* "The love of glory is but an airy lust." We may gild the cloud with colors of silver and gold, but we cannot empty it of the pollution that floats in its bosom. It is freighted with the elements of selfishness, cruelty and crime; and their poison mingles with every cup of ambition, and turns its glory to ashes. . . .

What is the business of war? It is to kill human beings. This is the deliberate calculation. To this end look all the preparations. The rifle and the musket, the bayonet and the sword, the bowie knife, the revolver, the cannon, the cartridge, the practice and drill of the soldier — all these are ingeniously contrived and elaborately executed to do well and surely this one end aim of the battle. Is not this a serious business? is it not an awful business? *prima facie,* is it not horribly wicked business? Without some high absolving reason, can it be right? Is it any thing less than wanton, wholesale murder that will cry unto heaven in the day of judgment against the soul that is guilty of it? If A take the life of B, except in pure self defence, it is murder in the eye of all civilized law and punishable as such. But it is not a crime because civil law declares it to be such, — it is a crime because the curse of God is upon it — and though the erring and often blind judgment of man should acquit the murderer of his deed, it cannot wash out the stain from his conscience. It will remain. — In the book of God's remembrance it is written, and will forever stand. . . .

"Christ in the Camp"

Throughout both North and South, the Civil War became an occasion for serious attention to religion. Pietistic impulses played heavily in southern soldiers' lives from the start of the conflict, but beginning in 1862, more and more reports appeared to document revivals of unusual force, especially among Confederate troops within the Army of Northern Virginia. By 1863 and 1864, a heightened spirit of religious fervor had spread throughout the Confederate forces as a whole. A few years after the war, a particularly interesting account of the revivals was provided by J. William Jones, a Baptist minister who served first as both an enlisted man and then a chaplain in the Army of Northern Virginia. Jones's writing about revival was part of his strategy to promote the Confederate "lost cause." Jones served as the secretary-treasurer of the Southern Historical Society, edited the organization's official publication, published Robert E. Lee's memoirs, and served nearly two decades as the chaplain-general of the United Confederate Veterans. Very much an apology for the Confederate cause, Jones's Christ in the Camp *(1888) nonetheless provided a full account of how the war had served, at least for some of the soldiers, to heighten receptivity for the Christian message.*

But, in pointing out the instrumentalities which God blessed to the spiritual good of our brave men, their own *eagerness to hear the Gospel* must not be overlooked. Indeed I believe that the desire of these men to listen to the Gospel and to receive religious instruction has never been surpassed. Let us visit some of these camps, and mingle in some of these scenes of worship, and if I shall be able to picture them as I saw them, I can give a far more vivid idea of them than by the recital of the detailed facts and figures.

It matters not what day in the week it may be, or what hour of the day, you have only to pass the word around that there will be preaching at such a point, and there will promptly assemble a large crowd of eager listeners. No appointment for weeks, or days, or hours ahead is necessary. No church-bell summons, to gorgeous houses of worship, elegant ladies or fashionably attired men. But a few taps of the drum, a few strains of the bugle, or, better still, the singing of some old, familiar hymn, serves as a "church call" well understood, and from every part of the camp weather-beaten soldiers, in faded and tattered uniforms, hasten to the selected spot and gather close around the preacher, who, with "Nature's great temple" for his church, and the blue canopy of heaven for his

---

[Source: J. William Jones, *Christ in the Camp; or Religion in Lee's Army* (Richmond, VA: B. F. Johnson, 1888), pp. 242-45.]

"sounding board," is fortunate if he have so much as a barrel or well-rounded stump for a pulpit.

But I proposed to take you, kind reader, to some of our meetings. Let us first visit the battered old town of Fredericksburg in the early weeks of 1863. We enter at sundown, just as the regiments of Barksdale's Brigade of heroic Mississippians are returning to their quarters front "dress parade," and we pause to gaze with admiration on the men who, on that bleak December morning, held the town with such tenacity against Burnside's mighty hosts until "Marse Robert" had formed on the hills beyond his lines of Gray, against which the waves of Blue surged in vain.

Soon we hear the familiar command, "Break ranks," and immediately the streets are filled with soldiers eagerly running in a given direction.

"What does this mean?" a stranger would inquire. "Is 'Old John Robinson' about to have a performance of his circus? Has 'Wyman, the great magician,' come to town? Are the 'Negro Minstrels' about to exhibit? What means this eager running?" Ask one of the men, and he will scarcely pause as he replies: "We are trying to get into the church before all of the seats are taken."

Yes! the house of God is the goal they seek, and long before the appointed hour the spacious Episcopal church, kindly tendered for the purpose by its rector, is filled — nay, *packed* — to its utmost capacity — lower floor, galleries, aisles, chancel, pulpit-steps and vestibule — while hundreds turn disappointed away unable to find even standing-room. The great revival has begun, and this brigade and all of the surrounding brigades are stirred with a desire to hear the Gospel, rarely equalled.

Enter, if you can make your way through the crowd, and mingle with that vast congregation of worshippers. They do not spend their time while waiting for the coming of the preacher in idle gossip, or a listless staring at every new comer, but a clear voice strikes some familiar hymn, around which cluster hallowed memories of home, and of the dear old church far away — the whole congregation join in the hymn, and there arises a volume of sacred song that seems almost ready to take the roof off of the house. I may be an "old fogy," but I declare I would not give one of those old songs which "the boys" used to sing "with the spirit and the understanding," and into which they threw their souls, for all of the "classic music" which grand organ and "quartette choir" ever rendered.

The song ceases, and one of the men leads in prayer. *And he prays.* He does not tell the Lord the news of the day, or recount to him the history of the country. He does not make "a stump-speech to the Lord" on the war — its causes, its progress, or its prospects. But, from the depths of a heart that feels its needs, he tells of present wants, asks for present blessings, and begs for the Holy Spirit in His convicting, converting power. I have rarely, if ever, heard such prayers as some of these men used to make. I remember that Brother Owen, the

Methodist chaplain who had the general conduct of these meetings, used to keep an accurate list of the men who professed conversion in the brigade, and from this list they were called on to lead in prayer.

I never heard of one who refused, and as a rule they made tender, earnest, appropriate prayers.

But presently some man in a tattered jacket gets up to speak, and the stranger might ask: "What business has he to speak in one of these meetings?" Listen, and you will soon see. As in simple, earnest style, he tells something of his own experience, or exhorts his comrades to come to Christ, you hear indeed

> "Words that breathe
> And thoughts that burn,"

and you feel that if eloquence is "logic set on fire," then that soldier is eloquent beyond almost any man you ever heard. The crowd seems thrilled by the power of his burning words and the momentous truth he utters. . . .

I remember that I preached to this vast congregation the very night before Hooker crossed the river, bringing on the battles of Second Fredericksburg and Chancellorsville — that, in my closing appeal, I urged them to accept Christ then and there, because they did not know but that they were hearing their "last invitation," and that sure enough we were aroused before day the next morning by the crossing of the enemy, and in the battles which followed, many of these noble fellows *were* called to the judgment-bar of God. And so, when the preacher stood up before these congregations of veterans, his very soul was stirred within him, and he "determined to know nothing among them save Jesus Christ and Him crucified." . . . If a man had any capacity whatever to preach, it would be developed under circumstances which would have stirred an angel's heart; and if he knew anything about the Gospel at all, he would tell it to these congregations.

And so our preacher, whoever he may be, tells "the old, old story of Jesus and His love." He has throughout the undivided attention of the crowd; there are tears in eyes "unused to the melting mood;" and when at the close of the sermon the invitation is given, and some stirring hymn is sung, there will be 20, 50, 100, or even as many as 200, to ask an interest in the prayers of God's people, or profess their faith in Jesus.

Military Rule

In the closing days of the Civil War and for some years thereafter, the South was a conquered country, subject to military rule and military occupation. So also, the South's churches bowed before military might and arbitrary order. Liberties, whether civil or religious, always suffer in time of war as the urgencies of the moment override the niceties which, in calmer times, would be conceded as the rights of all. Three separate orders given in three Confederate states reveal the temper of those abnormal times, two of the orders issued during the war, the third some five months after the surrender. That third order, directing (Episcopal) Bishop Richard H. Wilmer (1816-1900) of Alabama to include prayers for the president of the United States in all regular services, resulted in the temporary closing of all Episcopal churches in the state. Wilmer protested directly to President Andrew Johnson who ordered that the churches be reopened forthwith and Bishop Wilmer fully reinstated.

1.
Special Order, No. 31

Headquarters U. S. Forces
Natchez, Miss., June 18, 1864

II. The Colonel commanding this district having been officially notified that the pastors of many churches in this city neglect to make any public recognition of allegiance under which they live, and to which they are indebted for protection, and further, that the regular form of prayer for "the President of the United States, and all others in authority," prescribed by the ritual in some churches, and by established custom in others, has been omitted in the stated services of churches of all denominations, it is hereby

Ordered, That hereafter, the ministers of such churches as may have the prescribed form of prayer for the President of the United States, shall be read at each and every service in which it is required by the rubrics — and that those of other denominations, which have no such form — shall on like occasions pronounce a prayer appropriate to the time, and expressive of the proper spirit toward the Chief Magistrate of the United States. Any minister failing to comply with these orders, will be immediately prohibited from exercising the functions of his office in this city — and render himself liable to be sent beyond the lines of the United States forces.

[Source: Walter L. Fleming, ed., *Documentary History of Reconstruction* (Cleveland: Arthur H. Clark, 1906), I, pp. 221-26.]

2.
General Order No. 3

Norfolk, Va., Feb. 11, 1864

All places of public worship in Norfolk and Portsmouth are hereby placed under the control of the provost marshals of Norfolk and Portsmouth respectively, who shall see the pulpits properly filled by displacing, when necessary, the present incumbents, and substituting men of known loyalty and the same sectarian denomination, either military or civil subject to the approval of the commanding general. They shall see that all churches are open free to all officers and soldiers, white or colored, at the usual hour of worship, and at other times, if desired; and they shall see that no insult or indignity be offered to them, either by word, look, or gesture on the part of the congregation. The necessary expenses will be levied as far as possible, in accordance with the previous usages or regulations of each congregation respectively.

3.
General Order No. 38

Headquarters Department of Alabama
Mobile, Ala., Sept. 20, 1865

The Protestant Episcopal Church of the United States has established a form of prayer to be used for "the President of the United States and all in civil authority." During the continuance of the late wicked and groundless rebellion the prayer was changed for one for the President of the Confederate States, and so altered, was used in the Protestant Churches of the Diocese of Alabama.

Since the "lapse" of the Confederate government, and the restoration of authority of the United States over the late rebellious States, the prayer for the President has been altogether omitted in the Episcopal Churches of Alabama.

This omission was recommended by the Rt. Rev. Richard Wilmer, Bishop of Alabama, in a letter to the clergy and laity, dated June 20, 1865. The advice of the bishop to omit this prayer, and its omission by the clergy, is not only a violation of the canons of the church, but shows a factious and disloyal spirit, and is a marked insult to every loyal citizen within the department. Such men are unsafe public teachers, and not to be trusted in places of power and influence over public opinion.

It is, therefore, ordered, pursuant to the directions of Major-General Thomas, commanding the military division of Tennessee, that said Richard Wilmer, bishop of the Protestant Episcopal Church of the Diocese of Alabama, and the Protestant Episcopal clergy of said diocese be, and they are hereby suspended from their functions, and forbidden to preach, or perform divine service; and that their places of worship be closed until such time as said bishop and clergy show a sincere return to their allegiance to the government of the United States, and give evidence of a loyal and patriotic spirit by offering to resume the use of the prayer for the President of the United States and all in civil authority, and by taking the amnesty oath prescribed by the President.

This prohibition shall continue in each individual case until special application is made through the military channels to these headquarters for permission to preach and perform divine service, and until such application is approved at these or superior headquarters.

District commanders are required to see that this order is carried into effect.

By order of Major-General Chas. R. Woods.

Territory Conquered

Even before the war ended, northern churchmen called for the conquered South to become the converted South: converted by the "free churches" and the "full gospel" of northern religion — especially Congregationalism. Lyman Abbott (1835-1922), editor, lecturer, and popular Congregational preacher, was to dominate much northern Protestant thinking for half a century. Here, as a twenty-nine-year-old contributor to a New Haven periodical, Abbott declared that the war's terrible devastation must be followed by a moral and ecclesiastical reconstruction. It is clear, however, that Abbott saw such reconstruction as primarily a northern, not a southern responsibility. "We cannot trust those that have preached their congregations into rebellion to preach them back again."

At the commencement of this war we were often sneeringly asked the question — "Suppose you conquer the South, what are you going to do with it?" This question, impertinent then, becomes pertinent now. A considerable part of the South is conquered. The Federal flag floats in triumph over the principal parts of Missouri, Arkansas, Tennessee, and Louisiana. United States laws are enforced, United States Courts administer justice, United States authority is recognized and submitted to. And now the question does arise, full of perplexity, what are we going to do with the conquered territory?

[Source: Lyman Abbott, "Southern Evangelization," in *The New Englander*, 23 (1864), 699, 700-702, 702-3, 706-7.]

For it is apparent to the dullest of vision that we must do something. To conquer alone is not enough. It is impossible permanently to substitute military rule for civil authority, or make the President a permanent autocrat of the subjugated territory. All military governorships are temporary expedients; — doubtful ones at that. Where the Confederate authority has been destroyed, there the Federal authority must be restored in its *legitimate* and *constitutional* forms. Where the political and social despotism of the slave oligarchy has been destroyed, a permanent republicanism must be reorganized. Destruction must be followed by reconstruction. The history of liberty teaches us this necessity. . . .

Let us learn then a lesson from the experience of the past. To fight, to die even, for liberty, is not enough. When the enemies of the Republic have been conquered in battle, the *preparation* for the nation's work has been done; that is all. It then remains to enter upon the territory emancipated by the sword, and there establish in a permanent form the living institutions of freedom. We have not only to conquer the South, — we have also to convert it. We have not only to occupy it by bayonets and bullets, — but also by ideas and institutions. We have not only to destroy slavery, — we must also organize freedom. If we fail in our second task, success in the first will be of little use. The political problems involved in the delicate and difficult work of reconstruction are already engaging the attention of our wisest statesmen, as well they may. But, as we hope to show, there are religious problems connected with this subject which demand the attention of the church and ministry. To these we desire briefly to advert; — rather to provoke attention to the problem than to offer any satisfactory solution of it. . . .

Two conditions are absolutely essential to the perpetuity of republican institutions: popular intelligence and popular morality. In other words, before any people are competent to govern themselves successfully, they must possess intelligence and sound morals. Hence two institutions are essential to their preservation: common schools and Christian churches. Free institutions without general intelligence can exist only in name. There is no despotism so cruel and remorseless as that of an unreasoning mob. Men who do not know how to govern themselves cannot know how to govern a great country. The ignorance of the masses, and the consequent power of the few, alone made this rebellion possible. The power has been taken from the few. It remains to give knowledge to the masses. But knowledge alone is not enough. For, while intelligence tends to make *men* free, it does not suffice to constitute a free *State*. And it is not enough to emancipate individuals from iniquitous thraldom. That liberty may be permanent, it must be organic. Heads, legs, arms, trunks, gathered in an indiscriminate pile from the battle-field, cannot make a single man. They must be united by sinews and ligaments, inspired with life, and governed by one dominant head. So a mass of individuals, however free, gathered together, do not constitute a free Republic. Individualism is the characteristic of simple barbarism, not of republican civilization. They must be bound together by ties of interest and affection, inspired with one common national life, and possessed of one central government. How to harmonize individual liberty with the cohesion necessary to secure the preservation of the State, is the problem of republicanism. It is a problem which can never be solved without the aid of the Christian religion.

Thus to constitute a permanently free State, men must be taught not only their rights, but also their duties and their obligations. Submission must be inculcated, conscience must be educated, a generous love must be inspired. To establish liberty it is not enough to strike in sunder with the sword the chains which bind men. They must be bound together not, indeed, with handcuffs, as in a chain-gang, but with bands more enduring, because wrought of God, — bands of duty and affection. Thus the gospel is needed to prepare the way for true freedom. In truth, the principles of religion underlie republicanism. Religion teaches man that he is a son of God, and thus makes him unwilling to be a slave of man. She educates him to yield a willing submission to the sovereign power of God, and so renders it more easy for him to obey the reasonable requirements of his earthly superiors. And she inspires him with a universal affection for the human race, and so makes it possible for him to administer government in peace and amity with his fellows. . . .

We have thus endeavored to show, that to perpetuate Republicanism in the South we must follow the terrible devastations of war, with the more grateful, though no less difficult, work of reconstruction. And that to this reconstruction, the establishment of free churches and the proclamation of a full gospel is absolutely essential. Let us add that the Christian churches of the North alone can do this indispensable work. Government cannot. For though religious institutions are essential to the Republic, the Republic cannot establish religious institutions. Church and State are forever divorced in America. And God forever avert the day when the churches of America shall lapse into the hands of the politicians! Then *all* will be gone. Nor can we trust to the return of the exiled ministry, and the resurrection of the dead churches. We cannot transform the old schools of slavery and treason into schools of loyalty and liberty. We cannot trust those who have preached their congregations into rebellion to preach them back again. . . .

Now too is the time to commence this work. While society is fermenting, and institutions are being created, and customs are being established, and public opinion is forming, and governments are in process of organization, is the time to impress upon this new organization its permanent character. While nature was in chaos God fashioned and formed it as it is. While the metal is molten is the time to stamp and mold it. The Egyptian husbandman, while the waters still overflowed the banks of the Nile, was accustomed in olden times to go out in his boat and drop the seed upon the surface of the waters, that it might enter the softened and prepared soil. While the deluge of waters still overflows the fair fields of the South, is the very time for the Christian husbandman to sow the good seed, that when the waters shall retire it may be found already germinating — its growth beginning.

Theological Reflection

John Rice

When at the start of the Civil War, northern religious publications came out strongly for the Union, they were matched in intensity by Southerners who did the same for the Confederacy. Predictably, great controversy was engendered by these contradictory sentiments. John Rice contributed to the controversy among American Presbyterians when he responded at length to opinions published in the Biblical Repertory and Princeton Review *during the early years of the war. Rice's spirited rejoinder included a defense of Southern slavery as a direct product of God's providential action. Such reflections about the nature of providence were very common during the War, though Rice's particular interpretation of providence was a view that others, not least African Americans, hotly contested.*

. . . It was at last made perfectly manifest, not only by their utter inability to discover the way, but by the fearful failure of the experiment, on a small scale, in the British West Indies, that the problem of slavery could not be solved by any scheme of abolition, emancipation or colonization. The two first could only complicate it, while the last was utterly insufficient. Still, the slaves continued to multiply, and the danger of over population grew apace.

When hope began to depart, and the evils of shutting up slavery within narrow limits began in some measure to be realized, the providence of God opened the door of safety, by the operation of causes originating at points distant from each other by the whole length of the continent and the width of the broad Atlantic. The invention of the cotton-gin in Connecticut, and the spinning-jenny in Britain, almost simultaneously with the opening for settlement of the vast region of the South suited to the production of cotton, were

---

[Source: John Rice, "The Princeton Review on the State of the Country," *Southern Presbyterian Review* 14 (April 1861): 31-33.]

the instruments by which the safety-valve of the huge machinery was raised. These things came just when Southern Christians and statesmen were at their wit's end. The hope of relief from emancipation had faded away, and all were dreading a terrible explosion from the pent-up elements of unknown power confined within limits too strait for them. From that day to this, amazing progress and prosperity have blessed the Southern States, threatened only by the foolish and wicked meddling of men, like silly boys, who know nothing of the nature and powers of the vast machinery which they so recklessly handle, the explosion of which would as surely cause their destruction as that of the men to whom God in His providence, has committed its guidance and control. The South has great reason to be thankful that the great enginery that propels the bark which contains her social fortunes is so hard to disarrange, else ruin might have ensued long ago. We have before intimated our belief that one-half as much reckless and wicked interference with the social machinery of the North would, in much less time than thirty years, have produced an explosion, scattering it to the four winds of heaven. Its fragments could only be cemented again by the blood of untold thousands of people, and under the iron sceptre of a single despot.

The lesson which the South has learned from this whole history is, never to consent that her social system should be confined and restrained by any other limits than such as the God of nature interposes; and, above all, not to submit to the imposition of such restraints by another section of the country, whose fortunes are not embarked in the same vessel, whose motives can only be a spurious, fanatical philanthropy, or the lust of power; and whose domination, from the nature of the case, can be nothing but a fearful and hateful tyranny, not of one man, but of a many-headed monster. . . .

Charles Pettit McIlvaine (1799-1873)

As presiding bishop of the Episcopal Church, Charles Pettit McIlvaine felt compelled during the second year of the conflict to compose a pastoral letter to his fellow-Episcopalians. During an earlier period of service as chaplain and professor at West Point, McIlvaine had presided over revivals where, among others, Leonidas Polk was converted. It was one of the many strange signs in a very unusual time that in his letter from 1862 McIlvaine took aim at Polk, who meanwhile had become an Episcopal bishop in Louisiana but then returned to his older profession to take up a commission in the South-

[Source: Charles Pettit McIlvaine, *Pastoral Letter of the Bishops of the Protestant Episcopal Church in the United States of America* (New York: Baker & Godwin, 1862), pp. 4-7.]

> *ern army. McIlvaine's letter represented a contemporary application of the "jeremiad," a style of sermon perfected by early American Puritans. In traditional fashion, McIlvaine's "jeremiad" called upon his people to repent of their sins as a response to the crises, difficulties, and destruction brought on by the war.*

Returning to this great rebellion, with all its retinue of cost and sacrifice, of tribulation and anguish, of darkness and death, there are two aspects in which we must contemplate it, *namely:* as it comes *by the agency of man,* and as it comes *from the Providence of God.*

We desire *first,* to call your attention to it as it proceeds from *the Providence of God.* So comprehensive is that Providence that it embraces all worlds and all nations; while so minute is it that not a sparrow falleth without the knowledge and will of our Father in Heaven. In its vast counsels, this deep affliction has its place. God's hand is in it. His power rules it. It is His visitation and chastening for the sins of this nation. Who can doubt it? Just as the personal affliction of any of you is God's visitation to turn him from the world and sin, unto Himself; so is this national calamity most certainly His judgment upon this nation for its good. And we trust, dear brethren, we are in no danger of seeming, by such interpretation of our distresses, to excuse, in any degree, such agency as men have had in bringing them upon us. God's Providence has no interference with man's responsibility. He works by man, but so that it is still man that wills and works. The captivities of God's chosen people were, as His Word declares, His judgments upon them for their sins; while the nations that carried them captive were visited of God for heinous guilt in so doing. St. Peter declares that our Lord was "delivered" unto death "by the determinate counsel and forknowledge of God;" and that, nevertheless, it was *"by wicked hands"* that He was "crucified and slain." Thus we need to be under no temptation to diminish our estimate of the present dispensation of sorrow, as coming from the hand of God, for the punishment of our sins, whatever the agency of men therein. It is our duty, as Christians and as patriots, so to consider it, that it may do us the good for which it is sent, and may the sooner be taken away.

It is not possible for us, in this address, to set before you, in detail, or in their true proportions, all the national and other sins which make us, as a people, deserve, and need, the chastisements of a holy God. It needs no Daniel, inspired from on high, to discover them. Surely you must all be painfully familiar with many of them, in the profaneness of speech with which God's name and majesty are assailed; in the neglect of public worship which so dishonors His holy day; in the ungodliness of life which erects its example so conspicuously; and especially in the one great sin for which Jerusalem was given over to be trodden down by the heathen, and the people of Israel have ever since been wanderers and a by-word among the nations, *namely,* the rejection, whether in positive infidelity, or only in practical unbelief, of God's great gift of grace and mercy, His beloved Son, our Lord Jesus Christ, to be a sacrifice of propitiation for our sins, and an all-sufficient and all-glorious Saviour of our souls.

But there is a passage in the Scriptures which is of great use as a guide in this consideration of national sinfulness. It is a warning to the nation of Israel, and found in the eighth chapter of the book of Deuteronomy, as follows: "Beware that thou forget not the Lord thy God, in not keeping His commandments, and His judgments, and His statutes, which I command thee this day, lest when thou hast eaten and art full, and hast built goodly houses and hast dwelt therein, and when thy herds and thy flocks multiply, and thy silver and thy fold is multiplied, and all that thou hast is multiplied, then thy heart be lifted up, and thou forget the Lord thy God; for it is He that giveth thee power to get wealth. And it shall be, that if thou do at all forget the Lord thy God — as the nations which the Lord destroyeth before your face, so shall ye perish, because ye would not be obedient to the voice of the Lord your God."

Now it was because that nation was guilty of precisely such self-glorying, and such forgetfulness of its indebtedness to God and dependence on His favor, as this warning describes, that the grievous calamities which so fill its history, before the advent of Christ, were brought upon it. And it is because there is so much agreement between this description and the aspect which we, as a people, have presented before God, that we place the passage before you.

Marvellously have we been prospered in every thing pertaining to national prosperity, riches, and strength. God has loaded us with benefits; and with our benefits have grown our ingratitude, our self-dependence, and self-sufficiency, our pride, our vain-glorying, and that sad deficiency, so much felt, in the representative acts and voices of the nation as to all adequate acknowledgment of God and of the Gospel of Christ. Let us mark the words of the prophet Jeremiah: "Let not the wise man glory in his wisdom, neither let the mighty man glory in his might; let not the rich man glory in his riches; but let him that glorieth, glory in this, that he understandeth and knoweth me that I am the Lord which exercise loving-kindness, judgment, and righteousness in the earth." — (Jer. ix.; 23, 24.) How remarkably do these words exhibit our sin as a nation! How seldom, in any thing of a representative character, or any thing that speaks for the nation, especially in the counsels of our chosen rulers, or in the enactments of our legislatures, do we see any such reference to God, as is here required as the basis on which He blesses a nation! How literally have we gloried in our wisdom, and power, and wealth; and said in our hearts, *Our power and our hand have gotten us all these things!*

Dear brethren, can we consider these things, so palpable to every eye, and not acknowledge that we deserve God's anger, and need, for our good, His chastening Providence? Is it wonderful that this tribulation hath come upon us? O, that when thus His judgments are upon the land, the inhabitants may learn righteousness! We exhort you, brethren, that, as citizens and as Christians, you will take these things seriously to heart. Search and try yourselves, that you may duly humble yourselves under God's mighty hand, and He may, in due time, exalt us out of the present distress. Such a spirit of humiliation, taking wide possession of the people, especially of those who, as members of the Church of Christ, profess to be His disciples — above all, such a spirit appearing among those whose official position makes their words and acts of eminent weight and responsibility in determining the nation's standing before God — would more encourage us concerning the prospect of a happy removal of our national afflictions, a happy future of stability in our civil institutions, and of peace in the whole land, than if many signal victories were given to our honored armies. Let us pray earnestly and constantly for that spirit, which, above all things, is a nation's wealth, and strength, and praise. "The Lord's hand is not shortened," that it cannot thus bless us. "His ear is not heavy, that it cannot hear" us when we seek so great a blessing. He is "able to do exceeding abundantly above all that we ask or think;" and prayer is the arm that places our wants on His mighty power.

The *Christian Examiner*

Well into the nineteenth century, New England offered the United States more learned religious commentary on all manner of subjects than did any other region of the country. During the Civil War that commentary did not let up. One particularly interesting reflection on the ways of God with the United States came at the end of the war from a Unitarian periodical published in Boston, the Christian Examiner. *In an anonymous essay on the victory of the Union (much applauded) and the assassination of Abraham Lincoln (much bemoaned), a different reading of providence appeared than John Rice had held up early in the contest. What makes the essay in the* Christian Examiner *of particular interest is that, although Boston Unitarians had begun to give up notions of a transcendent deity who intervened in the daily affairs of society, the Unitarian author of this account did in fact return to those older habits of mind as he interpreted the meaning of the war.*

There is one thing which has made this revolution we have witnessed a very different matter from the ordinary difficulties and struggles by which nations are

[Source: Anonymous, "The Nation's Triumph, and its Sacrifice," *Christian Examiner* 78 (May 1865): 438-41.]

tried. The revolution to be wrought was not only a political, but a moral revolution. It had all to be wrought out in the minds and hearts of the people as we went along. And though an intelligent people may travel fast at such a time, yet there is danger, as in the march of a great army, that the van will get out of communication with the rear, and so, great dangerous spaces be left in the ranks. Then how much this danger is increased by the mere scale of things on which the work must be done, — a country so vast in its breadth from east to west, from Atlantic to Pacific shore; so sharply cut by belts of climate and population as you pass from north to south; a population so great and so changing, — the losses by war, gigantic as they were, being more than made up by immigration: such multitudes of citizens of foreign birth, who had no knowledge of our institutions, and little sympathy with us: such sharp divisions on every point of public policy; such eager dissension and rivalry on all matters of humanity, justice, and public right. Then this war was not a mere rivalry of two great sections; it was not a mere and simple controversy to preserve the national existence and honor: but it had sprung from the shock of moral controversies and ideas. It involved a moral revolution in men's ways of thinking and living. By the appointment of Providence, it carried along with it one of the great social revolutions of all history, — the emancipation of a race in bondage, a change in the whole political, social, and economical condition of four millions of a half-barbarian population. Only when we get a little way off from this turbulent time, in the coming years of quietness and peace, shall we begin to understand how vast is the change we are even now passing through.

Perhaps no man ever felt with a keener and deeper sense of personal responsibility his own position as chief and most responsible actor in such a time. And what, next after the profound and religious sense of duty which has moved him, we have to admire in the late President, is the steady patience with which he has set himself to study and understand the real facts of the time. He has not sought the interpretation of them in books or theories; but he has studied the facts themselves at first hand, or as reflected in the minds of the living actors in them. This enormous and complicated case, involving the institutions, the hopes, the future of a great nation, he has studied with the same careful, resolute, and patient attention which a lawyer gives to a very intricate case in court. Such a case — so vast in its interests, so complicated in its facts, so confused by the passions and prejudices of its witnesses, so august in the tribunal of its decision — was put into the hands of the shrewd, patient, sagacious, and intelligent, but not over-learned, country lawyer, to whom we committed it four years and a half ago. And steadily, month by month, in the best judgment of the world, the nation has been justified in the confidence it twice reposed in him.

Had he the fault of over-leniency and careless trust? For himself, it is too late to answer that question now. And yet it is hard to see how any ordinary prudence of self-protection would have saved him from a plot so deliberately laid and so coolly executed. The murder of that Friday night stands as one of the great crimes of history, — as a crime solitary and unexampled yet in the life of our nation. But, in the particular shape it took, it is hard to see how any greater political severity, or any different dealing with armed and rebellious populations over the border, would have been any defence. It would appear that the danger had been just as great for weeks back, — perhaps, for months, — and was no more likely to be shunned in one course of action than another. The one unpardonable thing in the eye of the fanatics and assassins who sought his life has been, that he was the successful head of a nation victorious in its defence from treason. Doubtless there are many at the South, desperate men, homeless, reckless, ruined by the war, their towns and homes devastated by fire, their property gone by pillage, the order of society in which they had bound up their ambitious hope and pride wrecked and overthrown in the storm of this great revolution. Doubtless there are many such, ready for any crime, and hungry only for revenge against those they fancy the authors of their ruin. We might have thought it less strange if the President's life had fallen by the hand of such, rather than by the dissolute and self-willed youth with whom murder was a theatrical ambition and a melodramatic scene. Such crimes are the natural progeny and the curse of war; especially of civil war, in which a man stakes not only some particular interest or fancied honor of his nation, but his life, his home, his property, his all. But it was not from such a source. It was from the impotent, blind, fanatic hate which seeks only vengeance on the head that has brought calamity and defeat to its ambitions and its dreams. For the President there would have been no escape by any excess of severity in dealing with a crushed and defeated population. And therefore we remember, not in regret, but only with gratitude and honor, the leniency and mercy which he was so anxious to cherish as the heart of all his public policy.

The tragedy of Good Friday has inaugurated a new era of public feeling. A gloomier, sterner temper than has possessed us in the darkest moments of the war pervades these hours of returning and victorious peace. How different it all was up to the time that deadly blow was struck, and how eagerly the popular heart responded to the language of mercy and good-will from the Chief Magistrate of the nation, we have already seen. The contrast is strikingly told in these words of a resolution passed at San Francisco:

"Before his death, peace was possible. All the atmosphere was filled with generous emotions and kind sympathy. Now, peace means subjugation. God have mercy on the souls of the rebel chiefs!

We say nothing of the obvious injustice of holding a whole class or population guilty of an act done by a single desperate hand, or even of a plot which must have been shared by many conspirators. Nor do we anticipate what terms of peace are likely to be made or altered, now that the nation's confidence has been so insulted and betrayed. But we note the remarkable fact, that neither defeat, nor delay, nor all the costs and sufferings of this four-years' war, have ever moved the popular heart to so deep a resentment, or to a feeling so near to vindictiveness and revenge. Nothing in these latter days has been more striking than the prompt and eager response to every word that has spoken of treason as a crime, and has denounced the punishment due to those who have assailed the nation's life. Secession and State rights might have been a dangerous doctrine before; but there was at least charity for those who held it in sincerity, and a disposition to forget and forgive what they had been madly led to attempt in support of it. But now that heresy, if not actually regarded as a crime, is looked on as an extenuation and defence of crime.

Horace Bushnell

At the same time that the Christian Examiner *was trying to provide a providential reading of the war, others were pursuing the same goal differently. The Hartford, Connecticut, pastor, Horace Bushnell (1802-76), returned to his alma mater, Yale, to deliver a commencement oration in July of 1865. But no college in America could think of honoring its graduates in that year without also honoring — and mourning — its dead. In the American Revolution the nation was born; in the Civil War the nation was reborn. The rebirth was even bloodier than the birth, but it is important for us all to remember, Bushnell noted, that now our unity as a nation has been "cemented and forever sanctified."*

According to the true economy of the world, so many of its grandest and most noble benefits have and are to have a tragic origin, and to come as outgrowths only of blood. Whether it be that sin is in the world, and the whole creation groaneth in the necessary throes of its demonized life, we need not stay to inquire; for sin would be in the world and the demonizing spell would be upon it. Such was, and was to be, and is, the economy of it. Common life, the world's great life, is in the large way tragic. As the mild benignity and peaceful reign of Christ begins at the principle: "without shedding of blood, there is no remission," so, without shedding of blood, there is almost nothing great in the world, or to be expected for it. For the life is in the blood, — all life; and it is put flowing within, partly for the serving of a nobler use in flowing out on fit occasion,

---

[Source: Horace Bushnell, "Our Obligations to the Dead," in *Building Eras in Religion* (New York: Charles Scribner's Sons, 1910), pp. 325-28.]

to quicken and consecrate whatever it touches. God could not plan a Peace-Society world, to live in the sweet amenities, and grow great and happy by simply thriving and feeding. There must be bleeding also. Sentiments must be born that are children of thunder; there must be heroes and heroic nationalities, and martyr testimonies, else there will be only mediocrities, insipidities, common-place men, and common-place writings, — a sordid and mean peace, liberties without a pulse, and epics that are only eclogues [country poems].

And here it is that the dead of our war have done for us a work so precious, which is all their own, — they have bled for us; and by this simple sacrifice of blood they have opened for us a new great chapter of life. We were living before in trade and commerce, bragging of our new cities and our census reports, and our liberties that were also consciously mocked by our hypocrisies; having only the possibilities of great inspirations and not the fact, materialized more and more evidently in our habits and sentiments, strong principally in our discords and the impetuosity of our projects for money. But the blood of our dead has touched our souls with thoughts more serious and deeper, and begotten, as I trust, somewhat of that high-bred inspiration which is itself the possibility of genius, and of a true public greatness. Saying nothing then for the present of our victors and victories, let us see what we have gotten by the blood of our slain.

And first of all, in this blood our unity is cemented and forever sanctified. Something was gained for us here, at the beginning, by our sacrifices in the fields of our Revolution, — something, but not all. Had it not been for this common bleeding of the States in their common cause, it is doubtful whether our Constitution could ever have been carried. The discords of the Convention were imminent, as we know, and were only surmounted by compromises that left them still existing. They were simply kenneled under the Constitution and not reconciled, as began to be evident shortly in the doctrines of state sovereignty, and state nullification, here and there asserted. We had not bled enough, as yet, to merge our colonial distinctions and make us a proper nation. Our battles had not been upon a scale to thoroughly mass our feeling, or gulf us in a common cause and life. Against the state-rights doctrines, the logic of our Constitution was decisive, and they were refuted a thousand times over. But such things do not go by argument. No argument transmutes a discord, or composes a unity where there was none. The matter wanted here was blood, not logic, and this we now have on a scale large enough to meet our necessity. True it is blood on one side, and blood on the other, — all the better for that; for bad bleeding kills, and righteous bleeding sanctifies and quickens. The state-rights doctrine is now fairly bled away, and the unity died for, in a way of such prodigious devotion, is forever sealed and glorified.

3. Meditations on the Nation under God

John Brown (1800-1859)

John Brown earned his reputation as one of the most violent opponents of slavery by combating slave interests in the Kansas Territory. In May 1856, Brown and a small band killed five proslavery settlers in their sleep in Kansas. A little more than three years later on October 16, 1859, he raided the federal armory in Harpers Ferry, Virginia on October 16, 1859, with the hope that the weapons "liberated" in that raid could be used by slaves to gain their freedom. The raid was a failure, in the sense that no uprising occurred, Brown was soon captured, and in December of that same year he was hung. But the raid was a success, in the sense that Brown had hoped to increase abolitionist pressure on the nation as a whole, and the controversy surrounding his raid and execution did exactly that. According to Brown himself, whose religious convictions had been shaped by evangelical and Calvinist influences, his activities stemmed completely from religious motivations. In particular, he believed that the United States could become God's agent for the return of Jesus Christ. Brown's plan for slaves to revolt against their masters was, in his view, a way of fulfilling God's plan for America. This position he maintained to the end of his life, as the following letter, written mere days before his execution, indicates.

Jail, Charlestown, Wednesday, Nov. 23, 1859.

Rev. McFarland — Dear friend,

Although you write to me as a stranger, the spirit you show towards me and the cause for which I am in bonds makes me feel towards you as a dear

---

[Source: Richard D. Webb, ed., *The Life and Letters of Captain John Brown* (London: Smith, Elder, and Co., 1861), pp. 273-74.]

friend. I would be glad to have you or any of my liberty-loving ministerial friends here, to talk and pray with me. I am not a stranger to the way of salvation by Christ. From my youth I have studied much on that subject, and at one time hoped to be a minister myself; but God had another work for me to do. To me it is given, in behalf of Christ not only to believe on him, but also to suffer for his sake. But, while I trust that I have some experimental and saving knowledge of religion, it would be a great pleasure to me to have some one better qualified than myself to lead my mind in prayer and meditation, now that my time is so near a close. You may wonder, are there no ministers of the gospel here? I answer, No. There are no ministers of Christ here. These ministers who profess to be Christian and hold slaves or advocate slavery, I cannot abide them. My knees will not bend in prayer with them, while their hands are stained with the blood of souls. The subject you mention as having been preaching on, the day before you wrote to me, is one which I have often thought of since my imprisonment. I think I feel as happy as Paul did when he lay in prison. He knew, if they killed him, it would greatly advance the cause of Christ; that was the reason he rejoiced so. On that same ground "I do rejoice, yea, and will rejoice." Let them hang me; I

John Brown
(Library of Congress)

forgive them, and may God forgive them, for they know not what they do. I have no regret for the transaction for which I am condemned. I went against the laws of men, it is true; but "whether it be right to obey God or men, judge ye." Christ told me to remember them that are in bonds as bound with them, to do towards them as I would wish them to do towards me in similar circumstances. My conscience bade me do that. I tried to do it, but failed. Therefore I have no regret on that score. I have no sorrow either as to the result, only for my poor wife and children. They have suffered much, and it is hard to leave them uncared for. But God will be a husband to the widow, and a father to the fatherless.

I have frequently been in Wooster; and if any of my old friends from about Akron are there, you can show them this letter. I have but a few more days, and I feel anxious to be away, "where the wicked cease from troubling, and the weary are at rest." Farewell.

Your friend, and the friend of all friends of liberty,

JOHN BROWN.

Philip Schaff

A nation of no long history, of no jingle culture, of varied race, language, and religion had spent four years tearing itself apart. Was there any reason whatsoever to expect greatness from such a land, such a people? Answers to that question had to come more from faith and religious hope than from experience and worldly calculation. The answer of Philip Schaff (1819-93), theologian and church historian of the German Reformed seminary in Mercersburg, Pennsylvania, was delivered in Europe in 1865. America is not a moral and spiritual chaos, Schaff argued, though he admitted that much would suggest the contrary. Rather, America is "a sound and robust national organism" which, as it faces a great future, is "daunted by no obstacle," not even by this prolonged and cruel conflict itself.

I am, it is true, very well aware that in every country all healthy conditions and institutions must assume a form agreeable to the natural development of its history, and that it is an idle undertaking to transplant foreign manners and customs, unmodified, to our own soil. But on the other hand, you will not deny, that not only the past but also the present is a book of instruction, warning, and encouragement for all that are willing to read it. Ought America, the land of the West,

---

[Source: "Dr. Schaff's Lectures on America Delivered in Europe, 1865" (trans. C. C. Starbuck), in the *Christian Intelligencer*, 38, no. 9 (Mar. 1, 1866), unpaged.]

Julia Ward Howe (1819-1910), author of the "Battle Hymn of the Republic"
and leader in woman's suffrage movement.
Picture taken in Newport, Rhode Island, in 1905.
(Keystone-Mast Collection, University of California, Riverside)

whither points the course of the sun and of civilization, to be an exception to this? The nations and churches of the old and of the new world are now, through a thousand channels of intercourse, continually drawing nearer together, and ought more and more to learn to understand, to value and to love each other better, and thereby advance the coming of that great crowning era, where there shall be one flock and one Shepherd, in the fullest sense of that prophetic word.

Among all the countries of the earth, America appears least of all to present the image of a harmonious whole. . . . Viewed cursorily and from without, it appears an impenetrable spiritual, moral, and religious chaos, a veritable *Tohuwabohu* [Hebrew, a great void]. It is a land of antitheses and antagonisms, like no other, and affords sufficient material for the most diverse impressions and judgments, from enthusiastic eulogy to the most utterly scornful censure. It is an arena and smelting crucible of all nationalities, churches, and sects, where the noblest and basest elements of the old world ferment confusedly together. New York, for instance, is as much Irish, German, and French, as an Anglo-American city, and in heterogeneousness of composition more cosmopolitan than even London or Paris.

But the very fact that America can not only endure without harm such an uninterrupted stream of the immigration of nations from the East, but can, without difficulty and with incredible rapidity, denationalize it and assimilate it unto itself; and that, in cases innumerable, out of men who, in Europe, had appeared pecuniarily or morally lost beyond hope, it makes useful citizens and earnest Christians — this very circumstance bears witness to the existence of a sound and robust national organism, which in impregnable faith in a great future is daunted by no obstacle, and welcomes immigrants from all lands to the development and administration of its inexhaustible resources for the good of mankind.

Abraham Lincoln (1809-65)

In the final decade of Lincoln's life, hope mixed with sorrow. No churchman, Lincoln nonetheless had a profound sense of human destiny and human tragedy. In a series of documents extending from 1855 to 1865, one observes a spiritual wrestling with realities as momentous as they were inescapable. Not only was a nation divided, but so were its churches, so was its moral purpose, so were its prayers. Lincoln, who has been called "the spiritual center of American history" (Sidney E. Mead), reluctantly concluded that "these are not . . . the days of miracles."

1. Letter to Joshua F. Speed

SPRINGFIELD AUGUST 24, 1855.

Dear Speed: You know what a poor correspondent I am. Ever since I received your very agreeable letter of the 22d of May I have been intending to write you an answer to it. You suggest that in political action, now, you and I would differ. I suppose we would; not quite as much, however, as you may think. You know I dislike slavery, and you fully admit the abstract wrong of it. So far there is no cause of difference. But you say that sooner than yield your legal right to the slave, especially at the bidding of those who are not themselves interested, you would see the Union dissolved. I am not aware that any one is bidding you yield that right; very certainly I am not. I leave that matter entirely to yourself. I also acknowledge your rights and my obligations under the Constitution in regard to your slaves. I confess I hate to see the poor creatures hunted down and caught and carried back to their stripes and unrequited toil; but I bite my lips and keep quiet. In 1841 you and I had together a tedious low-water trip on a steamboat from Louisville to St. Louis. You may remember, as I well do, that from Louisville to the mouth of the

[Source: J. G. Nicolay and John Hay, eds., *Complete Works of Abraham Lincoln* (New York: Lamb Publishing Co., 1905): (1) II, 281-87; (2) VIII, 28-29; (3) VIII, 52-53; (4) VIII, 235-37; (5) X, 109-10; (6) XI, 45-47.]

Ohio there were on board ten or a dozen slaves shackled together with irons. That sight was a continued torment to me, and I see something like it every time I touch the Ohio or any other slave border. It is not fair for you to assume that I have no interest in a thing which has, and continually exercises, the power of making me miserable. You ought rather to appreciate how much the great body

President Abraham Lincoln, 1864. Mathew Brady Collection.
(National Archives and Records Administration)

of the Northern people do crucify their feelings, in order to maintain their loyalty to the Constitution and the Union. I do oppose the extension of slavery because my judgment and feeling so prompt me, and I am under no obligations to the contrary. If for this you and I must differ, differ we must. You say, if you were President, you would send an army and hang the leaders of the Missouri outrages upon the Kansas elections; still, if Kansas fairly votes herself a slave State she must be admitted, or the Union must be dissolved. But how if she votes herself a slave State unfairly, that is, by the very means for which you say you would hang men? Must she still be admitted, or the Union dissolved? That will be the phase of the question when it first becomes a practical one. In your assumption that there may be a fair decision of the slavery question in Kansas, I plainly see you and I would differ about the Nebraska law. I look upon that enactment not as a law, but as a violence from the beginning. It was conceived in violence, is maintained in violence, and is being executed in violence. I say it was conceived in violence, because the destruction of the Missouri Compromise, under the circumstances, was nothing less than violence. It was passed in violence, because it could not have passed at all but for the votes of many members in violence of the known will of their constituents. It is maintained in violence, because the elections since clearly demand its repeal; and the demand is openly disregarded.

You say men ought to be hung for the way they are executing the law; I say the way it is being executed is quite as good as any of its antecedents. It is being executed in the precise way which was intended from the first, else why does no Nebraska man express astonishment or condemnation? Poor Reeder is the only public man who has been silly enough to believe that anything like fairness was ever intended, and he has been bravely undeceived.

That Kansas will form a slave constitution, and with it will ask to be admitted into the Union, I take to be already a settled question, and so settled by the very means you so pointedly condemn. By every principle of law ever held by any court North or South, every negro taken to Kansas is free; yet, in utter disregard of this, — in the spirit of violence merely, — that beautiful legislature gravely passes a law to hang any man who shall venture to inform a negro of his legal rights. This is the subject and real object of the law. If, like Haman, they should hang upon the gallows of their own building, I shall not be among the mourners for their fate. In my humble sphere, I shall advocate the restoration of the Missouri Compromise so long as Kansas remains a Territory, and when, by all these foul means, it seeks to come into the Union as a slave State, I shall oppose it. I am very loath in any case to withhold my assent to the enjoyment of property acquired or located in good faith; but I do not admit that good faith in taking a negro to Kansas to be held in slavery is a probability with any man. Any man who has sense enough to be the controller of his own property has too much sense to misunderstand the outrageous character of the whole Nebraska business. But I digress. In my opposition to the admission of Kansas I shall have some company, but we may be beaten. If we are, I shall not on that account attempt to dissolve the Union. I think it probable, however, we shall be beaten. Standing as a unit among yourselves, you can, directly and indirectly, bribe enough of our men to carry the day, as you could on the open proposition to establish a monarchy. Get hold of some man in the North whose position and ability is such that he can make the support of your measure, whatever it may be, a Democratic party necessity, and the thing is done. Apropos of this, let me tell you an anecdote. Douglas introduced the Nebraska bill in January. In February afterward there was a called session of the Illinois legislature. Of the one hundred members composing the two branches of that body, about seventy were Democrats. These latter held a caucus, in which the Nebraska bill was talked of, if not formally discussed. It was thereby discovered that just three, and no more, were in favor of the measure. In a day or two Douglas's orders came on to have resolutions passed approving the bill; and they were passed by large majorities!!! The truth of this is vouched for by a bolting Democratic member. The masses, too, Democratic as well as Whig, were even nearer unanimous against it; but, as soon as the party necessity of supporting it became apparent, the way the Democrats began to see the wisdom and justice of it was perfectly astonishing.

You say that if Kansas fairly votes herself a free State, as a Christian you will rejoice at it. All decent slaveholders talk that way, and I do not doubt their candor. But they never vote that way. Although in a private letter or conversation you will express your preference that Kansas shall be free, you would vote for no man for Congress who would say the same thing publicly. No such man could be elected from any district in a slave State. You think Stringfellow and company ought to be hung; and yet at the next presidential election you will vote for the exact type and representative of Stringfellow. The slave-breeders and slave-traders are a small, odious, and detested class among you; and yet in politics they dictate the course of all of you, and are as completely your masters as you are the master of your own negroes. You inquire where I now stand. That is a disputed point. I think I am a Whig; but others say there are no Whigs, and that I am an Abolitionist. When I was at Washington, I voted for the Wilmot proviso as good as forty times; and I never heard of any one attempting to unwhig me for that. I now do no more than oppose the extension of slavery. I am not a Know-nothing; that is certain. How could I be? How can any one who abhors the oppression of negroes be in favor of degrading classes of white people? Our progress in degeneracy appears to me to be pretty rapid. As a nation we began by declaring that "all men are created equal." We now practically read it "all men are created equal, except negroes." When the Know-nothings get control, it will read "all men are created equal, except negroes and foreigners and Catholics." When it comes to this, I shall prefer emigrating to some country where they make no pretense of loving liberty, — to Russia, for instance, where despotism can be taken pure, and without the base alloy of hypocrisy.

2. Reply to a Committee from the Religious Denominations of Chicago, asking the President to issue a Proclamation of Emancipation, September 13, 1862.

The subject presented in the memorial is one upon which I have thought much for weeks past, and I may even say for months. I am approached with the most opposite opinions and advice, and that by religious men who are equally certain that they represent the divine will. I am sure that either the one or the other class is mistaken in that belief, and perhaps in some respects both. I hope it will not be irreverent for me to say that if it is probable that God would reveal his will to others on a point so connected with my duty, it might be supposed he would reveal it directly to me; for, unless I am more deceived in myself than I often am, it is my earnest desire to know the will of Providence in this matter. And if I can learn what it is, I will do it.

These are not, however, the days of miracles, and I suppose it will be granted that I am not to expect a direct revelation. I must study the plain physical facts of the case, ascertain what is possible, and learn what appears to be wise and right.

3. Meditation on the Divine Will, September [30?], 1862

The will of God prevails. In great contests each party claims to act in accordance with the will of God. Both may be, and one must be, wrong. God cannot be for and against the same thing at the same time. In the present civil war it is quite possible that God's purpose is something different from the purpose of either party; and yet the human instrumentalities, working just as they do, are the best adaptation to effect his purpose. I am almost ready to say that this is probably true; that God wills this contest, and wills that it shall not end yet. By his mere great power on the minds of the now contestants, he could have either saved or destroyed the Union without a human contest. Yet the contest began. And, having begun, he could give the final victory to either side any day. Yet the contest proceeds.

4. Proclamation Appointing a National Fast-Day, March 30, 1863, by the President of the United States of America: A Proclamation.

Whereas, the Senate of the United States, devoutly recognizing the supreme authority and just government of Almighty God in all the affairs of men and of nations, has by a resolution requested the President to designate and set apart a day for national prayer and humiliation:

And whereas, it is the duty of nations as well as of men to own their dependence upon the overruling power of God; to confess their sins and transgressions in humble sorrow, yet with assured hope that genuine repentance will lead to mercy and pardon; and to recognize the sublime truth, announced in the Holy Scriptures and proven by all history, that those nations only are blessed whose God is the Lord:

And insomuch as we know that by his divine law nations, like individuals, are subjected to punishments and chastisements in this world, may we not justly fear that the awful calamity of civil war which now desolates the land may be but a punishment inflicted upon us for our presumptuous sins, to the needful end of our national reformation as a whole people? We have been the recipients of the choicest bounties of Heaven. We have been preserved, these many years, in peace and prosperity. We have grown in numbers, wealth, and power as no other nation has ever grown; but we have forgotten God. We have forgotten the gracious hand which preserved us in peace, and multiplied and enriched and strengthened us; and we have vainly imagined, in the deceitfulness of our hearts, that all these blessings were produced by some superior wisdom and virtue of our own. Intoxicated with unbroken success, we have become too self-sufficient to feel the necessity of redeeming and preserving grace, too proud to pray to the God that made us:

It behooves us, then, to humble ourselves before the offended Power, to confess our national sins, and to pray for clemency and forgiveness:

Now, therefore, in compliance with the request, and fully concurring in the views, of the Senate, I do by this my proclamation designate and set apart Thursday the 30th day of April, 1863, as a day of national humiliation, fasting, and prayer. And I do hereby request all the people to abstain on that day from their ordinary secular pursuits, and to unite at their several places of public worship and their respective homes in keeping the day holy to the Lord, and devoted to the humble discharge of the religious duties proper to that solemn occasion. All this being done in sincerity and truth, let us then rest humbly in the hope authorized by the divine teachings, that the united cry of the nation will be heard on high, and answered with blessings no less than the pardon of our national sins, and the restoration of our now divided and suffering country to its former happy condition of unity and peace.

In witness whereof, I have hereunto set my hand, and caused the seal of the United States to be affixed.

5. Letter to Dr. Ide and Others[1]

EXECUTIVE MANSION, MAY 30, 1864

In response to the preamble and resolutions of the American Baptist Home Mission Society, which you did me the honor to present, I can only thank you for thus adding to the effective and almost unanimous support which the Christian communities are so zealously giving to the country and to liberty. Indeed, it is difficult to conceive how it could be otherwise with any one professing Christianity, or even having ordinary perceptions of right and wrong. To read in the Bible, as the word of God himself, that "In the sweat of *thy* face shalt thou eat bread," and to preach therefrom that, "In the sweat of *other men's* faces shalt thou eat bread," to my mind can scarcely be reconciled with honest sincerity. When brought to my final reckoning, may I have to answer for robbing no man of his goods; yet more tolerable even this, than for robbing one of himself and all that was his. When, a year or two ago, those professedly holy men of the South met in the semblance of prayer and devotion, and, in the name of him who said, "As ye would all men should do unto you, do ye even so unto them," appealed to the Christian world to aid them in doing to a whole race of men as they would have no man do unto themselves, to my thinking they contemned and insulted God and his church far more than did Satan when he tempted the Saviour with the kingdoms of the earth. The devil's attempt was no more false, and far less hypocritical. But let me forbear, remembering it is also written, "Judge not lest ye be judged."

A. LINCOLN.

6. From the Second Inaugural Address, March 4, 1865

Neither party expected for the war the magnitude or the duration which it has already attained. Neither anticipated that the cause of the conflict might cease with, or even before, the conflict itself should cease. Each looked for an easier triumph, and a result less fundamental and astounding. Both read the same Bible, and pray to the same God; and each invokes his aid against the other. It may seem strange that any men should dare to ask a just God's assistance in wringing their bread from the sweat of other men's faces; but let us judge not, that we be not judged. The prayers of both could not be answered — that of neither has been answered fully.

The Almighty has his own purposes. "Woe unto the world because of of-

1. Committee composed of Rev. Dr. Ide, Hon. J. R. Doolittle, and Hon. A. Hubbell. [Note provided by editors Nicolay and Hay.]

fenses! for it must needs be that offenses come; but woe to that man by whom the offense cometh." If we shall suppose that American slavery is one of those offenses which, in the providence of God, must needs come, but which, having continued through his appointed time, he now wills to remove, and that he gives to both North and South this terrible war, as the woe due to those by whom the offense came, shall we discern therein any departure from those divine attributes which the believers in a living God always ascribe to him? Fondly do we hope — fervently do we pray — that this mighty scourge of war may speedily pass away. Yet, if God wills that it continue until all the wealth piled by the bondsman's two hundred and fifty years of unrequited toil shall be sunk, and until every drop of blood drawn with the lash shall be paid by another drawn with the sword, as was said three thousand years ago, so still it must be said, "The judgments of the Lord are true and righteous altogether."

With malice toward none; with charity for all; with firmness in the right, as God gives us to see the right, let us strive on to finish the work we are in; to bind up the nation's wounds; to care for him who shall have borne the battle, and for his widow, and his orphan — to do all which may achieve and cherish a just and lasting peace among ourselves, and with all nations.

Charles Hodge

Hodge, who was introduced above (p. 413), wrote with feeling about the war on several occasions. One of his most memorable essays appeared as a eulogy to Abraham Lincoln in July 1865. Much that Hodge said was conventional, including what he concluded about the workings of divine providence. Yet in the care with which he explored the concept of providence itself, and also in his awareness of the social conditioning that shaped attitudes in the war, Hodge's meditation came closer to apprehending the actual complexities of the time than did most of his peers.

The scriptural doctrine of Providence assumes: 1. The real existence of the external world. 2. The efficiency of secondary causes. That is, that created minds as agents, originate their own acts; and that material substances have properties or forces inhering in them, which make them the efficient and necessary antecedents of their effects. 3. That all events, whether in nature or history (supernatural events excepted), have their proximate and adequate causes in the agency and properties of created substances, spiritual or material. 4. That God,

---

[Source: Charles Hodge, "President Lincoln," *Biblical Repertory and Princeton Review* 37 (July 1865): 435-36, 450-51.]

as an infinite and omnipresent spirit, is not a mere spectator of the world, looking on as a mechanist upon the machine which he has constructed; nor is he the only efficient cause, so that all effects are to be referred to his agency, and so that the laws of nature are only the uniform methods of his operation; but he is everywhere present upholding all things by the word of his power, and controlling, guiding, and directing the action of second causes, so that all events occur according to the counsel of his will. An abundant harvest is proximately due to the operation of second causes, but God so determines and directs those causes as to secure the designed result. The prosperity of individuals, of communities, and of nations, is due to secondary causes, but those causes are so determined by God, that he is to be acknowledged as the Giver of all good. This is equally true of all events, whether prosperous or adverse, whether in themselves good or evil. Nothing happens by necessity or by chance. God governs all his creatures and all their actions. This universal and absolute control of Divine Providence is, on the one hand, consistent with the character of God, so that he is, in no sense, the author of sin; and, on the other hand, with the nature of his creatures. He governs free agents with certainty, but without destroying their liberty, and material causes, without superseding their efficiency.

It is impossible to express or to conceive the importance of these familiar principles of scriptural truth. They are not the discoveries of human reason; neither philosophy nor science (when divorced from the Bible) even accepts them. They are however the foundation of all religion, of all order, of all Christian civilization; and the only ground of confidence or hope.

Every great event therefore is to be viewed in two different aspects: first as the effect of natural causes; and secondly, as a design and result of God's providence. The interpretation of Divine providence is indeed often a matter of great difficulty and responsibility. It requires humility and caution. Some of his dispensations are, as to their design, perfectly clear, others are doubtful, and others to us and for the present inscrutable. In one thing however we are safe; we have a right to infer that the actual consequences of any event, whether great or small, are its designed consequences; whether intended in judgment or mercy to those affected by them must be determined partly by their nature, partly by their attendant circumstances, and partly by the course of subsequent events. Why the Reformation was suppressed in Italy and Spain, and allowed to succeed in Northern Germany and Great Britain, we cannot even now determine, but it is none the less our duty to recognize these events as due to the ordering providence of God, and to study them as such.

No Christian can look upon the events of the last four years without being deeply impressed with the conviction that they have been ordered by God to produce great and lasting changes in the state of the country, and probably of the world. Few periods of equal extent in the history of our race are likely to prove more influential in controlling the destinies of men. Standing, as we now

Charles Hodge
(Princeton Theological Seminary)

do, at the close of one stage at least of this great epoch, it becomes us to look back and to look around us, that we may in some measure understand what God has wrought. . . .

Another prominent feature of Mr. Lincoln's administration was a spirit of conciliation. From first to last he endeavoured to persuade the revolted States to return to their allegiance, in order to save them from the miseries of war. And in the process of reconstruction his ruling idea was to disturb as little as possible existing relations, to inflict as few penalties as possible, and to restore all rights and privileges as fully and as rapidly as was consistent with public safety. He made a clear distinction between sin and sinners, between the offence and the offenders. This is a distinction which is not commonly made, for the obvious reason that generally there is no legitimate ground for it. In ordinary cases of theft and murder all the criminality and turpitude which belong to the offence attach also to the offender. But in other cases, especially in the offences of nations or communities, the distinction is legitimate and important. Idolatry is a great crime; it is apostasy from God. It is denounced in the Bible as the greatest of all sins; it is declared to be always inexcusable. And yet no man can doubt that had we been born in India or Africa, we too would have been idolaters. Popery, the worship of the Virgin Mary, the adoration of the Host, are justly regarded by all Protestants as great offences against God and Christ. But had we been born in Italy or Spain, we too had been papists. Slavery, as it existed at the South (meaning by slavery the whole system of slave laws there in force) is also a great moral evil. And yet had we been born and educated under that system, we doubtless would either have acquiesced in it or defended it. Rebellion is a great crime (unless for just cause,) and the rebellion of the South was wanton and wicked; yet we must be strong in our self-conceit if we take for granted that had we been South Carolinians or Georgians, we should have resisted the overwhelming tide of popular feeling. This is not apologizing for idolatry, popery, slavery, or rebellion. It is only saying in other words what our blessed Lord himself says, when he declares it will be more tolerable in the day of judgment for the heathen than for us. This is true, not because heathenism is not the sum and essence of all moral evil, but because there is in such cases a great distinction between the criminality of an offence in itself considered, and the responsibility of the offender. The reason for this is obvious. A man's character, his opinions, feelings, and conduct are determined in part by the inward principles of his nature, and largely by the external influences to which he is subject. If kept in ignorance of the truth; if error is constantly inculcated, and all the power of education and example be brought to bear in favour of evil, it is almost unavoidable that the judgment will be perverted and the mind corrupted. Men thus brought up to regard idolatry, popery, slavery, or any other form of evil to be right, and surrounded by those who support and defend it, will not, by a righteous judge, as our Lord teaches, be dealt with according to the heinousness of the offence in itself considered, but according to the circumstances and opportunities of the offender. That Mr. Lincoln recognized this obvious principle of justice is plain from his official declarations and acts. . . .

4. After the War

"Welcome to the Ransomed"

Emancipation Celebrated

The Emancipation Proclamation issued on January 1, 1863, had no immedi-
ate effect, of course, in those areas still under Southern control or still being
contested by opposing armies. In the District of Columbia itself, however,
emancipation was immediate. Daniel A. Payne (1811-93), of black and In-
dian ancestry, moved briefly in Lutheran and Presbyterian circles before be-
coming in 1852 a bishop in the African Methodist Episcopal Church. From
1863 to 1876 Payne also served as president of Wilberforce University (Ohio),
this position reflecting his strong commitment to an educated black clergy. In
the excerpt below, the AME bishop loses no time in urging freed fellow blacks
to make their emancipation from slavery also the occasion for an emancipa-
tion from sin.

We are gathered to celebrate the emancipation, yea, rather, the *Redemption* of
the enslaved people of the District of Columbia, the exact number of whom we
have no means of ascertaining, because, since the benevolent intention of Congress became manifest, many have been removed by their owners beyond the
reach of this beneficent act.

Our pleasing task then, is to welcome to the Churches, the homesteads,
and circles of free colored Americans, those who remain to enjoy *the boon of*
holy Freedom.

[Source: "Welcome to the Ransomed," in Daniel A. Payne, *Sermons and Addresses, 1853-1891*
(New York: Arno Press, 1972), pp. 6-7 of this sermon.]

Brethren, sisters, friends, we say welcome to our Churches, welcome to our homesteads, welcome to our social circles.

Enter the great family of Holy Freedom; not to *lounge in sinful indolence,* not to *degrade yourselves by vice,* nor to *corrupt society by licentiousness,* neither to *offend the laws by crime,* but to the *enjoyment of a well regulated liberty,* the offspring of generous laws; of law as just as generous, as righteous as just — a liberty to be *perpetuated* by equitable law, and sanctioned by the divine; for law is never equitable, righteous, just, until it harmonizes with the will of Him, who is "*King* of kings, and *Lord* of lords," and who commanded Israel to *have but one law for the home-born* and the *stranger.*

We repeat ourselves, welcome then *ye ransomed ones;* welcome *not* to indolence, to vice, licentiousness, and crime, but to a well-regulated liberty, sanctioned by the Divine, maintained by the Human law.

Welcome to habits of industry and thrift — to duties of religion and piety — to obligations of law, order, government — of government divine, of government human: these two, though not one, are inseparable. The man who refuses to obey divine law, will never obey human laws. *The divine first,* the *human next.* The latter is the consequence of the former, and follows it as light does the rising sun.

We invite you to our Churches, because we desire you to be religious; to be more than religious; we urge you *to be godly.* We entreat you to never be content until you are emancipated from sin, from sin without, and from sin within you. But this kind of freedom is attained only through the faith of Jesus, love for Jesus, obedience to Jesus. As certain as the American Congress has *ransomed* you, so certain, yea, more certainly has Jesus redeemed you from the guilt and power of sin by his own precious blood.

As you are now free in body, so now seek to be free in soul and spirit, from sin and Satan. The *noblest freeman is he whom Christ makes free.*

Aid Solicited

Committed to both an evangelical and an abolitionist stance, the American Missionary Association — largely Congregational in membership — took the welfare of the freed black as its major concern. Both during the Civil War and after, the Association understood "welfare" in the broadest terms: food, clothing, shelter, education, and a surrounding, sustaining Christian community to help the newly "ransomed" reach their full potential. Only then could the lie be given to the many who contended "that the negroes are an improvident race, unfit to take care of themselves."

[Source: *The American Missionary,* ser. 2, 7 (Jan., 1863), 13.]

Appeal for the Freedmen

By a Committee appointed at the Annual Meeting of the American Missionary Association, October 16, 1862

In the providence of God, tens of thousands of freed slaves are now waiting, in various parts of the South, for the privileges which freedom confers, and slavery has denied them. The number is constantly increasing, and within a few months, or weeks, it is probable that hundreds of thousands will be looking to their friends for aid. And what class of people ever presented a better claim to charity? Indeed it hardly deserves the name of charity, to supply their wants. They only ask a little interest on a long standing debt. We have all reaped the fruits of their unpaid toil.

Their first wants are physical. Many of them have escaped, and will escape from their bondage in a very destitute condition. They need clothes, and bedding, and some shelter from the storm. This want will be temporary: they will soon be able to supply themselves. But for a few months they must have help.

They need education. Few of them can read, and still fewer can write. They need day schools and evening schools, for children and adults. Every family should at once be supplied with the Bible, and the mass of them should be taught to read it.

They need the preaching of the Gospel. Many of their own number are exhorters and preachers: but need teachers who can "expound unto them the way of God more perfectly."

They need assistance in organizing themselves into schools, Sabbath schools, congregations and churches. And they need intelligent friends and counselors, to guard them against the insults, impositions, immoralities and various abuses of those who hate them, and are interested to prove that the negroes are an improvident race, unfit to take care of themselves.

For every thousand of these emancipated people there should be at least one able, experienced, faithful missionary, to preach to them, to teach, to organize, and counsel them; and he should be assisted by several subordinate teachers. If a million should be emancipated within a few months, a thousand teachers will be needed, besides the requisite clothing, houses, school-houses, books and churches. Very inferior accommodations will satisfy them at first, but in some shape these must be provided.

These wants should be met at once. Never again will they welcome so heartily, appreciate so gratefully, and improve so satisfactorily these advantages, as on their first escape from the house of bondage. Such an inviting, promising field has rarely, if ever, been open to the Christian world. No time should be lost; already our work lags behind the demand. The missionaries and the teachers will be found when the call is made, if they can be sustained;

and to support a thousand missionaries and the requisite number of teachers will cost less than the support of a single regiment of cavalry. Shall it be said that the good people of the United States cannot do so much in this important work, without diminishing their contributions to other benevolent objects? We dare not ask for less. To say nothing of our obligations to these oppressed people, we owe it to ourselves, and to our country, if the President's proclamation is to be carried out, to see to it that it does not work disastrously, or fail of its legitimate fruits, for want of efficient co-operation on the part of the christian community.

Education Offered

In addition to the religiously-sponsored American Missionary Association, the Freedmen's Bureau, sponsored by the federal government, came into existence in 1865 and lasted until 1872. Its first and only head, General Oliver O. Howard (1830-1909), played a leading role in the creation of Howard University in Washington, D.C.; he also served as its first president, from 1869 to 1874. In his autobiography, Howard reveals the extent to which religion was involved here, just as it was in virtually every other effort to educate America's postwar blacks. Religion not only helped bring the educational institutions into being but also provided the leadership, the funding, and the curricular direction, the latter often being heavily theological in character.

Each denomination desired to have, here and there, a college of its own. Such institutions the founders and patrons were eager to make different from the simple primary or grammar schools; these, it was hoped and believed, would be eventually absorbed in each State in a great free school system. The educators naturally wished to put a moral and Christian stamp upon their students, especially upon those who would become instructors of colored youth. My own strong wish was ever to lay permanent substructures and build thereon as rapidly as possible, in order to give as many good teachers, professional men, and leaders to the rising generation of freedmen as we could, during the few years of Governmental control.

One of the institutions for the higher education of the negro which has maintained ample proportions and also bears my own name, warrants me in giving somewhat in detail its origin and my connection with it.

The latter part of 1866, a few gentlemen, at the instance of Rev. F. B. Mor-

---

[Source: *Autobiography of Oliver Otis Howard* (New York: Baker & Taylor Co., 1907), II, pp. 395-97.]

ris, who held an important Governmental office at the capital, and was a benevolent and scholarly man, came together at the house of Mr. A. Brewster, on K Street, Washington.

There had been two or three of such informal meetings, consisting mainly of residents of Washington, when Senators Wilson and Pomeroy, B. C. Cook, Member of the House, and myself were invited to this respectable self-constituted council, November 20, 1866. Nearly all of the dozen or more gentlemen who were present, and among them Rev. Dr. C. B. Boynton, the pastor of the Congregational Church of the city, were Congregationalists. A preliminary organization was already in existence. The subject under discussion for this time was a place for a theological school for the colored preachers and those who were to become such, that their teachings should be of value. Mr. H. D. Nichols moved that the new institution be entitled "Howard Theological Seminary." That name was adopted. Mr. Morris and some others were in the outset in favor of connecting with the seminary some industrial features; and, to show my good will, I made the same offer, being authorized by the law, that I had

School for freedmen and -women, Vicksburg, Mississippi, 1866
(Library of Congress)

been making to other educational associations, that if they would furnish a proper lot, I would cause to be erected thereon, by the [Freedmen's] Bureau, a suitable building. I believed it wiser not to use my name, but it was remarked sportively "there are other Howards."

At a meeting December 4, 1866, there was in ideas and proposals considerable progress manifested. At first, I had desired delay, thinking that the time was hardly ripe for a large institution at the capital, but, seeing the enthusiasm and fixed purpose of this body of some fourteen gentlemen, a few of whom I now observed were Presbyterians and two or three of other persuasions, I participated in their discussions. "Howard Normal and Theological Institute for the Education of Teachers and Preachers," was the new title adopted.

On January 8, 1867, at another gathering, Dr. Boynton was elected the president of the preliminary board. At this session my brother, General C. H. Howard, then assistant commissioner of the district and vicinity, moved a committee to plan a law department — a medical department having already been favorably canvassed. Thus, little by little, the idea of a university grew upon the preliminary board, the project of an institution which should have many separate departments acting together under one board of trustees. At this January sitting, an important committee was named to obtain a charter. . . . The charter was easily obtained, having seventeen charter members. The incorporation title was: "An Act to incorporate the Howard University in the District of Columbia." It was approved by the President of the United States March 2, 1867.

Optimism Tempered

Some denominations created their own agencies or bureaus to assist and nurture those Americans suddenly left to fend for themselves. The Freedmen's Aid Society, organized by the Methodist Episcopal Church (North) in 1866, saw its challenge in these terms: "The emancipation of four million of slaves has opened at our very door a wide field calling alike for mission and educational work. It has devolved upon the Church a fearful responsibility." In assuming that fearful responsibility, white northern Methodists reported their early efforts (1868) in optimistic and confident terms. Eight years later (1875), however, the enormity of the tasks weighed more heavily as the sad realization dawned that "we have been able to contribute so little. . . ."

[Source: *Reports of the Freedmen's Aid Society of the Methodist Episcopal Church . . .* (Cincinnati: Western Methodist Book Concern, 1893), pp. 6, 11 (1868); pp. 3-4 (1875).]

1. 1868

The South being thrown open to a loyal and liberty-loving ministry, Christians who had remembered those in bonds, who had prayed for, and in all proper ways labored for the overthrow of slavery, could carry or send to the millions degraded by it the means of mental and moral elevation. The Church, called to give the Gospel to every creature, must, if faithful to her trust, enter the open door, and use every efficient means to hasten the evangelization of the South. The school was found to be invaluable as an auxiliary to the missions among the Freedmen. They were every-where found anxious to have the Gospel preached to them by missionaries from the North, and to have Churches planted among them, but they were more anxious to have schools for themselves and their children.

The dawn of their freedom kindled within them a passion to learn to read and write, and a people whose incapacity to learn had been urged as a plea for their servitude, welcomed the teacher as first among their benefactors. The efforts of the undenominational commissions could not directly promote the missionary work; their agents and teachers were not chosen with reference to evangelical sentiments and experimental godliness; their schools were not designedly located so as to favor the spread of the Gospel; even where they had Sunday schools they were conducted so as to insure only temporary results. The control of the educational work connected with missions was as necessary to success as the work itself, and this necessity, seen alike by every denomination that entered the inviting field presented by the South, was the chief cause of the organization of denominational societies. . . .

It is a gratifying fact, and one that indicates the missionary character of our enterprise, that nearly a score of our teachers are ministers of the Gospel, who have been drawn to this field of labor because it furnishes such rare facilities for doing good both to the bodies and the souls of men. These teach school during the week and preach on the Sabbath, and thus carry forward in harmony this great movement for the intellectual and moral elevation of the race. All our teachers labor in the Sunday as well as in the day schools, and are preparing the thousands of ignorant and degraded children for usefulness on earth and happiness in heaven. We have been exceedingly fortunate in the selection of our laborers, for they have almost invariably been good scholars and successful teachers, and have been drawn to this work by love to Jesus and fallen humanity. The school-house, occupied as a meeting-house for religious worship as it usually is by our missionaries, and also by our teachers for Sunday school and the instruction of the children during the week, becomes to the South, as elsewhere, the true symbol of a high Christian civilization. These humble buildings in which the children are taught, are scarcely less the temples of the living God than the temples of science — for in them immortals pass into a higher spiritual as well as intellectual life.

2. 1875

The retrospection of our past efforts in behalf of this injured people awakens mingled emotions of gratitude and sadness: gratitude, that we have been enabled to accomplish so much in an enterprise so intimately connected with the safety of the nation, the elevation of man, and the prosperity of the Church, sadness, that, amid such general desolation, resulting from ignorance, superstition, crime, and slavery, we have been able to contribute so little to the relief and elevation of millions in our midst, suffering the accumulated wrongs of ages.

The work upon which this Society has entered is a gigantic one, and taxes to the utmost the energies and the benevolence of the nation. It is the Christian training of five millions of people, one-eighth of our entire population, and through these the elevation of hundreds of millions of incoming generations. They are now freemen and citizens, endowed with the rights and privileges of citizenship. It must not be forgotten that they were emancipated in ignorance, degradation, and poverty, and are what centuries of wrong and oppression have made them; and it is equally clear that the act of emancipation conferred no preparation for this new condition of life, into which, totally disqualified, they have been thrust. President Lincoln, with a dash of his pen, struck the fetters from the bodies of these four millions of slaves, but their minds were still left in the chains of ignorance, and the iron of slavery had entered into their souls. Emancipation was one of the grandest acts of the nineteenth century, and thrilled with joy the hearts of the people; and forever honored will be the noble men that participated in its achievement; but emancipation is not complete in itself; it presupposes and demands preparation. The nation has emancipated this people; but it has done it at its peril, unless it pushes more vigorously the work of Christian education. We insist upon it that the part we took in emancipation binds us with solemn obligations to educate, for education is the only completion of emancipation; and we are urged to complete this work by every consideration that induced us to commence it. To have emancipated and left these millions in ignorance and degradation would have been a work of doubtful philanthropy, and would have partaken more of the character of crime than of charity. To neglect the preparation of this people would be to perpetuate the wrongs inflicted by slavery, increase the peril of the nation, bring disgrace upon the Church, and provoke the just judgments of heaven. Giving freedom, and preparing its recipients for it, must go hand in hand, else this blood-bought boon is not worth the terrible price it cost.

Hopes Destroyed

After the end of Reconstruction in 1876, the South witnessed a dramatic rise
in the number of violent acts committed against African Americans. While
the adoption of the Thirteenth, Fourteenth, and Fifteenth Amendments to
the Constitution — which abolished slavery, guaranteed basic equality of all
races under the law, and gave all male citizens the right to vote — seemed to
signal the dawning of a new era, local southern governments found ways to
circumvent federal mandates for racial equality. One of these means was
extra-legal execution known as lynching. Although some Native Americans
and Hispanics, as well as a few whites, were lynched, overwhelmingly Afri-
can Americans were the target. In response to a steadily rising number of in-
cidents, defenders of black rights tried to take action. One of the most effec-
tive of these resisters was Ida B. Wells, who had been born into a slave family
in 1862 in Holly Springs, Mississippi. Wells was a member of the African
Methodist Episcopal Church who witnessed first hand the erosion of
African-American rights that had been supposedly secured by the Civil War.
Wells became an anti-lynching activist in 1892 when three of her friends
were strung up near Memphis. For the next years, Wells campaigned tire-
lessly against lynchings and the political forces that supported them. She
published at least three books on the subject from 1892 to 1900; the excerpts
that follow are from A Red Record *(1894).*

When asked what concerted action had been taken by churches and great moral
agencies in America to put down Lynch Law, I was compelled in truth to say
that no such action had occurred, that pulpit, press and moral agencies in the
main were silent and for reasons known to themselves, ignored the awful conditions which to the English people appeared so abhorent. Then the question
was asked what the great moral reformers like Miss Frances Willard and Mr.
Moody[2] had done to suppress Lynch Law and again I answered — nothing.
That Mr. Moody had never said a word against lynching in any of his trips to
the South, or in the North either, so far as was known, and that Miss Willard's
only public utterance on the situation had condoned lynching and other unjust
practices of the South against the Negro. When proof of these statements was

2. Rev. Dwight L. Moody, an internationally recognized evangelist from Northfield, Massachusetts, is perhaps best known as the founder of the Chicago Bible Institute (now the Moody
Bible Institute).

[Source: Ida B. Wells, *A Red Record: Tabulated Statistics and Alleged Cause of Lynchings in*
the United States, 1892-1893-1894 (1894), as found in Jacqueline Jones Royster, ed., *Southern*
Horrors and Other Writings: The Anti-Lynching Campaign of Ida B. Wells, 1892-1900
(Boston: Bedford, 1997), 140-41, 154-55.]

demanded, I sent a letter containing a copy of the New York Voice, Oct. 23, 1890, in which appeared Miss Willard's own words of wholesale slander against the colored race and condonation of Southern white people's outrages against us. My letter in part reads as follows:

> But Miss Willard, the great temperance leader, went even further in putting the seal of her approval upon the southerners' method of dealing with the Negro. In October, 1890, the Women's Christian Temperance Union held its national meeting at Atlanta, Georgia. It was the first time in the history of the organization that it had gone south for a national meeting, and met the southerners, in their own homes. They were welcomed with open arms. The governor of the state and the legislature gave special audiences in the halls of state legislation to the temperance workers. They set out to capture the northerners to their way of seeing things, and without troubling to hear the Negro side of the question, these temperance people accepted the white man's story of the problem with which he had to deal. State organizers were appointed that year, who had gone through the southern states since then, but in obedience to southern prejudices have confined their work to white persons only. It is only after Negroes are in prison for crimes that efforts of these temperance women are exerted without regard to "race, color, or previous condition." No "ounce of prevention" is used in their case; they are black, and if these women went among the Negroes for this work, the whites would not receive them. Except here and there, are found no temperance workers of the Negro race; "the great dark-faced mobs" are left the easy prey of the saloonkeepers.

We demand a fair trial by law for those accused of crime, and punishment by law after honest conviction. No maudlin sympathy for criminals is solicited, but we do ask that the law shall punish all alike. We earnestly desire those that control the forces which make public sentiment to join with us in the demand. Surely the humanitarian spirit of this country which reaches out to denounce the treatment of the Russian Jews, the Armenian Christians, the laboring poor of Europe, the Siberian exiles and the native women of India — will not longer refuse to lift its voice on this subject. If it were known that the cannibals or the savage Indians had burned three human beings alive in the past two years, the whole of Christendom would be roused, to devise ways and means to put a stop to it. Can you remain silent and inactive when such things are done in our own community and country? Is your duty to humanity in the United States less binding?

What can you do, reader, to prevent lynching, to thwart anarchy and promote law and order throughout our land?

1st. You can help disseminate the facts contained in this book by bringing them to the knowledge of every one with whom you come in contact, to the end that public sentiment may be revolutionized. Let the facts speak for themselves, with you as a medium.

2d. You can be instrumental in having churches, missionary societies, Y. M. C. A.'s, W. C. T. U.'s and all Christian and moral forces in connection with your religious and social life, pass resolutions of condemnation and protest every time a lynching takes place; and see that they are sent to the place where these outrages occur.

3d. Bring to the intelligent consideration of Southern people the refusal of capital to invest where lawlessness and mob violence hold sway. Many labor organizations have declared by resolution that they would avoid lynch infested localities as they would the pestilence when seeking new homes. If the South wishes to build up its waste places quickly, there is no better way than to uphold the majesty of the law by enforcing obedience to the same, and meting out the same punishment to all classes of criminals, white as well as black. "Equality before the law," must become a fact as well as a theory before America is truly the "land of the free and the home of the brave."

4th. Think and act on independent lines in this behalf, remembering that after all, it is the white man's civilization and the white man's government which are on trial. This crusade will determine whether that civilization can maintain itself by itself, or whether anarchy shall prevail; whether this Nation shall write itself down a success at self government, or in deepest humiliation admit its failure complete; whether the precepts and theories of Christianity are professed and practiced by American white people as Golden Rules of thought and action, or adopted as a system of morals to be preached to heathen until they attain to the intelligence which needs the system of Lynch Law. . . .

The Task

Unity Maintained

As a denomination primarily of the northeastern United States, Congregationalism easily avoided any division along political or sectional lines. But what of denominations with major memberships in both South and North? When a nation divided, must not a church suffer schism also? Remarkably, the Protestant Episcopal Church managed to keep its organizational integ-

---

[Source: "The Next General Convention," in *The American Quarterly Church Review, and Ecclesiastical Register,* 17, no. 3 (Oct., 1865), 452-53, 454.]

rity intact. Meeting in a national or General Convention every three years, Episcopalians in 1859, in 1862, and in 1865 avoided rupture, even while the "Sects about us are falling to pieces." In the excerpt below, the editor of an Episcopal journal reviews in 1865 the two previous conventions as he offers hope for the approaching one.

It is a great point, and let it never be forgotten, that up to the breaking out of the Civil War in 1861, no sectional feuds or animosities had disturbed our peace, or alienated the hearts of brethren. Even at the General Convention of 1859, held in the city of Richmond, when the mutterings of the storm began to be heard, and when sagacious men saw the cloud in the distant horizon, already bigger than a man's hand, and knew what it meant, unless God, in His mercy, should avert the awful judgment, still the members of that Convention, from the East and the West, the North and the South, only clung the closer to each other, and religiously vowed fidelity to one another, and to Christ, and to His Church, with a deeper solemnity. And, in the last General Convention, in this city of New York, in 1862, when the vials of wrath were pouring out their fury, and the brethren came together once more, to counsel and pray for the peace and prosperity of Israel, who can ever forget the impressiveness of that scene, when the seats appointed for the Southern brethren were found to be vacant? And yet the names of the absent Tribes were, as usual, officially called. Eyes wet with tears, and faces filled with sorrow, told unerringly where all hearts were, at that Convention. As little was done as possible, even in the legislation of the Church. Every thing was left undone that could be, in testimony of the hope and the belief that these broken ranks would be filled again; at any rate, that the bonds of Unity were not as yet hopelessly broken. . . .

And now, another Convention is close upon us. Whatever fears we may have formerly entertained as to its results, and as to its influence on the welfare of the Church and the well-being of the Nation, those fears are passing away. As this mighty nation is to be One Nation, and as we are to be One People and not many peoples, so, unless God's wrath is to be visited upon us for our unfaithfulness, we are to be yet again One Church, knit more firmly than ever before together, to do one great blessed work, for CHRIST, for this nation, and for the world. The Sects about us are falling to pieces. Even the most conservative of them are rending to fragments with their internal feuds and animosities, their mutual criminations and recriminations, their fierce and angry fanatical passions. So, for GOD's sake, and the Church's sake, and for the souls of men, let it not be among us.

Division Hardened

Methodists, on the other hand, did divide along geographical lines in 1844, the critical issue being sharply divergent attitudes toward slavery among Methodists in the North from those in the South. But since slavery was officially abolished by the Emancipation Proclamation during the war, what now prevented Methodists North and South from coming together again? The answer, of course, is that much prevented such a reunion, including a deep bitterness which many southern Methodists felt against what they viewed as northern intrusion, condescension, and radicalism. The following document, a pastoral letter from the bishops of the Methodist Episcopal Church, South, shows the lines of separation hardened and any loving reconciliation a distant dream.

[1865] The abolition, . . . of the institution of domestic slavery in the United States does not affect the question that was prominent in our separation in 1844. Nor is this the only difference or principal one between us and [the Northern Methodist Church]. While testifying with pleasure to the nobler conduct and sentiments of many brethren among them, we must express with regret our apprehension that a large portion, if not a majority, of Northern Methodists have become incurably radical. They teach for doctrine the commandments of men. They preach another gospel. They have incorporated social dogmas and political tests into their church creeds. They have gone on to impose conditions upon discipleship that Christ did not impose. Their pulpits are perverted to agitations and questions not healthful to personal piety, but promotive of political and ecclesiastical discord. . . . Without such a change as we see no immediate prospect of, in their tone and temper and practice, we can anticipate no good result from even entertaining the subject of reunion with them. . . . Preach Christ and Him crucified. Do not preach politics. You have no commission to preach politics. The divinity of the Church is never more strikingly displayed than when it holds on its even, straightforward way in the midst of worldly commotions. . . .

The conduct of certain Northern Methodist bishops and preachers in taking advantage of the confusion incident to a state of war to intrude themselves into several of our houses of worship, and in continuing to hold these places against the wishes and protests of the congregations and rightful owners, causes us sorrow and pain, not only as working an injury to us, but as presenting to the world a spectacle ill calculated to make an impression favorable to

[Source: Walter L. Fleming, *Documentary History of Reconstruction* (Cleveland: Arthur H. Clark Co., 1907), II, pp. 233-34.]

Christianity. They are not only using, to our deprivation and exclusion, churches and parsonages which we have builded, but have proceeded to set up a claim to them as their property; by what shadow of right, legal or moral, we are at a loss to conceive. We advise our brethren who suffer these evils to bear them patiently, to cleave closely together and not indulge in any vindictive measures or tempers. A plain statement of the case, and an appeal to the justice of those in authority cannot fail to defeat such scandalous designs, and secure us the full restoration of all our rights.

While some talk of the reunion of the two Churches, we forewarn you of a systematic attempt, already inaugurated, and of which the foregoing is only an instance, to disturb and if possible disintegrate and then absorb our membership individually. In the meeting [1864] of their bishops and missionary secretaries, alluded to, it was resolved to send preachers and plant societies in our midst wherever there is an opening. Their policy is evidently our division and ecclesiastical devastation. Against all this be on your guard.

Lost Cause Affirmed

After Lee's surrender at Appomattox Courthouse, white southerners found themselves a defeated people. Many whites in the South saw Reconstruction as an imposition on their way of life; and even before the last federal troops withdrew from southern posts in 1877, a strongly pro-Confederate interpretation of the Civil War emerged. As various organizations emerged to celebrate the glory of the Confederate enterprise, southern divines provided a religious basis for nostalgia. Among the most significant was J. William Jones (see above, p. 547). Jones's Christ in the Camp *(1888) provided much information about revivals in the Army of Northern Virginia, but served even more powerfully as a way of praising and defending the Confederacy itself. The selections below illustrate general hagiography (= veneration of the saints) for Confederate officials and the more specific praise for General Stonewall Jackson.*

No army, with whose history I am acquainted, at least, was ever blessed with so large a proportion of high officers who were earnest Christian men, as the Army of Northern Virginia.

We had at first such specimens of the Christian soldier as R. E. Lee, Stonewall Jackson, D. H. Hill, T. R. Cobb, A. H. Colquitt, Kirby Smith, J. E. B. Stuart,

---

[Source: J. William Jones, *Christ in the Camp; or Religion in Lee's Army* (Richmond, VA: B. F. Johnson, 1888), pp. 42, 82-83.]

W. N. Pendleton, John B. Gordon, C. A. Evans, A. M. Scales, "Willie" Pegram, Lewis Minor Coleman, Thos. H. Carter, Carter Braxton, Charles S. Venable, and a host of others too numerous to mention. And during the war Generals Ewell, Pender, Hood, R. H. Anderson, Rodes, Paxton, W. H. S. Baylor, Colonel Lamar, and a number of others of our best officers professed faith in Christ.

Nor was the example of these noble men merely *negative* — many of them were *active* workers for the Master, and did not hesitate, upon all proper occasions, to "stand up for Jesus."

OUR CHRISTIAN PRESIDENT, JEFFERSON DAVIS, was always outspoken on the side of evangelical religion, and manifested the deepest interest in all efforts for the spiritual good of the soldiers. His fast-day and thanksgiving-day proclamations were not only beautiful specimens of the chaste style and classic English for which this great man is remarkable, but they also breathed a spirit of humble, devout piety, which did not fail to have its influence on the armies of the Confederacy.

He said to Rev. A. E. Dickinson, who was then superintendent of the Virginia Baptist Colportage Board, which resolved in June, 1861, to send to labor in the army its band of nearly one hundred trained colporters: "I most cordially sympathize with this movement. We have but little to hope for, if we do not realize our dependence upon heaven's blessing and seek the guidance of God's truth."

The piety of STONEWALL JACKSON has become as historic as his wonderful military career. But, as it was my privilege to see a good deal of him, and to learn from those intimate with him much of his inner life; and as his Christian character is well worthy of earnest study, and of admiring imitation, I give a somewhat extended sketch of it.

I first came into personal contact with him on the 4th of July, 1861, while our army was drawn up in line of battle at Darkesville, to meet General Patterson. The skill and tact with which he had reduced the high-spirited young men who rushed to Harper's Ferry at the first tap of the drum into the respectable "Army of the Shenandoah," which he turned over to General Johnston on the 23rd of May, 1861, and the ability and stern courage with which he had checked Patterson's advance at Falling Waters, had won for him some reputation, and I was anxious to see him.

A colporter (good brother C. F. Fry) had sent me word that he desired permission to enter our lines to distribute Bibles and tracts. With the freedom with which in our army the humblest private could approach the highest officer I at once went to General Jackson for the permit. I have a vivid recollection of how he impressed me. Dressed in a simple Virginia uniform, apparently about thirty-seven years old, six feet high, medium size, grey eyes that seemed to look through you, light brown hair and a countenance in which deep benevolence seemed mingled with uncompromising sternness, he seemed to me to have about him nothing at all of the "pomp and circumstance of war," but every element which enters into the skilful leader, and the indomitable, energetic soldier who was always ready for the fight. Stating to him my mission, he at once replied in pleasant tones, and with a smile of peculiar sweetness: "Certainly, sir; it will give me great pleasure to grant all such permits. I am glad that you came to me, and I shall be glad to be introduced to the colporter."

Afterward introducing my friend, Jackson said to him: "You are more than welcome to my camp, and it will give me great pleasure to help you in your work in every way in my power. I am more anxious than I can express that my men should be not only good soldiers of their country, but also good soldiers of the Cross." We lingered for some time in an exceedingly pleasant conversation about the religious welfare of the army, and when I turned away, with a very courteous invitation to call on him again, I felt that I had met a man of deep-toned piety, who carried his religion into every affair of life, and who was destined to make his mark in the war.

Jackson had become a Christian some time before; but it was not until the 22nd of November, 1851, that he made public profession of religion and united with the Presbyterian Church in Lexington, then under the care of the venerable and beloved Rev. Dr. W. S. White, whose death in 1871 was so widely lamented.

African Americans Organized

Reconstruction failed in the effort to ensure equal opportunity as free citizens for the freedmen and freedwomen of the South. Yet despite disappointment in that failure, African Americans nonetheless did achieve a considerable measure of success in efforts to organize churches for their own benefit. Among the most important of the largely black denominations that burgeoned after the War was the African Methodist Episcopal Church. Its leading figure for many decades was Bishop Daniel Alexander Payne (see above, p. 579). When in 1890, Payne looked back over the history of his denomination, he was gratified to be able to tell a story of achievement against obstacles. Payne's recital of names that are now mostly lost to history offers an important reminder concerning how important ordinary people going about ordinary tasks have always been for the progress of churches and religious organizations.

[Source: Daniel Alexander Payne, "Organization Essential to Success for Quarto-Centennial of African Methodism in the South" (1890), in Payne, *Sermons and Addresses, 1853-1891* (New York: Arno, 1972), 38-40.]

For Quarto-Centennial of African Methodism in the South.

The word Organization is generic and therefore may be applied to any body of men, or women, associated under a written constitution for the accomplishment of some one or more specific purpose; . . . But whenever a number of men and woman associate for the public worship of the living God, in the house of God, which is the Church of the living God, the ground and pillar of the truth, it may be called an Ecclesiastical Organization, proven to every body and recognized by the common people as the Church. . . .

Many, if not all of these denominal organizations are the offsprings of internal troubles, quarrels and schisms. In like manner the African Methodist Episcopal Church was born into this world.

a. Her first appearance was in Philadelphia in 1816.

b. Her second appearance was in Charleston, S. C., in 1817-18.

c. In Philadelphia the movement was led by Richard Allen and Daniel Coker, of Baltimore, Md.

d. In Charleston the movement was led by Morris Brown and Henry Drayton, of Charleston, S. C. This organization embraced about one thousand persons (1817). In 1822 it numbered about three thousand. The leaders of these three thousand were Morris Brown, Henry Drayton, Charles Carr, Amos Cunckshanks, Marcus Brown, Smart Simpson, Harry Bull, John B. Matthews, James Eden, London Turpin, and Aleck Houlston. This band, or little church, was well organized, and had acquired a building lot upon which a commodious but plain house of worship was built. They also owned their own burial ground, or field of graves. Happy among themselves, they were at peace and concord with one another up to 1822. When the contemplated insurrection led by Denmark Vesy, a slave man, was discovered, in destroying which, the civil authorities of the city and state deemed it wise to crush the little band of christians. None of these religious leaders were implicated in the contemplated insurrection. But the love of freedom and the right to worship God according to one's own conscience led Henry Drayton, Charles Carr, father of the gifted and devout Joseph M. Carr; Marcus Brown, and Amos Cunckshanks to follow Morris Brown to Philadelphia. James Eden with a majority of the most intelligent united themselves with the Scotch Presbyterian Church, which was at that time located at the corner of Meeting and Tradd streets, next to the then princely mansion of Nathaniel Russell, esq., the father-in-law of Bishop Theodore Dehone. James Eden, perhaps the most intelligent of those who became members of the Scotch Presbyterian Church, subsequently sailed with the first emmigrants from Charleston to Liberia, where he lived many years, and died respected and lamented by all who knew him. Thus was the African M. E. Church in South Carolina blotted from the pages of Ecclesiastical History. But after the lapse of sixty-eight years we are here assembled to celebrate the

Quarto-Centenary of her Renaiscence in South Carolina, and of the expansion into Georgia, Florida, Alabama and Tennessee.

When, how and by whom has her present condition been brought into existence? In the spring of 1863 the Rev. C. C. Leigh, a white preacher of the Methodist Episcopal Church visited the Baltimore Annual Conference then in session in Baltimore, Md., and desired to know whether I could send two missionaries to take charge of the social, moral and religious interests of the Freedmen in South Carolina, who were like sheep without a shepherd. I told him I believed I could. Then said I to him, "how soon do you want them?" He said, "within ten days." In about ten days Rev. James Lynch, born in the city of Baltimore and a member of the Baltimore Conference, also Rev. James D. S. Hall of the New York Conference (then stationed in Sullivan street A. M. E. Church) were sent into these regions. They landed at Port Royal and immediately commenced operations on that island and at Beaufort, afterwards at Charleston, and after that James Lynch organized a little band at Savannah, Ga.

The two James were very unlike each other. James Lynch was always hopeful, James Hall was always fearful of coming evil; Lynch was the bold lion, Hall the timid sheep; Hall was the witty Irishman, Lynch the sagacious statesman; Lynch was born to be the skillful organizer, Hall the trembling follower, ready to run away from the ranks at the barking of a rat-tarrier, or the howling of a bull-dog. Each of these missionaries worked successfully, according to their heaven bestowed ability, and made it possible for the organization of the South Carolina Conference on Monday morning, May 16, 1865. That took place in the Colored Presbyterian Church, Calhoun street. The two itinerant elders were James Lynch and James A. Handy; the two licentiates were James H. A. Johnson and Theophilus G. Stewart — these licentiates from the North were subsequently ordained deacons. A local preacher named William Bently constituted the five persons present at the opening of the South Carolina Conference. Subsequently Elder R. H. Cain from the New York Conference, Elder Anthony L. Stanford and George A. Rue from the New England Conference were added. The natives of the state who joined the South Carolina Conference were Charles L. Bradwell, N. Murphy, Robert Taylor and Richard Vanderhorse. The whole number of persons within the boundaries of the South Carolina Conference was supposed to be about 4000. That number embraced North Carolina, South Carolina and Georgia, along the coasts and all the islands. Reports on temperance, education and missions were discussed and adopted; an Historic and Literary Society was formed, also a Preachers' Aid Society. Thus equipped the South Carolina Conference, like an armed ship launched, was sent forth to conquer the lands of the South.

Suggested Reading (Chapter Six)

After many years of unjustified neglect, scholarship on almost all aspects of religion and the sectional crises leading to Civil War is now at high tide. For the most comprehensive effort to date, see the essays in Randall M. Miller, Harry S. Stout, and Charles Reagan Wilson, eds., *Religion and the American Civil War* (1998). A well-illustrated, popularized rendition that also ranges widely was presented by *Christian History* (no. 33, 1992) as "The Untold Story of Christianity and the Civil War."

For considerations of race, abolition, and religious arguments about slavery, H. Shelton Smith's *In His Image, But . . . : Racism in Southern Religion, 1780-1910* (1972) was a pioneering effort that has been profitably expanded by several other authors and teams of scholars, including John R. McKivigan, *The War Against Proslavery Religion* (1984), Eugene D. Genovese, *"Slavery Ordained of God": The Southern Slaveholders' View of Biblical History and Modern Politics* (1985), James Oscar Farmer, Jr., *The Metaphysical Confederacy: James Henley Thornwell and the Synthesis of Southern Values* (1986), Larry E. Tise, *Proslavery: A History of the Defense of Slavery in America, 1701-1840* (1987), and John R. McKivigan and Mitchell Snay, eds., *Religion and the Antebellum Debate over Slavery* (1998).

Distinctly religious elements that shaped Southern culture and so led on to the Confederacy are well treated in Anne C. Loveland, *Southern Evangelicals and the Social Order, 1800-1860* (1980), Drew Gilpin Faust, *The Creation of Confederate Nationalism: Ideology and Identity in the Civil War South* (1988), Elizabeth Fox-Genovese, *Within the Plantation Household: Black and White Women of the Old South* (1988), Eugene D. Genovese, *The Slaveholders' Dilemma: Freedom and Progress in Southern Conservative Thought, 1820-1860* (1991), Mitchell Snay, *Gospel of Disunion: Religion and Separatism in the Antebellum South* (1993), and Kenneth Startup, *The Root of All Evil: The Protestant Clergy and the Economic Mind of the Old South* (1997).

There is not as much assessment of religious contributions to Northern sectional culture, although Richard J. Carwardine's *Evangelicals and Politics in Antebellum America* (1993) is a magisterial effort, and Mark Y. Hanley's *Beyond a Christian Commonwealth: The Protestant Quarrel with the American Republic, 1830-1860* (1994) shows how conflicted religious opinion could be on nationalistic issues. A fine set of primary sources, drawn from South and North, has been presented by David B. Chesebrough, ed., *God Ordained This War: Sermons on the Sectional Crisis, 1830-1865* (1991).

General histories of the Civil War that include full treatment of religion include Phillip Shaw Paludan, *"A People's Contest": The Union and Civil War, 1861-1865* (1988), Charles Royster, *The Destructive War* (1993), Allen C. Guelzo,

The Crisis of the American Republic: A History of the Civil War and Reconstruction Era (1995), and James McPherson, *For Cause and Comrades: Why Men Fought in the Civil War* (1997).

The "church history" of the Civil War was well treated in several older studies, including Lewis G. Vander Velde, *The Presbyterian Churches and the Federal Union, 1861-1869* (1932), and James W. Silver, *Confederate Morale and Church Propaganda* (1967 [1957]). More recent attention to that same history includes expert scholarship on religion in the armies: Gardiner H. Shattuck, Jr., *A Shield and Hiding Place: The Religious Life of the Civil War Armies* (1987), and Steven E. Woodworth, *While God Is Marching On: The Religious World of Civil War Soldiers* (2001); and equally fine efforts on how the war was interpreted: James H. Moorhead, *American Apocalypse: Yankee Protestants and the Civil War, 1860-1869* (1978), Judith Conrad Wimmer, "American Catholic Interpretation of the Civil War" (Ph.D. diss., Drew University, 1980), and Eugene D. Genovese, *Consuming Fire: The Fall of the Confederacy in the Mind of the White Christian South* (1999).

On the way that the destructiveness of the Civil War turned some intellectuals (mostly in the North) away from traditional religion, there has been especially careful work by George M. Fredrickson, *The Inner Civil War: Modern Intellectuals and the Crisis of the Union* (1965), Anne C. Rose, *Victorian America and the Civil War* (1992), and Louis Menand, *The Metaphysical Club: A Story of Ideas in America* (2001). The role of religion in shoring up a defeated, but unbowed Southern culture has been carefully examined in Charles R. Wilson, *Baptized in Blood: The Religion of the Lost Cause, 1865-1920* (1980), and Gaines M. Foster, *Ghosts of the Confederacy: Defeat, the Lost Cause, and the Emergence of the New South, 1865-1913* (1987).

The religion of Abraham Lincoln is a topic of perennial interest which, it is gratifying to note, has been coming ever closer to verified history as opposed to sanctimonious myth. See, in particular, William J. Wolf, *The Almost Chosen People: A Study of the Religion of Abraham Lincoln* (1959), David Hein, "Lincoln's Theology and Political Ethics," in *Essays on Lincoln's Faith and Politics*, ed. Kenneth W. Thompson (1983), Allen C. Guelzo, *Abraham Lincoln: Redeemer President* (1999), William Lee Miller, *Lincoln's Virtues: An Ethical Biography* (2002), and Stewart Winger, *Lincoln, Religion, and Romantic Cultural Politics* (2003). And for reactions to Lincoln's assassination, there is very useful material in David B. Chesebrough, *"No Sorrow like Our Sorrow": Northern Protestant Ministers and the Assassination of Lincoln* (1994). Philip Schaff's wide-ranging achievements as theologian, historian, and churchman are the subject of Henry W. Bowden, ed., *A Century of Church History: The Legacy of Philip Schaff* (1988), Stephen R. Graham, *Cosmos in the Chaos: Philip Schaff's Interpretation of Nineteenth-Century American Religion* (1995), and Gary K. Pranger, *Philip Schaff (1819-1893): Portrait of an Immigrant Theologian* (1997). Most biographies of John Brown include treatment of his religious beliefs, including Stephen B. Oates, *To Purge This Land With Blood: A Biography of John Brown* (1970).

Contributions toward understanding the role of religious organizations in the period immediately after the war have been made for African Americans by James T. Campbell, *Sons of Zion: The African Methodist Episcopal Church in the United States and South Africa* (1998), and for Baptists in the South by Paul Harvey, *Redeeming the South: Religious Cultures and Racial Identities Among Southern Baptists, 1865-1925* (1997).

Index

Page numbers in italics indicate illustrations.